Federal Lending
and Loan Insurance

NATIONAL BUREAU OF ECONOMIC RESEARCH
FINANCIAL RESEARCH PROGRAM

Federal Lending
and Loan Insurance

BY

R. J. SAULNIER
HAROLD G. HALCROW
NEIL H. JACOBY

A STUDY BY THE

NATIONAL BUREAU OF ECONOMIC RESEARCH, NEW YORK

PUBLISHED BY

PRINCETON UNIVERSITY PRESS, PRINCETON

1958

Printed in the United States of America
by Princeton University Press at Princeton, New Jersey

RELATION OF THE DIRECTORS
TO THE WORK AND PUBLICATIONS
OF THE NATIONAL BUREAU OF ECONOMIC RESEARCH

1. The object of the National Bureau of Economic Research is to ascertain and to present to the public important economic facts and their interpretation in a scientific and impartial manner. The Board of Directors is charged with the responsibility of ensuring that the work of the National Bureau is carried on in strict conformity with this object.

2. To this end the Board of Directors shall appoint one or more Directors of Research.

3. The Director or Directors of Research shall submit to the members of the Board, or to its Executive Committee, for their formal adoption, all specific proposals concerning researches to be instituted.

4. No report shall be published until the Director or Directors of Research shall have submitted to the board a summary drawing attention to the character of the data and their utilization in the report, the nature and treatment of the problems involved, the main conclusions and such other information as in their opinion would serve to determine the suitability of the report for publication in accordance with the principles of the National Bureau.

5. A copy of any manuscript proposed for publication shall also be submitted to each member of the Board. For each manuscript to be so submitted a special committee shall be appointed by the President, or at his designation by the Executive Director, consisting of three Directors selected as nearly as may be one from each general division of the Board. The names of the special manuscript committee shall be stated to each Director when the summary and report described in paragraph (4) are sent to him. It shall be the duty of each member of the committee to read the manuscript. If each member of the special committee signifies his approval within thirty days, the manuscript may be published. If each member of the special committee has not signified his approval within thirty days of the transmittal of the report and manuscript, the Director shall then notify each member of the Board, requesting approval or disapproval of publication, and thirty additional days shall be granted for this purpose. The manuscript shall then not be published unless at least a majority of the entire Board and a two-thirds majority of those members of the Board who shall have voted on the proposal within the time fixed for the receipt of votes on the publication proposed shall have approved.

6. No manuscript may be published, though approved by each member of the special committee, until forty-five days have elapsed from the transmittal of the summary and report. The interval is allowed for the receipt of any memorandum of dissent or reservation, together with a brief statement of his reasons, that any member may wish to express; and such a memorandum of dissent or reservation shall be published with the manuscript if he so desires. Publication does not, however, imply that each member of the Board has read the manuscript, or that either members of the Board in general, or of the special committee, have passed upon its validity in every detail.

7. A copy of this resolution shall, unless otherwise determined by the Board, be printed in each copy of every National Bureau book.

(Resolution adopted October 25, 1926 and revised February 6, 1933 and February 24, 1941)

PREFACE

THIS study of federal credit programs was started in 1951 and put into preliminary draft form in late 1952. Following suggestions received from National Bureau staff members, and from a sizable number of readers outside that group, the preliminary manuscript was extensively reorganized, resulting in the present version.

Several factors combined to cause this long interval between the completion of the first draft and the circulation of the present version. First, the team of collaborators—Professor Harold G. Halcrow of the University of Connecticut, Professor Neil H. Jacoby of the University of California at Los Angeles, and myself—was dispersed in 1952, two of us entering public service. The situation was saved only by the fact that we were able to delegate much of the work to two of our principal assistants—Catherine Martin and Mary Phelps. This was concluded with what we regard as the happiest of results. Second, delays caused by revisions in a manuscript of this sort tend to pyramid. Certainly they did so in this case, in which the reorganization of the study took so much time that it was necessary to bring many of the series up to date, which in turn was a time-consuming process.

The authors are indebted to many others for assistance received at various stages of the study's preparation. Professor George K. Brinegar of the University of Connecticut worked continuously with Dr. Halcrow; and Dr. Jacoby and I had the help of Henry K. Krauskopf, now of Quinnipiac College, in developing estimates of the volume and outstanding amount of federal credit aids and in completing the special analyses of RFC's business lending programs. In my studies of housing credit I benefited greatly from the assistance of Gerald Sirkin and Philip Golden. Our indebtedness to Catherine P. Martin, who designed plans for the compilation of many of the statistical materials on which the study is based, and supervised much of their compilation and processing, and to Mary Phelps, who edited all, and redrafted much, of the text, has been acknowledged above. Heavy as are our obligations to these able assistants, it is understood, of course, that the collaborators themselves are wholly responsible for the accuracy of the facts presented and for the interpretations placed upon them. Since the manuscript was first circulated in mimeographed form in early 1953, the authors have had the benefit of a number of suggestions aimed at improving its factual and analytical parts. Among these the comments of Geoffrey H. Moore and George Stigler of the National Bureau's staff, Earl Rolph of the University of California at Berkeley, Fred E. Case and J. Fred Weston of the University of California at Los Angeles, Morris A. Copeland of Cornell University, Lewis H. Kimmel of the Brookings Institution, have been especially helpful.

No study of this kind could be made without the full cooperation of the federal agencies involved, and we have been fortunate in having this help in full measure. The list of agencies that provided us with special tabulations is a long one and perhaps may be omitted here in view of the fact that specific acknowledgments of sources are made in the text. We are deeply grateful to all the agencies, but I should like especially to express our gratitude to the Board and Staff of the now liquidated Reconstruction Finance Corporation, particularly to Robert W. Benner, Chief of the Economic Analysis Staff, through whose good offices we put together a more complete account and appraisal of the business lending activities of that agency than has previously been available.

The work was undertaken in 1951 under a grant of funds from the Trustees of the Banking Research Fund of the Association of Reserve City Bankers. It is a pleasure to record the National Bureau's appreciation of this support of its Financial Research Program

R. J. SAULNIER

On leave, Director, Financial Research Program,
National Bureau of Economic Research and
Professor of Economics, Barnard College,
Columbia University

May 14, 1956

CONTENTS

CONTENTS

TABLES

xvii

TABLES

CHARTS

CHARTS

Federal Lending
and Loan Insurance

PART I

CHAPTER 1

The Nature and Scope of Federal Credit Activities

THE present study is directed to one aspect of the rising tide of governmental activities, namely, to the extension of credit by the federal government and to government insurance or guarantee of loans made by private financial agencies. Its purposes are to show how the various credit programs developed and where they stand today, to describe the services they offer, to record the experience of the federal government as a lender, and to analyze the impact of its credit activities on private finance and on the economy generally. These four objectives provide the subject matter of Chapters 2 through 5, respectively, of Part I. In Part II, Chapters 6 through 8, we deal separately with the programs in agriculture, business, and housing, giving for each of these areas a more detailed account of the services rendered, the experience encountered, and the effects of the program. Tables giving a still more detailed breakdown of data on lending programs are given in Appendix A, and technical treatments of the business lending programs of the Reconstruction Finance Corporation and the Veterans' Administration are given in Appendixes B and C.

Scope of the Study

The first, and in many ways the most troublesome, task of the study was to set conceptually satisfying and practical limits to its scope. Difficulties were inevitable, perhaps, in view of the variety and complexity of the activities that come within the general range of the investigation, and their unusually ramifying nature. It was essential, however, to set definite limits to the scope of the study, even though they necessarily have an arbitrary cast.

First, the study excludes credit programs of state governments and also of international agencies, even those in which the United States government plays a prominent role. State programs are not too numerous to deal with, but data on them are so fragmentary that they had to be ruled out; international agency programs were excluded for the obvious reason that to cover them would carry the investigation too far afield from the activities of the federal government.

Second was the question presented by domestic agencies only quasi-public in nature. Naturally, the study covers all direct credit agencies of the federal government; besides, it includes all those having a special financial or administrative connection with the federal government, whether or not federal funds are presently invested in them. The latter—for example, the district Federal Reserve banks, federal land banks, and federal home loan banks—are termed federally sponsored agencies, though the label does not fit all of them equally well. They include agencies that are in some respects private or cooperative in ownership and organization but that operate in part with Treasury funds; and agencies that, although no longer using Treasury funds, are specially connected with some federal agency through the latter's power to appoint policy-making officers and in some cases to review policy decisions. In most tabulations, data will be given separately for the federal and the federally sponsored agencies.

Third, the limits of the study are defined in terms of the types of activities as well as of the types of agencies covered. Programs under which privately made loans are insured or guaranteed are included, in addition to those in which credits are extended directly by the federal government. Federal purchases of stock or shares aimed mainly at aiding financial institutions have been included, but only where they are clearly a close substitute for financial aid through loans. These three main categories of financial assistance are shown separately in most tabulations.

Among the excluded programs are a number in which the extension of credit—usually on an accounts receivable basis—was only incidental to some other activity, such as when the U.S. Commercial Company gave open book credit during World War II in connection with its sales of commodities, or when the U.S. Housing Corporation, after the earlier war, took back receivables in selling government-owned housing. But assets such as the real estate sales contracts taken by Home Owners' Loan Corporation in its sales of foreclosed real estate have been included as credit extensions, on the ground that here the deferred payment sales were an integral and major part of what was essentially a program of financial aid.

Loans made indirectly—as when the federal intermediate credit banks discount paper for production credit associations, enabling the latter to extend credit to farmers—are covered, as well as those going directly to the ultimate borrower; but double counting that

4

might arise from such transactions has been rigorously avoided. Interagency loans—such as purchase by the Treasury of debentures of the RFC—have been excluded, also to avoid double counting.

Loans made under participation agreements with private institutions are included as direct loans when the credit has actually been extended; during the time when there is merely a commitment outstanding under which a federal agency is obligated to take up all or some portion of a loan at the option of the private lender, the amount of the obligation is regarded as a loan guarantee. Grant-in-aid programs, of course, are excluded, and it is perhaps equally obvious that loan or guarantee programs that are not fully self-supporting cannot be excluded, both for conceptual and for practical reasons.

Several special problems encountered in defining the area of study require comment. First, the decision was made to exclude loans by United States agencies to foreign governments, on the ground that these would lead too far afield from the first and central purpose: examining federal financial aids to business, agriculture, and homeowners. Furthermore, to have included, say, the Treasury's British loan authorized in 1946 would have raised the question of covering lend-lease transactions and the complex series of intergovernmental loans that were extended during and after World War I. To embrace these within the scope of the study would have been quite impractical.

But excluding all loans by federal agencies to foreign governments is not an easy matter. Some of this lending, specifically that which is conducted as part of the regular programs of the Export-Import Bank, could not be fully separated from lending to foreign private concerns and to domestic concerns engaged in foreign trade, and had to be included in the tabulations. It was feasible, however, to exclude credits extended to foreign governments by the Foreign Operations Administration and its predecessors (either directly or through the facilities of the Export-Import Bank) and by the RFC.

Next, there is the controversial matter of direct and guaranteed loans by the Commodity Credit Corporation. These might have been excluded on the ground that they are a means for carrying out a price support program and are not primarily a form of credit assistance. On the other hand, to exclude them would be objectionable, since the amounts involved are appreciable in certain years. The procedure adopted was a compromise: CCC loans are included, as a separate item, in the quantitative series on loans to agriculture

(Chapter 2); but they are dealt with only superficially in the text, since to treat them fully would carry the discussion far from its central focus.

Finally, discounts by the Federal Reserve Banks for their member banks (but not the direct loans of the Reserve Banks to business concerns) have been excluded both from the quantitative measures of credit activity and from the descriptive and analytical portions of the text. To include credits made by the Federal Reserve Banks purely in the exercise of their duties as central banks would have brought the whole field of monetary and credit policy within the scope of the study. The decision against doing so does not in any way imply, of course, that the Reserve Banks do not exercise a powerful effect, as credit agencies, on the economy. It is believed, however, that for analytical purposes the influence of Federal Reserve operations on the economy, and similarly the influence of what are termed here the credit programs of the federal government, are better viewed separately than when merged into a single aggregate.

In all of the instances cited above, the basic decision was made on conceptual grounds or for the practical reason that to include certain programs would have widened the scope of the study beyond manageable limits. In certain other cases programs have been excluded for practical reasons of a more mundane character, namely, the impossibility of compiling adequate data on them. It may be hard to believe that there should be no means of determining, even after persistent inquiry, how much was disbursed under federal programs that involved millions of dollars, but this is the case. It is perhaps small comfort to be able to report that the totals involved are not so large as to affect the conclusions of the study on the economic effects of federal credit activities.

In order to afford a quick view of the field of study, all agencies whose activities have been included are shown in Table 1, classified in three ways: (1) according to whether they were active or inactive as of the end of 1953; (2) whether they are direct federal agencies—designated F—or federally sponsored agencies—designated FS; and (3) according to the sector of the economy—agriculture, business, financial institutions, housing, minor governmental units, or miscellaneous—which they mainly serve. This table is followed by two listings, one of the specific programs covered in the study and the other of programs that for indicated reasons have been excluded.

TABLE 1

Federal and Federally Sponsored Credit Agencies, Classified by Economic Sector They Mainly Serve and by Active or Inactive Status as of December 31, 1953

Agriculture	*Business*
ACTIVE	**ACTIVE**
Banks for Cooperatives and Central Bank for Cooperatives (FS 1933)	Army and Navy Depts. (F 1942)
Commodity Credit Corp. (F 1933)	Atomic Energy Commission (F 1951)
Farmers Home Adm. (F 1946)	Dept. of Airforce (F 1951)
Federal Farm Mortgage Corp. (F 1934)	Dept. of Commerce (F 1951)
Federal Intermediate Credit Banks (FS 1923)	Export-Import Bank of Washington (F 1934)
Federal Land Banks (FS 1917)	Federal Reserve Banks (FS 1934)
Production Credit Corps. (FS 1933)	General Services Adm. (F 1951)
Rural Electrification Adm. (F 1935)	Maritime Adm. (F 1950)
	Small Business Adm. (F 1953) (also Misc.)
	Virgin Islands Corp. (F 1949) (also Agric.)
INACTIVE	**INACTIVE**
Agricultural Marketing Act Revolving Fund, FCA (F 1929)	Defense Materials Procurement Agency (F 1951)
Crop Production and Seed Loan Office, Dept. of Agriculture (F 1918)	Director General of Railroads (F 1919)
Electric Home and Farm Authority (F 1935)	Interstate Commerce Commission (F 1920)
Electric Home and Farm Authority, Inc. (F 1934)	Reconstruction Finance Corp. (F 1932) (also Agric., Financial Inst., Minor Govt. Units, and Misc.)
Emergency Crop and Feed Loan Div., FCA (F 1933)	Smaller War Plants Corp. (F 1942)
Farm Security Adm. (F 1937)	U.S. Maritime Commission (F 1936)
Farmers Seed Loan Office (F 1931)	U.S. Shipping Board (F 1921)
Land Bank Commissioner (F 1933)	U.S. Shipping Board Bureau (F 1933)
Regional Agricultural Credit Corps. (F 1932)	
Resettlement Adm. (F 1935)	
Rural Rehabilitation Div., Federal Emergency Relief Adm. (F 1934)	
Tennessee Valley Associated Cooperatives, Inc. (F 1934)	
War Finance Corp. (F 1918) (also Business and Financial Inst.)	

(*Continued on next page*)

TABLE 1 *(continued)*

Financial Institutions	Housing	Minor Governmental Units	Miscellaneous
ACTIVE	ACTIVE	ACTIVE	ACTIVE
Federal Home Loan Banks (FS 1932) Treasury Dept. (F 1933) (also Misc.)	Federal Housing Adm. (F 1934) (also Financial Inst.) Federal National Mortgage Assn. (F 1938)	Housing and Home Finance Agency (F 1950) (also Business, Housing, and Misc.) Public Housing Adm. (F 1947)	Bureau of Indian Affairs, Dept. of Interior (F 1911) Puerto Rico Reconstruction Adm. (F 1936) Veterans' Adm. (F 1930) (also Agric., Business, and Housing)
	INACTIVE	INACTIVE	
	Defense Homes Corp. (F 1941) Home Owners' Loan Corp. (F 1933) (also Financial Inst.) RFC Mortgage Company (F 1935)	Bureau of Community Facilities (F 1942) Community Facilities Service, GSA (F 1949) Federal Emergency Adm. of Public Works (F 1933) (also Business) Federal Public Housing Authority (F 1942) Inland and Coastwise Waterways Service, War Dept. (F 1921) Inland Waterways Corp. (F 1924) Public Works Adm. (F 1939) (also Business) Tennessee Valley Authority (F 1934) U.S. Housing Authority (F 1937)	INACTIVE Disaster Loan Corp. (F 1937) Federal Security Agency, Office of Education (F 1942) Prencinradio, Inc. (F 1943) U.S. Veterans' Bureau (F 1920)

F indicates direct federal agencies.

FS indicates federally sponsored agencies.

Date in parentheses is the year in which the agency in question was established or the year in which the earliest of its credit programs covered in this study (whether currently active or inactive) was initiated. Where a currently active agency was preceded by one or more now inactive agencies, the latter are included in the "inactive" group; where an agency currently inactive was preceded by one or more other agencies, also inactive, the agency and its predecessors are listed as inactive. The classification of agencies as active or inactive has reference exclusively to their credit-granting activities. Inactive agencies are those not now extending credits, though some of them have loans still outstanding; many of them are still quite active in functions other than credit extension.

NATURE AND SCOPE

I. PROGRAMS INCLUDED IN THE TABULATIONS

* For programs excluded, see List II, pages 19-25.
** See page 5.

Agency	Type or Purpose of Program	Economic Sector Served

A. Direct Agencies of the Federal Government

ATOMIC ENERGY COMMISSION
Guarantee of loans under Sec. 301 of the Defense Production Act of 1950 — Business

BUREAU OF COMMUNITY FACILITIES
Federal Works Agency (transferred as Community Facilities Service to the General Services Administration; currently administered by Housing and Home Finance Agency)

Lanham Act loans for construction of community facilities in connection with defense housing projects — Minor Governmental Units

*BUREAU OF INDIAN AFFAIRS
Department of the Interior
Loans to encourage industry and self-support among Indians, made under yearly appropriations beginning in 1911 (data available only since June 30, 1934) — Miscellaneous

Loans for educational purposes under act of June 18, 1934 — Miscellaneous

Loans to Indians and Indian organizations (including tribes, credit associations, and cooperative associations) from a revolving fund established under acts of June 18, 1934 and June 28, 1936 — Miscellaneous

Loans for emergency relief and rehabilitation — Miscellaneous

**COMMODITY CREDIT CORPORATION
Loans to finance the marketing of agricultural commodities — Agriculture
Loans for the construction or expansion of farm storage facilities — Agriculture
Guarantee of loans for the marketing of agricultural commodities — Agriculture

DEFENSE HOMES CORPORATION
Federal Public Housing Authority of the National Housing Agency
Loans for housing in defense areas — Housing

DEPARTMENT OF AIRFORCE
Guarantee of loans under Sec. 301 of the Defense Production Act of 1950 — Business

*DEPARTMENT OF ARMY
Loans to war contractors for production purposes during World War II — Business

(Continued on next page)

9

I. PROGRAMS INCLUDED IN THE TABULATIONS (*continued*)

Agency	Type or Purpose of Program	Economic Sector Served
*DEPARTMENT OF ARMY (*cont.*)		
	Purchases of loans guaranteed under Regulation V during World War II	Business
	Purchases of loans guaranteed under Sec. 301 of the Defense Production Act of 1950	Business
	Guarantee of loans to war contractors under Regulation V during World War II	Business
	Guarantee of loans under Sec. 301 of the Defense Production Act of 1950	Business
DEPARTMENT OF COMMERCE		
	Guarantee of loans under Sec. 301 of the Defense Production Act of 1950	Business
*DEPARTMENT OF NAVY		
	Purchases of loans guaranteed under Regulation V during World War II	Business
	Purchases of loans guaranteed under Sec. 301 of the Defense Production Act of 1950	Business
	Guarantee of loans to war contractors under Regulation V during World War II	Business
	Guarantee of loans under Sec. 301 of the Defense Production Act of 1950	Business
*DIRECTOR GENERAL OF RAILROADS and the INTERSTATE COMMERCE COMMISSION		
	Operating loans to railroads under Sec. 7 of the Federal Control Act of 1918 and Sec. 207 of the Transportation Act of 1920	Business
	Equipment trust notes taken by Director General after World War I	Business
	ICC loans to railroads under Sec. 210 of the Transportation Act of 1920	Business
DISASTER LOAN CORPORATION (transferred to RFC in 1945)		
	Loans to victims of floods and other catastrophes	Miscellaneous
ELECTRIC HOME AND FARM AUTHORITY (successor to Electric Home and Farm Authority, Inc.; transferred to RFC in 1942)		
	Loans for sale and installation of electrical and gas facilities and equipment	Agriculture
EXPORT–IMPORT BANK OF WASHINGTON		
	Loans to finance exports and imports and to assist in reconstruction, development, and stabilization of foreign economies	Business
	Loans and participation loans under Sec. 302 of the Defense Production Act of 1950, to private business concerns operating in foreign countries	Business

(*Continued on next page*)

10

I. PROGRAMS INCLUDED IN THE TABULATIONS (*continued*)

Agency / Type or Purpose of Program	Economic Sector Served
FARM CREDIT ADMINISTRATION, AGRICULTURAL MARKETING ACT REVOLVING FUND (formerly administered by Federal Farm Board)	
Loans to cooperative associations to finance construction or purchase of physical facilities or to refinance debt incurred in acquiring such facilities	Agriculture
Marketing and operating loans to farmers' cooperatives	Agriculture
Loans to stabilization corporations to support commodity prices	Agriculture
FARM CREDIT ADMINISTRATION, EMERGENCY CROP AND FEED LOAN DIVISION (successor to Crop Production and Seed Loan Office, Department of Agriculture; currently administered by the Farmers Home Administration)	
Operating loans to owners of small farms in drought- and flood-damaged areas and for other emergency purposes	Agriculture
Orchard rehabilitation loans	Agriculture
FARMERS HOME ADMINISTRATION (successor to the Farm Security Administration, the Resettlement Administration, and the Rural Rehabilitation Division, Federal Emergency Relief Administration)	
Loans to facilitate the purchase, enlargement, and development of family-type farms	Agriculture
Loans to finance construction or repair of farm houses and buildings	Agriculture
Receivables from individuals purchasing surplus property of rural rehabilitation projects	Agriculture
Operating and production loans to farmers and stockmen	Agriculture
Water facilities loans to farmers, ranchers, and cooperatives	Agriculture
Loans to cooperative associations for rehabilitation purposes	Agriculture
Production disaster and economic emergency loans	Agriculture
Insurance of mortgage loans for the purchase, enlargement, and development of family-type farms	Agriculture
FARMERS SEED LOAN OFFICE (transferred to the Farmers Home Administration)	
Loans to farmers and stockmen to purchase stock in agricultural credit and livestock loan corporations (1931)	Agriculture
FEDERAL FARM MORTGAGE CORPORATION (Land Bank Commissioner)	
Farm mortgage loans	Agriculture
Credit extended in connection with the sale of properties acquired through foreclosure	Agriculture

(*Continued on next page*)

11

I. PROGRAMS INCLUDED IN THE TABULATIONS (*continued*)

Agency	Type or Purpose of Program	Economic Sector Served
FEDERAL HOUSING ADMINISTRATION		
	Credit extended in connection with the sale of properties acquired through foreclosure	Housing
	Purchases of defaulted Title I notes and of mortgages assigned under various insurance funds	Housing
	Loans to financial institutions insured under Title I, Sec. 2 as authorized by Sec. 3 of Title I of the National Housing Act	Financial Institutions
	Insurance of property improvement loans under the National Housing Act of 1934	Housing
	Insurance of home mortgage loans under the 1934 Act and its wartime and postwar provisions	Housing
	Insurance of mortgage loans on cooperative housing projects, beginning 1950	Housing
	Insurance of mortgage loans on rental housing projects under the 1934 act and its wartime and postwar provisions	Housing
	Insurance of short-term loans to finance production of prefabricated houses after World War II	Housing
	Insurance of mortgage loans on publicly constructed housing sold after World War II	Housing
	Insurance of mortgage loans for housing in critical defense areas after 1951	Housing
FEDERAL NATIONAL MORTGAGE ASSOCIATION		
	Purchases of FHA-insured and VA-guaranteed mortgage loans; before 1948, restricted to mortgages secured by properties constructed after January 1, 1937	Housing
	Mortgage loans, made under FHA insurance, on rental-housing projects	Housing
	Mortgage loans, made under FHA insurance, on Alaskan properties	Housing
FEDERAL SECURITY AGENCY Office of Education (currently administered by the Department of Health, Education, and Welfare)		
	Loans to students enrolled in accelerated courses during the war emergency period	Miscellaneous
*****GENERAL SERVICES ADMINISTRATION**		
	Guarantee of loans under Sec. 301 of the Defense Production Act of 1950 and letters of credit issued to finance the overseas procurement of essential commodities under Sec. 303 (transferred from Defense Materials Procurement Agency)	Business
HOME OWNERS' LOAN CORPORATION		
	Loans to refinance defaulted or distressed mortgages of homeowners, and credit extended in connection with the sale of properties acquired through foreclosure	Housing

(*Continued on next page*)

I. PROGRAMS INCLUDED IN THE TABULATIONS *(continued)*

Agency	Type or Purpose of Program	Economic Sector Served
HOME OWNERS' LOAN CORPORATION *(cont.)*	Purchases of shares of insured federal and state savings and loan associations	Financial Institutions
HOUSING AND HOME FINANCE AGENCY		
Office of the Administrator	Loans to Alaska Housing Authority for residential construction and property improvement	Housing
	Loans to communities and local public agencies for slum clearance and urban redevelopment	Minor Governmental Units
	Loans to local communities in critical defense areas for construction of community facilities	Minor Governmental Units
	Loans made under the War Mobilization and Reconversion Act of 1944 and Public Law 352 for advance planning of large-scale public works	Minor Governmental Units
	Loans to manufacturers of prefabricated housing under Housing Act of 1948 and Public Law 139 of 1950 (transferred from RFC)	Minor Governmental Units
	Loans to educational institutions for housing facilities for students and faculty	Miscellaneous
*INLAND WATERWAYS CORPORATION (successor to Inland and Coastwise Waterways Service, War Department)	Loans to states, municipalities, and transportation companies for construction of terminal facilities	Minor Governmental Units
*MARITIME ADMINISTRATION (successor to the U.S. Shipping Board; the U.S. Shipping Board Bureau; and the U.S. Maritime Commission)	Construction loans to American shipowners	Business
	Sales of ships on a deferred payment basis	Business
	Insurance of mortgage loans to U.S. shipowners	Business
PRENCINRADIO, INCORPORATED	Loans to radio stations in Uruguay	Miscellaneous
	Advances through the Banco de Mexico as trustee to finance the purchase of motion picture production equipment	Miscellaneous
*PUBLIC HOUSING ADMINISTRATION (successor to the Federal Public Housing Authority and the U.S. Housing Authority)	Loans to local housing authorities for low-rent housing and slum clearance projects	Minor Governmental Units
	Guarantee of short-term notes and long-term obligations sold to private investors by local housing authorities to finance construction and operating costs of PHA-approved low-rent housing projects	Minor Governmental Units

(Continued on next page)

13

I. PROGRAMS INCLUDED IN THE TABULATIONS (*continued*)

Agency	Type or Purpose of Program	Economic Sector Served

PUBLIC WORKS ADMINISTRATION
Federal Works Agency (successor to the
Federal Emergency Administration of
Public Works)

	Maintenance and operating loans to railroads	Business
	Loans to states, municipalities, other public bodies, and private firms for construction of civic buildings and other community facilities	Minor Governmental Units
	Loans to limited dividend housing corporations and to states, municipalities, etc., for low-cost housing	Minor Governmental Units

PUERTO RICO RECONSTRUCTION ADMINISTRATION

	Rural rehabilitation loans to individuals and cooperative associations	Miscellaneous

*RECONSTRUCTION FINANCE CORPORATION

	Loans to finance storage and marketing of agricultural commodities and for livestock marketing	Agriculture
	Loans to finance exports of agricultural surpluses	Agriculture
	Loans to railroads	Business
	Loans, and participations in loans, to business enterprises, including those engaged in defense production	Business
	Loans to the fishing industry	Business
	Loans for mining, milling, and smelting of ores, including such loans to aid in national defense	Business
	Loans to processors or distributors of farm products subject to processing taxes	Business
	Loans to business through mortgage loan companies and banks	Business
	Loans and participations in loans, to prefabricated housing manufacturers.	Business
	Loans on rationed articles and commodities	Business
	Contract Settlement Act loans	Business
	Loans, and participations in loans, under commitments outstanding when the Smaller War Plants Corporation was dissolved	Business
	Loans, and participations in loans, to business enterprises under Sec. 302 and Sec. 714 of the Defense Production Act of 1950	Business
	Loans to aid in civilian defense as authorized under Sec. 409 of the Federal Civil Defense Act	Business
	Loans to banks and trust companies, savings and loan associations, insurance companies, mortgage loan companies, credit unions, joint stock land banks, and agricultural and livestock credit corporations	Financial Institutions
	Loans to aid in reorganization of closed banks and trust companies	Financial Institutions
	Construction loans to public agencies, including those for defense projects	Minor Governmental Units

(*Continued on next page*)

I. PROGRAMS INCLUDED IN THE TABULATIONS (*continued*)

Agency	Type or Purpose of Program	Economic Sector Served
RECONSTRUCTION FINANCE CORPORATION (*cont.*)		
	Loans to establish state funds for securing repayment of deposits of public moneys in banks and other depositories	Minor Governmental Units
	Loans to refinance obligations of public school districts	Minor Governmental Units
	Loans for payment of teachers' salaries	Minor Governmental Units
	Loans for self-liquidating public works	Minor Governmental Units
	Loans to drainage, levee, and similar districts	Minor Governmental Units
	Loans for relief and work relief under the Emergency Relief and Construction Act of 1932 as amended	Minor Governmental Units
	Loans to repair damage caused by floods, tornadoes, and other catastrophes	Miscellaneous
	Deferred participations in business loans, including loans to aid in national defense	Business
	Deferred participations in Contract Settlement Act loans	Business
	Deferred participations in loans made in connection with the transfer of certain functions of the SWPC to the RFC	Business
	Deferred participations in loans authorized under Secs. 302 and 714 of the Defense Production Act of 1950	Business
	Deferred participations in loans for civilian defense authorized under Sec. 409 of the Federal Civil Defense Act	Business
	Subscriptions to or loans on preferred stock, and purchases of capital notes and debentures, of banks and trust companies	Financial Institutions
	Subscriptions to or loans on preferred stock of insurance companies	Financial Institutions
RFC MORTGAGE COMPANY (subsidiary of RFC)		
	Mortgage loans, and participations in loans, for construction or refinancing of income-producing (mainly large residential) properties	Housing
	Loans to distressed holders of first mortgage bonds or certificates on income-producing properties	Housing
	Loans made under FHA insurance, and participations in such loans, for low-cost housing	Housing
	Loans, and participation loans, to owners of business properties adversely affected by war conditions, to assist in meeting debt service and other carrying charges	Housing
	Purchases of FHA-insured and VA-guaranteed mortgages on residential properties; after establishment of FNMA, purchases confined to mortgages secured by properties constructed before January 1, 1937	Housing

(*Continued on next page*)

I. PROGRAMS INCLUDED IN THE TABULATIONS (*continued*)

Agency	Type or Purpose of Program	Economic Sector Served
RFC MORTGAGE COMPANY (*cont.*) (subsidiary of RFC)		
	Purchases of mortgages on income-producing (mainly large residential) properties	Housing
REGIONAL AGRICULTURAL CREDIT CORPORATIONS (transferred to Farmers Home Administration)		
	Short-term production loans to farmers and stockmen	Agriculture
RURAL ELECTRIFICATION ADMINISTRATION		
	Loans for construction of electric facilities, purchase and installation of electrical appliances and plumbing and construction or expansion of telephone facilities in rural areas	Agriculture
*SMALL BUSINESS ADMINISTRATION		
	Loans to victims of floods or other disasters	Miscellaneous
SMALLER WAR PLANTS CORPORATION (transferred to RFC)		
	Loans, and participations in loans, to business concerns engaged in production of war goods and essential civilian goods	Business
TENNESSEE VALLEY ASSOCIATED COOPERATIVES, INC.		
	Loans to assist in development of cooperatives in the Tennessee Valley	Agriculture
	Purchases of shares in Tennessee Valley cooperatives	Agriculture
*TENNESSEE VALLEY AUTHORITY		
	Loans to municipalities and cooperative wholesale power distribution companies for the acquisition and operation of power plants and distribution facilities	Minor Governmental Units
*TREASURY DEPARTMENT		
	Loans to District of Columbia for civilian defense during World War II	Miscellaneous
	Loans to District of Columbia for construction of public works	Miscellaneous
	Purchases of shares of federal savings and loan associations	Financial Institutions
*U.S. MARITIME COMMISSION (now Maritime Administration, which see)		
	Guarantee of loans to war contractors under Regulation V during World War II	Business
*VETERANS' ADMINISTRATION (successor to U.S. Veterans' Bureau)		
	Loans for purchase, construction, or improvement of rural and farm dwellings	Housing
	Credit extended in connection with the sale of properties acquired through foreclosure	Housing

(*Continued on next page*)

I. PROGRAMS INCLUDED IN THE TABULATIONS (*continued*)

Agency	Type or Purpose of Program	Economic Sector Served

VETERANS' ADMINISTRATION
(successor to U.S. Veterans' Bureau) (*cont.*)

	Loans to policy holders of U.S. Government and National Service Life Insurance	Miscellaneous
	Guarantee of loans to veterans for the purchase or improvement of farm properties	Agriculture
	Guarantee of loans to veterans for the establishment or expansion of businesses	Business
	Guarantee of home mortgage loans to veterans	Housing

VIRGIN ISLANDS CORPORATION
Department of the Interior

	Loans to aid agriculture in the Virgin Islands	Agriculture
	Loans to aid business in the Virgin Islands	Business

WAR FINANCE CORPORATION

	Loans to cattle raisers under Sec. 9 of the War Finance Corporation Act of 1918	Agriculture
	Loans to livestock loan companies, cooperative associations, banks, and financial institutions under Sec. 24 of the Agricultural Credits Act of 1921	Agriculture
	Loans through banks to public utilities, industrial corporations, railroads, and canning companies under Sec. 9 of the War Finance Corporation Act	Business
	Export advances mainly under Secs. 21 and 22 of the Agricultural Credits Act	Business
	Loans to banks and building and loan associations under Secs. 7 and 8 of the War Finance Corporation Act	Financial Institutions

B. *Federally Sponsored Agencies*

BANKS FOR COOPERATIVES and the
CENTRAL BANK FOR COOPERATIVES

	Operating loans to cooperative associations, and loans to finance the marketing of farm products and for the construction or acquisition of marketing facilities	Agriculture

FEDERAL HOME LOAN BANKS

	Loans to savings and loan, building and loan, and homestead associations, savings and cooperative banks, and insurance companies that are members of the Federal Home Loan Bank system	Financial Institutions

FEDERAL INTERMEDIATE CREDIT BANKS

	Loans to, and discounts for, production credit associations, agricultural and livestock credit corporations, and commercial banks making farm production loans	Agriculture
	Loans to farmers' cooperative associations for production and general farm operating purposes	Agriculture

(*Continued on next page*)

I. PROGRAMS INCLUDED IN THE TABULATIONS (*continued*)

Agency	Type or Purpose of Program	Economic Sector Served
FEDERAL LAND BANKS		
	Mortgage loans secured by farm real estate	Agriculture
	Credit extended in connection with the sale of properties acquired through foreclosure	Agriculture
*FEDERAL RESERVE BANKS		
	Loans, and participations in loans, to industrial and commercial businesses for working capital under Sec. 13b of the Federal Reserve Act (beginning 1934)	Business
PRODUCTION CREDIT CORPORATIONS		
	Purchases of Class A stock of production credit associations	Agriculture

II. PROGRAMS EXCLUDED FROM THE TABULATIONS

† For programs included, see List I, pages 9-18.

Agency	Excluded Program or Activity	Reason for Exclusion

A. Direct Agencies of the Federal Government

ALASKA PUBLIC WORKS
Department of the Interior

	Partly repayable advances to territorial governments or other public bodies for public works	Approximates more closely a grant than a loan function

†BUREAU OF INDIAN AFFAIRS
Department of the Interior

	Livestock loans made in kind	Data not available

DEFENSE MINERALS EXPLORATION
ADMINISTRATION
Department of the Interior

	Advances for costs incurred in development and production of strategic minerals and metals under Section 303(a) of the Defense Production Act of 1950	Lending incidental to developing new sources of mineral supply

DEFENSE SUPPLIES CORPORATION

	Loans to aid in producing supplies or facilities (or obtaining manpower resources therefor) necessary to the war effort	Lending incidental to procurement and stockpiling functions; apparently not a programmed activity

†DEPARTMENT OF ARMY

	Credit extended in connection with the disposition of World War I surplus	Credit incidental to liquidation operations

†DEPARTMENT OF NAVY

	Credit extended in connection with the disposition of World War I surplus	Credit incidental to liquidation operations

†DIRECTOR GENERAL OF RAILROADS

	Operating loans to railroads under Section 12 of the Federal Control Act of 1918	Annual data not available

FOREIGN OPERATIONS ADMINISTRATION
(successor to the Mutual Security Agency,
the Economic Cooperation Administration,
the Technical Cooperation Administration,
and the Institute of Inter-American Affairs)

	Loans to foreign governments for economic, technical, and military procurement purposes considered essential to the mutual security and defense program as authorized under the Economic Cooperation Act, the Mutual Security Acts, and the Mutual Defense Assistance Act	Loans only to foreign countries or their agents

(Continued on next page)

II. PROGRAMS EXCLUDED FROM THE TABULATIONS *(continued)*

Agency	Excluded Program or Activity	Reason for Exclusion

FOREIGN OPERATIONS ADMINISTRATION *(cont.)*

Currency transfer guarantees in connection with approved foreign investments of American firms — Guarantees relate to non-lending activities

Guarantees against loss from expropriation or confiscation of approved foreign industrial investments of American firms as authorized by Sec. 111(b)(3) of the Economic Cooperation Act of 1948, as amended and Sec. 520 of the Mutual Security Act of 1951, as amended — Guarantees relate to non-lending activities

†GENERAL SERVICES ADMINISTRATION

Advances to contractors for materials procurement and expansion of productive capacity — Lending incidental to stockpiling activities

Notes receivable financing in connection with sale of government-owned surplus property — Lending incidental to liquidation operations

Guarantees, to producers, of sales of machine tools manufactured under pool order agreements — Guarantees relate to non-lending activities

Guarantees of recovery of construction costs in expanding defense plant capacity — Guarantees relate to non-lending activities

Investment in securities of public power and irrigation projects (transferred from the Federal Works Agency in 1940) — Avoidance of double counting

†INLAND WATERWAYS CORPORATION

Credit extended in connection with the disposition of the Corporation's real property — Credit incidental to liquidation operations

†MARITIME ADMINISTRATION

Loans by the U.S. Emergency Fleet Corporation for housing of shipyard workers as authorized by the act of March 1, 1918 — Annual data not available

Loans to transportation and public utility companies for expanding facilities in the vicinity of shipyards during World War I — Annual data not available

Loans to contractors for repairs and other miscellaneous purposes — Annual data not available

NATIONAL CAPITAL PLANNING COMMISSION
(successor to the National Capital Park and Planning Commission and the National Capital Park Commission)

Loan for the acquisition of land in Washington, D.C. and its environs (embracing the states of Virginia and Maryland) to provide a comprehensive park, parkway, and playground system for the city as set forth in the George Washington Memorial Parkway Act of May 29, 1930 — Annual data not available

(Continued on next page)

II. PROGRAMS EXCLUDED FROM THE TABULATIONS (*continued*)

Agency	Excluded Program or Activity	Reason for Exclusion
†PUBLIC HOUSING ADMINISTRATION	Credit extended in connection with the disposition of emergency housing erected under: (a) public war housing program of the Lanham Act; (b) veterans re-use housing program of the Lanham Act; (c) homes conversion program; (d) subsistence homesteads and greentowns programs transferred from Farm Security Administration; (e) farm labor camp program transferred from Farmers Home Administration; (f) PWA program; (g) Surplus Property Act loans in connection with the disposition of World War II surplus	Credit incidental to liquidation of government-owned properties
PUERTO RICAN HURRICANE RELIEF LOAN SECTION Department of the Interior (successor to the Puerto Rican Hurricane Relief Commission)	Loans to inhabitants of Puerto Rico for relief from 1928 hurricane damage	Annual data not available
†RECONSTRUCTION FINANCE CORPORATION	Loans to foreign governments	Foreign loans
	Loans to other federal agencies	Interagency activity
	Purchases from Public Works Administration of securities of municipalities and of railroads	Interagency activity
RUBBER DEVELOPMENT CORPORATION	Loans to producers of natural rubber for increasing supply during World War II	Lending incidental to stockpiling operations
†SMALL BUSINESS ADMINISTRATION	Loans, and participations in loans, to small business concerns for working capital expansion, and other purposes	Agency organized in 1953; no disbursements under this program by end of that year
SPRUCE PRODUCTION CORPORATION	Advances in connection with procurement of war supplies	Lending incidental to procurement activities
STATE DEPARTMENT	Loans to indigent Americans stranded abroad	Annual data not available
†TENNESSEE VALLEY AUTHORITY	Credit extended in connection with the sale of Norris village	Credit incidental to liquidation of government-owned property
†TREASURY DEPARTMENT	Loans to foreign governments	Foreign loans
	Loans to other foreign agencies	Interagency activity
	Advances to Federal Reserve Banks for industrial loans	Avoidance of double counting

(*Continued on next page*)

II. PROGRAMS EXCLUDED FROM THE TABULATIONS (*continued*)

Agency	Excluded Program or Activity	Reason for Exclusion
U.S. COMMERCIAL COMPANY	Loans in connection with the prevention of Axis control of world markets and sources of raw materials	Lending incidental to procurement activities
U.S. HOUSING CORPORATION	Credit extended in connection with the disposition of government-owned housing undertaken during World War I	Credit incidental to liquidation of government-owned assets
U.S. INFORMATION AGENCY (formerly administered by the State Department)	Guarantees of convertibility of receipts from the production and distribution of informational media in foreign countries as authorized under the Economic Cooperation Act of 1948 and the Mutual Security Act of 1951	Guarantees relate to non-lending activities
†VETERANS' ADMINISTRATION	Loans arising from federal guarantees of premium payments on private commercial life insurance held by servicemen as authorized by the Soldiers' and Sailors' Civil Relief Act	Annual data not available
	Loans to disabled veterans enrolled in vocational rehabilitation courses	Annual data not available

B. Federally Sponsored Agencies

Agency	Excluded Program or Activity	Reason for Exclusion
FEDERAL DEPOSIT INSURANCE CORPORATION	Loans to, or purchases of assets from, an insured bank to facilitate a merger or consolidation and thereby to reduce the probable loss to the Corporation	Loans incidental to liquidation operations
	Loans to, or purchases of assets from, closed or reopened insured banks in the interest of providing adequate local banking services	Loans incidental to liquidation operations
†FEDERAL INTERMEDIATE CREDIT BANKS	Loans to, and discounts for, regional agricultural credit corporations and the central and regional banks for cooperatives	Avoidance of double counting; separate series given for RACC's and BC's
†FEDERAL RESERVE BANKS	Advances to, and discounts for, member banks	Involves monetary and credit policies beyond scope of present study

(*Continued on next page*)

II. PROGRAMS EXCLUDED FROM THE TABULATIONS *(continued)*

Agency	Excluded Program or Activity	Reason for Exclusion
FEDERAL SAVINGS AND LOAN INSURANCE CORPORATION	Advances in the form of reimbursable contributions to distressed thrift and home-financing institutions	Loans incidental to liquidation operations and carry only a contingent repayment commitment
PRODUCTION CREDIT ASSOCIATIONS	Loans for general farm operating and production purposes	Avoidance of double counting. Discounts for, and loans to, PCA's are included under FICB data (see preceding list, section B)

Major Issues Raised by Federal Credit Programs

Although no position is taken in this study on the policy issues raised by federal credit-granting and related activities, the data and analyses which it presents should clarify certain vital aspects of these problems. The major issues involved are the following.

CREDIT EXTENSION AS A FUNCTION OF GOVERNMENT

Perhaps the paramount issue is whether it is appropriate at all for the federal government to engage in direct lending or in credit-insuring or guaranteeing activities. Different people, with different conceptions of the proper role of government in the social and economic process, can take quite widely separated views on this essentially controversial question. But it should be clear to all that the question cannot be debated fairly unless the precise nature and objectives of the various credit programs are understood. The fact is that the programs represent attempts to solve a number of different types of problems, and one's views as to whether they are a proper function of government may well vary from one to another. What have these purposes been?

The most familiar was to counteract depression. To some extent federal lending was used for that purpose directly after World War I, but not until the thirties was it employed extensively to that end, notably in the operations of the Reconstruction Finance Corporation. It was thought that this agency, set up in 1932, could counteract depression by extending credit to businesses in key sectors of the economy: specifically, by aiding commercial banks and insurance companies, and certain large and ramifying businesses such as railroads. The inadequacy of that policy was soon recognized, however, and the scope of RFC's lending authority was widened to accommodate any enterprise in which there was an apparent need for credit, provided there was some prospect that the loan would increase employment and provided there was sufficient security to assure its repayment. With the improvement in economic conditions after the mid-thirties the counter-cyclical objective of federal lending tended to be displaced by other purposes, but it came to the surface again in 1937–1938 and in 1949–1950 as the demand for financial assistance from concerns experiencing economic adversity increased sharply.

The second major objective of federal credit programs has been to provide needed credit services which are held to be unavailable, for one reason or another, through the private financial system. This is the "gap" basis of governmental action, and it has been present to some degree in nearly all federal programs. It is related to the counter-cyclical purpose in the sense that gaps are likely to appear most exigent during depression conditions, but it goes further. The argument is frequently made that some sort of federal action is needed, even in times of economic prosperity, to supply credit to small or beginning enterprises, on the ground that their needs are inadequately met through private financial channels. Sections of the text dealing with the services of federal and federally sponsored agencies present much data useful in appraising the extent to which the various programs have filled gaps in the credit system, and for judging the merits of the arguments that revolve about these activities.

Emergency conditions have provided a third basis for federal extension of credit. In a sense, they too are gaps, but here there is no thought that private financial agencies should provide the needed credit services. The most familiar emergency credit programs arise from war conditions; others are called into action by calamities of nature—floods, tornadoes, and the like. RFC loans to war contractors, the guarantee under Regulation V of similar loans made by private lenders, and RFC's wartime programs of small loans to finance mineral exploration and of loans to dealers whose inventories were frozen in connection with the control of strategic materials exemplify the first; RFC's disaster loans and orchard rehabilitation loans exemplify the second. Clearly, one's views as to the need for particular programs of this type will depend on one's appraisal of the seriousness of the emergency and the merits of attempting to meet it by a credit program. And there is also the possibility to be kept in mind that a program may outlast the emergency conditions that brought it into being. One aim of the materials that follow is to show what types of services have been provided by the credit programs stemming from such emergencies.

A fourth general objective underlying federal credit activities is the desire to give preferential treatment to some group or industry. Falling within this category are direct loan and loan guarantee programs for veterans, loans to municipalities for low-rent housing, loans and loan insurance for the shipping industry, farm purchase loans for tenants and relocation loans for owners of underimproved farms, and loans for students, Indians, cooperative associations of various kinds, and persons displaced by such federal activities as slum clearance. These programs vary widely and are not always clearly separable from those intended to fill gaps in the private financial system or to meet emergency needs; yet they have two distinguishing characteristics: the service is available only to a specifically defined group—often only for specified purposes—and on terms which, by deliberate policy, are usually more liberal than could be had for comparable credits in the competitive market. Whether such programs are a proper function of the federal government is obviously not an economic question, but their cost and their economic effect is; accordingly, these aspects will be discussed at appropriate points.

THE EFFECT OF FEDERAL CREDIT PROGRAMS ON
THE ALLOCATION OF ECONOMIC RESOURCES

It is presumably possible for the federal government, by focusing credit on specific areas, to influence the allocation of economic resources among different sectors and groups. The second major issue raised by federal credit activities, therefore, is whether they have in fact, caused resources to be allocated through the community in a manner significantly different from what would have resulted if credit had been available only through the channels of private finance, and if so, whether the changes have promoted the general welfare. More resources may be held in agriculture, for example, than would otherwise be employed in that sector of the economy. More resources may be placed in the hands of small and medium-sized businesses than these firms would command if only the funds of private lenders were at their disposal. Specific industries, or industries located in specific regions of the country, may be stimulated to expand output over what would be produced if credit from public sources were unavailable. A much argued point is whether the federal government, through credit extensions, should allow further access to economic resources to firms which have not prospered and which, lacking this aid, might be forced to liquidate. Although it is not the purpose of the present study to judge whether the public interest is served by such reallocations of resources, the factual materials bearing on their nature and extent—presented especially in Chapters 3 and 5 of Part I—should permit more informed judgments to be made on them.

THE ECONOMIC IMPACT OF FEDERAL CREDIT ACTIVITIES

The third major question raised by federal credit activities concerns their broad economic and financial effect. For example, have they been effective in bringing about economic recovery when used for that purpose? Have they had undesirable inflationary or deflationary effects? Have they been effectively coordinated with the stabilization activities of other agencies of government?

This range of questions is dealt with for all credit programs as a whole in Chapter 5 of Part I, and for the programs affecting the specific areas of agriculture, business, and housing in Chapters 6, 7, and 8 (Part II). They are exceedingly troublesome questions, for there is no fully satisfactory measure of the impact of federal credit activities on economy. Credit programs produce their effects simultaneously with those of other forces, and it is never possible to determine exactly what part of the joint effect may be attributed solely to them. However, the general quality of their effect can be ascertained; and it can be determined whether they have been effectively coordinated with the programs of other governmental agencies, or have been to an appreciable extent in conflict with them. This much the study attempts to do.

THE ORGANIZATION OF FEDERAL CREDIT AGENCIES

Finally, the possibility that federal credit programs have conflicted with other programs aimed at influencing economic activity raises questions as to how government should be organized to administer credit activities. This issue, also, involves more than purely economic considerations. Hence the present study cannot undertake to provide answers; but it may clarify certain aspects of the organizational problem by revealing the variety of programs involved and by showing how they differ, one from another, in terms of the credit services which they offer. Only with these facts in mind can specific reorganization proposals be properly evaluated.

CHAPTER 2

The Growth and Present Position of Federal Credit Programs

THE growth of federal credit programs has been so rapid that they now constitute what is in fact a second financial system, operating in part competitively with private finance and in part supporting and complementing the private financial system. The object of the present chapter is to give a brief factual account of the growth of these programs and to show their importance, especially from the standpoint of the amounts involved, relative to the activities of private lenders. Major subgroupings will be followed through but otherwise details will be kept to a minimum. The tabulations will distinguish between (a) programs administered by direct agencies of the federal government and by those that are quasi-public in nature, (b) direct government lending and the insurance or guarantee of loans made by private institutions, and (c) financial services rendered to different major sectors of the economy. A more detailed account of the growth of credit programs in the agriculture, business, and housing sectors is given in Part II, Chapters 6, 7, and 8, respectively.

The Growth of Federal Credit Programs

The statistical history of federal credit programs can be told most effectively when divided into two periods, 1917–1931 and 1932–1953. The activities were of relatively modest size in the first period and consisted mainly of lending by federally sponsored agencies; it was not until after 1932 that direct agencies of the federal government came into action as major instruments of policy, raising to a billion a year and more the volume of credit extended by all agencies. Also, it was only after 1932 that the insurance or guarantee of privately made loans was employed to supplement direct federal lending. The broad outlines of this statistical record are shown in Charts 1 and 2, the former showing the amount of credit outstanding and the latter the volume extended during each year.[1]

[1] The amounts entered under the basic categories in charts and tables of federal credit activities are as follows:

Loans cover (a) the full amounts of loans extended by specified federal and federally sponsored agencies; (b) the amounts disbursed to private lenders by federal

BEFORE 1932

For purposes of this account, federal credit activities n garded as originating in 1917. At that time they consisted of lending by the federal land banks, and only about $ was outstanding (Chart 1). This was a modest beginning; but steep growth followed. By the mid-twenties additional agencies, also of the federally sponsored type—the federal intermediate credit banks— were active, and some agencies of the federal government itself had entered the field; outstandings by then had reached $1.5 billion. This increase resulted largely from the refinancing of farm loans in the agricultural crisis following World War I and from loans to railroads as they were returned to private control after wartime nationalization.

The episode was short-lived, however, and from 1924 through 1929 the curve of total outstandings traced a level course. In fact, the holdings of direct federal agencies began to decline as early as 1922, and only the continued increase in outstandings of federally sponsored agencies kept up the total. But with provision of new credit for farm production purposes and price support in the Agricultural Marketing Act of 1929 the outstandings of direct federal agencies rose markedly, and total federal holdings reached $2.0 billion at the end of 1931, with direct agencies of the government accounting for the lesser share, about one-third.

As we shall see, the course and tempo of development then altered radically.

FROM 1932 THROUGH 1953

Picking the story up with the activities of federally sponsored agencies in 1932, it will be observed (Chart 1) that outstandings rose quickly to around $2.5 billion and stayed close to that level until 1942, when they began to decline. This wartime reduction in

---

agencies in purchasing outstanding loans made under federal insurance or guarantee; and (c) the amounts disbursed on loans made in participation with private lenders, mainly by direct federal agencies but also by the Federal Reserve Banks.

Loan insurance covers the full amounts of loans extended by private lenders and insured by federal agencies. *Loan guarantees* cover (a) the amounts federally guaranteed, ranging from 100 percent to seldom lower than 50 percent of a privately made loan; and (b) the amounts of the federal shares authorized under deferred participations, where the government stands ready to take up an agreed percentage of a privately made loan.

Stock purchases, included if identifiable as primarily credit aid, cover the amount of federal funds invested.

CHART 1

Federal Lending and Loan Insurance or Guarantees: Outstandings at Year Ends, 1917–1953

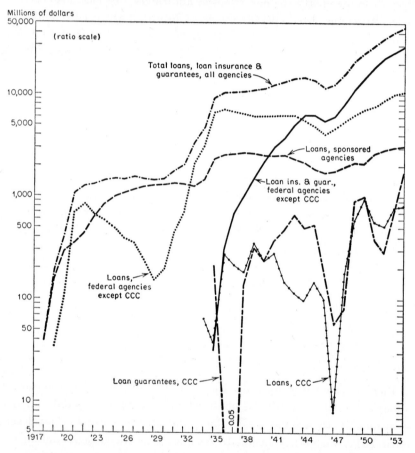

Stock purchases primarily for credit aid are included with loans; for further details, see Chapter 2, footnote 1. Data except for CCC are from Tables A-1 and A-2. Series for the Commodity Credit Corporation refer to its direct loans on commodities for price support purposes and (since 1949) for construction of storage facilities, or to its guarantees of similar loans made by other lenders, and are as given by the Department of Agriculture in "Agricultural Finance Review," Vol. 17, November 1954, pp. 92ff., with the 1933 direct loan figure from "Agricultural Statistics, 1952," p. 726.

CHART 2

Federal Lending and Loan Insurance or Guarantees: Annual Volume, 1917–1953

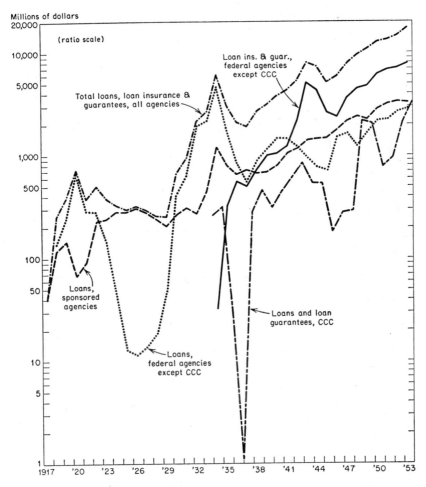

Stock purchases primarily for credit aid are included with loans; for further details, see Chapter 2, footnote 1. Data except for CCC refer to calendar year and are from Tables A-1 and A-2. Amounts of commodity and storage facility loans by the Commodity Credit Corporation, combined with amounts of similar loans made by other lenders under CCC guarantee, are shown for fiscal years, as supplied by the agency; calendar-year amounts for inclusion in the total line were estimated by linear interpolation (1933–1938) or were taken from data published annually by the Department of Agriculture in "Agricultural Statistics," adjusted in some years to exclude commodity purchases or loans not fully processed.

outstandings reflects the fact that they consisted mostly of farmers' obligations to federal land banks and that the farm prosperity of the war years made it possible to retire much of the long-term farm debt. After 1945, however, the curve is on the rise again—largely because of increased land bank activity, loans by the banks for co-operatives, and Federal Home Loan Bank loans to member institutions, mainly savings and loan associations—and by the end of 1953 it reached $3.1 billion.

Outstandings of agencies belonging wholly within the federal government, which at the end of 1931 had amounted to less than $720 million, in one year's time increased to $2.1 billion; and by the end of 1934 they had been swelled, in the government's massive effort to forestall economic depression and to moderate its impact on farmers, business concerns, and homeowners, to $6.5 billion. Equally significant, at no time except during World War II has the curve of outstandings shown more than a slight tendency to retreat. It makes little difference to this general account whether we include or exclude Commodity Credit Corporation loans in connection with farm price support. Although important in the sector they serve, they have formed only a minor part of total outstandings and guarantees of all the federal agencies combined.

There has been far less stability in the history of loan insurance and guarantees, programs which in recent years have added spectacularly to the scope of federal credit aid. Beginning with a modest $1 billion in the mid-thirties, outstandings increased more or less regularly until by 1950 they approached $19 billion and at the end of 1953 were about $30 billion. Though these amounts are not in all aspects commensurable with the totals for direct loans, they mark an area of federal protection and influence so large as to dominate the entire present picture of government credit activities.

In short, the recent record (1946 through 1953) shows slow but steady increase in the outstandings of loans by federally sponsored agencies, a more rapid increase in those of the strictly federal agencies, and, most striking of all, a continued sharp rise in the curve of federal insurance and guarantees.

The Relative Importance of Federal Lending

How important has federal credit been within the nation's total debt? A broad answer to this question is given in Table 2, which collects the available information on all components except the debt

TABLE 2

Outstanding Amounts of Direct Loans Held by Federal and Federally
Sponsored Agencies Compared with Net Private and Net State
and Local Debt at Decennial Years, 1920–1950

(*dollar figures in billions*)

	1920	*1930*	*1940*	*1950*
*Outstanding amounts of direct loans*a	$ 1.0	$ 1.8	$ 7.9	$ 10.2
Federal agencies	0.7	0.4	5.4	7.6
Federally sponsored agencies	0.3	1.3	2.4	2.6
Net private and net state and local				
*government debt*b	*86.6*	*136.3*	*113.2*	*190.0*
Net private debt	80.7	122.2	96.7	169.3
Net state and local government debt	5.9	14.1	16.5	20.7
Ratio of federal loans to net private				
and net state and local government debt	1.2%	1.3%	7.0%	5.4%
Federal agencies	0.8	0.3	4.8	4.0
Federally sponsored agencies	0.4	1.0	2.2	1.4

a Based on data in Tables A-1 and A-2. Amounts will not always add to totals
due to rounding.

b Data are from the *Survey of Current Business* (Department of Commerce),
September 1953, Table 1, p. 14. Net private debt includes the mortgage and nonmortgage obligations of individuals and noncorporate businesses, and the long-
term debt of corporate borrowers. Data for state and local government debt are
as of June 30 of each year; other data are for the year end.

owed by the federal government. The table shows at ten-year intervals
since 1920 the total amount owed by private borrowers and state
and local governments, and measures against that total the amounts
owed to federal and federally sponsored agencies under their direct
loan programs.

It will be seen at once that the high point in the relative importance
of the federal programs was reached in 1940, when outstanding loans
of agencies of the federal government itself accounted for 4.8 percent,
and such loans together with those of federally sponsored agencies,
for 7.0 percent, of the total net debt of individuals, businesses, and
state and local governments. These percentages were somewhat lower
in 1950, despite the increased dollar amount of federal outstandings,
for the reason that the volume of nonfederal debt grew much more
rapidly in the decade 1940–1950 than the volume of credit obtained
from federal and federally sponsored agencies. It is instructive also
to observe that over the three decades up to 1950 the growth in
relative importance was greater for the federal than for the federally

sponsored agencies. For strictly federal agencies the ratio of their outstandings to total net debt increased fivefold; for the quasi-public agencies, only three and a half times.

A different perspective is provided by Table 3, which distributes outstanding loans made under federal programs by major sector of the economy served (excluding miscellaneous programs), and compares them at ten-year intervals with the corresponding amounts for the chief types of private institutional lenders—commercial banks, mutual savings banks, insurance companies, and savings and loan associations. Again it is in 1940 that the over-all importance of federal lending appears relatively highest. In that year the outstandings of federal and federally sponsored agencies combined were one-seventh as large as the total for private lending institutions—the ratio having increased more than fivefold from 1920 to 1940. The decline in the ratio that occurred between 1940 and 1950 was due, as the absolute figures show, to the far more rapid growth of private institutional than of public lending.

The table also reveals that over-all figures comparing the amount of federal credit outstanding with that extended by private agencies mask important differences among different sectors of the economy. In agriculture and in lending to financial institutions, the programs of federal and federally sponsored agencies have attained substantial importance relative to private lending. For business, for minor governmental units, and for urban housing, outright federal lending has been minor as compared to financing by private institutions. These contrasts reveal how important it is, in judging the relative position of federal credit programs, to look separately at the different sectors of the economy to which their services are directed. Accordingly, we turn to the fields of agriculture, business, and urban housing.

AGRICULTURE

Of the $7.7 billion of farm mortgage debt outstanding on January 1, 1954 federal and federally sponsored agencies—the Farmers Home Administration, the Federal Farm Mortgage Corporation, and the federal land banks—accounted for 19 percent, which was higher than the comparable figures for 1920 and 1930 but only about one-half that for 1940, when they held more than 40 percent of the mortgage debt of farm enterprises (Chart 3). The reduction of their percentage share between 1940 and 1954 was due both to a decline

TABLE 3

Outstanding Amounts of Direct Loans Held by Federal and Federally Sponsored Agencies Compared with the Outstanding Amounts of Loans and Securities Held by Private Institutional Lenders at Decennial Years, 1920-1950, by Sector of Economy Served

(dollar figures in millions)

Year and Type of Lender	Agriculture[a]	Business[b]	Financial Institutions[c]	Urban Housing[d]	Minor Governmental Units[e]	Total[f]
1920 Federal agencies	$ 5	$ 680	..	..	..	$ 684
Federally sponsored agencies	350	..	..	..	..	350
Private institutions	6,523	24,594	$ 55[g]	$ 6,503	$ 1,903	39,578
1930 Federal agencies	243	125	..	..	1	369
Federally sponsored agencies	1,339	..	..	..	..	1,339
Private institutions	5,143	31,979	480	22,047	3,879	63,528
1940 Federal agencies	1,481	842	172	2,227	533	5,255
Federally sponsored agencies	2,237	9	201	..	..	2,448
Private institutions	2,544	24,651	77	18,478	7,486	53,236
1950 Federal agencies	2,157	3,199	h	1,543	503	7,402
Federally sponsored agencies	1,815	3	816	..	..	2,634
Private institutions	4,888	59,871	181	49,709	11,353	126,002
Holdings of Federal and Federally Sponsored Agencies as Percentages of the Holdings of Private Institutions						
1920 Federal agencies	0.1%	2.8%	..	..	..	1.7%
Federally sponsored agencies	5.4	..	..	..	..	0.9
1930 Federal agencies	4.7	0.4	..	..	i	0.6
Federally sponsored agencies	26.0	..	..	..	..	2.1
1940 Federal agencies	58.2	3.4	223.4%	12.1%	7.1%	9.9
Federally sponsored agencies	87.9	i	261.0	..	..	4.6
1950 Federal agencies	44.1	5.3	i	3.1	4.4	5.9
Federally sponsored agencies	37.1	i	450.8	..	..	2.1

(continued on next page)

TABLE 3 (continued)

a Outstandings of private institutions include farm real estate loans of open state and national banks in 1920 and 1930, of all insured commercial banks in 1940, and of all operating banks in 1950; farm real estate loans of life insurance companies; and non-real-estate loans of all operating banks to farmers (information not being available on loans to agricultural cooperatives, and CCC-guaranteed loans being excluded).

Sources: For federal and federally sponsored agencies, Table A-3 and A-4. For private institutions, *Agricultural Statistics, 1952*, Department of Agriculture, pp. 721 and 732, and *Agricultural Statistics, 1953*, p. 634.

b Outstandings of private institutions cover, for commercial and mutual savings banks in continental United States, their commercial and industrial loans (including open market paper), loans to security brokers and dealers, holdings of bonds, notes, debentures, and stock of domestic and foreign corporations, and holdings of Federal Reserve bank stock; for insurance companies (legal reserve life, fraternal life, fire and marine, and casualty and surety), their holdings of corporate bonds and stocks (railroads, public utilities, and industrials); and the business investments of savings and loan associations.

Sources: For federal and federally sponsored agencies, Table A-5. For the various private institutions, as follows: Banks, from the *Annual Reports* of the Comptroller of the Currency and the *Federal Reserve Bulletins*, except that the commercial bank data for 1920

and 1930 are NBER estimates obtained by inflating the data on business loans and discounts and business securities of national banks by the ratio of total loans and discounts of national to all banks and of total securities of national to all banks; data for 1940 and 1950 were adjusted for Federal Reserve Bank paid-in capital. Legal reserve life insurance companies, from the *Life Insurance Fact Book, 1954* (Institute of Life Insurance). Fire and marine and casualty and surety insurance companies, from "The Changing Importance of Institutional Investors in the American Capital Market," by Charles H. Schmidt and Eleanor J. Stockwell, in *Law and Contemporary Problems* (Duke University, School of Law), Vol. 17, No. 1, Winter 1952, p. 12. Fraternal life companies, for 1920–1940 from *A Study of Saving in the United States* by R. W. Goldsmith (Princeton University Press, 1955), Vol. 1, Table I-10, p. 462; and for 1950, estimated from the *Fraternal Monitor* (May 1951). Savings and loan associations, for 1920 and 1930 from Goldsmith, *op.cit.*, Tables J-2 and J-5, pp. 436 and 441, and for 1940 and 1950 from *Trends in the Savings and Loan Field, 1951*, Home Loan Bank Board, p. 4.

c Outstandings of private institutions include loans to banks by commercial and mutual savings banks, and advances to savings and loan associations other than those made by the Federal Home Loan banks.

Sources: For federal and federally sponsored agencies, Table A-6. For private institutions, as in note b above.

(continued on next page)

TABLE 3 (continued)

a Outstandings of private institutions include nonfarm real estate loans of commercial and mutual savings banks; nonfarm mortgages of legal reserve life insurance companies; total real estate mortgages of fraternal life, fire and marine, and casualty and surety companies; and net mortgage loans and real estate sales contracts (except in 1920 and 1930) of savings and loan associations.

Sources: For federal agencies, Table A-7. For private institutions, as in note b above, except that data for commercial and mutual savings banks for 1920–1940 were estimated by linear interpolation of June 30 holdings.

e Outstandings of private institutions include obligations of states and political subdivisions held by com-

mercial and mutual savings banks and by all insurance companies mentioned above.

Sources: For federal agencies, Table A-8. For private institutions, as in note b above.

f The estimates given in this column for the loan and security holdings of private financial institutions account for the following proportions of net private and net state and local government debt shown in Table 2: 46 percent in 1920; 47 percent in 1930 and 1940; and 66 percent in 1950.

g Represents borrowings of savings and loan associations only. Data for loans to banks were not available.

h Less than $500,000.

i Less than 0.05 percent.

CHART 3

Distribution of Farm Mortgage Debt among Principal Public and Private Lenders, Selected Years, 1910–1954

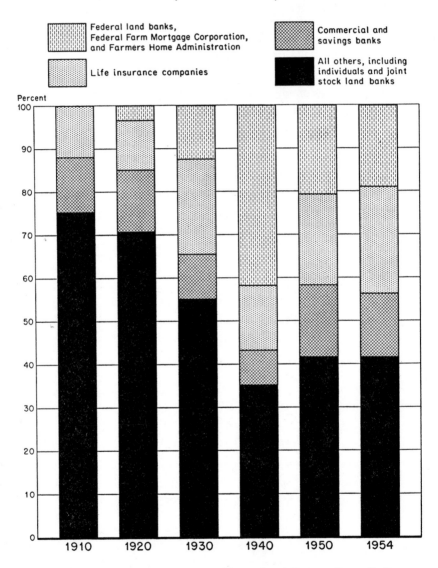

Data as of January 1 each year, from "Agricultural Finance Review" (Department of Agriculture, Agricultural Research Service), Vol. 17, November 1954, Table 1, p. 83.

in the dollar volume of their outstanding loans and to increased farm mortgage lending by private agencies and individuals.

Before 1933 the land banks were the only federal source of farm mortgage funds and accounted for comparatively small proportions of outstandings, ranging from 3.5 percent on January 1, 1920 to 13.5 percent at the beginning of 1933.[2] Through emergency programs undertaken during 1933 and 1934, which broadened the lending powers of the land banks and provided loan funds to the Land Bank Commissioner through the Federal Farm Mortgage Corporation, the proportion of credit extended to farmers by federal and federally sponsored agencies greatly increased. Land bank and Land Bank Commissioner loans accounted for 60 percent of the total dollar volume of farm mortgage recordings during the two-year period 1934–1935, when large numbers of farm mortgages were refinanced.[3]

The refinancing program tapered off in 1936, and from 1937 through 1953 only 12 percent of the total volume of farm mortgage recordings was supplied through the land bank system.[4] From 1938 on, the lending programs of the Farm Security Administration and its successor, the Farmers Home Administration, provided mortgage funds to farmers unable to obtain credit from other sources. Such loans, involving relatively high risks, have never represented more than 4 percent of the farm mortgage debt held by private and public lenders.

Regional differences in the sources of long-term farm credit are shown in Table 4, which distributes the farm mortgage credit outstanding in the several Farm Credit Administration districts on January 1, 1954 as among major types of lenders. Federal and federally sponsored agencies were most important in the New Orleans district (Alabama, Mississippi, Louisiana), where they accounted for 32 percent of the farm mortgage debt, and least important in the Berkeley district (the southern part of the Far West), where their mortgage credits accounted for only 11 percent of the total outstanding.

Turning to the short-term side of the farm credit market, we may note that at the beginning of 1954, 45 percent of the $6.2 billion of institutionally held non-real-estate debt owed by farmers con-

[2] *Agricultural Statistics, 1952*, Department of Agriculture, Table 727, p. 721.
[3] *Ibid.*, Table 728, p. 722.
[4] *Agricultural Finance Review* (Department of Agriculture, Agricultural Research Service), Vol. 17, November 1954, Table 8, p. 89.

TABLE 4

Distribution of Farm Mortgage Debt as of January 1, 1954 among Principal Public and Private Lenders, by Farm Credit District

Farm Credit District[a]	Federal and Federally Sponsored Agencies[b]	Life Insurance Companies	All Operating Banks	Others[c]
Springfield	15.6%	6.8%	21.5%	56.1%
Baltimore	12.4	7.2	32.0	48.4
Columbia	21.9	16.4	15.6	46.1
Louisville	12.7	23.2	27.6	36.5
New Orleans	32.3	19.5	15.1	33.1
St. Louis	20.1	38.4	14.5	27.0
St. Paul	19.6	14.0	17.4	49.0
Omaha	24.8	42.3	8.2	24.7
Wichita	19.3	36.3	6.4	38.0
Houston	25.3	42.2	5.5	27.0
Berkeley	11.1	15.9	12.1	60.9
Spokane	18.8	20.2	5.9	55.1

Computed from data in *Agricultural Finance Review* (Department of Agriculture, Agricultural Research Service), Vol. 17, November 1954, Table 3, p. 84. Bank loans are classified according to location of bank and are not strictly comparable with the data for other lenders, where the classification is by location of mortgaged farms.

a States included in the farm credit districts are as follows: *Springfield*—Maine, New Hampshire, Vermont, Massachusetts, Rhode Island, Connecticut, New York, and New Jersey; *Baltimore*—Pennsylvania, Maryland and the District of Columbia, Delaware, Virginia, and West Virginia; *Columbia*—North and South Carolina, Georgia, and Florida; *Louisville*—Indiana, Ohio, Kentucky, and Tennessee; *New Orleans*—Alabama, Mississippi, and Louisiana; *St. Louis*—Illinois, Missouri, and Arkansas; *St. Paul*—Michigan, Wisconsin, Minnesota, and North Dakota; *Omaha*—Iowa, Nebraska, South Dakota, and Wyoming; *Wichita*—Kansas, Oklahoma, Colorado, and New Mexico; *Houston*—Texas; *Berkeley*—Utah, Arizona, Nevada, and California; *Spokane*—Montana, Idaho, Washington, and Oregon.

b Covers the federal land banks, the Federal Farm Mortgage Corporation, and the Farmers Home Administration.

c Refers to individuals and miscellaneous institutions.

sisted of loans made independently by banks, and another 28 percent consisted of bank loans under CCC guarantee. The remainder was held by federal and federally sponsored agencies: production credit associations (9 percent), the Farmers Home Administration (6 percent), the Commodity Credit Corporation (direct loans, 11 percent), and the federal intermediate credit banks (1 percent, in the form of advances to private lending institutions).[5]

Production credit associations are perhaps the most interesting of these institutions for purposes of this study, since their services come closest to duplicating those available through private channels. The relative positions of PCA's and of banks in short-term farm credit are shown in Table 5 on two different bases: (1) according to the amount of institutionally held credit, apart from loans and loan guarantees in connection with CCC's price support program; and (2) according to the number of farmers served by each. As to amount, for the country as a whole in July 1954 the banks held 71 percent and PCA's 16 percent, with other public or quasi-public agencies accounting for the rest. Regionally, the relative importance of PCA's was lowest in the Omaha credit district (Iowa, Nebraska, South Dakota, and Wyoming) and highest in the Columbia district (the Carolinas, Georgia, and Florida), a contrast reflected also in the number of farm borrowers served.

The shares of the non-real-estate farm credit market served by banks and by federal and federally sponsored agencies have changed considerably over time. Until 1930 commercial banks served practically the entire market. It is true that the emergency crop and feed loan program of the federal government was important in some areas during the twenties; loans to cattle raisers, livestock loan companies, and other private financing institutions were made by the War Finance Corporation during 1918–1928; and from 1923 the federal intermediate credit banks made loans to, and discounts for, private financing institutions serving individual farmers. Yet at the end of 1929 these programs accounted for only about 2 percent of the short-term farm credit outstanding.

Chart 4 shows the changes thereafter. On January 1, 1935—after the introduction of emergency relief programs in 1932 and 1933, the creation of the production credit associations and the CCC in 1933, and the expansion of the disaster loan and emergency crop and feed loan programs in 1933 and 1934—credit supplied directly by federal and federally sponsored agencies represented 30 percent of all short-term farm credit outstanding. During the next two years their percentage share again increased markedly. By January 1, 1937, when short-term farm lending by banks had fallen to 25 percent of what it was in 1929, over half of the outstanding non-real-estate farm credit

[5] *Ibid.*, p. 92.

TABLE 5

Percentages of Outstanding Non-Real-Estate Loans to Farmers
Held by Banks and by PCA's as of July 1, 1954, and
Percentages of Farmers Obtaining Bank and
PCA Loans in 1951, by Farm Credit District

(*dollar figures in millions*)

FARM CREDIT DISTRICT[a]	NON-REAL-ESTATE DEBT, JULY 1, 1954 *Percentage Held by:*			PROPORTION OF FARMERS IN 1951 USING:	
	Banks	*PCA's*	*Total*[b]	*Bank Credit*[c]	*PCA Credit*
Springfield	68%	22%	$207	26.2%	7.6%
Baltimore	70	20	186	16.8	3.9
Columbia	53	31	284	26.5	7.5
Louisville	71	22	394	34.4	5.5
New Orleans	53	27	236	19.0	5.1
St. Louis	74	16	500	47.3	5.2
St. Paul	77	11	445	46.0	4.2
Omaha	84	8	576	63.8	2.8
Wichita	76	10	502	54.7	3.7
Houston	63	17	467	46.6	6.1
Berkeley	80	11	405	30.5	4.8
Spokane	63	23	288	39.8	6.4
United States	71%	16%	$4,489	36.9%	5.3%

Data for outstandings, which exclude bank and PCA loans guaranteed by the Commodity Credit Corporation in connection with price support, are from *Agricultural Finance Review* (Department of Agriculture, Agricultural Research Service), Vol. 17, November 1954, pp. 94–96. Data on number of farmers financed are from *Agricultural Credit and Related Data, 1953*, Agricultural Commission of the American Bankers Association, pp. 18ff.

a For a listing of states included in each farm credit district, see Table 4, note a. The bank series are classified according to location of bank; others, by location of security or borrower.

b Covers non-real-estate loans to farmers in continental United States (i.e. exclusive of loans to farmers' cooperatives) made by all operating banks, production credit associations, the Farmers Home Administration and its predecessors (including outstandings on loans made by the Emergency Crop and Feed Loan Division of the Farm Credit Administration and by the regional agricultural credit corporations), and private financing agencies (i.e. livestock loan companies and agricultural credit corporations) discounting with the federal intermediate credit banks. CCC direct loans, as well as guarantees, are excluded.

c Refers to all commercial banks.

was in the hands of the public agencies. The PCA's held 8 percent and the Resettlement Administration (one of the predecessors of the Farmers Home Administration) held 10 percent. Lending under the emergency crop and feed loan program and under the CCC direct loan program represented 13 percent and 16 percent, respectively,

CHART 4

Comparative Holdings of Non-Real-Estate Farm Debt by Banks,
by the Commodity Credit Corporation, and by Other Federal
and Federally Sponsored Agencies, 1930–1954

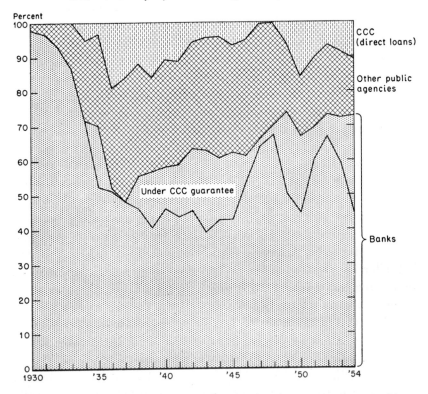

Data, as of January 1, are as given by the Department of Agriculture in "Agricultural Statistics, 1952," pp. 726 and 732, and "Agricultural Finance Review," Vol. 17, November 1954, pp. 92ff., and exclude loans to cooperatives.

Holdings of "other" public agencies are shown inclusive of loans under Commodity Credit Corporation guarantee, and refer to non-real-estate loans of the federal intermediate credit banks (to private institutions), production credit associations, the Emergency Crop and Feed Loan program, the regional agricultural credit corporations, and the Farmers Home Administration.

of total outstandings, while loans of the federal intermediate credit banks and regional agricultural credit corporations comprised the remaining 5 percent.

From 1938 through 1953, however—apart from CCC guarantees —the holdings of commercial banks grew more rapidly than the combined holdings of the federal and federally sponsored agencies, some of which had been curtailed or placed in liquidation. As a result, the publicly held share of short-term farm credit outstanding stood at 27 percent in January 1954, and the bank share (nonguaranteed) at 45 percent. Among the federal and federally sponsored agencies, the holdings of PCA's had held fairly constant at about 10 percent, whereas the holdings of the Farmers Home Administration, the FICB's, and the CCC had been reduced in relative importance.

Credit from federal agencies is of importance also in financing cooperatives, including those engaged in the marketing and processing of agricultural commodities and services and those organized for the special purpose of providing electric power and telephone services in rural areas. Table 6 shows the small amounts of such credit that were outstanding through 1935, the year the rural electrification program was introduced, and then the almost uninterrupted increase to the present level of $2.5 billion. Nearly four-fifths of that amount represents lending to electric cooperatives and is directly administered by the government. The financial aid to marketing cooperatives consisted at first (1930–1933) largely of loans from the Agricultural Marketing Act revolving fund, also a direct federal activity; but after the creation of the central Bank for Cooperatives and the twelve regional banks (1933) the holdings of federally sponsored agencies became relatively more important, ranging from 53 percent of total outstanding loans to marketing cooperatives at the end of 1934 to more than 90 percent at the end of 1946. Direct loans of the Commodity Credit Corporation have been important in some years, but only at the end of 1948 did they account for more than half of the amount owed by marketing cooperatives to federal and federally sponsored agencies.

Information showing the relative importance of public and private credit in the area of cooperatives is available for two dates, 1936 and 1954. A nationwide survey of farmers' groups in 1936 revealed that 31 percent of the amount owed by marketing and purchasing cooperatives had been supplied by the banks for cooperatives, and 46 percent by commercial banks, with the balance from a variety of sources.[6] Another nationwide survey in 1954 showed that the banks for cooperatives were supplying more than one-half of the credit used by cooperatives. This survey covered 632 cooperatives. The sources of credit for these cooperatives, in terms of reported outstanding bor-

[6] *A Statistical Handbook of Farmers' Cooperatives*, Farm Credit Administration, Bulletin 26, November 1938, pp. 180ff.

TABLE 6

Distribution of Outstanding Amounts of Loans to Farmers' Cooperative Associations among Federal and Federally Sponsored Agencies, 1929–1953

(*dollar figures in millions*)

END OF YEAR	FEDERALLY SPONSORED AGENCIES Loans to Marketing and Processing Cooperatives[a]	FEDERAL AGENCIES Loans to Marketing and Processing Coops.[b]	Loans to Rural Electric Coops.[c]	TOTAL
1929	64.2%	35.8%	..	$ 41
1930	32.0	68.0	..	201
1931	22.4	77.6	..	201
1932	5.8	94.2	..	169
1933	17.7	82.3	..	192
1934	53.0	47.0	..	117
1935	54.3	45.7	[d]	97
1936	52.8	45.4	1.8%	135
1937	54.6	27.1	18.3	164
1938	36.1	31.5	32.4	245
1939	25.9	18.0	56.1	301
1940	21.0	15.0	64.0	363
1941	30.0	10.1	59.9	508
1942	37.2	8.5	54.3	604
1943	40.9	6.4	52.7	628
1944	36.4	5.1	58.5	590
1945	28.0	3.6	68.4	572
1946	29.2	2.0	68.7	741
1947	23.7	16.1	60.2	1,179
1948	18.9	22.3	58.8	1,638
1949	17.0	13.1	69.9	1,791
1950	17.7	7.0	75.3	1,971
1951	18.5	9.2	72.3	2,312
1952	16.3	12.6	71.1	2,576
1953	14.9	6.0	79.1	2,505

Computed from Table 14 of the *Agricultural Finance Review* (Department of Agriculture, Agricultural Research Service), Vol. 17, November 1954, p. 93.

[a] Covers loans for production and general farm operating purposes made by the federal intermediate credit banks, 1929–1953, and loans made by the central and regional banks for cooperatives for operating purposes, the marketing of commodities, and construction or acquisition of marketing facilities, 1933–1953 (including CCC-guaranteed loans in 1941 through 1947).

[b] Represents loans for marketing and operating purposes made from the Agricultural Marketing Act revolving fund, 1929–1952; loans to cooperatives for rehabilitation purposes, and to water-facility cooperatives and defense relocation corporations, made by the Farmers Home Administration and its predecessors, 1937–1953; and loans to farm marketing cooperatives by the Commodity Credit Corporation, 1936–1953. But FHA loans in 1934–1936 are excluded for lack of annual data.

[c] Refers to loans made by the Rural Electrification Administration to electric or telephone cooperatives for construction of electric facilities, purchase and installation of electrical appliances and plumbing, and construction or expansion of telephone facilities.

[d] Less than 0.05 percent.

45

rowings at the close of fiscal years ending in 1954, were as follows :[7]

Lenders	Percent of Total
Banks for cooperatives	57.8
Commercial banks	10.3
Marketing and supply companies	1.6
Regional marketing and purchasing cooperatives	2.8
Individuals	4.0
Insurance companies	4.7
Certificates of indebtedness (usually members)	16.5
Miscellaneous sources	2.3
Total	100.0

A rough method of gauging the relative importance of public and private credit in financing rural electrification is to compare the number of customers served by organizations borrowing from the Rural Electrification Administration—public power districts, states and municipalities, and private power companies—with the total number of farms receiving central-station electricity. According to the annual survey conducted by REA, 4,888,460 farms (as defined in the 1950 census) were receiving central-station electricity on June 30, 1953.[8] At that time REA borrowers were serving 3,951,940 rural customers, of which about two-thirds were classed as farmers. Hence rural electric cooperatives (which represent more than 90 percent of REA borrowers) were serving about half of the farms in the United States receiving central-station electricity.

In 1949 the REA began a program for financing the construction and expansion of telephone facilities in rural areas. Loan allocations under this program through June 30, 1953 provided facilities for 302,597 subscribers; among them were 163,000 new subscribers, representing 5 percent of the 1950 census estimate of farms without telephones (3,322,554).[9]

A few federal agencies besides those already mentioned were active in extending credit to the agricultural sector during the 1930's. Among them were the Reconstruction Finance Corporation, which

---

[7] Based on survey by Farmer Cooperative Service, U.S. Department of Agriculture.

[8] *Report of the Administrator of the Rural Electrification Administration, 1953*, pp. 1, 14, and 15.

[9] *Ibid.*, p. 9, and *Agricultural Statistics, 1953*, Department of Agriculture, pp. 545 and 729.

disbursed $67 million in loans to private institutions for financing exports of surplus agricultural commodities and for financing the storage and marketing of farm commodities and livestock, and the Electric Home and Farm Authority, which discounted about $50 million of dealer paper originating in the sale or installation of electrical and gas appliances and equipment for farm use. And from World War II through 1953 the Veterans' Administration and the Farmers Home Administration insured or guaranteed, to a total of $180 million, loans for purchase or improvement of farm properties. All in all, federal lending in the agriculture sector has tended since the thirties to approach and even surpass the amounts advanced by private lending institutions. In 1950, federal farm credit outstanding totaled four-fifths of the amount held by commercial banks and life insurance companies as recorded in Table 3, but the comparison is marred by lack of information on loans to cooperatives by the private lenders. At a very rough estimate, their inclusion would lower the ratio of publicly to privately held farm credit in 1950 from four-fifths to about three-fourths.[10]

BUSINESS

It was shown in Table 3, above, that outstanding federal loans to business at the end of 1950 amounted to about 5 percent of the aggregate debt owed by business to major private financial institutions. Another indication that extensions of credit to business by federal and federally sponsored agencies have been comparatively unimportant on an over-all basis is given in Table 7, in which the out-

[10] Nearly one-half of the farm credit outstanding under federal programs at the end of 1950 represented loans to cooperatives, with the major share comprised of borrowings from REA by electric cooperatives. In its 1936 survey of farmers' cooperatives, cited above, the Farm Credit Administration found that outstanding commercial bank borrowings by marketing and processing cooperatives were 50 percent more than such credit held by the federally sponsored banks for cooperatives, which would indicate, if applicable to 1950, that about $525 million should be added to the total for holdings of private lending institutions in Table 3. That would be the only considerable addition, since rural electric cooperatives are almost entirely financed by REA. Thus the total for outstanding loans of commercial banks and life insurance companies both to farmers and to cooperatives in 1950 would probably not exceed $5.5 billion, with public holdings just short of $4 billion, or about 73 percent as large.

Confining the comparison to credit extended to farmers, the FCA reports that the combined holdings of the federal land banks, production credit associations, Federal Farm Mortgage Corporation, Farmers Home Administration, and federal intermediate credit banks at the beginning of 1950 were slightly less than one-half the amount held by commercial banks and life insurance companies. A similar relationship is indicated by the 1950 data in Table 3 after adjustment of holdings of public agencies to exclude loans to cooperatives.

47

TABLE 7

Outstanding Amounts of Federally Supplied Credit to Business as Percentages of Outstanding Net Business Debt, 1929–1953

(dollar figures in billions)

END OF YEAR	NET BUSINESS DEBT[a]	FEDERAL CREDIT AS % OF NET BUSINESS DEBT	
		Direct Loans[b]	Direct Loans, Loan Insurance, and Guarantees[c]
1929	$111	0.1%	0.1%
1930	112	0.1	0.1
1931	104	0.1	0.1
1932	96	0.5	0.5
1933	90	0.6	0.6
1934	87	0.8	0.8
1935	85	0.9	0.9
1936	85	0.8	0.8
1937	85	0.8	0.8
1938	82	0.9	0.9
1939	81	0.9	1.0
1940	81	1.1	1.1
1941	84	1.1	1.1
1942	81	1.4	2.3
1943	81	1.5	3.6
1944	82	1.4	3.3
1945	83	1.1	1.8
1946	89	2.0	2.5
1947	101	2.6	2.9
1948	110	2.8	3.1
1949	115	2.8	3.0
1950	132	2.4	2.6
1951	147	2.3	2.8
1952	161	2.2	2.7
1953	169	2.2	2.7

Outstanding amounts of federally supplied credit are from Table A-5, and outstanding net business debt was estimated from the *Survey of Current Business* (Department of Commerce), September 1953, pp. 17–19, and the October 1954 issue, pp. 18 and 19.

a Refers to net corporate long-term debt (excluding home mortgages), net corporate notes and accounts payable, and nonfarm debt owed by individual and noncorporate borrowers, other than consumer installment debt and mortgage debt on one- to four-family homes. Current estimates of total residential and commercial nonfarm mortgage debt of corporate borrowers were reduced by the yearly percentage relationship between home mortgage and total mortgage debt owed by corporations as shown by data published in the July 1944 and September 1945 issues of the *Survey*.

b Covers outstandings on direct loans made by the Director General of the Railroads and the Interstate Commerce Commission, the Maritime Administration and its predecessors, the War Finance Corporation, the Reconstruction Finance

(continued on next page)

TABLE 7 (*continued*)

Corporation, the Public Works Administration, the Export-Import Bank of Washington, the Smaller War Plants Corporation, the Departments of Army and Navy, the Housing and Home Finance Agency, and the Virgin Islands Corporation, and by the federally sponsored Federal Reserve Banks.

c In addition to the outstandings on loans made by agencies listed in note b, this series includes outstanding commitments of the RFC for deferred participations, and the outstanding amounts of guarantees or insurance on loans guaranteed or insured by the Maritime Administration and the Veterans' Administration or under the World War II Regulation V and the Defense Production Act of 1950 loan guarantee programs.

standing amounts of federally supplied credit are expressed as percentages of the net business debt outstanding at year ends, 1929 through 1953 (i.e. the aggregate net private nonfarm debt exclusive of loans on one- to four-family residences, consumer installment debt, and short-term corporate debt other than notes and accounts payable). Throughout this period, outstanding federal loans amounted to no more than 3 percent of the total owed by individuals and corporate and noncorporate borrowers. Governmental insurance and guarantee of private loans to business has also been small; even when the Regulation V loan guarantee program was most active (1943 and 1944), only 2 percent of the net business debt was federally protected.

It would appear that the proportions of the business population served by federal credit agencies have been equally small. From the beginning of its business loan operations in 1934 through June 30, 1953 the RFC authorized nearly 60,000 direct and participation loans to business enterprises; but the number of borrowers was less than that, because of cancellations and of repeat borrowers. During the same period the Export-Import Bank authorized about 500 loans, of which an estimated one-tenth may have involved American business firms. Under its ship construction loan program, which began in the early twenties, the Maritime Administration and its predecessors extended credits to only a handful of merchant shipbuilders and operators; and from 1934 to mid-1953 the industrial loans approved by the Federal Reserve Banks numbered only 3,758.[11] Even the V-loan program, which involved federal guarantees of war production loans totaling more than $10.5 billion, made credit available to only 4,864 business firms during 1942–1946.[12] From September 1942 through 1945, 4,487 loans were authorized by the Smaller War

[11] *Federal Reserve Bulletin*, June 1954, p. 603.
[12] Susan S. Burr and Elizabeth B. Sette, *A Statistical Study of Regulation V Loans*, Board of Governors of the Federal Reserve System, 1950, Table 4, p. 21.

Plants Corporation, another wartime agency.[13] The only federal program which directly touched a substantial number of enterprises —mainly very small, new ventures—was the business loan guarantee and insurance program of the Veterans' Administration. Up to mid-1953 a total of 205,450 VA-guaranteed business loans had been closed.[14]

On the basis of the above inventory it may be estimated that perhaps 280,000 enterprises benefited from federal or federally sponsored credit services at one time or another during the past twenty years. This number forms only about 7 percent of the more than four million operating business firms in the United States as of June 30, 1953. Admittedly the two measures correspond only roughly. The former includes some authorizations later canceled, concerns number of loans rather than number of different borrowers, covers a span of years, and includes some firms no longer in existence, whereas the latter characterizes one point in time and strongly reflects the increase in new business formations after World War II. To some extent these differences are counterbalancing: an estimate of about 5 percent for the proportion of business firms in the United States served by federal credit agencies seems reasonable.

Private financial institutions have served the credit needs of a vastly larger segment of the American business population. At the end of 1939, approximately 1,200,000 business firms were indebted to private institutional lenders, mainly commercial banks.[15] In 1946, member banks in the Federal Reserve system alone had an estimated 673,000 loans outstanding to business concerns.[16] If the businesses that have obtained credit from commercial finance companies, life insurance companies, and other types of private agencies were added to those served by the commercial banking system, the smallness of the number of firms—perhaps 280,000—that have been served by public agencies would appear even more striking.

HOUSING

Federal credit programs in the urban housing field consist prima-

[13] Douglas R. Fuller, *Government Financing of Private Enterprise*, Stanford University Press, 1948, Table 6, p. 151.

[14] *Loan Guaranty*, Veterans' Administration, June 1953.

[15] Neil H. Jacoby and Raymond J. Saulnier, *Business Finance and Banking* (National Bureau of Economic Research, Financial Research Program, 1947), p. 42.

[16] Albert R. Koch, "Business Loans of Member Banks," *Federal Reserve Bulletin*, March 1947, p. 253.

rily of the insurance or guarantee of loans extended privately for the construction, purchase, or repair of homes and apartment dwellings. In addition, during the thirties the federal government refinanced distressed mortgages on a large scale, and currently as well as during those years has been extending credits to home financing institutions, purchasing and making secondary distributions of insured and guaranteed mortgages, lending directly to mortgagees where credit is unavailable locally, and making loans to local governments, authorities, or other bodies for low-rent housing projects. Credit aid to urban housing, except for the direct loans to home financing institutions, has been administered by strictly federal rather than sponsored agencies.

It will be clear from Table 8 that the FHA-insured loan plays a prominent part in the financing of home repair and modernization.

TABLE 8

Outstanding Consumer Installment Loans for Home Modernization and Repair Held by Private Financial Institutions, and Proportion FHA-Insured, 1939–1953

(*dollar figures in millions*)

End of Year	Home Repair and Modernization Loans[a]	Estimated Percent FHA-Insured[b]
1939	$ 298	43%
1940	371	46
1941	376	55
1942	255	76
1943	130	98
1944	119	78
1945	182	62
1946	405	51
1947	718	57
1948	843	72
1949	887	72
1950	1,006	68
1951	1,090	71
1952	1,406	65
1953	1,649	68

Data for home repair and modernization loans are from the *Federal Reserve Bulletin*, April 1953, pp. 346 and 347, and March 1955, p. 310; those for FHA-insured home improvement loans were compiled from the *Annual Reports* of the Federal Housing Administration and of the Housing and Home Finance Agency.

a Covers only repair and modernization loans on owner-occupied homes. Refers to outstanding amounts of loans held by commercial and mutual savings banks, sales and consumer finance companies, credit unions, industrial loan companies,

(*continued on next page*)

TABLE 8 (*continued*)

savings and loan associations, and other lending institutions holding consumer installment loans.

ᵇ The underlying data for FHA-insured loans are estimates of outstanding net proceeds of single family home improvement loans derived by applying to total average year-end outstandings on all property improvement loans the percentages of annual volume used for the improvement of single family dwellings.

It is estimated that since 1939, the first year in which data necessary for the calculation are available, FHA-insured loans for the improvement of single family homes have represented at least 40 percent of the amounts outstanding on all loans for the repair and modernization of owner-occupied dwellings; in some years, particularly during the period of wartime controls, FHA-insured loans accounted for more than three-fourths of total outstandings. Though data for other types of properties are lacking, it is known that the insured loan plays a smaller part in the improvement of business structures and multifamily and farm dwellings than of one-family homes.

Somewhat greater accuracy is possible in measuring the importance of federal loan insurance and guarantees in the vastly larger residential mortgage field. Figures showing the proportion of building starts and of mortgage recordings which involved either VA or FHA financing are given in Table 9. There was little thought, when the FHA mortgage insurance program was initiated in 1934, that it would assume the importance that it has now attained. It is no exaggeration, however, to say that at the present time the insured or guaranteed loan plays a leading role in the mortgage financing of residential properties and that through these government programs the entire structure of housing credit has been brought under federal influence. As Table 9 shows, about two-thirds of the multiunit residential construction starts during the post-World War II period involved insured or guaranteed financing, and from two-fifths to one-half of the smaller structures started carried this protection. After 1951 the percentage of multifamily residences started with FHA-insured loans dropped sharply, and was slightly more than 25 percent in 1953. The proportion of one- and two-family homes financed with VA-guaranteed and FHA-insured loans continued to represent about two-fifths of such units under construction. On a different basis of measurement—mortgage recordings up to $20,000 size, which include transfers of existing properties as well as the financing of new construction—insured and guaranteed loans in 1953 accounted for roughly three-tenths of the dollar volume of transactions.

TABLE 9

Relative Importance of FHA-Insured and of VA-Guaranteed Loans in
Nonfarm Residential Construction and Financing, 1935–1953

| | PERCENTAGE OF DWELLING UNITS IN PRIVATE NONFARM STARTS FINANCED WITH: | | | | | PERCENTAGE DISTRIBUTION OF DOLLAR VOLUME OF NONFARM HOME MORTGAGE RECORDINGS OF $20,000 OR LESS | | |
| | VA-Guaranteed Loans | | FHA-Insured Loans | | | | | |
YEAR	1- and 2-Family Houses^c	Total	1- and 2-Family Houses^d	Multi-family Dwellings^e	Total	FHA-Insured	VA-Guaranteed	Conventional
1935	..	..	7%	5%	6%	†	...	†
1936	..	..	18	5	16	†	...	†
1937	..	..	19	11	18	†	...	†
1938	..	..	32	19	30	†	...	†
1939	..	..	37	21	34	20%	...	80%
1940	..	..	37	9	34	19	...	81
1941	..	..	38	10	36	19	...	81
1942	..	..	56	46	55	25	...	75
1943	..	..	76	98	80	20	...	80
1944	..	..	65	89	67	15	...	85
1945	3%	3%	20	15	20	8	3%g	88
1946	14	13	11	6	10	4	22	74
1947	27	25	23	63	27	8	28	64
1948	13	12	28	68	32	18	16	66
1949	13	11	32	62	36	19	12	69
1950	17	15	31	76	36	15	19	66
1951	16	15	22	65	26	12	22	66
1952	14	13	25	37	26	11	15	74
1953	16	15	23	26	24	12	16	73

(continued on next page)

TABLE 9 (*continued*)

Compiled from *Housing Statistics*, Housing and Home Finance Agency, January 1954, pp. 24 and 26, the *Sixth Annual Report* of the Housing and Home Finance Agency, 1952, Table 4, p. 221, and *Annual Reports* and specially supplied data of the Federal Housing Administration. The Bureau of Labor Statistics series on total starts divides structures by size into one- and two-family homes, and all others. The VA data, and the FHA data after partial adjustment, have slightly different coverage, as noted under c, d, and e below.

a The underlying data were estimated by HHFA on the basis of dwelling units in homes securing first mortgages guaranteed by the VA through 1950; thereafter they represent units in houses meeting VA first compliance inspection.

b The underlying data represent dwelling units in houses and housing projects meeting FHA first compliance inspection.

c Represents dwelling units in total VA starts as a percentage of units in privately financed one- and two-family houses. However, the proportion of VA guarantees for multifamily structures, being restricted to dwelling units owned and occupied by a veteran, has been very small.

d Data were supplied by the FHA and cover units in one- and two-family houses financed under Sections 2, 8, 203, 603, and 903 of the National Housing Act, and in one-family houses financed under Sections 207, 213, 608, 611, 803, and 908. Two-family houses of the project type are excluded for lack of information.

e Data were supplied by the FHA and cover three- to four-family houses insured under Sections 203 and 603, and structures of two-family size or larger in rental and cooperative projects insured under Sections 207, 213, 608, 803, and 908.

f Not available.

g Includes recordings made during 1944.

The relative frequency with which insured and conventional loans are used in financing small residential properties is shown in Chart 5.

CHART 5

Proportion of Insured and of Conventional Mortgages for New vs. Existing Homes and Metropolitan vs. Smaller Communities

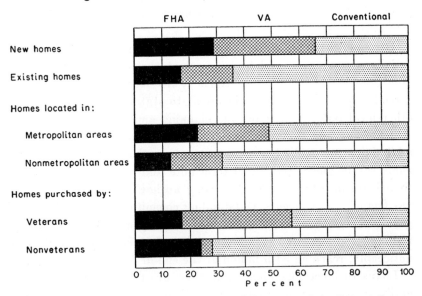

Data are from a sample survey by the Board of Governors of the Federal Reserve System of 1,368 persons who purchased one- and two-family nonfarm dwellings for owner occupancy between October 12, 1950 and March 15, 1951. See "Federal Reserve Bulletin," July 1951, Tables 13, 21, and 23, pp. 788, 795, and 796.

Federally protected financing, particularly VA-guaranteed loans, is more important than purely private financing in connection with new construction, but less so in the transfer of existing structures; in metropolitan areas, insured or guaranteed loans are as frequent as conventional loans, but outside the large cities conventional loans predominate.

Direct loans by federal agencies have been extended in the housing field both for refinancing and new money purposes. At the end of 1935 the outstanding loans of the Home Owners' Loan Corporation, mainly for refinancing, were second only to the amounts held by savings and loan associations, and accounted for nearly one-fifth of the total outstanding mortgage debt on one- to four-family homes.[17] Although unimportant nationally, direct lending by federal agencies

[17] *Housing Statistics*, Housing and Home Finance Agency, January 1954, p. 20.

to homeowners and to private builders has been significant in some cases at the local level. During 1941–1944, the Defense Homes Corporation advanced slightly less than $1 million for the construction of housing in defense areas, and since 1950 the Veterans' Administration has closed about $290 million in loans to veterans for home purchase or construction in localities, mainly rural, where VA-guaranteed credits at maximum permissible interest rates were unavailable from private sources.

Through the operations of the Public Housing Administration and its predecessors, and to some extent through programs of the Housing and Home Finance Agency, the federal government has extended nearly $3.7 billion in credit to states, municipalities, and other local public bodies for the planning and construction of low-rent housing and slum clearance projects. In addition to advancing $3.6 billion for public housing construction, the Public Housing Administration guarantees short-term note and bond obligations sold to private investors by local housing authorities with which PHA has financing agreements. Outstanding commitments under this program averaged about $230 million over the years 1940–1949; as a result of the increased building activity of 1950, commitments rose noticeably, reaching $1.9 billion at the end of 1953.

Loans to home financing institutions are made through the federally sponsored Home Loan Banks. From 1932 through 1944 borrowings by member institutions, principally savings and loan associations, were relatively small; but the funds advanced from 1945 through 1953 totaled $4 billion, nearly three times the total disbursements made through 1944.

Finally, the federal government has provided facilities for the purchase and secondary distribution of mortgages covered by federal insurance or guarantee. Through June 30, 1947, when its activities were discontinued, the RFC Mortgage Company disbursed $496 million, of which $393 million represented purchases of federally insured home and project mortgages. The Federal National Mortgage Association, set up in 1938, purchased $1.3 billion in FHA-insured home and housing project mortgages, and $2.6 billion in VA-guaranteed mortgages, through December 31, 1953. Some indication of the role of federal agencies in the secondary market for insured loans is given by Table 10, which weighs their purchases and sales of FHA-insured home mortgages against those of private financial institutions over the years. In the total volume of purchases

TABLE 10

Relative Importance of Federal Agencies and Private
Financial Institutions in the Secondary Market for
FHA-Insured Home Mortgages, 1935–1953

	MORTGAGES PURCHASED		MORTGAGES SOLD	
YEAR	Federal Agencies[a]	Private In- stitutions[b]	Federal Agencies[a]	Private In- stitutions[b]
1935–1936	15.8%	84.2%	0.1%	99.9%
1937	24.9	75.1	5.6	94.4
1938	28.3	71.7	5.3	94.7
1939	28.4	71.6	2.9	97.1
1940	15.9	84.1	1.4	98.6
1941	12.9	87.1	1.1	98.9
1942	8.1	91.9	2.0	98.0
1943	7.0	93.0	26.3	73.7
1944	10.4	89.6	3.0	97.0
1945	4.4	95.6	21.8	78.2
1946	0.3	99.7	8.7	91.3
1947	0.1	99.9	0.7	99.3
1948	11.7	88.3	0.1	99.9
1949	23.6	76.4	0.1	99.9
1950	5.8	94.2	14.9	85.1
1951	3.0	97.0	5.9	94.1
1952	10.1	89.9	2.7	97.3
1953	19.8	80.2	1.5	98.5

Data are from the *Annual Reports* of the Federal Housing Administration and the Housing and Home Finance Agency, and refer to the face amount of mortgages insured under Sections 8, 203, 603, 603–610, 611 and 903 of the National Housing Act.

[a] Covers transactions of the RFC Mortgage Company, the Federal National Mortgage Association, the U.S. Housing Corporation, and (in 1938) the Federal Deposit Insurance Corporation.

[b] Refers to activities of state and national banks, savings banks, savings and loan associations, insurance companies, mortgage companies, investment and finance companies, endowed institutions, and other similar investment groups or funds.

and sales in the secondary mortgage market, the activities of federal agencies have been relatively unimportant. Mortgages purchased by federal agencies comprised 20 percent or more of the total dollar volume only in the last half of the thirties and in 1949.

OTHER AREAS SERVED

Among the lending programs of federal agencies that fall outside the scope of agriculture, business, and housing are such diverse activities as the disaster loan programs of the Reconstruction

Finance Corporation and the Disaster Loan Corporation, loans to Indians and Indian organizations by the Bureau of Indian Affairs, loans for economic improvement by the Puerto Rico Reconstruction Administration, loans to students by the Federal Security Agency, or loans to holders of government life insurance by the Veterans' Administration. Even in the aggregate, however, these have not been large; estimated disbursements under these miscellaneous programs, some of which began as early as 1911, totaled less than $800 million through the end of 1953.

Loans to state and local authorities for purposes other than housing construction warrant separate mention. Through December 1953, funds totaling upwards of $1.8 billion had been advanced by federal agencies such as the Inland Waterways Corporation (during the twenties); the RFC, the Public Works Administration, and the Tennessee Valley Authority (during the thirties); and, more recently, the Housing and Home Finance Agency—principally for financing the construction of public works and other community facilities.

To banks and other private financial institutions, credit has been extended not only in the housing field (through Home Loan Bank loans to mortgage lending institutions) but for more general purposes. After World War I, the War Finance Corporation advanced about $5 million in loans to banks and building and loan associations. From 1932 through the end of World War II, mainly during the depression years, the RFC disbursed more than $2.7 billion in loans, and $1.2 billion for stock subscriptions, to banks, insurance companies, and other financial institutions. During the same period the Home Owners' Loan Corporation and the Treasury Department invested nearly $275 million in shares of federal- and state-insured savings and loan associations.

CHAPTER 3

Services and Credit Terms of Federal Credit Agencies

THE purpose of the present chapter is to give a brief description of the various credit services provided by the federal government. With more detailed accounts reserved for Part II (in which Chapters 6, 7, and 8 are devoted in turn to the credit services available to agriculture, business, and urban real estate), the focus here is on the broad, distinguishing features of federal credit programs as a whole, and, especially, on points of similarity and difference among specific programs.

Perhaps the most important feature in which the various credit programs of the federal government differ is the directness of the intervention involved. On this ground one can distinguish sharply between the programs developed in agriculture and in housing and those directed to the assistance of business concerns. In agriculture and urban housing, intervention has been relatively indirect, though the specific methods pursued in the two fields have been quite different. In aiding business, on the other hand, the federal government has, in most cases, employed techniques of direct intervention.

In agriculture, much (though not all) of the government's aid has been given principally through the medium of farmer-owned, cooperative credit institutions. These have operated initially with federal funds but under plans to eliminate government capital, and with a few exceptions this goal has been achieved. The agencies concerned—federal land banks, federal intermediate credit banks, production credit corporations, production credit associations, and banks for cooperatives—are federally sponsored institutions in the language of this study; not only do they closely resemble private financial institutions in organization and management, but in some cases they serve markets that are broadly similar to those served by private finance. Indeed, it is in the agricultural areas that competition between private finance and the federal government is closest and most extensive.

In the housing field, direct intervention has been minimized by using chiefly (though, again, not exclusively) the technique of loan insurance or guaranty. The hand of the federal government is felt less directly by private finance when the government insures or guarantees a loan than when it is the sole maker of the loan.

Federal credit programs in the business field have been of a quite different character. In this area the government has made no effort to sponsor specialized credit institutions of the cooperative type, though there have been discussions from time to time of the desirability of regional investment companies. And although the technique of loan insurance and loan guarantees has been employed, notably in the guarantee of war and defense production loans, for the most part federal credit programs designed to aid business have consisted of direct loans made under circumstances in which the hand of the federal government has been obvious. It is perhaps this feature which has made them more controversial than the programs pursued in aid of agriculture and of urban housing, despite their small volume in comparison to the total of credit to business.

There is no great difficulty in explaining why federal credit programs have taken such different turns in these three areas. In agriculture, a tradition of cooperatively organized enterprises was already of long standing, here and abroad, when the federal land bank system was set up in 1917. At that time, two types of agencies were established under the Federal Farm Loan Act: the federal land banks, organized on a cooperative basis, and the joint stock land banks, intended to be privately owned and operated. A need was felt for agencies to supplement private lending institutions, and in a spirit of compromise the two types were established, one wholly private and the other aided by federal subsidy.

It is also understandable that federal aid to homeowners followed the course described above. The need in this case was not for the creation of new institutions to fill a gap in credit supply but rather to induce existing institutions to increase their investments in the home mortgage field. Thus financial aid took the form of offering loan insurance as a protection to private lenders. Criticism of the program was held to a relatively minor amount by the indirectness of the federal government's approach.

The situation was quite different when the programs of credit assistance to business were initiated. For the most part these were designed hastily to meet dire emergencies, when there was neither the opportunity to create institutions of the federally sponsored type, nor the practical possibility of inducing an increased flow of private investment funds under the protection of loan insurance. Techniques of the latter type were used later, but not in the critical days of the early thirties. The firms needing aid at that time were unable to borrow from private financing institutions and probably could not have borrowed even under the protective cloak of a loan guarantee. To some extent this situation was altered in later years, which accounts for the growth of the Reconstruction Finance Corporation's participation lending and, more recently, the Small Business Administration's emphasis on its participation program. But in the early thirties the federal government had no choice except to establish agencies that would make loans directly to business concerns or to stay out of the field altogether.

We may turn now to a comparison of the various services that have been available under federal credit programs.

Agriculture

Whereas federal credit services in the business and urban housing sectors of the economy have been directed to rather limited segments of the market, the federal government has made a full line of credit services available to farmers. Long-term mortgage credit has been obtainable since 1917 through the farmer-owned federal land banks, and short-term production credit since 1933 through local production credit associations, also farmer-owned. These two credit systems lend to farmers of good and often superior credit standing, but other programs are available to assist borrowers less well situated. The Farmers Home Administration offers short- and long-term credit to farmers unable to obtain financing from private sources and in the 1930's other agencies, notably the office of the Land Bank Commissioner, acting for the Federal Farm Mortgage Corporation, supplied large amounts of mortgage credit to farmers experiencing acute difficulties as a result of agricultural depression. Finally, specialized credit services are available to farmers' marketing, processing, and purchasing cooperatives through the banks for cooperatives and to electric light and power cooperatives through the Rural Electrification Administration. A view of the current organization of federal and federally sponsored farm credit agencies and the amount of their credit outstanding on January 1, 1953 is given in Table 11.

The federal land banks, one of which is located in each of the twelve districts of the Farm Credit Administration, were the first of the federally sponsored farm credit agencies to be established. Operating since 1917 through a system of national farm loan asso-

61

TABLE 11

Federal and Federally Sponsored Agricultural Credit Agencies: Organization as of January 1953

(*data on amounts outstanding for January 1, 1953*)

Agricultural Credit Group
(Assistant to Secretary of Agriculture)

Farm Credit Administration		*Farmers Home Administration*		*Rural Electrification Administration*
		Real Estate Loans	*Non-Real-Estate Loans*	
12 federal land banks	Central bank and 12 district banks for cooperatives ($419 million outstanding)	($193 million direct farm ownership loans; $52 million insured farm ownership loans; $70 million farm housing loans outstanding)	($294 million production and subsistence loans; $29 million disaster, fur and orchard loans; $30 million emergency crop and feed loans and $8 million loans to cooperatives and defense relocation corporations outstanding)	(1,019 REA-financed systems in operation; $2.2 billion advanced; 3.9 million consumers connected as of January 1, 1953)
1,164 national farm loan associations ($1,078 million exclusive of purchase money mortgages and real estate sales contracts)	12 federal intermediate credit banks[a]			
	12 production credit corporations			
	499 production credit associations ($606 million outstanding)			

[a] In addition to serving as a major source of financing for PCA's, the intermediate credit banks make advances to privately capitalized credit corporations ($91 million outstanding) and also may make production loans directly ($2 million outstanding). Organizationally, the intermediate credit banks are a separate service in the Farm Credit Administration from the production credit service.

From *Agricultural Statistics, 1953* (Department of Agriculture), pp. 652–663 *passim*; covers United States and possessions. Outstandings refer to amounts owed by ultimate borrowers (i.e. interagency loans are excluded). Besides those shown, the Federal Farm Mortgage Corporation, from whose funds Land Bank Commissioner loans were made until the program went into liquidation in 1947, had $23 million outstanding.

ciations, which are local farmer-owned institutions now totaling around 1,200, the district banks are at present entirely farmer-owned, though subject to fairly direct and extensive federal control and supervision. They make amortized, long-term mortgage loans (with maturities usually of twenty to thirty-three years) to farm and ranch operators and in special cases to livestock corporations. Perhaps the most interesting feature of the system is that land bank loans must meet credit standards roughly comparable with those employed by private lending institutions.

The cooperative feature of the land bank system is devised along lines that were without a close precedent when first put into effect and have never been exactly duplicated elsewhere in federal credit programs. The farmer who wishes to borrow deals directly with his local national farm loan association and is required to purchase stock in it (which generally has been dividend-paying) equal to 5 percent of the amount borrowed. The association, in turn, makes an equivalent investment in land bank stock, and the loan is made by the land bank, with the endorsement of the local association, under a risk-sharing arrangement which in most cases provides for a division of losses about equally between the two institutions. The land banks were originally provided with capital by the federal government, but under the mutuality feature described they have been able to retire all government capital. From time to time an individual land bank may employ federal funds, but the system is to all intents and purposes now wholly farmer-owned.

Because land bank loans are screened much like those by private agencies, the markets served by the two systems are roughly comparable. Yet there are certain features of land bank policy that reflect the semipublic nature of the banks. Most obvious, perhaps, is the fact that interest rates on land bank mortgage loans are identical throughout given districts and vary only moderately over the country as a whole. In 1953, for example, they were 4 percent in all districts except Springfield, Baltimore, and Columbia, where they were 4½ or 5 percent.[1] There are no differences in rates within districts on loans of different amounts, a practice quite at variance with the methods of private finance, where rates commonly vary with loan size and with the type and quality of the collateral.

[1] *Annual Report* of the Farm Credit Administration, 1952–1953, p. 64.

63

Secondly, the rates charged by the land banks have been, on the average, lower than those available through private financial channels. Thus, in 1953 the average contract rate on farm mortgage loans for all private lenders was 4.7 percent, in contrast to the 4 percent rate available in nine of the twelve farm credit districts.[2]

Other things equal, uniform or nearly uniform interest rates quoted below the going market level are destined to claim for the lender an increasing share of the market; this has been the case in the farm mortgage field, though other factors as well have affected the competitive position of the land banks. For example, the land banks have been limited by Congress, or by their own administrative decisions, as to the amounts that may be loaned in given situations. From 1917 to 1933 they could not loan more than 50 percent of the current market value of the land plus 20 percent of the current value of the farm's permanent, insured improvements. Under that fairly restrictive limitation, the program accounted for a relatively small portion of farm mortgage lending. In 1933 and 1934, steps were taken to make land bank credit more readily available for refinancing defaulted or distressed farm mortgages. First, the Emergency Farm Mortgage Act of 1933 authorized the land banks to make loans directly to farmers, not only where existing national farm loan associations were unable to accept applications because of their financial condition, but even in areas where associations had not been organized. Second, $200 million was made available to the Land Bank Commissioner (the officer of the Farm Credit Administration having direct responsibility for the land bank program) for emergency loans, a program designed to aid the most distressed farmers, and which was expanded in 1934 with the establishment of the Federal Farm Mortgage Corporation. Under it, loans could be made up to 75 percent of a farm's normal agricultural value, defined as the amount a typical purchaser would be justified in paying for the farm under conditions of customary agricultural use, average yields, and farm product prices such as might prevail in years reasonably free of inflation and deflation.[3] Thus Commissioner loans, as they were called, could be secured by first mortgages on farms not up to land bank standards; and, further, they could be made on second

[2] *Agricultural Finance Review* (Agricultural Research Service), Vol. 16, November 1953, Table 2, p. 92.

[3] In general the period from 1909 to 1914 was accepted as representing normality for farm product prices, although in some cases allowances were made for commodity prospects and for other conditions and prospects in particular regions.

mortgages supplemental to regular land bank loans. Commissioner loans were first available to farmers at a 5 percent rate, but this was lowered to 4 percent from mid-1937 to the end of 1939 and lowered again, to 3½ percent, in 1940–1944. The rate was adjusted back to 4 percent in 1945. Contract terms were set at forty years, and the loans were made repayable over their term by fixed annual or semiannual installments.

Appraisal of regular land bank loans, too, was put on the normal agricultural value basis in 1933, and the interest rate was lowered from 4½ to 3½ percent in mid-1935 and remained there through mid-1944.

The Land Bank Commissioner was also authorized by Congress in 1935 to make loans to part-time farmers on what was termed a "prudent investment value" basis. The intention was to give special assistance to farmers who were supplementing their farm income by means of off-farm work and so to strengthen a group of farm borrowers regarded as being especially hard-pressed. In all, around 5,300 such loans were made during the period of the program, from early 1935 through mid-1946.

As a result of liberalization in appraisal policies, low interest charges, and the adoption of emergency measures which made it possible for farmers' debts to be scaled down to the point where they could be refinanced with district land banks or with the Land Bank Commissioner, the proportion of all farm mortgage credit extended by federal and federally sponsored agencies increased greatly during the mid-thirties.

In 1945 the limit on land bank mortgage loans was increased to 65 percent of a farm's normal agricultural value. By then, however, inflationary trends were evident in the farm economy and the appraisal method employing normal agricultural value was more restrictive than a method employing current value. As a result the land banks in recent years have had a surplus of loanable funds. As would be expected, the appraisal policy has had the effect in some districts of limiting land bank lending to well-established farmers whose mortgage requirements were modest compared with the collateral they could offer.

The second farm credit network developed by the federal government is the production credit system, consisting of: local production credit associations, presently numbering around 500, from which farmers may obtain short-term production loans; the federal inter-

65

mediate credit banks, district banks from which a good part of the funds loaned by local associations are obtained; and the production credit corporations, one in each farm credit district, through which the federal government provides equity funds to local associations. As in the land bank system, there is a cooperative element in the production credit system, though it has not been carried as far: farmers borrowing from local associations are required to purchase capital stock in their association (usually a dividend-paying investment) equaling at least 5 percent of the amount borrowed, but the PCA's do not, in turn, buy stock in the FICB's. Stock purchases by farmer borrowers have enabled the PCA's to retire virtually all government capital.

There is somewhat greater variability in the rates charged by PCA's than in those charged by the land banks; furthermore, PCA rates are relatively close to those charged by commercial banks, with which they are in close competition. In 1951, for example, PCA loans carried contract interest rates of between 4½ and 6 percent, and in 1952 and 1953 the range had been raised to from 5 to 6¾ percent. In a certain sense, this relatively high level of rates symbolizes the fact that PCA's do not operate as emergency lending institutions. Indeed their average loan is so large in comparison to the average commercial bank loan that there is strong reason for believing that PCA's serve farmers who are on the whole operating larger, and presumably better established and more profitable, farms. The average PCA loan in 1950 was around $3,700 and an average commercial bank farm production loan was around $2,300; in some farm credit districts, the difference was even greater.

Loans made by the production credit associations are usually secured by a first lien on crops, livestock, or equipment and are generally written on a basis which requires repayment or extension within one year. It was calculated that, taking account of both interest and other charges, the average total cost of PCA loans to borrowers was 6.4 percent during the calendar year 1952.[4]

The resources of the local PCA's are obtained largely, as has been indicated, from district federal intermediate credit banks. The latter discount notes not only for the PCA's but for federally sponsored banks for cooperatives and also for private financial institutions, though the great bulk of their activity is in the discounting of PCA paper. Just under 85 percent of the total credit extended by the

[4] *Annual Report* of the Farm Credit Administration, 1952–1953, p. 31.

FICB's through mid-1953 went to the local PCA's.[5] For the most part these loans mature in one year, but the term may extend up to three years. The discount rates are determined by reference to the cost of money to the intermediate credit bank, which raises its funds mainly through the sale of debentures in the open investment markets. In mid-1953 the cost of intermediate credit bank borrowing for the PCA's was between $2\frac{1}{2}$ and 3 percent with some variation from one district to another.

A third federally sponsored farm credit system—the central and regional banks for cooperatives—lends to cooperatives engaged in marketing agricultural products, purchasing farm supplies, or furnishing farm business services. Three kinds of loans are provided. Long-term facility loans for the construction or acquisition of buildings or equipment for storing or marketing of farm commodities and food products are made on first mortgage security, usually at the same interest rate as on land bank mortgage loans and with a similar cooperative arrangement (i.e. the borrower must purchase stock in the lending bank, or make a guaranty fund payment, equal to 5 percent of the loan). Short-term, operating capital loans, which may or may not be secured, are available at rates of 3 to $3\frac{1}{2}$ percent (1954), with a stock purchase or guaranty fund payment equal to 5 percent of the loan amount. Commodity loans secured by first liens or other title to storable commodities are made to mature at the end of the current marketing year or season and have carried relatively low interest rates: $1\frac{1}{2}$ percent during most of the forties, $2\frac{3}{4}$ to $3\frac{1}{4}$ percent (depending on the credit district) in 1954, with a stock purchase or guaranty fund payment equal to 1 percent of the loan.

Evidence by which to compare public and private lending to farm cooperative associations is limited as to area and time, but there are some indications (as will be seen in Chapter 6) that the federally sponsored banks have tended to serve more the larger associations borrowing comparatively large amounts, and constituting presumably better than average credit risks. This may be due to the relatively large resources of the public banks for cooperatives as compared with local, private banking institutions and to the fact that the commercial banks, unlike the banks for cooperatives, cannot (with but few exceptions) make loans in excess of 10 percent of their capital.

5 *Ibid.*, p. 36.

Also serving cooperative enterprises, but lacking the cooperative feature of the banks for cooperatives and other federally sponsored farm credit agencies, is the Rural Electrification Administration, a direct agency of the federal government. The REA extends mortgage loans to persons, corporations, states, territories, municipalities, public utility districts, and cooperative, nonprofit or limited dividend associations, to finance generating plants and electric transmission and distribution lines for furnishing electric service to persons in rural areas not receiving central station electric service. REA loaned to 1,080 borrowers from 1935 to mid-1953, and over nine-tenths of them were cooperatives.[6] Loans for telephone facilities were authorized on October 28, 1949 and had been made to 112 cooperatives and 107 commercial companies as of June 30, 1953. The credit policy has been a liberal one: the interest rate is currently at 2 percent, and loans are made in amounts up to 100 percent of the cost of constructing the facilities involved. The basic policy of REA has been to extend service throughout each area entered, even though certain of the power lines may prove unprofitable, the aim being to serve farm families in outlying districts as well as those located near the main lines.

With the exception of the so-called Commissioner loans and some of the REA loans, all of the programs described above have served borrowers equally well or better established creditwise than the average client of private lending institutions. The federal government has also extended credit to farmers unable to borrow from private agencies of finance. One such program is that of the Farmers Home Administration, which was formed in 1946 in a reorganization of the Farm Security Administration and which has operated as a direct lending and loan-insuring agency in the long- and short-term fields. In addition to farm mortgage loans to farmers unable to obtain credit from other sources, the program has made disaster loans (in designated areas) to enable farmers suffering losses from drought, flood, or other disaster to continue production; supplied credit for the development of water facilities; and relieved conditions of acute economic distress, as with the livestock loans of 1953. In 1949 the agency was authorized to make loans for the construction and repair of farm houses and other farm buildings, where such credit was unobtainable from private sources.

Interest rates and other contract terms on Farmers Home Ad-

[6] *Agricultural Statistics, 1953* (Department of Agriculture), p. 662.

ministration loans have varied according to the purpose, water facility and disaster loans being made in 1952 at 3 percent, real estate loans at 4 percent, and the production and subsistence and fur and orchard loans at 5 percent. Farm ownership loans have been made for as long as forty years on an amortized basis in amounts not to exceed $12,000; farm housing loans have also been made for long terms, ranging up to thirty-three years. Water facility loans have had a maximum limit of $100,000 (but have averaged much less), and have been made for terms up to twenty years. Production and subsistence loans have been made for terms up to seven years and on a basis which requires repayment coincidental with the receipt of income. Disaster loans and the fur and orchard loans have been made up to five to ten years. In general, the loan contracts have been designed to meet the special circumstances that gave rise to the programs.

Since 1947, when a program of mortgage insurance became active, the Farmers Home Administration has insured loans made by private lenders, and has made direct loans to help tenants to become farm owners, to finance farm enlargement, to finance farm capital improvements, and to aid in project liquidation. The loans made or insured under this program have been smaller than the usual farm mortgage loans made by private lenders and have been made for the most part in areas of relatively low income. As of January 1953 over half of the agency's $258 million of farm ownership and farm housing loans outstanding in continental United States were in the twelve southern states extending from the Carolinas to Texas.[7]

Similarly, farmers obtaining non-real-estate loans from the Farmers Home Administration have for the most part been those faced with emergency situations arising from crop failure, low farm product prices, and other adversities. It should be mentioned, finally, that in addition to its lending services the Farmers Home Administration has aided borrowers in farm and home planning through its advisory services.

Business

Federal credit programs for business, in contrast to those for agriculture, have almost all been administered through agencies that are integral parts of the federal establishment. The only exceptions are a program of industrial loans begun in the mid-1930's and a guar-

[7] *Agricultural Finance Review*, Vol. 16, November 1953, p. 93.

antee program during and after World War II, both involving the Federal Reserve Banks. Yet this directness of action through its own agencies has not brought the federal government into such close competition with private financial institutions as have the quasi-public programs in agriculture. For one thing, its business loans have been directed predominantly to concerns which, either because they were newly established or had encountered some special difficulty, have been unable to obtain private credit of the type, or in the amount, which they sought; second, the extensive use of the technique of loan guarantees and the sharing of loans with private banking institutions has given the business lending programs a less abrasive effect as far as private lenders are concerned.

The limited line of credit services available to business through federal agencies contrasts both with the completeness and variety of those in agriculture and with the broad array of credits conventionally employed by business concerns. Short-term working capital loans from banks and long-term debt financing obtained through the open market, and, particularly for small and medium-sized firms, trade or mercantile credit obtained from suppliers, have been the traditional sources of funds for business, types of credit offered seldom or not at all in federal business lending programs. The latter have operated mainly in the comparatively small field of intermediate-term loans, with maturities ranging from one to ten years. Term lending has been more widely practiced by private lending institutions during the past fifteen years or so than before, which accounts in good part for the somewhat more intense competitive relationship between public and private credit agencies at the end of the thirties and in the postwar period than prevailed when the federal government's programs were started in the early thirties. A brief description of federal credit services to business follows, treating separately of the direct lending programs and of the programs in which federal agencies function in collaboration with private lenders.

The principal agencies through which the federal government has made direct loans to business firms have been the Reconstruction Finance Corporation, the Federal Reserve Banks, the Export-Import Bank of Washington, the Maritime Administration, and the Small Business Administration (formed in 1953 on the termination of RFC).

RFC, at first narrowly restricted by law in its lending field and credit standards, in 1934 received very broad powers to aid all types of businesses unable to obtain credit from private sources. In volume of direct business loans its program was by far the most important of those named, totaling $15 billion from 1934 through 1953. Export-Import Bank loans financing foreign trade with United States firms, extended partly to help reconstruct and stabilize foreign economies or facilitate lend-lease termination, were second in volume, totaling $4.6 billion from 1934 through 1953. The Federal Reserve Banks have extended working capital loans, comparatively small in total volume, where unavailable from private lenders; and the Maritime Administration has financed the construction or reconditioning of American-owned vessels, especially for use in foreign service.

The predominantly medium-term character of federal loans to business has been mentioned. For instance, about 70 percent of the total amount loaned by RFC carried maturities of 4 years, 7 months or longer.[8] Though some Export-Import Bank loans were for as much as twenty years, about 70 percent of the bank's loans outstanding at the end of 1953 had original maturities of ten years or less. Federal Reserve working capital loans were of shorter contract length, not exceeding five years.

On the average the loans have been of medium size, as compared to business term loans of private lenders, which suggests that medium-sized businesses have been the main group of borrowers served. The average size of commercial bank business term loans made during 1946 was about $27,000.[9] Since about half of the total amount was in very large loans, it is apparent from the smallness of the average that the great majority of the bank term loans were small loans, to small firms. In contrast, the average size of direct business loans made by RFC during 1934–1951 was some $70,000,[10] and of industrial loans approved by the Federal Reserve Banks through 1950, about $175,000.[11]

RFC maintained a uniform interest rate for all types and sizes

[8] See Table B-2. In comparison, 46 percent of all commercial bank credit to business outstanding in 1946 had been written for terms of five years or less (Duncan McC. Holthausen, "Term Lending to Business by Commercial Banks in 1946," *Federal Reserve Bulletin*, May 1947, Table 14, p. 513).

[9] From a sample survey of member banks in the Federal Reserve system (Holthausen, *op.cit.*, Table 6, p. 505). An estimated 119,000 loans with maturities of one year or more were made, totaling $3.2 billion exclusive of repayments during the year.

[10] See Table B-1.

[11] *Federal Reserve Bulletin*, December 1951, p. 1541. Up to December 31, 1950, 3,698 applications had been approved for a total of $651,389,000.

of loans and in all regions; adjusted from time to time—from 6 to 5 percent in 1935, to 4 percent in 1939, and to 5 percent in 1950—usually it was below the average bank rates on roughly comparable credit. Interest charges on Export-Import Bank loans varied rather widely, with rates of $3\frac{1}{2}$ to 4 percent the most frequent for loans outstanding in 1953. The Maritime Administration discriminated in favor of ships used in foreign service, these having credit available at $3\frac{1}{2}$ percent as compared with $5\frac{1}{4}$ percent for ships used in domestic service. Rates on Federal Reserve Bank working capital loans ranged from 4 to 6 percent when the program was most active.

The stated policy of federal agencies supplying business credit has been to lend only where credit was unavailable from private sources. At the same time, federal statutes have embodied credit standards limiting the agencies' operations. The RFC Act required that loans should be "so secured or of such sound value as reasonably to assure repayment," and RFC in practice required the borrower to provide collateral security adequate in its estimation to protect the loan. Not that the current market value of collateral had to equal or excel the amount of a loan; rather, the long-run anticipated value should exceed it. Similar provisions for the other business lending agencies, as well, show that Congress has not viewed business credit programs as disguised grants, but has intended that normal banking measures be taken to assure their repayment; and in practice, collateral has been required.

The fact that the Reconstruction Finance Corporation regarded its business loans as sufficiently secured to assure repayment did not necessarily mean that the loan was of such high standing that it should have been available through private sources. In the first place, a private banking institution might well have questioned the adequacy or acceptability of the collateral regarded as sufficient by RFC. Moreover, the legal framework within which banking institutions operate, the policy of bank examining authorities, the liquidity needs imposed by slender capital resources and high ratios of demand deposits to total liabilities, unfamiliarity with a particular type of credit, and other such factors may affect the availability of bank credit. At any rate, it seems clear that RFC undertook to make loans involving higher risks than many banks could or would assume. Broadly speaking, the same appears true of other federal business lending agencies.

Unlike the federal loan programs in agriculture and in housing, which in several outstanding cases were introduced and administered in large part with the object of relieving financial institutions of illiquid assets and loans of dubious quality, federal business credit programs have tended to avoid the policy of "bailing out" private credit institutions. Nonetheless, a fairly substantial part of the funds advanced by federal agencies to business was used to pay existing debt.

Finally, federal loans to business have been used rather extensively to finance new businesses and firms establishing themselves in new industries. In this respect the programs differ from those pursued in other sectors of the economy and, to a very considerable extent, from the activities of commercial banking institutions.

COLLABORATIVE FINANCING ARRANGEMENTS
BETWEEN PUBLIC AND PRIVATE AGENCIES

In every one of the federal business lending programs an effort has been made to extend credit, whenever possible, under some form of collaborative arrangement with private financing institutions. To do so was not possible in all cases, but the participation of private lenders has been obtained in a high proportion of all loans. The RFC did it through entering into immediate or deferred participations with private lenders, and this technique has been continued, with somewhat greater emphasis, by the Small Business Administration. Furthermore, for roughly two years beginning in March 1945, the RFC offered automatic guarantees to commercial banks under its so-called blanket participation agreements, which provided that a commercial bank was automatically assured of a deferred participation by RFC of up to 75 percent of the amount of any business loan which it made in conformity with RFC statutory loan restrictions and subject to certain size limitations. The Federal Reserve Banks and the Export-Import Bank have also made a special point of participation with private agencies. In amount, however, the most extensive program of this type was that under which the War and Navy Departments and the U.S. Maritime Commission, through the Federal Reserve Banks as agents, guaranteed loans to war contractors under Regulation V, working capital loans for the transition from defense to civilian activities, and loans to release funds tied up in terminated government contracts.

The fees charged for guarantee or deferred participation commitments have varied considerably on different types of transactions. In the case of the RFC the portion protected varied from 50 to 90 percent of the total loan amount, with the fee charged for the guarantee commitment being graduated, at first, from a lower limit of ½ percent, depending upon the duration of the proposed guarantee; during the thirties the fees were raised, then lowered, and finally in 1950 they were sharply raised, to a flat 2 percent. Most of the industrial advances which carried Federal Reserve Bank guarantees involved protection of 50 percent of the loan amount, and commitment fees ranged from ½ to 2 percent in the early years of the program and from ½ to 1¼ percent after 1945.

A special study of loans made by private lenders with immediate or deferred RFC participation revealed that they were predominantly of medium and large size, averaging about twice the size of loans made wholly by RFC and well over three times the size of term loans made independently by banks. The banks involved were usually institutions of medium and large size, located in cities of medium or large populations. Only a small fraction of the banks eligible for RFC participation chose to use it; 99 banks accounted for roughly a third of the number and half of the amount of loans involving RFC participation. The fact that a quarter of the participation loans were for amounts which exceeded the legal loan limit of the bank involved suggests that the opportunity of making larger loans than the statutes or the diversification policies of bank managements would ordinarily permit was a major reason why RFC collaboration was sought out.

Special interest attaches to the program initiated in 1944 under which the Veterans' Administration guarantees up to 50 percent of the amount of a business loan made to an eligible veteran provided the guarantee does not exceed $4,000 on a loan secured by real estate or $2,000 on a loan secured by other collateral or unsecured. This program is distinctive in that VA was not given the authority to lend directly to business but only to guarantee loans made by private institutions, and in that the program was unrestricted as among eligible borrowers. The business loans guaranteed by VA have consisted mainly of credits to very small firms, made in relatively small amounts, and on maturities that run in the neighborhood of three years. They have been marked by an unusually high application to the financing of new businesses and have probably served to attract considerably more funds into this area than would otherwise have been directed to it.

Housing

The federal credit aids available to homeowners, home financing institutions, and builders are also fairly limited in scope and variety; but whereas the narrowly focused programs of credit aid to business have had little influence outside of the immediate area to which they have been directed, the impact of federal housing credit programs has been felt throughout the housing field. The general arrangement of the program through which credit aids to housing are currently administered is shown in Table 12.

The Home Loan Bank system—which consists of the Home Loan Bank Board, the eleven Home Loan Banks, the Federal Savings and Loan Insurance Corporation and the member savings and loan associations (all those federally chartered and state associations choosing to affiliate themselves)—was the first of the housing credit programs to be established. It was set up in 1932 to provide credit to home financing institutions on a plan similar in some respects to that by which commercial banks obtain credit through the Federal Reserve Banks. The facilities of the Home Loan Banks have been used extensively: in mid-1936, 64 percent of the eligible members were indebted to the Home Loan Banks; at the end of 1949, 47 percent and at the end of 1953, 52 percent.[12] Although the Home Loan Banks were set up with the immediate object of aiding home financing institutions hard hit by depression, the bulk of their lending came in the housing boom which followed World War II. The system was designed for ultimate ownership by the member associations using its facilities, and at the present time all federal capital has been eliminated. Borrowing members have been required to hold Federal Home Loan Bank stock equal to one-twelfth of the amount of their indebtedness to a district bank or to 1 percent of their home loan outstandings. The advances outstanding at the end of 1953 were divided about equally as between those having maturities of one year or less and those extending for longer periods of time, up to ten years. Interest rates ranged in the various districts during 1953 from 2¾ to 3½ percent; and the system has always provided that the charge to a nonmember borrower should be at least ½ percent, but not more than 1 percent higher than the rate charged to a member.

12 *Sixth Annual Report*, Federal Home Loan Bank Board, 1938, p. 112; *Fourth Annual Report*, Housing and Home Finance Agency, 1950, p. 173; and *Seventh Annual Report* (*id.*), 1953, pp. 136 and 143.

TABLE 12

Federal Housing Finance Agencies: Organization as of the End of 1953

(amounts of transactions through December 31, 1953, or of outstandings on that date)

Housing and Home Finance Agency (Office of the Administrator)			Veterans' Administration
Home Loan Bank Board *Federal Home Loan Banks* ($952 million of loans to member institutions outstanding) *Federal Housing Administration* ($33 billion of insurance written on residential mortgage and property improvement loans) *Federal National Mortgage Assn.* ($3.9 billion of FHA-insured and VA-guaranteed mortgages purchased, $1.0 billion sold) *Public Housing Administration* ($667 million of loans and investments, advances, and other credits outstanding, mainly to local authorities, and guarantee commitments of $1.7 billion for local authorities)a	*Division of Community Facilities and Special Operations* *College Housing Program* ($29 million of loans made) *Defense Community Facilities* ($2.8 million of applications approved for loan funds that are sole responsibility of HHFA and $0.9 million that are joint responsibility of HHFA and Dept. of Health, Educ. and Welfare)	*Division of Slum Clearance and Urban Redevelopment* *Slum Clearance and Urban Redevelopment* ($7.6 million in preliminary and final planning and $30.8 million in project loans disbursed)	*Loan Guaranty Program* ($21.5 billion of guarantees written on home loans) ($289 million of direct home loans closed)

From *Seventh Annual Report* of the Housing and Home Finance Agency, 1953, *passim*, and *Loan Guaranty*, Veterans' Administration, December 1953, pp. 69 and 75.

In basic tables (Appendix A) and in general sections of the text, classification of loan programs by economic sector served refers to the immediate recipient of credit, so that the FHA, defense community facilities, and slum clearance programs are under "minor governmental units," the federal home loan bank program under "financial institutions," and college housing under "miscellaneous." Here such programs are included to give a functional view of federal credit activities affecting housing. Excluded because in liquidation are: the prefabricated housing, first and second advance planning, and Alaska housing programs of the Division of Community Facilities of the HHFA.

a As of June 30, 1953.

The Home Loan Banks are also responsible for the supervision and examination of member associations, and the Federal Savings and Loan Insurance Corporation provides insurance of shares in member savings and loan associations. While the facilities of the federal intermediate credit banks in agriculture and of the Federal Reserve Banks in commercial banking resemble the Home Loan Bank system in several significant respects, the latter provides, within the scope of its own operations, a set of federal financial aids unmatched in coverage by those developed for any other sector of the economy.

In contrast to the Home Loan Bank system, which was conceived and has operated as a permanent agency for strengthening the network of savings and loan associations, the Home Owners' Loan Corporation was created as a temporary agency to refinance home mortgage loans in default as a result of deep depression, and which would wind up its operations as quickly as possible. This, too, was the history of the corporation, though the conclusion of its affairs perhaps took longer than was at first expected.

The need for the services of the corporation was dramatically proven when within four months of its establishment in 1933 over 400,000 applications for refinancing home mortgage loans were received. Altogether, 1,017,821 loans, for a total of $3.1 billion, were made; it is estimated that 21 percent of all homeowners eligible for HOLC assistance actually received it. It was this unprecedented refinancing operation—comparable only with the Land Bank Commissioner program in agriculture—that was the substance of HOLC's activities.

Although the HOLC was designed to refinance defaulted mortgages for distressed mortgagors generally, the fact is that the individuals who availed themselves of its assistance came mainly from a middle income group. It was in the intermediate zone of property values— from $3,000 to $8,000—that HOLC activities were concentrated, at least in the New York region, where it was possible to study the loan characteristics in detail. Little more than 40 percent of all the properties in the New York region in the mid-thirties fell within that price class, but over 60 percent of HOLC properties were found there. This fact is especially interesting because, as will be seen below, mortgage loan insurance too has served mainly a middle section of the housing market.

The loan insurance and guarantee programs of the federal government consist of the Federal Housing Administration's facilities for insuring home modernization and repair loans and long-term residential mortgages, and the Veterans' Administration's program of guarantees of loans on owner-occupied residences. The FHA programs were started in 1934 to offset the effects of economic depression on the construction industry and, incidentally, to encourage the adoption of methods of home financing that would help avoid a repetition of the mortgage collapse of the early thirties.

The insurance of property improvement loans, which got under way first, was intended to be temporary, but the program is still in effect; under it, approved lending institutions have been insured, at no cost to them or to the borrowers, up to 20 percent (later, 10 percent) of the aggregate amount they loaned. In 1939 a fee intended to put the program on a self-supporting and permanent basis was established; and in 1954, after exposure of widespread abuses in the program, a principle of loss-sharing between the federal government and lending institution was introduced.

The property improvement loan insurance program was launched with considerable, and sometimes spectacular, publicity and soon reached sizable proportions. In the first three years well over a million loans were insured, and by the end of 1953 nearly 16,600,000 loans, with net proceeds over $7.4 billion, had been insured.[13] As of 1953, insurance was available under the Title I program for loans to repair, alter, or improve existing residential and other structures, single or multifamily, in amounts up to $10,000 and for terms mainly of three years.

Most of the insured property improvement loans—in fact, three-quarters of them, by amount, during 1934–1953—were made by commercial banks, though a variety of financial institutions have participated in the program.[14] The insured loans have been predominantly small, with terms averaging eighteen months, and for the most part have been for the improvement of one-family structures, though very early in the program some emphasis was placed on loans for the improvement of small commercial buildings.

One of the most interesting aspects of the Title I program is that it is frequently credited with having introduced banking institutions to, or at least encouraged them to extend their activities in, the

[13] *Seventh Annual Report,* Housing and Home Finance Agency, 1953, Table 61, p. 297.

[14] *Sixth* . . . and *Seventh Annual Reports,* Housing and Home Finance Agency, 1952, p. 337, 1953, p. 304.

installment financing field. The loans have almost all been of the installment credit type, involving some down payment and repayment in equal monthly amounts.

Turning to the main field of housing finance, home mortgages: more than the fact that federal insurance and guarantee programs now in effect provide protection for approximately one-third of the mortgages on small residential structures in the United States, a summary of the particular services rendered, and borrowers and lenders affected, will suggest the influence such programs have exerted on the home mortgage market. Under FHA, lenders are insured for the full amount of their mortgage loans in return for a premium charge which is paid into an insurance fund. Losses are met out of these funds, but should they prove insufficient the federal government would be responsible for the full amount of the loss. Under VA, which is a nonfunded plan, approved lenders are guaranteed at no cost up to 60 percent of the amount of the loan which they made to an eligible veteran, but the guaranteed portion may not exceed $7,500. Under either agency's program, to qualify for protection the loan must be made within terms specified by the guaranteeing agency. These encompass the interest rate charged, the maximum ratio of loan amount to value of underlying security, and the maximum maturity. All loan contracts must provide for full repayment by maturity and must permit the mortgagor to repay in advance of maturity without penalty. The two schemes vary somewhat with respect to the liens that can be taken: FHA loans must be of a first mortgage type, but second mortgages may be guaranteed under VA. Finally, only when the properties being financed meet certain physical specifications laid down by the insuring and guaranteeing agency is loan protection granted.

Perhaps the most interesting fact about the federal programs of loan insurance is that they have been employed mainly by a middle class of home buyers. Between October 1950 and March 1951, for example, FHA insured 27 percent and VA guaranteed 30 percent of the loans given on homes costing between $10,000 and $12,500. In the lower and higher price brackets of houses the incidence of federal insurance or guarantee activity was substantially lower. Thus, only 10 percent of the loans on houses costing less than $5,000 were financed through FHA, and only 11 percent were guaranteed by the VA; similarly, only 19 percent of the houses costing $15,000 and over were financed by loans carrying FHA insurance, and VA

79

guarantees aided in the purchase of but 8 percent.[15] Conventional lending (that is, lending without benefit of federal insurance or guarantee) was more important as a financing technique in the lower and upper grades of construction.

The terms on which home mortgage loans are made under the protection of federal insurance or guarantee are naturally more liberal than those characteristic of conventional lending, and in general the loans guaranteed by VA are more liberal than those insured by FHA. In a comparison of loan-to-value ratios for loans on single family, owner-occupied homes acquired during 1949 and the first half of 1950, well over half of the conventional loans had loan-to-value ratios lower than 65 percent, as against less than a tenth of the federally protected loans. About seven out of ten VA-guaranteed loans were in amounts equaling 90 percent or more of the value of the property; but of FHA-insured and conventional loans, only about one in ten had such a liberal ratio.[16] As to contract maturity, periods of about twenty years have been characteristic for both agencies. Among the conventional home loans of private lenders, only those by life insurance companies show more than a small frequency of such long terms (31 percent).[17] The Housing Act of 1954 liberalized FHA loans on one- to four-family properties to the extent of permitting loans up to 30 years with amounts loaned equal to 95 percent of the first $9,000 of value of the property and 75 percent of the excess of value over that amount.

Probably the most active recent controversy in the mortgage insurance and guarantee field has concerned the interest rates at which federally protected loans can be made. The specification of maximum rates on FHA-insured home mortgages at $4\frac{1}{4}$ percent in the early fifties required either that funds be diverted from investment in such loans or that mortgages be sold at discounts to the lenders. This situation was temporarily remedied in early 1953 when interest rates were raised to $4\frac{1}{2}$ percent. Similarly the maximum rate on VA-guaranteed loans was raised in May 1953 from 4 to $4\frac{1}{2}$ percent.

Extensive use of the loan insurance facilities of the federal government has also been made in the apartment house field. There are no

15 Data are for purchases of new and existing one- and two-family nonfarm homes for owner occupancy, from a sample survey by the Board of Governors of the Federal Reserve System. See *Federal Reserve Bulletin*, July 1951, Table 19, p. 793.

16 *Housing Research*, Housing and Home Finance Agency, Winter 1951–52, Table 1, p. 9.

17 See footnotes 23 and 24, Chapter 8.

systematic data with which to describe the units that are built outside of the FHA insurance system, but it is probably safe to say that they consist either of very low-cost structures which fail to conform to FHA standards, or are luxury apartments in which the cost per dwelling unit is so high that the FHA financing would have little practical value.

Under the FHA program, there is provision for the insurance of loans on rental properties and also for those operated on the cooperative plan, and over the years special provisions have been made for the insurance of loans for war or defense production needs. It is primarily in connection with the latter programs that the terms of loan insurance were deliberately made liberal and that allegations of abuse have been most frequently heard. The institutions making use of the project mortgage programs are primarily commercial banks and savings banks. These institutions originated 73 percent of the total insured project mortgages in 1953, as compared with 4 percent for insurance companies and 12 percent for mortgage companies. However, at the end of 1953 banks held only 50 percent of the total outstanding compared with 36 percent for insurance companies and 6 percent for mortgage companies, indicating that the banks (commercial banks, at least) and mortgage companies tended to sell their holdings in part to the longer-term investors.[18]

There has been considerable interest since the early thirties in establishing secondary mortgage market facilities within the federal government. The RFC Mortgage Company, a subsidiary of RFC created in 1935 primarily to make direct loans on income properties, soon after became also a secondary market facility in the home mortgage field, with authority to purchase and sell FHA-insured home and housing project mortgages, and later, VA-guaranteed home mortgages.

This operation was discontinued in June 1947, and on July 1, 1948 the Federal National Mortgage Association, the so-called "Fanny May," which had been set up in 1938 to provide a market for FHA-insured home mortgages, was authorized to purchase VA-guaranteed home mortgages. Later it was authorized to conduct operations in all types of FHA-insured mortgages. Through December 31, 1953, it had purchased $3.9 billion of mortgages and at that time was holding about $2.5 billion.[19]

[18] *Seventh Annual Report,* Housing and Home Finance Agency, 1953, Table 49, p. 278.
[19] *Housing Statistics* (Housing and Home Finance Agency), January 1954, p. 67.

FNMA was reorganized under the Housing Act of 1954 with the object of making it eventually a privately owned institution by the device of requiring stock purchase by the users on the pattern of the federal land banks. In addition, its powers were widened so that it might serve as a secondary facility in the sense of providing liquidity for holders of existing insured and guaranteed mortgages.

Since the expiration of the HOLC the federal government has been involved but little in the direct extension of credit to homeowners. FHA direct loans have been incidental to disposing of foreclosed properties acquired through its loan insurance responsibilities. After 1950, a VA program supplied home loans to veterans in areas where VA-guaranteed loans were unavailable from private sources on what are determined to be reasonable terms.

The Voluntary Home Mortgage Credit Program authorized by the Housing Act of 1954 is specifically designed to obviate the need for direct lending such as practiced by the Veterans' Administration.

CHAPTER 4

Lending Experience of Federal Credit Agencies

THE variety of federal lending and of loan insurance programs is such that it is exceedingly difficult to generalize concerning the credit experience of the government. A few facts, however, stand out clearly. First, it is fairly well established that the federal government had an exceptionally favorable record in those programs in which it refinanced debts that were in default during the economic depression of the thirties. The outstanding examples are the home mortgage refunding operations of the Home Owners' Loan Corporation and the farm mortgage refinancing carried out by the Land Bank Commissioner, both in the thirties. We shall come at a later point to the details concerning these programs; mainly, the explanation for the favorable credit experience is that the borrowers for the most part were only temporarily embarrassed and economic recovery rather quickly put them back on their feet.

A second conclusion, equally well-established, seems to be that the federal government has had an unfavorable credit experience when it has attempted to supply credit, sometimes during depression but even during periods of general economic prosperity, to business firms and farm enterprises unable—because of their newness, or owing to some weakness in financing position or management—to find financing on reasonable terms through private lenders. Large parts of the Reconstruction Finance Corporation's activities and certain of the programs in the agricultural field fall within this category.

Third and last, it is generally clear that the cooperative financial institutions sponsored by the federal government have fared well as lenders; indeed, they have shown a tendency to become more and more like private institutions, with which they often compete closely, and have registered a broadly comparable credit experience.

Default and Loss Experience

The general observations concerning loan experience may be illustrated by reference to those programs on which sufficient data are available to permit at least rough appraisals of default and loss experience.

83

In agriculture this includes the experience of the federal land banks, the so-called Commissioner loans, the loans made since 1933 by the production credit associations, and the activities of the banks for cooperatives, the Rural Electrification Administration, and the Farmers Home Administration. The federal land banks have been active over a long period of time, and it is therefore possible to examine their experience under different economic conditions. From their establishment in 1917 until 1929, the twelve district banks had a largely favorable experience; indeed, it was slightly more favorable than the experience of life insurance companies. The percentage of their outstanding loans that were delinquent was around 5 percent over this period, and less than 3 percent of the loans made through the end of 1929 ended in foreclosure. Recoveries on properties sold during the period equaled 88 percent of the banks' investment in them and total losses on mortgage loans and real estate investments amounted to about 3 percent of loan extinguishments or 0.13 percent of cumulative outstanding loan balances.

Compared with the experience of the land banks, the record of a group of fifteen large life insurance companies during the twenties was considerably less favorable. At the end of 1929, the value of the properties which they held as a result of foreclosure amounted to 7.6 percent of their total farm mortgage investment, compared to 2.5 percent for the land banks. On the other hand, the life insurance companies recovered a larger percentage of their investment in foreclosed properties. Thirteen companies reported that they recovered about 95 percent of their total investment in properties sold in 1928 and 1929, compared with the 88 percent cited for land banks. Since the land banks were permitted during the twenties to lend up to 50 percent of the appraised value of land plus 20 percent of the value of insured permanent improvements, they were not compelled to follow a rigidly conservative lending program; but the evidence indicates that they did in fact lend conservatively and that they managed, by and large, to build a record that was somewhat better than that of typical private institutions.

As might be expected, delinquencies on the mortgage loan accounts of the land banks increased sharply in the decade 1930–1940, but not more so than the delinquencies on loans of private institutions. By the beginning of 1933, about half of the loans held by the land banks were delinquent or had been extended in order to prevent default;

land bank foreclosures averaged somewhat under 10,000 per year for the decade 1930–1940, compared with a cumulative total of less than 15,000 for the whole history of the land bank system up to 1930. This was not an unusual record, however, considering the fact that fifteen of the largest life insurance companies were forced to foreclose by 1937 on more than one-third of the loans that they had outstanding in 1928. Also, the loss experience of the land banks was severe, especially during the latter part of the decade. Throughout the period 1930–1940 total losses incurred on mortgage loans and real estate transactions averaged 0.70 percent of year-end loan balances. Finally, the available evidence suggests that in the thirties, as in the predepression years, life insurance companies were more successful than the land banks in disposing of farm properties. From 1930 to 1937, land bank recoveries averaged about 75 percent of the total cost of acquired properties, compared to nearly 90 percent for thirteen large insurance companies.

Between 1940 and 1953 there were virtually no delinquencies or foreclosures, and losses on real estate and mortgage transactions were negligible both for public and private institutions. The delinquency ratio of the land banks was reduced to the 5 percent level characteristic of the years before 1930; foreclosures declined from 859 in the fiscal year 1944 to 20 in fiscal 1953; and after 1948, recoveries on farms sold exceeded the land banks' investment in them.

The Land Bank Commissioner program (set up in 1933 with the idea of providing credit to farmers which could not be had through the facilities of the land bank system nor through the channels of private finance) was distinctly an emergency program, and the expectation from the beginning was for substantial losses. The Commissioner was authorized to make first mortgage loans to borrowers whose credit needs were not being met by the land banks or by private banking institutions, and second mortgage loans to supplement borrowing from the land banks. As might be imagined, many of the first mortgage loans involved the refinancing of defaulted loans held by the land banks. Moreover, the Federal Farm Mortgage Corporation, from whose funds Commissioner loans were made, followed a liberal policy in resetting and extending loans, provided the borrower was making a reasonable effort to carry them. As a result, from 1933 through 1940 the corporation's farm real estate acquisitions totaled about 10 percent of the total amount loaned. By the end of 1940, three-fourths of the acquired properties had been sold and about 72 percent of the corporation's investment in them had been recovered. Moreover, as of this date the losses on Commissioner loans were 0.42 percent of cumulative outstanding loan balances, compared to 0.51 percent for the land banks. The two are not in every way comparable, because the bulk of the Commissioner loans were made during the very bottom of the depression and had the full advantage of the recovery that followed, whereas the land bank experience reflected lending in the late twenties as well as in the early years of the thirties. Yet the comparison is instructive.

From 1941 on, experience under the Commissioner program paralleled that of other farm mortgage lenders. Delinquencies declined from about 25 percent of outstandings in 1939–1940 to 8 percent in 1945–1947. The percentage of investment recovered on properties sold increased from 70.4 percent in 1940 to 89.6 percent in 1946. Total losses from 1941 to 1951 on property acquired and subsequently sold equaled 0.57 percent of the cumulative amount of outstanding loans.

Experience with Land Bank Commissioner loans was far more favorable than had been anticipated. Furthermore, on the whole it was better than the experience of other federal programs designed to relieve distressed borrowers during the early thirties, primarily because Commissioner loans were made on a long-term basis, with liberal amortization requirements, and had the advantage of a subsequent long period of recovery. Loans that were made on shorter term, and which came to maturity before economic recovery had had its full effect, had a much less favorable record.

The relatively favorable experience of the programs designed to help borrowers who, by and large, could meet the credit standards of private finance but were unable to borrow because of inadequate credit facilities is well illustrated by the history of the production credit associations. The losses incurred by these cooperative financing agencies varied widely from one district to another, and among individual associations, but over all the record was approximately the same as that of commercial banks operating under similar conditions. Net losses for PCA's averaged about one-half of one percent of yearly outstanding loan balances in 1936–1940, compared to 0.58 percent for country national banks. From 1941 to 1946, both PCA's and country national banks reported recoveries in excess of losses in some years and for the remaining years, small net losses in relation to yearly outstandings. At the end of 1950 the loss rates for both PCA's and banks were less than 0.10 percent. Over the entire twenty-year history of the PCA's net losses and provision for losses have amounted to only 0.14 percent of total cash advanced under loan contracts, exclusive of renewals. This percentage has varied from a low of 0.08 percent in the Midwest (the Louisville, St. Louis, and Wichita farm credit districts) to a high of 0.33 percent in the northeastern section of the country.

Similarly, favorable records of loan experience have been built by the banks for cooperatives. The total net losses of these institutions have been only 0.13 percent of the cumulative outstanding loan balances, or 0.07 percent of the total amount of loans made from the beginning in 1933 through 1953. Like the land banks and the PCA's, the banks for cooperatives incurred much higher losses in the 1930's than during the years following 1940. At the end of 1941 the cumulative net losses were 0.2 percent of the loans made to that date and 0.29 percent of cumulative outstandings.

The REA has had very few losses on its loans made to local cooperative power and light companies. Through June 30, 1953, only two loans resulted in loss, and in both cases the amounts were small.

The heaviest losses in the agricultural field have come in those programs, currently administered by the Farmers Home Administration, in which credit was extended for general farm operating and production or emergency and disaster purposes, either on the security of farm real estate or on relatively short term. The credit programs of the Farmers Home Administration and its predecessors were specifically designed to assist low-income farmers, farm tenants, or farm laborers who could not obtain financing from private sources at reasonable rates of interest. It was to be expected, therefore, that losses under them would be substantial. The available evidence indicates that losses actually incurred to mid-1953 on all except the farm ownership and farm housing programs have not fallen short of expectations. Thus, the over-all loss rate in relation to the $2.9 billion loaned by the FHA since 1946 and by its predecessors as far back as 1918 was 5.3 percent, and nearly 7 percent if the total amount of interest written off is also included.[1]

However, losses through the FHA real estate credit program were not unduly severe. Amounts written off (including accounts on which judgments were pending) under the Bankhead-Jones farm tenant purchase program equaled only 0.32 percent of the $428 million ad-

[1] *Report of the Administrator of the Farmers Home Administration,* 1953, p. 32.

vanced from 1937 to mid-1953. No losses were reported as of June 30, 1953 for the farm housing program authorized under Title V of the Housing Act of 1949, nor for the farm ownership insured loan program set up in October 1947. Over its four years of operation, loans under the former totaled $81 million, of which more than 85 percent was still outstanding as of mid-1953. In addition, grants totaling about $364,000 were made from November 1949 to mid-1953. At the end of 1952, FHA contributions to delinquent accounts, as provided under the enabling legislation, amounted to nearly $54,-000, covering both interest and principal installments.[2] Under the farm-ownership insured loan program only about 10 percent of the $64 million extended to farmers by private lenders through June 30, 1953 had been repaid. In summary, FHA's experience with its real estate credit programs was fairly successful up to 1953, as compared with the record of the land banks or the Land Bank Commissioner, a comparison in which allowance should be made for the fact that the program has operated since its beginning in a favorable economic climate.

Experience under FHA's various non-real-estate credit programs, and those of its predecessors, is not easily summarized from the information available in published reports. Additional recoveries on certain programs under liquidation, such as the rural rehabilitation loan programs of the Farm Security Administration and the emergency crop and feed loan program of the Farm Credit Administration, are still anticipated. To date, however, principal charged off on rural rehabilitation loans represented 7.0 percent of about $1 billion advanced from 1934 through November 1, 1946, when the program was discontinued.[3] The heaviest losses were experienced in the emergency crop and feed loan program, which began in 1918 as a means of giving temporary relief to farmers suffering from production disasters. Through June 30, 1953, principal charged off represented 13.5 percent of total loans made, and as of that date nearly $24 million of the $576 million extended before the program was discontinued in November 1946, remained unpaid.[4]

The record of the FHA with its production and subsistence, water facilities, and disaster loan programs has been more satisfactory.

[2] *Ibid.*, p. 23.

[3] Compiled from the *Report of the Administrator of the Farmers Home Administration, 1953*, p. 22.

[4] *Ibid.*, p. 22, and *Agricultural Finance Review* (Agricultural Research Service), Vol. 16, November 1953, p. 105.

From 1946 through mid-1953 only 0.25 percent of the $614 million advanced for production and subsistence loans had been written off or was in process of judgment. Less than 6 percent of the matured principal of such loans was unpaid as of June 30, 1953.[5] The water facilities loan program, begun in 1937 by the Farm Security Administration and continued by the Farmers Home Administration, has shown the most favorable record. Disbursements through mid-1953 were only about $28 million; write-offs and judgments in process accounted for less than 0.04 percent of this amount; and repayments of principal were slightly in excess of the total amount of matured principal.[6] The outcome of the disaster loan program (including fur and orchard loans) is by its very nature unpredictable. Losses to June 30, 1953 had been moderate. Less than 0.01 percent of the $129 million advanced from 1949 to mid-1953 was written off, but nearly $80,000 or 0.06 percent was in process of judgment. About 9 percent of the matured principal was unrepaid, and more than 40 percent of these short-term credits were still outstanding, as of June 30, 1953.[7]

On balance, the Farmers Home Administration has experienced severe losses in providing non-real-estate credit to farmers. To mid-1953 the over-all loss rate on loans for general farm operating and production purposes—covering rural rehabilitation, production and subsistence, and water facilities programs—was 4.4 percent, and the combined loss rate for loans of the emergency type, such as the disaster loan and emergency crop and feed programs, was in excess of 10 percent.

BUSINESS

The experience of federal and federally sponsored agencies in lending to business enterprises has been approximately what would have been expected considering the nature of the programs. That of the Reconstruction Finance Corporation comes to mind first, of course, but it bears very close similarities to the program of industrial advances carried on by the Federal Reserve Banks and the two may be considered together. Both programs were devised to provide intermediate-term credit to business concerns unable to meet the credit standards of private agencies; both, furthermore, were most active during the thirties, in the years of most severe economic depression, that of the RFC beginning in 1932 and of the Federal Reserve Banks

5 *Ibid.*, p. 22. 6 *Ibid.*, p. 23. 7 *Ibid.*, pp. 22 and 30.

in 1934. As might be expected, the records achieved by the two agencies were distinctly less favorable than those characteristic of private financing institutions; indeed, their losses were greater than could be sustained by private agencies functioning under the requirement of earning a reasonable return on invested capital.

Up to the end of 1951 the RFC had incurred losses equal to about 2 percent of all disbursements on loans extinguished to that date; and over its entire history somewhat less than 10 percent of the number of loans extinguished had involved some loss. A fair comparison of RFC experience with that of commercial banking institutions is not easily made, since there was always a tendency for the better loans in the portfolio of the federal agency to be taken over by private financing institutions. The RFC, accordingly, was left with an adverse selection of credit risks. For what it is worth, however, it may be pointed out that at the end of 1951, 13 percent of RFC loans then outstanding were delinquent, whereas during 1951 less than 1 percent of all bank loans were classified as substandard by supervisory agencies.

The experience of the industrial loan program of the Federal Reserve Banks can best be described (for reasons that will appear) in terms of its activity during the period before 1941 when the depression forced many small business firms to utilize the credit services of the program in financing their working capital needs. Up to December 31, 1940 just over 2,000 loans had been made—slightly more than one-half in cooperation with banks and other financial institutions, and the remainder as direct loans. Losses were subsequently charged off on 4 percent of the former and on 6 percent of the latter. In anticipation of severe losses, the Federal Reserve Banks had set up reserves which, in addition to a small amount of losses charged off as of that date, amounted to about 5 percent of total loan advances through the end of 1940. During the late forties and early fifties, there were both substantial recoveries on loans previously charged off and withdrawals from reserves. In addition, fewer loans were made, although average loan size increased. The banks were also more thorough in their investigation of prospective borrowers. All things considered, therefore, it seems reasonable to evaluate the loss experience of the program by reference to the loan advances made through 1940. On this basis, net losses actually charged off to the end of 1951 represented 3 percent of total advances from 1934 to the end of 1940, a rate that is slightly higher than the over-all loss ratio of the RFC program. However, if the highly favorable lending operations of recent years are taken into consideration, net losses through December 31, 1951 form only 0.6 percent of the total amount of loans extinguished to that date.

The close relationship between the loss experience of a federal credit agency and the type of credit function which it is called upon to perform is vividly illustrated in the case of the RFC. Nearly two-thirds of the RFC business loans extinguished with loss were made to newly established firms. It is also quite clear from an examination of RFC loan experience—given in greater detail in Part II and in Appendix B—that a factor closely connected with loss experience has been the availability of information concerning the financial condition of the borrower. The proportion of loan extinguishments involving some loss was significantly higher for those loans on which the credit files were inadequate than for other loans. Absence of information on the previous financial condition of the borrower might reflect the fact that the enterprise was new and to all intents and purposes had no previous experience. Alternatively, it might result from an even more ominous condition, namely, inadequate management of the enterprise. In any case, either because of the newness of the firm or the inadequacy of its management, this characteristic was closely associated with unfavorable experience.

Four other business lending programs may be mentioned. These are the program of the VA under which small loans to veterans for business purposes were insured or guaranteed, the very large program under which guarantees were provided for loans for war production purposes, the lending program of the Export-Import Bank, and the modest loan program of the Maritime Administration for ship purchase and construction. The last two may be dismissed briefly with the observation that losses have been negligible. Credit extended by the Maritime Administration, it should be borne in mind, had not the character of a general lending program but rather was a financing arrangement that was only part of a broad program for advancement of the merchant marine. More interest attaches to the VA program of business loan guarantees and the Regulation V program. The VA program began in late 1944 and up to December 25, 1954, 8 percent of the guaranteed loans extinguished involved the payment by the VA of some claim to the financing institution that made the loan. These claims rose sharply in 1947–1949, owing in part to adverse economic conditions, but receded thereafter. Data on loss ratios are not available, but it is likely that they would be comparable to the RFC ratio of 2 percent; in fact, through December 25, 1954 net claims paid by the VA equaled less than 3 percent of the total principal collected on guaranteed loans repaid in full. As a more or less regular matter the delinquency ratio under the program has been in the neighborhood of 5 percent, which is probably higher than that of commercial banks, though bank data for a direct comparison are lacking.

The Regulation V program was established when it became clear that producers having war contracts during World War II would find it difficult to obtain the necessary short- and medium-term financing through private financing channels. It was felt at the time that the risks involved in these operations exceeded those that could properly be undertaken by private financing institutions, and accordingly a program was put together along the lines described in the preceding chapter. As will be recalled, the loans were exclusively for working capital purposes, there being an over-all prohibition against the guarantee of loans for plant and facilities. The record of the program shows that 1.8 percent of the guaranteed loans were extinguished with some loss, but as these were mainly small credits to small manufacturing plants they accounted for only 0.6 percent of the total amount of loans authorized under the guarantee program. Furthermore, settlements were so favorable that the estimated extent of loss on the program has been put at 0.06 percent of the aggregate loan authorizations. All things considered, the loans as a group produced a loss ratio very much lower than was expected.

HOUSING

The similarity between the lending experience of public and private agencies when the two operate under comparable circumstances is again evident in the record of the Home Owners' Loan Corporation. The corporation was established in 1933 to refinance defaulted home mortgages held by private financing institutions. Nearly 20 percent of the more than one million mortgages refinanced were eventually foreclosed by HOLC, but this is not an extraordinary record when it is recalled that 20.9 percent of the home mortgage loans made by major life insurance companies in the period 1925–1929 ended in foreclosure.

HOLC's record was very much better on loans made in connection with the sale of its foreclosed properties. Only about 2 percent of these so-called "vendee" accounts ended in foreclosure, a result which compares very closely with the life insurance company foreclosure rate of 1.8 percent on loans made in the years 1935–1939. A further point of similarity between the experience of the HOLC and that of private lenders is the regional variation in foreclosure rates. The HOLC rates in New York, New Jersey, and Massachusetts were as high as 40 percent, whereas the over-all rate was approximately 20 percent. The experience of private lenders, in particular the life insurance companies, was also distinctly less favorable in the New England and Middle Atlantic states than elsewhere. As a general rule, foreclosures were more frequent for both the HOLC and the life insurance companies on loans secured by properties located in highly industrialized and heavily populated areas.

In contrast to the HOLC, whose activities were directed to the relief of distressed homeowners, the RFC Mortgage Company operated in a much broader area, supplying credit on a mortgage basis directly to business firms (such as owners of apartments and commercial buildings), and purchasing such loans and also FHA-insured home mortgage loans from private lenders. The company's record makes it possible, therefore, to compare within one agency's experience the performance of loans secured by commercial and industrial properties with that of loans secured by small residential dwellings. Through June 30, 1946, just a year before its dissolution, the RFC Mortgage Company had foreclosed or charged off nearly 9 percent of the credit it had extended to business firms, directly or through loan purchases, since 1935. For the same period of lending, only 5 percent of the amount of FHA-insured home loans purchased had been so extinguished (through September 1952). Though these figures do not measure ultimate loss, they illustrate a fact common among both public and private lending agencies in the housing field, namely, that the experience on loans secured by small, medium-priced, owner-occupied homes was much more favorable than that on loans secured by income-producing properties, particularly apartment house structures. The record of the RFC Mortgage Company's refinancing activities was even more satisfactory where purchases of VA-guaranteed mortgages were involved. Through September 30, 1952, less than 3 percent of them, by amount, had ended in foreclosure.

The different experience with small home loans as against those on larger residential properties is vividly illustrated in the record of the Federal National Mortgage Association, an agency empowered to purchase both VA-guaranteed and FHA-insured loans. Through December 31, 1953, less than 1 percent of FNMA's total purchases of federally protected home mortgage loans, but fully 10 percent of the FHA-insured housing project loans purchased, were terminated by foreclosure.

The loan insurance and guarantee programs of the Federal Housing Administration and the Veterans' Administration also illustrate the relatively low risk associated with the financing of small homes designed for owner occupancy. For example, through insuring loans for the repair, alteration, or improvement of properties—mainly single family homes—the FHA has paid claims from the beginning of the program through 1953 equal to only 2 percent of the net proceeds of loans insured. Furthermore, recoveries have amounted to at least 40 percent of the claims paid to that date. With home mortgages, experience for both the FHA and the VA has also been exceedingly favorable. Over the years 1934–1953 foreclosures represented only about 0.5 percent of both the number and original amount of FHA loans insured; and under the VA home mortgage guarantee program, claim payments through 1953 were made on only 0.6 percent of the loans, and the amount paid (less recoveries) represented a similarly small fraction of the amount of the guaranteed loans. In contrast, nearly 4 percent of the number and 3 percent of the original amount of FHA-insured multi-unit housing project loans since 1934 have been terminated by foreclosure.

Earnings and Net Operating Results

Besides the foreclosure and loss data obtainable from loan records, a means of revealing the experience of federal and federally sponsored agencies is to examine whether their operations have been self-supporting. Analyses of this type are in most instances quite complicated, since they call for a full accounting of all costs associated with a particular program and only in very rare cases are the data available for making such a record. Nevertheless, it is possible, by examining each program separately, to approximate an answer to the question whether federal lending programs have been self-sustaining.

In the field of agriculture attention is first directed to the operations of the federal land banks. Through June 30, 1954 the land banks reported cumulative net earnings of $371 million. However, if a 2 percent charge were made for the interest-free capital supplied by the government through subscriptions to their capital stock and contributions to their paid-in surplus, net earnings of the land banks would be reduced by almost one-fifth. The provision of interest-free capital was not the only basis on which financial assistance was made available. The land banks were also remunerated by the Treasury to the extent of $277 million for the reduction in interest rates which they made in 1933–1944 at the direction of Congress. If this reimbursement is deducted from the net income remaining after the charge for government-supplied funds, it appears that the program as a whole has been barely self-supporting.

The experience of the Land Bank Commissioner is in striking contrast to that of the land banks. In the emergency lending through the Commissioner the estimated cost of government-supplied capital, assuming an interest rate of 2 percent, was about $39 million and the reimbursement received by the program for its interest rate reductions was $57 million. Net earnings from 1933 to mid-1954 exceeded the combined cost of such federal assistance by 50 percent. On balance, therefore, the program may be considered as having been self-supporting. This result is surprising in view of the fact that the Commissioner loan program was intended to provide credit in high-risk areas where private capital and the capital of the land banks was unavailable or in short supply. Nevertheless, it is another indication of the remarkably good over-all record of long-term mortgage lenders whose activities were directed to areas of severe mortgage distress and whose operations were initiated at the trough of the real estate cycle.

Similarly, the production credit system has apparently been self-supporting. The production credit associations, through the purchase of their class A stock by the production credit corporations, were supplied with interest-free capital which, at a 2 percent charge, would have cost about $20 million to mid-1954. However, the cumulated net earnings of $90.8 million reported by the PCA's from 1934 to mid-1954 easily covered that cost. In addition to the capital supplied by the PCC's, the PCA's also obtain loan funds by borrowing from, or discounting their loans with, the federal intermediate credit banks; the latter, in turn, extend the major part of their credit to PCA's, and therefore can be treated as part of the production credit system. From 1923 to mid-1954 the cost to the FICB's of the interest-free capital which they employed would be $37 million at an interest rate of

2 percent. The banks, however, were required to pay franchise taxes to the government amounting to $9.2 million from the date of their organization to June 30, 1954. After offsetting this amount against the estimated interest cost of federal capital, the position of the banks, which reported cumulated earned surplus of $30.1 million to June 30, 1954, with $17.0 million in reserves, is highly favorable. Thus the system as a whole can be regarded as being more than self-supporting through mid-1954.

Generally speaking, the banks for cooperatives have struck a rough balance between their net profit and the estimated cost of federal assistance. From 1933 through June 30, 1954, their cumulated net profit was $78.4 million, against which an estimated $67 million, at an assumed rate of 2 percent, should be charged for the interest-free capital provided by the Treasury.

A comparable analysis of the operations of the Rural Electrification Administration and of the Farmers Home Administration is not possible. For the former it is known that federal aid has involved the payment of REA administrative expenses, which amounted to $76.8 million through mid-1953, and the provision of low-cost capital at rates which have sometimes been higher than the interest rates paid by REA borrowers. As to the FHA, it is clear that various programs administered by this agency and its predecessors have not been self-sustaining, though the amount of federal subsidy entailed is unknown. Moreover, the FHA has performed a wide variety of services for its borrowers in addition to its credit extensions, and in some cases has extended grants as well as loans to the same individual. At least part of the cost of such services and of the grant program would have to be considered in determining the amount of federal assistance given to the loan program. The most that can be said is that through mid-1953 cumulative interest payments and repayments of principal have almost struck a balance with the total amount advanced under all programs.

The lending programs of federal and federally sponsored agencies in the business field have exhibited varying degrees of self-sufficiency. The lending activities of the Export-Import Bank, and presumably the loan-guaranteeing activities under Regulation V, were definitely self-supporting. Through June 30, 1954 the Export-Import Bank reported cumulated net earnings in excess of $300 million, against which only the cost of funds borrowed from the Treasury since 1945 had been charged. However, net income to date would still be sizable

96

even if adjusted for the full cost of all Treasury borrowings from the beginning of operations in 1934.

From April 1942 to December 31, 1949, the net revenue from the V-loan guarantee program amounted to over $23 million. Although no charges had been made as of the end of 1949 for administrative expenditures, it may be inferred that the program was at least a self-sustaining, if not a profitable, one.

The business loan program of the RFC has been conducted at a concealed subsidy—a fact which was clearly faced by both the RFC management and the Congress, particularly during the later years of the corporation's life. There were no restrictions placed upon the income and cost structure of RFC lending activities, either by congressional directive or by the RFC Act itself. A recommendation was made by a special subcommittee of the Senate Committee on Banking and Currency in 1948 that "under normal conditions the (lending) activities should be conducted so as to make them self-sustaining insofar as it is possible."[8] Two years later evidence was presented in Senate hearings to show that RFC was not currently operating on a self-supporting basis from the taxpayers' standpoint. The subcommittee studying RFC in 1950 found that lending operations in fiscal 1949 (for all programs combined) would show a net loss of $6.5 million, instead of the published profit of about $5.2 million, if a deduction was made for interest on cost-free capital supplied by the Treasury, and on earned surplus not paid back into the Treasury. In its defense, the RFC maintained that the use of interest-free capital had been intended by Congress as a subsidy to small borrowers.

Apparently the RFC earned a small net profit on a full-cost basis from its combined lending programs during the five-year period after World War II, but there is reason to believe that the operating results of the business loan program compare unfavorably with the over-all record. During fiscal 1949 and during the first nine months of fiscal 1950, for example, according to estimates prepared for the Fulbright Subcommittee the RFC operated at a net deficit of $8.0 million and of $5.6 million, respectively, if the proportionate share of all expenses such as interest on cost-free capital and surplus is charged against the gross income from business loans. Moreover, during the twenty-one months ending March 31, 1950, the relation

8 Senate Report 974, 80th Cong., 2nd sess., March 1948. Committee on Banking and Currency, *Report on the Operations of the Reconstruction Finance Corporation* to accompany S. 2287.

97

of costs to income was less satisfactory for deferred participation loans than for direct business loans (including immediate participations). Unfortunately, the accounting methods used by the RFC in its published financial statements do not permit this kind of analysis for the years after 1950; but even lacking the precision of detailed calculations, examination of the reported figures, with rough allowance for a full-cost basis, suggests that at best only a small net profit was realized on the business loan program from 1951 through June 30, 1953.

Only limited evidence on earnings is available for the industrial loan program of the Federal Reserve Banks. During the early years of the program, operations were highly unprofitable, if the cost of the Treasury funds employed is included with the realized and anticipated losses on loans as operating expense. At the end of 1940, the estimated net deficit of the program was nearly $2 million; but a decade later, through substantial recoveries on losses previously charged off and because of reductions in the provision for anticipated losses during the World War II and postwar period, the program showed a modest profit.

The last program for consideration in the field of federal credit to business—a loan guarantee and insurance program of the Veterans' Administration—was designed from its beginning in 1944 as a subsidy to eligible veterans in need of bank credit for financing small business ventures. From 1944 to the end of 1952, estimated total expenses of the business loan guarantee program were in the neighborhood of $25 million. Had a self-supporting operation been intended, to achieve it the VA would have had to charge premiums equal to about 5 percent of the total principal amount loaned, or to 15 percent of the guaranteed portion, on all loans disbursed up to the end of 1952.

The records of federal credit agencies in the housing field also provide evidence as to whether federal lending programs have been self-supporting. Through March 31, 1951, by which time operations had virtually ceased, the Home Owners' Loan Corporation reported that it had earned a net income of $352 million exclusive of losses, and that losses on loans charged off were $338 million. The small indicated profit, however, might be transformed into a small loss if the costs of Treasury-supplied funds and of other services supplied by the government such as the free use of the mails were taken into account. Considering the highly speculative nature of such cost adjustments, a less harsh conclusion may be more just. Perhaps the tentative evaluation of the operations of HOLC should be that the program from its initiation in the depths of the depression to its final termination in 1951 struck an approximate balance between income and cost.

From the fragmentary published materials on the financial outcome of the RFC Mortgage Company operations, it would appear that this agency, like the HOLC, successfully balanced income against outgo. Cumulative earned surplus up to the time of its dissolution in 1947 was about $4 million and was probably adequate to absorb the costs of funds supplied, or of the exemptions and privileges allowed by the government.

The Federal National Mortgage Association has presumably also been self-supporting. Through December 31, 1953 a net income of $140.4 million had been earned, out of which $92.4 had been paid in dividends to the Reconstruction Finance Corporation and in dividends and interest to the Treasury on capital advances. Nearly three-fourths of the balance had been set aside as reserves for losses, but the reserve accumulation, although apparently adequate for a portfolio consisting entirely of insured or guaranteed loans, was low by conventional standards, amounting to less than 2 percent of FNMA's outstanding mortgage portfolio at the end of 1953.

Similarly, the financial record of the Federal Housing Administration has been one of income exceeding expense, although reserve accumulations have been relatively modest compared to the total unpaid balances of insured loans still outstanding. Thus, the combined net income of all FHA programs through June 30, 1953, exceeded the federal government's contribution to the programs by $301 million. In view of the magnitude of its operations, however, the FHA's earnings record to date after allowance for federal contributions has been relatively low, forming only 0.91 percent of the volume of insurance written through the end of 1953.

The loan guarantee and insurance program of the Veterans' Administration in the housing field, on the other hand, has not operated without federal subsidy, since no premiums have been charged for the services granted. It is impossible to determine from data presently available the extent of federal assistance to date, or even the exact amount of income and operating costs associated with this program as distinct from the other loan programs of the VA. However, estimates developed from information supplied by the VA place the cost of administering the home loan program (including gratuity payments, net claim payments, salaries, and other operating expenses) at just under $430 million through December 1952.

Surveying the major areas of federal credit programs—agriculture, business, and housing—it is found that most of the programs have been self-supporting, at least from a long-range point of view. An element of subsidy has been present only in those programs which served a particular class of borrower such as low-income farmers, veterans, or small business firms. On the other hand, it is clear that no program, except possibly that of the Export-Import Bank, has realized profits at a level which would be considered satisfactory by the conventional standards of the private financial system.

CHAPTER 5

The Economic Significance of Federal Lending and Loan Insurance

AT THE END of 1953 there was outstanding in the public's hands nearly $43 billion of credit extended or underwritten by federal or federally sponsored agencies (Table 13). About two-thirds of this amount consisted of the insured or guaranteed portions of federally protected private loans. About 69 percent of the $43 billion total loaned or insured or guaranteed had been extended to homeowners, 12 percent to farmers and farm financing institutions, and 10 percent to business enterprises. This vast pool of obligations represented the accumulated flow—net of debt retirements and repayments—of over thirty-five years of federal credit activity. During most of this period the trend of the annual volume of loans made or insured by federal agencies has been strongly upward; federal credit activities have grown faster than the value of gross national product or the credit activities of private financial institutions. The volume of operations reached a new high during 1953, the last year under study, when loans made, insured, or guaranteed by federal and federally sponsored agencies totaled nearly $14 billion.

If one aggregates the amount of credit extended since 1917, without deduction of repayments or retirements, it is found that the gross volume of loans made, guaranteed, or insured, and stocks and shares purchased by federal and federally sponsored agencies amounts to $138.7 billion. Of this sum, the share of federal agencies consists of $37.5 billion of direct loans, $62.9 billion of loan insurance or guarantee commitments, and $1.5 billion of stocks purchased; $36.8 billion of direct loans and stock purchases were made by federally sponsored agencies.

What have been the effects upon the American economy of these large federal lending and loan insurance and guaranty operations? Their magnitude suggests that their influence has been profound, though the analysis of these effects is complicated by the fact that the programs have operated under widely varying economic conditions and differed widely as to objectives and administration.[1]

---

[1] Federal credit has not been the subject of extensive economic analysis. Apart from discussions of particular agencies, and incidental references to federal lend-

TABLE 13

Volume of Federal Lending and Loan Insurance Extended during 1953, and Amount Outstanding at Year End, by Type of Agency and Sector of the Economy

(dollar figures in millions)

	AGRICULTURE		BUSINESS		HOUSING		OTHER[a]		TOTAL	
	Amt.	Percent	Amt.	Percent	Amt.	Percent	Amt.	Percent	Amt.	Percent
EXTENDED DURING 1953										
Federal agencies										
Loans	$ 458	15.4%	$ 821	28.9%	$ 723	11.0%	$ 835	53.4%	$ 2,838	20.3%
Loan ins. & guaranty	12	0.4	1,996	70.3	5,851	89.0	b	b	7,860	56.3
Stock & share purch.	..	..	..	..	..	..	..	..	..	..
Federally sponsored agencies										
Loans	2,509	84.2	22	0.8	..	..	728	46.6	3,258	23.3
Stock purchase	1	c	..	..	..	..	..	..	1	c
Total	2,980	100.0	2,839	100.0	6,575	100.0	1,562	100.0	13,957	100.0
Percent of total	21.4%		20.3%		47.1%		11.2%		100.0%	
OUTSTANDING END OF 1953										
Federal agencies										
Loans	2,790	55.1	3,755	83.0	3,003	10.2	965	24.8	10,514	24.5
Loan ins. & guaranty	124	2.4	765	16.9	26,504	89.8	1,933	49.7	29,327	68.2
Stock & share purch.	..	..	..	..	..	..	41	1.1	41	0.1
Federally sponsored agencies										
Loans	2,148	42.4	2	c	..	..	952	24.4	3,102	7.2
Stock purchase	5	0.1	..	..	..	..	..	..	5	c
Total	5,068	100.0	4,522	100.0	29,508	100.0	3,891	100.0	42,988	100.0
Percent of total	11.8%		10.5%		68.6%		9.1%		100.0%	

Computed from Tables A-1 and A-8. For amounts included under the several categories of credit activity, see Chapter 2, footnote 1. Amounts will not always add to totals due to rounding; percentage distributions were computed before rounding.

a Includes financial institutions, minor governmental units, and miscellaneous groups.
b Not available.
c Less than 0.05 per cent.

Some programs have been designed to stimulate economic recovery generally; others have been intended to divert resources to particular segments of the economy. Many have had unforeseen and unintended economic consequences. In the wake of all of them have followed material changes in the credit practices of, and markets served by, private financial institutions. The present chapter seeks to analyze these relationships, grouping them into three broad categories:[2]

First, aggregative economic relationships, or the relations between federal lending and loan insuring on the one hand and the general level of prices and the over-all physical volume of production on the other. In this analysis, the policies implied by federal lending and loan insuring operations will be compared with federal policy in expenditure and fiscal operations, with monetary policy, and with private credit activities.

Second, resource-allocational effects, by which is meant changes in the patterns of resource-use that have been induced by federal credit activities, both as between and within major sectors of the economy. For present purposes it is convenient to distinguish between the agricultural, housing, and business sectors, which appear to have been the segments most profoundly affected by federal lending and loan insuring activities. An attempt has been made to appraise the influence of the federal programs on the physical volume of production, the level of costs and prices, and the debt-equity relationships within each of these sectors.

Third, the institutional effects of federal credit programs on the private financial system, by which is meant the effects on the volume of credit extended and methods of operation of private financial institutions, their credit practices, and the economic functions that they perform.

ing and loan insurance in treatments of monetary and fiscal policy, the articles by Neil H. Jacoby on "Government Loan Agencies and Commercial Banking," *American Economic Review* (Vol. XXXII, No. 1, March 1942, pp. 250-260), and by Robert Friedman, Jr. on "Federal Credit Agencies and the Structure of Money Markets, Interest Rates, and the Availability of Capital," *Quarterly Journal of Economics* (Vol. LXIX, No. 3, August 1955, pp. 421-444), appear to be the only efforts to assess its over-all economic effects, and they have focused attention only upon the relation between federal lending and the banking system.

2 For brevity, the phrase "loan insuring" will often be used to cover guarantees as well as insurance; also for simplicity of presentation, stock and share purchases are grouped with and treated as similar to long-term direct loans. For more exact definition of terms and of amounts included, see Chapter 2, footnote 1.

Aggregative Economic Relationships

PROBLEMS OF MEASUREMENT

The difficulty of determining the precise effect of federal loans and loan insurance on gross national product is readily seen if one poses the question: How much would GNP have been in recent years if there had been no federal lending or loan insurance programs? Clearly, the effect of a given volume of federal lending or loan insurance on GNP will depend upon where and how the funds involved were obtained, and how they influenced the expenditures of the borrowers. To simplify the analysis and the exposition, possible differences in the effects of loan insurance and of direct lending will for the moment be disregarded.

The effect on GNP of a net increase of, say, $1 million in the outstanding credit of federal agencies will depend principally on the following: (1) the extent to which the net change in total public and private credit outstanding is different than it would have been had not an increase in public credit occurred; that is, the extent to which the new public credit substituted for, augmented, or reduced private credit;[3] (2) the extent to which aggregate federal expenditures were different than they would have been in the absence of an increase in public credit; that is, the degree to which federal credit substituted for federal grants, subsidies, or other expenditures (as when a guaranteed loan finances defense plant construction that would otherwise have involved federal outlays); (3) the extent to which the federal credit was financed by taxes, by a reduction of federal deposit balances, by the sale of securities to the banking system, or by sales of securities to the public, and, if the latter, what the public would have done with its funds if it had not utilized them to purchase federal securities; (4) the degree to which borrowers from federal agencies utilized the proceeds of loans to refund outstanding indebtedness or to increase their deposit balances, rather than to acquire additional noncash assets; and (5) the degree to which borrowers repaid loans by liquidating noncash assets, instead of drawing on idle balances.

Since it is not possible to obtain accurate and comprehensive measures of these factors, any simple comparison of the magnitude of federal credit operations with gross national product is subject

---

[3] Although federal credit is at times extended to borrowers who would otherwise obtain it from private sources, private agencies sometimes grant additional credit on the basis of federal loans.

to serious qualification if it be taken to measure directly the effect of these operations on GNP. Yet certain inferences can reasonably be drawn from such a comparison, and we shall proceed along that line. First, however, it is necessary to consider (a) whether it is essential in this connection to differentiate between direct federal lending and loan insurance, and (b) whether the volume of credit should be measured in terms of net or gross flow.

There are a number of reasons for believing that, in some circumstances, the expenditure-generating effects per dollar of federal loan insurance have been at least equal to those of direct federal lending. For example, if the Reconstruction Finance Corporation stood ready to make a direct loan to a business enterprise, it would also be willing to guarantee the major part of a similar or larger loan made by a commercial bank. Loan guarantees were administered by RFC strictly as alternatives to direct loans. Indeed, the expansionary effects on expenditures per dollar of loan guaranty usually exceeded those of direct lending by RFC, because the amount disbursed by a private lender under RFC protection was often larger than what would have been loaned directly by RFC without the participation of a commercial bank.[4]

With respect to the federal guaranty under Regulation V of loans to businesses engaged in war production, the similarity of the effects of federal loan guarantees and direct federal loans is less clear. There was no legal requirement in this case that the credit should be unavailable to a business before the guaranty could be extended; and there is evidence that a considerable fraction of V-loan credit would have been extended by commercial banks in the absence of a federal guaranty.

A similar observation may be made with respect to the home mortgage loans insured by the Federal Housing Administration and the Veterans' Administration, which have composed the bulk of all federal loan insurance activities. Federal loan insurance has undoubtedly increased the volume of home mortgage lending,[5] and its expansive influence upon aggregate housing expenditures has been at least as much as, and probably more than, it would have been if federal

---

[4] In addition, federal loan guaranty or insurance does not require the immediate disbursement of federal funds and cannot, therefore, have a deflationary effect on expenditures by impinging on tax funds.

[5] Our data show only the amount of the liability of each federal agency on an insured loan, thus understating the economic impact of loan insurance by ignoring the part of such credit carried at private risk.

agencies had stood ready to make home mortgage loans directly.[6] Yet the influence on housing expenditures per dollar of federal insurance has probably been less than the impact on business and agricultural spending per dollar of direct federal lending or of loan insurance in those sectors of the economy, because a larger proportion of home mortgage lending would have occurred in the absence of any federal action. For this reason, it is probably incorrect to add federal home loan insurance to direct federal loans, in attempting to determine the impact of federal credit programs on GNP, unless one reduces somehow the amount of home mortgage loan insurance involved. Unfortunately, we have not been able to develop a satisfactory method of determining how, or to what extent, the figures should be deflated; our series will include the uncorrected amounts.

Regarding the relative merits of measures of the net or gross flow of credit: there is strong support for the view that the net flow, or change in the level of outstandings, provides the best gauge of the impact of federal credit on the economy. The argument is that only the net difference (positive or negative) between loan disbursements and repayments exerts a thrust (expansive or contractive) upon aggregate expenditures.[7] On the other hand, it is sometimes argued that the gross flow, i.e., the annual volume of loans made, and of loan insurance granted, is a superior measure of economic impact, because disbursements of loans may be expected to increase business and consumer expenditures, whereas repayments of direct or insured loans are unlikely to entail a proportionate reduction. In other words, it is more likely that borrowers contracting new loans will add to their expenditures than that those making repayments on old loans will reduce them.[8] There is the further consideration that repayments are usually scheduled by existing contracts, and are not susceptible to immediate alteration, so that public control of federal

[6] Federal loan insurance probably resulted in larger expenditures on housing than direct federal loans of the same type would have produced, in so far as competition among private lenders resulted in greater promotional effort and in expansion of the market.

[7] See Gottfried Haberler's *Consumer Instalment Credit and Economic Fluctuations* (National Bureau of Economic Research, Financial Research Program, 1942), Chapter 3, p. 79, especially.

[8] Repayments undoubtedly exert some contractive influence on the expenditure rates of debtors, especially when loans are repaid in lump sums rather than amortized over a period of years. Because the timing of the reductions in the expenditures of borrowers will differ from the timing of their repayments, loan disbursements in a given period cannot be compared with repayments in the same period to determine the net effect of credit operations on aggregate expenditures in that period.

lending or loan insurance in the interest of economic stability must rely mainly on adjustments in the volume of credits extended.

Each of the two measures—volume of credits extended and change in outstandings—possesses validity for particular purposes, with the choice between them turning principally on what one believes to be the effects of repayments on the expenditures of borrowers. In recent years repayments have grown so large (nearly $10 billion in 1953) that it would be difficult to ignore them.[9] We shall, therefore, utilize both measures in our analysis, and consider the relationship of each to GNP. In addition we shall treat a rise in net lending in the same way as a rise in gross lending, without regard to whether the net rises from a negative to a smaller negative figure, from a negative to a positive figure, or from a positive to a larger positive figure; likewise with declines.

RELATION OF FEDERAL CREDIT PROGRAMS
TO GROSS NATIONAL PRODUCT

The most generous measure of the importance of federal lending and loan insurance programs in the national economy is the annual ratio of the gross volume of these operations to GNP. By this measure, federal credit activities were less than 1 percent of GNP in every year from 1919 through 1930, rose to 3.7 percent in 1932, and continued (except in 1934, when they rose to nearly 9 percent of GNP) to hold about that relative position through 1953 (Table 14). Although its high level in the early thirties was never subsequently regained, the ratio has shown no tendency to decline secularly and may be said to have been a factor of considerable importance relative to the aggregate expenditures of the economy for nearly two decades.

The conclusions reached are not greatly different when one employs the more conservative measure of the importance of federal credit activities in the economy, the ratio to GNP of the net change in outstandings of federal loans and loan insurance. Through 1931,

9 Over the whole period 1917–1953, loan repayments and expirations of insurance have amounted to 69 percent of the volume of credit extended: the ratio of repayments and other reductions in outstandings to advances has been much lower during years of rapid rise in credit operations (for example, 13 percent in 1920 and 27 percent in 1934) than in years of shrinking operations (for example, 114 percent in 1944 and 136 percent in 1945). For each dollar of net increase in outstandings over a given period, federal agencies typically have extended about three dollars of credit services, concurrently receiving around two dollars in repayments.

TABLE 14

Federal Loans and Loan Insurance in Relation to Gross National Product, 1919–1953

(dollar figures in millions)

YEAR	GROSS NATIONAL PRODUCT	VOLUME EXTENDED DURING THE YEAR		OUTSTANDINGS AT YEAR END	NET CHANGE IN OUTSTANDINGS		REPAYMENTS OF LOANS AND EXPIRATIONS OF INSURANCE
		Amount	As Percentage of GNP		Amount	As Percentage of GNP	
1919	$ 75,027	$ 386	0.51%	$ 395	$ 205	0.27%	$ 181
1920	86,815	733	0.84	1,034	639	0.74	94
1921	71,081	379	0.53	1,260	226	0.32	153
1922	71,825	506	0.70	1,303	43	0.06	463
1923	83,711	382	0.46	1,431	128	0.15	254
1924	84,954	325	0.38	1,487	56	0.07	269
1925	88,530	294	0.33	1,476	−11	−0.01	305
1926	95,021	320	0.34	1,527	52	0.05	268
1927	93,409	292	0.31	1,474	−53	−0.06	345
1928	95,537	258	0.27	1,438	−36	−0.04	294
1929	104,436a	250	0.24	1,486	48	0.05	202
1930	91,105	667	0.73	1,779	293	0.32	374
1931	76,271	943	1.24	2,031	252	0.33	691
1932	58,466	2,175	3.72	3,324	1,293	2.21	882
1933	55,964	2,550	4.56	4,574	1,250	2.23	1,300
1934	64,975	5,827	8.97	8,830	4,256	6.55	1,571
1935	72,502	2,827	3.90	10,019	1,189	1.64	1,638
1936	82,743	2,031	2.45	10,101	82	0.10	1,949
1937	90,780	1,746	1.92	10,106	5	0.01	1,741
1938	85,227	2,250	2.64	10,215	109	0.13	2,141
1939	91,095	2,781	3.05	10,832	617	0.68	2,164

(continued on next page)

TABLE 14 (continued)
(dollar figures in millions)

YEAR	GROSS NATIONAL PRODUCT	VOLUME EXTENDED DURING THE YEAR		OUTSTANDINGS AT YEAR END	NET CHANGE IN OUTSTANDINGS		REPAYMENTS OF LOANS AND EXPIRATIONS OF INSURANCE
		Amount	As Percentage of GNP		Amount	As Percentage of GNP	
1940	100,618	3,260	3.24	11,749	917	0.91	2,343
1941	125,822	3,663	2.91	12,534	785	0.62	2,878
1942	159,133	4,522	2.84	13,598	1,064	0.67	3,458
1943	192,513	7,440	3.86	13,958	360	0.19	7,080
1944	211,393	6,482	3.07	13,079	−879	−0.42	7,361
1945	213,558	4,775	2.24	11,345	−1,734	−0.81	6,509
1946	209,246	5,658	2.70	12,520	1,175	0.56	4,483
1947	232,228	7,438	3.20	15,699	3,179	1.37	4,259
1948	257,325	8,108	3.15	19,636	3,937	1.53	4,171
1949	257,301	8,603	3.34	23,559	3,953	1.54	4,650
1950	285,067	11,154	3.91	28,936	5,377	1.89	5,777
1951	328,232	12,234	3.73	34,620	5,684	1.73	6,550
1952	346,095	13,144	3.80	38,817	4,197	1.21	8,947
1953	364,857	13,957	3.83	42,988	4,171	1.14	9,786

Volume of loans (including stock purchases) and loan insurance extended by federal and federally sponsored agencies, and amounts outstanding at year end, from Tables A-1 and A-2. Gross national product (in current dollars) for 1929-1953 from *National Income Supplement, 1954, Survey of Current Business* (Department of Commerce), Table 2, p. 162; for 1919-1928 estimated by Simon Kuznets in *Supplement to Summary Volume on Capital Formation and Financing* (unpublished), Part A: Annual Estimates, 1919-1953, Variant III.

a Kuznets' figure, comparable with earlier years, is $101,465 million.

109

annual net changes in outstandings amounted to well under 1 percent of GNP, but the percentage rose in 1932 to 2.2 and reached a peak of 6.6 percent in 1934. Thereafter the ratio fell, stood for a decade at less than 1 percent, and then increased to between 1 and 2 percent in the years 1947–1953. However, the increase during this last period should be discounted at least in part, and the ratios for 1936–1943 and for 1946 regarded as rather lower than those given, since in those years the net increase in FHA (and VA) home mortgage loan insurance was large in relation to the net increase in outstandings. The figures on net flow bear out the previous observation that the year 1934 probably witnessed the peak of the influence of federal credit programs on the economy.

Have federal lending and loan insuring activities tended to amplify or to dampen business fluctuations in the past twenty years? The analysis may begin with the thirties, since federal credit programs were too small in the twenties to have an appreciable weight in general economic conditions. The major economic decline of the early thirties extended from a peak in June 1929 to a trough in March 1933, according to the National Bureau's business cycle chronology. On a calendar-year basis, GNP fell sharply in each year of the period 1930–1932 (Chart 6). Although the gross and net annual volume of federal loans[10] began to rise steeply in 1930, in absolute terms the increase was not sharp until 1932. Between 1931 and 1932 GNP declined $17.8 billion, while the gross flow of federal credit increased $1.2 billion and the net $1.0 billion. The gross and net flow did not change much between 1932 and 1933, while GNP declined only $2.5 billion. Between 1933 and 1934 an expansion in GNP of $9.0 billion was realized. It is significant that the 1933–1934 increase in gross volume of federal loans and loan insurance, $3.3 billion, was more than a third as large as the increase in GNP, and the figure is not much smaller when taken net of repayments. Federal credit programs appear to have been an important instrument for the revival of the economy in these years, operating influentially as a counter-cyclical measure.

The stimulating effect of federal credit programs diminished after 1934, as both the gross and net volume of loans and loan insurance declined. In 1936 and 1937 repayments virtually equaled new loans

[10] Unfortunately, not enough quarterly data on federal loans and loan insurance programs are available to make the more precise study of their cyclical influence that such materials would permit.

and in 1937–1938 the increase in new loans barely exceeded the increase in repayments. This withdrawal, on net balance, of federal credit supports to spending may have contributed to, though it could not have been a principal cause of, the short but severe downturn in general economic activity from mid-1937 to mid-1938. Furthermore, although the revival in 1938 and the subsequent economic upswing, which lasted through World War II, coincided with an expansion of federal lending and loan insurance programs, neither could have been much affected by it. The economy during these years was dominated by the enormous rise in federal military expenditures. The net flow of funds from the federal loan and loan insurance programs reached a peak in 1942, the gross flow in 1943. The decline to 1945 was due, in the main, to the tapering-off of federal guarantees of war production loans under Regulation V.

By 1946, however, the postwar readjustment had been completed and a construction boom was under way. In every year since 1946 the net flow of federal loans and loan insurance has been substantial, and in 1950–1953, despite a rapidly rising volume of repayments, the annual dollar volume approached or exceeded that of 1934, the peak depression year. Coming as they did in a period of high-level employment of economic resources due principally to other causes, these increases in federal credit programs, while relatively small compared with the increases in GNP, nevertheless must have contributed appreciably to the price inflation of that period.

Additional light may be shed on the relation of federal credit programs to general business conditions by considering the extent to which the directions of change in GNP, on the one hand, and in gross and net credit flow, on the other, have been concurrent or divergent (Table 15). It appears that the gross volume of federal credit has increased not only in every year that GNP declined, but also in a substantial majority of the years when GNP increased. On the average, the annual increase in gross volume was about the same when GNP rose as when it fell, and in any case small relative to the changes in GNP. However, the gross volume of credit has frequently increased substantially during the initial year of revival (i.e., 1933–1934, 1938–1939, 1946–1947, and 1949–1950) and it is reasonable to call such increases counter-cyclical. On this basis the gross volume moved in a counter-cyclical direction 15 years out of 24 since 1929, and the average annual increase during the 11 years of contraction or initial revival in GNP was $1.12 billion, or ten

CHART 6

Annual Volume and Year-End Outstandings of Federal Loans and Loan Insurance, and National Product, 1917–1953

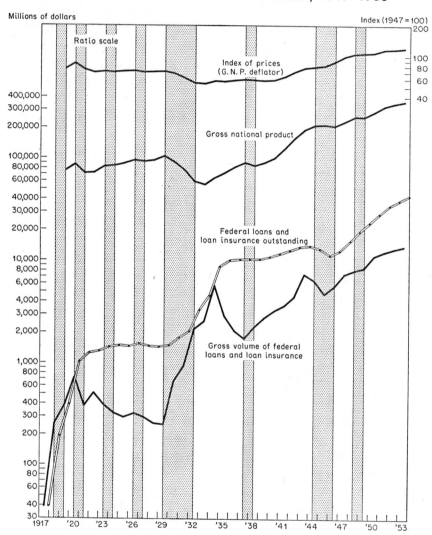

For data of lending and loan insuring by federal and federally sponsored agencies, and of gross national product, see Table 14. Price index is from the sources cited there for GNP, with the Kuznets series, 1919–1928, lowered by its 1929 ratio to the Commerce series (the latter, from Table 41 of the 1954 Supplement referred to).

Shaded areas denote periods of contraction in business activity, as defined by National Bureau of Economic Research reference dates.

CHART 6 (concluded)

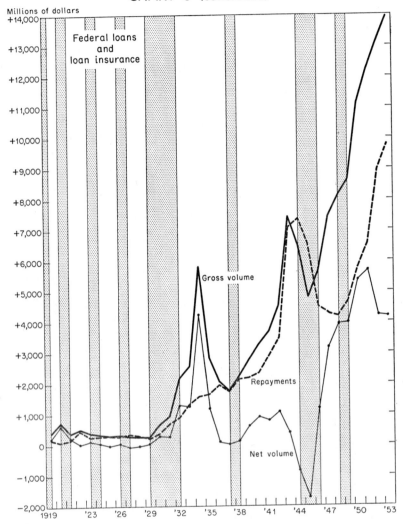

Millions of dollars

Federal loans and loan insurance

Gross volume

Repayments

Net volume

times the average annual increase during the remaining 13 years of expansion in GNP ($0.12 billion).

In terms of the *net* volume of loans and loan insurance the counter-cyclical record is somewhat better. Net volume rose more often than not when GNP declined and fell more often than not when GNP rose. Like gross volume, it rose during each of the four years of initial revival in GNP, and especially rapidly in three of them. On the average the net volume increased one billion dollars per year during years of contraction or initial revival, declined one-half billion dol-

113

TABLE 15

Year-to-Year Change in Volume of Federal Loans and Loan Insurance, in Relation to Changes in Gross National Product, 1929–1953

(billions of dollars)

YEARS WHEN GNP DECLINED[a]

	Change in GNP	Change in Federal Credit	
		Gross Volume	Net Volume
1929–30	−13.33	+0.42	+0.24
1930–31	−14.83	+0.28	−0.04
1931–32	−17.80	+1.23	+1.04
1932–33	−2.50	+0.38	−0.04
1937–38	−5.55	+0.50	+0.10
1945–46	−4.31	+0.88	+2.91
1948–49	−0.02	+0.50	+0.02
Average	−8.33	+0.60	+0.60
Number of			
Increases	0	7	5
Decreases	7	0	2

YEARS WHEN GNP INCREASED[a]

	Change in GNP	Change in Federal Credit	
		Gross Volume	Net Volume
1933–34	+9.01	+3.28	+3.01
1934–35	+7.53	−3.00	−3.07
1935–36	+10.24	−0.80	−1.11
1936–37	+8.04	−0.28	−0.08
1938–39	+5.87	+0.53	+0.51
1939–40	+9.52	+0.48	+0.30
1940–41	+25.20	+0.40	−0.13
1941–42	+33.31	+0.86	+0.28
1942–43	+33.38	+2.92	−0.70
1943–44	+18.88	−0.96	−1.24
1944–45	+2.16	−1.71	−0.86
1946–47	+22.98	+1.78	+2.00
1947–48	+25.10	+0.67	+0.76
1949–50	+27.77	+2.55	+1.42
1950–51	+43.16	+1.08	+0.31
1951–52	+17.86	+0.91	−1.49
1952–53	+18.76	+0.81	−0.03
Average	+18.75	+0.56	−0.01
Number of			
Increases	17	12	8
Decreases	0	5	9

Source: Table 14.

[a] With two exceptions (1932–1933 and 1944–1945) these correspond to years of contraction and expansion, respectively, according to the National Bureau's business cycle chronology.

114

lars per year during years of expansion. It would seem therefore that loan repayments, which constitute the difference between gross and net, have imparted some degree of counter-cyclical behavior to the lending programs—presumably by increasing more rapidly in good times than in bad.[11] Consequently, it is difficult to credit more than a part of this modest record to the conscious management of the program. But this was hardly to be expected, in view of the fact that unified management of the programs to promote economic stabilization has not been a major objective.

To summarize: Before 1932, neither the annual volume, nor the net change in outstandings, of federal loans and loan insurance was large enough, relative to GNP, to have exerted a significant influence on the general business situation; however, they appear to have imparted an upthrust to economic activity during the revival from the Great Depression. They were about neutral in their effects from 1936 to the end of World War II, but thereafter they contributed appreciably to the postwar inflationary boom. In the aggregate, federal programs of lending and loan insurance have a mixed record in their influence on business cycles; they have operated at times in a stabilizing, and at other times in a destabilizing, direction.[12] On balance, however, the programs have operated more often than not to offset a contracting or depressed level of economic activity and to give a stimulus to economic activity in the early stages of recovery movement, especially when account is taken of the volume of loan repayments as well as new loans made.

MOVEMENTS OF THE MAJOR COMPONENTS OF
FEDERAL LOANS AND LOAN INSURANCE

It may be useful to inquire also whether broad components of federal credit services—for example, the activities of direct federal

11 The difference in the counter-cyclical record of the gross and net figures is due primarily to the large volume of repayments during World War II (1940–1946) and the Korean War (1950–1953). It is interesting, however, to note W. Braddock Hickman's similar finding in his study of corporate bond financing. New money offerings exhibit a moderately regular inverse conformity to business cycles, repayments a fairly regular positive conformity; as a result the difference, the net change in outstandings, shows a markedly inverse association with business cycles. See The Volume of Corporate Bond Financing since 1900 (Princeton University Press for the National Bureau of Economic Research, 1953), pp. 116–123, 152–154.

12 These conclusions regarding the cyclical effects of federal loans and loan insurance correspond in most respects to those reached by Beryl W. Sprinkel regarding the credit operations of the RFC. See his "Economic Consequences of the FRC," Journal of Business, Vol. XXV, No. 4, October 1952, pp. 218f.

agencies as distinct from those of federally sponsored agencies, or direct lending regarded separately from loan insuring, or programs directed to different major sectors of the economy—have been mutually reinforcing or offsetting in their relationship to business fluctuations.

Loans by direct federal agencies have passed through five rather well-defined cycles. The first reached a peak at a volume of $666 million in 1920, in the post-World War I readjustment period; the second reached a peak at $4.6 billion in 1934; the third peak occurred at $1.4 billion in 1940, following the sharp recession of 1937–1938; the fourth peak was $1.6 billion in 1947, the immediate post-World War II readjustment period; after dropping in 1948, the volume rose steadily and stood at $2.8 billion in 1953 (Chart 7).

Loan insurance activities of direct federal agencies date only from 1934, and reveal two major peaks in volume. The first occurred during 1943 at a level of $5.1 billion, and reflected principally the V-loan guarantees extended by federal military procurement agencies. The second was reached during 1953, with a volume of $7.9 billion, largely in consequence of FHA and VA insurance or guarantee of home mortgage loans. Until 1949 the gross volume of the two types of credit services of direct federal agencies moved oppositely as often as concurrently; thereafter, they rose together. The net volumes have, if anything, been less closely correlated than the gross.

Federally sponsored agencies have not offered loan insurance services, and their annual volume of direct loans has fluctuated less widely than that of federal agencies. For the federally sponsored agencies, which have been managed more like private financing institutions, there were two definite peaks in loan volume. The first came during 1934, when $1.2 billion was loaned, mainly by federal land banks; the second came in 1952, with a figure of $3.3 billion, largely as a result of loans to farmers and farmer cooperatives.

Since 1930, the gross volume of credit services furnished by the two types of agencies have moved concurrently in seven of every ten years, but the net volumes moved in opposite directions in six out of ten years. When loans and loan insurance are compared without regard to type of agency, both their gross and net volumes show movements of similar direction in about two years of every three in the period after 1934 (when federal loan insurance began).

Thus in many years the activities of federal and federally sponsored agencies diverged, and there were frequent divergencies, too, in the movements of direct loans and loan insurance. In such instances, of course, the programs tended to offset rather than to reinforce one another's economic effects. Can we then discern any differences among them in the degree to which they may have promoted economic stability? Tables 16 and 17 summarize the evidence. Of the three major categories of activity, direct lending by direct agencies of the federal government has shown the strongest tendency to rise during contractions and early expansions; indeed, loans by federally sponsored agencies and loan insurance have moved in a pro-cyclical direction more often than not. The net volumes show a more consistent counter-cyclical behavior; loans by federal agencies, and even the loans of federally sponsored agencies and loan insurance, taken on a net basis, show a preponderance of counter-cyclical movements.

Attention is now turned to the movements of the federal credit services directed to different sectors of the economy—agriculture, business, finance, and housing. Up to 1930, the preponderance of all federal programs served agriculture; hence any intersector comparison can begin only with the thirties. During 1930–1934 the annual volumes of federal credit to all sectors reached peak levels, that for business coming in 1932, for other sectors in 1934 (Chart 8). After general declines through 1936, the patterns vary markedly: in credit aid to agriculture, an almost uninterrupted growth; to business, violent swings, with high peaks early in World War II and in the Korean conflict; to housing, rises through 1941, declines during the war, and then steep rises through 1950; to financial institutions, an irregular flow except for sustained rises from 1943 through 1948. After the counter-cyclical effort of the early thirties, the relationship between business fluctuations and the course of federal credit aids to the several sectors is rather mixed. Most notable from a counter-cyclical standpoint were the increases in the volume of credit for housing during the recessions of 1937 and 1945–1946, an increase in lending to business antedating and accompanying the 1937 recession, and an increase in lending to financial institutions following the contraction in 1949. Taking the record as a whole, it is the gross volume of credit aid to housing that has most often moved counter-cyclically, while aid to agriculture, business, and financial institutions has moved in pro-cyclical fashion about as often as not (Tables 17 and 18).

The net volume of credit extended to the several sectors shows

117

CHART 7

Lending and Loan Insuring by Federal and by Federally Sponsored Agencies: Annual Volume and Year-End Outstandings, 1917–1953

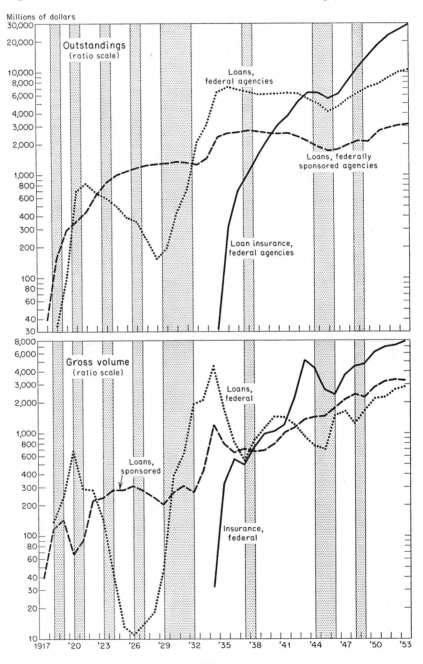

CHART 7 (concluded)

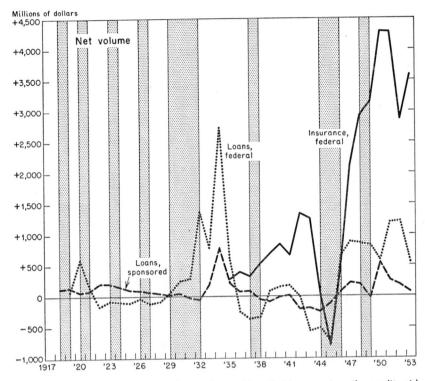

From Tables A-1 and A-2. Stock purchases identifiable as primarily credit aid are included; for other details, see Chapter 2, footnote 1.

Shaded areas denote periods of contraction in business activity, as defined by National Bureau of Economic Research reference dates.

more consistent counter-cyclical performance than the gross volume. Indeed, in the case of housing, when we allow increases in the first year of a recovery to be reckoned as counter-cyclical, only three instances of "pro-cyclical" movement appear in the twenty-year record, the three being increases in 1939–1940, 1947–1948, and 1952–1953. On this basis, too, counter-cyclical changes outnumber pro-cyclical three to one in the agricultural sector, and nearly three to two in the business sector. In the financial sector the pro- and counter-cyclical changes are equally divided.

RELATION TO FEDERAL EXPENDITURES

Expenditures of the federal government, including grants, subsidies, and investments, are often alternative methods of achieving

TABLE 16

Year-to-Year Change in Volume of Federal Credit, by Type of Agency or Activity, in Relation to Changes in Gross National Product, 1929–1953

(billions of dollars)

| | | CHANGE IN FEDERAL CREDIT | | | | |
| | | Gross Volume | | | Net Volume | | |
	CHANGE IN GNP	Loans, Federal	Loans, Sponsored	Loan Insurance	Loans, Federal	Loans, Sponsored	Loan Insurance
		Years When GNP Declined[a]					
1929–30	−13.33	+0.35	+0.06	..	+0.20	+0.04	..
1930–31	−14.83	+0.23	+0.04	..	+0.04	−0.08	..
1931–32	−17.80	+1.27	−0.04	..	+1.08	−0.03	..
1932–33	−2.50	−0.07	+0.17	..	−0.57	+0.26	..
1937–38	−5.55	+0.37	−0.04	+0.23	+0.30	−0.13	+0.20
1945–46	−4.31	+0.80	+0.31	−0.22	+1.36	+0.19	+1.40
1948–49	−0.02	+0.41	−0.19	+0.27	−0.03	−0.21	+0.22
Average	−8.33	+0.48	+0.04	+0.09[b]	+0.34	+0.01	+0.61[b]
Number of							
Increases	0	6	4	2	5	3	3
Decreases	7	1	3	1	2	4	0

(*continued on next page*)

TABLE 16 (continued)

	CHANGE IN GNP	CHANGE IN FEDERAL CREDIT					
		Gross Volume			Net Volume		
		Loans, Federal	Loans, Sponsored	Loan Insurance	Loans, Federal	Loans, Sponsored	Loan Insurance
Years When GNP Increased[a]							
1933–34	+9.01	+2.05	+0.68	..	+1.94	+0.59	..
1934–35	+7.53	−2.34	−0.34	+0.29	−2.11	−0.57	..
1935–36	+10.24	−0.86	−0.13	+0.24	−0.87	−0.15	+0.12
1936–37	+8.04	−0.25	+0.06	−0.06	−0.12	+0.02	−0.08
1938–39	+5.87	+0.27	+0.02	+0.26	+0.43	−0.05	+0.17
1939–40	+9.52	+0.31	+0.11	+0.05	+0.05	+0.09	+0.16
1940–41	+25.20	+0.04	+0.21	+0.17	+0.03	+0.02	−0.18
1941–42	+33.31	−0.23	+0.13	+0.97	−0.18	−0.23	+0.67
1942–43	+33.38	−0.27	+0.25	+2.95	−0.56	+0.03	−0.08
1943–44	+18.88	−0.18	+0.05	−0.82	−0.04	−0.07	−1.26
1944–45	+2.16	−0.05	+0.03	−1.69	−0.20	+0.14	−0.81
1946–47	+22.98	+0.10	+0.38	+1.29	+0.24	+0.15	+1.56
1947–48	+25.10	−0.36	+0.25	+0.79	−0.02	−0.03	+0.79
1949–50	+27.77	+0.51	+0.60	+1.44	−0.26	+0.58	+1.13
1950–51	+43.16	+0.06	+0.38	+0.64	+0.62	−0.30	−0.01
1951–52	+17.86	+0.42	+0.12	+0.37	+0.02	−0.07	−1.42
1952–53	+18.76	+0.19	−0.05	+0.67	−0.67	−0.11	+0.73
Average	+18.75	−0.03	+0.16	+0.47[c]	−0.10	+0.002	+0.10[d]
Number of							
Increases	17	9	14	13	8	8	8
Decreases	0	8	3	3	9	9	7

Source: Tables A-1 and A-2; for GNP, Table 14.
a See note a, Table 15.
b Based on 3 items.
c Based on 16 items.
d Based on 15 items.

TABLE 17

Pro- and Counter-Cyclical Changes in Federal Lending and Loan Insurance,
Federal Expenditures and Deficit, and Federal Reserve Bank Credit,
1929–1953

	Counter-Cyclical[a] (1)	Pro-Cyclical[b] (2)	Counter-Cyclical Modified[c] (3)	Pro-Cyclical Modified[c] (4)	TOTAL (5)
			NUMBER OF YEAR-TO-YEAR CHANGES THAT ARE:		
All loans and loan insurance					
Gross volume	12	12	16	8	24
Net volume	14	10	18	6	24
Loans and loan insurance, by type					
Gross volume					
Loans, federally sponsored agencies	7	17	11	13	24
Loans, federal agencies	14	10	18	6	24
Loan insurance, federal agencies	5	14	8	11	19[d]
Net volume					
Loans, federally sponsored agencies	12	12	14	10	24
Loans, federal agencies	14	10	16	8	24
Loan insurance, federal agencies	10	8	13	5	18[e]
Loans and loan insurance, by economic sector					
Gross volume					
Housing	12	8	16	4	20[f]
Agriculture	10	14	14	10	24
Business	14	10	12	12	24
Financial institutions	8	13	10	11	21[g]
Net volume					
Housing	13	7	17	3	20[f]
Agriculture	14	10	18	6	24
Business	14	10	14	10	24
Financial institutions	10	11	10	11	21[g]
Federal expenditures					
Full period	11	13	11	13	24
Excluding war periods[h]	10	7	10	7	17
Federal deficit					
Full period	13	11	13	11	24
Excluding war periods[h]	11	6	11	6	17
Federal Reserve Bank credit					
Full period	8	16	10	14	24
Excluding war periods[h]	6	11	8	9	17

Source: Tables 15, 16, 18, and 20.
[a] Increase when GNP declined and decrease when GNP increased.
[b] Increase when GNP increased and decrease when GNP declined.
[c] Same as columns (1) and (2) except that during first year of expansion in GNP (1933–1934, 1938–1939, 1946–1947, 1949–1950) increases are counter-cyclical and decreases are pro-cyclical.
[d] 1933–1953 only.　　　　[e] 1934–1953 only.　　　　[f] 1933–1953 only.
[g] 1932–1953 only.　　　　[h] I.e. excluding 1940–1945, and 1950–1952.

the same results that may be brought about by loans or loan insurance or guaranty. The Public Works Administration, for example, employed loans and grants during the thirties to finance public works in the interests of expanding employment. Both devices may stimulate increased production and employment during periods of unemployment; both may tend to inflate prices during periods of full employment. The effect on GNP of a dollar of federal loans or loan insurance is probably greater in most instances than that of a dollar of outright federal expenditure, because the loan or loan insurance is more likely to be accompanied by an equity investment by the borrower. (However, federal grants to states or municipalities, if conditioned upon matching expenditures by the grantee, also have a multiplied effect upon aggregate GNP.) Hence, it is pertinent to inquire into the importance of federal credit programs relative to federal expenditures, and to determine the extent to which the lending and loan insuring activities and the federal expenditure programs have reinforced or offset each other in their cyclical effects. Two types of comparison may usefully be made; first, between the gross flow of federal loans and loan insurance and the annual amount of federal expenditures; second, between the net flow of federal loans and loan insurance and the amount of surplus or deficit in the conventional federal budget.[13] The first is a comparison of gross amounts of funds injected into the economy; the second, a comparison of their net impact, when repayments of loans are assumed to have effects on private expenditures analogous to payments of federal taxes.

A comparison of the annual volume of loans extended and loan insurance commitments made with the annual volume of budget expenditures indicates that credit programs have been a factor of material importance in the financial activities of the national government since 1920, and that they were of vital importance during the depression years 1933 and 1934 (Table 19). Credit volume amounted to 51 percent of federal budget expenditures during 1933 and 78 percent during 1934. During the remainder of the thirties, annual extensions of loans and loan insurance were about one-fifth to three-tenths the amount of federal expenditures, and they main-

[13] Expenditures and surpluses or deficits in the conventional federal budget are used, despite their many ambiguities, in preference to (1) the consolidated cash budget, or (2) federal purchase of goods and services and surplus or deficit on income and product transactions, because only the conventional budget provided, throughout the period under study, a widely known measure of fiscal policy.

CHART 8

Major Sectors of the Economy: Annual Volume of Federal Loans and Loan Insurance Utilized, and Year-End Outstandings, 1920–1953

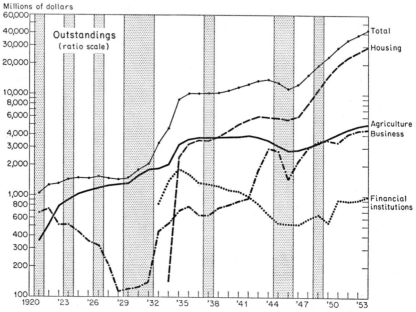

Covers lending and loan insuring by federal and federally sponsored agencies, from Tables A-1 through A-8. Total includes loans to minor governmental units and loans for miscellaneous purposes, as well as the components shown. Stock purchases identifiable as primarily credit aid are included; for other details, see Chapter 2, footnote 1.

Shaded areas denote periods of contraction in business activity, as defined by National Bureau of Economic Research reference dates.

(continued on next page)

tained this level of relative importance again during the postwar years 1947–1953.

If the annual changes in the amounts of federal loans and loan insurance outstanding at year ends are compared with the annual surpluses or deficits in the conventional federal budget, on the assumption that the net deficit and the net flow of credit are more meaningful measures of their relative importance to the economy, federal credit programs assume an even greater significance. During the 36-year period 1918–1953 there were six years during which the net flows of credit were significantly greater than the amount of surplus or deficit in the federal budget. Ignoring the years before

CHART 8 (continued)

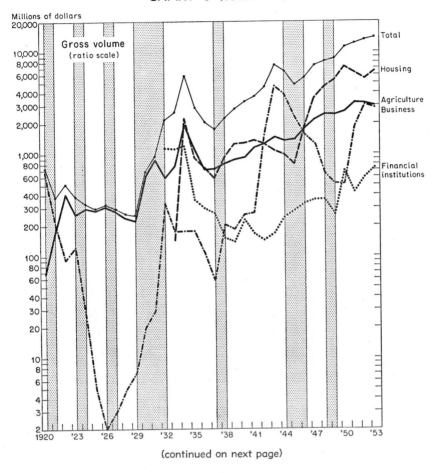

Millions of dollars

(continued on next page)

1930, in which both magnitudes were too small for meaningful comparison, it is found that during the depression years 1932–1935 the net flow of credit equaled about half the amount of budget deficits and in the single year 1934 the net flow exceeded the amount of the budget deficit (Table 19). This suggests that during 1934 federal credit programs may have made a greater contribution to economic recovery than did federal fiscal operations. In the postwar years 1947–1951 outstanding federal loans and loan insurance (mainly the latter) increased by amounts that were as large as, and sometimes larger than, the budgetary surpluses or deficits, suggesting that credit programs may have made a major contribution toward the postwar inflationary boom; in 1952 and 1953 the increases in

CHART 8 (concluded): Federal Loans and Loan Insurance Utilized by Major Sectors

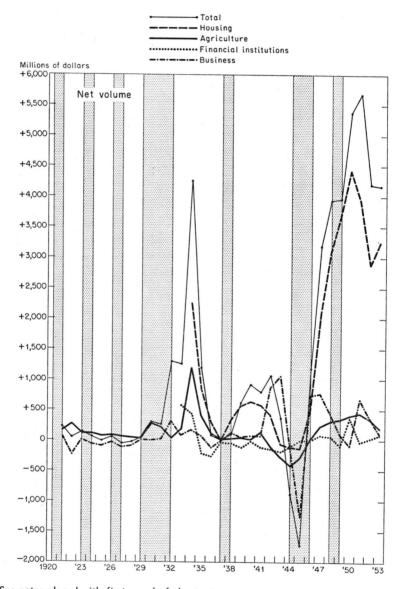

Total
Housing
Agriculture
Financial institutions
Business

Millions of dollars

Net volume

See notes placed with first panel of chart.

outstanding federal credit were smaller than, but nevertheless substantial relative to, the current budgetary deficits.[14]

Have federal lending and loan insuring activities been harmonious with federal fiscal policies in their cyclical impact upon the economy? Although an over-all counter-cyclical policy was not deliberately pursued before the Great Depression and since then has not always been the major criterion in either the fiscal policy or the credit programs of the federal government, it is instructive to observe whether federal activities have tended to help or hinder stability. A strategy of general economic stabilization would call for concurrent reductions or concurrent increases, at appropriate times, in both federal expenditures and the volume of loans and loan insurance extended. Thus one test of past experience is to determine the number of years in which the directions of annual change in the gross flows of federal credit aids and of federal expenditures matched or diverged. Over the 36-year period 1918–1953 such changes were concurrent in 22 years and divergent in 14 years. Although concurrent movements outnumbered divergent movements, the degree of concurrence is not impressive. During the contraction of 1929–1932 and the beginning of recovery afterward, federal credit volume and federal expenditures rose together; but while expenditures rose irregularly from 1934 through 1937, credit programs contracted (Chart 9). In the 1937–1938 recession, federal credit and expenditures both rose, and by roughly the same amount. After the war, the gross volume of federal credit rose not only in the brief contractions but through the entire expansionary period, while expenditures contracted at first, then rose, mainly under defense requirements.

An illuminating comparison may be made between net credit flow and the size of the budgetary surplus or deficit. If federal credit programs were to contribute to economic stability, reductions in the net flow of loans and loan insurance simultaneous with reductions in the budgetary deficit (or increases in the surplus) would occur at appropriate times (e.g., when GNP was at a "high" level and rising), and increases in the net credit flow would coincide with increases in the deficit at other times (e.g., when GNP was falling or at a "low" level). Tables 15 and 20 enable us to observe how frequently the

14 Use of the consolidated cash budget, instead of the conventional budget, would not significantly alter the findings. The difference between the two was not considerable until after 1935, when social security trust funds began to build up; and federal deficits were sizable in most years thereafter, whether measured on a conventional or a consolidated cash basis.

TABLE 18

Year-to-Year Change in Volume of Federal Credit, by Economic Sector, in Relation to Changes in Gross National Product, 1929–1953

(*billions of dollars*)

| | CHANGE IN FEDERAL CREDIT EXTENDED TO: | | | | | | | |
| | Gross Volume | | | | Net Volume | | | |
	Housing	Agri-culture	Busi-ness	Finan-cial Insti-tutions	Housing	Agri-culture	Busi-ness	Finan-cial Insti-tutions
	Years when GNP Declined[a]							
1929–30	..	+0.40	+0.01	..	..	+0.24	−0.002	..
1930–31	..	+0.26	+0.01	..	..	−0.05	+0.01	..
1931–32	..	−0.30	+0.31	..	..	−0.18	+0.30	..
1932–33	..	+0.17	−0.16	−0.003	..	+0.15	−0.23	−0.28
1937–38	+0.35	+0.10	+0.14	−0.11	+0.34	+0.01	+0.12	−0.02
1945–46	+1.12	+0.40	−0.72	+0.05	+0.59	+0.30	+1.99	+0.001
1948–49	+0.75	−0.01	−0.13	−0.10	+0.58	+0.03	−0.35	−0.15
Average	+0.74b	+0.15	−0.08	−0.04c	+0.50b	+0.07	+0.26	−0.11c
Number of								
Increases	3	5	4	1	3	5	4	1
Decreases	0	2	3	3	0	2	3	3

(continued on next page)

TABLE 18 (continued)

| | CHANGE IN FEDERAL CREDIT EXTENDED TO: | | | | | | | |
| | Gross Volume | | | | Net Volume | | | |
	Housing	Agri-culture	Busi-ness	Financial Institutions	Housing	Agri-culture	Busi-ness	Financial Institutions
	Years when GNP Increased[a]							
1933-34	+2.13	+1.18	+0.001	+0.08	+2.11	+1.02	+0.09	−0.12
1934-35	−1.35	−0.85	−0.001	+0.84	−1.44	−0.80	−0.10	−0.65
1935-36	−0.20	−0.39	−0.07	−0.06	−0.52	−0.30	−0.20	−0.06
1936-37	−0.14	+0.01	−0.05	−0.03	−0.31	−0.09	+0.12	+0.24
1938-39	+0.34	+0.07	−0.02	−0.01	+0.23	+0.01	−0.07	−0.06
1939-40	+0.02	+0.05	+0.07	+0.09	+0.07	+0.03	+0.02	+0.09
1940-41	+0.08	+0.25	+0.01	−0.06	−0.06	+0.13	−0.01	−0.09
1941-42	−0.08	+0.09	+1.28	−0.02	−0.15	−0.24	+0.81	−0.03
1942-43	−0.21	+0.19	+3.09	+0.02	−0.49	−0.17	+0.19	−0.03
1943-44	−0.09	−0.10	−0.75	+0.07	−0.05	−0.14	−1.24	+0.07
1944-45	−0.20	+0.03	−1.59	+0.04	−0.02	+0.13	−1.08	+0.11
1946-47	+1.65	+0.40	−0.32	+0.03	+1.64	+0.22	+0.04	+0.07
1947-48	+1.03	+0.25	−0.62	+0.004	+1.02	+0.08	−0.34	−0.02
1949-50	+1.86	+0.18	−0.001	+0.42	+0.74	+0.07	−0.18	+0.47
1950-51	−0.93	+0.59	+1.36	−0.25	−0.48	+0.03	+0.77	−0.40
1951-52	−0.79	−0.02	+1.19	+0.16	−1.07	−0.10	−0.32	+0.05
1952-53	+1.10	−0.19	−0.23	+0.14	+0.38	−0.15	−0.24	+0.06
Average	+0.25	+0.10	+0.20	−0.01	+0.09	−0.02	−0.10	−0.02
Number of								
Increases	8	12	7	10	7	8	7	8
Decreases	9	5	10	7	10	9	10	9

Source: Tables A-1 through A-8.
b Based on 3 items.

a See note a, Table 15.
c Based on 4 items.

TABLE 19

Federal Loans and Loan Insurance, Federal Expenditures, Budgetary Surpluses or Deficits, and Federal Reserve Bank Credit, 1918–1953

YEAR	FEDERAL EXPENDITURES (million dollars)	FEDERAL SURPLUS (+) OR DEFICIT (−) (million dollars)	VOLUME OF FEDERAL CREDIT AS A PERCENTAGE OF FEDERAL EXPENDITURES	NET CHANGE IN FEDERAL CREDIT OUTSTANDING AS A PERCENTAGE OF BUDGET SURPLUS OR DEFICIT[a]		FEDERAL RESERVE BANK CREDIT	
				Years of Surplus	Years of Deficit	Outstanding at Year End (million dollars)	Net Change (million dollars)
1918	18,127	−13,420	1.4%	...	−1.1%	2,498	+1,327
1919	11,730	−4,960	3.3	...	−4.1	3,292	+794
1920	5,064	+1,368	14.5	+46.7%	...	3,355	+63
1921	4,705	+267	8.1	+84.6	...	1,563	−1,792
1922	3,553	+113	14.2	+38.1	...	1,405	−158
1923	3,718	+387	10.3	+33.1	...	1,238	−167
1924	3,345	+567	9.7	+9.9	...	1,302	+64
1925	3,600	+220	8.2	−5.0	...	1,459	+157
1926	3,614	+470	8.9	+11.1	...	1,381	−78
1927	3,605	+483	8.1	−11.0	...	1,655	+274
1928	3,755	+165	6.9	−21.8	...	1,809	+154
1929	3,798	+445	6.6	+10.8	...	1,583	−226
1930	3,809	+145	17.5	+202.1	...	1,373	−210
1931	5,001	−2,333	18.9	...	−10.8	1,853	+480
1932	5,083	−3,145	42.8	...	−41.1	2,145	+292
1933	5,017	−2,543	50.8	...	−49.2	2,688	+543
1934	7,495	−4,064	77.7	...	−104.7	2,463	−225
1935	6,646	−2,854	42.5	...	−41.7	2,486	+23
1936	8,539	−4,206	23.8	...	−1.9	2,500	+14
1937	7,635	−1,888	22.9	...	−0.3	2,612	+112
1938	8,220	−2,670	27.4	...	−4.1	2,601	−11
1939	9,151	−4,300	30.4	...	−14.3	2,593	−8

(continued on next page)

TABLE 19 (continued)

YEAR	FEDERAL EXPENDITURES (million dollars)	FEDERAL SURPLUS (+) OR DEFICIT (−) (million dollars)	VOLUME OF FEDERAL CREDIT AS A PERCENTAGE OF FEDERAL EXPENDITURES	NET CHANGE IN FEDERAL CREDIT OUTSTANDING AS A PERCENTAGE OF BUDGET SURPLUS OR DEFICIT[a]		FEDERAL RESERVE BANK CREDIT	
				Years of Surplus	Years of Deficit	Outstanding at Year End (million dollars)	Net Change (million dollars)
1940	9,645	−3,934	33.8	..	−23.3	2,274	−319
1941	20,229	−11,762	18.1	..	−6.7	2,361	+87
1942	57,542	−41,461	7.9	..	−2.6	6,679	+4,318
1943	89,918	−55,691	8.3	..	−0.6	12,239	+5,560
1944	96,896	−53,650	6.7	..	+1.6	19,745	+7,506
1945	87,271	−43,594	5.5	..	+4.0	25,091	+5,346
1946	41,080	−2,512	13.8	..	−46.8	24,093	−998
1947	37,955	+2,434	19.6	+130.6	..	23,181	−912
1948	35,623	+5,241	22.8	+75.1	..	24,097	+916
1949	41,106	−3,592	20.9	..	−110.1	19,499	−4,598
1950	37,728	−422	29.6	..	−1,274.2	22,216	+2,717
1951	56,337	−3,358	21.7	..	−169.3	25,009	+2,793
1952	70,682	−5,842	18.6	..	−71.8	25,825	+816
1953	72,997	−9,157	19.1	..	−45.5	26,880	+1,055

a Minus sign indicates positive change over a deficit, or negative change over a surplus. Plus sign indicates positive change over a surplus, or negative change over a deficit.

Source: Federal credit series computed from Tables A-1 and A-2. Federal expenditures and budgetary surplus or deficit for 1918–1932 (estimated on a calendar-year basis from monthly figures) are from the Annual Reports of the Secretary of the Treasury; and for 1933–1953 (calendar years) are from the Treasury Bulletin, February 1954, p. 5, and April 1954, p. 1. Federal Reserve Bank credit through 1941 is from Banking and Monetary Statistics (Board of Governors of the Federal Reserve System, 1943), Table 102, pp. 373–377; for 1942–1953, from Federal Reserve Bulletins.

CHART 9

Annual Volume of Federal Lending and Loan Insuring, Federal Budget Expenditures, and National Product, 1920–1953

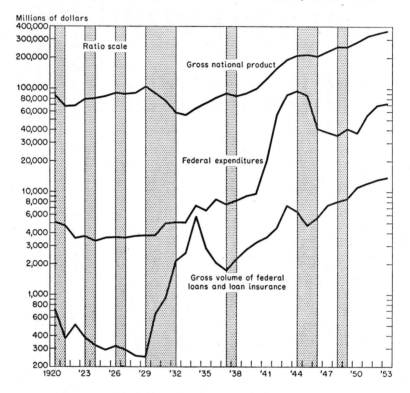

Series on gross and net volume of lending and loan insuring by federal and federally sponsored agencies, and gross national product, are from Table 14; on federal expenditures and budgetary deficit or surplus, from Table 19.

Shaded areas denote periods of contraction in business activity, as defined by National Bureau of Economic Research reference dates.

changes in net loan volume and in the deficit have moved in like direction, and to judge at least roughly whether the movements were favorable or unfavorable for economic stability. The results are tallied in the following scheme, in which an increase in net lending or in the deficit is termed counter-cyclical if it occurs when GNP is falling or is in the initial year of recovery, while decreases are counter-cyclical when GNP is rising (beyond the initial recovery year). The two factors have moved together in a "counter-cyclical" direction somewhat less than half the time, and on the occasions

132

CHART 9 (concluded)

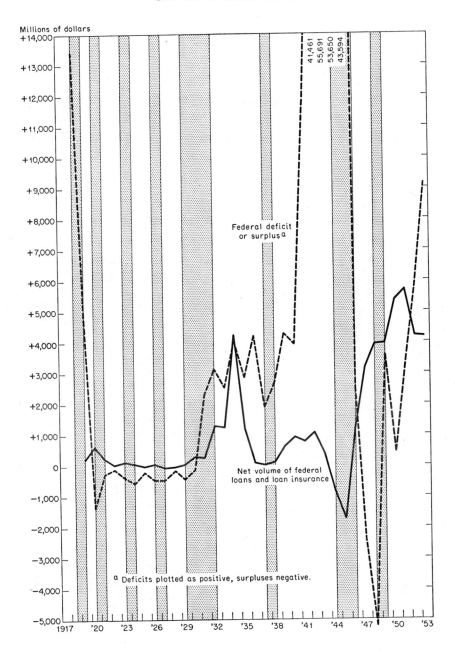

Millions of dollars

41,461
55,691
53,650
43,594

Federal deficit
or surplus[a]

Net volume of federal
loans and loan insurance

[a] Deficits plotted as positive, surpluses negative.

1917 '20 '23 '26 '29 '32 '35 '38 '41 '44 '47 '50 '53

TABLE 20

Year-to-Year Change in Federal Expenditures, Federal Deficit, and Federal Reserve Bank Credit, in Relation to Changes in Gross National Product, 1929–1953

(billions of dollars)

	YEARS WHEN GNP DECLINED[a]				YEARS WHEN GNP INCREASED[a]		
	Change in:				Change in:		
	Federal Expenditures	Federal Deficit[b]	Federal Reserve Bank Credit[b]		Federal Expenditures	Federal Deficit[b]	Federal Reserve Bank Credit
1929–30	+0.01	+0.30	+0.02	1933–34	+2.48	+1.52	−0.77
1930–31	+1.19	+2.48	+0.69	1934–35	−0.85	−1.21	+0.25
1931–32	+0.08	+0.81	−0.19	1935–36	+1.89	+1.35	−0.01
1932–33	−0.07	−0.60	+0.25	1936–37	−0.90	−2.32	+0.10
1937–38	+0.58	+0.78	−0.12	1938–39	+0.93	+1.63	+0.003
1945–46	−46.19	−41.08	−6.34	1939–40	+0.49	−0.37	−0.31
1948–49	+5.48	+8.83	−5.51	1940–41	+10.58	+7.83	+0.41
				1941–42	+37.31	+29.70	+4.23
				1942–43	+32.38	+14.23	+1.24
				1943–44	+6.98	−2.04	+1.95
				1944–45	−9.62	−10.06	−2.16
				1946–47	−3.12	−4.95	+0.09
				1947–48	−2.33	−2.81	+1.88
Average	−5.56	−4.07	−1.60				
Average, excl. 1945–46	+1.21	+2.10	−0.81				

(continued on next page)

134

TABLE 20 (continued)
(billions of dollars)

YEARS WHEN GNP DECLINED[a]

	Change in:		
	Federal Expenditures	Federal Deficit[b]	Federal Reserve Bank Credit[c]
Number of			
Increases	5	5	3
Decreases	2	2	4

YEARS WHEN GNP INCREASED[a]

	Change in:		
	Federal Expenditures	Federal Deficit[b]	Federal Reserve Bank Credit[c]
1949–50	−3.38	−3.17	+7.32
1950–51	+18.61	+2.94	+0.08
1951–52	+14.34	+2.48	−1.98
1952–53	+2.32	+3.32	+0.24
Average	+6.36	+2.24	+0.74
Average, excl. 1940–45 & 1950–52	−0.25	−0.70	+0.87
Number of			
Increases[d]	11(5)	9(4)	12(7)
Decreases[d]	6(5)	8(6)	5(3)

Source: Table 19.

a See note a, Table A-15.

b I.e., an increase (+) means an increase in the deficit, or a decrease in the surplus, or a change from surplus to deficit. A decrease (−) means a decrease in the deficit, or an increase in the surplus, or a change from deficit to surplus.

c I.e., an increase (+) means an increase in the net change in credit outstanding.

d Numbers in parentheses exclude war periods, i.e. 1940–1945 and 1950–1952.

YEAR-TO-YEAR CHANGE IN NET FEDERAL LENDING AND LOAN INSURANCE AND IN FEDERAL DEFICIT	PEACETIME: 1929–1939 1945–1949, 1952–1953				WARTIME: 1940–1945, 1950–1952	1929–1953
	Years When GNP Declined	Years When GNP Increased		Total	Years When GNP Increased	
		Initial Year[a]	Other Years			
Lending rose, deficit rose	4	2	–	6	2	8
Lending fell, deficit fell	1	–	2	3	2	5
Lending fell, deficit rose	1	–	2	3	3	6
Lending rose, deficit fell	1	2	2	5	–	5
Lending and deficit counter-cyclical	4	2[b]	2	8	2	10
Lending and deficit pro-cyclical	1	–	–	1	2	3
Lending counter-, deficit pro-cyclical	1	2[b]	2	5	3	8
Lending pro-, deficit counter-cyclical	1	–	2	3	–	3
Total	7	4	6	17	7	24

[a] 1933–1934, 1938–1939, 1946–1947, 1949–1950.
[b] Rise in lending or in deficit is termed counter-cyclical.

when the two moved in opposite directions, net lending moved "counter-cyclically" more frequently than the deficit did.

RELATION TO FEDERAL RESERVE CREDIT

An inquiry into the economic repercussions of federal credit activities should examine the relationships between such programs and monetary policies. Of special interest is the question whether movements in federal credit-granting activities and movements in credit made available by the central banking system have been reinforcing or divergent. A pertinent comparison lies between the annual net flow of federal credit and the annual net change in Federal Reserve Bank credit outstanding, because the latter provides the best objective measure of central bank influences upon the availability of credit from the commercial banking system. If economic stabilization were a major objective, central banking policy would normally require a progressive reduction in Federal Reserve Bank credit during advanced stages of economic upswings, and sharp increases in the net volume of such credit during the early stages of downswings; and federal credit policy would require concurrent changes in the net volume of loans and loan insurance. Actually, the directions of change in the two series were concurrent in only one-third of the 36 years embraced within the period 1918–1953 (Chart 10). Cyclical movements in the net volume of federal loans and loan insurance since 1929 may be compared with movements in the net volume of Federal Reserve Bank credit in Tables 15 and 20.

The net volume of federal agency credit rose markedly during and and after World War I 1917–1920, but declined sharply in 1921 (Chart 10). The net volume of central bank credit reached a peak in 1918, and was cut back drastically during 1918–1921, rising sharply the following year. Thereafter, changes in both series were comparatively minor until the onset of the Great Depression, when both series rose. Beginning in 1934, central bank credit was reduced and little change was experienced until the exigencies of financing World War II brought a vast increase during the years 1942–1944. The net volume of agency credit diminished sharply in 1935, rose again during 1938–1941. During the years 1943–1945 it declined, principally in response to a reduction of guarantees of defense loans, and by roughly the same amount that reserve bank credit increased. There was a sharp contrast between the reduction in the net advances of central banking credit in 1945–1946 and 1948–1949, in an effort to curb price inflation, and the large annual increases in federal agency credits outstanding. Since 1949 the two types of credit have followed quite similar courses.

On the whole, as the accompanying tabulation illustrates, federal

YEAR-TO-YEAR CHANGE IN NET FEDERAL LENDING AND LOAN INSURANCE AND IN NET FEDERAL RESERVE BANK CREDIT	PEACETIME: 1929–1939 1945–1949, 1952–1953				WARTIME: 1940–1945, 1950–1952	
	Years When GNP Declined	Years When GNP Increased			Years When GNP Increased	1929–1953
		Initial Year[a]	Other Years	Total		
Lending rose, bank credit rose	1	3	1	5	2	7
Lending fell, bank credit fell	–		1	1	2	3
Lending fell, bank credit rose	2		3	5	3	8
Lending rose, bank credit fell	4	1	1	6	–	6
Lending and bank credit counter-cyclical	1	3[b]	1	5	2	7
Lending and bank credit pro-cyclical	–	–	1	1	2	3
Lending counter-, bank credit pro-cyclical	4	1[b]	3	8	3	11
Lending pro-, bank credit counter-cyclical	2	–	1	3	–	3
Total	7	4	6	17	7	24

a 1933–1934, 1938–1939, 1946–1947, 1949–1950.
b Rise in lending or in bank credit is termed counter-cyclical.

137

CHART 10

Federal Loans and Loan Insurance, and Federal Reserve Bank Credit: Outstandings at Year Ends, and Net Volume during Year, 1917–1953

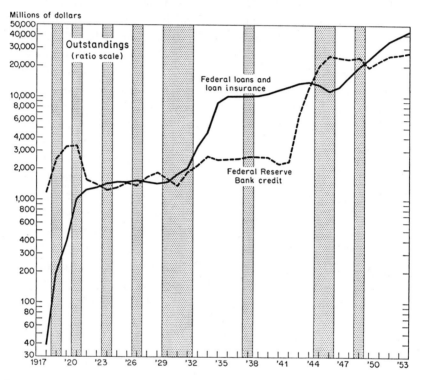

Series on loans and loan insurance by federal and federally sponsored agencies are from Table 14; on Federal Reserve Bank credit, from Table 19.

Shaded areas denote periods of contraction in business activity, as defined by National Bureau of Economic Research reference dates.

loan and loan insurance policy shows less correlation with monetary policy than with fiscal policy. Indeed, counter-cyclical movements have been appreciably more frequent in the behavior of federal lending and loan insurance than of federal reserve bank credit, during both expansions and contractions in Gross National Product. Divergence between these policies under some circumstances may be defended, of course, but the record reflects defects in federal monetary policies as well as inadequacies in the management of the credit programs of federal agencies.

138

CHART 10 (concluded)

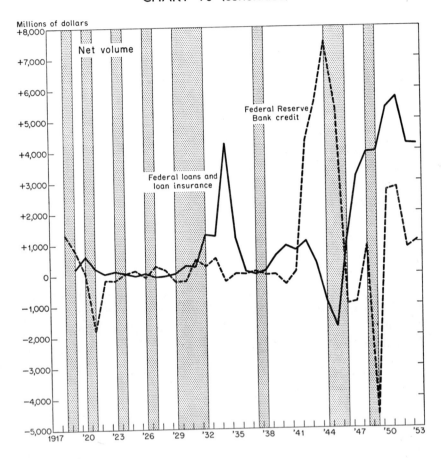

SUMMARY

A summary of the foregoing materials on the relations of federal credit programs to aggregate economic activity may be convenient. Gauged by its relation to gross national product, federal credit first became a significant factor in the economy in 1932. In that year the volume of federal credit extended rose from under 1 percent to 3.7 percent of GNP; in no subsequent year up to 1953 did it decline to less than 2 percent. Federal loans emerged as a major economic force, consciously and deliberately employed to affect the level of economic activity, during the Great Depression. The combined lending operations of public agencies during the early thirties apparently made a positive contribution to reemployment which matched, if it did not outweigh, the contributions of federal expenditures.

This appears to have been the only period in American history in which federal credit aids were consciously used as the instrumentality, pre-eminent over both fiscal and monetary measures, to combat depression.

The annual volume of federal loans and loan insurance ran between one-fifth and three-tenths of the amount of federal expenditures during most of the thirties and during the postwar years 1947–1953; in 1933 and 1934, on the other hand, it reached 51 and 78 percent, respectively, indicating the vital role of credit in the New Deal effort to restore prosperity. During the Great Depression and in the postwar years 1947–1953, federal credit operations appear to have been at least as influential as determinants of total demand as were federal fiscal operations. However, the record does not reveal effective counter-cyclical coordination between federal financial policy in the two spheres; reductions in the net flow of loans and loan insurance have accompanied increases in budgetary deficits nearly as often as not, and conversely.[14] Similarly, federal credit programs do not appear to have been effectively meshed with federal monetary policies to assist economic stabilization, a result which of course may be due to errors or to emphasis on aims other than stabilization in the management of either program. Stabilization would appear to require concurrent changes in both the net flow of Reserve Bank credit and in the net flow of loans and loan insurance by federal agencies; however, the record reveals more years of divergent than of concurrent movement.

The relations of federal lending and loan insurance operations to other federal financial activities—expenditures, budgetary surpluses or deficits, and central bank credit—and the relations of all of these magnitudes to general economic activity, represented by GNP and by the business cycle chronology, have been considered. The salient figures for such comparisons are summarized in Table 21, which presents net changes in the various series during the expansion or contraction phases of business cycles over the period 1927–1953. They reveal vividly how checkered has been the record of consistency between federal credit activities and fiscal and central banking activities, on the one hand, and between all these operations and business cycle behavior, on the other hand. The principal generalization

[15] Occasionally, of course, there may be good reasons for such inconsistency. For example, at the end of World War II (1945–1946) a decline in the federal deficit was almost inevitable, and the increase in lending that occurred then can easily be reconciled with the requirements of economic stability.

TABLE 21

Changes in Federal Lending and Related Series during Business Cycles, 1927–1953
(billions of dollars)

		RISE OR FALL IN				
		Federal Lending		Federal Reserve Bank Creditd	Federal Expendituerese	Federal Deficitf
BUSINESS CYCLE	GNPa	Grossb	Netc			
EXPANSIONS						
1927–1929	+8.06g	—0.04	+0.10	—0.50	+0.19g	+0.04g
1932–1937	+32.31	—0.43	—1.29	—0.18	+2.55	—1.26
1938–1944	+126.17	+4.23	—0.99	+7.52	+88.68	+50.98
1946–1948	+48.08	+2.45	+2.76	+1.91	—5.46	—7.75
1949–1953	+107.56	+5.35	+0.22	+5.65	+31.89	+5.57
CONTRACTIONS						
1929–1932	—45.97	+1.93	+1.24	+0.52	+1.29g	+3.59g
1937–1938	—5.55	+0.50	+0.10	—0.12	+0.59	+0.78
1944–1946	—2.15	—0.82	+2.05	—8.50	—55.82	—51.14
1948–1949	—0.02	+0.49	+0.02	—5.51	+5.48	+8.83

a Data for 1927–1929 represent change in GNP as estimated by Simon Kuznets in *Supplement to Summary Volume on Capital Formation and Financing* (unpublished), Part A: Annual Estimates, 1919–1953, Variant III; other data represent changes in Department of Commerce estimates of GNP as given in *National Income Supplement, 1954, Survey of Current Business*, Table 2, p. 162.

b Represents changes in volume of direct loans and of stock and share purchases made by federal and federally sponsored agencies, and in amounts of loan insurance or guaranty extended annually by federal agencies; from Tables A-1 and A-2.

c Represents changes in the net flow of direct loans and of stock and share purchases made by federal and federally sponsored agencies and of loan insurance or guarantees extended by federal agencies; from Tables A-1 and A-2.

d Represents change in the net flow of Federal Reserve Bank credit. Basic figures for 1927–1941 are from *Banking and Monetary Statistics* (Board of Governors of the Federal Reserve System, 1943) Table 102, pp. 375ff., and for 1942–1953, from *Federal Reserve Bulletins*.

e Data for 1927–1932 represent changes in calendar-year expenditures for general, special, and trust accounts (as compiled from unrevised monthly Daily Statement figures given in the *Annual Reports* of the Secretary of the Treasury) and are not strictly comparable with data from 1933 forward, which represent changes in calendar-year expenditures for general and special accounts (as given in *Treasury Bulletin*, February 1954, p. 5, and April 1954, p. 1).

f Positive quantities indicate a rise in the deficit or fall in surplus; negative quantities, a fall in the deficit or rise in surplus. Figures were obtained from sources cited in note e above, and therefore the data for 1927–1932 have somewhat broader coverage than those for subsequent periods.

g Not comparable with data for other periods.

that appears to be warranted from this record is that diversity of movement and a lack of counter-cyclical coordination has characterized federal financial operations in the past.

One characteristic of federal credit programs has been that, once set in motion, they have tended, in the aggregate, to expand irrespective of general economic conditions. Consequently, aggregate federal loans and loan insurance continued to rise through the late thirties and early forties, through economic recession and expansion alike. The most important unstabilizing effects were experienced during the post-World War II boom, when, largely as a result of federal insurance and guaranty of home mortgage loans, federal credit operations were working counter to federal fiscal and monetary policies. The reason, perhaps, is that some programs have objectives apart from stabilization and also that aggregate federal credit is a mosaic of many pieces: each particular program has been designed to accomplish some special purpose and has been managed with that end in view, often without regard to its effects on over-all economic stability. Yet in the aggregate the programs have at times exerted a profound influence on prices and production.

Resource-Allocational Effects

Federal programs of lending, loan guaranty, and loan insurance have undoubtedly influenced the pattern as well as the aggregate amount of investment in the American economy. Yet the identification and measurement of this influence is exceedingly difficult. The availability of credit service is only one of many factors that determine the structure of resource use; underlying conditions of demand and supply, including technological changes, have had a far greater weight. Equally important, federal credit aids have formed only a minor fraction of aggregate available financial services, private financial enterprise having supplied the preponderance of this service in all major sectors of the economy, especially in the business sector. The influences of federal credit aids upon the structure of investment are therefore subtle and difficult to trace clearly.

Nevertheless, it is possible to point to certain changes in the physical activities of the economy presumably due to the operation of federal credit programs. These are now described briefly for the agricultural, business, and housing sectors of the economy (fuller treatments being reserved for Part II), with emphasis upon employment and physical output, the prices of products, the incomes and financial position of producers, and regional shifts in economic activity.

AGRICULTURE

Although the relationship cannot be rigorously demonstrated, federal agricultural credit programs appear to have lowered the cost and increased the supply of credit to agriculturists. Thus they have tended to bring about a somewhat greater allocation of economic resources to farming than would otherwise have occurred. There is some reason for believing that the effects of the consequent expansion in the supply of agricultural products were such, given the relatively inelastic demand for farm products, as to reduce somewhat the percentage of the national income received by farmers, especially during the thirties, when nonagricultural employment opportunities were relatively unfavorable.

Apart from their effects upon agriculture's relative position in the economy as a whole, public farm credit aids have produced internal adjustments within this sector of the economy. Thus, the policies of the federal agencies worked toward greater uniformity throughout the nation in the costs of both mortgage and production credit. They reduced farm credit costs, especially in the South and West where loan rates have traditionally been the highest. The fact that the largest proportions of delinquencies and foreclosures on farm loans took place in the Old South and the West (particularly, the northern Great Plains) during the thirties suggests that federal credit aids were particularly potent in promoting the shift of economic resources into farming enterprises in these regions.

BUSINESS

Relative to the total amount of credit utilized by business enterprises, loans and loan insurance by public agencies directly serving businesses have been of minor importance. It follows that federal credit programs for business probably have not had important direct effects upon the aggregate amount of business employment and production.[15] Yet federal agencies of business credit have had significant selective effects in stimulating investment in business firms of particular types and industries, notably the following: ocean shipping, railroad transport, and foreign trade enterprises; new enterprises, firms in comparatively unfamiliar lines of trade, and concerns which were "marginal" from a banking point of view. However, whether these resource-allocational effects have been socially beneficial is an issue beyond the scope of this study.

[15] Federal credit aids to agriculture and housing have probably had more influence, indirectly, on business markets and employment than have the programs directly serving businesses.

143

The principal objective of federal housing credit programs since 1934 has been to increase the volume of construction activity. The weight of evidence regarding Title I insurance of loans for home repair and modernization during the thirties is that the program had little influence in initiating the recovery of such expenditures, although it contributed in some degree to their increase once recovery was under way. This conclusion also appears to stand in reference to the federal home loan insurance program, which was launched in earnest in 1935.

An analysis of the effects of the liberal credit terms made available to home buyers after World War II through FHA and VA home mortgage insurance, and Federal National Mortgage Association purchases of home mortgages from private lenders, is more complex. A comparison of the physical dimensions of the home building booms that followed World Wars I and II, after allowance for changes in population and rates of family formation, strongly suggests that residential construction was actually less during the years following World War II than would have been expected on the basis of post-World War I experience. Moreover, comparisons of the post-World War II movements of indices of residential construction costs with those of commercial and industrial construction and of prices of semimanufactured goods generally leads to a conclusion that a considerable part of the effect of federal credit aid programs in this period was to raise the cost of home construction and the prices of existing homes above the levels that would otherwise have prevailed. Thus, it would appear that a material part of the impact of federal credit aids on housing was dissipated after 1946 in price inflation rather than being utilized in the generation of increased physical activity.

Apart from their resource-allocational effects, federal housing credit aids appear to have done the following: first, promoted a decrease in the average size of homes and in the number of rooms per home, a trend in keeping with urbanization and the decline in average family size up to World War II; second, stimulated multi-unit projects developed on a cooperative ownership basis; and third, increased the scale of operations of home building enterprises, thus promoting production efficiency.

Effects on Credit Markets and Lending Practices

It appears probable that the institutional effects of federal credit programs have exceeded in their importance either the aggregative or resource-allocational effects of these programs upon the American economy. Even at those times or in those sectors of the economy where federal credit aids seem to have had but slight direct influence upon the physical volume of activity, they often have modified the markets, practices, and economic functions of the private financial system in profound and enduring ways.

AGRICULTURE

Federal land banks have tended not only to lower the price of mortgage credit to farmers but also to liberalize maturity provisions and loan size. In many years they have functioned as leaders in farm mortgage markets, setting terms and conditions which private lenders were compelled to meet if they were to retain their relative market positions. Also in farm production credit, though to a lesser degree, the production credit associations have been market leaders, in a field formerly served exclusively by commercial banks. The result has been, in part, that commercial banks and life insurance companies have yielded market position to the publicly sponsored agencies; in part, that they have lowered the interest charges and lengthened the maturities of their farm loans. These effects of federal agencies on farm credit markets occurred mainly during a long period of decline in the structure of interest rates. Events might, of course, have taken a quite different direction if federal agencies had pursued the same policies in an economic environment marked by a stable or rising structure of investment returns.

BUSINESS

Federal credit and capital were used with dramatic effects during the thirties to maintain the solvency and enhance the risk-taking ability of private institutions financing business, notably through the RFC bank loans and capital programs. Although federal credit activities have undoubtedly exerted a net expansive influence upon the loan markets of banks and insurance companies, they have also operated in certain respects to compete with, and to restrict, the markets of private credit institutions by making relatively high-risk loans at rates less than those necessary to cover the full costs of such operations. They have often set rates which private institutions were unable to meet, mainly because of the tendency of public agencies to standardize their charges, irrespective of the size, term to maturity, risk, or administrative cost involved in a business loan. On the other hand, federal business credit programs have involved mainly a use of amortized, term loans, and they have promoted the use of this kind of credit by commercial banks. Public lending agencies serving business have thus tended to influence private business credit practices in the same way that federal programs for housing finance have tended to lengthen maturities and to promote the use of amortized loans in the home mortgage market.

HOUSING

Federal housing credit agencies have exerted a persistent downward pressure on mortgage loan rates, one of their principal objects having been to reduce the costs of home mortgage credit. Yet a comparison of the trend of mortgage interest rates with the yields of corporate bonds suggests that the influence of federal housing credit programs has been minor in comparison with the long-term decline in the whole interest rate structure. The facts also show that regional differences in rates charged on home mortgage loans have diminished markedly; since this does not appear to be true of regional differences in the rates carried by bank loans to business, the trend to greater regional uniformity may perhaps be attributed to federal home loan insurance programs. It is much clearer that federal credit programs in the housing field have lengthened the terms to maturity of mortgage loans, have helped to increase their loan-to-value ratios, and, as noted previously, have greatly encouraged the practice of periodic amortization, although they did not originate that practice.

When the influence of federal guarantees and insurance on the volume of nonfarm home mortgage debt is tested by comparing the movement of such debt with the movement of consumer installment sales credit, it is found that between 1935 and 1941 and again in the postwar years, uninsured installment sales credit rose more rapidly. The stimulative influence of federal insurance on mortgage loan volume was substantial; but it is easily exaggerated. Broadly speaking, federal loan insurance has not much influenced the distribution of mortgage lending among types of institutions, as is demonstrated by the minor shifts since 1935 in the relative positions

146

of commercial banks, mutual savings banks, life insurance companies, and savings and loan associations.

In conclusion, federal credit programs have displayed, during a long period of falling interest rates, a pervasive tendency to reduce the costs of credit to borrowers, to increase the ratio of debt to equity, to lengthen the final maturities of loans, and to promote the principle of periodic amortization of loans. Thus, they have tended on the whole to cause private lending agencies to liberalize their credit terms and to readjust their credit practices.

PART II

CHAPTER 6

Agricultural Credit Programs

FEDERAL credit services to agriculture are more complete than those made available to any other sector of the economy. Mortgage loans and short-term production credit are provided through two separate systems of cooperatively organized district banks and local lending associations. A third set of quasi-public district banks extends credit to private cooperative associations marketing farm products or purchasing farm supplies. These wide-reaching enterprises of federally sponsored agencies will be described, in the order given, as to organization, services provided, and lending experience; and where possible, their experience will be put in comparison with that of private lending institutions in the same markets. Next the more specialized programs of direct agencies of the federal government, usually reaching markets not served by private lenders, will be reviewed. Finally, we try to assess the economic impact of federal lending to agriculture.

The Land Bank System

ORGANIZATION

Shortly before 1916 three states, Minnesota, North Dakota, and South Dakota, set up government banks for making farm loans. In the federal sphere, going back a considerable distance, the credit sales of public lands in the early nineteenth century might be regarded as the start of farm credit activities. No advance of funds was involved therein, however. It was the establishment of the federal land bank system in 1916, or rather the first loans made by the land banks, in 1917, that marked the beginning of systematic participation of the federal government in cash lending activities.[1]

Proposals for a system of banks that would specialize in providing long-term farm mortgage credit had been studied for a number of years prior to 1917. Several commissions were organized to explore alternative approaches to its solution. Among these were two groups, one appointed by President Wilson in 1913, which made careful studies of the governmental and cooperative land bank systems of

---

[1] An extensive account of federal intervention in the farm and urban real estate credit markets is given by Miles L. Colean in *The Impact of Government on Real Estate Finance in the United States* (National Bureau of Economic Research, Financial Research Program, 1950).

Europe, with the object of borrowing from their experience such ideas concerning organization and operating policies as might be useful in the United States.[2]

Support was expressed in some quarters at that time for a system of privately organized and financed land banks and in others for a cooperative land bank system with government sponsorship and financial aid. As a result, the Federal Farm Loan Act of 1916 (39 Stat. 362; 12 U.S.C. 641-1012) created two types of banks: the joint stock land banks, which were privately incorporated and financed, and the federal land banks, whose original capital was supplied in the main by the federal government and which were made subject to close government direction and supervision.

The joint stock land banks had a relatively short and not altogether distinguished history. Eighty-eight of them were chartered, all by 1931; but widespread defaults on their loans and the difficulties that they experienced in raising funds in the private capital markets led to their being, in effect, placed in liquidation under the terms of Section 29 of the Emergency Farm Mortgage Act of 1933 (48 Stat. 46; 12 U.S.C. 810). This act prohibited the joint stock land banks from issuing additional tax-exempt bonds or from making additional loans except to refinance outstanding accounts or in connection with the sale of owned real estate. The liquidation of the remaining three banks was completed in 1951. The banks were financed in the main by the sale of tax-exempt securities, but since none of these were ever owned by the United States government, and because the government permitted the banks autonomy in their management and operation, we shall not regard them as federal credit agencies, either direct or sponsored.

The federal land banks, on the other hand, obviously fall within the scope of our study. They were organized almost exclusively with government capital, and provision was made for their direct supervision by the Federal Farm Loan Board, a direct agency of the federal government. Besides providing virtually all of the $9 million of original capital of the twelve banks ($750,000 per bank), the government subscribed an additional $125 million of capital under an amendment to the Federal Farm Loan Act, approved January 23, 1932 (47 Stat. 12; 12 U.S.C. 698), and approximately $189

---

[2] The development of the federal land bank system and other government credit agencies is described in *Financial Statements of Certain Government Agencies,* S. Doc. 172, Part I, 76th Cong., 3rd sess., 1940.

million under the Emergency Farm Mortgage Act of 1933. The latter amount, a subscription to paid-in surplus, was advanced to enable the land banks to make extensions and deferments of defaulted farm loans.

The retirement of government capital from the land banks was envisaged in a plan requiring the borrowing members of the local national farm loan associations, which were organized under the 1916 act, to buy stock in their respective associations in an amount equal to 5 percent of the mortgage loan for which they were applying, and requiring the associations, in turn, to buy an equal amount of stock in the land banks of their respective districts. It was further required that when association-subscribed capital reached $750,000 in an individual district bank, not less than 25 percent of any additional capital funds obtained in that way must be used to retire government capital at par. By the end of March 1934 all of the original government capital of the banks had been retired; and the subscriptions of $125 million to capital and $189 million to paid-in surplus which were made by the government during the depression years of the early thirties were retired by June 30, 1947. It should be noted, however, that at that time the latter amounts were set up in the Treasury as a revolving fund, with the understanding that they would be made available to the banks in case of need. Public Laws 146 and 759 returned the money in the revolving fund to the Treasury, the transfers being made in 1949 and 1951.

The essentially governmental character of the land banks is established by the fact that the federal government has from the beginning had a decisive hand in the selection of their officers and has exercised close supervision over their operations. Under the Farm Loan Act of 1916, over-all administration was provided for by the Federal Farm Loan Board, an agency of the Treasury with the Secretary of the Treasury, ex officio, as its chairman and with the remaining four members—later six—appointed by the President. District farm credit boards of seven members each were also formed, and the Federal Farm Loan Board was given an important part in their selection. The district boards, in turn, were given responsibility for directing the affairs of the land banks, and later of other federal farm credit agencies as these were created.

In the 1933 reorganization of federal farm credit activities the functions of the Federal Farm Loan Board were transferred to the Farm Credit Administration, which held an independent status until

1939, when it was made part of the Department of Agriculture. The independence of the land bank system was re-established by the Farm Credit Act of 1953, under which the Farm Credit Administration again became an independent agency in the executive department of the government. The 1953 act also established a thirteen-member Federal Farm Credit Board to direct the Farm Credit Administration, which continues to supervise and coordinate the activities of the land banks and of other federally sponsored agricultural credit institutions. Further, it required that such institutions if supplied with government capital pay franchise taxes.

The Emergency Farm Mortgage Act of 1933 and the Federal Farm Mortgage Corporation Act of 1934 set up arrangements by which land bank facilities were used in an emergency farm mortgage lending program utilizing funds provided by direct agencies of the federal government—first, by the Reconstruction Finance Corporation, then by the Federal Farm Mortgage Corporation, specially created to alleviate the farm mortgage distress of that time. The resulting Land Bank Commissioner loans, as they were called, will be referred to occasionally in this section and dealt with more fully later, when the programs of direct federal agencies are reviewed.

SERVICES

The role and significance of the federal land bank system has varied considerably from year to year. From 1917 to 1932 the land banks served only a relatively small proportion of the total farm mortgage market (Table 22). Their peak lending of $224 million in 1922 was not quite 9 percent of all farm mortgage loans recorded in that year. Their functions were expanded in 1933 and 1934, however, as part of a federal program designed to make additional credit available to farmers. Under the Emergency Farm Mortgage Act of 1933, the land banks were permitted to make direct loans to farmers in areas where national farm loan associations had not been organized or where existing associations were unable to accept additional applications. In addition, $200 million was made available to the Land Bank Commissioner for emergency loans to farmers, a program expanded in 1934 with the establishment of the Federal Farm Mortgage Corporation, with funds from which Commissioner loans were to be made. As a result mainly of these efforts to facilitate the refinancing of farmers' debts, the land banks from their regular funds supplied 40 percent of all farm mortgage credit extended in

TABLE 22

Farm Mortgage Loans Made by Federal Land Banks, Land Bank Commissioner, Farmers Home Administration and Joint Stock Land Banks and Estimated Amount of Farm Mortgages Recorded by Other Lenders, 1910–1953

(in millions)

| YEAR ENDED DEC. 31 | LOANS MADE[a] | | | | MORTGAGES RECORDED[b] | | | TOTAL ALL LENDERS |
	Federal Land Banks	Federal Farm Mtg. Corp.[c]	Farmers Home Administration[d]	Joint Stock Land Banks[e]	Individuals[f]	Banks & Trust Companies[g]	Insurance Companies[h]	
1910	...	...	...	...	$ 936.8	$207.7	$105.4	$1,249.9
1911	...	...	...	...	970.9	234.6	121.3	1,326.8
1912	...	...	...	...	977.5	252.1	143.7	1,373.3
1913	...	...	...	...	1,038.1	252.5	110.5	1,401.1
1914	...	...	...	...	1,006.7	270.4	120.4	1,397.5
1915	...	...	...	...	989.7	313.7	184.3	1,487.7
1916	...	...	...	...	1,147.5	454.7	235.1	1,837.3
1917	$ 39.1	...	...	$ 1.9	1,301.3	404.2	259.7	2,006.2
1918	118.1	...	...	6.6	1,348.7	316.8	161.5	1,951.7
1919	145.0	...	...	53.0	1,991.2	540.5	214.1	2,943.8
1920	67.0	...	...	19.3	2,489.5	663.2	386.8	3,625.8
1921	91.0	...	...	9.3	1,531.0	654.5	292.8	2,578.7
1922	224.3	...	...	138.7	1,224.0	578.1	340.9	2,506.0
1923	190.3	...	...	189.7	1,115.7	546.5	451.6	2,493.7
1924	162.5	...	...	74.6	1,014.1	475.7	346.1	2,073.0
1925	124.8	...	...	131.4	1,100.3	476.0	347.6	2,180.2
1926	129.0	...	...	123.0	1,012.6	433.4	335.1	2,033.1
1927	138.4	...	...	83.7	905.6	397.3	250.6	1,775.6
1928	100.6	...	...	40.6	902.2	398.2	223.2	1,664.8
1929	63.0	...	...	18.2	834.6	343.5	203.4	1,462.7

(Continued on next page)

TABLE 22 (continued)

(in millions)

YEAR ENDED DEC. 31	LOANS MADE^a				MORTGAGES RECORDED^b			TOTAL ALL LENDERS
	Federal Land Banks	Federal Farm Mtg. Corp.^c	Farmers Home Administration^d	Joint Stock Land Banks^e	Individuals^f	Banks & Trust Companies^g	Insurance Companies^h	
1930	47.1	..	..	5.2	783.4	355.2	173.7	1,364.6
1931	41.8	..	..	5.4	697.6	327.6	127.5	1,199.9
1932	27.5	..	..	2.2	535.5	263.3	74.8	903.3
1933	151.6	$ 70.8	..	0.7	386.7	167.1	46.0	823.0
1934	730.1	553.0	..	..	353.2	130.6	53.4	1,820.4
1935	247.6	195.9	..	..	363.7	176.5	78.0	1,061.7
1936	108.6	76.9	..	..	315.7	186.1	115.1	802.4
1937	62.8	39.7	..	..	314.2	212.8	128.2	757.7
1938	51.2	29.2	$10.2	..	285.3	209.9	137.4	723.2
1939	51.5	27.2	26.3	..	268.2	217.8	138.0	729.0
1940	63.9	36.4	39.1	..	267.7	219.8	145.6	772.5
1941	64.7	37.3	59.6	..	290.6	221.3	160.5	834.0
1942	53.6	28.2	34.9	..	300.5	191.0	154.6	762.8
1943	61.2	30.1	31.9	..	392.4	233.1	167.1	915.8
1944	69.4	34.5	36.4	..	414.6	255.3	160.8	971.0
1945	91.9	28.7	16.6	..	459.3	312.8	145.1	1,054.4
1946	128.6	14.6	47.3	..	573.8	521.9	200.0	1,486.2
1947	137.3	10.3	26.1	..	548.4	487.1	230.9	1,440.1
1948	148.6	[i]	18.8	..	564.1	436.4	259.1	1,427.0
1949	180.6	[i]	15.1	..	539.4	396.5	276.9	1,408.5
1950	203.1	[i]	42.8	..	590.3	471.6	348.0	1,655.9
1951	211.4	0.1	45.3	..	673.5	458.4	381.6	1,770.2
1952	251.6	[i]	47.7	..	649.0	483.7	345.6	1,777.6
1953	286.1	[i]	30.5	..	658.5	484.0	394.5	1,853.6

(continued on next page)

TABLE 22 (*continued*)

From *Farm Mortgage Loans Made and Farm Mortgages Recorded by Principal Lenders* (Farm Credit Administration, Economic and Credit Analysis Division), June 1954, p. 4. U.S. possessions not included.

a Refers to regular mortgage loans only exclusive of purchase-money mortgages and sales contracts. Data for the joint stock land banks for 1917–1920 were partially estimated by the Bureau of Agricultural Economics.

b Estimates for the years 1910 through 1933 were prepared by the Bureau of Agricultural Economics, those for 1936 to date were prepared by the Farm Credit Administration, and those for 1934 and 1935 were prepared jointly by the two agencies.

c The authority to make Land Bank Commissioner loans expired July 1, 1947, except for the limited purpose of refinancing loans previously made.

d Covers tenant purchase, farm enlargement, farm development, and project liquidation farm ownership loans, and similar loans made from state corporation trust funds. Figures represent amounts obligated, except that for project liquidation loans they refer to the amount advanced. Data for 1944 include all project liquidation loans made from inception of program through December 31, 1944. Data for 1950–1953 include

farm housing loans made from beginning of program in November 1949.

e Placed in liquidation May 12, 1933. Loans made after that date are included with mortgages recorded by individuals.

f Refers to individual lenders, administrators, executors, and guardians; mortgage and investment companies; savings and loan associations; state and local governmental agencies; production credit associations, religious, educational, civic, and fraternal organizations; and any other lender not specifically mentioned.

g Covers both commercial and savings banks. The period 1911–1935 includes all such banks whether open or closed. From 1936 to date, receivers or conservators of banks are included with "individuals."

h Data for the years 1910–1935 exclude mortgages recorded in the New England states, which were too few to classify separately and are included with the recordings shown for "other" lenders. Data for the years 1936 to date, however, include recordings in the New England states. Recordings are mainly those of life companies, but they also include those of any other types of insurance companies.

i Less than $50,000.

157

1934; and with inclusion of the Commissioner loans made from specially provided funds, 60 percent of all farm mortgage credit extended during 1934–1935 was loaned by or arranged through the land bank system (Table 22). The refinancing program tapered off in 1936, and from 1937 through 1953 (the Commissioner program was discontinued on July 1, 1947) only about 12 percent of the total volume of farm mortgages recorded was made through the land banks.

In 1945 the land banks were authorized to lend up to 65 percent of the normal agricultural value of farm property. The allowable percentage represented a liberalization; but the new method of valuation—based on anticipated farm performance assuming average yields and assuming price conditions as in a period like 1909–1914, which was not markedly either deflationary or inflationary—proved restrictive in the period of rising land values that ensued. It required the land banks to appraise farms more conservatively than most other lenders. Thus the banks in recent years have had a surplus of loanable funds, and in some farm credit districts have been restricted to dealing only with relatively well-established farmers.

The proportion of total farm mortgage debt held by the federal land banks has varied widely as a result of the changing role of their loan program (Table 23). Before 1933 they accounted for relatively small proportions, ranging from 3.5 percent in 1920 to 13.5 percent in 1932. By the end of 1936, however, they held more than $2.1 billion, or 30 percent of the $7.2 billion farm mortgage debt; their holdings together with the Land Bank Commissioner loans held by the Federal Farm Mortgage Corporation comprised more than 40 percent of the total. The proportion held by the land banks remained close to 30 percent through 1943, then declined continuously until the end of 1953, when of the $7.7 billion outstanding the federal land banks held only 15.3 percent, Commissioner loans outstanding having meanwhile declined to minute percentages of the total after 1947 as new loans ceased to be made.

Land bank loans have usually been written with maturities of from twenty to thirty-three years, on an amortized basis. The Federal Farm Loan Act originally provided for terms varying from five to forty years, the loans to be fully amortized. An amendment to the act adopted in 1920 provided that the borrower or mortgagor, upon any regular installment date, might make any number of advance payments on a portion of the loan or pay the entire principal of the

TABLE 23

Farm Mortgage Holdings of the Principal Public and Private Lenders, 1909–1953

(in thousands)

End of Year	Total^a	Federal Land Banks	Federal Farm Mortgage Corporation^b	Farmers Home Administration^c	Joint Stock Land Banks^d	Individuals & Miscellaneous	Banks & Trust Companies^e	Life Insurance Companies
1909	$ 3,207,863	...	...	...	...	$2,414,654	$ 406,248	$ 386,961
1910	3,522,121	...	...	...	...	2,621,099	477,568	423,454
1911	3,929,758	...	...	...	...	2,869,805	580,300	479,653
1912	4,347,679	...	...	...	...	3,123,769	673,752	550,158
1913	4,707,358	...	...	...	...	3,386,109	723,787	597,462
1914	4,990,785	...	...	...	...	3,574,690	746,111	669,984
1915	5,256,425	...	...	...	...	3,714,585	776,269	765,571
1916	5,825,851	...	...	...	...	4,030,717	933,990	861,144
1917	6,536,860	$ 39,112	...	...	$ 1,888	4,531,777	1,008,492	955,591
1918	7,137,365	156,214	...	...	8,384	4,924,364	1,030,240	1,018,163
1919	8,448,772	293,595	...	...	60,038	5,915,930	1,204,383	974,826
1920	10,221,126	349,679	...	...	77,959	7,140,227	1,447,483	1,205,778
1921	10,702,257	432,523	...	...	85,017	7,212,345	1,540,005	1,432,367
1922	10,785,621	639,486	...	...	218,775	6,864,690	1,506,467	1,556,203
1923	10,664,919	797,785	...	...	392,639	6,294,244	1,388,106	1,792,145
1924	9,912,650	923,077	...	...	446,429	5,400,064	1,200,456	1,942,624
1925	9,713,213	998,552	...	...	545,559	4,960,341	1,178,460	2,030,301
1926	9,658,422	1,068,642	...	...	632,476	4,690,045	1,143,595	2,123,664
1927	9,756,957	1,144,984	...	...	669,798	4,672,227	1,097,085	2,172,863
1928	9,756,559	1,182,813	...	...	656,516	4,731,626	1,046,624	2,138,980
1929	9,630,768	1,201,732	...	...	637,789	4,675,340	997,468	2,118,439

(continued on next page)

TABLE 23 (continued)

(Farm mortgage holdings, in thousands)

End of Year	Total a	Federal Land Banks	Federal Farm Mortgage Corporation b	Farmers Home Administration c	Joint Stock Land Banks	Individuals & Miscellaneous	Banks & Trust Companies e	Life Insurance Companies
1930	$ 9,398,088	$1,197,063	...	...	$605,858	$4,561,244	$ 946,876	$2,087,047
1931	9,093,983	1,180,992	...	...	552,180	4,384,062	940,135	2,036,614
1932	8,466,418	1,147,014	...	...	474,954	4,057,049	889,083	1,898,318
1933	7,685,203	1,257,825	$ 70,738	...	412,346	3,535,644	710,863	1,697,787
1934	7,584,459	1,947,442	616,737	...	277,020	2,942,856	498,842	1,301,562
1935	7,422,701	2,113,502	794,147	...	200,617	2,714,641	487,505	1,112,289
1936	7,153,963	2,147,768	841,251	...	162,786	2,499,009	487,534	1,015,615
1937	6,954,884	2,126,610	824,151	...	133,554	2,380,562	501,450	988,557
1938	6,779,318	2,088,478	774,377	$10,218	114,992	2,289,038	519,276	982,939
1939	6,586,399	2,009,820	713,290	31,927	91,726	2,221,176	534,170	984,290
1940	6,493,527	1,957,184	685,149	65,294	73,455	2,152,558	543,408	1,016,479
1941	6,376,080	1,880,784	634,885	114,533	55,919	2,091,581	535,212	1,063,166
1942	5,956,458	1,718,240	543,895	157,463	37,015	1,980,230	476,676	1,042,939
1943	5,395,671	1,452,886	429,751	171,763	10,097	1,896,080	448,433	986,661
1944	4,940,915	1,209,676	347,307	193,377	5,455	1,797,243	449,582	938,275
1945	4,760,464	1,078,952	239,365	181,861	3,208	1,858,517	507,298	891,263
1946	4,896,970	976,748	146,621	189,300	1,641	2,010,766	683,229	888,665
1947	5,064,245	888,933	107,066	195,069	645	2,072,170	840,647	959,715
1948	5,288,331	868,156	77,920	188,893	462	2,215,674	900,843	1,036,383
1949	5,579,278	906,077	58,650	188,855	270	2,315,956	937,144	1,172,326
1950	6,071,345	947,431	44,008	214,047	0	2,501,734	1,008,359	1,355,766
1951	6,588,270	994,128	32,778	233,374	0	2,740,026	1,046,923	1,541,041
1952	7,154,038	1,071,358	23,899	257,936	0	2,980,585	1,105,096	1,715,164
1953	7,656,186	1,169,418	17,628	268,060	0	3,177,223	1,131,214	1,892,643

(continued on next page)

TABLE 23 (continued)

From *Agricultural Statistics 1952* (Department of Agriculture), Table 727, p. 721, and *Agricultural Finance Review* (Agricultural Research Service), Vol. 17, November 1954, Table 1, p. 83. U.S. possessions not included.

a Data for federal land banks, Federal Farm Mortgage Corporation, joint stock land banks and life insurance companies in 1929–1953 include regular mortgages, purchase-money mortgages, and sales contracts; before 1929, regular mortgages only. Federal land banks and FFMC mortgages in process of foreclosure were estimated for 1950 and 1951.

b Loans held by the Federal Farm Mortgage Corporation were made on its behalf by the Land Bank Commissioner. Authority to make new loans expired July 1, 1947.

c Before 1941, covers tenant purchase loans only. Beginning with 1941, also includes farm development (special real estate) loans; beginning with 1943, farm enlargement loans; beginning with 1944, project liquidation loans; and beginning with 1950, farm housing loans. Loans made for these purposes from state corporation trust funds are also included. Loans insured by Farmers Home Administration are not included.

d Liquidation of the joint stock land banks began May 12, 1933, and was completed April 26, 1951. Data for banks in receivership are also included.

e Data for 1934–1946 refer to insured commercial banks; before 1934, to open state and national banks and from 1947 to date, to all operating commercial and savings banks.

loan. As a result of the increase in delinquencies in the early 1930's the act was further amended to provide adjustment or deferments in the repayment schedule. Authority was given to the bank directors, with approval of the Farm Credit Administration, to extend the unpaid balances and to accept as payments installments sufficient to extinguish the debt within an agreed period of not more than forty years.

The importance of these deferment and extension provisions can scarcely be overestimated. On the average, more than one out of every four land bank loans outstanding over the period 1931 to 1940 had been delinquent or extended. The delinquency rate (i.e. the number of loans delinquent or extended during the year as a percentage of the number of loans outstanding at year end) more than doubled between 1931 and 1932, rising from about 23 percent in 1931 to nearly 50 percent at the end of 1932. It stayed close to the peak through 1933, dropped quickly to 27 percent at the end of 1935, and remained above 20 percent through 1940.[3] Although the number of loans delinquent or extended declined sharply during the forties, in recent years it has been around 4 or 5 percent of the total number of loans outstanding. On January 1, 1954, for example, 4.9

3 Donald C. Horton, Harald C. Larsen, and Norman J. Wall, *Farm-Mortgage Credit Facilities in the United States* (Department of Agriculture, Misc. Pub. 478, 1942), Table 32, p. 100.

percent of the number of land bank loans outstanding had extensions or delinquent installments.[4]

The interest rates charged on land bank loans have been relatively low—4 percent in 1954 in all districts except Springfield, Baltimore, and Columbia, which compares with an average for all farm mortgage lenders of 4.7 percent. In contrast to the rates of most private lenders, they have not varied with loan size. Rates of 4½ percent were authorized by Congress from July 11, 1933 to June 30, 1935 (a reduction from the pre-depression rate) and of 3½ percent from July 1, 1935 to June 30, 1944.[5] Rates were at 4 percent in all districts from 1944 to 1954 except at the Federal Land Banks of Springfield and of Baltimore, which increased interest rates to 4½ percent as of January 1, 1949 and October 1, 1951, respectively. The Federal Land Bank of Columbia increased the interest rate to 4½ percent on August 1, 1948 and to 5 percent on July 1, 1951. In comparison, the average interest rate on all farm mortgage loans reached a high of 6.4 percent on January 1, 1923, dropping to 6.0 percent in 1929 and to 4.4 percent in 1942. From this point the average rate increased to 4.6 percent in 1946 and to 4.7 percent by January 1, 1953.[6] Thus land bank loans, on the average, have carried an interest rate about 0.5 percent to 1.5 percent lower— depending on the year—than the average for all farm mortgage lenders.

Land bank interest rates have been relatively lower in the western and southern parts of the United States than in the central and eastern sections of the country. Between 1933 and 1944, while the reduced rates were in effect, the average farm mortgage interest rate in the North Central states declined from about 5.7 percent on January 1, 1933 to about 4.2 percent in 1944, whereas in the South Atlantic region the average went from 6.3 percent to 4.6 percent and in the Rocky Mountain region from 6.7 percent to 4.5 percent.[7] During the period 1944 to 1953 while the land bank rate was 4 percent (with the exceptions noted above), the average rate on all farm mortgage loans was about 4.3 percent in the North Central states, but about 5.0 percent in the South Atlantic and East South

[4] *Agricultural Finance Review* (Department of Agriculture, Agricultural Research Service), Vol. 17, November 1954, p. 88.

[5] From *Annual Reports* of the Farm Credit Administration.

[6] *Agricultural Statistics, 1952* (Department of Agriculture), Table 720, p. 715, and *Agricultural Statistics, 1953*, Table 728, p. 629.

[7] *Ibid.*

Central states and about 4.7 percent in the Mountain and Pacific Coast areas. The percentage of the total farm mortgage debt held by federal land banks has varied to some extent from one region of the country to another, as is indicated in Table 24; but more striking are the regional variations for other lenders. At the beginning of 1954 the Farmers Home Administration held 13 percent of the total farm mortgage debt in the New Orleans district, for example, but only 1.2 percent in the Berkeley district. Private lenders also vary in

TABLE 24

Distribution of Farm Mortgage Debt as of January 1, 1954
among the Principal Public and Private Lenders
by Farm Credit District

Farm Credit District[a]	Federal Land Banks	Federal Farm Mtg. Corp.	Farmers Home Adm.	Life Insurance Cos.	All Operating Banks	Others[b]
Springfield	13.4%	0.3%	1.9%	6.8%	21.5%	56.1%
Baltimore	8.9	0.1	3.4	7.2	32.0	48.4
Columbia	13.6	0.3	8.0	16.4	15.6	46.1
Louisville	10.0	0.1	2.6	23.2	27.6	36.5
New Orleans	19.2	0.2	12.9	19.5	15.1	33.1
St. Louis	15.8	0.2	4.1	38.4	14.5	27.0
St. Paul	16.8	0.5	2.3	14.0	17.4	49.0
Omaha	22.6	0.2	2.0	42.3	8.2	24.7
Wichita	15.2	0.1	4.0	36.3	6.4	38.0
Houston	21.6	0.3	3.4	42.2	5.5	27.0
Berkeley	9.7	0.2	1.2	15.9	12.1	60.9
Spokane	15.3	0.2	3.3	20.2	5.9	55.1
United States	15.3	0.2	3.5	24.7	14.8	41.5

Compiled from *Agricultural Finance Review* (Agricultural Research Service), Vol. 17, November 1954, Table 3, p. 84. Bank loans are classified according to location of bank and are not strictly comparable with the data for other lenders, where the classification is by location of mortgaged farms.

[a] States included in the farm credit districts are as follows: *Springfield*—Maine, New Hampshire, Vermont, Massachusetts, Rhode Island, Connecticut, New York, New Jersey; *Baltimore*—Pennsylvania, Maryland, District of Columbia, Delaware, Virginia, West Virginia; *Columbia*—North and South Carolina, Georgia, Florida; *Louisville*—Indiana, Ohio, Kentucky, Tennessee; *New Orleans*—Alabama, Mississippi, Louisiana; *St. Louis*—Illinois, Missouri, Arkansas; *St. Paul*—Michigan, Wisconsin, Minnesota, North Dakota; *Omaha*—Iowa, Nebraska, South Dakota, Wyoming; *Wichita*—Kansas, Oklahoma, Colorado, New Mexico; *Houston*—Texas; *Berkeley*—Utah, Arizona, Nevada, California; *Spokane*—Montana, Idaho, Washington, Oregon.

[b] Refers to individuals and miscellaneous institutions.

importance regionally; indeed, the variability was greater at the end of 1953 for banks and insurance companies than for the land banks. Worthy of special note, perhaps, is the fact that insurance company lending has tended to be concentrated in the general region of the Corn Belt and the southwestern wheat, cattle, and cotton areas—in the Omaha, St. Louis, Wichita, and Houston farm credit districts.

The land banks have made their facilities available to all farmers who could fulfill their equity requirements, but the basis on which they are directed by law to appraise farm properties—that is, the limitation of land bank loans (since 1945) to 65 percent of the normal agricultural value of the farm—has restricted their lending to a considerably smaller percentage of the market value of the farm than for other lenders.[8] As a result, land bank loans have averaged considerably smaller than those of insurance companies, although larger than those of banks and of individuals and others. According to estimates of the Farm Credit Administration, the average size of mortgage loans made during 1942–1947 was as follows: land banks, $4,100; Land Bank Commissioner, $1,400; insurance companies, $7,200; banks, $3,000; individuals and miscellaneous, $3,100.[9]

Further information on the distribution of the farm mortgage credit market among land banks and other major lenders shows that commercial banks have their largest shares of total outstandings in counties where (1) farms are of moderate size; (2) land is a relatively unimportant component of total assets; (3) dairy and miscellaneous products are more important than crops and livestock in total farm output; and (4) home consumption of farm products and earnings from off-farm work are relatively high.[10] Insurance companies, on the other hand, tend to hold their greatest shares of outstanding farm mortgage debt in counties where (1) farms are large; (2) land is a relatively important component of total assets, and the bulk of the acreage is in cropland; (3) crop and livestock sales are high compared with sales of dairy and miscellaneous products; and (4)

[8] Cf. John I. Smith, "Federal Land Bank Dilemma," *Farm Policy Forum*, Vol. 3, No. 3, March 1950, pp. 9–14.

[9] See *Farm-Mortgage Loans and Their Distribution by Lender Groups, 1940–48*, by Harold T. Lingard (Department of Agriculture, Circular 812, August 1949), pp. 28f.

[10] Donald C. Horton, *Patterns of Farm Financial Structure* (Princeton University Press for the National Bureau of Economic Research, 1957), pp. 120f.

home consumption of farm products and earnings from off-farm work are relatively low.

Land banks hold a somewhat higher share of the farm mortgage debt in counties where the operator interest in farms is low (which tend also to rank low in frequency of mortgage use) than elsewhere. Insurance companies show the same pattern, more markedly. No evidence is discernible, however, that either they or the land banks tend to concentrate their lending in areas of either high or low ratios of debt to equity.

Whereas private lending agencies tend to show some degree of specialization—regional, or otherwise—in their lending, the federal land banks are almost equally active in all areas of the market. As was seen in Table 24, their relative importance as holders of long-term farm loans does not vary as greatly by regions as that of banks or insurance companies. The share of total farm mortgage debt held by land banks appears to have varied but little as between areas differing in size of farm, in frequency of mortgage use, and in the intensity of mortgage credit use as measured by ratios of debt to equity.

EXPERIENCE

Federal land bank experience (apart from Commissioner loans) illustrates long-term lending to farmers who in most cases would have been able to obtain financing from private sources. Thus it affords, over a long span of activity, opportunities for comparison with the experience of private institutions lending in the same market. Three periods should be distinguished in federal land bank experience: (1) the pre-depression years, extending from the establishment of the system in 1917 to 1929; (2) the depression and recovery period from 1930 to 1940; and (3) the war and postwar period, running from 1941 to 1954.

During the 1920's the land banks encountered no serious trouble: delinquencies averaged about 5 percent of the total number of loans outstanding, acquisitions of farms were relatively infrequent, and the losses on properties sold were small. To the end of 1929 only about 2.8 percent of all loans made went to foreclosure, and at the end of 1929 land bank farm holdings amounted to not quite 2.5 percent of their total farm mortgage investment. About half the acquired farms had been sold by the end of 1929, and 88 percent of the investment in them had been recovered. The total loss on loan and real estate transactions, plus net charge-offs against farms still held, came to about 3 percent of the total amount of loans extinguished during the period, equivalent to an annual charge of about 0.13 percent on loans outstanding.

Life insurance companies, on the other hand, ran into somewhat more trouble during the twenties. They had acquired a sizable amount of farm mortgage loans by the end of World War I, often at relatively inflated values. Fifteen large life insurance companies, for example, doubled their farm mortgage investment from 1920 to 1929. Although until 1926 they made few foreclosures, by the time their peak investment was reached in 1929 their total farm property holdings (including farms owned, farms sold but with title retained, and farms on which foreclosure was pending) amounted to 7.6 percent of their total farm mortgage investment.[11] However, the life insurance companies recovered a larger percentage of their investment in acquired properties than did the land banks. In 1928 about 7 percent, and in 1929 about 5 percent, of the farms owned by thirteen life insurance companies were sold, with average recoveries of 94.4 percent and 96.0 percent, respectively.[12]

After 1929, farm mortgage delinquencies for all public and private lenders became much more general. Whereas only about 5.5 percent of the land bank mortgages outstanding at the end of 1929 had been delinquent at some time during that year, by the beginning of 1933 almost half the mortgages were delinquent or had been extended.[13] Delinquencies remained at a relatively high level for some years, and were particularly numerous in the Columbia and New Orleans credit districts and in the St. Paul district, covering the major northwest spring wheat area.[14]

[11] Data from *Résumé of Farm Loan Experience, 1928–1937*, Farm Mortgage Conference of Life Insurance Companies, December 1939. The insurance companies composing the Farm Mortgage Conference held 71 percent of the farm mortgage and land investment of life insurance companies at the end of 1928 and 70 percent at the beginning of 1937.

[12] The relatively low recovery ratio of the land banks (88 percent) may be due to the fact that in this period they sold a higher proportion of the foreclosed properties that they held than did the life insurance companies.

[13] Before 1932, any federal land bank loan with matured interest or principal unpaid was considered delinquent, but after 1932 land banks had the privilege of extending such loans. To assure comparability, delinquency after 1932 is defined to include both delinquent loans on which no extensions had been granted and loans that had been extended, even though the latter were not still delinquent.

[14] See Horton, Larsen, and Wall, *op.cit.*, Table 32, p. 100.

By 1932 delinquencies among farm mortgages of ten of the leading life insurance companies were about as extensive as among those of the land banks (Table 25). On the other hand, in the years after 1933 life insurance company delinquencies declined more rapidly, in

TABLE 25

Delinquency Status of Farm Mortgage Loans Held by 10
Life Insurance Companies at Year Ends, 1932–1937

Status of Mortgage	1932a	1933	1934	1935	1936	1937
Nondelinquent	55%	55%	63%	72%	79%	85%
Delinquent						
More than 90 days	29	32	24	18	12	9
Less than 90 days	9	6	4	2	2	2
In foreclosure						
Not subject to redemption	7	7	5	4	4	2
Subject to redemption			4	4	3	2
Total	100	100	100	100	100	100

From *Resume of Farm Loan Experience, 1928–37* (Farm Mortgage Conference of Life Insurance Companies, December 1939), p. 20.
a Refers to March 31, 1933, the date when delinquency figures were first collected.

part because the land banks refinanced around $260 million of the $1.5 billion of farm mortgage loans held by the fifteen companies at the end of 1929, and in part because about $572 million of the principal amount of the mortgages held by the companies had passed into their real estate accounts between 1928 and 1937 through foreclosure.

Although it was the policy of most farm mortgage lenders—especially the land banks and the insurance companies—to exhaust other means of settlement before resorting to foreclosure, lenders' acquisitions of farm real estate increased rapidly after 1930. During the eleven years from 1930 to 1940 the land banks acquired an average of 9,300 farms *per year*, as compared with a total of about 14,000 farms acquired through 1929.[15] In 1936, alone, 14,652 farms were acquired.[16] Foreclosures by life insurance companies were also

[15] *Annual Reports* of the Federal Farm Loan Board, 1929–1932, and of the Farm Credit Administration, 1934–1940.
[16] *Annual Report*, Farm Credit Administration, 1938, p. 21.

frequent. Of the mortgages held by fifteen life insurance companies at the beginning of 1928, and which were not in foreclosure then, more than one-third, comprising 41 percent of the amount held, had been foreclosed by 1937 or were in the process of being foreclosed.[17]

Foreclosure data for commercial banks and other lenders are not as complete, but show their acquisitions of farms to have been less extensive than those of the land banks and insurance companies. At the end of 1937, insured commercial banks held only $56 million of acquired farm real estate, which compares with $132 million for the federal land banks and Federal Farm Mortgage Corporation, and $612 million for the life insurance companies.[18] One of the reasons for the relatively light acquisitions by commercial banks in the 1930's was their heavy liquidation of farm mortgage loans in the twenties, somewhat before the onset of the most severe farm difficulties. In 1925–1929 the average annual number of distress transfers of farms was 6.2 percent of the number of mortgaged farms in 1925; during 1930–1934, on the other hand, distress transfers were 9.5 percent of the number of mortgaged farms in 1930.[19]

The peak of foreclosures by federal land banks came several years after the peak for other lenders, with sharp increases in 1935 and 1936, just as the foreclosures of insurance companies and most other lenders were declining (Table 26). In 1934 and the first part of

TABLE 26

Indexes of the Number of Farm Foreclosure Sales
for Selected Lenders, 1934–1939
(*1934–1939 average = 100*)

Type of Lender	1934	1935	1936	1937	1938	1939
Federal Land Banks and Land Bank Commissioner	38.2	95.9	127.6	106.5	108.9	124.4
Individuals	148.5	123.4	106.1	86.6	74.9	59.7
Commercial banks	119.0	119.0	111.3	98.1	83.5	69.4
Insurance companies	185.7	135.9	99.8	68.7	58.6	50.8
Miscellaneous	167.8	150.8	104.5	74.6	55.4	46.9
All lenders	131.1	123.1	109.9	87.3	77.4	70.8

From *Farm-Mortgage Credit Facilities in the United States* by Donald C. Horton, Harald C. Larsen, and Norman J. Wall (Department of Agriculture, Misc. Pub. 478, 1942), Table 11, p. 41.

[17] *Résumé of Farm Loan Experience, 1928–1937*, p. 8.
[18] *Agricultural Statistics, 1952*, Department of Agriculture, Table 754, p. 751.
[19] Horton et al., *op.cit.*, Table 9, p. 39.

1935, the land banks and the Land Bank Commissioner were closing large numbers of refinancing loans, and foreclosures were infrequent; the 1936 rise in foreclosures reflects the accumulation of delinquencies in the immediately previous years, and the rises in 1938 and 1939 reflect the larger number of federal land bank loans then outstanding.

During the thirties there were three or four distinct areas in which farm mortgage delinquencies and foreclosures were especially heavy. The largest of these was in the northern Great Plains—the Dakotas, Montana, Wyoming, Colorado, Nebraska, and Kansas—stretching east to cover parts of Minnesota, Wisconsin, and northern Iowa. A second and considerably smaller area was in southern Iowa and northern Missouri. The third was centered in the eastern Cotton Belt, particularly in Georgia and South Carolina. As Table 27

TABLE 27

Estimated Number of Farm Foreclosure Sales, 1934–1939,
per 1,000 Farms Mortgaged on January 1, 1935,
by Farm Credit District

Farm Credit Districta	1934	1935	1936	1937	1938	1939
Springfield	18.7	16.2	14.0	13.9	12.9	12.0
Baltimore	24.3	26.0	25.9	20.2	15.0	14.4
Columbia	32.9	26.6	26.1	15.7	12.8	10.9
Louisville	22.7	18.4	13.3	9.2	7.9	6.5
New Orleans	17.8	21.2	18.5	11.1	7.7	7.2
St. Louis	39.5	36.1	29.6	24.8	19.9	15.5
St. Paul	22.8	23.6	25.6	23.1	23.8	24.3
Omaha	48.7	42.5	37.0	30.1	30.4	29.8
Wichita	40.6	38.1	30.0	26.5	26.1	25.6
Houston	19.8	22.3	18.8	13.2	12.6	10.6
Berkeley	16.4	11.4	10.8	9.8	7.7	7.5
Spokane	21.2	22.8	25.3	22.1	13.2	8.2
United States	27.8	26.1	23.3	18.5	16.4	15.0

From *Farm-Mortgage Credit Facilities in the United States* by Donald C. Horton, Harald C. Larsen, and Norman J. Wall (Department of Agriculture, Misc. Pub. 478, 1942), Table 10, p. 40.

a For a listing of states included in each farm credit district, see Table 24, note a.

shows, foreclosures of farms were relatively high in the St. Louis, St. Paul, Omaha, and Wichita farm credit districts, which include the first two of the mortgage distress areas. Furthermore, foreclosure rates in the Omaha and Wichita districts remained well above the national average throughout 1934–1939, whereas in the St. Paul district they reached their peak in 1936 and the trend in the St. Louis district was downward throughout the period. Foreclosures in the Columbia district were higher than the national average during 1934–1936 but declined to less than the national average in the years following.[20]

The heavier occurrence of farm mortgage distress in certain major areas naturally affected the experience of private lending agencies. The fact that farm mortgage holdings of life insurance companies were concentrated in the Corn Belt and Northern Plains meant that the companies suffered a particularly adverse effect. At the end of 1937, 65 percent of the farm mortgage and land investment of seventeen leading companies was secured by properties in Ohio, Indiana, Illinois, Minnesota, Iowa, Missouri, and Nebraska.[21] If Kansas and the Dakotas are included, the area contains 77 percent of their total investment; and the ten Cotton Belt states from North Carolina to Texas contained another 15 percent of the farm mortgage investment of these companies. This concentration in areas of especially heavy distress doubtless explains their relatively adverse experience.

On the other hand, as had been the case in the twenties, so in the thirties insurance companies appear to have recovered a larger percentage of their investment in acquired farms disposed of than did the federal land banks (Table 28). The most likely explanation of this difference is that the land banks followed a policy of disposing of properties as soon as possible after acquisition, whereas the life insurance companies held theirs for somewhat longer periods.[22]

[20] For more extensive discussion of the location of areas of farm mortgage distress see *Mortgage Lending Experience in Agriculture* by Lawrence A. Jones and David Durand (Princeton University Press for the National Bureau of Economic Research, 1954), Chapter 1.

[21] *Résumé of Farm Loan Experience, 1928–1937*, pp. 6–8.

[22] Sixty-three percent of the total book value of farm real estate held by twenty-six large life insurance companies at the end of 1938 had been acquired before 1935. See *Operating Results and Investments of the Twenty-Six Largest Legal Reserve Life Insurance Companies in the United States, 1929–38*, a report submitted by the Securities and Exchange Commission to the Temporary National Economic Committee, Hearings before the Temporary National Economic Committee, 76th Cong., 3rd sess., February 1940, Part 10-A, p. 182.

TABLE 28

Percentage of Cost Recovered through Sales of Farm Properties by
Federal Land Banks and by 13 Life Insurance Companies, 1927–1940

Year	Federal Land Banks[a]	Life Insurance Companies[b]
1927	93.1%	c
1928	87.3	94.4%
1929	84.8	96.0
1930	78.9	91.2
1931	70.2	78.3
1932	66.0	87.6
1933	84.7	91.7
1934	86.3	93.1
1935	77.9	92.5
1936	74.3	89.6
1937	76.6	88.9
1938	72.4	c
1939	69.4	c
1940	67.2	c

a From *Farm-Mortgage Credit Facilities in the United States* by Donald C.
Horton, Harald C. Larsen, and Norman J. Wall (Department of Agriculture,
Misc. Pub. 478, 1942), Table 36, p. 106. Through 1934 the cost figure covers only
unpaid loan balances at date of acquisition; from 1935 through 1940, cost also
includes accrued interest to date of acquisition as well as expenses for operation
and maintenance. Figures for 1927–1932 reflect net disposals of real estate,
sheriff's certificates, etc. (i.e. total disposals less reacquisitions).

b Data from *Résumé of Farm Loan Experience, 1928–1937* (Farm Mortgage
Conference of Life Insurance Companies, 1939), p. 96. In addition to capital investment at time of acquisition, cost includes maintenance, improvements, and
taxes and is net of income earned from operation.

c Data unavailable.

Losses on real estate and mortgage loan transactions of the land
banks (including, from 1935 on, allocations to reserves set aside for
valuation adjustments) are presented in Table 29. When these
amounts are cumulated and expressed as a percentage of cumulated
year-end outstandings of mortgage loans, one obtains a measure of
the charge that would have been required against outstandings to
cover all losses. This would have been 0.13 percent from the beginning of the system to the end of 1929 and 0.51 percent to the end
of 1940 (Table 29). The charge that it would have been necessary
to make against any one year's holdings in order to cover that year's
losses is, of course, a more variable figure, ranging from nearly 1.00
percent to as low as 0.40 percent.

TABLE 29

Federal Land Bank Loss Rates, 1929–1940

Year	Cumulative Losses to End of Year as a Percentage of Cumulated Year-End Outstandings[a]	Annual Losses as a Percentage of Year-End Outstandings[a]
1929	0.13%[b]	0.42%
1930	.16	.40
1931	.21	.60
1932	.27	.95
1933	.29	.52
1934	.29	.26
1935	.34	.70
1936	.38	.73
1937	.41	.76
1938	.46	.93
1939	.49	.94
1940	.51	.80

Data for losses in 1929–1935 are from *Farm-Mortgage Credit Facilities in the United States* by Donald C. Horton, Harald C. Larsen, and Norman J. Wall (Department of Agriculture, Misc. Pub. 478, 1942), p. 106; losses in 1936–1940 and total amounts of loans outstanding are from the *Annual Reports* of the Farm Credit Administration.

a Losses also include: throughout, charge-offs of principal and interest on mortgage loans; from 1935 through 1937, net increases in valuation reserves maintained against farms owned outright or in process of acquirement; and from 1938 on, net increases in valuation reserves covering both loans and real estate transactions. Losses are given net of recoveries from national farm loan associations resulting from their endorsement of loans.

b From year of organization.

In the period 1941–1954, land bank delinquencies declined to relatively low levels; foreclosures became rare after 1943, and losses on disposals of farm real estate dwindled and disappeared (Table 30). Data gathered from a selected group of life insurance companies show somewhat similar trends. After 1943, foreclosures by the reporting companies practically ceased—only a fraction of 1 percent of the life insurance mortgages made after 1931 resulted in foreclosure—and recoveries on properties sold exceeded the total investment in them. The few farm foreclosures which occurred after World War II were largely on loans made by individuals and banks. In 1950, for example, of 1,214 farm foreclosures, 62 percent were by individuals, 27 percent by banks, 4 percent were divided about equally between the land banks and the Federal Farm Mortgage Corpora-

TABLE 30

Loan Experience of the Federal Land Banks, 1940–1954

(*dollar figures in thousands*)

YEARs a	DELINQUENT LOANSb AS A PERCENTAGE OF ALL LOANS OUTSTANDING	FARM REAL ESTATE ACQUISITIONS Number	FARM REAL ESTATE ACQUISITIONS Investmentc	FARM REAL ESTATE DISPOSALS Investment at Time of Disposald	FARM REAL ESTATE DISPOSALS Proceeds of Sales	FARM REAL ESTATE DISPOSALS Proceeds as a Percentage of Investment
1940	22.2%	6,063	$25,790	$42,083	$28,274	67.2%
1941	15.8	4,874	19,828	54,477	37,693	69.2
1942	11.0	3,480	14,330	46,000	33,119	72.0
1943c	9.2	950	4,259	19,359	15,506	80.1
1944	6.5	859	3,926	16,519	15,041	91.0
1945	5.3	368	1,582	8,747	8,627	98.6
1946	4.4	163	745	3,366	3,319	98.6
1947	4.0	57	199	927	916	98.9
1948	4.0	36	126	262	275	105.1
1949	4.3	16	52	87	99	113.6
1950	4.8	22	78	62	71	107.4e
1951	4.3	27	62	78	90	115.0e
1952	3.8	23	73	56	61	103.1
1953	3.8	20	42	87	94	108.3
1954	4.0	38	123	68	69	103.1

From *Annual Reports* of the Farm Credit Administration, 1940–1954.

a Calendar years 1940–1942; fiscal years ending June 30, 1943–1954.

b Covers both delinquent and extended loans.

c Covers unpaid loan balances, accrued interest to date of acquisition, and subsequent operation and maintenance costs.

d Data for delinquent loans cover the year ending June 30, 1943; data for acquisitions and disposals are for the six months ending June 30, 1943.

e Excludes data for disposals in the New Orleans district, where investment is carried at $1 on the land bank's statement of condition. Percentages based on the amounts shown in the two preceding columns would be 115.3 in 1950 and 114.7 in 1951.

tion, on the one hand, and life insurance companies on the other, and 7 percent were by other lenders.[23]

The quantity reflecting the experience of a lender most fully is the difference between over-all costs and revenues. In the case of public or quasi-public institutions, the calculation should include some estimate for costs of government-supplied capital that were not borne by the institution itself.

From 1917 through 1947 the federal government provided the land banks with 1,608 million "dollar-years" of interest-free capital through capital stock subscription. An additional 1,723 million dollar-years of interest-free capital in the form of paid-in surplus was provided in connection with mortgage extensions and deferments.[24] A total of about 5 million dollar-years of capital was provided through Treasury deposits during 1918–1923; and in 1934, $168 million was deposited in the land banks when they were designated as federal government depositories. Under a different type of aid, the land banks issued a total of $333 million of bonds in 1933 and 1934 on which interest was guaranteed by the federal government; but the authority to issue such bonds was discontinued in early 1934 and those issued were retired before the end of the year.

If an interest rate of 2 percent is assigned to interest-free capital, the value to the land banks of this assistance is estimated at about $67 million, which is not quite one-fifth of their cumulative net earnings—dividends to NFLA's and others of $115 million, legal reserve of $107 million, surplus reserve of $119 million, and earned surplus of $30 million—through mid-1954. In addition, as an aid to farm mortgage borrowers, the land banks received direct reimbursement from the Treasury, of $277 million, to compensate them for the interest rate reductions to borrowers which were made at the direction of Congress in the years 1933–1934. Also a certain amount of indirect aid was extended through the Federal Farm Mortgage Corporation's purchases of land bank bonds. It is difficult to determine the degree of financial benefit received from the latter source, though it doubtless reduced the cost of borrowed funds for the land banks. At any rate, it seems probable that earnings somewhat ex-

[23] *Agricultural Finance Review*, Vol. 14, November 1951, p. 59.

[24] "Dollar-years" of capital were calculated by adding the amounts of capital stock in the land banks held by the government at year ends over the given period. This slightly overstates that capital contribution where the government's holdings of capital stock were increased during the year and understates it where holdings were decreased during the year.

ceeded the full costs of operation over the long run, and that the regular land bank program has been self-sustaining.

The Production Credit System

ORGANIZATION

Establishment of a federally sponsored farm production credit system began shortly after World War I when, largely as a result of postwar price disturbances, the federal intermediate credit banks were created under the Agricultural Credits Act of 1923 (42 Stat. 1454; 12 U.S.C. 1021-1022). The $60 million of original capital, $5 million for each of the twelve banks, was subscribed by the federal government and is still in use by them. An additional $40 million was provided by Congress in the Federal Farm Mortgage Corporation Act of 1934 (48 Stat. 348; 12 U.S.C. 1041) as a revolving fund for subscription, when needed, to their capital or paid-in surplus. (From 1940 to 1948 no government capital was in use except the original $60 million. Intermittently after June 1948 federal subscriptions to surplus of several of the banks were made, totaling $14 million, of which $11 million was repaid by mid-1954.)

These banks were set up along lines suggested in joint congressional hearings on the postwar financial problems of agriculture. Their initial purpose was to liberalize farm production credit by making loans to commercial banks, agricultural credit corporations, livestock corporations, and other private financing agencies. Although they languished in this capacity, through developments arising in the agricultural crisis of the early thirties the intermediate credit banks later became a significant factor in the farm credit market.

The specialized wholly private agricultural credit corporations to which the federal intermediate credit banks were originally empowered to lend (as well as to commercial banks and other lenders) never developed to any great degree, and many were liquidated in the latter part of the twenties and early thirties. In 1932 the Reconstruction Finance Corporation was authorized by the Emergency Relief and Construction Act (50 Stat. 704; 12 U.S.C. 1148) to establish and finance, as direct federal agencies, regional agricultural credit corporations, one in each farm credit district, to fill what was regarded as a gap in farm credit facilities. The regional corporations were, in turn, empowered to obtain additional funds by borrowing from the federal intermediate credit banks, the RFC, and the Federal Reserve Banks. This arrangement continued until May 27, 1933, when the responsibility for supervising the regional corporations was transferred to the Farm Credit Administration by Executive Order 6084 (of March 27, 1933), and during 1933–1935 the corporations made farm production loans totaling about $450 million. But meanwhile the Farm Credit Act of 1933 made new arrangements that largely eliminated the need for the RACC's; and in the Farm Credit Act of 1937 (12 U.S.C. 1148b, 1148c, 1148d) Congress provided for their consolidation or merger. The last remaining corporation, the Regional Agricultural Credit Corporation of Washington, D.C., was dissolved by Public Law 38 approved April 6, 1949 and its functions and assets were transferred to the Secretary of Agriculture, who in turn delegated those functions to the Farmers Home Administration.

The Farm Credit Act of 1933 (48 Stat. 257; 12 U.S.C. 1131 et seq.) authorized the establishment of twelve production credit corporations (PCC's), one in each farm credit district, and the chartering, through these district corporations, of local production credit associations. The PCC's were provided with a fund of $120 million and empowered to act for the federal government in making subscriptions to the Class A stock of the local associations; in addition, they were given broad supervisory powers over the associations.[25] This act completed the design for the system as it operates today. About 500 local associations extend production credit to farmers, drawing part of their equity funds from the twelve production credit corporations and obtaining short-term financing from the twelve intermediate credit banks.

The federal intermediate credit banks, much like the federal land banks, obtain their lending funds primarily through the issuance and sale to the investing public of consolidated collateral trust debentures and through borrowings from commercial banks. The United States government assumes no liability for any obligations of the intermediate credit banks. Yet although they finance their lending activities otherwise than by the use of public funds, it seems appropriate to include the intermediate credit banks among federally sponsored credit agencies by reason of their being wholly govern-

[25] The Farm Credit Act of 1953 stressed the formulation of plans for the retirement of government capital in the PCC's and eventual payment of supervisory costs.

ment-owned.[26] In addition, their semipublic status is heightened by the degree of control which the federal government exercises over their policies and operations. The same district farm credit boards which direct the federal land banks direct the activities of the intermediate credit banks; of the seven members of each of the boards, two (formerly four) are appointed by the Governor of the Farm Credit Administration; the others are elected by the national farm loan associations and by the PCA's and cooperatives borrowing from the bank for cooperatives. Thus, by virtue of both the government capital which they use and their administrative relation to a direct agency of the federal government, the intermediate credit banks may be regarded as falling within the scope of our study as federally sponsored institutions. The same applies to the twelve production credit corporations.

Unlike the national farm loan associations, which function merely as intermediaries between farmer-member borrowers and the federal land banks, production credit associations were organized actually to extend credit to farmers; in turn, the associations obtain short-term credit from the federal intermediate credit bank of their district. The extent to which the PCA's are permitted to use the facilities of the intermediate credit banks depends, in the main, on the quality of the paper which they originate and the amount of their net worth; the latter, in turn, is accumulated out of earnings, out of the subscriptions to their Class A (nonvoting) capital stock by the production credit corporations and others,[27] and by the required purchase of the Class B stock by member-borrowers. In this way, their lending capacity is very definitely influenced by the availability of federal financial assistance.

Provision for the retirement of PCC-held Class A stock was made by the 1933 act, similar to that made by the 1916 act for the land banks. As of June 30, 1954, 354 of the then 498 local production credit associations were wholly member-owned; most of the remaining associations had made substantial progress in retiring corporation-owned stock, so that the PCA's as a whole were using only $3.6 million of production credit corporation capital, whereas during

[26] The Farm Credit Act of 1953 requires the Federal Farm Credit Board to develop a plan for retiring all government-owned capital in the intermediate credit banks.

[27] The Farm Credit Act of 1953 authorizes issuance of Class C stock for sale to PCC's and investors.

the thirties the PCC investment had amounted at its peak to $90 million.[28]

The use of government capital in all PCA's when they were originated, the continued use of federal capital by a few associations, their dependence on the federal intermediate credit banks, and their close supervision by the production credit corporations justify their inclusion within the scope of this study as federally sponsored lending agencies. They are so treated in the present chapter and elsewhere, except that in over-all measures of the volume of government activity in farm lending they have been excluded to avoid double counting. The great bulk of their paper is discounted with the federal intermediate credit banks, and it is in that account that PCA lending, as part of total federal credit activity, is registered.

SERVICES

The PCA's, operating locally, make short-term production loans to farmers at interest rates that in 1954 varied, as among different regions and individual associations, from 5 to 6¼ percent. The borrowing farmer is required to purchase Class B stock equal to at least 5 percent of his loan, in the PCA from which he borrows; and a loan servicing fee, variable with the size of the loan, is charged.

The production credit used by agriculture is of short term, extending for periods of 30 days to five years; with maturities of from six months to a year the most common. The security may be the borrower's note or may be a lien on farm machinery or livestock or against crops or other produce. Typically, farmers borrow on this basis to cover seasonal expenses, but production credit may also be used to finance certain farm operations that extend over more than one season.

It is estimated that there was about $7.0 billion of short-term farm loans, mainly for production purposes, outstanding at the end of 1953.[29] Of this amount, according to Agricultural Research

[28] *Annual Report* of the Farm Credit Administration, 1953–1954, pp. 24f. Government capital retired by the PCC's has been set aside in the Treasury in a revolving fund which may be made available to PCA's in time of need as directed by the Governor of the Farm Credit Administration. As of June 30, 1954 repayments totaled $58 million, which, together with the return of $30 million to the Treasury in 1949, as required by Public Law 860, reduced government-owned capital of the corporations to $32 million, of which only $3.6 million was invested in PCA capital stock (*ibid.*, p. 34).

[29] The figure represents total non-real-estate farm credit as given in the *Balance Sheet of Agriculture, 1954* ($9.4 billion) less loans made or guaranteed by the Commodity Credit Corporation ($673 million in direct loans outstanding, $1,727 million in privately made loans guaranteed by CCC). The loans made or

Service estimates, about $3.2 billion, or 46 percent, was held by individuals, merchants, dealers, and other miscellaneous lenders. About $2.8 billion, or 40 percent of the total, was held by commercial banks. PCA's held 8 percent and the Farmers Home Administration (a direct federal agency making loans of an emergency character) 6 percent, and a negligible fraction consisted of intermediate credit bank loans to farm lending institutions other than PCA's.

The importance of PCA's as a source of production credit varies regionally. In the Omaha farm credit district, for example, PCA's held only 9 percent of the combined holdings of PCA's and commercial banks on January 1, 1954, but in the Columbia district PCA's held 35 percent, about one-half as much as the commercial banks (Table 31).

TABLE 31

Outstandings of Commercial Bank Non-Real-Estate Farm Loans and of PCA Loans, January 1, 1954, by Farm Credit District

(dollar figures in thousands)

FARM CREDIT DISTRICTa	NON-REAL-ESTATE BANK LOANS	PCA LOANS	PERCENTAGE DISTRIBUTION	
			Banks	*PCA's*
Springfield	$ 127,572	$ 39,415	76%	24%
Baltimore	119,355	32,241	79	21
Columbia	87,140	46,326	65	35
Louisville	246,371	70,492	78	22
New Orleans	77,380	27,412	74	26
St. Louis	317,276	51,723	86	14
St. Paul	311,834	44,176	88	12
Omaha	411,524	42,240	91	9
Wichita	329,610	43,521	88	12
Houston	233,340	59,426	80	20
Berkeley	303,101	34,155	90	10
Spokane	137,963	50,659	73	27
United States	$2,702,466	$541,786	83%	17%

From *Agricultural Credit and Related Data 1954* (Agricultural Commission, American Bankers Association), Table 4, pp. 16 f. Bank data represent the holdings of insured commercial banks exclusive of loans guaranteed by the Commodity Credit Corporation and are classified according to location of banks; PCA data, which also exclude CCC-guaranteed loans, are classified according to the location of the borrower.

a For a listing of states included in each farm credit district, see Table 24, note a.

guaranteed by the CCC were for the marketing or storing of farm products under price support, and their credit terms differed from those characterizing production loans. Nearly all the CCC-guaranteed loans were held by commercial banks. See the *Balance Sheet of Agriculture, 1954* (Department of Agriculture, Agricultural Research Service), Table 19, p. 25, and *Agricultural Finance Review* (*id.*), Vol. 17, November 1954, Table 13, p. 92.

The figures below (for source, see Table 5 in Chapter 2) show that 36.9 percent of the farmers in the United States obtained non-real-estate loans from commercial banks in 1951 and 5.3 percent from PCA's. However, the relative frequency of borrowing varied widely in different parts of the country; for instance, in the Baltimore district only 16.8 percent of all farmers borrowed from banks and only 3.9 percent from PCA's; in contrast, in the Omaha district 63.8 percent used banks and 2.8 percent the PCA's.

Farm Credit District	Percentage of Farmers Obtaining Non-Real-Estate Loans from Commercial Banks	Percentage of Farmers Obtaining Loans from PCA's
Springfield	26.2%	7.6%
Baltimore	16.8	3.9
Columbia	26.5	7.5
Louisville	34.4	5.5
New Orleans	19.0	5.1
St. Louis	47.3	5.2
St. Paul	46.0	4.2
Omaha	63.8	2.8
Wichita	54.7	3.7
Houston	46.6	6.1
Berkeley	30.5	4.8
Spokane	39.8	6.4
United States	36.9%	5.3%

The shares of the farm production credit market served by banks and by public agencies have changed considerably since 1930. Until then, banks served virtually the entire market. But an expansion of the disaster loan and emergency crop and feed loan programs during 1933 and 1934, and the rapid growth of the depression-born PCA system, brought the public share of institutionally held short-term farm credit (apart from loans in connection with price support made by the Commodity Credit Corporation or made by other lenders under CCC guarantee) to 34 percent in January 1935 and to 43 percent at the beginning of 1937 (Table 32). The share of public agencies remained between 40 and 45 percent through the end of 1944, dropped to 31 percent at the end of 1947, and continued to decline through 1951, standing at 23 percent in January 1952 and 27 percent in January 1954.

The relative position of banks and PCA's in the farm production credit market has fluctuated within a narrower range. By the beginning of 1938, PCA holdings were one-fifth as large as the comparable bank holdings, and from then through 1953 this ratio remained fairly constant, ranging no lower than about one-sixth (Table 32).

In the main PCA borrowers are such as would meet the credit standards of commercial banks and other private lending institutions. This is by no means conclusively demonstrated by data on the size distribution of PCA loans, but the fact that a fairly high proportion of the total amount loaned has been advanced in individual amounts exceeding $2,000 strongly suggests that the loans have gone to well-established farm operators (Table 33). Although only 35 percent of the total number of loans paid or renewed during the year ending June 30, 1950 were in amounts of more than $2,000, such loans were estimated to account for 84 percent of the total amount loaned. The largest 5.6 percent of the loans made involved an estimated 42.5 percent of the total amount loaned, meaning that a large proportion of PCA funds went to rather large commercial farmers. In 1950 the average PCA loan was larger than the average non-real-estate loan of commercial banks (Table 34), which suggests that the farms served by PCA's are probably as large as, perhaps larger than, those obtaining their production financing from commercial banks.

The average PCA loan increased every year from 1936 through 1950, with the exception of 1949, and in 1950 was almost four times as large as it had been in 1936 (Table 35). The Department of Agriculture estimate of farm production expenses in the United States was $5,563 million in 1936 as compared with $19,704 million in 1950,[30] almost a fourfold increase. Since the total number of farms declined during this period, the average expense per farm probably increased by more than four times. Thus the increase in average size of PCA loans reflected the increase in average size of business, and the increased mechanization of agriculture.

The average cost of borrowing money from PCA's as indicated by data on the gross loan income of individual PCA's, has varied from year to year and among the various districts. During 1938–1939 and again from 1940 to 1946, when PCA interest rates were uniform at 4½ percent throughout the United States, there was a substantial reduction in loan service fees and gross loan income fell

[30] *Agricultural Outlook Charts, 1954,* Department of Agriculture, Bureau of Agricultural Economics, p. 14.

TABLE 32

Non-Real-Estate Farm Loans Outstanding at Year Ends 1928–1953 and Made during Years 1929–1952, for Specified Lenders

YEAR	ALL OPERATING BANKS[a]	PRODUCTION CREDIT ASSOCIATIONS[b]	FED. INT. CREDIT BANKS[c]	FARMERS HOME ADMINISTRATION		
				Production and Subsistence Loans[d]	Production Emergency and Economic Emergency Loans[e]	Emergency Crop and Feed Loans[f]
			Outstanding December 31 (*in thousands*)			
1928	$2,596,491		$43,884			$ 2,246g
1929	2,490,742		47,283			7,976g
1930	2,109,050		62,462			8,946g
1931	1,649,855		71,960			49,769
1932	1,272,211		79,658			90,353
1933	913,204	$ 27	60,382		$ 24,373	90,863
1934	627,878	60,459	55,083	$ 5,600h	144,615	111,238
1935	735,257	93,400	46,518	62,900h	87,087	172,470
1936	620,866	104,481	40,508	131,600h	43,394	164,762
1937	682,545	136,918	39,974	118,017	25,282	171,983
1938	788,716	146,825	32,612	169,148	15,588	170,952
1939	900,079	153,425	32,316	242,452	11,080	167,795
1940	983,774	170,686	32,371	286,930	8,005	167,862
1941	1,073,198	185,611	37,382	317,475	5,854	163,792
1942	924,236	182,658	37,854	367,945	5,531	155,456
1943	935,764	196,637	33,882	342,798	3,991	146,181
1944	948,829	188,306	29,792	303,050	32,751	138,068
1945	1,033,800	194,788	26,487	279,175	13,618	128,901
1946	1,289,105	230,022	31,701	282,381	7,388	116,733
1947	1,592,762	289,077	37,916	264,879	3,695	105,913
1948	1,945,598	366,822	55,750	252,512	2,634	90,048
1949	2,048,819	387,454	50,825	267,160	3,073	71,186
1950	2,524,153	450,673	62,073	259,585	12,771	53,283
1951	3,120,196	561,371	77,841	253,189	20,110	38,191
1952	3,195,058	599,295	82,931	291,375	28,739	27,919
1953	2,762,562	541,786	63,557	318,938	50,792	19,946

TABLE 32 (continued)

Made during Year Ending December 31 (in thousands)

YEAR	ALL OPERATING BANKSa	PRODUCTION CREDIT ASSOCIATIONSb	FED. INT. CREDIT BANKSc	FARMERS HOME ADMINISTRATION		
				Production and Subsistence Loansd	Production Emergency and Economic Emergency Loanse	Emergency Crop and Feed Loansf
1929	..	..	$ 90,591	..	..	$ 5,760
1930	..	..	103,906	..	..	5,340
1931	..	..	118,381	..	..	55,788
1932	..	..	148,624	..	$ 24,597	64,205
1933	$ 27	..	140,526	..	223,089	57,376
1934	106,812	..	124,429	h	140,585	70,471
1935	194,959	..	116,187	h	90,655	96,382
1936	226,915	..	105,587	h	34,667	16,135
1937	284,886	..	100,983	$158,142k	18,603	31,815
1938	301,022	..	88,698	80,290	5,718	19,196
1939	319,401	..	85,382	108,943	4,664	14,567
1940	347,145	i	87,314j	92,200	4,804	18,963
1941	414,815	..	100,697j	103,797	6,759	16,891
1942	474,009	..	106,881j	163,110	7,759	18,411
1943	497,178	..	91,790j	123,548	73,961	17,232
1944	485,750	..	79,266j	63,222	17,038	17,087
1945	509,579	..	73,039	72,450	9,913	15,085
1946	607,482	..	84,892	107,767	1,932	15,642
1947	747,967	..	107,545	93,668	77	..
1948	915,812	..	158,777	85,088	1,084	..
1949	946,440	..	154,635	98,252	10,814	..
1950	1,065,745	..	169,455	95,811	30,080	..
1951	1,310,034	..	216,394	113,329	20,820	..
1952	1,330,320	..	212,147	139,040	38,104	..

(continued on next page)

183

TABLE 32 (continued)

Data for PCA's and FHA are from *Agricultural Statistics 1952* (Department of Agriculture), Table 732, pp. 726f., and *Agricultural Statistics 1953*, Table 741, pp. 638f., with outstandings for 1953 from *Agricultural Finance Review* (Department of Agriculture, Agricultural Research Service), Vol. 17, November 1954, p. 92; see also notes a and c below.

a From *Agricultural Statistics 1952*, Table 734, p. 732, and *Agriculture Statistics 1953*, Table 743, p. 644; excludes loans made under Commodity Credit Corporation guarantee in connection with price support for farm commodities.

b Excludes CCC-guaranteed loans. Beginning 1946, also excludes loans held by associations in liquidation.

c From *Agricultural Statistics 1952*, Table 732, p. 726 (for 1928–1932 outstandings and 1929–1933 volume), and *Agricultural Finance Review*, November 1954, p. 92 (for other years). Represents loans to, and discounts for, private financing institutions extending short-term production credit to farmers. Outstanding loans under CCC guarantee (1940–1944) are excluded as pertaining to a price support rather than a credit aid program; so are outstandings and volume of loans to the banks for cooperatives, in connection with farm marketing. Loans to PCA's and regional agricultural credit corporations, whose production loans to farmers appear in the PCA and FHA series here, are excluded to avoid double counting. Loans made include renewals.

d Also includes rural rehabilitation, water facility, construction, and wartime adjustment loans, and such loans from state corporation trust funds except for January 1, 1938–March 31, 1942.

e Covers flood and windstorm restoration, flood damage, fur, and orchard loans, and (from 1949 on) production emergency loans; also regional agricultural credit corporation loans (from 1932 on). Outstandings in 1953 also include economic emergency and special livestock loans.

f Also includes drought relief and orchard rehabilitation loans.

g As of July 1.

h Represents amounts obligated; data for actual advances are unavailable.

i Data unavailable.

j Includes an unspecified amount of CCC-guaranteed loans.

k Cumulative from inception of programs.

TABLE 33

Size Distribution of PCA Loans Paid or Renewed during the Year Ending June 30, 1950

Size of Loan	Number	Amount
$500 or less	26.5%	2.3%
$501–1,000	19.2	4.3
$1,001–2,000	19.3	9.0
$2,001–5,000	21.2	22.7
$5,001–10,000	8.2	19.2
Over $10,000	5.6	42.5
Total	100.0%	100.0%

Covers 282,030, loans, totaling $955,932,000. From *Risk Problems of Production Credit Associations* (Farm Credit Administration, Bulletin CR-5), January 1952, p. 56.

TABLE 34

Average Size of Farm Production Loans Made by Commercial Banks
and by PCA's in 1950, by Farm Credit District

Farm Credit Districta	Average Bank Loan	Average PCA Loan
Springfield	$1,860	$2,959
Baltimore	1,549	2,712
Columbia	1,068	1,569
Louisville	1,197	2,425
New Orleans	1,088	2,173
St. Louis	1,863	3,579
St. Paul	1,586	2,930
Omaha	3,670	9,278
Wichita	3,926	7,219
Houston	2,035	6,275
Berkeley	9,136	10,266
Spokane	2,937	7,960
United States	$2,293	$3,717

From *Agricultural Credit and Related Data, 1952* (Agricultural Commission, the American Bankers Association), Table 5, pp. 18f.
a For a listing of states included in each farm credit district, see Table 24, note a. Bank data are classified according to location of bank; PCA data, by location of security or borrower.

from $6.34 per hundred dollars of average loan balance outstanding in 1937 to $5.30 per hundred in 1946 (Table 36). In 1947, original differences in interest rates were introduced and on January 1, 1948 individual associations were authorized to charge different rates. As a result, many PCA's raised rates and greater differences developed among districts. Between 1947 and 1950 the average gross loan income increased from $5.38 per hundred dollars of average loan balance outstanding to $6.07 per hundred, and the spread among districts widened.

Table 37 shows interest rate differences among individual PCA's in 1950. For example, 35 PCA's had gross incomes of $7.50 or more per hundred dollars of outstandings and 13 had gross loan incomes of less than $5.00 per hundred. These variations result from differences in patronage refund policy and in loan costs among individual PCA's.

EXPERIENCE

Loss experience on PCA loans has been about the same, over similar periods, as that of commercial banks. From the organization of the PCA's in 1933 through the end of 1952, net losses and provision for

185

TABLE 35

Average Size of PCA Loans, 1936-1950, and Median Size in Selected Years, by Farm Credit District

YEAR	FARM CREDIT DISTRICT[a]												UNITED STATES
	1	2	3	4	5	6	7	8	9	10	11	12	
Average Size of Loan													
1936	$1,280	$ 824	$ 335	$ 576	$ 570	$ 546	$ 541	$1,274	$1,458	$1,808	$ 4,443	$4,081	$ 972
1937	1,338	941	404	761	698	798	698	1,505	1,871	2,654	4,533	4,587	1,166
1938	1,395	1,004	476	833	692	910	751	2,320	2,050	2,663	4,551	4,498	1,242
1939	1,412	1,081	523	915	773	1,165	796	2,819	2,468	2,891	4,750	4,859	1,368
1940	1,418	1,215	566	970	865	1,271	975	2,926	2,826	3,135	4,995	5,101	1,514
1941	1,572	1,440	652	1,141	1,008	1,553	1,211	3,431	3,265	3,284	5,633	5,566	1,803
1942	1,659	1,572	788	1,384	1,113	1,810	1,396	3,528	3,622	3,494	6,424	5,563	2,023
1943	1,838	1,637	862	1,567	1,090	1,970	1,586	4,940	3,518	3,602	7,141	5,850	2,172
1944	1,965	1,908	998	1,565	1,225	1,909	1,658	4,583	3,597	3,743	8,011	5,623	2,246
1945	2,132	2,087	1,102	1,630	1,287	2,098	1,874	5,196	3,962	3,796	8,413	5,923	2,411
1946	2,550	2,480	1,222	1,858	1,394	2,337	2,129	5,773	4,653	4,352	9,153	6,339	2,691
1947	2,813	2,691	1,337	2,158	1,520	2,649	2,416	7,099	5,390	4,787	9,776	6,703	3,016
1948	3,083	2,620	1,378	2,398	1,939	3,124	2,659	7,907	6,414	5,286	10,388	7,071	3,369
1949	2,890	2,783	1,449	2,280	1,971	3,099	2,649	7,919	6,272	6,069	9,527	7,042	3,326
1950	2,959	3,070	1,569	2,425	2,173	3,580	2,931	9,278	7,219	6,275	10,266	7,960	3,734
Median Size of Loan[b]													
1939	678	466	243	461	226	464	518	958	602	595	1,750	1,559	442
1943	931	661	360	719	313	732	826	1,637	1,132	983	2,200	1,948	675
1946	1,293	788	455	836	388	901	1,040	1,975	1,381	1,176	3,351	2,457	828
1950	1,836	1,120	666	1,238	473	1,331	1,771	3,850	2,900	1,873	3,868	3,346	1,221

From *Risk Problems of Production Credit Associations* (Farm Credit Administration, Bulletin CR-5), January 1952, Table A, p. 55.

a For a listing of states included in each farm credit district (number 1 designating the Springfield district and following in order through number 12—Spokane), see Table 24, note a.

b Median size of loans repaid or renewed based on total amount advanced. Data for 1939 and 1943 are for calendar years and data for 1946 and 1950 are for fiscal years ended June 30.

TABLE 36

PCA Gross Loan Income per $100 Average Loan Balance, 1936–1950, by Farm Credit District

YEAR	FARM CREDIT DISTRICT[a]												UNITED STATES
	1	2	3	4	5	6	7	8	9	10	11	12	
1936	$5.60	$6.15	$7.65	$6.43	$7.26	$6.79	$6.17	$5.62	$5.93	$6.88	$5.68	$5.71	$6.30
1937	5.56	6.61	8.27	6.52	8.59	6.69	6.29	5.71	5.93	5.95	5.82	5.73	6.34
1938	5.40	6.29	7.22	6.37	7.55	6.54	6.11	5.69	6.01	5.89	5.68	5.60	6.13
1939	5.10	6.13	6.83	5.89	7.00	5.97	5.91	5.34	5.70	5.67	5.48	5.48	5.84
1940	4.88	5.82	6.50	5.60	6.54	5.77	5.61	5.06	5.35	5.36	5.27	5.18	5.56
1941	4.81	5.56	6.39	5.49	6.17	5.56	5.47	4.94	5.22	5.16	5.20	5.21	5.42
1942	4.76	5.27	6.03	5.37	5.81	5.44	5.28	4.86	5.18	5.06	5.08	4.96	5.26
1943	4.76	5.41	6.06	5.28	5.89	5.37	5.05	4.77	5.14	5.11	5.04	4.99	5.24
1944	4.73	5.38	5.89	5.26	5.77	5.34	5.07	4.76	5.14	5.23	4.99	5.04	5.24
1945	4.71	5.36	5.92	5.30	5.82	5.32	5.10	4.75	5.24	5.46	5.02	5.04	5.28
1946	4.71	5.32	5.93	5.32	5.82	5.39	5.19	4.75	5.20	5.51	5.01	4.98	5.30
1947	4.70	5.27	6.07	5.33	6.01	5.53	5.22	4.74	5.18	5.69	5.20	5.05	5.38
1948	5.07	5.52	6.55	5.53	6.28	5.86	5.56	4.64	5.31	6.15	5.26	5.40	5.64
1949	5.45	5.86	7.15	5.95	6.54	6.23	6.13	5.29	5.57	6.63	5.32	5.58	6.04
1950	5.58	5.88	7.25	5.97	6.64	6.26	6.17	5.31	5.60	6.56	5.43	5.58	6.07

From *Risk Problems of Production Credit Associations* (Farm Credit Administration, Bulletin CR-5), January 1952, Table 12, p. 30. Gross loan income consists of gross interest on loans (less patronage refunds) and loan service fees, including fees paid for abstracts, filing, etc.

a For a listing of states included in each farm credit district (number 1 designating the Springfield district and following in order through number 12—Spokane), see Table 24, note a.

TABLE 37

Distribution of PCA's in the Several Farm Credit Districts by Gross Loan Income per $100 of Average Loan Balance in 1950

FARM CREDIT DISTRICT	GROSS LOAN INCOME PER $100 AVERAGE LOAN BALANCE								TOTAL
	Less than $5.00	$5.00–5.49	$5.50–5.99	$6.00–6.49	$6.50–6.99	$7.00–7.49	$7.50–7.99	$8.00–and over	
Springfield	1	8	23	2	1	..	..	..	35
Baltimore	..	4	20	9	3	..	..	..	36
Columbia	..	..	1	12	26	29	12	7	87
Louisville	1	2	17	17	3	..	..	..	40
New Orleans	..	..	5	4	10	6	1	..	26
St. Louis	..	4	11	12	4	8	4	2	45
St. Paul	..	1	9	41	2	1	..	..	54
Omaha	4	11	23	2	..	..	..	..	40
Wichita	..	11	25	5	..	..	..	..	41
Houston	1	4	3	6	8	5	3	6	36
Berkeley	6	7	14	3	..	..	..	..	30
Spokane	..	9	16	3	2	..	..	..	30
United States	13	61	167	116	59	49	20	15	500

From *Risk Problems of Production Credit Associations* (Farm Credit Administration, Bulletin CR-5), January 1952, Table 13, p. 30. Gross loan income consist of gross interest on loans (less patronage refunds) and loan service fees, including fees paid for abstracts, filing, etc.

a For a listing of states included in each farm credit district, see Table 24, note a.

estimated losses have amounted to $12.8 million out of a total of $9.1 billion loaned (i.e. cash advanced excluding renewals), or approximately 0.14 percent. The rate has varied considerably from year to year. Net loans averaged about 0.50 percent of average yearly outstandings in the period 1936–1940, turned to net recoveries of about 0.13 percent in 1941–1943, and fell back to a loss rate of around 0.10 percent in the period 1944–1950. The changes in loss rates for country banks, as will be seen in Table 38, followed roughly the same pattern.

TABLE 38

Loss Rates on PCA Loans and on Loans of National Banks
and of Country National Banks, 1936–1950

Year	Total Losses of All National Banks[a]	Net Losses of Country National Banks[b]	Net Losses of PCA's[c]
1936	1.87%	1.37%	0.68%
1937	0.82	0.48	0.28
1938	0.95	0.42	0.88
1939	0.74	0.33	0.46
1940	0.58	0.31	0.22
1941	0.44	0.16	−0.14
1942	0.42	0.05	−0.12
1943	0.43	−0.15	−0.12
1944	0.36	−0.22	0.06
1945	0.21	−0.19	0.03
1946	0.26	−0.12	0.06
1947	0.34	0.06	0.10
1948	0.21	0.10	0.11
1949	..	0.18	0.22
1950	..	0.09	0.08

From *Risk Problems of Production Credit Associations* (Farm Credit Administration, Bulletin CR-5), January 1952, Table 4, p. 8. *Minus sign* indicates net recoveries.

Bank data are not limited to short-term farm production loans comparable with those of PCA's but include nonfarm and long-term loans as well; and the bank series exclude losses by banks placed in receivership or trusteeship, whereas PCA data cover both inactive and active associations.

a Calendar-year losses (before deduction for recoveries) as percentage of December 31 outstandings.

b For 1936 and 1937 fiscal-year losses as percentage of June 30 outstandings; thereafter, refers to calendar-year losses and December 31 outstandings. Except for 1936 and 1937 (when banks in 14 to 21 cities with less than three banks are included) the data are restricted to national banks other than those in reserve or central reserve cities.

c Actual plus estimated net losses for calendar year as percentage of average of month-end balances, with the 1949 and 1950 losses of taxable PCA's adjusted for the "general provision for undetermined losses."

Loss experience among PCA's has varied widely from one farm credit district to another and among individual associations in the different districts.[31] Net loans and provisions for losses in percent of total cash advanced through 1952 varied from a high of 0.33 percent in the Springfield district to a low of 0.08 percent in the Louisville, St. Louis, and Wichita districts. In this connection it is interesting to note that several districts with relatively good records—St. Paul, Wichita, St. Louis, and Columbia—showed less favorable experience in the land bank program. Probably what this difference in federal experience with long- and with short-term farm lending signifies is that certain areas have had highly variable records, ranging from the very unfavorable, where climatic and economic conditions are adverse, to the unusually favorable, when these conditions have turned to the other extreme.

The progress made by the PCA's toward achieving the goal of member ownership has been mentioned and is worth considering here for its bearing on capital position. Progress by five-year periods is shown in the following tabulation.[32] By mid-1954, seven out of

	JUNE 30, 1944	JUNE 30, 1949	JUNE 30, 1954
		(in millions)	
Member-owned capital stock	$ 28.2	$ 62.0	$ 93.7
PCC-owned capital stock	64.0	25.0	3.6
Total accumulated earnings	30.5	54.4	90.8
Total net worth	$122.7	$141.4	$188.1
PCC-owned capital stock as a percentage of total net worth	52.2%	17.7%	1.9%

every ten PCA's were wholly member-owned, and the PCA capital stock held by the government through the PCC's—$3.6 million—was only 4 percent as large as the peak PCC investment, $90 million, during the thirties.

The use of earnings and the proceeds of sale of Class A stock to farmer-borrowers to retire government capital has prevented the PCA's, however, from adding rapidly to their capital accounts. At the end of fiscal 1954, for example, total capital stock was only

[31] See *Risk Problems of Production Credit Associations* (Farm Credit Administration, Bulletin CR-5, January 1952), pp. 3–5, and the *Annual Report* of the Farm Credit Administration, 1952–1953, p. 93.

[32] *Annual Report* of the Farm Credit Administration, 1953–1954, p. 25.

about 6 percent more than at the end of fiscal 1944, whereas the total amount of loans outstanding had increased nearly threefold. Most of the funds used to retire government capital were returned to a revolving fund which might be called upon to strengthen the associations' capital position in time of need; but apart from that recourse, the capital position of many PCA's was not such as to enable them independently to weather a prolonged period of adverse loan experience.

The most inclusive measure of lending experience is the relation between over-all costs and revenues. Has the production credit system been self-supporting, when full costs including those for capital supplied interest-free by the government are considered?

Through June 30, 1954 the government had furnished a total of 1.9 billion dollar-years of interest-free capital to the PCC's, and over the same period the PCA's have employed 1.0 billion dollar-years of government capital through the PCC holdings of their Class A stock.

No dividends were paid by PCA's on this government-provided capital until 1940, but a total of $475,000 was paid between that date and June 30, 1954. If the PCA's had been required to pay 2 percent interest for the use of these funds, the total interest outlay during the period would have been about $20 million, as compared with net accumulated earnings for the PCA's, as of June 30, 1954, of $90.8 million.

In addition to the capital received from the PCC's, PCA's have obtained substantial amounts of funds by borrowing from the federal intermediate credit banks; while the latter make some advances to other types of lenders, the bulk of their credit is extended to the PCA's and most of the financial assistance they have received from the federal government may, therefore, properly be considered an item of cost to the production credit system. From their establishment in 1923 to June 30, 1954 the intermediate credit banks have employed upwards of 1.8 billion dollar-years of interest-free capital from the government. At an interest rate of 2 percent this would have cost about $37 million. Against that cost, however, should be set the franchise taxes paid to the government by the banks from date of organization to 1923 through June 30, 1954, amounting to $9,216,586; and the earned surplus which the banks had accumulated as of June 30, 1954 amounted to $30.1 million and reserves for contingencies to $17.0 million. On balance, therefore, the production credit system as a whole would seem to have been more than self-sustaining through mid-1954.

Banks for Cooperatives

ORGANIZATION

A significant extension of the scope of government activity in the farm credit field occurred after the first World War when, as a means of moderating the impact of the postwar decline in farm prices the War Finance Corporation was empowered during 1921 and 1922 to make loans for the marketing of farm products and livestock. That agency was placed in liquidation in 1929; and in the same year, under the Agricultural Marketing Act (46 Stat. 11, 12 U.S.C. 1141 *et seq.*), an Agricultural Marketing Revolving Fund of $500 million was created and placed under the administration of a newly formed Federal Farm Board. The act authorized the board to extend marketing and operating loans to cooperative associations, and also loans to finance the construction or purchase of physical facilities, or to refinance debt incurred in connection with the acquisition of such facilities, with the general object of improving the marketing of farm commodities and the food products derived therefrom. Loans to stabilization corporations, essentially for the purpose of supporting the prices of basic farm commodities, were also authorized.

Loans to cooperatives under the 1929 act were never very important, however, and the functions of the board in making such loans were transferred in 1933 to newly created district banks for cooperatives. These banks were placed under the district farm credit boards, and the Central Bank for Cooperatives under a separate board, and have continued as the main instrument of governmental financial aid to agricultural marketing cooperatives.[33] Loans previously made by the Revolving Fund to cooperatives were liquidated and the program of loans for stabilization corporations was discontinued altogether.[34]

[33] Another agency affecting farm marketing credit is the Commodity Credit Corporation, which in connection with its price support program extends or guarantees credit for storage facilities and marketing of specified farm products. The amounts involved have been shown in Chapter 2 (Charts 1 and 2); but the program will not be further considered, since our focus is on programs whose primary activity is credit aid.

[34] It was in this reorganization of federal farm credit agencies, carried through under Executive Order No. 6084, dated March 27, 1933, that the Federal Farm Board was transformed into the Farm Credit Administration.

192

The initial capital of the twelve district banks for cooperatives and for the Central Bank for Cooperatives was provided by the Farm Credit Administration from funds made available through the Agricultural Marketing Act revolving fund,[35] and provision was made for additional subscriptions to stock by borrowing cooperatives or for payment of an equivalent amount into a guaranty fund by a cooperative not authorized to purchase stock. The banks obtain the major part of their loan funds by borrowing from, or discounting with, the federal intermediate credit banks and commercial banks, and another source of funds is the sale of collateral trust debentures issued by the Central Bank. In most cases the loans to cooperatives are made by the district banks, but loans to associations of national or broad regional scope may be, and are, made by the Central Bank for Cooperatives, in some cases with participation by the district banks. Supervision over the whole system is exercised by the Cooperative Bank Service of the Farm Credit Administration, and the district banks have as boards of directors the same district farm credit boards as direct the activities of the federal land banks, the intermediate credit banks, and the production credit corporations. Like these institutions, the banks for cooperatives are treated in this study as federally sponsored agencies.

SERVICES

Three kinds of loans are made to eligible farmer cooperatives engaged in marketing agricultural products, purchasing farm supplies, and furnishing farm business services: (1) facility loans for constructing or acquiring buildings, equipment, or other goods to facilitate the storing, handling, or marketing of farm commodities and food products; (2) short-term operating loans on inventories, receivables, payrolls, and supplies; and (3) commodity loans to facilitate the marketing of farm commodities and the buying of farm supplies. Facility loans may be made for the construction of storage facilities for commodities assigned to the Commodity Credit Corporation.

Facility loans are secured by first mortgages and have been limited to 60 percent of the value of the property and to a twenty-year term. Usually, the loans are amortized, and the interest rate must generally conform to that charged by the land banks on farm mortgage loans,

35 The Farm Credit Act of 1953 provides for retirement of the government-supplied capital.

which was 4 to 4½ percent in 1954.[36] Also a borrowing cooperative is required to purchase stock in the bank equal to 5 percent of the loan or to pay an equivalent amount into a guaranty fund. The bank is pledged to return the stock or the interest in the guaranty fund to the cooperative when the loan is repaid, if requested to do so.

Commodity loans are secured by first liens on storable commodities, warehouse receipts, and other title documents representing agricultural products and supplies. According to law, loans cannot exceed 75 percent of the market value of unhedged commodities, and 90 percent of the value of hedged commodities; in practice, cooperatives usually borrow less than the maximum, and the actual amount of loan extended also depends on the cooperative's financial condition and operating record. The loans usually mature at the end of the marketing year or season. For several years interest rates were about 1½ percent per year, but in 1954 the range by farm credit districts was from 2¾ to 3¼ percent. The equivalent of one percent of a commodity loan must go toward the purchase of capital stock or into a guaranty fund.

Operating capital loans are made for short periods of time and may or may not be secured. They carried an interest rate of 2½ percent for several years and ranged from 3 percent to 3½ percent in 1954. Five percent of the loan is allocated to stock purchase or guaranty fund payment.

The heaviest borrowers from the banks for cooperatives have been the cooperatives handling farm products, including grains, fruits and vegetables (except citrus fruits), and cotton fibers, and those handling farm supplies, including petroleum products. Of the $6.5 billion in credit extended from 1933 through June 30, 1954 cooperatives handling cotton fibers received $1.4 billion, grain marketing associations $1.3 billion, farm supply associations $746 million, and associations marketing and processing fruits and vegetables exclusive of citrus fruits $709 million.[37]

Although information is not complete, it appears that the businesses borrowing from the banks for cooperatives are somewhat larger than those borrowing from commercial banks. Thus, a 1936 survey found that 57 percent of the marketing and purchasing cooperatives borrowing from commercial banks, as against 44

[36] For 1941–1944 and in 1946 and 1947, the interest rate on facility loans was 3½ percent; in all other years the rate was 4 percent. For a discussion of interest rates on land bank loans see pp. 162–163.

[37] *Annual Report* of the Farm Credit Administration, 1953–1954, p. 42.

percent of those borrowing from the banks for cooperatives, had total sales in 1936 of less than $100,000; and 6.3 percent of the cooperatives with sales of $1,000,000 or over borrowed from the banks for cooperatives, as against only 3.4 percent from commercial banks.[38] Further evidence to this same general effect is supplied by a 1950 survey of Minnesota cooperatives,[39] where it was found that the average loan made to local associations and minor federations by the banks for cooperatives was twice as large as the average commercial bank loan to such concerns. Regional cooperatives showed the opposite pattern; but those borrowing from the banks for cooperatives more frequently obtained more than one loan, so that the average amount of total credit obtained was higher for them—over half again higher—than for regional associations borrowing from commercial banks.

EXPERIENCE

Like the land banks and PCA's, the banks for cooperatives had much higher losses in the thirties than in the forties. At the end of 1941, cumulative net losses on assets acquired in liquidation of loans totaled $1.4 million, which was equivalent to 0.20 percent of all loans made since the organization of the banks or 0.29 percent of cumulative outstandings based on average month-end balances. After 1941, losses declined to relatively low amounts. During the fiscal years 1943 and 1944 small net recoveries were realized on assets previously acquired, and from 1945 through June 30, 1954 total net losses on assets acquired were $2.8 million. Total net losses from time of organization through June 30, 1954 were $4.0 million,[40] equivalent to a loss rate of 0.06 percent of the total amount of loans made or 0.12 percent of cumulative outstandings based on an average of month-end balances.

Government aid to the banks for cooperatives consisted primarily of 3.3 billion dollar-years of interest-free capital up to June 30, 1954. With an assumed interest rate of 2 percent this amount of capital would have cost about $67 million. In comparison, the net profit of the banks from their organization to June 30, 1954 was

38 *A Statistical Handbook of Farmers Cooperatives,* Bulletin 26, Farm Credit Administration, November 1938, Table 118, p. 178.

39 E. Fred Koller, T. W. Manning and O. B. Jesness, *Statistics of Farmers' Cooperatives in Minnesota, 1950,* University of Minnesota Agricultural Experiment Station Bulletin 412, June 1952, Table 56, p. 64.

40 *Annual Reports* of the Farm Credit Administration, 1952–1953 (p. 43) and 1953–1954 (p. 106).

$78.4 million, with allocation of $50.0 million to earned surplus, $20.3 million to legal reserve and $8.1 million to reserve for contingencies,[41] so that cumulative profit easily covered the cost of government-supplied capital at the interest rate assumed.

Federal Farm Mortgage Corporation

ORGANIZATION AND SERVICES

In the farm mortgage distress of the early thirties a direct agency of the federal government was created to extend emergency credit, utilizing land bank facilities but not limited to land bank standards. The genesis of the organization goes back to the Emergency Farm Mortgage Act of 1933, which set up a fund of $200 million (made available through the RFC) for mortgage loans on farm real estate to be extended by the Land Bank Commissioner in cases where the restrictions surrounding the operations of the land banks prohibited them from lending. The fund proved inadequate, however, and in 1934 the Federal Farm Mortgage Corporation was formed (by the act of that name: 48 Stat. 344; 12 U.S.C. 1020 *et seq.*) to take up the mortgage loan assets that had already been acquired by the Commissioner, to make such further loans as could be financed through the original $200 million fund, and to make additional loans from the proceeds of sales of fully guaranteed bonds, of which the corporation was authorized to have up to $2 billion outstanding.

The Commissioner was authorized to lend up to 75 percent of a farm's normal agricultural value (that is, its value assuming average yields and under price relationships comparable to those in 1909–1914), whereas regular land bank loans were limited to 50 percent of the value of the land plus 20 percent for buildings. Commissioner loans were secured either by first mortgages on farms involving risks considered too great for the land banks or by second mortgages supplemental to land bank loans. Under a May 1935 amendment of the Emergency Farm Mortgage Act of 1933, the Commissioner was also authorized to make loans to persons receiving part of their income from nonfarm sources—provided the joint income from all sources would support the farm family, maintain the farm, and service the mortgage loan—where the property offered as security was valued at an amount representing a prudent investment. This special, "prudent investment value" program was a relatively small

[41] *Annual Report* of the Farm Credit Administration, 1953–1954, p. 101.

proportion of total Commissioner activity. Altogether, from May 1935 through June 30, 1946 only 5,307 of these loans, for about $12 million, were made. During the same period, approximately 261,000 loans of all kinds were closed under the Commissioner program for an aggregate amount of more than $470 million.

The main program began swiftly and attained large volume in the depression period. Between May 1, 1933 and December 31, 1936, $898 million was loaned, of which about $337 million was secured by first mortgages and the balance by second mortgages. Most of the second mortgage loans—almost $500 million—were made as joint land bank (first mortgage) and Commissioner (second mortgage) loans, and the balance as second mortgage loans subject to existing land bank loans. After 1936 the volume of Land Bank Commissioner lending declined rapidly, and from 1937 to the termination of the program on July 1, 1947 only $320 million was loaned, somewhat more than one-third of the amount loaned during 1933–1935.

Commissioner loans secured by second mortgages were made in practically all instances on properties acceptable for land bank first mortgage loans, but the first mortgage Commissioner loans went characteristically where the risk of lending was considered too great for the land bank system. Among these were loans on nonsustaining farm units where the operator placed substantial reliance on income earned off the farm, loans to irrigation, drainage, and levee districts of uncertain strength, loans to farmers in areas subject to excessive field or stream erosion or in areas where the type of agriculture was undergoing considerable change, and loans on farms which, while yielding the operator sufficient income to carry the loan, had such limited sale or rental prospects that losses would almost inevitably ensue in the event of foreclosure.

The average maturity of both first and second mortgage Commissioner loans made in the 1933–1935 period was about thirteen years, with annual principal payments beginning after the third year. As a result of delinquency and collection experience during this period, however, it was decided to reset many of the loans for longer terms, thus providing more liberal amortization schedules. By December 31, 1940 approximately 135,000 loans, representing three-tenths of the total number of loans outstanding on that date had been reset.[42]

[42] *Eighth Annual Report* of the Farm Credit Administration, 1940, p. 57.

The greatest concentration of delinquencies in the 1930's was along the one-hundredth meridian—in eastern Montana, North Dakota, South Dakota, Nebraska, Kansas, and Oklahoma—and the resetting of Commissioner loans in these states generally ran above the national average. For most of the area west of the Mississippi, with the exception of Texas, almost half of the first mortgage loans had been reset by the end of 1940. By the end of 1940, of the $1 billion loaned under the Commissioner program 24 percent had been reset, 3.6 percent had been extended one or more times, and 1 percent had been deferred.[43] Among the loans outstanding at the end of 1940 about 25 percent were delinquent or extended, which compares with 22 percent for regular land bank loans (Table 30, above).

It was the policy of the Federal Farm Mortgage Corporation during the thirties not to foreclose if the borrower was making a reasonable effort to carry the loan, was applying the proceeds of farm production over and above necessary living expenses to the payment of obligations, and was taking care of the property, all provided he had the capacity to support a reasonable debt burden under normal conditions. As a result, from 1933 through 1940 the corporation acquired only $108 million of property, about 10 percent of the total amount loaned. It was FFMC's policy to sell foreclosed properties as soon as possible, and by the end of 1940 about 76 percent of the total number of properties acquired had been sold for an average recovery of 71.8 percent of the investment. This represented a total loss of $22.2 million—equivalent to a charge of about 0.42 percent on cumulative outstandings. In comparison, the land banks had a loss of 0.51 percent on the basis of cumulative outstandings. Almost certainly, a less liberal policy on the part of FFMC in the resetting, extension, deferment, and foreclosure of loans would have resulted in higher losses.

From 1941 to 1954, trends in loan delinquency, property acquisition, and losses under the Commissioner program corresponded with those of other farm mortgage lenders. The percentage of loans delinquent declined from about 25 percent in 1939–1940 to about 7.6 percent during 1945–1947. Although acquisitions were fairly frequent in 1942–1944—about $32 million as compared with about $34 million in 1939 alone—the recovery rate rose steadily from 70.4 percent in 1940 to 89.6 percent in 1946, the year before the program

[43] Horton et al., *op.cit.*, p. 120.

was terminated. Total losses from 1941 to 1951 on property acquired were about $15.8 million, a loss rate equal to 0.57 percent of cumulative outstandings. For the entire span of the program from 1933 to 1951, losses on farms acquired were $38.0 million, about 3.12 percent of the total amount loaned. The increase in agricultural income and appreciation in property values that occurred after 1941 naturally resulted in much lower losses than would otherwise have been sustained.

It is possible to estimate roughly the relationship between over-all costs and revenues, including among expenses the cost of government-supplied capital for which the corporation was not required to pay interest. Direct government aid to the FFMC through mid-1954 included some 1.9 billion dollar-years of interest-free capital, beginning with the capital subscription of $200 million in 1934. At an interest rate of 2 percent, this would have cost the corporation about $39 million. Moreover, like the land banks, the FFMC received a reimbursement—$57 million—from the Treasury for interest rate reductions passed on to borrowers. In comparison, the cumulative earnings of the FFMC on June 30, 1954 consisted of $145.5 million —$129 million in dividends paid to the Treasury and an earned surplus of $16.5 million. The corporation also had the benefit of a federal guarantee of the interest and principal of its bonds, and this indirect aid was doubtless an appreciable advantage in its financing program. Even so, it appears that up to mid-1954, and with but a small amount of mortgages remaining to be extinguished, the Commissioner loan program had been more than self-supporting.

Farmers Home Administration

ORGANIZATION

Among direct agencies operated by the federal government to supply credit to farm operators, the most important in recent years has been the Farmers Home Administration, serving both the long-term mortgage and the short-term production-credit fields. In addition the Farmers Home Administration makes disaster loans to enable farmers who have suffered losses from natural or economic disasters to continue their production, and supplies credit for such special purposes as the development of water facilities.

A new and significant chapter in the history of federal lending activities began in 1935 with the establishment of the Resettlement Administration. This action, which was taken under Executive Orders

7027 and 7200 (April 30, 1935), combined in one agency the responsibility for the resettlement of low-income farm families that was shared among various agencies and the conduct of a rehabilitation program that was started with grants made by the Federal Emergency Relief Administration under the Federal Emergency Relief Administration Act of 1933 (49 Stat. 115). All of the duties and powers of the Resettlement Administration were transferred on January 1, 1937 to the Secretary of Agriculture by Executive Orders 7530 and 7557; and on September 1, 1937 its name was changed to the Farm Security Administration.

The Resettlement Administration was called upon to carry out not only approved projects involving the resettlement of low-income farm families, but also projects related to soil erosion, stream pollution, reforestation, flood control, etc., and to make direct rehabilitation loans to farm families. These loans could be made either to finance current operations or to refinance existing debt; furthermore, small grants could be made for the alleviation of distress among farm families. Loans to cooperatives were also extended under the rehabilitation program. The scope of lending was further broadened when the Farm Security Administration was authorized to make loans to farm tenants, laborers, and sharecroppers for the purchase of farms (Bankhead-Jones Farm Tenant Act of 1937: 50 Stat. 522; 7 U.S.C., Sup. 1000-1006).

Another step in the reorganization of these activities came in 1946 when the Farmers Home Administration Act of 1946 (60 Stat. 1062; 7 U.S.C. 1001 note) was passed. As a division of the Department of Agriculture, the new agency assumed the functions that had been performed up to that time by the Farm Security Administration and by the Emergency Crop and Feed Loan Division of the Farm Credit Administration. Under the powers granted in the 1946 act, the Farmers Home Administration is authorized to make operating or production loans to farmers or stockmen; to finance the purchase, improvement, or enlargement of family-size farms; to insure mortgages made by private lenders where the purpose is similar to that of the farm ownership loan program; and to make water facility and disaster loans.

In Title V of the Housing Act of 1949 (Public Law 171, 81st Cong.) financial and technical assistance was made available, through the FHA, to farm owners to provide themselves and their tenants with "decent" and "adequate" housing and farm buildings. In July

1953 a special program of loans to livestock operators in need of temporary financing because of drought or the decline in cattle prices was authorized. At the same time the FHA was authorized to make loans in areas in which economic disaster caused a critical need for agricultural credit that could not be met through established channels (including the regular programs of FHA). Such loans could be made only in areas declared by the President to be disaster areas under Public Law 875. Areas for economic disaster loans were first authorized late in October 1953. Also in recent changes the water facilities loan program was expanded to include various soil conservation facilities and practices, and in other ways; and a corresponding program of loan insurance was inaugurated. For the farm ownership program, authority to lend on second mortgage security was given.

FARM MORTGAGE SERVICES

Because its basic purpose has been to provide credit to farmers unable to qualify for loans from private lenders the Farmers Home Administration, like its predecessors, the Farm Security Administration and the Resettlement Administration, has had to ration loans among applicants, in contrast to the land banks, which have often had a surplus of loanable funds. The Farmers Home Administration mortgage program is designed to provide credit to low-income, small-scale farmers with little equity, on terms more favorable than offered by other lenders. To a considerable degree, this has meant that the Farmers Home Administration has not competed directly with private farm mortgage lenders, for the reason that these lenders would ordinarily not be serving the same market, even at higher rates.

Among the different types of farm mortgage loans made by the FHA and its predecessors, several come under the general category of farm ownership loans: (1) tenant purchase loans, authorized under the Bankhead-Jones Farm Tenant Act of 1937 (Public Law 210, 75th Cong.), to be made to tenants, farm laborers, or sharecroppers to enable them to buy farms and make necessary repairs and improvements on them; (2) rural rehabilitation loans (to cooperatives and projects), begun under the Resettlement Administration, and loans for financing, refinancing, redeeming, or repurchasing farms lost or in danger of being lost through foreclosure; (3) farm development and farm enlargement loans, directed to the problem of underdeveloped or inadequate farms; and (4) construction and improvement loans, authorized in October 1949, under which—through a "lease and purchase contract" (known as a 171 contract)—unimproved land is sold to a farmer who agrees to improve it under the supervision of, and with a loan provided by, FHA. In addition a farm housing loan program was begun under Title V of the Housing Act of 1949, making FHA credit and technical assistance available to farm owners for construction or repair of farm houses and buildings.

Loans under the tenant purchase program have been made on exceptionally liberal terms—3 percent interest originally (later 3½, then 4 percent), and thirty- to forty-year maturities—and have in some instances provided for the deferral of interest and principal when borrowers have been hard pressed to make their payments. Naturally, therefore, the limiting factor in the program has been the amount of funds available and the screening of applicants by the lending agency. Some limitations are effected also through the size of loans permitted. The average size of all loans approved from the beginning of the program through June 30, 1940 was $5,733.[44] But in five successive appropriation acts, beginning with that of 1941, Congress adopted the so-called Tarver limit, which provided that no loan might be made for the purchase of a farm that was of greater value than the average of all farms of thirty acres or more in the same county in which the farm was located. This limit varied considerably from county to county but was less than $4,000 in 35 percent of all counties in the United States and in 60 percent of all the counties in the South, which was fairly restrictive of the program.[45] As a result of this and other limitations on the amount that could be loaned in particular counties, the Farm Security Administration was unable to use, and returned to the Treasury, one-fourth of the 1944 appropriation.

Section 505(b) of the Servicemen's Readjustment Act of 1944 made veterans of World War II eligible for tenant purchase loans, and in the appropriations act of 1946 Congress earmarked for veterans $15 million of the $35 million appropriated for the program, to be distributed without regard to the Tarver limit or related limitations.

In 1946 the Farmers Home Administration Act made several im-

[44] Horton et al., op.cit. p. 139.
[45] Cf. Edward C. Banfield, "Ten Years of the Farm Tenant Purchase Program," *Journal of Farm Economics*, Vol. XXXI, No. 3, August 1949, pp. 474f.

portant changes in the program: (1) it provided federal insurance of privately made loans similar to FHA farm ownership loans, if a down payment of at least 10 percent had been made; (2) it increased the interest rate on direct farm ownership loans to 3½ percent and set the rate on insured loans at 2½ percent interest plus 1 percent charge for insurance and administration; (3) eligibility and preference was given to veterans of all wars; (4) limits on the distribution of loan funds among states were retained but each state was given a minimum of $100,000, with preference for veterans; (5) it authorized loans to farm owners (as well as to tenants and laborers) for repair, improvement, and enlargement of farms of less than family size and for refinancing loans made for that purpose; (6) it substituted for the Tarver limit a provision that loans should be limited to not more than the average value of an efficient family type farm in the county, as determined by the Secretary of Agriculture; and (7) it converted its variable payment plan to a conventional arrangement for prepayment.

After the 1946 revisions, the average size of FHA loan increased but the number of new borrowers being served declined (Table 39). From 1945 through 1952 the total outstandings of FHA's farm ownership loans—including farm purchase, farm enlargement, and farm development (special real estate) loans—remained at about the same level, averaging $190 million over the eight-year period. On the other hand, the corresponding loan insurance program expanded, and new borrowers under the housing loan program outnumbered those coming under both the direct and insured farm ownership programs (Table 39).

The Farmers Home Administration direct farm ownership and housing loans have been concentrated rather heavily in regions containing a relatively large number of low-income farms, while the insured loans have been more widely distributed. Out of $190 million of direct farm ownership loans outstanding on July 1, 1954 over $95 million was in the twelve southern states from the Carolinas to Texas,[46] while only $2.4 million was in the New England States. Not quite $60 million was in the fifteen states comprising the Middle Atlantic and North Central regions. Of the amount of insured loans outstanding on January 1, 1953, 30 percent was in the twelve southern states, and about half in the North Central group. Of the amount of direct farm housing loans, more than half was in the twelve southern states.

[46] *Agricultural Finance Review*, Vol. 17, November 1954, p. 86.

TABLE 39

Farmers Home Administration Real Estate Loans, and Insurance of Loans, to Individuals, 1938–1952

(dollar figures in thousands)

YEAR	FARM OWNERSHIP LOANS[a]			FARM OWNERSHIP LOAN INSURANCE[b]			FARM HOUSING LOANS		
	Number of New Borrowers	Volume during Year[c]	Out-standings Dec. 31	Number of New Borrowers	Volume during Year[d]	Out-standings Dec. 31[e]	Number of New Borrowers	Volume during Year	Out-standings Dec. 31
1938	2,028	$10,275	$ 10,275	…	…	…	…	…	…
1939	4,622	26,576	32,301	…	…	…	…	…	…
1940	7,025	39,713	66,286	…	…	…	…	…	…
1941	11,689	60,663	116,610	…	…	…	…	…	…
1942	7,680	35,695	160,258	…	…	…	…	…	…
1943	5,139	32,531	174,946	…	…	…	…	…	…
1944	6,755[f]	36,385[f]	196,815[f]	…	…	…	…	…	…
1945	2,713	16,767	185,060	…	…	…	…	…	…
1946	6,807	47,725	192,620	…	…	…	…	…	…
1947	3,364	26,359	198,279	…	…	…	…	…	…
1948	2,518	19,250	192,506	646[g]	4,623[g]	4,559	…	…	…
1949	1,839	15,396	192,457	1,727	12,324	16,700	…	…	…
1950	1,496	14,693	191,454	2,504	19,398	29,359	6,423[h]	29,077[h]	26,782
1951	1,969	22,298	190,282	1,376	11,981	43,084	4,853	23,789	47,631
1952	1,753	22,521	193,123	1,211	12,185	51,599	4,657	26,332	69,680

(continued on next page)

TABLE 39 (continued)

From *Agricultural Statistics, 1953* (Department of Agriculture), Table 755, p. 657.

a Covers tenant purchase, farm enlargement, and farm development (special real estate) loans; project liquidation loans; and similar loans from state corporation trust funds.

b Covers tenant purchase, farm enlargement, and farm development loans privately made under FHA insurance.

c For project liquidation loans, represents amounts advanced; for all other loans, amounts obligated. Includes supplemental loans to borrowers who received an initial loan in a prior year.

d Represents amount obligated. Includes supplemental loans to borrowers who received an initial loan in a prior year.

e For 1948 and 1949, represents amounts obligated less principal repayments; for 1950–1952, loan advances less principal repayments. From data as of January 1 of following year.

f Includes project liquidation loans advanced from inception of program through 1944.

g Loans obligated from beginning of program in October 1947 through December 1948.

h Loans obligated from beginning of program in November 1949 through December 1950.

NON-REAL-ESTATE CREDIT SERVICES

Non-real-estate credit programs for farmer-borrowers unable to obtain credit from other sources were grouped under the Farmers Home Administration in 1946. Emergency crop and feed loans made under the Farm Credit Administration since 1933 and the operating loans under the rural rehabilitation program of the Farm Security Administration (earlier, of the Resettlement Administration) were discontinued at that time, and the functions of these two programs were placed in the new production and subsistence loan program of the Farmers Home Administration. The water facilities loan program—chiefly for irrigation in the West, until broadened in 1954 to include soil conservation as well, and on a nationwide basis—was continued, along with the disaster loan program.

Of the programs carried on between 1946 and 1953, the production and subsistence loan program has been by far the largest (Table 32, ante). Under this program, a total of $614 million was advanced from November 1, 1946 to June 30, 1953, and $373 million in principal and $32 million in interest had been repaid. In comparison, loan advances under the disaster loan program (including fur and orchard loans) from April 1949, when Public Law 38 (81st Cong.) redefined it, through June 30, 1953 totaled only about $129 million, and advances under the water facilities program from its initiation in 1937 totaled only $28 million.[47]

In contrast to the farmers obtaining short-term credit from banks or from PCA's, non-real-estate borrowers under the Farmers Home Administration have usually been faced with an emergency situation; that is, a compelling need for operating funds arising from such circumstances as low yields or crop failure, low farm product prices, or personal or family adversities. Besides extending credit, the Farmers Home Administration staff aids borrowers in farm and home planning and budgeting, in carrying out programs of farm enlargement and improvement, and in becoming more efficient producers. As would be expected, those borrowing from the FHA for reasons of personal or family adversity have been widely distributed geographically and by type of farm, whereas those borrowing because of low yields or crop failure have been concentrated in high-risk areas such as the southern Cotton Belt and parts of the Great Plains. On July 1, 1954, for example, $88 million of the $365 million of production and subsistence loans outstanding[48] in the United States was in the five states of Georgia, Mississippi, Arkansas, Oklahoma, and Texas. More than $62 million of the $106 million of disaster loans outstanding[49] was in Texas, Oklahoma, Arkansas, and Missouri. About $7 million of the $18 million emergency crop and feed loans outstanding was in North and South Dakota.

EXPERIENCE

Experience under the farm ownership program has naturally been greatly affected by the fact that farm prices and income have moved generally upward since its beginning. From 1937 through June 30, 1953, a total of about $428 million of direct loans had been made by the FHA or its predecessor the Farm Security Administration: of this amount about $190 million was still outstanding; repayments of $237 million had been made, and $1,018,000—about 0.24 percent of the amount advanced—had been written off as losses and accounts

[47] *Report of the Administrator of the Farmers Home Administration, 1953,* pp. 22f.

[48] Also includes rural rehabilitation, water facility, construction, and wartime-adjustment loans, and such loans made from state corporation trust funds. See *Agricultural Finance Review,* Vol. 17, November 1954, p. 96.

[49] Now called "production and economic emergency loans." The figures are inclusive of special livestock, flood-damage, flood- and windstorm-restoration, fur, and orchard loans, and loans formerly made by the Regional Agricultural Credit Corporation.

totaling $323,000 were in process of judgment. The related insurance program and the farm housing loan program both began too recently to have produced meaningful experience data. From 1946 through mid-1953, $64 million of farm ownership loans by private lenders had been insured, and repayments of $7.5 million had been made.[50] From 1949 through mid-1953, $81 million in farm housing loans had been advanced by FHA to more than 16,300 farm owners; by June 30, 1953 about $10 million of principal had been repaid and $71 million was outstanding.

As to non-real-estate credit extended by the FHA and its predecessors, experience information is fullest for the oldest and largest of the programs, the composite known as production and subsistence loans. Up to November 1, 1946, when the rural rehabilitation and the emergency crop and feed loan programs were discontinued as separate undertakings and their functions delegated to FHA, these loans resulted in a considerably higher rate of loss than most other federal farm credit programs. Under the rural rehabilitation loan program as such a total of $1,005 million was loaned to farmers from 1934 through 1946. Collections of interest and principal amounted by June 30, 1953 to $1,012 million and about $46.1 million was still outstanding. However, the principal repayments which were received amounted to only 88.4 percent of the maturities. In the case of crop and feed loans, farmers borrowed about $576 million from 1918 to November 1, 1946, and by June 30, 1953 the principal paid back totaled $474 million or 82.4 percent of the amount advanced. On the production and subsistence loans made after November 1, 1946 (when FHA took over), by June 30, 1953, $614 million had been advanced, $373 million of principal had been repaid, $1,340,000 in principal had been written off, and $165,000 was under review.[51]

Experience under the disaster loan program is not easily summarized, but it is reasonable to expect that the over-all loss rate will be higher than that encountered in the production and subsistence programs. Loan operations are for the most part limited to counties designated by the Secretary of Agriculture as disaster areas, and the amounts obligated from year to year fluctuated widely, depending on the prevalence of flood, drought, insect infestations, and other types of disasters. From April 1949 through June 30, 1953,

[50] *Report of the Administrator of the Farmers Home Administration, 1953*, pp. 26f.
[51] *Report of the Administrator of Farmers Home Administration, 1953*, pp. 22 and 24f.

loan advances totaled $129 million, principal repayments $75 million; only $6,828 in principal had been written off and $79,660 was in process of judgment (together, 0.07 percent of total advanced).[52]

Loss rates on water facilities loans are lower than those for disaster and production and subsistence loans. Although these loans are restricted to cases where other financing is not available, they are made for specific production purposes, such as repair or development of irrigation facilities, by individual farmers or by groups of farmers. On June 30, 1953 the cumulative total of loan advances was $27.8 million and principal repayments were about $11 million. Only $6,541 in principal had been written off and $3,505 was under review. This loss rate, even including the amount under review, would be negligible—about 0.04 percent of total loan advances.[53]

It is not possible to make an accurate estimate of the amount of government aid extended in the programs collected within the Farmers Home Administration because services of a farm-home supervisory nature have been involved along with credit activities, and because of the wide variety of circumstances in which loans and grants were made. Generally speaking, it appears that the federal government has recovered the equivalent of the capital advanced in loan programs, but only if interest as well as principal repayments are regarded as offsets to the original capital investment. However, an added consideration is that a total of about $153 million in grants under the rural rehabilitation program was expended (1935 through 1946) and about $364,000 in farm housing grants (1949 through mid-1953).[54] Since loans and grants were sometimes made to the same individual, part of the grant program may be considered as a cost of the loan programs. Between 1945 (when debt settlement was authorized by Public Law 518) and June 30, 1953 the Farmers Home Administration, in settling debts under current and past programs on loans dating as far back as 1918, recovered $16 million on a principal balance of $48 million (with unpaid interest of $19.4 million); and unpaid balances in other cases totaling $105 million in principal and $40 million in interest were settled by cancellation.[55] The conclusion is that the programs as a whole have not been self-

[52] *Report of the Administrator of the Farmers Home Administration, 1953*, pp. 30f.

[53] *Ibid.*, p. 28.

[54] *Ibid.*, p. 23, and *Agricultural Statistics, 1947* (Department of Agriculture), Table 697, p. 598.

[55] *Ibid.*, p. 32.

supporting, although cumulative payments of interest and principal have come close to balancing the total principal amount advanced.

Veterans' Administration

The special provisions for veterans under the farm-ownership and farm housing loan programs of the Farmers Home Administration have been mentioned. In addition, the Veterans' Administration itself has been authorized since the end of World War II to guarantee or insure loans by other lenders to veterans for the purchase, construction, or improvement of farm properties.

The number and amount of farm loans guaranteed or insured by the Veterans' Administration increased rapidly in 1946 and 1947 and then declined. As will be seen from Table 40, while only 1,064 loans were insured or guaranteed in 1945, a total of 17,138 loans were insured or guaranteed in 1946. Between 1945 and 1954 the average size of loan increased somewhat, from about $3,600 in 1945–1946 to about $4,400 in 1953–1954.

Rural Electrification Administration

ORGANIZATION AND SERVICES

Another direct farm lending agency of the federal government is the Rural Electrification Administration, through whose facilities mortgage credit with a maximum term of thirty-five years, and currently carrying interest rates of 2 percent, is made available in amounts up to 100 percent of the cost of constructing rural electrification facilities. Like the bank for cooperatives the REA was established to provide credit mainly to cooperative organizations, in this case those engaged in the generation and distribution of electric power. It also makes short-term loans to individuals for purchase and installation of electric appliances and plumbing and for wiring of homesteads, through buying consumer installment contracts made by REA-financed power distributors.[56] In October 1949, REA was

[56] A similar program was that of the Electric Home and Farm Authority. In 1933 Executive Order 6514 created the Electric Home and Farm Authority, Inc., a direct agency of the federal government, first organized as a Delaware corporation with the directors of the Tennessee Valley Authority also serving as its directors and with the object of increasing employment and stimulating the use of TVA-generated electric power. This was to be accomplished by providing facilities for discounting installment contracts arising out of the sale by accredited dealers, on a deferred payment basis, of electrical home appliances and equipment. In 1935 a new corporation—the Electric Home and Farm Authority, disassociated from TVA and related closely to the Rural Resettlement Adminis-

TABLE 40

Farm Loans Guaranteed or Insured by the Veterans' Administration, 1945–1954

(dollar figures in thousands)

YEAR	NUMBER OF LOANS MADE			TOTAL PRINCIPAL AMOUNT[a]	AMOUNT OF GUARANTY OR INSURANCE		
	Real Estate	Non-Real-Estate	Total		Real Estate	Non-Real-Estate	Total
1945	174[b]	890[b]	1,064	$ 3,585[b]	$ 390	$ 875	$ 1,265
1946	9,597[b]	7,541[b]	17,138	63,259[b]	22,141	7,685	29,826
1947	10,707	9,086	19,793	77,765	27,697	8,937	36,634
1948	5,290	5,118	10,408	42,004	13,704	4,857	18,561
1949	1,937	3,009	4,946	17,533	4,883	2,681	7,564
1950	2,003	3,155	5,158	19,400	5,364	2,603	7,967
1951	1,487	2,143	3,630	16,020	4,287	1,644	5,931
1952	613	1,332	1,945	7,892	1,804	811	2,615
1953	435	1,016	1,451	6,265	c	c	1,641
1954	457	967	1,424	6,464	c	c	1,830

From *Agricultural Statistics, 1953* (Department of Agriculture), Table 761, p. 661, and *Loan Guaranty* (Veterans' Administration), December 1953 and December 1954, pp. 53 and 57, respectively.

a Breakdown between real estate and non-real-estate loans is not available.
b Estimated.
c Not available.

authorized to make loans to telephone organizations, with preference to existing companies and cooperatives, for the expansion of telephone facilities in rural areas.

The REA was set up originally under Executive Order 7037 (dated May 11, 1935), issued under the authority of the Emergency Relief Appropriation Act of 1935 (49 Stat. 115). Its functions were redefined about four months later in Executive Order 7130 (August 7, 1935), and it was established as a permanent and independent agency by the Rural Electrification Act of 1936 (49 Stat. 1363; 7 U.S.C. 901 *et seq.*). Finally, it was transferred to the Department of Agriculture under the Reorganization Act of 1939 (53 Stat. 561).

The emphasis on lending to cooperatives is shown by the following distribution of borrowers under the Rural Electrification Act from the beginning through mid-1953:

Cooperatives	985
Public power districts	44
Other public bodies	26
Power companies	25
	1,080

The basic policy of REA, adopted in its formative period, has been to provide "area coverage": that is, once an area or locality has been entered, service is extended to cover all its parts, even though some of the projected power lines may prove unprofitable. The objective is to reach the so-called "fringe" areas and to serve relatively isolated farm families, as well as those located near the main power lines.

Congress has directed how the loan funds shall be allocated among the states. Under the original Rural Electrification Act, one-half of the amount authorized annually was allocated proportionately to the several states on the basis of the number of unelectrified farms when compared to the U.S. total. The remaining funds could be loaned as determined by the Administrator, except that not more

tration—was formed in the District of Columbia to take over the assets of EHFA and to widen the scope of its operations from a regional to a national basis. Seven of the eight directors of the new corporation were officers of the Reconstruction Finance Corporation and the other was the Rural Electrification Administrator. The operations of the agency were financed partly with government capital ($850,000) and partly with the proceeds of the sale to commercial banks of the corporation's notes, which, while unsecured, were issued under an RFC commitment to purchase them if not paid at maturity. Outstanding accounts of the Electric Home and Farm Authority were transferred in 1942 to RFC for liquidation.

than 10 percent of the remainder (after allocation of 50 percent on the basis of number of unelectrified farms) could be employed in any one state. When the REA was organized in 1935, approximately 11 percent of the farms in the United States were being served with central-station electricity, with the percentage varying from 36.7 percent in New England and 46.4 percent in the three Pacific Coast states to between 2 and 3 percent in the South Central or Cotton Belt states.[57] The allocation of REA funds according to the number of unelectrified farms in the various states has naturally resulted in a larger proportion of farmers being served by REA borrowers in the midwestern and southern states than in New England or on the Pacific Coast. Of the $2.5 billion loans made from organization to January 1, 1952, more than half of the total ($1.3 billion) had been loaned in twelve midwestern and southern states (Missouri, Texas, Minnesota, Iowa, North Dakota, Kentucky, Oklahoma, Wisconsin, Nebraska, Georgia, Kansas, and Tennessee), whereas less than one-twentieth of the total was loaned in the twelve states of the New England, Middle Atlantic, and Pacific Coast regions, as is shown in Table 41.

The most rapid development of the REA program has occurred since 1945. At the beginning of 1946 less than half a billion dollars had been advanced out of the loans made, whereas by the beginning of 1953 the total advanced was almost $2.2 billion, more than four times as much as was advanced through 1945.[58] By the end of fiscal 1953 a total of nearly $2.3 billion had been advanced to REA borrowers, and advances to telephone borrowers amounted to approximately $32 million.

As a result of this expansion, REA borrowers in recent years have served about half of the farms in the United States receiving central-station electric service. According to the annual REA survey of unelectrified farms, as of June 30, 1953, 4,888,460 farms (as defined in the 1950 census) or approximately 9 out of 10 farms in the United States were receiving central-station electric service.[59] About 54 percent of these were being served by REA borrowers. Of the total of 3,952,000 rural consumers being served by REA borrowers, approximately two-thirds were farmers.

[57] *Agricultural Statistics, 1953* (Department of Agriculture), Table 842, p. 731.
[58] *Ibid.*, Table 765, p. 663.
[59] *Report of the Administrator of the Rural Electrification Administration, 1953*, pp. 1, 14, and 15.

TABLE 41

Rural Electrification Administration Loans Classified by Purpose, 1935–1951

(dollar figures in thousands)

STATE AND TERRITORY	TOTAL LOANS		LOANS TO COOPERATIVE ASSOCIATIONS[a]		LOANS BY PURPOSE			MILES OF LINE PROVIDED FOR BY LOANS[c]	NUMBER OF CONSUMERS PROVIDED FOR BY LOANS[c]
	Number of Borrowers	Amount Approved	Number of Borrowers	Amount Approved	Line Construction and Working Capital	Generation and Transmission	Consumer Facilities[b]		
Maine	5	$ 2,129	5	$ 2,129	$ 1,800	$ 269	$ 60	933	4,234
New Hampshire	2	5,561	1	5,361	5,513	8	40	2,351	7,298
Vermont	3	3,572	3	3,572	3,359	150	63	1,976	5,927
Massachusetts	0	0	0	0	0	0	0	0	0
Rhode Island	0	0	0	0	0	0	0	0	0
Connecticut	0	0	0	0	0	0	0	0	0
New York	7	5,495	6	3,631	5,400	0	95	4,056	13,774
New Jersey	2	996	2	996	984	0	12	549	2,689
Pennsylvania	13	27,860	13	27,860	27,523	87	250	16,180	62,807
Ohio	29	49,332	28	47,597	47,259	1,775	298	28,432	113,469
Indiana	47	54,183	46	53,753	53,770	56	357	35,320	139,035
Illinois	28	77,015	27	76,934	71,759	4,886	370	44,057	133,118
Michigan	15	49,491	15	49,491	28,362	20,716	413	17,138	64,679
Wisconsin	31	90,886	30	90,795	41,412	48,813	661	29,948	83,478
Minnesota	54	130,364	52	129,389	106,876	22,228	1,260	77,454	186,561
Iowa	55	117,720	53	117,620	76,465	40,957	298	56,064	135,423
Missouri	49	195,069	48	195,034	135,024	59,353	692	79,908	244,472
North Dakota	25	97,626	24	97,013	68,289	28,925	412	49,966	64,634
South Dakota	34	74,744	34	74,744	63,344	11,302	98	44,345	67,139
Nebraska	36	90,155	11	23,994	75,996	13,581	578	53,040	96,397
Kansas	37	82,719	36	82,713	74,595	7,847	277	51,643	93,524

(continued on next page)

TABLE 41 (continued)
(dollar figures in thousands)

STATE AND TERRITORY	TOTAL LOANS		LOANS TO COOPERATIVE ASSOCIATIONS[a]		LOANS BY PURPOSE			MILES OF LINE PROVIDED FOR BY LOANS[c]	NUMBER OF CONSUMERS PROVIDED FOR BY LOANS[c]
	Number of Borrowers	Amount Approved	Number of Borrowers	Amount Approved	Line Construction and Working Capital	Generation and Transmission	Consumer Facilities[b]		
Delaware	1	$ 3,032	1	$ 3,032	$ 3,027	$ 0	$ 5	1,934	7,091
Maryland	2	12,735	2	12,735	10,535	2,200	0	5,195	25,114
Virginia	22	69,507	21	69,314	48,781	19,240	1,486	26,913	98,747
West Virginia	2	1,422	2	1,422	1,407	0	15	857	3,203
North Carolina	38	78,701	33	77,352	70,614	6,100	1,987	40,788	170,286
South Carolina	28	52,347	26	50,861	41,948	9,181	1,218	29,283	113,559
Georgia	46	85,385	45	85,278	79,483	4,037	1,865	58,928	221,176
Florida	17	32,908	15	32,695	27,860	3,861	1,187	18,082	55,664
Kentucky	28	97,757	27	97,755	82,954	14,450	353	45,519	191,136
Tennessee	33	81,807	22	75,920	81,388	264	155	41,102	247,281
Alabama	27	64,288	25	62,771	55,804	7,879	605	34,511	147,671
Mississippi	27	76,377	26	75,983	72,898	3,121	358	45,700	194,821
Arkansas	21	79,160	20	78,637	54,408	23,785	967	37,291	129,537
Louisiana	19	39,793	17	37,367	34,620	4,921	252	21,197	97,893
Oklahoma	28	97,614	27	97,429	82,003	15,258	353	55,983	131,082
Texas	98	180,604	97	179,568	159,949	18,699	1,956	127,974	308,180
Montana	25	37,339	25	37,339	34,743	2,461	135	21,612	35,574
Idaho	10	13,842	10	13,842	12,464	1,281	97	6,419	16,448
Wyoming	16	21,016	15	20,938	18,650	2,241	125	11,654	17,967
Colorado	23	49,496	22	49,367	43,744	5,592	160	25,712	58,875
New Mexico	17	42,204	16	42,069	31,517	9,372	1,315	16,307	39,934
Arizona	10	15,438	8	15,196	8,581	6,537	320	3,537	11,234
Utah	8	14,226	8	14,226	3,963	10,198	65	2,145	6,579
Nevada	2	364	0	0	279	75	10	165	745

(continued on next page)

TABLE 41 (continued)
(dollar figures in thousands)

STATE AND TERRITORY	TOTAL LOANS		LOANS TO COOPERATIVE ASSOCIATIONS[a]		LOANS BY PURPOSE			MILES OF LINE PROVIDED FOR BY LOANS[c]	NUMBER OF CONSUMERS PROVIDED FOR BY LOANS[c]
	Number of Borrowers	Amount Approved	Number of Borrowers	Amount Approved	Line Construction and Working Capital	Generation and Transmission	Consumer Facilities[b]		
Washington	24	$ 28,534	14	$ 19,356	$ 25,838	$ 2,617	$ 79	13,197	32,412
Oregon	17	27,117	16	26,692	23,297	3,731	89	9,276	28,466
California	8	11,394	6	5,369	9,905	1,477	12	3,167	23,211
Alaska	6	14,688	6	14,688	6,679	7,915	94	863	7,357
Virgin Islands	1	432	0	0	235	197	0	85	912
United States and territories	1,076	$2,484,444	986	$2,379,827	$2,015,304	$447,643	$21,497	1,298,756	3,940,813

From *Agricultural Statistics, 1952* (Department of Agriculture), Table 755, p. 752. State totals represent data for borrowers incorporated within the state.

a United States totals for other types of borrowers are: public power districts, 41 borrowers, $82,295,129; municipalities and other government authorities, 24 borrowers, $13,070,089; power companies, 25 borrowers, $9,251,731.

b Funds loaned to corporate borrowers for relending to individuals. Includes wiring, plumbing, and refrigeration installations.

c Includes miles energized and consumers connected.

Up to June 30, 1953, losses had been taken on only two loans made by the Rural Electrification Administration: one was foreclosed as a result of damage caused by a hurricane and resulted in a loss of $28,550 of principal and $5,081 of interest; the other involved writing off an advance for engineering purposes when the borrowing cooperative was dissolved—before construction of facilities—on the entry of a private power company into the territory, which raised the loss figure to $45,000 (principal and interest).[60]

Government aid to the REA has consisted of: (1) the payment of administrative expenses, which amounted to $76,788,479 between 1935 and June 30, 1953, and (2) the provision of low-cost capital. From 1935 to September 19, 1944 the REA borrowed from the Reconstruction Finance Corporation at an interest rate of 3 percent. As of June 30, 1947 the REA relationship with the RFC was discontinued and loan funds were thereafter borrowed from the U.S. Treasury. According to a memorandum of understanding between the Administrator of the REA and the Secretary of the Treasury, the interest paid to the Treasury by the REA was to be the average rate paid on all marketable securities outstanding at the beginning of the fiscal year, with a maximum of 2 percent. The rates paid by REA borrowers, which have generally been lower than those paid by public utility firms, have sometimes been above, and sometimes below, the rate of interest paid by REA for its funds.

Impact of the Programs on Agriculture

The credit services offered by federal and federally sponsored agencies in the field of agriculture have had important and far-reaching impacts on agriculture and agricultural lenders. Government credit programs have affected the flow of resources into agriculture, and their allocation within agriculture and as between agriculture and the rest of the economy, producing results that may be read in terms of the amount of capital employed, farm employment, and agricultural output. Further, federal and federally sponsored agencies, by establishing what has often been a different pattern of interest rates, equity requirements, and other loan terms, have had an important impact on other agricultural lenders. In some cases they have functioned in a complementary, and sometimes in a

[60] *Report of the Administrator of the Rural Electrification Administration, 1953*, pp. 32 and 34.

competitive relation with private agencies. These principal effects are discussed below.

Since the demand for credit by farmers is affected by the level of farm prices and other business conditions, as well as by their own debt, and savings-asset position, no close relationship has been found between changes in the amount of credit used by farmers and changes in the aggregate volume of agricultural output. During World War II, for example, agricultural output increased by about one-fifth while the total amount of farm mortgage credit and of non-real-estate credit outstanding declined.[61] From the beginning of 1946 to 1953, on the other hand, total farm debt rose more rapidly than the volume of agricultural output. Farm mortgage debt increased then by about 50 percent and non-real-estate debt more than doubled, whereas agricultural output increased at a notably slower rate. Changes in the volume and distribution of farm debt often reflect ownership changes, and although the normal effect of increased use of credit is to raise farm output, and of decreased credit use to lower it, these effects have not been precisely measured. Farm management specialists working with production functions or production responses are just beginning to attack this quantitative problem.

Stringent credit conditions (like adverse terms of trade for farmers) affect farm output by restricting the employment of factors used in farm production, particularly hired labor, machinery, and supplies. This can be seen most clearly perhaps in the period of declining farm income and tightening credit conditions during 1929–1933, when the index of farm prices (1910–1914 = 100) fell from 148 to 70, going as low as 65 in 1932.[62] The volume of farm mortgages made or recorded dropped from $1,463 million in 1929 to $823 million in 1933, and the amount of non-real-estate farm credit outstanding dropped from about $2,684 million on January 1, 1929 to about $1,401 million on January 1, 1934.[63] The total acreage of crops planted increased somewhat during these years—rising from 363 million to 373 million acres—and the number of people employed in agriculture dropped only slightly—from 12.8

[61] *Agricultural Outlook Charts, 1954* (Department of Agriculture, Bureau of Agricultural Economics), October 1953, pp. 32 and 40.
[62] *Agricultural Outlook Charts 1954*, p. 11.
[63] *Agricultural Statistics, 1952*, Tables 728 and 732, pp. 722 and 726.

million in 1929 to 12.7 million in 1933, or by one percent.[64] The index of power and machinery used on farms dropped by about 10 percent.[65] But farmers' expenditures on labor, machinery, and supplies fell sharply. The number of hired laborers employed declined by about one-seventh (from 3.4 million in 1929 to 2.9 million in 1933)[66] and farm wage rates dropped by more than 50 percent.[67] Farm machinery prices declined by less than 10 percent,[68] but expenditures on motor vehicles and machinery, including repair parts for machinery, fell by more than 70 percent.[69] The number of tractors purchased by farmers declined from 137,000 in 1929 to 25,000 in 1932, a drop of more than 80 percent.[70] The total amount of farm equipment and related products sold for use in the United States dropped from $458 million in 1929 to $302 million in 1935;[71] the value of total farm equipment manufactured fell from $606 million in 1929 to $214 million in 1931, or by more than 65 percent.[72] Expenditures on several other items used in farm production, such as costs of operating motor vehicles, seeds, twine, electricity, and other items consumed in day-to-day farm operations, did not decline proportionately. Fertilizer prices, however, declined from an index of 131 in 1929 to 96 in 1934 (1910–1914 = 100), a drop of about 27 percent;[73] and the tonnage of commercial fertilizer consumed declined from 8,208,000 in 1929 to 4,545,000 in 1932, a drop of about 45 percent.[74] Although declining prices for farm products were the chief motivating force in bringing about these declines in employment

[64] *Ibid.*, Table 664, p. 644, and *Agricultural Statistics, 1953*, Table 665, p. 565.

[65] Martin R. Cooper, Glen T. Barton, and Albert P. Brodell, *Progress of Farm Mechanization*, Department of Agriculture, Misc. Pub. 630, 1947, p. 81. The index number measures volume in terms of 1935–1939 average dollars, 1870 = 100.

[66] *Agricultural Statistics, 1953*, Table 665, p. 565.

[67] *Farm Wage Rates, Farm Employment and Related Data*, Department of Agriculture, Bureau of Agricultural Economics, 1943, pp. 3f. The index of farm wage rates (1910–1914 = 100) was 187 in 1929 and 89 in 1933. With 1929 = 100, wage rates were 48 in 1933. See also *Agricultural Statistics, 1952*, Table 659, p. 639.

[68] *Agricultural Statistics, 1952*, Table 696, p. 684.

[69] Calculated from data on machinery manufactured, prices of machinery and equipment, and value of farm equipment and machinery sold in the United States from 1929 to 1931. *Agricultural Statistics, 1945*, Tables 590, 592, and 593, pp. 454ff.

[70] *Ibid.*, Table 591, p. 454.

[71] *Ibid.*, p. 456. Census was not taken during 1932–1934. Includes plows and listers, harrows, rollers and pulverizers, planting machinery, cultivators and weeders, harvesting machinery, machines for preparing crops for market or use, tractor and tractor engines, internal combustion engines, horse-drawn vehicles, sprayers and dusters, elevators and blowers, hand tools, dairy equipment, poultry equipment, barn and barnyard equipment, and miscellaneous.

[72] *Ibid.*, p. 456.   [73] *Ibid.*, p. 429.

[74] *Ibid.*, p. 467.

of the various factors or resources, the stringency of credit was no doubt a contributing influence.

Even here, however, the effect of credit changes on aggregate agricultural output would not be great. The Bureau of Agricultural Economics index of "total inputs" used in farm production (1935–1939 = 100) declined only moderately from 107 in 1931 to 101 in 1933, 96 in 1934 and back to 99 in 1935. In years of credit stringency (as during declines in farm product prices) farmers postpone expenditures on machinery and equipment, buildings, and other capital investments and tend to "make do."[75] At such times, changes in the index of agricultural output are apt to be small (but not insignificant) in comparison with changes in the indexes of farmer expenditures on certain factors, particularly hired labor, machinery, fertilizer and supplies.

An increase in the supply of credit will lead to a greater increase in output if the funds made available are expended on machinery and equipment, fertilizer and supplies, than if the funds merely finance ownership changes of resources already employed in agriculture. An expansion in farm mortgage credit that merely facilitates transfers of land in a rising land market will have little if any effect on output, whereas expansion of credit to overcome some of the adverse effects of "capital rationing" on efficiency[76] will have greater effects on output. In contrast to the trends of the early depression years from 1929 to 1933, there was a marked increase in the use of fertilizer and in purchases of machinery, motor vehicles, and farm supplies during most of the period after 1932 (except for the effect of shortages during the war), and a pronounced upward trend after 1946. The amount of fertilizer used increased from 4,545,000 tons in 1932 to 8,656,000 tons in 1940 and to 22,700,000 tons in 1952.[77] The amount spent on the operation of tractors, motor vehicles, and trucks used in farm work increased from $384 million in 1932 to $584 mil-

[75] Cf. J. K. Galbraith and J. D. Black, "The Maintenance of Agricultural Production During Depression: The Explanations Reviewed," *Journal of Political Economy*, June 1938, pp. 205-223, and D. Gale Johnson, "The Nature of the Supply Function for Agricultural Products," *American Economic Review*, September 1950, pp. 539-564.

[76] Capital rationing in agriculture is defined as a situation in which the rate of return on additional capital invested would be greater than the interest rate, or the marginal cost of capital, but the farmer because of caution or inability to borrow does not borrow or invest the additional funds. Cf. Harold G. Halcrow, *Agricultural Policy of the United States* (New York: Prentice-Hall, 1953), pp. 116, 117, 338-340.

[77] *Agricultural Statistics, 1952*, Table 710, p. 705 and *Agricultural Statistics, 1953*, Table 719, p. 621.

lion in 1940 and to $2,131 million in 1952.[78] Between 1932 and 1940, and again between 1946 and 1952, there was a high positive correlation between the amount of farm credit used and farm production expenditures.

The chief direct effects of federal credit programs on farm output, to the extent that these effects can be measured from percent of the market served, have come as a result of the expansion in land bank lending in 1934 and 1935 and the later expansion in production credit and rural electrification. Important indirect effects have come from the increased competition among lenders stimulated by federal lending agencies, including the important effect of the joint stock land banks in the 1920's. During the twenties, lending by the federal land banks, which amounted to not quite 13 percent of the total farm mortgage debt outstanding by the end of the period, probably had more indirect than direct effect on farm output. During the thirties the refinancing programs of the land banks and the Land Bank Commissioner exerted the dominant, direct influences on farm output attributed to credit extensions. In 1934–1935, $1.7 billion of farm mortgages were made under these two programs, consisting of a relatively few new loans and extensive refinancing (about one-fourth of the cases involving a scale-down of old indebtedness). Later, during the period 1937–1949, federal farm mortgage loans extended did not equal the amount paid off, and by January 1, 1951 the outstandings of the federal land banks and the Federal Farm Mortgage Corporation (holder of the Commissioner loans) were about $991 million, which compares with $2,642 million on January 1, 1941 and a high of $2,989 million on January 1, 1937. During the period after 1936, and particularly after 1946, such direct output-increasing effect as came from federal credit programs (excluding the price-support operation of the Commodity Credit Corporation) must be attributed mainly to the federally sponsored PCA's and to the Rural Electrification Administration.

EFFECTS ON THE AGRICULTURAL CREDIT MARKET

Additional imputations about the effects of federal farm credit programs on farm output, the capital structure of agriculture, and other lenders may be drawn from a study of the impact of the programs on the agricultural credit market. We seek to appraise the

[78] *Agricultural Statistics, 1952*, Table 705, p. 701 and *Agricultural Statistics, 1953*, Table 713, p. 617.

effect of each of the major programs—mortgage credit, production credit, credit for farmers' marketing cooperatives, and credit for rural electrification—especially on interest rates, equity requirements, and other loan terms in the field of agriculture.

FARM MORTGAGE CREDIT

The most striking effect of federal lending in the farm mortgage field arose out of actions taken in 1934 and 1935. In 1934, 70 percent, and in 1935, 42 percent of the farm mortgages recorded were made by the federal land banks and the Land Bank Commissioner, as contrasted with only 3.0 percent in 1932, when all federal farm mortgage credit was provided by the land banks.[79] The increase in the total volume of farm mortgage credit extended in these years— from $903 million in 1932 to $1,820 million in 1934—was due entirely to the land bank and Commissioner programs, the activity of other lenders having decreased.

A major effect of this large volume of mortgage re-financing— done on terms that were much more liberal than those required by other lenders or previously by the land banks themselves—was a change in the ownership of farm debt, giving other holders of farm debt, especially mortgage debt, an opportunity to liquidate their investments. From the passage of the emergency legislation in 1933 to the end of the year, the land banks had received 502,470 applications under the regular and Commissioner programs for an amount of $2.1 billion—a total larger than applied for in the previous sixteen years.[80] During the four years from 1933 to 1936 the land banks closed 314,045 loans for an amount of $1.2 billion, and Commissioner loans brought the amount to more than $2 billion. During 1934 alone the combined programs loaned well over $1 billion. Afterward, from the beginning of 1937 to the end of 1940 their loans totaled only some $360 million. That land bank credit was largely used to refinance existing indebtedness is documented in Table 42, where it is shown that during the peak of loan operations in 1934 about 88 percent of the total extended under the regular program was for such purposes. The next largest use was to buy land and to redeem farm property from foreclosure. During 1934 only 2.4 percent of the total went for general agricultural uses including buildings and improvements. But such credit usage would have been

---

[79] *Agricultural Finance Review*, Vol. 16, November 1953, p. 98.

[80] *Annual Report* of the Farm Credit Administration for 1933, p. 8, and for 1952–1953, p. 69.

TABLE 42

Percentage of Proceeds of Federal Land Bank Loans Used for Given Purposes, 1917–1940

Year[a]	Refinancing Indebtedness	Purchase of Land and Redemption from Foreclosure	General Agricultural Uses Including Buildings and Improvements	National Farm Loan Association Stock[b]	Loan Fees[c]	All Purposes
1917–21	65.0%	18.0%	12.0%	5.0%	..	100.0%
1922	87.3	2.2	5.5	5.0	..	100.0
1923	84.6	3.8	6.6	5.0	..	100.0
1924	83.0	6.3	5.7	5.0	..	100.0
1925	78.5	9.5	7.0	5.0	..	100.0
1926	76.9	11.0	7.1	5.0	..	100.0
1927	80.4	8.7	5.9	5.0	..	100.0
1928	77.2	9.9	7.9	5.0	..	100.0
1929	74.0	14.0	7.0	5.0	..	100.0
1930	74.6	12.9	7.5	5.0	..	100.0
1931	79.8	8.6	6.6	5.0	..	100.0
1932	85.8	4.6	4.6	5.0	..	100.0
1933	86.8	3.3	3.8	5.0	1.1	100.0
1934	88.0	3.3	2.4	5.0	1.3	100.0
1935	d	d	d	d	d	d
1936	77.8	13.6	2.5	5.0	1.1	100.0
1937	69.2	21.4	3.3	5.0	1.1	100.0
1938	69.6	20.5	3.8	5.0	1.1	100.0
1939	67.3	22.7	4.0	5.0	1.0	100.0
1940	67.3	21.8	5.0	5.0	0.9	100.0

From *Farm-Mortgage Credit Facilities in the United States*, by Donald C. Horton, Harald C. Larsen, and Norman J. Wall (Department of Agriculture, Misc. Pub. 478, 1942), Table 28, p. 94.

[a] Period 1917–21 is from organization through October 31, 1921. The years 1922 through 1926 refer to periods of twelve months ended October 31, and 1927 is a fourteen-month period ended December 31, 1927.

[b] Borrowers have been required to purchase stock in the federal land bank or national farm loan association equal to 5 percent of the loan.

[c] Statutes provide that borrowers may arrange with federal land bank making the loan to advance loan fees, such advance to be made a part of the face amount of the loan.

[d] Unavailable.

affected secondarily, since a farmer who improved his capital position by means of a land bank loan could more likely obtain additional funds for production purposes.

To what extent did the refinancing involve change in the ownership of farm mortgage debt rather than further extension of credit where the land banks already held mortgages? Scattered sources give an approximate idea. It is known that during 1933–1936 about two-thirds of the combined proceeds of land bank and Commissioner loans went to refinance farm mortgage indebtedness.[81] Nearly half of the amount of mortgage debt refinanced in 1936 (i.e. nearly one-third of the total amount loaned) had been owed to life insurance companies, commercial banks, and the joint stock land banks, and the other half to the federal land banks and to miscellaneous private lenders.[82] The latter may have accounted for roughly 30 percent of the mortgage refinancing, or 20 percent of the total amount loaned.[83] Thus the available data suggest that at least one-half of the funds made available through the land bank and Commissioner loan programs during 1933–1936 went to liquidate the farm mortgage investments of private lending institutions and individuals, transferring the long-term debt of the farms involved, upon new terms, to the portfolios of the land banks and the Federal Farm Mortgage Corporation. Similarly, indications are that over the long run, from 1917 through 1953, upwards of two-fifth of the total funds loaned by the land banks and FFMC represented their assumption of farm mortgage debt previously held by private lenders.

Geographically, the impact of the land bank and Commissioner programs centered most heavily in the North Central states. This is indicated in Table 43, where it is shown that 66 percent of the loans closed during 1933–1936 were in the East and West North Central regions. In comparison, during earlier periods the volume of loans made—substantially smaller in aggregate amount—had been less concentrated regionally. The concentration in the East North Central and still more in the West North Central states during 1933–1936, with the latter group receiving 42 percent of the total, is perhaps accounted for by the fact that at the beginning of 1933 an estimated 55 percent of the farm mortgage debt of the United States was in the two regions combined, and that the western part was a major farm mortgage trouble spot of the nation.[84]

The purpose of Congress in establishing the land bank system was

---

[81] Horton et al., *op.cit.*, p. 23.
[82] *Annual Report* of the Farm Credit Administration, 1936, pp. 122 and 157.
[83] In 1941, 13.3 percent of the loan proceeds were used to refinance land bank and Land Bank Commissioner loans and 22.0 percent to refinance mortgages held by individuals and other miscellaneous lenders. See *Annual Report* of the Farm Credit Administration, 1941, p. 149, footnote 2.
[84] See *Mortgage Lending Experience in Agriculture*, by Lawrence A. Jones and David Durand (Princeton University Press for the National Bureau of Economic Research, 1954), Chapters 1 and 2.

TABLE 43

Regional Distribution of Amount of Federal Land Bank Loans Made,
Four-Year Periods 1917–1940

Region[a]	1917–20	1921–24	1925–28	1929–32	1933–36	1937–4
New England	1.9%	1.6%	1.9%	2.7%	1.0%	1.9%
Middle Atlantic	2.7	3.4	4.9	5.9	2.5	4.9
East North Central	10.0	13.4	17.5	16.4	23.4	20.6
West North Central	29.9	23.2	25.7	25.8	42.3	28.2
South Atlantic	8.6	10.3	7.7	4.5	5.0	5.7
East South Central	9.0	13.1	10.4	7.6	3.8	6.8
West South Central	17.3	17.5	19.7	22.0	10.1	13.6
Mountain	11.0	10.7	6.1	8.1	3.5	6.1
Pacific	9.6	6.7	6.0	7.0	8.4	12.2
United States	100.0%	100.0%	100.0%	100.0%	100.0%	100.0%

From *Farm-Mortgage Credit Facilities in the United States*, by Donald C. Horton, Harald
C. Larsen, and Norman J. Wall (Department of Agriculture, Misc. Pub. 478, 1942), Tabl
27, p. 93.

[a] States included in the regions are as follows: *New England*—Maine, New Hampshire
Vermont, Massachusetts, Rhode Island, Connecticut; *Middle Atlantic*—New York, New
Jersey, Pennsylvania; *East North Central*—Ohio, Indiana, Illinois, Michigan, Wisconsin; *Wes
North Central*—Minnesota, Iowa, Missouri, North Dakota, South Dakota, Nebraska, Kansas
South Atlantic—Delaware, Maryland, District of Columbia, West Virginia, Virginia, Nortl
Carolina, South Carolina, Georgia, Florida; *East South Central*—Kentucky, Tennessee, Ala
bama, Mississippi; *West South Central*—Arkansas, Louisiana, Oklahoma, Texas; *Mountain*—
Montana, Idaho, Wyoming, Colorado, New Mexico, Arizona, Utah, Nevada; *Pacific*—Washing-
ton, Oregon, California.

to provide cheaper and more adequate sources of farm mortgage
credit and thereby to encourage owner operation of farms. The
land bank program introduced and encouraged long-term amortized
mortgage lending at relatively low interest rates, and helped to
protect farmer ownership by the large-scale refinancing program
of 1934 and 1935. But the limitations on the amount that could
be loaned an individual borrower became progressively more restrictive after about 1940 as land prices moved upward and away from
the valuations fixed according to "normal agricultural value." How
have these limitations affected owner operation of farms? The effect
would be to give little aid in establishing farm ownership to those
who have small amounts of equity, since when land prices are high
the limitation to 65 percent of normal agricultural value restricts
the amount that can be loaned to a proportion of the sale price
considerably smaller than that. It is reported, for example, that on
the first 66 farm purchases financed by the Federal Land Bank of
St. Louis after July 1, 1947, the bank advanced a total of $159,500

on the total sale price of $748,650.[85] After deducting $9,000 for loan expense and stock purchases the borrowers had loans representing about 20 percent of the purchase prices. Although this is a small sample, the suggestion is implicit that land bank financing would have been generally restricted to those who had substantial equities.

The impact of the farm mortgage programs now under the Farmers Home Administration has been mainly confined to low-income farmers who could not get credit elsewhere. From 1937 through June 30, 1953 about $428 million of direct farm-ownership loans were made by the Farm Security Administration and then the FHA; and from October 1947 through mid-1953 similar loans of private lenders totaling about $64 million were insured by the FHA.[86] Through these programs approximately 76,000 farm families were helped to acquire farms or increase the size of their holdings, a number equal to about 3 percent of the not quite two-and-a-half million tenant farmers in the United States in 1940. About 10 percent of the loans (6,285 between 1939 and 1948) were made on family farm units created out of larger plantation holdings in the Cotton Belt states.[87]

Whereas land bank loans were larger for refinancing, most of the funds loaned by FSA and FHA—apparently more than two-thirds of the total—have been used for purchasing farms,[88] although the trend in recent years has been toward fewer loans for farm purchase and more funds for farm enlargement and development. Again in contrast with the land bank program, the largest part of the funds were disbursed in the southern states, as was shown earlier in the chapter in describing FHA credit services. A shift in appraisals was made in 1952, from historical averages of commodity prices and operating costs based on 1935–1939 conditions to appraisals based on recommendations of the Agricultural Research Service (then the

[85] See "Federal Land Bank Dilemma," by John I. Smith, *Farm Policy Forum*, March 1950, pp. 9–14.

[86] *Annual Report* of the Administrator of the Farmers Home Administration, 1953.

[87] See *The Land Is Mine*, by Paul V. Maris (Department of Agriculture, Monograph 8, November 1951), p. 8.

[88] In 1941, for instance, almost 70 percent of the funds advanced under the tenant purchase (farm ownership) program were for farm purchase, and in 1947 about 76 percent of the funds were so used. See "Ten Years of the Farm Tenant Purchase Program," by Edward C. Banfield, *Journal of Farm Economics*, August 1949, p. 474.

Bureau of Agricultural Economics) keyed to project levels of the economy.

The impact of the Farmers Home Administration farm ownership program on assets and income of borrowers was summarized in 1951 through a review of all loans made in 1939 and 1944.[89] The loans were amortized for forty years, but by the end of 1949, 65 percent of the 4,204 loans made in 1939 has been repaid and about two-thirds of the others were ahead of schedule in their repayment. Of the 5,402 families receiving ownership loans in 1944, 32 percent had repaid in full by 1949 and more than half the others were ahead of schedule. Among the 1939 borrowers still active in the program in 1949 (i.e. excluding those who had repaid in full), production per acre had increased by an average of 24 percent. Cash income from farming had increased from $855 per borrower in 1938 to $3,677 in 1949—a 66 percent gain after adjustment for changes in prices received for farm products—and net worth had increased from $1,528 to $8,473. Among the 1944 borrowers still active in the program, production per acre had increased by an average of 39 percent, cash income had increased from $1,725 per borrower to $3,260, and net worth from $2,276 to $6,345. These increases in productivity were relatively greater than the increases in the regional and national averages for agriculture as a whole. Also, although this was a period of general increases in cash farm income, the increases cited are considerably greater than the national average. Comparable data are not available on the borrowers who had repaid their loans in full, but doubtless the rate of increase in output, income, and net worth would be relatively greater for them than for those who were still paying on loans of similar type.

Turning again to changes of wider scope: The second major financial effect of the farm mortgage program was to reduce mortgage carrying charges for many farmers. A federal land bank borrower, for example, was given the privilege, during the five-year period ending July 10, 1938, of deferring his principal payments if he was not in default on any other covenant of his mortgage. In addition, about 150,000 of the more than 620,000 refinancing loans closed by the federal land banks or the Land Bank Commissioner from May 1, 1933 through December 31, 1940 involved scale-downs of other indebtedness.[90] These debt reductions aggregated more than

---

[89] *Annual Report of the Administrator of the Farmers Home Administration,* 1951, p. 27f.
[90] Horton et al., *op.cit.,* p. 49f.

$200 million, or about one-third of the original indebtedness. In many instances they involved the writing off of past-due interest and the reduction of both real estate and non-real-estate indebtedness.

The Farm Security Administration also helped refinance farm debt. According to data compiled by that agency from reports submitted by state adjustment committees covering the period from September 1, 1935 to October 31, 1940, 230,936 applications for debt adjustment were considered by the committees, a number equal to about 3.4 percent of the total number of farm operators reported in the 1935 census. More than half of the cases (135,100) were adjusted, involving total indebtedness of about $423 million and a debt reduction of about $96 million, or 22.7 percent of the original amount. In addition, adjustments of $15 million on original indebtedness of about $22 million were made in 105 group cases including farmers' cooperatives and other business organizations. This debt adjustment program resulted in 101,004 loans by various credit agencies, distributed as follows:[91]

Lender Groups	Number of Loans
Federal land banks	12,802
Land Bank Commissioner	4,793
Production credit associations	1,920
Farm Security Administration	67,731
Insurance companies	535
Local banks	3,225
Individuals	7,122
Others	2,876
Total	101,004

During the years 1932–1934 the interest rates charged by all major farm mortgage lenders decreased significantly, with the land banks leading the field in the downward trend. The average contract interest rate on farm mortgages recorded by all lenders, which was 6.38 percent in 1932—just about what it had been in 1920 (6.40%) —fell to 5.84 percent by 1933 and to 5.33 percent by 1934.[92] The contract interest rate of the land banks in effect on January 1, 1933 was 5½ percent in all districts except the Columbia and New Orleans districts and the island of Puerto Rico, where the contract rate was 6 percent. Specific acts of Congress provided that the interest rates actually paid on loans through national farm loan associations be reduced to 4½ percent per year for all interest payable on install-

91 *Ibid.*, pp. 50ff.
92 *Ibid.*, Table 68, pp. 229–231.

ment dates within the period July 11, 1933 to June 30, 1935, and to 3½ percent per year for all interest payable on installment dates within the period July 1, 1935 through June 30, 1944 irrespective of the contract rate of the individual mortgages. This loss in interest income was reimbursed to the federal land banks by the Treasury. On July 1, 1944, a 4 percent interest rate was established voluntarily by the land banks for all loans outstanding at higher rates which were made through national farm loan associations. With the exception of the Federal Land Banks of Springfield, Baltimore, and Columbia, which have raised rates to 4½, 4½, and 5 percent, respectively, the contract rate has been 4 percent during recent years.

The contract interest rates on all Land Bank Commissioner loans during the entire period of the program was 5 percent. By acts of Congress, the interest rate was reduced to 4 percent on installments due on or after July 22, 1937 and before July 1, 1940, and to 3½ percent for installment dates occurring on or after July 1, 1940 and before July 1, 1944; and a 4 percent rate was in effect from July 1, 1944 through June 30, 1945.

Naturally, the interest rate policy in land bank and Commissioner lending had a marked effect on the rates charged by private lenders. During 1932–1935 the average contract interest rate on farm mortgages recorded declined from 5.87 percent to 5.53 percent for insurance companies, from 6.83 percent to 6.28 percent for banks, from 6.15 percent to 5.74 percent for individuals, and from 6.64 percent to 6.01 percent for other lenders.[93] Furthermore, the reductions were general over the country, although there was a tendency for them to be somewhat greater in those regions, such as the Mountain and West South Central States, where rates had previously been highest. How far these interest rate reductions were due to the competitive practices of the land banks, however, and how far to general economic conditions cannot be determined. Interest rates also declined on nonfarm mortgage loans: the average interest rate on nonfarm home mortgage loans made by life insurance companies, commercial banks, and savings and loan associations averaged about 1.5 percentage points lower in the period 1940–1947 than in 1930–1934.[94]

[93] *Ibid.*, Table 68, pp. 229–231.
[94] From National Bureau of Economic Research sample surveys. See *Urban Mortgage Lending: Comparative Markets and Experience*, by J. E. Morton (Princeton University Press for the National Bureau of Economic Research, 1956), Chart 6 and Table C-5, pp. 91 and 176.

Finally, the wider use of the amortized farm mortgage during the depression can probably be attributed in large part to the influence of the land banks, in whose lending it was a standard practice, although some influence may have been exerted by nonfarm mortgage financing, where the amortized loan also was becoming more general.

After 1936 the impact of land bank lending diminished as its volume declined and stabilized at around 10 to 13 percent of the total amount of farm mortgages made; and particularly after 1940 the role of the land banks changed. As land values rose, the statutory limitation of their loans to 65 percent of the value of the farm as it would be appraised under more representative price conditions was increasingly restrictive, and the influence of the land banks became that of a relatively conservative element in the farm mortgage market.

PRODUCTION CREDIT

The federally sponsored production credit system, although playing a much less spectacular role during the depression years of the thirties than the land bank system, has had an important effect on loan terms in the farm production credit field. The credit services provided by PCA's are similar to the short-term non-real-estate credit services provided by banks and have affected competitively the activities of commercial banks and other non-real-estate lenders in the farm credit market.

The PCA interest rate, which was uniform up to 1947 (except that in Puerto Rico it was one-half of one percent higher than elsewhere), and which had only slight regional differentials subsequently, doubtless affected the terms on which credit was extended by private lenders. The impact of the production credit program differed widely, however, from one part of the country to another, as is indicated by the variations in the percent of the market served by PCA's. In Iowa in 1951, for example, only 2.2 percent of the farmers borrowed from PCA's, whereas 65.7 percent borrowed from commercial banks.[95] By way of contrast, in Vermont in 1951 about 12.3 percent of the farmers borrowed from PCA's and 29.0 percent from commercial banks, and in West Virginia the percentages were 1.6 and 9.6, respectively. Yet the full impact of the PCA's cannot be assessed by reference to the percentage of the credit market that

[95] *Agricultural Credit and Related Data, 1953* (Agricultural Commission, American Bankers Association), Table 5, pp. 18f.

they serve. The mere fact of their existence as an alternative source of credit doubtless caused private lenders to offer loans on more liberal terms than would otherwise have been the case.

Among the credit programs merged under the Farmers Home Administration, those other than the farm ownership program—that is, emergency crop and feed loans, disaster loans, and production and subsistence loans—come largely (but not entirely) within the field of non-real-estate credit. In the main they have been non-competitive with the activities of other lenders, since the general policy has been to lend only to farmers regularly or temporarily unable to get credit elsewhere. It seems likely that these programs, being restricted to special groups of borrowers, have had little effect on the loan terms of other lenders. Essentially, the Farmers Home Administration programs are outside the mainstream of farm production credit. Their chief effect would be to carry low-income farmers and farmers in disaster areas through periods of adversity, and if they affected the farm credit market, it would be through the possibility that such farmers might become or remain users of credit supplied through ordinary channels.

Production and subsistence loans, or rehabilitation loans as they were called under the Farm Security Administration, have represented by far the largest part of the Farmers Home Administration program and no doubt have had important effects on the income and bargaining position of the borrowing farmers. By the end of 1942, more than a million farmers had received rehabilitation loans from the Farm Security Administration.[96] Loans outstanding amounted to about one-fifth of the short-term farm debt held by the major credit institutions. Between 1944 and 1952 an average of just under $100 million was extended annually. The production and subsistence loans are intended to help farmers build up their productive assets and living necessities so that labor and management skills can be used most effectively; and after a few years borrowers are expected to develop their farms to the point where they can qualify for credit from local banks or PCA's. The number and proportion reaching that status will vary, of course, from year to year. In 1950, for example, 59,000 farmers, about one-fourth of all active borrowers, repaid their operating loans in full. In about 4 percent of the cases

[96] *Agricultural Statistics, 1943* (Department of Agriculture), p. 461. The figure inclusive of water facility loans is used, since they are not separable in the other data quoted.

final payment was made from the proceeds of loans obtained from banks or PCA's.[97]

CREDIT FOR FARMERS' COOPERATIVES

The major effect of the banks for cooperatives has been to decrease the cost of borrowing for farmers' cooperatives and thus, presumably, to stimulate their growth. That the existence of the banks for cooperatives has been felt by other lenders is indicated by the fact that the federally sponsored banks have served about one-half of the credit market originating with farmers' cooperatives. The services provided by the banks have been used most heavily by the medium-sized and largest cooperatives, rather than the small-scale enterprises, and accordingly it is the private lenders serving these groups that have been most acutely affected.

CREDIT FOR RURAL ELECTRIFICATION

The REA program accelerated rural electrification not only through the rapid expansion of REA facilities but probably also by stimulating private utilities to undertake more extensive expansion programs than they would otherwise have attempted. As of June 30, 1953, REA electrification loans approved total $2.7 billion and the advances to borrowers totaled $2.3 billion. Approximately 1.3 million miles of lines were energized and almost 3.9 million consumers were connected, of whom more than 2.5 million were farmers, these being about half of the farmers using central-station power in the United States. Private utilities were doubtless stimulated by REA to accelerate their own rural electrification programs and to reconstruct generating capacity to provide electricity at wholesale to REA cooperatives. Thus, on the assumption that REA facilities did not displace private utilities, it is almost certain that the demand for credit by private utility companies was increased over what it might otherwise have been.

Further, the provision of central-station electrical power, by making possible a technological revolution in agriculture, probably extended the base for the profitable employment of borrowed funds. The average investment in wiring and electric appliances is unknown, but studies made by the REA indicate that it is approximately $2,000 per farm. If this figure is correct, the direct capital invest-

[97] *Annual Report of the Administrator of the Farmers Home Administration, 1950*, p. 8.

ment on farms from services provided by REA borrowers would total more than $5 billion, and possibly as much as $2 billion more would be added for investments made by other consumers. Thus, there has been a far-reaching impact from the REA program both on agriculture and on agricultural lenders.

The direct impact of the REA program differed considerably from one part of the country to another because its funds were allocated among states largely according to the number of unelectrified farms. The southern and midwestern areas receiving the greater part of the credit have been delineated earlier, in describing the agency's services.

CONCLUSION

The agricultural credit programs of the federal government lowered the cost of credit to farmers, farm cooperatives, and rural electrification cooperatives, and have had a general output-increasing effect on resource allocation among farms. The refinancing program undertaken by the land bank system in the 1930's brought relief to both farmer-borrowers and farm-mortgage lenders. Since then the federal land banks have been restricted to serving a smaller percentage of the markets and have been more conservative lenders as the result of statutory limitations on the amounts that could be extended to individual borrowers. The growth in the production credit system, particularly since 1940, has provided an alternative source of credit to farmers, and has had an important effect on the terms on which production credit is made available to farmers. The programs of the Farmers Home Administration have provided credit to some farmers who could not obtain it from other sources, although the programs have touched only a small percentage of the farm population. The program of the banks for cooperatives has provided a cheaper source of credit for cooperative associations and thus has probably contributed to their growth. Likewise REA credit has stimulated the growth of rural electrification, with indirect effects on farm output.

In many respects the agricultural credit programs have brought about important institutional effects. Thus, the policies of the public agencies worked toward greater uniformity in both mortgage and production credit costs throughout the nation, bringing the largest relative reductions in the costs of farm credit in the South and the West. Federal land banks have tended not only to lower the price of mortgage credit to farmers but also to lengthen the terms to maturity that were available. They functioned as leaders in farm mortgage markets, setting terms and conditions that private lenders were compelled to meet if they were to retain their positions in the market. To a lesser degree, the PCA's have likewise been aggressive market leaders in the field of production credit, encroaching upon the markets formerly served exclusively by nongovernmental lenders. In part commercial banks and life insurance companies have yielded market position to the publicly sponsored agencies; in part, however, they have met the increasingly liberal terms with loans carrying lower interest charges and longer maturities than formerly. These effects of public agencies on farm credit markets occurred mainly during a period of secular decline in the structure of interest rates outside of agriculture. The course of events might have been quite different in a different economic environment. Finally, the federal and federally sponsored agencies constitute an organization in being that can be used and has been used to help facilitate national credit policies on interest rates and other loan terms, and thus affect the amount and type of credit available in the economy.

CHAPTER 7

Federal Lending and Loan Insurance Programs for Business and Financial Institutions

Development of the Programs

WHEREAS World War II was to bring federal credit programs to bear on a vast scale and in a wide range of industries, only limited segments of business received such aid in the earlier world war. The War Finance Corporation, established in 1918, helped finance certain essential war industries. The Director General of Railroads in 1919 and the Interstate Commerce Commission in 1920 were empowered to lend to railroads, which from 1918 through February 1920 were under federal operation. Specifically, financial assistance to the railroads consisted of operating loans made by the Director General out of a $500 million revolving fund, notes taken in payment for capital improvements and purchases of rolling stock, and certain loans made on the cessation of federal control, from a $300 million revolving fund set up under the Transportation Act of 1920 and administered by the Interstate Commerce Commission. New loans by the War Finance Corporation ceased after 1922, and new loans by the ICC, after 1924. There remained a program of loans for shipping.

Legislative action designed to promote United States shipping began with the Shipping Act of 1916 (34 Stat. 728), which created the U.S. Shipping Board. During World War I the board's efforts to increase the U.S. merchant fleet were carried out through a subsidiary, the Emergency Fleet Corporation, and after the war a revolving fund of $125 million was established by the Merchant Marine Act of 1920 (41 Stat. 988) to finance ship construction in domestic yards. The Merchant Marine Act of 1928 (45 Stat. 689) reaffirmed the policy of financial aid to shipping concerns and supplemented it with a system of mail contract subsidies; but the Merchant Marine Act of 1936 (49 Stat. 1985; 46 U.S.C. 1111), which established the U.S. Maritime Commission as an independent agency in the Executive Branch, constituted a reorientation of policy. The commission sought to stimulate shipbuilding by a system of direct subsidies intended to make up the difference between domestic and foreign cost of ship operation, and by an indirect subsidy program under which the commission produced and sold merchant vessels to American shipowners at prices below their actual cost in order to equalize the cost differential between domestic and foreign-built ships. The commission was also authorized to insure mortgages on all types of vessels owned by United States citizens and to make direct loans to shipping interests. Under Reorganization Plan 21 of 1950, the U.S. Maritime Commission was reorganized as the Maritime Administration and transferred to the Department of Commerce.

Meanwhile the depression of the early thirties had brought federal credit activity into other areas of business, with the establishment of the Reconstruction Finance Corporation in 1932—like all the foregoing organizations, a direct agency of the federal government. At first the authority conferred by the RFC Act (47 Stat. 5; 15 U.S.C. 601 *et seq.*) was of limited scope, directed mainly at the assistance of financial institutions (including banks and insurance companies) and of railroads. It was thought that aid to these strategic enterprises, many of which were under severe pressure at the time, would forestall the spread of unemployment. However, as financial and industrial difficulties became more insistent the need for a full-scale business lending program gathered force. A policy of aid granted at key points—at the top, as it were, of the economic pyramid—was replaced by a policy of supplying credit to business concerns generally. In 1934 the RFC was authorized to make loans directly to business where funds were not available from private lenders, and the Federal Reserve Banks were empowered, under Section 13b of the Federal Reserve Act, to undertake a similar program of direct lending.[1] The various extensions and revisions of RFC's lending authority and the precise nature of the financial assistance extended are described at some length in Appendix B. In compact form the variety of RFC's credit activities—through which from 1934 till its dissolution in 1953 the corporation disbursed $15 billion in direct business lending alone, apart from its loan

---

[1] Section 13b of the Federal Reserve Act and Section 5d of the Reconstruction Finance Act were both added to the original statutes by acts of June 19, 1934 (44 Stat. 1105, Ch. 653, and 48 Stat. 1108-1109, respectively).

It is interesting to note that in the hearings that prefaced the adoption of Section 13b the Federal Reserve authorities sponsored a more novel arrangement which would have provided for the extension of business credits by federally sponsored "industrial banks."

guaranteeing functions—has been shown in the listing in Chapter 1.

In the field of business lending, the year 1934 was notable also for the establishment of the Export-Import Bank of Washington. The bank was set up under Section 2 of Title I of the National Industrial Recovery Act (48 Stat. 195) with the specific purpose of helping finance trade between the United States and Soviet Russia. The bank did no business, however, on the ground that it could not do so as long as the settlement of debts and claims between the United States and the Soviet Union was still pending, and another institution, the Export-Import Bank of Washington, D.C., was also created in 1934. The initial purpose of this second bank was to promote trade between the United States and Cuba, but its functions were later extended to all countries except the Soviet Union. With the breakdown of debt settlement negotiations between the United States and Russia in 1935, the second bank was discontinued and all operations were concentrated in the Export-Import Bank of Washington. Over the years the Export-Import Bank has functioned primarily to finance exports of agricultural and industrial equipment, notably heavy machinery. Volumewise, among public institutions lending to business in the period under review it was second only to RFC, with loans financing trade with American firms totaling $4.6 billion from 1934 through 1953. Its original common stock of $1 million was subscribed by the Treasury, and preferred stock in much larger amount was taken up by the Reconstruction Finance Corporation. The Export-Import Bank Act of 1945 increased the bank's capitalization to $1 billion wholly subscribed by the Treasury. Not only by the source of its funds but also in management the bank is directly attached to the federal government, its original board of trustees and currently its president being appointed directly by the President.

The prospect of very large amounts of war production work on a basis that presented difficult credit problems led to an important innovation in finance early in World War II. This was Regulation V of the Board of Governors of the Federal Reserve System under which the War and Navy Departments and the U.S. Maritime Commission guaranteed loans to war contractors by any lending agency, including the Federal Reserve Banks and the RFC. The regulation was issued April 6, 1942 under Executive Order 9112, dated March 26, 1942, and the program which it authorized was carried out by the Federal Reserve Banks as agents for the contracting services. The loans made under this original regulation were known as V loans; subsequently (September 1, 1943) the regulation was amended to permit the guarantee of loans made partially to replenish working capital upon the termination of war contracts, the so-called VT loan; and finally (September 1944) it was revised to permit the guarantee of loans exclusively to liquidate working capital tied up in terminated government contracts, the so-called T loans (authorized by the Contract Settlement Act of 1944).[2] Also under the revised authority of 1944, loans for production purposes or for a combination of production and termination financing purposes were made available, known as 1944-V loans.

This program carried into a new field, and extended to a very large volume of financing operations, the procedures of loan insurance first developed for real estate mortgages. Its effect, of course, was to meet enormous financing needs without recourse to direct government financing, though the inapplicability of the program to the financing of plant and equipment forced the government to enter that field through other and more direct measures, such as the construction and leasing of facilities by the Defense Plants Corporation and the direct extension of credits by the RFC and the Smaller War Plants Corporation.

In 1944 the Veterans' Administration was empowered to guarantee small term loans to veterans for establishing or expanding a business, and in December 1945 a reserve account form of loan insurance was added to the program.

The Defense Production Act of 1950 (64 Stat. 932) placed renewed emphasis on lending and loan guaranteeing activities related to the government's procurement and stock-piling operations for national defense. Both the RFC and the Export-Import Bank were directed by Executive Order 10281 of August 27, 1951 to make loans and to participate with other lenders in making loans to private business enterprises for plant expansion, technological development, and production of essential materials (including metals and minerals) upon certification of essentiality by the Defense Production Administration—currently the Office of Defense Mobilization—or any other designated federal agency, as provided by Sections 302 and 304 of the Defense Production Act of 1950. Guarantees by government pro-

---

[2] A summary of the programs is given in "Financing War Production and Contract Terminations under Regulation V," in the *Federal Reserve Bulletin*, March 1946, pp. 240–248, and in the technical paper "A Statistical Study of Regulation V Loans," by Susan S. Burr and Elizabeth B. Sette (Board of Governors of the Federal Reserve System, 1950).

curement agencies of such loans made by public or private financing institutions were also authorized, by Section 301 of the act, using the facilities of the Federal Reserve Banks and under the conditions and terms established by Regulation V of World War II.

The legislation terminating the lending powers of the RFC (Public Law 163, 83rd Cong., July 30, 1953) also provided for the creation of the Small Business Administration to make loans—including immediate and deferred participation loans—to small business firms, and to make disaster loans.

Federal financial aid to business firms, in contrast with that to farmers and homeowners, has been extended almost entirely through direct rather than federally sponsored agencies. The Federal Reserve Banks are the only quasi-public agency involved; and although their services as agents for various federal agencies in the Regulation V and Defense Production Act programs were administratively important, loans to business from their own funds have been of comparatively small volume. Chart 11 makes that plain, and shows how the credit of the federal agencies lending to business was concentrated in a relatively few years: 1919–1921, 1932–1935, 1942–1947, and 1952–1953. Chart 12 shows the shifting importance of the major agencies, with RFC supplying in 1932–1935 and during World War II nearly two-thirds of the total disbursed, whereas in 1946 and 1947, and again in 1952–1953, the Export-Import Bank accounted for upwards of three-fourths of the total.

The course of federal credit activities directed to the financial sector of the economy (apart from Federal Reserve Bank credit to member banks of the Federal Reserve System)[3] has been uneven, as Chart 13 shows. The first noteworthy phase was short-lived, being restricted to the early 1930's. In this period RFC loans were made on a large scale mainly to banks and insurance companies, primarily to alleviate distress caused by depression conditions. Almost concurrently, the RFC carried out a substantial program of stock purchases in banks and insurance companies, and lesser programs of the same type were directed to the financial assistance of savings and loan associations by the United States Treasury and, after 1934,

[3] Advances to, and rediscounts for, member banks are not regarded as coming within the scope of the present study because, as was pointed out in Chapter 1, in connection with them the primary purpose of the Federal Reserve Banks is to influence general credit conditions through changes in member bank reserve balances and not to provide a financing service in a sense comparable to what is aimed at by the various agencies whose activities are included in our study.

by the Home Owners' Loan Corporation (the two combined accounting for about one-seventh of the associations' total capital investment in 1932–1935).

In the second phase the principal activity consisted of lending by the federally sponsored Federal Home Loan Banks to their member institutions, mainly savings and loan associations. Quite in contrast to the programs of the early thirties, which had as their object the support of faltering financial institutions, Home Loan Bank loans to member institutions in recent years have served mainly to enable prospering savings and loan associations to increase their lending activity during a period of general economic expansion. Since 1950, federal assistance to financial institutions has consisted exclusively of these loans by the Federal Home Loan Banks, now almost altogether owned by their member associations.

Home Loan Bank lending ultimately affects the housing sector of the economy and will be discussed in the next chapter. With no other public or quasi-public agency currently extending credit to financial institutions (apart from the excluded Federal Reserve operations), the two following sections—on credit services and on lending experience—will be limited to federal financial activities in the field of business.

Services and Credit Terms

American business enterprises have traditionally made use of a number of different credit services, for each of which there has existed one or more supplying institutions and a more or less well-developed market. Among these services have been long-term loans, usually secured by mortgage or pledge of real estate or securities by the borrower; medium-term loans, running from one to ten years to maturity, and either secured or unsecured; short-term loans of less than one year's duration, usually unsecured and used principally for the conduct of current operations; trade or mercantile credit, obtained from suppliers and repayable within short periods of time. In addition, American businesses have used a limited amount of credit insurance, supplied by specialized underwriters and, in a somewhat different form, by factoring and commercial financing houses that purchase business accounts receivable without recourse.[4]

[4] For a description of these business credit services and markets as of around 1946, see *Business Finance and Banking* by Neil H. Jacoby and Raymond J. Saulnier (National Bureau of Economic Research, Financial Research Program, 1947).

CHART 11

Federal Credit for Business, 1918–1953

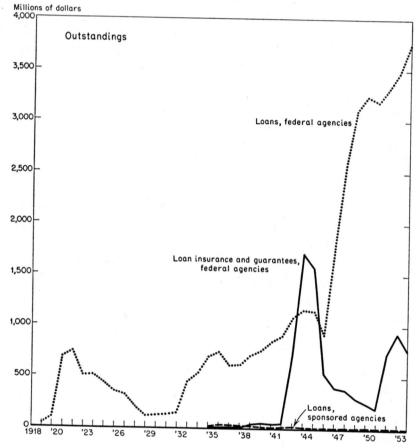

Millions of dollars

Outstandings

Loans, federal agencies

Loan insurance and guarantees, federal agencies

Loans, sponsored agencies

The task of comparing the credit services available through federal agencies with those customarily obtained from private financial institutions is considerably simplified by the fact that public agencies have confined their business credit activities preponderantly to lending on medium term and to the guaranty and insurance of such loans made by private financial institutions. In this connection it may be asked: What types of credit services have been provided and to what types of businesses? What unusual or unique economic functions have been served by federal credits to business? How have public and private agencies cooperated in business credit activities?

In dealing with these questions, attention will be focused upon the

CHART 11 (concluded)

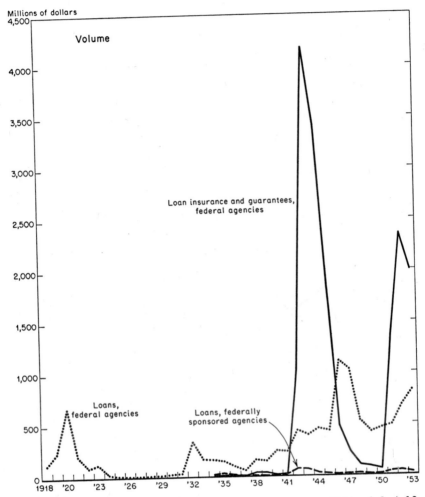

Millions of dollars

Volume

Loan insurance and guarantees, federal agencies

Loans, federal agencies

Loans, federally sponsored agencies

From Table A-5. For data on the components of the series, see Tables A-9, A-10, A-12 to A-14, A-16, A-18, A-21, A-27, A-30, A-32, and A-33.

operations of the five major federal agencies and one federally sponsored agency having active business credit programs in the early 1950's; namely, the Reconstruction Finance Corporation,[5] the Veterans' Administration, the Export-Import Bank, the Maritime Ad-

[5] Public Law 163, 83rd Congress, enacted July 30, 1953, terminated all lending powers of the RFC under Section 4 of the RFC Act as amended, effective September 28, 1953. Executive Order 10489 transferred all powers, duties and functions of RFC under the Defense Production Act of 1950 to the Secretary of the Treasury, effective September 29, 1953.

CHART 12

Business Loans, Loan Guarantees, and Loan Insurance by Principal Federal and Federally Sponsored Agencies, 1932–1953

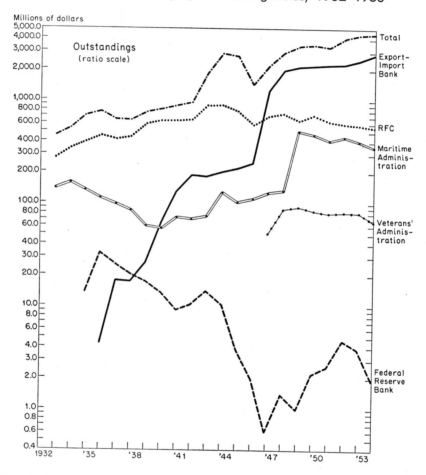

From Tables A-5, A-9, A-10, A-16, A-18, A-27, and A-30.

Total outstandings include, besides those of the federally sponsored Federal Reserve Banks and of the several direct federal agencies shown, those of the following direct agencies: the Director General of Railroads and the Interstate Commerce Commission in 1932–1953; the War Finance Corporation in 1932–1934; the Public Works Administration in 1934–1950; the Housing and Home Finance Agency in 1950–1953; the War and Navy Departments and U.S. Maritime Commission (including Regulation V and defense production guarantees) in 1942–1953; the Department of Commerce, the General Services Administration, and the Atomic Energy Commission (guarantees under the Defense Production Act of 1950) in 1951–1953. RFC totals include loans of the Smaller War Plants Corporation outstanding from 1942 on.

CHART 12 (concluded)

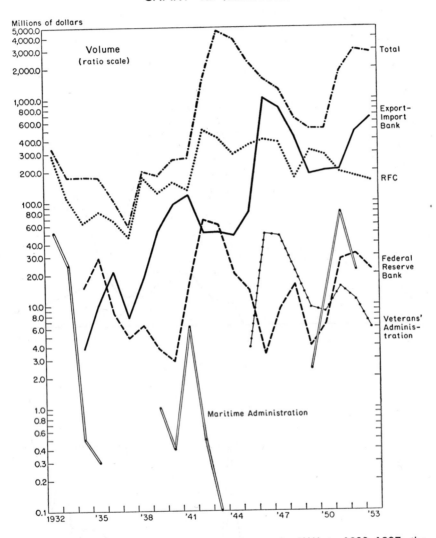

Total volume covers, besides the agencies shown: the PWA in 1933–1937; the HHFA in 1950–1953; the Department of Defense in 1942–1953; the War and Navy Departments and U.S. Maritime Commission in 1942–1946; and the Department of Commerce, the GSA, and the AEC in 1951–1953. RFC totals include loans of the Smaller War Plants Corporation for 1942 through 1946.

CHART 13

Federal Credit for Financial Institutions, 1918–1953

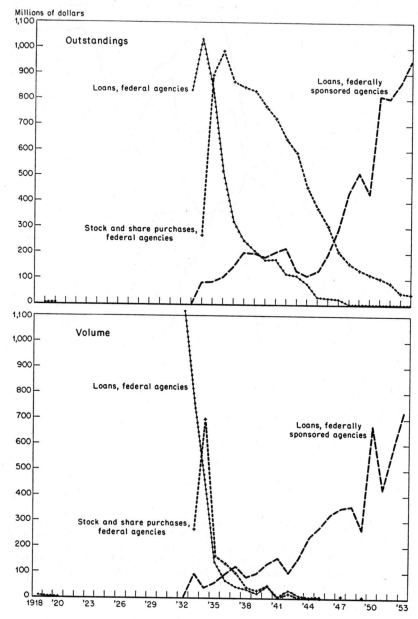

From Table A-6. For data on the components of the series, see Tables A-9, A-11, A-12, A-17 and A-19.

ministration, the Small Business Administration,[6] and the Federal Reserve Banks.

These six agencies offered one or more of three types of credit services, mainly within the medium-term credit field: (1) direct loans, (2) guarantees of parts of loans made by private lending institutions, and (3) insurance against loss on loans made by private agencies. All except the VA have had power to lend money directly to businesses. All of them have also been empowered to offer loan guarantees by agreeing to take up a specified part (ranging up to 90 percent) of business loans made by banks or other private institutions upon default or upon demand by the private lenders concerned. In addition, the Veterans' Administration has insured certain private lenders against loss—up to the limits of a reserve fund built up in a fashion similar to FHA Title I loan insurance reserves—on small term loans made to eligible veterans for business purposes. The volume of these various activities, and the outstanding amounts of loans and loan insurance or guaranty extended under them, were shown in Charts 11 and 12.

The federal agencies have also acted as advisers and clearinghouses of financial information for businesses, especially small firms, and have provided stand-by sources of credit. For example, RFC received and disposed of nearly 336,000 different inquiries from businesses during a sixteen-month period ending October 31, 1947. Among them 68,000 pertained to business loans and 197,000 to miscellaneous matters, such as financial, management, engineering and accounting advice, and RFC policies.[7] In many instances RFC referred inquiries to commercial banks or aided businessmen in framing their applications to commercial banks. In rendering such assistance and by serving as a *potential* source of credit the RFC, and other federal agencies that have performed similar functions,[8] undoubtedly exerted an im-

---

[6] The Small Business Administration began operations in October 1953 in accordance with the provisions of the Small Business Act of 1953 (Public Law 163). Therefore it seems appropriate to include it wherever possible in a discussion of credit terms and policies, at the same time noting that its lending program—in terms of loan disbursements—first became active in early 1954.

[7] *Hearings* before a Subcommittee of the Committee on Banking and Currency, U.S. Senate, on S. Res. 132, "A Resolution for an Inquiry into the Operation of the Reconstruction Finance Corporation and Its Subsidiaries," Part 2, 80th Cong., 2nd sess., January 1948, Exhibit 37, pp. 455ff.

[8] One of the responsibilities delegated to the newly formed Small Business Administration by the Congress was that of helping small business obtain competent management, technical, and production counsel and also a fair share of government procurement contracts. For a brief resume of progress under these

portant indirect influence on the business credit market, wholly apart from the loan funds disbursed or the insurance or guaranty commitments made.

CHARACTERISTICS OF THE BUSINESSES SERVED

Indirect but significant evidence on the size of the businesses served by federal credit programs is at hand in comparative data of loan size. Excepting small business loans guaranteed or insured by the Veterans' Administration, the loans made or protected by public agencies have been predominantly of medium size. The average size of bank term loans to business during 1946 was about $27,000.[9] In contrast, loans disbursed by the RFC during 1934–1951 averaged $72,300;[10] Export-Import Bank loan authorizations over the same period averaged more than $1 million;[11] the average amount of Federal Reserve Bank industrial loans approved through 1950 was $176,000;[12] and loans by the Smaller War Plants Corporation (September 1942 through December 1945) averaged $103,000.[13] Bank loans made with immediate or deferred participation by RFC (that is, those authorized up to mid-1947) averaged $138,700.[14]

The concentration of federal activities in the field of medium-sized loans is forcefully revealed in Table 44. Of commercial bank term loans to business firms in 1946, less than one-tenth were for individual amounts of $25,000 to $500,000. But considerably larger fractions of federal loans and guarantees were of that size—fractions ranging from one-third for direct business loans made by the RFC in 1934–1951 to more than three-fifths of all business loans approved by the Small Business Administration in the ten months to July 31, 1954.

programs through July 31, 1954 see the *Second Semi-Annual Report* of the Small Business Administration, of that date, pp. 53ff.

[9] Duncan McC. Holthausen, "Term Lending to Business by Commercial Banks in 1946," *Federal Reserve Bulletin*, May 1947, Table 6, p. 505. During the year ended November 20, 1946, an estimated 119,900 loans totaling $3,242 million were made.

[10] From the National Bureau of Economic Research sample survey of direct loans made under RFC's regular lending authority (i.e., apart from wartime powers), reported in Appendix B (Table B-1).

[11] *Semiannual Reports* of the bank.

[12] *Federal Reserve Bulletin*, December 1951, p. 1541. Up to December 31, 1950, 3,698 applications had been approved for a total amount of $651,389,000.

[13] Douglas R. Fuller, *Government Financing of Private Enterprise*, Stanford University Press, 1948, Table 6, p. 151.

[14] From Table B-36; based on the National Bureau of Economic Research compilation of all RFC participation loans except those made under blanket participation agreements or in the Small Loan Participation program.

TABLE 44

Size Distributions of RFC Business Loans, Small Business Administration Loans, Regulation V Loan Guarantees, and Commercial Bank Term Loans to Business

SIZE OF LOAN[a]	NUMBER OF LOANS					AMOUNT AUTHORIZED OR DISBURSED				
	Member Bank Loans	RFC Participations	RFC Direct Loans	Regulation V Loans	SBA Loans	Member Bank Loans	RFC Participations	RFC Direct Loans	Regulation V Loans	SBA Loans
Under $5,000	65.3%	11.1%	28.3%	10.5%	2.5%	4.1%	0.3%	1.0%	0.1%	0.2%
$5,000–9,999	13.9	13.5	14.5		8.6	3.2	0.8	1.3		1.3
10,000–24,999	10.7	22.3	21.7	8.7	25.4	5.1	3.0	4.2	0.2	8.3
25,000–49,999	4.1	16.4	13.2	12.3	21.8	4.2	4.7	5.7	0.5	14.8
50,000–99,999	2.5	16.5	12.0	36.1	26.1	5.0	9.6	9.8	5.0	36.0
100,000–499,999	2.4	15.8	8.2	12.5	15.6b	16.3	26.7	19.0	4.9	39.4b
500,000–999,999	0.6	2.2	1.1	19.9	…	12.4	11.7	9.5	89.3	…
1 million and over	0.5	2.1	1.0		…	49.8	43.2	49.5		…
Total	100.0%	100.0%	100.0%	100.0%	100.0%	100.0%	100.0%	100.0%	100.0%	100.0%

RFC direct loans refer to disbursements through December 1951 on loans authorized from 1934 through mid-1951, from Table B-2. RFC participations refer to authorizations from 1934 through mid-1947, from Table B-40. Bank term loans refer to transactions between November 1945 and November 1946 and cover amounts still outstanding at the latter time, from "Term Lending to Business by Commercial Banks in 1946," by Duncan McC. Holthausen, Federal Reserve Bulletin, May 1947, Table 6, p. 505. V-loan guarantees cover authorizations from 1942 through mid-1946 and refer to number of borrowers rather than of loans (with borrowers receiving a number of authorizations classified only once and then under the size class of their largest authorization), from A Statistical Study of Regulation V Loans, by Susan S. Burr and Elizabeth B. Sette (Board of Governors of the Federal Reserve System, 1950), Table 11, p. 35. Small Business Administration loans cover direct business loans and participations approved from September 28, 1953 through July 31, 1954, from the Second Semi-Annual Report of the Small Business Administration, July 31, 1954, p. 45.

a Distributions for RFC participation loans and for SBA loans are for the following class intervals: $5,000 and under; $5,001 to $10,000; $10,001 to $25,000, etc., to over $1 million. Size is based on amount authorized, except that bank loans are classified by size of outstanding balance.

b Covers loans up to $300,000.

These figures are impressive despite the imperfect comparability of the different loan groups.[15]

Outside the medium loan size range, differences between the public credit institutions and the commercial banks were greater in the small than in the large size ranges. Ninety percent of commercial bank term loans were in amounts under $25,000. The comparable figure for the Small Business Administration was only 37 percent; for RFC participations, 47 percent; for loans made solely by RFC, 65 percent. At the upper end of the size scale, the distribution by amount shows commercial banks and RFC each with about half their credit in loans of $1 million and over. The V-loan guarantee program, geared to aid large key war industries, extended 90 percent of its credit in amounts of $1 million or more; and virtually the entire portfolios of the Export-Import Bank and the Maritime Administration also consisted of very large loans.

It may be concluded, then, that with the single exception of the business loans guaranteed or insured by the Veterans' Administration—most of which were (for statutory reasons) concentrated within the $1,000 to $5,000 size bracket[16]—federal credit services have been directed to the middle ranges in the business-size spectrum. They have not been instrumentalities predominantly for the financing of small business. This conclusion is confirmed in the case of RFC by an analysis of the size of business firms receiving credit benefits, included in Appendix B. By and large, federal agencies have not found it feasible to make large numbers of small loans to small enterprises because of the high administrative costs per dollar of credit extended which such operations entail.[17]

Compared with the medium-term credits supplied by the commercial banking system, those provided by federal agencies have tended to be concentrated among manufacturing businesses. This has been true of all federal programs with the exception of the Veterans' Administration, which, being focused wholly on very small ventures, has been concentrated among retail trade and service

---

[15] For instance, all the SBA loans and guarantees and many of the RFC direct loans were made during the inflationary period from 1947 on, whereas the bank loans, the RFC participations, and the V-loan guarantees stem partly or entirely from earlier periods. V-loan data refer to number of borrowers rather than of loans and are biased upward as to size.

[16] See Appendix Table C-11 for a distribution of VA-guaranteed business loans made from May through October 1947 according to purchase price of assets acquired with the loan proceeds.

[17] See the testimony of an RFC official, footnote 59, Appendix B.

businesses where small size is characteristic.[18] Table 45 presents comparisons of RFC participation loans, RFC direct loans, Federal Reserve Bank industrial loans, Small Business Administration loans, and commercial bank term loans according to the industry of the borrower involved. Manufacturing firms formed about 9 percent of the total number of operating businesses in the United States in 1949. Yet as much as 60 percent of all RFC participation loans, 48 percent of RFC direct loans, and 57 percent of Federal Reserve Bank loans and of Small Business Administration loans were made to manufacturing enterprises; and in line with the special purpose of the program, more than nine out of every ten V-loan guarantees authorized from April 1942 to June 1946 applied to a manufacturing credit.[19] The majority of Export-Import Bank credits also went to finance capital goods exports by American manufacturing firms, even where the loan was made directly to a foreign government or corporation. On the other hand, only 14.6 percent of commercial bank term loans went to the manufacturing segment of business. Retail trade and service firms—which comprise 64 percent of all operating businesses in 1949—were numerically much more important users of commercial bank term credit and comparatively unimportant users of the credit services of federal agencies.

One reason is that the risks of term lending have been, on the average, greater with manufacturing than with trade, service, or financial firms because the commitment to fixed assets is relatively greater, the term to maturity of the required credit is longer, fluctuations of profits are wider, and the impacts of technological changes and economic fluctuations are more severe. A contributing factor was the very severe erosion of working capital suffered by many medium and small American manufacturing firms during the thirties. As a result, proportionately more manufacturing firms have been ultra-marginal to private lenders and have sought public credit.

GEOGRAPHICAL DISTRIBUTION OF CREDIT

Federal credit services appear to have exerted a pull on the regional distribution of economic resources generally toward the South Atlantic, Gulf, and Pacific Coastal regions, and away from the earlier-developed areas of the nation—New England, and the

[18] See Appendix Table C-17 for a distribution of VA-guaranteed business loans made in 1949–1950 by industry of borrower.
[19] Burr and Sette, op.cit., Table 8, p. 28.

TABLE 45

Industry Distributions of RFC Business Loans, Federal Reserve Bank Industrial Loans, and Small Business Administration Loans, with Those of Commercial Bank Term Loans and of All Operating Businesses

INDUSTRY	ALL U.S. BUSINESS FIRMS	NUMBER OF LOANS					AMOUNT AUTHORIZED OR DISBURSED			
		Member Bank Loans	RFC Participations	RFC Direct Loans	FRB Loans	SBA Loans	Member Bank Loans	RFC Participations	RFC Loans	SBA Loans
Manufacturing and mining[a]	8.9%	14.6%	60.4%	48.0%	57.0%	56.6%	52.0%	71.7%	76.2%	61.8%
Construction	8.4	5.3	6.9	6.3	3.0	5.0	1.4	7.0	3.0	5.2
Wholesale trade	5.1	6.8	4.9	4.6	11.0	}	4.9	6.5	1.4	}
Retail trade	42.7	37.3	13.3	15.5	21.0	21.0	9.0	2.4	2.8	14.5
Transportation, communications, and public utilities[b]	4.8	11.7	6.1	8.3	1.0	10.2	21.1	3.4	8.1	14.4
Services	21.5	16.7	3.9	14.6	5.0	5.4	5.1	1.1	3.0	3.3
Finance, insurance, and real estate[c]	8.7	0.2	3.3	0.5	..	..	1.6	6.7	5.1	..
All other[d]	e	7.4	1.3	2.1	2.0	1.8	4.9	1.2	0.4	0.8
Total	100.0%	100.0%	100.0%	100.0%	100.0%	100.0%	100.0%	100.0%	100.0%	100.0%

RFC direct loans refer to disbursements through December 1951 on loans authorized from 1934 through mid-1951, from Table B-7. RFC participations refer to authorizations from 1934 through mid-1947, from Table B-41. Bank loans refer to term loans outstanding November 20, 1946, from "Term Lending to Business by Commercial Banks in 1946," by Duncan McC. Holthausen, *Federal Reserve Bulletin*, May 1947, Table 2, p. 502. Federal Reserve Bank loans represent the number of applications from January 1, 1935 to May 1, 1940, from "Capital and Credit Requirements of Federal Reserve Industrial Loan Applicants," by Charles L. Merwin, Jr. and Charles H. Schmidt (National Bureau of Economic Research, Financial Research Program, mimeo., 1942), Table A-6, pp. A-7f. Small Business Administration loans, inclusive of immediate and deferred participations, are those approved from September 28, 1953 through July 31, 1954, from the *Second Semi-Annual Report* of the Small Business Administration, July 31, 1954, p. 47. Business firms are those in existence at the end of 1949, from *Survey of Current Business*, January 1952, p. 10.

a Predominantly manufacturing enterprises.
b Data for RFC direct loans exclude railroads.
c Data for banks exclude real estate firms.
d Includes forestry, fishing, and farming (mainly the latter two) for RFC and SBA; for banks, excludes farming but includes real estate and also a few cases unclassified by industry.
e Not covered in the Department of Commerce estimates of the business population.

Middle Atlantic and East North Central states. The tendency of federal business credit to finance firms in areas which are newly industrialized and have gained relatively most rapidly in population and economic wealth during the past generation is evident not only in RFC lending[20] but also in Federal Reserve Bank industrial loans (though not among privately made small business loans guaranteed or insured by the Veterans' Administration). This may betoken a relatively greater lack of private credit facilities in the regions of most rapid growth; it may indicate the presence in these areas of relatively more firms in new industries or other high risk situations. At any rate, disproportionately large numbers of RFC and Federal Reserve Bank loans to business were made in the capital deficit areas of the nation, and disproportionately small numbers in the capital surplus areas such as the New England, the Middle Atlantic, and the East North Central regions.

TERMS TO MATURITY

Federal business credit agencies have functioned predominantly in the medium-term market. At the inception of their business lending operations during the early thirties, RFC and the Federal Reserve Banks made, or facilitated the making, of business loans with longer maturities than were then commonly available from commercial banks, life insurance companies, or other private lenders.[21] After 1934 private lending agencies progressively entered the medium-term business credit market; federal agencies appear to have continued to operate in the more lengthy segment of the market, but this difference between public and private agencies is tending to lessen.

Business loans guaranteed by the Veterans' Administration brought the commercial banking system into a new type of credit operation, namely term lending to new and very small firms. Whereas probably more than three-quarters of the small business loans made by commercial banks are written to mature within a year, virtually no VA-guaranteed business loans have matured in less than ten months.[22]

20 See Appendix Table B-8, which compares the regional distribution of RFC direct business loans disbursed in 1934–1951 with that of all business loans held by commercial banks in 1941 and 1951 and of all operating businesses in 1948.

21 Cf. N. H. Jacoby and R. J. Saulnier, *Term Lending to Business* (National Bureau of Economic Research, Financial Research Program, 1942), pp. 24f.

22 See Appendix Table C-12 for a comparison of maturity of distributions for VA-guaranteed business loans and commercial bank term loans to small businesses. Appendix Table B-2 gives comparable data for RFC direct loans to business concerns.

251

Loans guaranteed under Regulation V had original maturities running over one year in about two-fifths of the cases,[23] and the Export-Import Bank has been concerned primarily with the provision of medium-term credit, nearly 70 percent of the loans outstanding at the end of 1953 having original maturities of ten years or less.[24]

CREDIT POLICIES

A basic policy of all federal agencies lending to business has been to provide credit only to firms unable to procure it from the usual sources on reasonable terms. The agencies interpreted this to mean an inability on the part of the prospective borrower to obtain funds at conventional rates from the commercial banks with which it ordinarily dealt, and they have faithfully sought to avoid making loans that such commercial banks would make.[25] This policy has defined in part the class of business borrowers with which federal agencies would deal—firms which were ultra-marginal credit risks or which lacked local banking connections.

Federal statutes have embodied other credit standards as well. The RFC statute required that loans should be "so secured or of such sound value as reasonably to assure repayment," and in practice the agency required that adequate collateral security be supplied. RFC totally eschewed unsecured lending.[26]

Industrial advances by the Federal Reserve Banks were also required to be "on a reasonable and sound basis," and this was interpreted by most banks to mean full collateralization. On V loans, the commercial bank concerned ordinarily relied on the government contract as collateral. Export-Import Bank loans usually involved collateral or endorsement, and the Maritime Administration's ship loans have been secured by first mortgages. By law, the Veterans' Administration might guarantee or insure a small business loan to a veteran only if the experience and ability of the veteran were such that there was a "reasonable likelihood" that he would be successful,

---

[23] Burr and Sette, op.cit., Table 18, p. 50.

[24] Seventeenth Semiannual Report, Export-Import Bank of Washington, July–December 1953, Appendix C.

[25] RFC and Federal Reserve Banks did not insist that credit be "unavailable" from other lenders than commercial banks, or from other commercial banks than those in the applicant's community. Nor did they require the applicant to show an inability to obtain equity funds.

[26] See Hearings before a Subcommittee of the Committee on Banking and Currency, 81st Cong., 2nd sess., May 8 and 9, 1950, on A Study of the Operations of the Reconstruction Finance Corporation pursuant to S. Res. 219. Analysis of Income and Costs, statement of Harvey L. Gunderson.

and only if the purchase price paid by the veteran for business property or for the cost of constructing such property did not exceed "the reasonable value thereof" as determined by a VA-designated appraiser.[27] The law also requires that realty loans be secured by a first mortgage, and that loans for machinery, equipment, working capital, good will, or intangibles be secured by personalty "to the extent legal and practicable." It is clear that Congress has intended that the normal banking measures be taken to assure repayment or recovery of funds disbursed.

The question naturally arises: If loans by federal agencies were supposed to be sufficiently secured to assure repayment, why were not the business enterprises using their services in a position to satisfy their requirements from private sources? Why did they come to federal agencies? One answer would seem to be that the adequacy of security is a matter open to a wide range of judgments; federal agencies were expected—and frequently were able—to take a more liberal view of the value of collateral than could private bankers.

Moreover, some firms which were unquestionably worthy of private credit lacked local banking facilities altogether, or lacked facilities that were adequate to their needs. A questionnaire mailed to more than 15,000 commercial banks by the Subcommittee of the Senate Committee on Banking and Currency investigating the RFC in 1947 brought forth these significant findings: Of the nearly 8,000 banks which responded, half reported that they had refused to make some business loans which appeared to be sound credit risks. Several reasons were given, of which the most frequent were: the loan exceeded the bank's legal limit; the requested maturity was too long; the bank lacked experience with the requested type of loan, or the applicant was launching a new enterprise.[28] Behind these reasons lay the restrictions on risk assumption imposed by banking laws and bank examining officers, and the need for liquidity imposed by the slender capital resources and the high ratio of demand deposits which characterize American banking. The inquiry indicated that ordinarily RFC did not make types of loans that banks were not making; rather, it took *higher risk* loans than many banks could,

[27] Veterans' Administration, *Lenders' Handbook*, December 1948, supplementary pp. 3.5f., citing 38 U.S.C. 694C.
[28] *Hearings* . . . on S. Res. 132, Part 1, 80th Cong., 1st. sess., December 1947, pp. 253ff.

or would, make.[29] The same appears to have been true of the working capital loans made by Federal Reserve Banks, the exporter credits of the Export-Import Bank, and the ship purchase or construction loans of the Maritime Administration. In the case of the Veterans' Administration, the existence of loan guaranty or insurance, by reducing exposure to risk of loss, doubtless induced many banks to make loans they would not otherwise have made.

In his study of the operations of Export-Import Bank from 1934 through 1947, Marsh reached the conclusion that the bank had faithfully followed the statutory injunction "not to compete with private capital," and had financed export transactions for which private credit was not available, either because of the high trading risk or the high risk of inability to transfer funds from the foreign buyer's country.[30]

Another business credit policy apparently followed by most federal agencies was not to lend money primarily for the purpose of enabling a firm to refund or repay other debts. Federal credit was supposed to fulfill the primary purpose of financing new activity, and not to bail out private credit institutions from loans of questionable collectibility.[31] Nevertheless, a material fraction of the funds provided by federal business credit agencies was used to repay or retire existing debt, sometimes in order to relieve a borrower's property of prior liens so that the federal agency itself could obtain a first lien. Thus, the proceeds of about one-fifth of RFC's direct business loans, aggregating more than one-third of the funds disbursed, were so utilized.[32] Comparison with an analysis of the use of the proceeds of commercial bank term loans to business firms

[29] This appears to have been the thought expressed by John D. Goodloe in testimony as chairman of RFC before the Special Subcommittee of the Senate Committee on Banking and Currency. He stated that apart from long-term credit to small firms "we know of no important general classification [of business] that is unable to obtain private credit. However, there will always be a lack of credit for concerns which fall within the lower level of desirability from the risk standpoint." Cf. *Hearings* just cited, p. 35.

[30] Donald B. Marsh, *The Export-Import Bank of Washington* (Department of Financial and Business Research, Chase National Bank of New York, mimeo., May 5, 1947), p. 43.

[31] The official instructions of RFC to its loan agency managers stated: "Generally, a loan should not be made for the primary purpose of discharging an existing indebtedness, except for the purpose of paying income taxes on a compromise basis. There may be circumstances, however, under which a reasonable portion of a loan may be used for discharging an indebtedness, but no part should be used to pay off a bank or other financial institution in liquidation or to reduce existing indebtedness of slow or questionable nature."

[32] See Appendix Table B-3.

outstanding June 30, 1941 indicates that RFC credits and private term credit were used for about the same purposes.[33]

Proportionately more of federal credit has performed the function of financing new ventures than of private credit. It is estimated that about one in seven of the direct business loans made by RFC went to enterprises that were yet to be established at time of loan authorization. Among these loans were such well-publicized venture financing operations as Kaiser Steel Company, Carthage Hydrocol Inc., and Lustron Corporation. RFC was also active in financing firms in relatively new industries—including motor courts, cold storage lockers, alfalfa dehydrators, and bottled gas—where private credit was difficult to obtain because of the novelty of the industry and the lack of data and experience for appraising risks. VA-guaranteed business loans were, of course, entirely for the purpose of enabling veterans to establish or expand their own businesses. Most veterans used the proceeds of loans to purchase going concerns or to expand established ventures; about 35 percent of the proceeds of loans closed between April 26 and October 25, 1947 were to start a business.[34]

CREDIT STANDARDS

In applying the statutory credit policies, federal business credit agencies have examined many more applications for loans, loan insurance, or loan guaranty than they have approved. Over the period 1934 to mid-1951, RFC received about 88,000 applications for business loans (covering both direct loans and participation loans exclusive of blanket participation agreements), of which it approved about 47,000, or 53 percent. The percentage of approvals to applications received rose as high as 74 percent during the first war year, 1942, and fell as low as 41 percent during 1949, reflecting variations in economic conditions, in the percentage of applications withdrawn, and in RFC's policy regarding acceptance of applications, as well as variations in the rigor with which applications were scrutinized.[35] Up to May 31, 1940, Federal Reserve Banks had approved only 2,900 or 30 percent of the 9,590 applications for business loans received by them.[36]

[33] Cf. N. H. Jacoby and R. J. Saulnier, *Term Lending to Business*, pp. 51f.
[34] See Appendix Table C-15.   [35] From material supplied by the RFC.
[36] Charles L. Merwin, Jr. and Charles H. Schmidt, *Capital and Credit Requirements of Federal Reserve Bank Industrial Loan Applicants* (National Bureau of Economic Research, Financial Research Program, mimeo., 1942), Tables A-2 and A-8, pp. A-3 and A-11.

In examining the differences in financial characteristics between samples of approved and rejected loan applicants for Federal Reserve Bank loans, Merwin and Schmidt found that the approved applicants ran larger in asset size, were more heavily weighted by manufacturing concerns, were somewhat more profitable (or less unprofitable), and were somewhat less indebted than were the rejected applicants.[37] Trends in financial ratios were less favorable for the rejected than for the approved applicants. This appears to indicate that the primary reason for rejecting applications was failure of the applicant to meet minimal financial standards of the Federal Reserve Banks; not availability of private credit, or other reasons. Systematic information as to why RFC, VA, and other federal agencies declined applications for credit services is not available, but scattered evidence suggests that failure to meet the credit standards of the public agency was predominant. Data on a small sample of applications rejected by RFC, for example, reveal that "insufficient collateral," "earning ability not demonstrated," "excessive debt retirement," "inexperienced management," "insufficient equity investment," and "promotional venture" were the reasons most frequently assigned.[38]

The financial trends and ratios of firms borrowing from RFC are known from a sample of the loans; and although comparable data for commercial bank term loans are lacking,[39] some inferences as to comparative credit standards may be drawn. Nearly half of the RFC loans were made to businesses whose current ratio (current assets/current liabilities) in the fiscal year preceding the date of loan application was less than the two-to-one standard generally regarded as minimal by commercial banks. Moreover, a fifth of the number and about one-third of the amount of RFC loans went to firms with a net-worth-to-debt ratio of *less* than one-to-one, whereas the average ratio for American business as a whole is about two-to-one.[40] Finally, about two-thirds of the number and amount of loans went to firms rated "good" or "fair" by Dun and Bradstreet, while

[37] *Ibid.*, p. 8.

[38] *Hearings* . . . on S. Res. 132, Part 2, 80th Cong., 2nd sess., January 1948, p. 459.

[39] The publications of Robert Morris Associates contain aggregates and averages of information about financial ratios and trends of samples of firms submitting their financial statements to commercial banks, but the statistics are not in a form which facilitates comparison with federal agency credit standards.

[40] Based on a distribution in which nearly 20 percent of the loans went to firms failing to report financial data of this type. Many of these doubtless had low net-worth-to-debt ratios. See Appendix Table B-10.

relatively few loans were made to firms rated "high." The conclusion appears justified that the preponderance of borrowers from RFC were at, or under, the margin of creditworthiness, when judged by the ordinary standards of commercial banks.

COOPERATIVE CREDIT ARRANGEMENTS

Part of the effort of public agencies to avoid competition with private credit institutions and to accelerate the flow of credit to business firms has taken the form of cooperative credit relationships. RFC policy was consistently directed toward inducing commercial banks to make business loans by its readiness to enter into immediate or deferred participations. In immediate participations, RFC and a commercial bank each advanced a specified part of the funds under a single loan agreement initiated by either lender. In deferred participations, a bank advanced the total amount of a loan from its own funds, and the RFC agreed to "take up," i.e. to purchase, a specified percentage of the loan upon demand by the bank, in effect guaranteeing to the bank repayment of that portion of the loan. Federal Reserve Banks have entered into similar cooperative arrangements with commercial banks.

The Export-Import Bank and commercial banks have cooperated in several ways. Export-Import Bank has supplied "supplementary credits," in which both it and a commercial bank have lent money to the same exporter; it has at all times made its current portfolio of loans available for purchase by private investors; commercial banks have participated in numerous credits arranged by it; finally, "agency agreements" have been made with commercial banks engaged in financing exports, whereunder the Export-Import Bank has agreed to "take out" or reimburse the lending bank for a specified proportion of the credit on demand—essentially a deferred participation or loan guarantee. Commercial bank credits disbursed at Export-Import Bank risk under agency agreements represented about 19 percent of the total of EIB loans and guarantees made from February 12, 1934 to December 31, 1946.[41]

The V-loan program and the business credit activities of the Veterans' Administration were, of course, entirely cooperative in character. Material on the characteristics of business loans made with RFC participation, of those made cooperatively by Federal Reserve

41 Cf. Marsh, *op.cit.*, pp. 44–47.

Banks, and of those guaranteed under Regulation V and under the VA program, follows.

Of the 47,000 business loans separately authorized by RFC under its regular and wartime powers from 1934 to mid-1951, some 15,100, or nearly one-third, involved cooperation with commercial banks. Another 11,100 participation loans were authorized under Blanket Participation Agreements arranged during the reconversion years 1945 and 1946. Our information on loan and borrower characteristics concerns mainly the ordinary (rather than the BPA) participations.

A study of the approximately 6,000 ordinary participation loans authorized during the thirteen years from 1934 through mid-1947 (a period for which information on the participating banks was readily available)—involving gross loan amounts of about $828 million for 2,018 different commercial banks—revealed these salient facts:[42]

1. The great majority of participations carried a deferred rather than an immediate commitment.

2. More participation loans involved an RFC risk of 75 percent of the total loan than any other percentage. The volume of participation lending would probably have been much less if RFC had not been the major partner in carrying the risks.

3. Participation loans were preponderantly of medium and large size; they averaged larger than loans made by RFC on its own account, and much larger than the term loans made by banks without participation. Clearly, they were not a device for financing small business.

4. The industrial and regional distributions of participation loans resembled those of direct RFC loans.

5. The banks which utilized participation facilities tended to be well-established institutions of medium and large size, with national charters or Federal Reserve membership, located in medium and large-sized cities. About one-eighth of the banks in the nation were involved. Participation was demonstrably not a measure utilized principally by small banks in small communities to aid in the meeting of local credit demands.

6. There was a considerable measure of concentration in the use of participation facilities: a third of the number and half of the

[42] See Appendix B for supporting tabular material and a more detailed treatment of the findings.

amount of loans authorized from 1934 through mid-1947 involved RFC participations with only 99 banks. On the other hand, more than half the banks that participated with RFC did so on only one occasion.

7. Because a quarter of the number of all participation loans were in amounts which exceeded the legal loan limit of the creditor bank, one may infer that an important motivation for banks in seeking RFC guarantees was the opportunity, when most of the risk on a business loan could be shifted to a public agency by paying a relatively small fee, to make larger loans than the regulatory laws or prudent bank management policies of asset diversification would otherwise permit.

The most important post-World War II venture of public agencies into the guaranteeing or insuring of business loans for commercial banks was the blanket participation (BPA) program, begun by RFC in March 1945 in an effort to provide ample reconversion credit and to forestall anticipated mass unemployment. A commercial bank that negotiated a blanket agreement with RFC was, in effect, automatically assured of a deferred participation by RFC of up to 75 percent of the amount of any business loan conforming to the statutory restrictions on RFC loans. Under blanket guarantees the volume of RFC participations greatly expanded. For the first time, federal guaranty reached banks in small communities,[43] and embraced loans of smaller average amount than had been made under ordinary participation arrangements, although they were not by any means small loans.[44] BPA demonstrated the potentialities of a streamlined governmental underwriting of business credit risks, and suggested some of the dangers as well, coming under criticism as an untimely stimulus to credit and an encouragement to loose lending practices. The program was withdrawn in January 1947.

With respect to a considerable proportion of regular participation loans, it appears that RFC functioned as a risk-distributing agency for banks of medium size. In an economy increasingly characterized by large enterprises with large credit requirements, and where the dominant pattern of banking is one of small-scale institutions with limited capital resources, it was perhaps natural that RFC participation should take on that emphasis. Partly to meet the problem of limiting the exposure to risk of loss for an individual

[43] See Appendix Table B-49.
[44] See Appendix Table B-48.

bank in meeting the credit demands of its area, commercial banks have developed an intricate set of correspondent relationships. Commercial bankers have contended that the correspondent banking system is an instrumentality capable of solving the problem of diversification of risks, and that a public credit agency for the purpose is unnecessary.

The preceding description of RFC participation credits and of the banks involved appears to apply in its major outlines to the participation loans made by Federal Reserve Banks. More than half of the number and two-thirds of the amount of Federal Reserve Bank loans and guarantee commitments to business represented loans made cooperatively with commercial banks and other financial institutions. In the majority of the loans, the commercial bank assumed between 20 and 50 percent of the liability for loss. Cooperative loans averaged larger in amount than the loans made by the Federal Reserve Banks alone. Each of the twelve Federal Reserve Banks was delegated authority to pass upon the creditworthiness of applicants and to work out the terms of its loans, subject only to broad regulations laid down by the Board of Governors of the Federal Reserve System. Hence there were material variations between Federal Reserve districts in the use of cooperative arrangements. On the whole, experience with cooperative loans proved somewhat better than with loans made solely by the Reserve Banks—a conclusion which might have been expected.

Measured by the volume of funds involved, the most extensive federal program of business loan guaranty was the V-loan program of World War II.[45] The armed services were authorized to guarantee loans made by private financial institutions to meet the working capital needs of businesses engaged in war production either as contractors or subcontractors; and the Board of Governors of the Federal Reserve System established a procedure under Regulation V by which the twelve Federal Reserve Banks administered the guarantees, as agents for the War and Navy Departments and the U.S. Maritime Commission. The purpose was to assure an adequate flow of credit to finance war production. Extensions of the regulation to apply to working capital needs as contracts terminated have already been described. Regulation V originally established a maximum interest rate of 5 percent on the loans to be guaranteed, which was reduced in September 1944 to 4½ percent. It provided for a maxi-

[45] Cf. *Federal Reserve Bulletin,* March 1946, pp. 240–248; also Burr and Sette, *op.cit.,* pp. 7ff.

mum guarantee of 90 percent, except in unusual cases, and the lending institution was charged a fee graduated upward as the guaranteed portion of the loan increased.

Authorizations under Regulation V from April 1942 to June 1946 totaled about $10.5 billion.[46] Most were revolving credits, so that although some authorizations were never disbursed but functioned as standby credits, others were used many times over, and the total of disbursements reached $12 billion. Some part of the credit undoubtedly would have been advanced without federal guarantee, because commercial banks shifted a material part of their lending for war purposes from an unguaranteed to a guaranteed basis after Regulation V was promulgated.[47] Even when guaranteed credit was at its peak, it represented only about two-thirds of all bank credit for war purposes, the banks having carried the risk of the other one-third themselves.

The concentration of V-loan guarantees with large banks was quite pronounced: only 10 percent of all commercial banks took part, and nearly all of them were of medium or large size.[48] In fact, 98 percent of all banks with deposits of $50 million or over, and 78 percent of those with deposits of $10 to $50 million had loans guaranteed under Regulation V, as against only 1 percent of the banks with deposits of under $1 million and 6 percent of those with deposits of from $1 to $2 million. The V-loan guarantee program bypassed the small bank, just as it bypassed small businesses.

Both in statutory conception and in actual operation, the business loan guaranty program of the Veterans' Administration has had a markedly different character from other federal programs of loan guaranty or insurance. The salient distinctions may be summarized as follows:

1. Unlike other federal business loan guaranteeing agencies, VA lacked the power to lend directly to business.

2. VA enforced no requirement that the borrower show unavailability of nonguaranteed credit from private sources, whereas other public agencies made the granting of credit or credit guaranty contingent upon a showing that the prospective borrowing business had been unable to obtain credit on reasonable terms from private sources.

3. Other federal business credit programs have been restricted to

---

[46] Burr and Sette, op.cit., Table 2, p. 14.
[47] Ibid., p. 19. [48] Ibid., Table 20, p. 52.

established or solvent firms, to firms engaged in exporting or some specified type of economic activity, or—as in the case of Federal Reserve Bank industrial loans—to the financing of working capital needs; but VA loans have been unrestricted in all these respects.

4. VA was forbidden by law to charge for its guaranty service on business credits, and the loans it could guarantee were held to a maximum interest rate (5.7 percent per annum for insured non-real-estate loans) that is low in relation to the high risks and administrative costs involved. Other federal business credit agencies have had broad administrative powers to determine charges for credit services (though in practice they have tended to standardize rates without distinction among borrowers and to vary rates rather infrequently through time).

5. VA guarantees have been limited to very small amounts—50 percent of the amount of a loan but not more than $2,000 in the case of loans not secured by real estate, or $4,000 in the case of real-estate-secured loans—whereas other public agencies have usually been permitted to make, guarantee, or insure loans of any amount.

6. The VA program has been more decentralized than that of any other public agency. More than seventy regional offices were operated at one time, each with power to approve loans finally for guaranty or insurance.

VA-guaranteed business loans have been preponderantly amortized term loans to very small firms. They averaged under $3,000 in amount, with an average VA liability of approximately $800.[49] They had a modal term to maturity of two and one-half to three years, and were amortized in equal monthly installments.[50] Nearly three-quarters of the loans closed during June and July 1947 were secured by liens on personal property employed in the business.[51]

Measured against private credit to businesses of fairly small size, VA guarantees appear quantitatively unimportant. From 1945 to December 1954, 217,764 loans, in an aggregate original amount of $588 million, had been disbursed; and about 57,000 loans, with balances estimated between $100 million and $150 million, were outstanding.[52] The number of "small business" loans held by Federal

[49] *Loan Guaranty*, Veterans' Administration, December 1954, p. 57.

[50] From Appendix Table C-12, which gives the maturity distribution of loans made between May and August 1947, and Table C-14, which gives the repayment schedule for loans closed in June and July 1947.

[51] See Appendix Table C-13.

[52] Compiled from data in *Loan Guaranty*, Veterans' Administration, December 1954, p. 57.

Reserve member banks in November 1946 is estimated at 514,000, and the amount outstanding, at $2.9 billion.[53] Yet VA guarantees might bulk large if they could be compared solely with private credit to similar borrowers: that is, new and extremely small firms. Their importance lies in the introduction of term lending into that market, and in inducing commercial banks to undertake and gain experience with such loans.

The pricing policies of federal business credit agencies contrast with those of private-lending institutions in certain distinctive characteristics. There has been evident, in the first place, a strong tendency to standardize the interest rate or commitment fee charged within each broad class of loans rather than to discriminate between borrowers and loans according to size, credit risk, and costs of loan administration. Secondly, there has been a tendency toward inflexibility of charges through time, instead of sensitive and frequent adjustment to changing supply-demand conditions in the money markets. Thirdly, the pricing policy has tended to consider only partial costs, with interest rates and commitment fees in many instances insufficient to defray the full cost of supplying the credit services if the cost of capital funds employed is included. Fourthly, in loan guaranty and insurance programs congressional as well as administrative actions have operated in the direction of reducing charges for business credit by private lending institutions, frequently below current market rates.

RFC, whose statute did not prescribe its customer charges, set a standard 5 percent rate on direct loans or immediate participations in 1935. This was reduced to 4 percent on April 1, 1939 and restored to the 5 percent rate on November 10, 1950, apparently in response to criticism that full costs were not being met. RFC's loan guarantee fees were originally graduated from ½ percent to about 2 percent, depending on duration; were shifted upward, then downward, and on November 10, 1950 were raised to a flat 2 percent.

Each Federal Reserve Bank has fixed its own rate for industrial loans and commitments, subject to approval by the Board of Gov-

[53] "Member Bank Loans to Small Business," by Charles H. Schmidt, *Federal Reserve Bulletin*, August 1947, p. 963. In the survey, the definition of small business covers manufacturing and mining firms with total assets of less than $750,000, wholesale trade concerns with assets under $250,000, and all other firms with assets under $50,000.

ernors of the Federal Reserve System. At the beginning, five of the banks announced a standard loan rate of 6 percent, one bank announced a standard rate of 5½ percent, and the remaining banks published rates varying from 4 to 6 or 5 to 6 percent.[54] Later the different banks tended to abandon the standard rate and to move toward a range of rates, until at the end of 1954 the published range of rates on loans was 2½ to 5 percent and 3½ to 5 percent for all banks excepting St. Louis, for which it was 3 to 5 percent and Atlanta and Kansas City, where it was 2¾ to 5 percent. The range of rates on loan guarantees at the end of 1954 was ½ to 1¼ percent or ½ to 1⅜ percent per annum of the amount of the Reserve Bank's commitment.[55] Despite these changes in pricing policy, recent charges only partially reflect the variation of individual loan risks and costs. As with RFC, changes in Federal Reserve Bank rates through time have been comparatively infrequent.

Congress fixed a maximum annual interest rate of 4 percent on business loans eligible for guarantee by the Veterans' Administration,[56] and a maximum rate of 5.7 percent on insured loans not secured by real estate—rates demonstrably below the competitive rate for loans of similar risk and administrative cost. It did not authorize the VA to make any charge whatever for business loan guaranty or insurance, so that these services represent an outright subsidy to the veteran borrower.

For Regulation V loans the Board of Governors of the Federal Reserve System limited the interest rate that could be charged by the lender to 5 percent and established a definite scale of charges to be made by Federal Reserve Banks for entering into contracts of loan guarantee.[57] The scale was altered twice. After September 11, 1944, the Reserve Banks were required to charge a fee of 10 percent of the total interest collected on a loan, when the percentage of the loan guaranteed was 60 percent or less. As the percentage of the

[54] *Banking and Monetary Statistics*, Board of Governors of the Federal Reserve System, 1943, Table 118, p. 446.

[55] *Federal Reserve Bulletin*, January 1955, p. 27.

[56] Congress amended the law effective August 10, 1948, to permit the Administrator, with the concurrence of the Secretary of the Treasury, to approve of rates up to 4½ percent. Effective May 5, 1953 the Veterans' Administration, with the approval of the Secretary of the Treasury, authorized an increase in the maximum interest rate to 4½ percent per annum.

[57] Burr and Sette, *op.cit.*, pp. 45f. The Reserve Board also limited the commitment fees that banks were permitted to charge business firms on the undisbursed portions of loans authorized by them.

loan covered by the guarantee rose, the fee ranged upward to a maximum of 50 percent of the interest charge when the fraction of the loan guaranteed was over 95 percent. The scale was applicable to all loans, irrespective of size, credit risk, or administrative costs.

Congress has fixed the maximum rate chargeable on ship construction loans by the Maritime Administration at $3\frac{1}{2}$ percent if the ship is to be used in foreign trade, and at $5\frac{1}{4}$ percent if in domestic trade. For its insurance of ship mortgage loans made by private lenders the agency has fixed a premium of between $\frac{1}{2}$ percent and 1 percent per annum of the insured amount of the loan.

Among the federal sources of business credit only the Export-Import Bank appears to have adopted a flexible interest rate policy. This was a matter of administrative decision; Congress left the bank's management free to establish its own scale of charges. Most loans to foreign governments have carried rates ranging from $2\frac{1}{2}$ to $3\frac{1}{2}$ percent per annum; loans to foreign or domestic business enterprises have been made at rates in the range of 4 to 5 percent; special exporter-importer credits have been extended at 6 percent.[58]

The implications of the standard loan rate policy followed by federal business credit agencies have received much attention from congressional committees and others. RFC's policy was examined intensively by a Senate subcommittee in 1947 at which time officers of the corporation testified that distinctions in rates as between sizes, maturities, and risk qualities were impractical.[59] The committee's report suggested that the managers of local RFC loan agencies, consulting their advisory committees of bankers and businessmen, should be free to set loan rates in the light of local conditions and without required adherence to a national standard rate.

The RFC standard loan rate policy was again examined in 1950 by a subcommittee of the Senate Committee on Banking and Currency which demonstrated the inverse relationship between lending costs and size of loan, which meant that at the standard rate, then 4 percent, the income from a relatively few large loans made up the losses on many smaller loans.[60] The corporation's loan rate policy was at variance, of course, with the customary practices of commercial banks, as is shown by comparison of average bank rates on

[58] *Twelfth Semiannual Report to Congress*, Export-Import Bank of Washington, January–June 1951, Appendix C, pp. 32–54.
[59] *Hearings . . . on S. Res. 132*, Part 1, 80th Cong., 1st sess., December 1947, p. 65.
[60] *Analysis of Income and Costs* (cited in footnote 26), p. 71.

business loans of different sizes with the RFC rate as of November 1946.[61]

Another implication of the comparatively inflexible interest rate policy of federal lending agencies is that public credit tended to become relatively more attractive during periods of economic expansion, when interest rates would tend to be rising. The opposite would be the case during periods of credit contraction. Thus the federal policy had a tendency of producing a perverse cyclical effect. Effective coordination of federal lending operations with over-all fiscal and monetary policies for economic stability would seem to imply a more flexible loan rate policy than that typically followed by federal agencies.

Credit Experience

With the exception of the Export-Import Bank, the default experience and loss experience of federal lending and loan guaranteeing programs for business have been unfavorable in comparison with those of private business credit institutions. However, this result was to be expected in view of the relatively high-risk financing in which federal agencies have engaged, and does not necessarily reflect adversely on the management of the programs. Certain of the activities for which Congress made the public agencies responsible were destined from the beginning to result in appreciable losses, a fact that should be kept in mind in appraising the credit experience of the public agencies.

It is important also to recognize the character of the economic environment in which the programs functioned and its relation to their default and loss experience. Economic expansion over most of the thirties and forties made many credits good which under depressed or even stable economic conditions would have resulted in losses. The experience records available to us fall within an unusually favorable period, from the mid-thirties to the early fifties. It would be an egregious error to regard that experience as characteristic of federal business credit agencies in all time and under all conditions.

DEFAULT RATIOS

Evidence on the extent of delinquency among active loans in the portfolios of federal agencies supplying credit service to business refers mainly to loans made after World War II. At the end of 1951

[61] See Appendix Table B-51.

about 87 percent of the number and 90 percent of the amount of the Reconstruction Finance Corporation's active business loans (about four-fifths of which dated from 1948 or later) were "in good standing"; the remainder were delinquent in some respect.[62] This record cannot be compared directly with the experience of commercial banks with term loans, but it is known that during 1951 less than 1 percent of the bank loans of all types appraised by bank examiners were classified as "substandard" in quality.[63] It would seem to follow that the RFC loans were of distinctly lower quality than those held by commercial banks.

Estimated default ratios (ratios of the number and amount of loans delinquent to the number and amount of active loans) for the RFC direct business loan portfolio at the end of 1951, by size of loan, term to maturity, size of borrower, industry of borrower, region of borrower, year borrowing firm was established, and principal use of proceeds are shown in Appendix Tables B-12 to B-14. Loan size appears to have had little relation to default experience, but it is interesting to observe that defaults were less frequent among the loans with longer maturities than among those made for shorter periods, possibly because the former were more conveniently related to the capacity of the borrowing firm to make repayments. By and large, the differences in delinquency ratios among various categories of loans were not marked. Higher than average default ratios were found for (1) loans with maturities of less than five years; (2) loans used principally to increase working capital or to retire debt; (3) loans to firms in the transportation, communications, and public utilities group; (4) to firms in the South Atlantic, East South Central, and Mountain regions; and (5) to firms with declining sales or profit trends. Loans to businesses in most asset-size classes under the $250,000 level had less than average delinquency, and the ratio for businesses just forming at time of loan or too young to show three-year financial trends was about average. The absence, in general, of marked differences in delinquency ratios is an interesting phenomenon, suggesting that RFC's credit standards were consistently applied to all groups of loans.

---

[62] Based on the National Bureau of Economic Research sample survey of RFC direct business loans exclusive of participations and national defense loans. For details, see Appendix Tables B-11 through B-16 and accompanying text.

[63] *Annual Report* of the Federal Deposit Insurance Corporation, December 31, 1951, Table 108, p. 154.

For business loans guaranteed by the Veterans' Administration, default ratios over the period 1946–1954 ranged from 1.4 percent in the first year to 9 percent in 1954:

End of Year	No. of VA-Protected Business Loans Outstanding	Default Ratio[a]
1946	41,875	1.4%
1947	68,972	4.5
1948	68,422	5.8
1949	63,446	6.0
1950	62,653	5.0
1951	94,236	4.1
1952	110,766	4.5
1953	80,102	7.5
1954	56,615	9.0

[a] Loans in default at year end plus cases for which claim payments were pending, as percentage of all active loans. From Appendix Table C-8.

In connection with the rise in the ratios from 1951 to 1954, the increase and then decrease in number of outstandings, exerting a downward and then heightening effect on the default ratio, should be borne in mind. We lack corresponding measures to make a comparison with non-VA-guaranteed commercial bank loans to businesses of comparably small size.

FREQUENCY OF LOSS

The frequency and the severity of loss are more important, of course, than the incidence of default in the description of loan experience. It is of interest to examine, first, the proportions of all loans extinguished which resulted in some loss to the agency and, secondly, to consider the ratio of the amount of realized net loss to the amount disbursed on extinguished loans.

It is estimated that RFC, from 1934 to the end of 1951, extinguished 9.3 percent of its business loans with some loss.[64] Loss frequency was distinctly high with loans to firms in the transportation, communications, and public utilities group (a result in which loans during 1945 and 1946 to small trucking enterprises played a large part); with loans in the Mountain and East South Central regions

[64] The figure refers to direct loans made under regular lending powers (i.e. national defense loans and loans made in participation with private lenders are excluded).

268

and in the territorial possessions; with loans used principally to purchase land or buildings or to purchase equipment; and with loans to firms just organizing at time of application and those too young to show three-year trends in financial condition.[65]

Among the VA-guaranteed small loans made after 1944 to veterans establishing or expanding a business, 7.5 percent of those extinguished by the end of 1954 were loss loans—that is, terminated with payment by VA of a claim by the private lending institution that made the loan.[66] The ratio had trended downward from about 15 percent in the early years.[67]

Information is available on Federal Reserve Bank loss experience with business loans up to December 31, 1940, by which time the great majority of the loans had been made. Funds had been disbursed on 2,027 loans, of which 1,132 were participations with commercial banks and other private financial institutions and 895 were made independently by the Federal Reserve Banks. In the first group losses were charged off, or provided for, on 4 percent of the total number; in the second group, on 6 percent. Federal Reserve Bank experience was thus more favorable than RFC's with respect to the relative frequency of loss; but undoubtedly (although documentation is lacking) both were unfavorable in comparison to commercial bank term lending.

It was to be expected that losses on loans guaranteed under Regulation V would be relatively small, because the government was the principal customer of the borrowing enterprises as well as the guarantor of their loans. Yet a number of "distress cases" arose, mainly as a result of problems such as poor management or high costs, and in a few cases because of unexpected contract cancellations. Some of the distress loans were liquidated through the joint efforts of the originating commercial bank and the Federal Reserve Bank of its district; yet 157 loans, totaling $66 million, were purchased by the Federal Reserve Banks as agents for the procurement agencies in fulfillment of their guarantees.[68] The loss loans numbered about 1.8 percent of all loans extinguished, and were of smaller average size than other V loans. Among industry groups of loans, those to manufacturers of aircraft and aircraft parts had a relatively poor record.

[65] See Appendix Tables B-24 through B-29.
[66] Up to December 25, 1954, 149,021 loans had been paid in full and 12,128 loans terminated by payment of a claim, for a total of 161,149 loans extinguished. See *Loan Guaranty*, Veterans' Administration, December 1954, p. 57.
[67] See Appendix Tables C-7 and C-9.   [68] Burr and Sette, *op.cit.*, p. 57.

No losses had been realized up to the end of 1951 on the comparatively few ship purchase and construction loans held by the Maritime Administration, although several loans were delinquent at that date. Willingness, under the broad purpose of advancing the merchant marine, to extend or renew loans not in current status may partly explain the favorable record, but data on that aspect are lacking.

EXTENT OF LOSS ON EXTINGUISHED LOANS

We turn to records of the amount of realized losses on extinguished loans. It is estimated that up to the end of 1951 the Reconstruction Finance Corporation's loss ratio slightly exceeded 2 percent, which is to say that the corporation lost two cents on every dollar of funds disbursed on all business loans extinguished by that date.[69] Comparable figures for commercial bank term loans are unavailable, but insured banks reported losses, charge-offs, and transfers to reserve accounts in 1951 amounting to less than one-half of 1 percent of loans and discounts of all types that were outstanding at the end of that year; which, since the weighted average maturity of the loans was probably under two years, implies a maximum loss of less than 1 percent of the amount extinguished during the year.[70]

RFC losses from the amount advanced on loans extinguished before 1952 appear to have been heaviest on loans to very small firms (with total assets under $25,000); to businesses just organizing at time of loan; to manufacturing firms in the petroleum, coal, chemicals, rubber group; and to firms in the Mountain region and the territorial possessions.[71]

The full amount of the losses realized on the small business loans guaranteed by the Veterans' Administration is not accurately known, because VA collects no data on the aggregate amount of repayments made by debtors nor on the lender's total loss, but accounts only for that part of the loss which was compensated by governmental guaranty or insurance. Up to December 25, 1954, VA had

[69] From the National Bureau of Economic Research sample survey of RFC direct business loans made under regular lending powers (i.e. excluding participation loans and national defense loans); see Appendix B, page B-97.

The Controller of RFC in 1950 estimated a higher loss ratio, about three cents on each dollar of investment, probably referring to loans inclusive of those made under wartime powers. See *Analysis of Income and Costs* (cited in footnote 26 above), pp. 86 and 92.

[70] *Annual Report* of the Federal Deposit Insurance Corporation, 1951, pp. 154 and 162.

[71] See Appendix Tables B-33 to B-35.

paid lenders' claims in the amount of $9,653,000, equal to 2.7 percent of the total original amount of loans that had been repaid in full or 1.6 percent of the total principal amount of all the loans guaranteed or insured to that date.[72] For RFC, estimated losses through 1951 in ratio to the amount of all business loans made were 1.3 percent,[73] a figure difficult to compare with the 1.6 percent for VA because the latter covers only the compensated portion of the total loss on the loans, because more of the credit extended under VA guarantee than of that advanced by RFC up to the given dates was still of unknown outcome, and for other reasons.

Like the RFC and VA business loan programs, that of the Federal Reserve Banks also produced losses of larger amount than are ordinarily encountered in private banking activities. According to an unpublished study by the Board of Governors of the Federal Reserve System, estimated net losses were approximately $1.9 million through 1951. Thus realized losses approximated 0.6 percent of the amount loaned through 1951 and as much as 3 percent of the amount loaned during 1934–1940, when loans were most numerous and were more in the nature of a credit aid to businesses generally than were the fewer, large loans made during and after the war. The FRB loss ratio on loans made through 1951 is below that for RFC (0.6 as against 1.3 percent) ; the fact that participation loans (with a comparatively good record as among the FRB loans) are covered in the ratio for the Reserve Banks but not for RFC may partly explain the difference. Extensive losses on certain large loans are the chief factor in the loss ratio for the FRB program. The record apparently varied considerably among the different reserve districts; losses on loans appear to have been comparatively heavy in those—such as New York, San Francisco, and Richmond—where the business lending programs were most active.[74] It should be reiterated that the inflationary boom of the forties affected the outcome of loans made then, and for earlier loss loans brought substantial recoveries, so that in more normal conditions the record would have been less favorable. At the end of 1940 the amount of money set aside by the Reserve

[72] *Loan Guaranty*, Veterans' Administration, December 1954, p. 57.
[73] Appendix Table B-33.
[74] From an unpublished study, "13b Loan Program of the Federal Reserve System, 1934-40," by Caroline H. Cagle, Division of Research and Statistics, Board of Governors of the Federal Reserve System; also "The Industrial Loans of the Federal Reserve Bank of New York," by Robert V. Rosa: unpublished address to the Sixth Annual Convention of the National Conference of Commercial Receivables Companies, October 17, 1950.

Banks as provision against business lending losses, together with amounts already charged off, approximated 5 percent of the credit advanced up to that date.

The loss ratios on loans guaranteed under Regulation V have been almost infinitesimal, owing to the unusual circumstances under which the guarantees were extended. By the end of 1949 the uncollected balance of loans purchased from commercial banks by the federal procurement agencies pursuant to their guarantees had been reduced to about $6 million. Guarantee agreements covering an additional $800,000 of loan balances were still outstanding on that date. It has been estimated that losses on the entire program will be about 0.06 percent of aggregate loan authorizations, and about 0.4 percent of the peak amount of guaranteed V-loan credit outstanding ($1.8 billion at the end of July 1944).[75]

Up to June 30, 1954 the Export-Import Bank reported losses of $496,068, representing less than 0.1 percent of cumulative gross income, and 0.01 percent of the total amount disbursed under all authorizations, since the establishment of the bank in 1934.[76]

REVENUES, COSTS, AND OPERATING RESULTS

A general picture of the operating results of federal business credit programs is difficult to form because information on the largest of them—that of the Reconstruction Finance Corporation—is deficient. The statements published by the agency itself relate to its combined programs for housing, railroads, and other segments of the economy as well as business, and the underlying accounts do not permit precise calculations for the business program alone. Moreover, they require adjustment to reflect operating results from the standpoint of the public: that is, to include the cost of interest-free capital supplied by the Treasury, and earned surplus not returned to the Treasury. Published statements show a net income of about $100 million from all RFC lending programs during the five years 1946–1950; estimates on a full-cost basis put the five-year profit for the combined programs at only about $21 million.[77] Estimates developed in congressional hearings in 1950, covering the business program alone for twenty-one months in fiscal 1949 and 1950, indicate a net

[75] Burr and Sette, *op.cit.*, p. 57.
[76] *Eighteenth Semiannual Report to Congress*, Export-Import Bank of Washington, January–June 1954, pp. 3 and 4.
[77] See page B-166.

deficit of $13.6 million after provision for losses and as adjusted to reflect the cost of all funds employed.[78]

For the similar but smaller program of the Federal Reserve Banks during the period when it reached the widest variety of businesses an unprofitable record is also indicated if allowance is made for realized and anticipated losses on loans and for interest on funds employed. From 1934 up to the end of 1940 the combined operating accounts of all twelve Reserve Banks for the industrial loan program could be summarized as follows:[79] The preceding figures suggest that up

(1) Gross earnings (interest, fees, etc.)		$7,411,733
(2) *Deduct*: Administrative expenses	$3,976,848	
Interest on funds supplied by U.S. Treasury (1¾ percent × $27.5 million × 5 years)	2,406,250	
Total expense		6,383,098
(3) Net income before losses		1,028,635
(4) Losses charged off		430,293
(5) Balance		598,342
(6) Estimated losses at December 31, 1940		2,447,459
(7) Estimated net deficit		($1,849,117)

to the end of 1940, Federal Reserve Bank charges would have had to be about 25 percent higher to have enabled the banks as a group to break even on the industrial loan program. By the end of 1951, recoveries on losses previously written off and withdrawals from allowances for estimated losses in consequence of the inflationary boom during and after World War II had eliminated the net deficit. The figures appearing above, however, appear to represent the normal results of the program in a stable economic environment.

This picture of the operating results of the Section 13b loan program in all Federal Reserve Banks finds confirmation in Rosa's analysis of the New York Federal Reserve Bank's experience. Rosa found that aggregate gross earnings were roughly double out-of-pocket administrative expenses, and that the balance of net income was just equal to realized losses. Provision for interest on funds employed, anticipated future losses, and overhead expense absorbed by

[78] See Appendix Table B-52.
[79] From an unpublished study by the Board of Governors of the Federal Reserve System.

the New York Federal Reserve Bank created a considerable deficit in the operation.[80]

Most successful of the federal agencies supplying business credit, from the point of view of operating net income, has been the Export-Import Bank. This institution has been required only since 1945 to pay interest on its Treasury borrowings. Yet its gross income from operations has been so large from the beginning that, if the bank had paid interest or dividends into the Treasury on all funds advanced to it since its establishment at a rate representing the interest cost of those funds to the Treasury, its earned surplus at the end of 1951 would still have amounted to $165.7 million as compared to the reported figure of $262 million as of that date.[81] From February 2, 1934 to June 30, 1954 operating results were as follows:[82]

(1) Gross income (interest, fees)		$563,191,520
(2) Expenses:		
(a) Administrative expense	$ 9,439,670	
(b) Interest paid U.S. Treasury	116,841,621[a]	
(c) Dividends paid U.S. Treasury	105,905,178	
Total		222,746,799
(3) Losses		496,068
(4) Net retained earnings		$330,508,983

[a] Represents interest paid on new borrowings from 1945 on.

The sources of the Export-Import Bank's profitability, in comparison with other public suppliers of credit to business, have been a very large average loan size and an exceedingly low administrative outlay arising from a compact, centralized operation. The remarkable record of profitability may also be attributed to the fact that the bank has been the sole and official foreign lending agency of the United States government; as such, it has been in a position to minimize risks and losses in ways not open to other federal credit agencies or to private institutions.

Operating results of the war loan guaranty program under Regulation V are not known precisely, because the expenditures of the Federal Reserve Board (as agent) and of the military procurement agencies (as loan guarantors) that were allocable to the administra-

[80] Rosa, op.cit., pp. 10f.

[81] Thirteenth Semiannual Report to Congress, Export-Import Bank of Washington, July–December 1951, p. 21.

[82] Eighteenth Semiannual Report to Congress, Export-Import Bank of Washington, January–June 1954, p. 4.

tion of the program are not available. Other gross revenue and expense items up to the end of 1949 were as follows:[83] Prima facie, it

(1) Gross income (guaranty and commitment fees and interest)		$35.0 million
(2) Expenses deductible:		
(a) Reimbursable expense of Reserve Banks	$3.6 million	
(b) Estimated losses	6.3	
(c) Paid to banks by guarantors	1.7	
Total		11.6
(3) Balance before FRB and military agency expenses:		$23.4 million

would appear that the V-loan program was at least self-supporting and possibly profitable to the government.

The guaranty and insurance of small business loans by the VA was frankly intended to be a subsidy to veterans who desired to enter business and showed reasonable likelihood of success; no charge was made for those services. Yet it is of interest to know the costs of the credit services, and what charge would have had to be made for them if they were priced at full cost. Although the Veterans' Administration has published no official statement of the costs of administering the loan guaranty and insurance programs, data made available by it make possible a rough estimate of its expenditures from the beginning of the program in 1944 up to the end of 1952. For the business loan program alone, the expenditures may be estimated as follows:[84]

(1) Gratuities of 4 percent paid veterans	$ 5,848,000
(2) Net cost of claims paid by the government	8,496,000
(3) Direct salary and other costs of loan origination	3,336,000[84]
(4) Direct salary and other costs of loan servicing and liquidation	5,679,000[84]
(5) Office and other overhead expenses	1,803,000[84]
Total expenses	$25,162,000

Up to the end of 1952, 198,134 individual business loans had been closed and disbursed in a total principal amount of $532,-

[83] Burr and Sette, op.cit., pp. 57f.
[84] Through 1952, total direct administrative costs charged to the loan guaranty program (including home, farm and business loans) was $70,374,244 and general administrative expenses including office and other overhead costs were estimated at 20 percent of total direct costs. About 75 percent of total costs charged to the loan guaranty program are assumed to have been expended in loan origination, and 25 percent in loan servicing and liquidation. Loan origination expenses are assumed to be allocable among the home, farm, and business loan programs in proportion to number of loans disbursed, and loan servicing and liquidation expenses in proportion to number of claims filed after default.

769,000, or an average amount per loan of $2,689.[85] Total expenses formed 4.72 percent of the aggregate principal amount of funds loaned, and 15.1 percent of the guaranty or insurance of all loans. The cost of guaranty or insurance has averaged about $127 per loan. In summary, it appears that the VA would have had to charge "premiums" of about 5 percent of the total principal amount of business loans disbursed, or of about 15 percent of the guaranteed portion of such loans, in order to break even on the operation.

Impact on Business Enterprises and Business Financing Institutions

RELATIVE MAGNITUDE OF PUBLIC AND
PRIVATE CREDIT AIDS TO BUSINESS

In comparison to the total amount of credit utilized by business, that supplied by public lending institutions has been small. Table 46 records year-end outstandings of business loans and loan guarantees by federal and federally sponsored agencies from 1918 through 1953, shows the percentage ratio of federal credit to the total debt owed by business corporations, and measures similarly the outstandings of the principal private lending institutions: for life insurance companies, their investments in stocks and bonds (mainly bonds) of business and industrial corporations; for commercial banks, their loans to, and investments in bond and security offerings of, commercial enterprises.[86] Through 1941 the ratio of federal business credit to total corporate debt never rose much above 1 percent. At its highest, in 1943 and 1949, it was only 3 percent. Life insurance companies and commercial banks were each supplying about eight eight times as much business credit as federal agencies at the end of 1953. There is to be observed, however, a mild secular uptrend in the relative importance of federal credit in the total debt of American business.

---

[85] *Finance, Guaranty of Loans*, Veterans' Administration, December 1952, p. 71.

[86] The data are not strictly comparable because of different definitions of business by the several types of lender and because total debt refers only to the net corporate long- and short-term debt exclusive of that owed by unincorporated businesses. Despite these deficiencies the comparisons are believed to be meaningful.

Inclusion of loan guarantees in the amount of federal credit causes some overlapping (from 1934 on) with the bank figures. Loan guarantees were important during World War II, and in 1943 and 1944 even exceeded federal loans. From 1946 through 1953 they comprised less than 20 percent of federal credit, or less. For series measuring federal credit both inclusive and exclusive of guarantees against a differently constructed debt total, see Table 7 in Chapter 2.

Only an incomplete picture of the relative importance of public and private credit to financial institutions can be given. Loans made directly by commercial banks to other banking institutions are reported regularly, but there are many other types of financial assistance furnished by one private agency to another on which information is lacking—for example, purchases of stock or shares.

Federal lending to financial institutions before 1932 was negligible; but in that year over $1 billion was advanced. By 1940, the debt of financial institutions to public agencies had been reduced to $373 million, yet was nearly five times as large as the combined total ($77 million) of loans to commercial banks and mutual savings banks held by other banks and of the amount owed by savings and loan associations apart from their indebtedness to the Federal Home Loan Banks (Table 3, Chapter 2). For financial institutions, therefore, loans of government agencies were for a time very much more important than their borrowing from private sources. By 1950, the indebtedness of private lending institutions to public agencies had all been retired (except for some $800 million of outstanding loans by the Home Loan Bank to savings and loan associations—ultimately, a credit aid to the housing sector, since the associations lend almost exclusively on mortgage security). Public holdings of stocks and shares of financial institutions were considerable in the late thirties and early forties (Chart 13, above). Their relative importance can be judged only for savings and loan associations. Government-supplied capital in 1940 was about 5.1 percent of the amount of the private savings capital then in use by the associations; in 1951, government contributions to capital had been entirely repaid.[87] As of the end of 1953, government capital (in the form of RFC investment in capital stock, notes, and debentures) had also been largely retired from banks, trust companies, and insurance companies.

It may be concluded that on an aggregate basis, federal credit to business has not been large enough to exert important over-all effects on employment and production, on the formation of new enterprises, on the size of the business population, or on the average asset-and-liability structure of American enterprises; and effect of governmental influence on the stability of the supply of business credit has been

[87] See Appendix Tables A-11 and A-19 for data on outstanding amounts of federally held savings and loan association shares. For data on outstanding amounts of private savings capital, see *Trends in the Savings and Loan Field*, 1951, p. 4.

TABLE 46

Outstanding Amounts of Federal Loans and Loan Guarantees to Business, of Life Insurance Company Business Investments, of Commercial Bank Business Loans and Securities, and Net Corporate Debt, 1918–1953

(dollar figures in millions)

END OF YEAR	NET CORPORATE DEBT^a	OUTSTANDING BUSINESS LOANS OR INVESTMENTS			AS PERCENTAGES OF NET CORPORATE DEBT		
		Federal Agencies^b	Life Insurance Companies^c	Commercial Banks^d	Federal Agencies	Life Insurance Companies	Commercial Banks
1918	$47,000	$ 30	$2,039	$13,900	0.1%	4.3%	29.6%
1919	53,300	94	2,044	16,400	0.2	3.8	30.8
1920	57,700	680	2,024	18,500	1.2	3.5	32.1
1921	57,000	740	2,030	17,400	1.3	3.6	30.5
1922	58,600	506	2,189	17,700	0.9	3.7	30.2
1923	62,600	508	2,408	18,900	0.8	3.8	30.2
1924	67,200	442	2,747	19,800	0.7	4.1	29.5
1925	72,700	353	3,103	20,900	0.5	4.3	28.7
1926	76,200	321	3,565	21,600	0.4	4.7	28.3
1927	81,200	204	4,043	22,100	0.3	5.0	27.2
1928	86,100	113	4,642	21,800	0.1	5.4	25.3
1929	88,900	120	4,995	20,700	0.1	5.6	23.3
1930	89,300	125	5,448	19,500	0.1	6.1	21.8
1931	83,500	140	5,663	16,300	0.2	6.8	19.5
1932	80,000	450	5,580	12,000	0.6	7.0	15.0
1933	76,900	533	5,388	9,800	0.7	7.0	12.7
1934	75,500	704	5,510	9,800	0.9	7.3	13.0
1935	74,800	773	5,897	10,600	1.0	7.9	14.2
1936	76,100	646	6,593	12,000	0.8	8.7	15.8
1937	75,800	642	7,111	12,200	0.8	9.4	16.1
1938	73,300	762	7,895	10,800	1.0	10.8	14.7
1939	73,500	815	8,538	10,300	1.1	11.6	14.0

(continued on next page)

278

(dollar figures in millions)

END OF YEAR	NET CORPORATE DEBT^a	OUTSTANDING BUSINESS LOANS OR INVESTMENTS			AS PERCENTAGES OF NET CORPORATE DEBT		
		Federal Agencies^b	Life Insurance Companies^c	Commercial Banks^d	Federal Agencies	Life Insurance Companies	Commercial Banks
1940	$ 75,600	$ 886	$ 9,250	$11,100	1.2%	12.2%	14.7%
1941	83,400	950	10,174	13,200	1.1	12.2	15.8
1942	91,600	1,823	10,315	11,800	2.0	11.3	12.9
1943	95,500	2,885	10,494	11,900	3.0	11.0	12.5
1944	94,100	2,711	10,715	12,900	2.9	11.4	13.7
1945	85,300	1,456	11,059	15,800	1.7	13.0	18.5
1946	93,500	2,191	13,024	19,100	2.3	13.9	20.4
1947	108,900	2,964	16,144	22,400	2.7	14.8	20.6
1948	117,800	3,402	20,322	23,500	2.9	17.3	19.9
1949	118,000	3,490	23,179	22,200	3.0	19.6	18.8
1950	142,100	3,393	25,403	27,700	2.4	17.9	19.5
1951	163,600	4,061	28,204	31,300	2.5	17.2	19.1
1952	171,700	4,410	31,646	28,500	2.6	18.4	16.6
1953	179,400	4,522	34,570	33,100	2.5	19.3	18.5

a Net corporate debt (both long- and short-term) as defined by the Department of Commerce, from *Survey of Current Business*, September 1953, Table 1, p. 14, and October 1954, Table 1, p. 14.

b Refers to direct loans and loan guarantees and insurance by federal agencies and direct loans to business by the Federal Reserve Banks. Data are from Appendix Table A-5.

c Represents investment of all United States life insurance companies in business and industrial bonds and stocks, from *Life Insurance Fact Book 1954* (Institute of Life Insurance), p. 67.

d Data for 1918-1941 were estimated by inflating National Bureau of Economic Research estimates of national bank business loan and security holdings by annual ratios of total assets of national banks to total assets of commercial banks in continental United States and converting midyear figures (1918-1938) to end-of-year figures by linear interpolation. Data for 1942-1953 were compiled from *Annual Reports* of the Comptroller of the Currency, *Federal Reserve Bulletins*, and *Trends in the Savings and Loan Field, 1953* (Home Loan Bank Board), p. 5, and reflect the following types of loans or securities held by commercial banks in continental United States: commercial and industrial loans (including open market paper), adjusted to exclude loans to savings and loan associations by deduction of "other borrowed money" reported in *Trends*; loans to brokers and dealers in securities; and all bonds, notes, debentures, and securities other than those of the United States government and of state and political subdivisions, with Federal Reserve Bank stock eliminated by deduction of FRB paid-in capital reported in *Federal Reserve Bulletins*.

through aid to lending institutions rather than to businesses directly. Federal lending programs in the business field appear, however, to have had a selective effect on the allocation of economic resources through aid to particular types of business firms.

SELECTIVE EFFECTS OF FEDERAL CREDIT
AIDS ON THE BUSINESS POPULATION

In the first place, federal agencies provided a very significant measure of assistance to firms in certain industries: notably, railroad transportation, ocean shipping, and foreign trade. Railroad loan programs have been conducted by several federal agencies since 1918; the merchant shipping industry has likewise received a considerable fraction of its credit from federal agencies; and foreign trading enterprises, and domestic manufacturing enterprises heavily dependent upon foreign markets, have been aided importantly by the Export-Import Bank. There is no means, however, of measuring precisely the effects of federal credit even in these areas where it has been of relatively great importance.

Second, federal loans and loan guarantees have provided significant assistance to new firms and new industries, helping them through periods of trial to the point where some have been able to obtain funds from private financial institutions. The Reconstruction Finance Corporation made many loans to firms in relatively unfamiliar lines, unable to obtain private credit for lack of data on which the private creditors could gauge the risks involved. This appears to have been true of RFC loans to motels, fresh-frozen food canning and packing firms, petro-chemical firms, and food locker enterprises. It was also true of Veterans' Administration guarantees and insurance of very small term loans to enable veterans to initiate or to purchase small enterprises.

Newly established and very small firms have been assisted not only through VA protection of privately made loans but also through financing by the RFC, Federal Reserve Banks, and the Smaller War Plants Corporation. Credit from private financial institutions has rarely been a factor in the financing of new, small ventures, because the risks have been considered too high to lie within the commercial banking range. Public agencies, however, have made a considerable number of such small business loans, have invited and occasionally received private institutional participation, and have to some extent loosened up the credit market for the new, small enterprise. They have shown that the risks of such lending may be kept within tolerable limits by taking appropriate collateral security. Undoubtedly, many bankers who gained familiarity with lending operations of that type through participation in a defense loan guaranteed by a federal agency have been led to continue them without federal cooperation.

Third, federal agencies have carried on a certain amount of marginal financing for firms which were financially weak but which appeared to have reasonable prospects of success and for profitable firms whose rapid market growth had outstripped their financial resources. Marginal financing was provided especially by the loans of Federal Reserve Banks to mercantile and manufacturing ventures and by the loans of the RFC. A large part of the guarantees of war production loans by the War and Navy Departments and the U.S. Maritime Commission were also of that character.

To summarize: although federal credit aids to business probably have not exerted a powerful influence on the aggregate of resources employed in business, they have significantly influenced the movement of resources into (or their retention in) a few established industries considered essential to national security, into certain comparatively new industries, and into firms whose financial conditions were marginal as regards the availability of credit from private financial institutions. Whether these resource-allocational effects have been socially beneficial on balance, and whether more efficient methods of achieving them might have been devised, are issues beyond the purview of this study.

EFFECTS ON BUSINESS FINANCING
INSTITUTIONS AND PRACTICES

The most significant effects of federal credit programs on the business sector of the economy appear to have been the institutional changes brought about in the markets, credit practices, and economic roles played by private business financing agencies. Furthermore, over a sufficiently long period of time, such institutional effects ultimately may produce material changes in the utilization of resources. We shall consider, in turn, the following institutional effects: first, the effects of federal aid to financial institutions on their risk-taking ability; second, the effects of federal business credit services on the size of the credit markets confronting private institutions; third, competitive relationships between federal agencies and private institutions in extending credit to business; fourth, effects of federal lending and loan guaranteeing operations on the term to maturity, collateral security requirements, and other terms of business credit.

1. Federal credit and capital to support commercial banks and life insurance companies maintained the solvency, enhanced the risk-taking ability, and strengthened private financial institutions during periods of severe economic strain. The most extensive and dramatic use of federal financial aid for these purposes was in the RFC bank loan and capital programs of 1932–1934. RFC loans to banks were of two types: "confidence" loans made to active banks for the purpose of enabling them to keep open, and liquidation loans to closed banks to facilitate an early discharge of their depositor claims. The first type of loan predominated up to March 1933, when the national "bank holiday" occurred; thereafter the second type of loan was most frequent. Between February 1932 and March 31, 1933, RFC authorized 10,178 loans to 6,100 banks and trust companies under which $1 billion was disbursed. The RFC also invested nearly $1.2 billion in preferred stock, capital notes, and debentures of 6,104 banks.[88]

2. Federal credit programs undoubtedly exerted a net expansive influence on the markets for private financing institutions, thereby increasing their earning power, equity investment, and financial strength. Federal credit maintained and supported private credit institutions by means of direct loans and by relieving them of assets believed to be illiquid or undesirable. By injecting credit into the economy at numerous points, federal agencies also raised the level of production and the demand for private credit. It is important to observe in this connection that federal credit aids to agriculture and to housing, as well as directly to business, have indirectly created new demands for loans by business firms from private financial institutions. Thus, federal financing of farmers enlarged the credit demands of food processors; and federal credit for home construction created needs for private bank loans among building contractors and building material and equipment manufacturers.

3. Although it is certain that federal credit activities have brought about a net expansion in the market for private business financing,

[88] Jesse H. Jones with Edward Angly, *Fifty Billion Dollars: My Thirteen Years with the RFC (1932–1945)*, Macmillan, 1951, pp. 25 and 614f. See Chapters I–V for an absorbing account of the circumstances under which these programs were executed. For an appraisal of the economic effects of the programs, see *The Reconstruction Finance Corporation, 1932–1941*, by James B. Eckert (unpublished dissertation, Cornell University, 1947), Chapter V.

they have also operated in certain respects to compete with, and to restrict the markets of, banks and other private lending agencies. The ways in which that influence took place are not immediately apparent, however, and require an understanding of the nature of competition in the rendering of credit services.

Competition in extending credit consists in offering loans at lower interest rates, in offering more favorable repayment or collateralization terms and conditions, in offering longer maturities on loans, or in providing borrowers with such ancillary services as accounting and financial advice, or general management counsel. The analysis of competition in credit markets is further complicated by the fact that borrowers differ with respect to the probability that they will repay their debts, and because of differences in size, financial strength, and probable future earning power. Even if the effective interest rates charged, the terms and conditions of loans, and the ancillary services offered by public and private lending institutions were identical, the two might still compete with each other in assuming risks of different magnitudes. Credit is a highly differentiated commodity, and borrowers are not influenced to select one rather than another lender merely by comparing nominal rates of interest.

With these considerations in mind, it becomes apparent how federal agencies may compete with private lenders, even though public agencies are debarred by statute from making loans to businesses to whom private credit is available. For example, RFC could make a business loan which, because of small amount, high risk, or large costs of loan administration, a commercial bank could not afford to make at less than 7 percent annual interest. RFC adopted a more or less standard rate: during most of its period of activity, 4 percent. By lending at this relatively low rate, RFC in effect underpriced the credit by charging less than its full cost. It would not necessarily eliminate RFC competition with a commercial bank for RFC to offer a participation in the loan to the bank, because a share in the loan might still not be profitable to the bank at the low interest rate fixed by RFC.

Neither do statutory measures for eliminating competition do away with the encroachment on private credit markets which occurs if federal agencies offer loans on more favorable terms (longer maturities, less burdensome collateral requirements, more lenient treatment of defaults, etc.) to relatively high-cost or high-risk borrowers at the same interest rates as are charged to low-cost or low-risk borrowers. The strong and pervasive tendency in public credit operations toward standard interest rates and terms of loans has been observed. Standard terms tend to make federal agencies the most attractive sources of credit to borrowers to whom private institutions can advance funds only at comparatively high interest rates and on closely restricted terms. It is in the high-risk segment of the credit market that the operations of federal agencies have cut most deeply into the potential loan markets of banks and other private lenders. To minimize this kind of competition between private and public credit agencies would require: first, changes in public policy permitting and encouraging banks to take longer risks and to charge commensurately higher interest rates;[89] second, policies of public credit agencies that gear their charges for loans to individual borrowers more closely to the actual risks and costs of loan administration, and abandonment of a standard loan rate; third, a policy of public credit agencies to offer commitments to purchase participations in the loans of private agencies for a fee measuring as accurately as possible the costs and risks involved, and to sell to private institutions their interests in loans originated by them.[90]

4. Another institutional effect of federal business credit programs has been an extension of the use of the amortized term loan, running for periods exceeding one year and repayable in periodic installments. It is notable that all of the federal agencies loaning money to business have extended term loans almost exclusively. The amortized term loan has been a development of the past twenty years. It has to a considerable extent replaced the traditional short-term, single payment, promissory note that was often paid up annually and renewed by the business borrower. A number of factors account for the development of term lending by commercial banks during the middle thirties; but the credit activities of the RFC and the Federal Reserve Banks in making term loans beginning in 1934 helped set the stage for an expansion of private financing of this type. Public

---

[89] Usury laws, strong banking conventions against high loan rates, and public supervision of banking which has discouraged risk assumption by banks, have all operated to cause banks to abdicate their position in the high-risk loan market. The problem is not strictly one of competition by the federal credit agencies; it is, rather, that public policy proscribes banking service in a particular segment of the business credit market, a segment where federal agencies then step in to meet the demand.

[90] See "Government Loan Agencies and Commercial Banking," by Neil H. Jacoby, *American Economic Review*, Vol. XXXII, No. 1, March 1942, pp. 258f. for a more complete discussion of these measures.

agencies facilitated the extension of bank term credits by offering to, and taking from, commercial banks substantial participations in term loans. The familiarity with medium-term loans gained by commercial bankers from observations of, or participation in, term credits of the public agencies was to a large extent responsible for private term lending.

A similar process may be observed in connection with the term credits granted by the Export-Import Bank after 1933 to finance the movement of American machinery and equipment into the hands of foreign enterprises and governments. Here again, medium- or long-term export credits have rarely been available from American commercial banks; yet a number of years are required before the earning power of exported equipment can produce the means of repaying its purchase price. Such long-term export credits were first provided by the Export-Import Bank.

The Veterans' Administration, through its guaranty or insurance of small-term loans made by commercial banks or other lending institutions to veterans to purchase or establish businesses, also pioneered in sponsoring the application of the amortized term loan principle to new and very small enterprises. As a result of a strong desire to assist returning veterans, and of the risk sharing undertaken by the VA, commercial banks were induced to enter a new field of lending. Many bankers gradually learned how to make these small business term loans safely and profitably.

Federal agencies have performed in the field of business credit an economic function similar to that discharged by them in the field of housing credit. They have tended to lengthen the maturities of loans and to broaden the use of the amortized loan. In this respect, they fostered an adjustment in the nature of business credit responsive to the increasing use of durable producers goods by business enterprise in the American economy. The term lending principle has brought commercial banks new problems of portfolio management and of liquidity maintenance; but undoubtedly it has helped business enterprises by relating repayments to earning power.

CHAPTER 8

Federal Lending and Loan Insurance Programs for Housing

In our basic series, federal credit aid to housing is limited to loans made for construction, purchase, or improvement of real estate (including insurance or guarantee, or purchase of such loans); it does not include financial assistance to state or city authorities for urban redevelopment projects and the like, nor aid to private financial institutions that supply housing credit. Descriptively, however, we depart from that limitation here in including aid extended to savings and loan associations by the Federal Home Loan Bank system. Among the principal private lending agencies extending long-term mortgage credit, savings and loan associations differ from the others (commercial banks, mutual savings banks, life insurance companies) in devoting their resources almost exclusively to that field, especially to home financing. When federal credit programs for housing arose during the Great Depression, the first step taken was to create a system of federally sponsored district banks that would supplement the investment resources of savings and loan associations and thus increase the supply of mortgage credit.

Development of Federal Agencies for Housing and Home Financing

The Federal Home Loan Bank Act of 1932 (47 Stat. 725; 12 U.S.C. 1421, *et seq.*), provided for the establishment of twelve Federal Home Loan Banks (now eleven) operating under a Home Loan Bank Board and financed by government capital—at its maximum amounting to nearly $125 million—and by funds which the banks were authorized to raise in the open markets from the sale of consolidated Federal Home Loan Bank obligations. The district banks were authorized to make loans to member associations, predominantly federally chartered savings and loan associations but also state-chartered associations and certain other types of mortgage lenders. A requirement that borrowing members purchase Home Loan Bank stock in an amount not less than $500 and equal to 1 percent of their outstanding balance of home loan[1] or one-twelfth of

[1] In June 1950, raised to 2 percent.

their outstanding indebtedness to the Home Loan Bank, whichever might be greater, provided means for the retirement of government capital in the district banks. Beginning in 1945 the banks gradually repurchased federally owned stock, so that by mid-1951 the capital stock was owned entirely by their member institutions.

The Home Owners' Loan Act of 1933 (48 Stat. 128; 12 U.S.C. 1461 et seq.) established the Home Owners' Loan Corporation for the purpose of refinancing defaulted home mortgages,[2] and also authorized the Federal Loan Bank Board to set up a system of federally chartered savings and loan associations. The HOLC was organized exclusively with government capital, and was authorized to obtain additional funds in the open market by issuing bonds whose interest, and later both principal and interest, were guaranteed by the federal government. It was placed under the supervision of the Federal Home Loan Bank Board.

The federal savings and loan associations provided for in the 1933 legislation were granted the privilege of borrowing from their district Home Loan Banks, and both the Treasury and later the HOLC were authorized to purchase their shares. Under this authority the Home Loan Banks made advances to federal- and state-chartered associations of more than $5 billion through 1953, and at that time had a balance of about $950 million of such advances outstanding. From 1935 until its liquidation in 1951 the HOLC purchased nearly $224 million of association shares, mainly those of federally chartered associations. Treasury purchases of shares in federal associations totaled something over $49 million, and were entirely extinguished by the end of 1949.

The next important step in the unfolding of federal policy in the field of housing and home finance was the passage on June 27, 1934 of the National Housing Act (48 Stat. 1246; 12 U.S.C. 1702). This provided for the establishment of two direct government agencies: the Federal Housing Administration, authorized to insure loans for the modernization and repair of residential property or for the construction or purchase of such property, and the Federal Savings and Loan Insurance Corporation, set up to do for the savings and loan group substantially what the Federal Deposit Insurance Corporation was authorized to do for commercial banks and mutual savings banks.

2 The organization, policies, and operation of the HOLC are described in detail by C. Lowell Harriss in *History and Policies of the Home Owners' Loan Corporation* (National Bureau of Economic Research, Financial Research Program, 1951).

These two steps represented quite different approaches to the problem of expanding and strengthening home mortgage credit facilities. The fundamental initial purpose of FHA was to promote employment in the construction industry by encouraging a freer flow of credit into the urban real estate market.[3] The insurance of home mortgage loans contributed to the stability of the institutions engaged in extending such credits, but at the outset its employment-increasing effect was the paramount objective.[4] While there was support for this approach, the savings and loan groups expressed little if any interest in such insurance. They expressed a preference for an agency similar to the FDIC which would attract savings to their institutions and stand ready to aid them in the event of difficulties. Accordingly the Federal Savings and Loan Insurance Corporation, as a means of supporting its share-insurance program, was authorized to extend financial aid to savings and loan associations that seemed likely to default on their obligations to shareholders, and also to associations already in default. Specifically, the corporation was empowered to make loans to distressed associations, to make cash contributions to them, or to purchase their assets for cash, all with the object of preventing defaults or restoring defaulted associations to operation. The corporation has so far used the contribution and asset-purchase methods of aiding institutions, rather than the loan-extension method. Since these activities are concerned exclusively with liquidation operations, and carry only a contingent repayment commitment, they are excluded from our compilation of data on direct lending.

In much of this early legislation there are evidences of the federal government's interest in establishing additional facilities for channeling funds into the financing of urban real estate. Thus the National Housing Act empowered the FHA to charter and supervise national mortgage associations and gave to the Reconstruction Finance Corporation the authority to provide funds to the FHA for establishing and operating such agencies. Also, a January 31, 1935 amendment of the RFC Act gave RFC the right to purchase stock

---

[3] See *Government Agencies of Consumer Instalment Credit*, by Joseph D. Coppock (National Bureau of Economic Research, Financial Research Program, 1940), pp. 22f.

[4] In addition to its power to insure lending institutions against losses on loans made for the repair and modernization of real property and on home mortgage loans, the FHA was also given the power to charter, and the responsibility of supervising, national mortgage associations. These associations would purchase insured mortgage loans, with funds obtained from open market sales of debentures.

in mortgage loan companies, among other types of corporations. In March 1935 action was taken under this amendment to provide a facility for financing multifamily residential and nonresidential properties: the establishment of the RFC Mortgage Company. The object of the new company was to make mortgage loans on structures having more than four apartments (or smaller properties ineligible for FHA-insured mortgage or HOLC financing) and other income-producing properties such as hotels and office buildings. The company was authorized to refinance existing first mortgage loans, make first mortgage loans in connection with the construction of new properties, make loans to holders of first mortgage bonds and first mortgage certificates in cases where the investor was found to be in need of such help, and, finally, to purchase FHA-insured mortgages. The latter function of the RFC Mortgage Company represented the government's effort to establish a secondary market for home mortgages.

A related development occurred in 1938 when, acting under powers granted in the National Housing Act of 1934 as amended, the Reconstruction Finance Corporation was directed by the President in February to organize a national mortgage association to purchase FHA-insured mortgages. The National Housing Act provided for such associations, but none had been formed privately. As a result, the National Mortgage Association of Washington, later named the Federal National Mortgage Association, was established with a capital stock of $10 million, the whole of which was purchased by the RFC. From time to time the resources of FNMA have been supplemented and the terms on which it may purchase loans altered; the most important extension of its activities came in 1948 when it was granted authority to purchase VA-guaranteed home mortgages as well as FHA-insured loans.

Federal intervention in the field of home finance was broadened, as World War II veterans returned to civilian life, with the passage of the Servicemen's Readjustment Act of 1944 (59 Stat. 626; 38 U.S.C. 693 et seq.). This far-reaching statute provided for Veterans' Administration guarantees of loans made by lending agencies to veterans for purchase or improvement of a home, farm, or business.

Under the Housing Act of 1954 (68 Stat. 613) the Federal National Mortgage Association was reorganized so that private capital could replace federal funds and the organization might be transformed into one fully capitalized by the mortgage lending institutions using its facilities. At the same time, the association was given the right to borrow up to $1 billion from the federal treasury, so that resources would not be lacking for the purchase of insured and guaranteed mortgages of all types in a period of financial stringency or for the support at any time of special programs of loan insurance or guarantee.

Volume and Relative Importance of Federal Credit

Federal credit aid for housing in the immediate sense—that is, aid to owners or purchasers of residential or commercial properties, as distinct from aid to financial institutions serving that sector or to urban redevelopment projects and the like—has been entirely the work of direct agencies of the government. Both direct lending and (increasingly through time) insurance or guarantee of loans have been the methods used.

Chart 14 shows two periods of intense activity in direct lending, 1934–1935 and 1949–1953. The first came when the Home Owners' Loan Corporation was refinancing large amounts of home mortgages, and the second when federally insured or guaranteed mortgages were being purchased on a large scale by the Federal National Mortgage Association. Throughout the period direct loans were made on a relatively modest scale by other agencies, namely the RFC Mortgage Company, the FHA, the VA, the Defense Homes Corporation, and the Housing and Home Finance Agency.

In contrast, the insurance and guarantee of privately made housing loans has grown steadily and in recent years quite steeply. The outstanding amounts of federal liability rose in every year from the beginning of the activity, and during 1947–1953 increased more than fivefold, to over $26 billion (Chart 14). The annual volume of insurance or guarantees, except for minor reductions during the war and in 1951 and 1952, also moved steadily upward. During 1953, the commitments made by federal agencies through insurance or guarantee of housing loans totaled about $5.9 billion.

The relative importance of the federal agencies' direct lending is shown in Chart 15 where it gives annually their percentage share of the estimated total mortgage debt on nonfarm residential structures. The imperfections of the measure[5] involve relatively small amounts

---

[5] Federal credit includes some loans on commercial (as well as residential) structures, by the RFC Mortgage Company; and it is not certain whether direct loans by the Defense Homes Corporation, HHFA, FHA, and VA are included in the debt total as well as in the federal share.

CHART 14

Federal Credit for Nonfarm Housing, 1933–1953

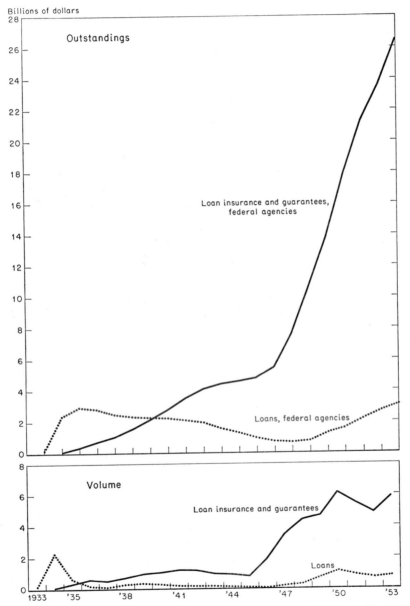

From Table A-7. For data on the components of the series, see Tables A-10, A-11, A-14, A-17, A-28, and A-30.

CHART 15

Ratios of Housing Loans Held by Federal Agencies and of
Outstanding Home Loans Insured by FHA or Guaranteed
by VA to Estimated Nonfarm Residential Mortgage
Debt, 1933–1952

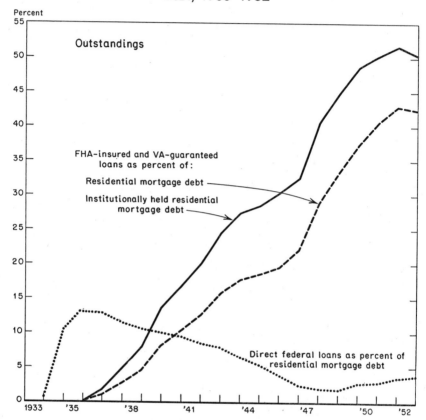

Federal agency direct housing loans are from Table A-7. FHA-insured outstandings for 1935–1938 were estimated as of June 30 from the "Annual Reports"
of the Federal Housing Administration (all other data are year-end figures). Data
for FHA, 1939–1952, and VA, 1945–1952, are from "Housing Statistics" (Housing and Home Finance Agency), January 1954, pp. 37 and 41; and for institutionally held and total nonfarm residential mortgage debt, from Table N-2 in
"Capital Formation in Residential Real Estate: Trends and Prospects," by Leo
Grebler, David M. Blank, and Louis Winnick (Princeton University Press for the
National Bureau of Economic Research, 1956).

The estimates of total residential debt cover loans on one- to four-family houses
and multifamily structures held by open and closed commercial banks, mutual
savings banks, open and closed savings and loan associations, life insurance and
other insurance companies, real estate and mortgage investment companies, the
Home Owners' Loan Corporation, the Federal National Mortgage Association, and
miscellaneous other institutions, as well as those held by individuals and other
noninstitutional investors.

and for present purposes can be ignored. Federal agencies held 13 percent of the residential mortgage debt in 1935—that share representing almost exclusively the activity of the HOLC—but in recent years only 3 to 4 percent.

The relative importance of government insurance and guarantee of loans is also shown in Chart 15, by measuring federally protected loans against the total residential mortgage debt and then against the part of it held by institutional lenders, both private and public (excluding HOLC). Outstandings of loans carrying federal protection steadily increased as against the amount of conventional loans, until by the end of 1952 about 40 percent of the total and 50 percent of the institutionally held debt was underwritten by the federal government.

Since federal protection does not always apply to the full amount of a loan, another way of measuring its relative importance is to compare the amount of the government's contingent liability actually in force with the debt total. This gives somewhat lower percentages, but still indicates a role of considerable importance: thus, in 1952 the liability of federal agencies for insured or guaranteed loans amounted to 34 percent of all nonfarm residential mortgage debt. In short, whatever measure is employed, it is seen that the federal government now has a large part of the urban mortgage debt under its insurance protection; naturally, through its influence on the contract terms of the protected loans, it exerts also a very considerable influence, as will be shown later, on the contract terms of that part of the mortgage debt which is written on an uninsured basis.

The federally sponsored Home Loan Bank system—consisting of the Home Loan Bank Board, the eleven district banks with their member institutions, and the Federal Savings and Loan Insurance Corporation—was formed with the immediate object of aiding savings and loan associations that had been adversely affected in the depression years of the early thirties by heavy demands on them for withdrawal of funds and by illiquidity of their investment holdings, and to provide a continuing pool of credit which would supplement, as circumstances might require, the associations' resources for investment in real estate markets.

Chart 16 traces the annual volume of Home Loan Bank advances to members[6] and of repayments, and also compares the outstanding

6 The membership at the end of 1953 consisted of 4,108 savings and loan associa-

CHART 16
Federal Home Loan Bank Lending Activity and Outstanding Mortgage Loans of Savings and Loan Associations, 1932–1953

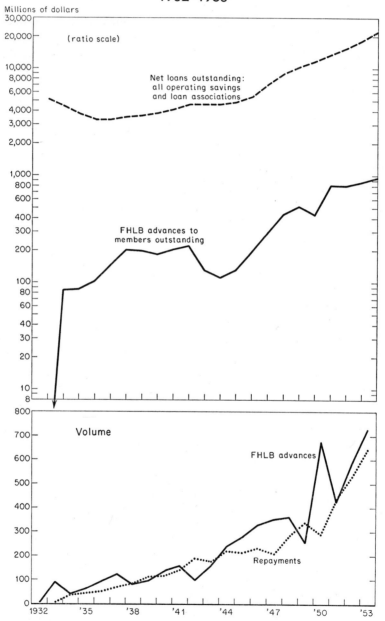

From "Housing Statistics" (Housing and Home Finance Agency), January 1954, p. 43, and "Trends in the Savings and Loan Field, 1953" (Home Loan Bank Board), Table 1, p. 4.

amounts of such advances with the outstanding loans of all operating savings and loan associations. Lending by the Home Loan Banks was negligible in the early thirties and reached a considerable volume only during the real estate credit expansion following World War II. The low level of borrowing which prevailed from 1932 through 1936 may be explained by the fact that the net loans of savings and loan associations declined in those years by somewhat more than did their private share capital.[7] Individual associations doubtless found themselves hard pressed at that time, but the group as a whole was holding less assets, on balance, year after year. Outstanding net loans of associations grew moderately in 1937 and 1938 but their increased demand for funds was apparently satisfied through the liquidation of owned real estate, a process which began in 1937 to provide substantial amounts of funds for the expansion of other types of assets.

Changes are shown for the period 1939–1953 in the unadjusted net sources and uses of funds account for all operating associations in Table 47. Through 1945 the growth of private share capital, plus the liquidation of owned real estate, exceeded by substantial amounts the net increase in mortgage holdings, and for that matter in the total assets of all associations, and Home Loan Bank advances were retired on balance by a small amount. In the three-year period 1946–1948 a rapid increase in mortgage loan holdings was financed with relatively small demands on the Home Loan Banks, mainly from increased private shareholder capital and by the liquidation of United States government securities. Heavy dependence on the Home Loan Banks did not come until 1950 when associations expanded their loan accounts by some $2 billion and their shareholder accounts by only $1.5 billion. By that time their holdings of government securities had been largely liquidated and there was an immediate and heavy draft on the Home Loan Banks for supplementary funds. Repayments on Home Loan Bank advances about equaled new advances in 1951 and 1952 but member associations were moderate net borrowers in 1953. The lending policy of the Home Loan Banks made it possible for the associations to participate more heavily than would

---

tions (about two-thirds of all operating associations), 23 mutual savings banks, and 3 insurance companies (*Seventh Annual Report*, Housing and Home Finance Agency, 1953, p. 143; *Trends in the Savings and Loan Field, 1953*, Home Loan Bank Board, p. 4).

[7] For selected data on the financial condition of savings and loan associations over the period 1932 to 1938 see *Trends in the Savings and Loan Field, 1954*, Home Loan Bank Board, p. 3.

TABLE 47

Sources and Uses of Funds of All Operating Savings and
Loan Associations, Selected Periods, 1939–1953

(*in millions*)

Sources and Uses	*1939–45*	*1946–48*	*1949*	*1950*	*1951–52*	*1953*
Uses of Funds						
First mortgage loans[a]	$1,762	$4,929	$1,311	$2,006	$4,714	$3,546
Owned real estate	−868	−21	3	6	0	−1
U.S. government securities	2,345	−965	7	27	302	132
Other assets[b]	84	379	279	191	735	381
Total Uses	$3,323	$4,322	$1,600	$2,230	$5,751	$4,058
Sources of Funds						
Private savings capital	$3,288	$3,599	$1,507	$1,507	$5,165	$3,635
FHLB advances	−8	310	−76	365	56	87
Reserves and undivided profits	129	323	140	174	381	244
Other liabilities and capital[c]	−86	90	29	184	149	92
Total Sources	$3,323	$4,322	$1,600	$2,230	$5,751	$4,058

Derived by taking the first differences between year-end balance sheet items of the year preceding and ending each period. A negative use is a source and a negative source is a use. Data are from *Trends in the Savings and Loan Field, 1954,* Home Loan Bank Board, Table 2, p. 4.

[a] Net of mortgage pledged shares.

[b] Includes real estate sold on contract, non-real-estate loans, FHLB stock and other investments, cash on hand and in banks, net fixed assets, and miscellaneous other assets.

[c] Includes U.S. government savings capital, other borrowed money, loans in process, permanent stock, deferred credits, and other liabilities.

otherwise have been possible in the real estate expansion which followed 1949.

The member associations of the Home Loan Bank system have used its facilities fairly widely; 2,147 of them (including one non-member noninsured state-chartered association and one insurance company) were indebted to the banks at the end of 1953—52 percent of the membership.[8] Dependence on FHLB funds varies among districts. At the end of 1952, for example, amounts owed by associations to the Cincinnati district bank equaled less than 2 percent of their total assets; in the San Francisco district, the corresponding ratio was nearly 6 percent. Puerto Rican associations, with FHLB advances equal to more than 8 percent of their total resources, were

[8] *Seventh Annual Report,* Housing and Home Finance Agency, 1953, pp. 136 and 143.

the most dependent of all.[9] Interestingly enough, it is the larger associations, as will be seen in Table 48, which have recently been most dependent on advances from the FHLB's.

Services

The credit extended by private agencies in the real estate market is of two types: long-term, or so-called permanent, mortgage credit extended to finance the purchase of new or existing structures; and short-term loans primarily to builders, to finance the construction process itself. There is a close connection between the two, since the proceeds of long-term financing are frequently employed in part to liquidate the short-term construction loans. Loans made to finance repair, alteration, or modernization of existing structures— usually on a medium- or short-term installment payment basis— complete the system of credits directly involved in the production and transfer of urban real estate. Certain additional types of credit are provided on a relatively minor scale, which nevertheless play a critical role in the real estate financing process. Credits are frequently advanced to finance holdings of mortgages that are passing from their originator (usually a builder, or a mortgage loan or investing company closely connected with a builder) to the hands of a long-term investing agency. These "warehousing" credits serve to bridge the time intervals required to find permanent financing for mortgages. They have been used for a number of years where an interregional flow of funds is involved, and more recently have also served to supplement with short-term credit, and presumably on a temporary basis, the flow of long-term funds available for mortgage investment.

Although some institutions engage in several of the operations, there is a fairly high degree of functional specialization among private real estate financing institutions. Insurance companies, savings banks, trust and pension funds, and other long-term investors are predominantly interested in permanent financing; commercial banks and savings and loan associations are to all intents and purposes the sole sources of construction financing, and commercial banks of warehousing credits; the placing of construction loans and

---

[9] From *Trends in the Savings and Loan Field, 1953*, Home Loan Bank Board, Tables 6 and 7, pp. 9–15. The percentages given measure outstanding FHLB advances to members against the assets of all operating associations in a district. When only member associations' assets are considered, the percentages are practically the same, since nonmember associations are comparatively of very small asset size.

TABLE 48

Number of FHLB-Member Savings and Loan Associations and Their Ratios of FHLB Borrowing to Total Assets, By Size Group, 1946 and 1952

TOTAL ASSET SIZE (000)	DECEMBER 31, 1946			DECEMBER 31, 1952		
	No. of Assns.	% Distribution Total Assets	FHLB Borrowings as % of Total Assets	No. of Assns.	% Distribution Total Assets	FHLB Borrowings as % of Total Assets
Less than $250	509	0.9%	2.33%	479	0.7%	3.77%
250–499.9	539	2.2	2.51	545	1.9	3.79
500–999.9	662	5.2	3.20	1,047	8.0	3.13
1,000–2,499	955	17.3	3.73	799	13.6	3.41
2,500–4,999	584	23.1	3.14	648	21.4	3.27
5,000–9,999	260	19.8	3.02	379	26.7	4.00
10,000–24,999	127	20.7	3.04	131	27.8	5.03
25,000 and over	25	10.8	2.86			
Total	3,661	100.0%	3.15%	4,028	100.0%	3.97%

From the Federal Home Loan Bank Administration's *Annual Report, Combined Financial Statements of Members of the Federal Home Loan Bank System,* 1946, Table 8, and the Home Loan Bank Board's *Combined Financial Statements of Members of the Federal Home Loan Bank System,* 1952, Table 3, p. 13.

mortgage loans, and in some cases the secondary distribution of the latter, and a certain amount of the arrangements for refinancing are handled by mortgage loan or investment companies, dealers, and brokers. In the aggregate these agencies comprise the private mortgage financing system.

Federal credit programs in the field of real estate financing do not reach directly into each area of financial service, yet their role is a strategic one. In many cases the availability of long-term financing is contingent upon the possibility of obtaining loan insurance or guarantee under one of the federal programs, and it is often true that the availability of permanent financing is a necessary prerequisite to the availability to construction or warehousing credit. Thus the system of loan insurance and loan guarantees support to a great extent the whole structure of mortgage credit. In addition, the federal government has extended substantial amounts of credit directly to the real estate market. The following sections describe in detail the services of the principal federal agencies involved, and compare them wherever possible with the services rendered independently by private lending agencies. We follow the order in which the main kinds of federal activity began: the refinancing of defaulted home mortgages by HOLC; credit support for privately made loans, begun by FHA and later augmented by the VA guaranty program; the activity of the RFC Mortgage Company and FNMA in the secondary market; and the VA direct loan program.

REFINANCING DEFAULTED HOME MORTGAGES:
THE HOME OWNERS' LOAN CORPORATION

The Home Owners' Loan Corporation was set up in June 1933 as a depression-alleviating device. The response was immediate and widespread: within four months it received something over 400,000 applications for the refinancing of home mortgage loans, and nearly 1,900,000 by mid-1935. It has been estimated that in twenty-five states applications for refinancing loans were received from one-half of all those homeowners potentially eligible for assistance—owner-occupants of one- to four-family nonfarm properties appraised by the HOLC at not over $20,000 and whose mortgages were in default.[10] Although a good many of the applications were ultimately withdrawn by the prospective borrower or rejected by the HOLC, 54 percent were accepted. Loans were made approximately—one million

[10] Harriss, *op.cit.*, Tables 1, 2, and 5, pp. 17, 21f., and 32f.

in number for a total of $3.1 billion—to an estimated 21 percent of all homeowners eligible for assistance. Other lending programs administered by HOLC were incidental to its major task of refinancing defaulted mortgages and will not be discussed in detail. Specifically, they consisted of (a) direct cash loans, either for the payment of taxes where a tax sale was imminent or for refinancing defaulted loans where a lender refused to accept HOLC bonds, (b) group or wholesale purchases of loans from banks in receivership, (c) direct advances for the maintenance or reconditioning of properties, and (d) direct credits to individuals in connection with the sale by HOLC of properties acquired through foreclosure—the so-called "vendee" loans.[11]

HOLC dealt entirely with distressed mortgagors, yet its services were employed more frequently by homeowners in what might be described as the middle income group. This point is not easily established, but it is strongly suggested by the data in Table 49, which show that a much lower proportion of HOLC borrowers in the New York region had incomes of under $1,200 annually than did a sample of families in Trenton, New Jersey, which can probably be taken as

TABLE 49

Income Distributions of HOLC Borrowers in the New York Region, 1933–1934, and of Families in Trenton, New Jersey, 1933

Annual Family Income	HOLC Borrowers[a]	Trenton, New Jersey Families[b]
Under $600	12.5%	36.2[c]%
600–1,199	29.2	28.7
1,200–1,799	28.5	17.7
1,800–2,399	15.8	7.8
2,400–2,999	7.5	5.2
3,000 and over	6.5	4.4
Total	100.0%	100.0%

[a] Based on a sample of HOLC loans made in New York, New Jersey, and Connecticut, from *History and Policies of the Home Owners' Loan Corporation*, by C. Lowell Harriss (National Bureau of Economic Research, Financial Research Program, 1951), Table 8, p. 51. Original data, referring mainly to 1933–1934, have been adjusted by assuming that the loans for which information was not available were distributed in the same proportion as the known cases.

[b] Based on a sample of families in Trenton, New Jersey, from *Changes in Income Distribution during the Great Depression*, by Horst Mendershausen (National Bureau of Economic Research, 1946), Appendix B.

[c] Includes families with no income.

[11] *Ibid.*, pp. 37, 38, 127ff., and 137ff.

broadly similar to the population from which HOLC borrowers in the New York region were drawn. More pertinent would be an income comparison of HOLC borrowers with the generality of mortgagors (rather than with the whole population), but requisite data are lacking.

Certain other facts also suggest that HOLC functioned most in the middle-income range. Only about 6 percent of the HOLC-financed New York region properties were valued at less than $3,000, as against 10 percent for all nonfarm, owner-occupied properties in that area; and only slightly more than 30 percent of the HOLC-financed New York region properties were valued at $8,000 or over, as contrasted with more than 45 percent for all owner-occupied dwellings. It was in the intermediate zone of property values—from $3,000 to $8,000—that HOLC was relatively most active: over 60 percent of the properties financed by the HOLC were in that range, as against about 40 percent of the comparable properties in the real estate market as a whole.[12]

Further evidence that those who received HOLC aid, even though they were in default on their mortgages, held an intermediate economic position with respect to the whole population is seen in the fact that the structures securing HOLC loans were far from inferior in quality. Thus, 87 percent of those refinanced by the HOLC in the New York region had central heating facilities and 84 percent had the same number of baths as families; 57 percent were less than fifteen years old, as compared with only 41.3 percent for all nonfarm owner-occupied properties in the area; and 77 percent had depreciated by less than 25 percent.[13]

Also, while HOLC loans were relatively modest in amount they were not notably smaller than home mortgage loans in general. Sample data indicate that the average size of such loans originated by life insurance companies during 1930–1934 was $5,500; by commercial banks, $4,300; and by savings and loan associations, $2,800.[14] The average size of HOLC loans made between August 1933 and June

12 *Ibid.*, Table 15, p. 58. Data were adjusted by assuming that the loans for which information was unavailable were distributed in the same proportions as the known cases.

13 *Ibid.*, Tables 11, 12, and 17, pp. 55, 56, and 60. Data were adjusted by distributing information-lacking loans in the same proportions as the known cases.

14 From *Urban Mortgage Lending: Comparative Markets and Experience*, by J. E. Morton (Princeton University Press for the National Bureau of Economic Research, 1956), Table 37, p. 94. Refers to loans on one- to four-family dwellings, without regard to owner occupancy.

1936 (that is, the average amount advanced in purchase of a defaulted mortgage) was about $3,000.[15] In general these facts suggest that the individuals aided by HOLC were drawn from the lower middle-income brackets of the population and that even among mortgagors generally, who would be expected to have a somewhat better than average income position in the community, they probably were not notably concentrated in the lower ranges. The credits advanced went, of course, to the financial institutions from whom the defaulted mortgages were purchased, but it is a matter of interest that they alleviated the financial circumstances of what might be described as a lower middle-income group.

LOAN INSURANCE AND GUARANTEES:
THE FHA AND VA PROGRAMS

No activity of government has made a greater impress on the private mortgage market than its loan insurance and guarantee programs. These consist primarily of the FHA's programs for insurance of home modernization and repair loans and for insurance of mortgages on one- to four-family and larger, so-called "project" dwellings, and the VA's program of guarantees of loans for the purchase or construction of owner-occupied residences.

Loans for home modernization and repair. At the same time that it provided for Federal Housing Administration insurance of home mortgage loans, the National Housing Act of 1934 authorized the program under which the FHA insures medium-term amortized loans for the modernization and repair of specified types of properties, the principal purpose being to stimulate expenditures for home improvement as a counter-cyclical measure. The program for insuring modernization loans (Title I program) was the first to get under way, and with the stimulus of considerable publicity it quickly grew to sizable dimensions: in the first three years of operation over a million loans were insured. At the outset loans made by eligible institutions for approved purposes were insured up to 20 percent of the aggregate amount loaned by the individual lender. Later, when it became clear that losses on the loans were relatively small, the percentage was reduced to 10; and in 1939 a fee for the insurance service was introduced and the program was put on a self-supporting and presumably permanent basis. After the disclosure of sometimes spectacular practices of fraud in connection with the contracts under

[15] Harriss, *op.cit.*, Table 4, p. 30.

which homeowners had borrowed money under this program, the Housing Act of 1954 provided that the lender assume up to 10 percent of the loss sustained on individual loans, thus introducing a new principle of loss sharing as between the federal government and the private lending institution.

From the beginning of the program to the end of 1953 nearly 16,600,000 loans, with net proceeds of over $7.4 billion, were insured.[16] In 1953, the following types of loans were eligible for insurance under Title I on the terms indicated:[17]

		MAXIMUM PERMISSIBLE		
TYPE OF LOAN	TYPE OF IMPROVEMENT	*Maturity*	*Amount*	*Annual Financing Charge*
Class 1 (a)	Repair, alteration, or improvement of *an existing structure*	3 years	$2,500	5% discount
Class 1 (b)	Repair, alteration, improvement, or conversion of *an existing multifamily structure*	7 years, 32 days	$10,000	5% discount if $2,500 or less; 4% if more
	Construction of *a new structure for:*			
Class 2 (a)	Nonfarm, nonresidential use	3 years, 32 days	$3,000	5% discount
Class 2 (b)	Farm, nonresidential use	7 years, 32 days or 15 years, 32 days, if secured by first lien	$3,000	5%, or 3.5% discount if maturity is over 7 years, 32 days

The Title I program has been widely used by financial institutions, mainly by commercial banks, which accounted for 76 percent of the net proceeds of loans insured in the years 1934–1953. Finance companies accounted for 20 percent and savings and loan associations for 4 percent of the loans insured.[18] For the most part, the loans have been of small amount and of relatively short term, usually three years or under; and during 1953, as in most other years, they were

---

16 *Seventh Annual Report*, Housing and Home Finance Agency, 1953, Table 61, p. 297.

17 *Ibid.*, p. 187.

18 *Sixth Annual Report*, Housing and Home Finance Agency, 1952, Tables 63 and 64, pp. 337f., and the agency's *Seventh Annual Report*, 1953, Tables 66 and 67, pp. 304f.

made predominantly for the improvement of single family properties.[19] The principal types of improvement for which loans in 1953 were made, given in descending order, were: insulation, heating, exterior finish, plumbing, interior finish, and roofing.[20]

Home mortgage loans. When the innovation of federal home mortgage insurance was launched in 1934 with the establishment of the Federal Housing Administration, the scale on which it would develop was neither intended nor foreseen. Today more than two-fifths of the outstanding home mortgage debt ($75.6 billion at the end of 1954) comprises loans made under conditions of federal insurance or guarantee;[21] and though estimates of debt on larger structures are not available, the evidence on nonfarm housing starts that was shown in Table 9 (Chapter 2) indicates that during the war and in 1947–1951 most apartment house projects, too, utilized federal credit support. It is not too much to say that through FHA and VA the entire structure of residential housing credit has been brought under federal influence.

Two measures are available of the extent to which various types of financial institutions extend mortgage credit on an insured basis, namely the proportions of all insured and guaranteed loans that are originated by the different types of agencies, and the proportions of the current mortgage holdings of major institutional lenders that consist of insured loans. Data on originations are given in Table 50 through mid-1954 for VA loans through 1953 for FHA. It should be borne in mind, of course, that an agency does not necessarily hold the same proportion of insured loans that it originates. Particularly, real estate and mortgage investment companies are major originators of loans but occupy a minor position as permanent investors.

As will be seen in Chart 17, insured mortgages comprise almost one-half of the combined residential mortgage holdings of the principal institutional lenders, but there are interesting differences among types of institutions in use of federal credit support; the relative unimportance of FHA insurance to savings and loan associations is perhaps the most notable.

Finally, the home mortgage market served by the federal programs may be described, and contrasted with the market served by the so-called conventional or uninsured loan, in terms of the bor-

---

[19] *Seventh Annual Report,* Housing and Home Finance Agency, 1953, pp. 306ff.
[20] *Ibid.,* Table 71, p. 308.
[21] *Savings and Loan Fact Book, 1955,* United States Savings and Loan League, p. 24.

TABLE 50

Type of Institution Originating FHA-Insured and
VA-Guaranteed Home Mortgage Loans
*(percentage distribution of cumulative
amount of loans made)*

Type of Institution	FHA 1935–1953	VA 1944 to mid-1954
Commercial banks	36.9%	25.9%
Mortgage and real estate companies	27.8	27.7
Savings and loan associations	10.4	27.6
Savings banks	4.6	11.8
Insurance companies	16.5	6.4
All others and individuals	3.8	0.6

For FHA, from the *Annual Reports* of the Federal Housing Administration
and of the Housing and Home Finance Agency; for VA, from *G.I. Loans—the
First Ten Years* (VA Pamphlet 4A-11), Chart 6, p. 31.

CHART 17

Insured and Guaranteed versus Conventional Residential
Mortgages: Holdings of Principal Private Lending
Institutions Compared, 1953

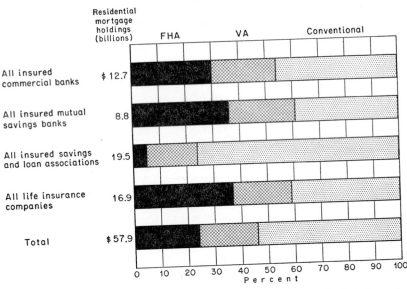

End-of-year data: for commercial banks and mutual savings banks, from the
"Annual Report" of the Federal Deposit Insurance Corporation, 1953, p. 101;
for federal savings and loan associations, from the "Seventh Annual Report" of
the Housing and Home Finance Agency, 1953, p. 153; and for life insurance
companies, from "Mortgage Investments of Life Insurance Companies" (Home
Loan Bank Board, 1953), p. 2.

rower's economic position—his income, the price of the house he buys, his occupational status—and of the terms on which credit is made available. Table 51 presents evidence on borrower characteristics, where it will be seen that the federal programs, particularly FHA, are employed with the greatest relative frequency by a

TABLE 51

Conventional versus Insured or Guaranteed First Mortgage Financing for Home Buyers Grouped by Price of House, Income, and Occupation, October 1950–March 1951

Characteristics of Property and Buyer	FHA- Insured	VA- Guaranteed	Conven- tional	Total
PURCHASE PRICE OF HOUSE				
Less than $5,000	10%	11%	79%	100%
5,000–7,499	15	26	59	100
7,500–9,999	26	31	43	100
10,000–12,499	27	30	43	100
12,500–14,999	16	29	55	100
15,000 and over	19	8	73	100
ANNUAL INCOME OF HOME BUYER				
Under $3,000	19	21	60	100
3,000–3,999	16	30	54	100
4,000–4,999	21	30	49	100
5,000–7,499	29	18	53	100
7,500 and over	15	13	72	100
OCCUPATIONAL STATUS OF HOME BUYER				
Professional and semi-professional	23	24	53	100
Managerial and self-employed	20	12	68	100
Clerical and sales	27	29	44	100
Skilled and semiskilled	19	27	54	100
Unskilled and service	10	20	70	100
Other	10	22	68	100

Data are for purchases during the period October 12, 1950 to March 15, 1951 of new and existing one- or two-family nonfarm dwellings for owner occupancy, from a nationwide sample survey conducted by National Analysts, Inc. for the Board of Governors of the Federal Reserve System. See *Federal Reserve Bulletin*, July 1951, Tables 9, 16, and 19, pp. 786, 790, and 793.

middle class of home buyers. Individuals both in the lowest and in the highest income brackets, those buying the least, and those buying the most, expensive home, and buyers in occupational groups consistent with these brackets of income and wealth are more frequently found borrowing on a conventional basis than are those in the in-between groups, where the dependence on FHA-insured or VA-guaranteed loans is greatest. The reasons differ for houses in the upper and lower price brackets. In the case of the more expensive dwellings, the fact that there is an upper limit on the amount of the loan that will be insured by FHA means that the loan-to-value ratio required under the insured loan is no more liberal than that which might be obtained on a conventional loan; and the fact that the percentage of the loan guaranteed by VA declines as loan size rises makes lenders less willing to assume the risks involved. At the other end of the price range, buyers able to purchase only the least expensive houses either cannot meet the standards set up for insured financing or are unable to find a willing lender at the maximum rates set by the insuring or guaranteeing authorities. This suggests that one of the principal effects of the maximum rate schedules on federally protected financing is largely to cut off this type of service from borrowers in the least favored economic positions. It is true also with apartment house projects that those of the more expensive type are predominantly financed by uninsured mortgage loans; the federal programs have been more prominent in projects built for war or defense housing purposes and for structures organized for ownership on a cooperative plan.

As for the terms on which home mortgage financing is available, there is considerable overlapping of markets as between the federally protected and the conventional loans but, as will be seen in Chart 18, clear differences are nonetheless evident: VA loans carry much the most liberal loan-to-value ratios, conventional loans are clearly the most conservative, and FHA loans are in an intermediate position. The availability of VA-guaranteed loans on which little or no down payment is made has been dependent on the condition of the money market in general and on the anti-inflationary policies of the government. In 1944–1946, no-down-payment loans accounted for nearly 60 percent of the total first mortgage home loans made under VA guaranty. During the recession of 1948–1949 and the period of credit controls in effect from July 1950 through 1952 their importance dropped considerably. In 1953 and especially in 1954 after a rise in the interest rate on federally protected loans to $4\frac{1}{2}$ percent, and some decline in yields on other types of investments, an increased volume of funds was attracted to the mortgage market. No-down-payment loans increased from less than 5 percent of total VA loans

CHART 18

Loan-to-Value Ratios of FHA-Insured, VA-Guaranteed,
and Conventional Loans, 1949–1950

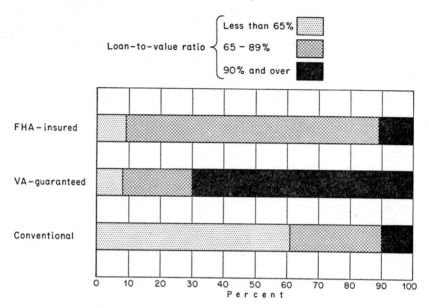

Data are for new owner-occupied one-family dwellings acquired during 1949 and the first half of 1950 as reported in the census Survey of Residential Financing. See "Housing Research" (Housing and Home Finance Agency), Winter 1951–1952, Table 1, p. 9.

closed in 1952 to 14.7 percent in 1954.[22] In addition, some so-called "negative down payment" loans began to appear, namely those on which the proceeds of the loan were enlarged to cover closing costs.

In original maturity provisions, however, FHA- and VA-protected loans differ little. In 1953 the average maturity for home loans closed under VA guaranty was about 21 years; for single family home loans insured by FHA under Section 203, the average maturity was 22 years in the case of new, and 20 years in the case of existing properties.[23]

Within the field of conventional lending, the policies of financial institutions differ, and it is of interest to compare the characteristics

[22] *G.I. Loans—the First Ten Years*, p. 20, and the *Annual Report* of the Administrator of Veterans Affairs, 1954, p. 95.

[23] Data for VA-guaranteed loans are for the fiscal year ending June 30, from the *Annual Report* of the Administrator of Veterans Affairs, 1954, p. 95. Data on FHA-insured loans are for the calendar year, from *Seventh Annual Report*, Housing and Home Finance Agency, 1953, Table 18, p. 228.

of conventional loans by particular types of lender with the characteristics of federally protected loans. Sample survey materials gathered by the National Bureau of Economic Research in 1947 afford data on the contract terms of conventional loans on one- to four-family residential structures that were held at that time by three of the principal institutional lenders.[24] Whereas less than 10 percent of the federally protected home loans analyzed in Chart 18 had loan-to-value ratios under 65 percent, the percentages of conventional home loans where the ratio was less than 60 percent were: for commercial banks, 67 percent; life insurance companies, 43 percent; savings and loan associations, 25 percent. Of the conventional loans held by savings and loan associations, only 7 percent had contract lengths of twenty years or more; of commercial bank loans, 1 percent; of life insurance company loans, 31 percent. To be compared with interest rates (in 1947) or 4 percent on VA-guaranteed home loans and 4.5 percent on FHA-insured loans are the following average current interest rates on conventional loans held: by savings and loan associations, 5.2 percent; by commercial banks, 4.7 percent; by life insurance companies, 4.6 percent. Thus in contract maturity and rate of interest the conventional loans of life insurance companies most nearly resembled federally protected loans, and in loan-to-value ratios the savings and loan associations, which made less use of federal protection than the other lenders, came closest in their conventional lending to matching the insured or guaranteed loans.

It would be a mistake to interpret the above data as evidences of differences in credit liberality without reference to the character and quality of the loans involved. The conventional loans made by life insurance companies on small residential dwellings also resemble FHA-insured loans fairly closely in certain other characteristics (size, for example) and in quality; the conventional loans of savings and loan associations and of commercial banks, on the other hand, are doubtless sufficiently different in character to warrant differences in the contract terms which they carry.

The fact that conventional loans often carry terms that are sub-

[24] Loans held by 24 large life insurance companies were sampled as of December 31, 1946; by 170 commercial banks, chiefly as of mid-1947; by 202 savings and loan associations, chiefly as of the fall of 1947. The survey is fully described in *Urban Mortgage Lending: Comparative Markets and Experience*, by J. E. Morton (Princeton University Press for the National Bureau of Economic Research, 1956), Chapter 4 and Appendix A.

stantially at variance with those available on federally protected credits, in some cases being more, and in other cases, less favorable to the mortgagor, is consistent, of course, with the facts reviewed above to the effect that insured and guaranteed loans (especially the former) are made predominantly to individuals occupying a middle position as regards income and value of home purchased. One would expect that loans made without insurance or guarantee to borrowers in a more favored economic status would carry more favorable contract conditions, and vice versa. In other words, a division of the market would seem to have been reached in which the federal programs reach a mass of standardized middle-quality credits and in which conventional lending supplies the needs of mortgagors who are distributed, in their economic and financial position, mainly on either side of the middle ground and who require a loan such as will deviate, in its terms, from the standard pattern.

Mortgages on multi-unit dwellings. Extensive use of the loan insurance facilities of the federal government was made in the apartment house or "project mortgage" field in the war years, when as much as 90 percent of the units constructed were started under, or in contemplation of, financing arrangements that involved FHA insurance. The percentage dropped sharply in 1945–1946, was above 60 throughout 1947–1951, years of high construction activity, but then again fell, to just over 25 in 1953 as building in the multi-unit field came to consist more of the higher-cost structures.

Relevant section numbers of the National Housing Act help in specifying briefly the projects carried out under FHA insurance. During 1952 the programs were concerned with rental projects (Section 207), cooperative housing (213), veterans' emergency rental housing (608), the disposition of existing publicly constructed housing (608, pursuant to 610), rental projects of twenty-five or more site-fabricated houses (611), military rental housing (803; Maybank-Wherry Bill), and rental projects in critical defense areas (908). In 1953 activity concerned mainly the Section 207, 213, and 803 projects. Section 608 insurance, which had earlier been of such importance, was terminated by the Housing Act of 1954 after the investigation of so-called overlending in that program. The same act severely restricted other elements of the program, and activity sharply declined.

The kinds of structures financed have varied somewhat from one insurance program to another: one-family structures of the row type and those that are detached or partly detached are most frequent with housing built in or near military installations for military personnel; in other rental project programs the structures consist mainly of the walk-up apartment type; cooperative housing projects are either elevator type or one-family (row, semidetached, or detached) houses. Military housing projects have been the largest, averaging about 300 units per project in 1950–1953, as against averages of about 165 units for cooperative housing and 90 units for Section 207 rental projects.[25]

Fair comparisons of monthly rental values in projects of different types are difficult to make, but it may be of interest to note that 77 percent of the dwelling units in cooperative housing projects for which insurance commitments were issued in 1953 carried monthly charges of $70 to $100, whereas only 35 percent of the units in Section 207 projects had rentals in that range.[26] Over half the units in Section 207 projects were planned to rent for $110 or more per month. The lowest proposed rents were those in the military and defense housing projects: 56 percent of the military units had monthly rentals of $60 to $80, and nearly 80 percent of the defense units were to rent at $80 to $100.[27]

Since the size of loan per unit and its ratio to the value of the property are limited, under the different programs, by statute or FHA regulation, data on these matters are difficult to interpret. Nearly all mortgages insured in 1953 under the cooperative housing program, and almost half in the case of military and defense housing, were in amounts of $8,000 or more per dwelling unit (specifically, 98, 46, and 45 percent). Besides giving rise to comparatively large loans, the cooperative and defense housing programs also involved the highest loan-to-value ratios, with 48 and 69 percent, respectively, of the mortgage loans insured in 1953 being for amounts equal to 85 percent or more of the replacement cost of the project.[28]

The extent to which various types of financial institutions participate as originators of insured project-mortgage loans, or as holders of such loans, or in their purchase and sale is summarized in Table 52. Commercial banks were the principal originators of FHA project mortgages in 1953, doubtless because of their role in financ-

25 Estimated from *Annual Reports* of the Housing and Home Finance Agency.
26 *Seventh Annual Report*, Housing and Home Finance Agency, 1953, Table 58, p. 292.
27 *Ibid.*, pp. 283 and 286.
28 *Ibid.*, Tables 55 and 56, pp. 287 and 290.

TABLE 52

Originations, Holdings, and Transfers of FHA-Insured Project Mortgages, 1953, by Principal Agencies

AGENCY	ORIGINATIONS DURING YEAR			HOLDINGS AT YEAR END		TRANSFERS DURING YEAR	
	Amount (000,000)	Percentage Distribution	Average Size (000)	Amount (000,000)	Percentage Distribution	Net Purchases (000,000)	Net Sales (000,000)
Commercial banks	$151	58%	$1,320	$ 552	13%	..	$284
Savings banks	38	15	1,533	1,469	35	$120	..
Insurance companies	10	4	1,156	1,502	36	63	1
Savings and loan assns.	10	4	1,476	29	1	..	..
Mortgage companies	32	12	676	240	6	..	42
Federal agency	2	1	703	104	2	72	..
All others	15	6	1,675	325	8	72	..
Total	$259	100%	..	$4,221	100%	..	..

Data are from *Seventh Annual Report, Housing and Home Finance Agency*, 1953, Tables 49 and 50, pp. 278 and 280. Commercial banks include state and national banks; insurance companies include life and other companies; federal agency operations are exclusively those of the Federal National Mortgage Association; "all others" include industrial banks, finance companies, investment companies, private and state benefit funds, and endowed institutions.

ing construction. Next were savings banks and mortgage investment companies; but their combined amount was less than half the total for commercial banks. Insurance companies and savings banks were the principal permanent holders of insured project mortgages.

SECONDARY MORTGAGE MARKET FACILITIES

The interest of the federal government in promoting new facilities in the secondary mortgage market, its action in 1935 empowering RFC to invest in the capital of privately formed national mortgage associations, and the failure of private initiative to create such associations have been described earlier. Accordingly a subsidiary agency, the RFC Mortgage Company, was authorized to serve as a secondary market facility in the home mortgage field by purchasing FHA-insured loans, in addition to its other services—chiefly, refinancing and construction loans on multifamily and commercial properties, and loans to distressed holders of first mortgage bonds and first mortgage certificates. During World War II other functions were added: lending to the Defense Homes Corporation; the purchase of FHA-insured, Title VI mortgages on war and defense housing; and the making of loans to defray taxes and other fixed charges on income properties in distress as a result of wartime restrictions and regulations. The RFC Mortgage Company operated from March 1935 until June 1947, when it was discontinued. By then it had disbursed, or committed itself subsequently to disburse, credits in the amount of $496 million.

The discontinuance of the RFC Mortgage Company was made possible mainly by the creation of the Federal National Mortgage Association, which was set up early in 1938 in order to provide a market for FHA-insured home mortgages. The association was subsequently authorized to conduct operations in VA-guaranteed mortgages and in all types of FHA-insured mortgages. FNMA operations can be described briefly: cumulatively through December 31, 1953 the agency had purchased $3.9 billion of mortgages and at that date was holding about $2.5 billion.[29] The difference between the two figures is accounted for by sales of mortgages, by repayments on those held, and by other credits. In the main, over the period 1938–1953, the discrepancy between purchases and sales was greatest with VA-guaranteed mortgages on single family and multifamily homes and with mortgages insured by FHA under Sections 8, 207, and 903.

29 *Ibid.*, Table 11a, p. 82.

313

Of VA single family loans, FNMA purchased $2,553 million worth and sold only $477 million, or less than one-fifth of the amount; of multifamily loans it purchased $9.1 million and sold less than one-tenth as much. Of nearly $29 million of Section 8 FHA-insured loans (for construction of one-family homes for families of low or moderate income) only one percent was sold; of $23 million Section 207 loans (rental housing project loans), less than 2 percent. Of Section 903 loans (for one- and two-family houses in critical defense areas)— a recently added program—FNMA purchased $268 million, and had sold less than one percent as much by the end of 1953. During 1953 its purchases of FHA-insured mortgages amounted to $355 million and its sales to $32 million; its purchases of VA-guaranteed mortgages, the overwhelming bulk of which were secured by single family homes, to $187 million, and its sales to $181 million.[30]

Unfortunately, it is not possible to contrast the characteristics of mortgages purchased by the Federal National Mortgage Association with those handled by the market without recourse to the federal credit agency: hence, not possible to determine whether the mortgages acquired by FNMA, and more particularly those which it holds for the longest periods of time, are relatively unattractive investments. However, in view of the fact that the mortgages in which it deals are either insured or guaranteed, there would seem to be no basis for presuming that they are of inferior credit quality. More likely, FNMA purchases, and finds it necessary to hold as a more or less permanent investment, loans in which the private market has the least interest because the costs involved in servicing them are high in relation to the interest income which they yield.

The FNMA was never empowered to act as a secondary mortgage market in the full sense of that term: its operations have always been confined to governmentally insured or guaranteed mortgages and exclude transactions in so-called conventional loans. At times its activity has been restricted to the purchase and sale of mortgages only at par and only where secured by new construction. The latter restriction was removed, however, by the Housing Act of 1954, which, through provisions described in the opening section of the chapter, effected a basic reorganization in the structure and functions of the FNMA. The history of the agency reveals clearly two distinct purposes: on the one hand, there has been pressure to use its facilities to underwrite special programs which would not be ex-

[30] *Loc.cit.*

314

pected to survive in the open financial market or which might need bolstering until the private lending industry could become favorably disposed. On the other hand, there has been an interest in designing the agency along lines enabling it to serve as lender of last resort for mortgage investors during a period of severe financial stringency. The Housing Act of 1954 made it possible for FNMA to perform both functions.

DIRECT FINANCING FOR HOMEOWNERS

Among direct lending activities of the federal government in real estate markets are certain operations of FHA and VA. The former may be ignored here since concerned entirely with financing the sale of properties acquired by FHA in foreclosure proceedings. The VA program, on the other hand, is directed specifically to supplying credit to homeowners where, for one reason or another, an inadequacy of private lending facilities is alleged.

The VA direct loan program was authorized by Congress in 1950, with resources of $150 million. Later a revolving fund was set up, consisting of the unreserved portion of the original allocation plus such funds as would become available from repayments or from sales of loans to private investors. On several occasions Congress then increased the revolving fund, adding $375 million, but subject to offset by the proceeds of loans sold to private investors. Up to the end of 1953, 42,102 loans, amounting to approximately $290 million, had been closed and fully disbursed. The average size was $6,874, as compared with $8,340 for VA-guaranteed home loans closed and fully disbursed by private lenders over the same period (August 1, 1950 to December 25, 1953).[31]

The program extends loans at 4½ percent (originally, 4 percent) in amounts of not more than $10,000 to veterans for home purchase or construction, or for construction or improvement of farm homes, provided the veteran furnishes evidence that he was unable to obtain a VA-guaranteed loan from a private lending institution in his locality at the specified maximum rate (4½ percent in May 1953). Since credit would most probably be unavailable in thinly populated places, a system of so-called eligible areas was conceived which embraced all or part of 2,600 of the 3,100 counties and independent cities in the United States in 1950. In 1952 all cities with 50,000 or more

31 Veterans' Administration, *Finance, Guaranty of Loans*, July 1950, p. 79, and *Loan Guaranty*, December 1953, pp. 69 and 75.

inhabitants in 1950 were removed and additional measures were taken to limit eligibility to smaller places.

Loans originating in smaller centers of population would very likely be smaller, on the average, than those secured by properties located in more heavily populated areas, a presumption that is borne out by the difference in average size between loans made directly by VA and those guaranteed. The size factor may partly account for the alleged unavailability of private funds, but other factors are doubtless also important, such as the relatively small number of loans available in a given area, and thus the relatively high cost of servicing loans and managing acquired properties. That loan size is insufficient to explain the lack of private credit would seem to be demonstrated by the fact that the average size of the direct loans which VA was able to sell to private lenders through the end of 1953 ($6,839) was only slightly larger than the average size of all direct loans closed up to that date ($6,740). Furthermore, there is no evidence that VA regional offices originating the largest direct loans have had any greater success in disposing of them to private lenders than the offices with a relatively low average size of loan. What factors were responsible for the unavailability of private investment funds in the first place, and subsequently in the failure of some, and success of other, regional VA offices in selling direct loans to private lenders, cannot be determined from available data. Nor can one determine how much of the requirement for home mortgage funds which was satisfied by direct government loans might have been made from private sources at an interest rate more nearly in line with the cost of administering a loan portfolio of this type.

Under the Housing Act of 1954 the Voluntary Home Mortgage Credit Program was created to facilitate private mortgage lending under federal insurance or guaranty in small communities and remote areas, as an alternative to federal mortgage lending of the kind undertaken by the VA. Under the supervision of the Administrator of the Housing and Home Finance Agency, regional committees composed of representatives of private lending agencies and builders refer credit needs not being met locally to private institutions in the region or elsewhere. As of early 1955 the program was only just organized and its effectiveness as yet unknown.

Experience

This section reviews the credit experience of the federal agencies that have made direct housing loans or loan purchases, and of the agencies that have insured or guaranteed such loans; and an attempt is made to determine whether the several programs have been self-supporting.

HOME OWNERS' LOAN CORPORATION[32]

The activities of the Home Owners' Loan Corporation consisted of two distinct operations: the refinancing of about one million distressed mortgage loans in the amount of $3 billion under its "original" lending program, and the so-called vendee loans which, in the amount of close to $600 million, financed the sale of properties acquired by HOLC through foreclosure of refinanced mortgages. Naturally the two programs involved quite different experience records: refinancing loans were made in depressed economic conditions to borrowers already in default and were destined to produce a substantial number of further defaults; vendee loans, on the other hand, were made under improved economic circumstances to individuals thought by HOLC to be capable of meeting their contract obligations. These expectations were borne out in experience: the foreclosure rate on HOLC refinancing loans was 19.1 percent; on vendee loans only about 2 percent (through March 1951, near the end of the program). Regional variation in foreclosure rates on vendee loans was slight, but on refinancing loans, marked, with foreclosures running as high as 40 percent, or thereabouts, in New York, New Jersey, and Massachusetts.

Though HOLC made its loans under conditions less favorable than those under which private mortgage lenders normally operate, its foreclosure experience conformed closely to that of private lenders. For example, 20.9 percent of the one- to four-family home mortgage loans made by major life insurance companies during the years 1925–1929, which are comparable with loans refinanced by HOLC at least in the sense that they were originated in about the same period, went to default before 1946 whereas only 1.8 percent of those made by the same companies in the years 1935–1939, when HOLC made most of its vendee loans, had gone to default and foreclosure by the end of 1946.[33] Even the exceptionally high rates which HOLC encountered in New York, Massachusetts, and New Jersey

---

[32] A full account of HOLC operations is given in Harriss, *op.cit.* The present discussion draws particularly on Chapters 6, 7, and 8 of that volume.

[33] Saulnier, *op.cit.*, Table 22, p. 84.

had their counterpart in the experience of private lenders, for it was in the New England and Middle Atlantic states that the life insurance companies experienced their highest foreclosure rates.

HOLC's studies reveal that although economic adversity was a major factor in its foreclosures—roughly 4,500 per month occurred during the contraction period extending from May 1937 to June 1938—moral factors were predominant. Thus, HOLC agents responsible for making foreclosure recommendations judged that in 45 percent of the foreclosures completed through mid-1944 the borrower had a reasonable chance to avoid default but lacked the determination to do so, and that in 22 percent of the cases properties were foreclosed because of the mortgagee's "obstinate refusal to pay." In only 18 percent of the cases were homes foreclosed because of "total inability to pay," though economic stringency doubtless played a part in the 11 percent of the cases foreclosed because of "abandonment of the property." Similar records for private lenders are not available, but it is perhaps reasonable to expect that economic rather than moral factors played the more important role in their case.

Much light is thrown on the question whether HOLC was a self-supporting undertaking from the financial viewpoint by published HOLC accounts, but not all that is needed to formulate a definitive answer. HOLC reported gross income through March 31, 1951 of $1,417 million and expenses (exclusive of losses) of $1,065 million. The $352 million difference was almost totally absorbed by HOLC's $338 million of recorded losses on loans (arising mainly from the sale of foreclosed properties); and the small indicated net profit was probably offset by costs of HOLC's operations borne by other agencies of government. For example, capital advances of $200 million were furnished by the Treasury, without interest charge; in addition, HOLC enjoyed free use of the mails and exemption from social security taxes.

In other words, a full-cost accounting would doubtless indicate a small over-all loss for the corporation. It should be borne in mind, in interpreting this result, that HOLC's losses were much affected by the directives it received from Congress; for example, on the policy to be followed in the disposition of foreclosed properties. A profit-seeking enterprise would presumably have conducted its affairs differently, and might in fact have turned what would appear to be a small loss (on a full-cost basis) into a modest profit. But these are highly speculative matters, and one is perhaps unjustified in saying more than that HOLC conducted its affairs so that at the end its over-all expenses and income were approximately in balance.

RFC MORTGAGE COMPANY

Unlike the HOLC, whose facilities were available only to distressed mortgagors, the RFC Mortgage Company[34] was constrained by Congress to lend only where the credit was financially sound, though unobtainable from private sources. The varied nature of the company's programs makes it difficult to describe its lending experience fairly, but the broad outlines can be indicated with some confidence.

The largest part, about $393 million, of the funds disbursed by the RFC Mortgage Company went for purchases of FHA-insured and VA-guaranteed loans—mainly home loans. Table 53 gives data

TABLE 53

RFC Mortgage Company Purchases of FHA- and VA-Protected
Loans, Cumulative through September 30, 1952
(*in thousands*)

	VA-Guaranteed	FHA-Insured
Authorized	$148,538	$332,088
Canceled	7,778	79,843
Purchased	140,759	252,245a
Repaid	33,560	27,649b
Sold	30,373	211,996c
Foreclosed	3,480	12,391
Other credits	96	..
Outstanding	73,250	209

Based on data made available by the RFC Mortgage Company.
a Also includes some loans and participations in loans on low-cost housing projects.
b Inferred from the difference between reported sales (through December 31, 1950) and the reported total of repayments and sales (through September 30, 1952).
c Sales through December 31, 1950.

of repayments, sales, and foreclosures on such loans through September 1952. Measured against the gross amount of loan purchases, the foreclosure rate on FHA-insured mortgages was about 5 percent; on VA-guaranteed, about 2.5 percent. Measured against net pur-

[34] This summary is based in large part on an unpublished National Bureau of Economic Research memorandum on the RFC Mortgage Company prepared by Donald T. Wood.

319

chases (loans purchased less loans sold), the foreclosure rate on VA loans was 3.2 percent, and on FHA loans nearly 31 percent—reflecting the greater proportion of FHA loans sold.

The second largest activity was lending and the purchasing of loans to finance new or existing income-producing properties. The record through June 1946 shows foreclosures and charge-offs amounting to about 9 percent of the $100 million advanced on commercial properties,[35] a figure not to be interpreted as a loss rate, but comparable in a rough way with the foregoing foreclosure rates on gross purchases, and indicating poorer experience with mortgages on business than on home properties.

Published materials on the financial outcome of RFC Mortgage Company operations are too fragmentary to form anything but the most tentative judgment as to whether the agency was self-supporting. It reported a net profit of $416,000 from March 1935 through the first half of 1939 (although operating at a net loss of $426,000 in 1935)[36] and a net profit of $1.7 million through March 31, 1943.[37] It seems not unreasonable, therefore, to interpret the $3.8 million of earned surplus reported on the March 31, 1947 balance sheet as the cumulative net profit of the company's operations to that date (Table 54). In a full accounting from the standpoint of the public, however, that figure would be reduced because of costs borne by other agencies. The company enjoyed tax exemption as well as a franking privilege, and presumably paid no return to the RFC on its capital stock (though interest—of unknown amount— was paid on funds borrowed from the RFC). If capital had been borrowed even at the rate of 1 percent per annum, its cost over the company's history would have nearly equaled the earned surplus at termination. Perhaps it can be said that this agency, like the HOLC, struck an approximate balance between income and expense over its whole period of operations.

FEDERAL NATIONAL MORTGAGE ASSOCIATION

The experience record of FNMA, in operations which have been

[35] *Federal Lending 1934–1948*, report of the Joint Committee on Reduction of Nonessential Federal Expenditures (S. Doc. 103, 80th Cong., 1st sess., July 1947), Table II, pp. 6ff.

[36] *Financial Statements of Certain Government Agencies, Letter from the Secretary of the Treasury . . . in response to Senate Resolution 150*, S. Doc. 172, 76th Cong., 3rd sess., Part 1, February 1940, p. 83.

[37] U.S. Congress, *Hearings* before the Joint Committee on Reduction of Nonessential Federal Expenditures pursuant to Section 601 of the Revenue Act of 1941, 78th Cong., 1st sess., Part 7, June 1943, pp. 2282 and 2305.

TABLE 54

Balance Sheet of the RFC Mortgage Company
as of March 31, 1947

ASSETS	
Deposits with the U.S. Treasury, etc.	$ 433,561
Loans	32,923,128
FHA debentures	8,925,950
Acquired security or collateral	1,869,966
Other assetsa	7,383,345
Total assets	$51,535,950
LIABILITIES	
Bonds, notes, and debentures	$21,072,071
Other liabilities	1,649,358
CAPITAL	
Capital stock	$25,000,000
Earned surplus	3,814,521
Total liabilities and capital	$51,535,950

From the *Daily Statement of the United States Treasury*, May 15, 1947, p. 13.
a Includes real estate valued at $6,757,229, net of depreciation.

restricted to the purchase and sale of federally protected mortgages,
is depicted in Tables 55 and 56. Through December 31, 1953, 1.1
percent of the amount of all mortgages purchased by the association and 1.5 percent of its net purchases (that is, purchases less
sales) had been foreclosed. At no time since FNMA's inception has
its cumulative foreclosure rate exceeded 1.1 percent of gross purchases or 2.8 percent of net purchases. This is a considerably better
record than that reported through September 30, 1952 for the RFC
Mortgage Company, but this is to be expected in view of the heavy
concentration of FNMA activities in the more recent, favorable
years.

There have been substantial differences in FNMA's foreclosure
record, however, among various types of mortgages. As Table 56
shows, the cumulative record through December 31, 1953 has been
very much better on VA than on FHA mortgages, 0.6 percent of the
former and 2.1 percent of the latter having ended in foreclosure.
Within the VA program, however, foreclosure experience has been
very unfavorable on Section 505 (a) loans (small second mortgages
taken in combination with an FHA loan), and within the FHA program, on Sections 210 (rental) and 608 (war housing) projects. In
the latter case, FNMA has had to foreclose on 15.9 percent of its
gross, and 36.5 percent of its net, purchases of mortgages.

TABLE 55

Federal National Mortgage Association: Mortgage Purchases, Repayments, Sales, Foreclosures, and Outstanding Portfolio, 1938-1953

(dollar figures in thousands)

YEAR	PURCHASES	REPAYMENTS	SALES	FORECLOSURES & ASSIGNMENTS	OUTSTANDING (year end)	FORECLOSURES AS PERCENTAGE OF: Purchases (cumulative)	Purchases Less Sales (cumulative)
1938	$ 82,166	$ 1,900	..	..	$ 80,266	0 %	0 %
1939	74,081	6,731	$ 351	$ 505	146,760	0.3	0.3
1940	48,041	12,614	6	1,081	181,100	0.8	0.8
1941	42,321	15,671	3	907	206,840	1.0	1.0
1942	23,179	18,779	..	311	210,929	1.0	1.0
1943	1,502	21,202	126,646	96	64,487	1.1	2.0
1944	200	12,238	11	15	52,423	1.1	2.0
1945	58	6,416	38,623	..	7,442	1.1	2.8
1946	32	1,881	2	..	5,591	1.1	2.8
1947	60	1,226	..	5	4,420	1.1	2.8
1948	197,945	3,071	..	..	199,294	0.6	1.0
1949	672,213	21,199	19,753	2,201	828,354	0.5	0.5
1950	1,044,294	44,279	469,382	12,323	1,346,664	0.8	1.1
1951	677,309	55,472	111,115	7,852	1,849,534	0.9	1.2
1952	537,872	78,891	55,921	10,927	2,241,667	1.1	1.4
1953	542,457	93,714	221,126	7,646	2,461,637	1.1	1.5
1938-53	3,943,730	395,284	1,042,039	43,869		1.1	1.5

Source: Covers FHA-insured and VA-guaranteed mortgages as detailed in Table 46. Data for 1938-1950 were supplied by FNMA and for 1951-1953 are from its *Semi-Annual Reports.*

TABLE 56

Federal National Mortgage Association: Purchases, Repayments, Sales, Foreclosures, 1938–1953, and Outstanding Portfolio as of December 31, 1953, for FHA-Insured and VA-Guaranteed Mortgages

(dollar figures in thousands)

TYPE OF MORTGAGE	PURCHASES	REPAYMENTS	SALES	FORECLOSURES & ASSIGNMENTS	OUTSTANDING	FORECLOSURES AS PERCENTAGE OF:	
						Purchases	Purchases Less Sales
FHA-Insured	$1,357,629	$165,437	$ 542,990	$28,167	$ 621,035	2.1%	3.5%
Title I							
Sec. 8	28,661	1,417	311	5	26,926	b	b
Title II							
Sec. 203	549,038	115,340	284,178	4,028	145,494	0.7	1.5
Sec. 207	23,233	4,932	413	1,292	16,597	5.6	5.7
Sec. 210	277	230	...	46	...	16.6	16.6
Sec. 213	16,273	289	...	...	15,984	0	0
Title VI							
Sec. 603	339,549	38,072	209,791	12,056	79,628	3.6	9.3
Sec. 608	66,311	794	37,330	10,564a	17,624	15.9	36.5
Title VIII							
Sec. 803	53,467	276	10,427	...	42,765	0	0
Title IX							
Sec. 903	268,194	4,059	540	176	263,419	0.1	0.1
Sec. 908	12,626	28	...	...	12,598	0	0
VA-Guaranteed	2,586,101	229,847	499,949	15,703	1,840,602	0.6	0.8
Sec. 501 (home)	2,552,813	226,530	484,321	15,447	1,826,512	0.6	0.7
Sec. 501 (multi)	9,076	832	743	...	7,501	0	0
Sec. 502	1,905	330	6	2	1,568	0.1	0.1
Sec. 505 (a)	22,307	2,155	14,879	254	5,021	1.1	3.4
Total	$3,943,730	$395,284	$1,042,939	$43,869	$2,461,637	1.1%	1.5%

(continued on next page)

TABLE 56 (continued)

Data for 1938–1950 were supplied by FNMA and for 1951–1953 are from the *Semi-Annual Reports* of FNMA. Amounts will not always add to totals due to rounding. See text footnote 41, below, for types of mortgages insurable by FHA under particular sections of the law. For VA, Section 502 relates to farm housing, and 505(a) to VA-guaranteed second mortgages, junior to an FHA-insured first mortgage.

a Includes four mortgages aggregating $520,000 assigned to FHA in lieu of foreclosure.

b Less than 0.05 percent.

The published records of FNMA indicate a substantial profit over its entire history. The balance sheet of FNMA on December 31, 1953 (Table 57) indicated an earned surplus of roughly $48 million; the net income earned to that date was reported as $140.4 million (Table 58), of which $91.0 million was paid out in dividends to the RFC or

TABLE 57

Balance Sheet of the Federal National Mortgage
Association, December 31, 1953
(*in thousands*)

ASSETS	
Mortgages and related receivables	$2,470,978
Assets acquired through foreclosure	1,133
Claims in process	2,385
Other assets	4,261
Total	$2,478,758
LIABILITIES	
Accounts payable and accrued liabilities	$ 1,492
Trust and deposit liabilities	8,227
INVESTMENT OF THE U.S. GOVERNMENT	
Notes payable to Administrator, HHFA	$2,375,000
Accrued interest	25,408
Capital stock held by Administrator, HHFA	20,000
Paid-in surplus	1,000
Retained earnings	47,630
Total liabilities and U.S. government investment	$2,478,758

From the *Semi-Annual Report* of the Federal National Mortgage Association, December 31, 1953, p. 1.

the Treasury. On that basis the association would seem to have been self-supporting, although at the end of 1953 its reserves for losses and its accumulated earned surplus (although improved over 1951) were still low by conventional standards. Reserves and earned surplus

TABLE 58

Income and Expense Statement of the Federal National
Mortgage Association, Cumulative
through December 31, 1953
(*in thousands*)

Income	
Interest earned	$358,449
Commitment fees earned, acquisition and service fees	16,073
Premiums earned	10,661
Other income	91
Total	$385,274
Expenses and Losses	
Interest expense	$164,092
Administrative expense	28,639
Mortgage servicing fees	44,266
Other expenses and losses	430
Sales discounts	7,440
Total	$244,867
Net Income	$140,407
ANALYSIS OF ACCUMULATED NET INCOME	
Dividends paid to RFC	$ 30,500
Dividends paid to U.S. Treasury	60,500
Interest on government investment in capital structure	1,358
Reserves for losses	35,682
Undistributed earned surplus	11,948
Other reserves	419
	$140,407

From the *Semi-Annual Report* of the Federal National Mortgage Association,
December 31, 1953, p. 2.

amply covered the amount of assets held as a result of foreclosure
and of "claims in process," but amounted to only less than 2 percent
of FNMA's mortgage portfolio of $2.5 billion. It must be borne in
mind, however, that the agency's portfolio consists altogether of
insured or guaranteed credits.

DIRECT LENDING BY THE FEDERAL HOUSING ADMINISTRATION
AND THE VETERANS' ADMINISTRATION

Credit has been extended by the Federal Housing Administration
to finance the sale of properties acquired under the terms of its
insurance when loans defaulted. The agency reported about $40

million of such advances were outstanding at the end of 1953. It has also held notes and mortgages (at the end of 1953 the amount outstanding was about $108 million) acquired as collateral when insured loans defaulted. Experience data are not available separately for those parts of FHA's operations; such losses as were sustained enter into the experience record of its various insurance programs, to be dealt with in the next section.

The record of the program under which the Veterans' Administration advanced nearly $290 million from 1950 through 1953 in home loans to veterans unable to obtain a VA-guaranteed loan from private institutions in the community is summarized in Table 59. Experience

TABLE 59

Status of the Direct Housing Loan Program of the Veterans'
Administration, through December 31, 1953
(*dollar figures in thousands*)

	Number	Amount
Loans closed and fully disbursed	42,102	$289,390
Loans terminated (all types)	2,198	14,706
By sale	1,658	11,339
By repayment in full	486	3,077
By foreclosure	25	138
By voluntary conveyance	29	152
Loans outstanding	39,904	274,684
Loans in default		
Total	1,284	a
Four or more installments	158	a

From *Loan Guaranty*, Veterans' Administration, December 1953, p. 75.
a Not available.

on terminated loans has so far been good, as would be expected from the favorable economic circumstances of the years covered. Most of the credit—$275 million of it—was still outstanding at the end of 1953.

PROGRAMS OF LOAN INSURANCE AND GUARANTEES

FHA insurance of loans for home modernization and repair. Title I (Classes 1a and 1b) insurance of loans for the alteration, repair, improvement, or conversion of existing structures was explicitly regarded at its inception in 1934 as a device for stimulating the building industry, and in order to gain its maximum effect no charge was made, either to the homeowner or to the insured lending institution, for the protection which it provided. Furthermore, the selection of risks was left largely to the discretion of the lender; it was expected that the risk-sharing principle of the program—under which the lender was originally insured up to 20 percent of the credit extended—would hold lending institutions to a sufficiently high standard of credit quality to protect the Federal Housing Administration from undue losses. The basis of the insurance has been changed from time to time, but its underlying character has not been altered. The first major change came in 1936 when protection was lowered to 10 percent of the aggregate net amount of loans insured; the second, in 1939 when FHA was empowered to charge fees; and the third in 1954 when the insured lender was required to assume 10 percent of the loss on defaulted loans.

Experience under the Title I program is summarized briefly in Table 60: claims paid since 1934 have been 2.0 percent of the net proceeds of the notes insured, and 40.9 percent of the amount of the claims paid has been subsequently recovered. This places the over-all losses incurred (net of recoveries and notes in process of collection) at less than 1.0 percent of notes insured,[38] though at times the cumulative loss rate has been considerably higher.

Available data fail to reveal any particular type of Title I note, or notes originating from any particular source, that have had a distinctly better or worse experience than others. There has been little regional spread in ratios of claims paid to notes insured (1934–1953); most states have had ratios of from 1.5 to 3.0 percent and with the exception of Alaska, Hawaii, and Guam, where the percentages were 1.1 or less, and of Vermont, where it was 6.0, all ratios fell between 1.47 and 3.75 percent.[39]

There has been some variation also in claims ratios according to the source of the notes: commercial banks, which financed 76 percent of the net proceeds of all notes insured in 1934–1953, had a ratio of 1.7 percent; finance companies, on the other hand, show a significantly worse figure—3.4 percent—and savings and loan associations the highly favorable ratio of 1.0 percent.[40] Little variation is found—probably none of significant amount—in the experience record of loans classified according to the proposed uses of the funds.

38 *Seventh Annual Report*, Housing and Home Finance Agency, 1953, p. 323.
39 *Ibid.*, Table 64, p. 302.
40 *Sixth Annual Report*, Housing and Home Finance Agency, 1952, Tables 63 and 64, pp. 337f., and *Seventh Annual Report*, Tables 66 and 67, pp. 304f.

TABLE 60

Selected Experience Data, FHA Title I, Property Improvement Loans, 1934–1953
(*dollar figures in millions*)

				PERCENTAGE RATIO OF:	
YEAR	NOTES INSURED (NET PROCEEDS)	CLAIMS PAID	RECOVERIES	Claims Paid to Notes Insured (cumulative)	Recoveries to Claims Paid
1934	$ 27.4	..	..	0 %	..
1935	201.3	$ 0.4	a	0.2	2.2%
1936	221.5	5.9	$ 0.3	1.4	4.8
1937	54.3	6.9	0.9	2.6	9.1
1938	150.7	6.0	1.6	2.9	14.6
1939	204.0	4.7	1.9	2.8	19.7
1940	241.7	6.5	1.9	2.8	21.7
1941	248.6	7.3	2.5	2.8	24.1
1942	141.2	7.1	2.8	3.0	26.6
1943	87.2	3.7	4.2	3.1	33.2
1944	113.9	1.9	3.6	3.0	39.1
1945	170.8	1.6	2.9	2.8	43.5
1946	320.6	2.4	3.1	2.5	47.2
1947	533.6	5.8	2.3	2.2	46.5
1948	621.6	14.3	2.5	2.2	40.9
1949	607.0	17.5	3.4	2.3	36.9
1950	700.2	18.2	5.2	2.4	35.5
1951	707.0	12.2	6.7	2.3	37.4
1952	848.3	11.5	7.5	2.2	39.8
1953	1,334.3	15.0	7.6	2.0	40.9
Total	$7,535.4	$149.1	$60.9	2.0%	40.9%

Based on Statement 3, p. 322, of the *Seventh Annual Report* of the Housing and Home Finance Agency, 1953. Amounts will not always add to totals due to rounding.
a Less than $50,000.

FHA insurance of home and project mortgages. FHA experience with the insurance of residential mortgage loans—which is customarily considered separately for mortgages of the "home" (1 to 4 dwelling units) and "project" (5 or more units) type—is summarized in Table 61 for the years 1934–1953.[41] Roughly 3.4 million

[41] Home mortgages include those made under Section 8 (new, one-family dwellings for low and moderate income families), Section 203 (new and existing 1–4 unit structures), Section 213 (single dwelling units in cooperative apartment projects released from blanket mortgages), Sections 603 and 603–610 (1–4 unit structures built under the War Housing and Veterans' Emergency Housing Pro-

home mortgages with an original amount of $20.8 billion were insured; just over 20,000 (0.6 percent), having an original amount of roughly $113 million (0.5 percent), were foreclosed by the mortgagees. Over the same period, 8,167 project mortgages, having an original amount slightly in excess of $4.6 billion, were insured; 3.7 percent of the number and 3.0 percent of the original amount of those loans, however, were foreclosed. In the home mortgage field, experience was much more favorable on Section 203 (nonwar) than on Section 603 (war housing) loans. The Section 207 program in the project mortgage field produced the worst record, with a foreclosure rate of 5.9 percent.

Some states have had a substantially better, and some a substantially worse, record than others in Section 203 loans, under which the bulk of FHA's nonwar home mortgage insurance has been written: for Massachusetts, New Hampshire, and Vermont, ratios of titles acquired to mortgages insured were over 1 percent, whereas for the District of Columbia, Nevada, and New Mexico they were under 0.1 percent.[42] State experience with Section 603 home mortgages was even more variable: ratios of title acquisitions to mortgages insured have varied from as high as 20 percent or more (Connecticut and West Virginia) to less than 1 percent (twenty other states and the District of Columbia).

Another aspect of FHA experience may be mentioned, namely the losses (through December 31, 1953) incurred on the disposition of properties and mortgage notes acquired as collateral in connection with defaults. Net losses on the insurance handled under the combined Title I Housing Insurance Fund, Mutual Mortgage Insurance Fund, War Housing Insurance Fund, and Housing Insurance Fund[43]

---

grams or permanent housing sold by the government), Section 611 (single units released from blanket mortgages on projects of 25 or more new, single family dwelling units produced under the Site Fabrication Program), and Section 903 (1–2 family dwellings in critical defense areas).

Project mortgages include those originated under Section 207 (rental projects of 12 or more dwelling units), Section 213 (cooperative housing projects), Sections 608 and 608–610 (housing produced under the War Housing and Veterans' Emergency Housing Programs, and government-built permanent housing sold to private owners), Section 611 (projects of 25 or more single family units produced under the Site Fabrication Program), Section 803 (military housing built under the Maybank-Wherry bill), and Section 908 (multifamily rental housing in critical defense areas).

42 *Seventh Annual Report*, Housing and Home Finance Agency, 1953, Table 14, p. 211.

43 See Table 62 and footnote 41 of this chapter for the programs to which the various funds relate.

TABLE 61

Number and Original Amount of Home and Project Mortgages Insured by FHA, 1934–1953, Terminated through Foreclosure, and Outstanding, December 31, 1953, by Section

(*dollar figures in thousands*)

TITLE AND SECTION OF NATIONAL HOUSING ACT	MORTGAGES INSURED, 1934–1953		MORTGAGES FORECLOSED[a]		In Percent of Loans Insured		MORTGAGES IN FORCE DECEMBER 31, 1953	
	Number	*Original Amount*	*Number*	*Amount*	*Number*	*Original Amount*	*Number*	*Original Amount*
HOME MORTGAGES								
I, 8	16,582	$ 81,854	61	$ 263	0.4%	0.3%	16,298	$ 80,577
II, 203	2,690,459	16,651,963	8,299	44,062	0.3	0.3	1,540,975	11,093,614
II, 213	6,237	59,881	...	...	0	0	6,226	59,780
VI, 603	624,652	3,645,260	11,759	68,922	1.9	1.9	323,630	2,147,264
VI, 603–610	3,362	16,103	13	42	0.4	0.3	2,979	14,590
VI, 611	75	556	...	...	0	0	72	534
IX, 903	35,466	310,621	3	36	b	b	35,305	309,116
Total	3,376,833	$20,766,238	20,135	$113,325	0.6%	0.5%	1,925,485	$13,705,474
RENTAL AND COOPERATIVE PROJECT MORTGAGES								
II, 207	618	$ 315,233	29	$ 18,659	4.7%	5.9%	266	$ 164,526
II, 213	145	242,192	3	3,284	2.1	1.4	103	182,924
VI, 608	7,046	3,439,679	269	117,921	3.8	3.4	6,522	3,234,424
VI, 608–610	23	8,360	...	...	0	0	18	6,617
VI, 611	25	11,991	...	...	0	0	6	2,686
VIII, 803	230	577,175	...	...	0	0	230	577,175
IX, 908	80	52,683	...	...	0	0	80	52,683
Total	8,167	$ 4,647,313	301	$139,863	3.7%	3.0%	7,225	$ 4,221,035

Data are from Tables 12 and 46 of the *Seventh Annual Report*, Housing and Home Finance Agency, 1953, pp. 207 and 275. See text footnote 41 of this chapter for types of mortgages insurable under particular sections of the law.

a Covers foreclosures in which properties are retained by the mortgagees or transferred to FHA, and also mortgages assigned to FHA in lieu of foreclosure.
b Less than 0.05 percent.

have totaled approximately $5.4 million, stemming mainly from, and divided about equally between, the Mutual Mortgage and the War Housing Funds: these losses have been under 10 percent of the amounts disbursed (in debentures, cash adjustments, liquidation profits, and other expenses) in connection with Title II properties (primarily Section 203) and less than 4 percent for Title VI projects (primarily Section 603 properties).[44]

Published summary reports permit only a limited analysis of the financial outcome of FHA operations. The basic statement in this connection is the income account of the various funds under which insurance is written, which shows that there was a net income through June 30, 1953 of $354 million for all funds combined (Table 62). The bulk of this was accounted for by the Mutual Mortgage, War Housing, and Title I Insurance Funds, whereas very small net incomes or deficits have been reported by the other, and smaller, funds. Losses and charge-offs have been highest in the Title I Insurance Fund for property improvement loans, where they equaled 20.2 percent of total income through mid-1953; it should be recalled that no fees were charged under that program until mid-1939. For all funds combined, losses and charge-offs equaled 3.3 percent of the total income earned to mid-1953, and they were 1.2 and 0.6 percent, respectively, for the War Housing and Mutual Mortgage Insurance Funds. Recoveries equal to 0.5 percent of total income were realized on the Housing Insurance Fund. In general, this confirms the observations based on foreclosure rates: experience has been least favorable in the war emergency housing programs and most favorable in those programs under which insurance has been provided for small, nonwar home mortgages, with the various apartment or project programs showing an intermediate record.

The disposition of FHA fund income is shown in Table 63. The bulk of the earnings have been retained in various funds as additions to capital—$146 million in earned surplus (after interfund transfers of $12 million) and $148 million in statutory reserves. The remainder—$47 million—was returned to mortgagors as participations in mutual fund earnings.

The retentions of income, along with the investment made in the several insurance programs by the United States government (either as allocations from the Treasury or as appropriations for salaries,

---

[44] See Statements 9, 14, 17, and 20 (pp. 331, 339, 346, and 352, respectively) of the report cited in footnote 42, above.

TABLE 62

Income and Expenses of Combined FHA Insurance Funds and of Component Funds, through June 30, 1953

(in thousands)

Income and Expenses	All FHA Funds	Title I Ins. Fund (property improvement)	Title I Housing Ins. Fund (Title I Sec. 8)	Mutual Mortgage Ins. Fund (Title II Secs. 203 and 207)a	Housing Ins. Fund (Title II Secs. 207, 210, & 213)a	War Housing Ins. Fund (Title VI Secs. 603, 608, 609 610, & 611)	Housing Inv. Ins. Fund (Title VII Sec. 710)	Military Housing Ins. Fund (Title VIII Sec. 803)	National Defense Housing Ins. Fund (Title IX Secs. 903 and 908)
INCOME									
Interest and dividends	$ 58,153	$ 3,079	$ 64	$ 41,055	$ 1,050	$ 12,075	$ 50	$ 653	$ 127
Ins. premiums and fees	708,374	96,740	1,152	381,679	12,121	204,219	..	9,660	2,804
Other	1,845	8	..	1,599	89	154	..	..	..
Total	768,372	99,822	1,216	424,333	13,260	216,448	50	10,313	2,931
EXPENSES									
Interest on debentures and Treas. funds	24,479	..	..	21,216	1,369	1,374	106	414	..
Adm. expense	306,397	21,086	1,186	198,759	11,472	68,054	41	3,164	2,634
Other expense	1,945	370	6	1,111	71	359	b	16	13
Losses and charge-offs	25,402	20,148	b	2,742	—72	2,585	b	—1	c
Total	358,223	41,604	1,192	223,829	12,840	72,372	147	3,593	2,647
Net increase (—) or decrease in valuation res.	—56,300	—35,241	—3	—267	—310	—20,477	..	..	..
Net income	353,849	22,977	20	200,237	109	123,599	—97	6,720	284

(continued on next page)

HOUSING

TABLE 62 (continued)

Statements in each case cover fund operations from their inception to June 30, 1953. Data are from the *Seventh Annual Report*, Housing and Home Finance Agency, 1953, pp. 320, 325, 330, 336, 344, 350, 356, 360, and 363. Negative loss indicates profit. Amounts will not always add to totals because of rounding. See footnote 41 of this chapter for types of mortgages insurable under particular sections of the law.

a Section 207 insurance was handled under the Mutual Mortgage Fund until February 1938, and afterward under the Housing Fund.

b Less than $500.

c Less than $500 profit.

TABLE 63

Disposition of Net Income of Combined FHA Insurance Funds, through June 30, 1953

Net income available for distribution	$353,849,212
Participations of mortgagors in mutual earnings	47,283,201
Allocations to statutory reserves	148,268,198
Earned surplus (gross)	158,297,813
(net)a	146,297,813

Based on Statement 2, p. 321, of the *Seventh Annual Report* of the Housing and Home Finance Agency, 1953.

a Adjustments are for allocations of $1 million to the Housing Insurance Fund from the general reinsurance reserve fund of the Mutual Mortgage Insurance Fund and of a similar amount to the Title I Housing Insurance Fund from the insurance reserve fund of the Title I Insurance Fund, and of $10 million to the National Defense Housing Insurance Fund from the insurance reserve fund of the War Housing Insurance Fund.

claims, and other expenses) and with liabilities of $250 million (including outstanding debentures of $79 million), yielded resources of $556 million for all FHA funds combined on June 30, 1953 as shown in the fund balance sheets in Table 64. The table understates the amount of the federal government's contributions to FHA programs, however, since it excludes additional allocations of $38.2 million made to FHA during the period of subsidized Title I operations ($19.1 million of which has been returned to the Treasury) and subsequent allocations to this and other funds amounting to $65.5 million ($43.9 million of which has been repaid). Adding the amount not repaid, $40.7 million, to the $12.0 million government investment recorded in Table 64 places the federal investment in the programs (disregarding any accrual of interest) at $53 million

333

TABLE 64

Assets, Capital, and Liabilities of Combined FHA Funds and of Component Funds, June 30, 1953

(*in thousands*)

Assets and Liabilities	All FHA Funds[a]	Title I Ins. Fund	Title I Housing Ins. Fund	Mutual Mortgage Ins. Fund	Housing Ins. Fund	War Housing Ins. Fund	Housing Inv. Ins. Fund	Military Housing Ins. Fund	National Defense Housing Ins. Fund
ASSETS									
Cash with U.S. Treasury	$ 55,870	$36,662	$ 310	$ 6,963	$ 650	$ 6,806	$ 57	$ 712	$ 472
Investments	344,093	..	957	234,304	5,028	78,640	952	12,768	11,443
Acquired collateral or security (net of reserves for losses)	107,663	14,766	21	1,217	1,600	90,058	..	..	..
Other assets	48,445[b]	8,694	7	7,775	2,584	29,232	1	76	15
Total	556,070	60,122	1,296	250,260	9,863	204,737	1,011	13,555	11,930
CAPITAL AND LIABILITIES									
Statutory reserves	148,268	..	..	148,268	..	..	..	..	..
Investment of U.S. govt.	12,000	..	1,000	..	1,000	..	..	..	10,000
Earned surplus	146,298	21,977	20	3,686	109	113,599	−96	6,720	284
Liabilities	249,504[c]	38,145	275	98,306	8,753	91,138	1,107	6,835	1,646
Total	556,070	60,122	1,296	250,260	9,863	204,737	1,011	13,555	11,930

Data are from the statements of financial condition given in the *Seventh Annual Report* of the Housing and Home Finance Agency, 1953, pp. 317, 324, 329, 335, 343, 348, 356, 359, and 362.

[a] Total assets and liabilities for all FHA funds exceed the sum of assets and liabilities for the component funds shown, by $3,296,575, because of interfund receivables and payables of $1,021,307 that should be eliminated from the separate fund accounts and because of $4,317,882 of assets and liabilities under an account not shown—the Administrative Expense Account.

[b] Includes loans receivable (net of reserves), $36.8 million; accounts and notes receivable, $9.9 million; accrued interest on U.S. government securities, $0.7 million; net fixed assets, $1.0 million; and a small amount of other assets held for mortgagors.

[c] Includes accounts payable, $4.9 million; accrued liabilities, $20.9 million; trust and deposit liabilities, $9.2 million; deferred and undistributed credits, $70 million; debentures, $79 million; and other liabilities, $66 million.

and indicates for all FHA funds combined a net income of $301 million in excess of federal contributions.[45]

This $0.3 billion excess of net income over federal contributions may be compared with the roughly $33 billion of insurance that has been written under all FHA programs combined since 1934. The fact that the programs have been self-sustaining on this accounting is commendable, but measured against the vast amount of insurance written and the amount of risks still outstanding, the margin—approximately 0.91 percent of the insurance written through the end of 1953 and 1.72 percent of the net balance of insured loans estimated by FHA to be outstanding on December 31, 1953—has been a narrow one.

VA guaranty of home mortgage loans. The outcome of the VA's program of home loan guarantees, which from its beginning to December 25, 1953 has guaranteed 3,196,355 home mortgage loans, is summarized in Table 65. Claims have been paid on 0.6 percent

TABLE 65

Status of VA-Guaranteed or -Insured Home Loans,
through December 25, 1953
(*dollar figures in millions*)

	Number	Original Principal Amount	Original Guaranty Amount
Loans closed	3,196,355	$21,544	$11,534
First mortgages	2,783,536	a	a
Second mortgages	412,819	a	a
Loans extinguished	473,349	a	1,220
By repayment in full	455,734	2,428	1,177
By payment of claim to mortgagee	17,615	a	43b
Loans outstanding	2,723,006	a	a
In default	28,301	a	a
Ratio of claims paid to loans closed	0.55%	a	0.37%
Ratio of loans in default to total outstanding	1.04%	a	a

Data from *Loan Guaranty*, Veterans' Administration, December 1953, p. 69.
a Not available.
b Represents amount of the claim paid to a mortgagee (i.e. the guaranteed portion of the unpaid loan balance, plus accrued interest and other admissible costs at time of filing claim).

45 An accounting of transactions during the subsidized Title I period is given in Statement 6, p. 327 of the *Seventh Annual Report* of the Housing and Home Finance Agency, 1953.

of all loans closed under the program, and cumulative claim payments equaled 0.4 percent—but after refunds and recoveries from the liquidation of collateral, 0.07 percent—of the total amount closed through the end of 1953.[46] The number of loans in default as a percentage of total loans outstanding was somewhat larger, of course, but it stood on December 25, 1953 at the unusually favorable level of 1.04 percent. The program has not been self-sustaining and was not intended to be. The cost of the program to the federal government through December 1952 has been estimated at just under $430 million, of which $343 million consisted of gratuities paid to veterans.[47]

Impact on Housing Production, Prices, and Financing

Because urban real estate markets are affected by a variety of factors other than the federal government's credit programs, definitive results cannot be expected in an attempt to measure the unique impact of these programs in the combined result. At a number of points, however, their impact can be determined, and it is possible in any case to test the leading aims or expectations that have been expressed. These concern mainly the effects of federal credit programs on the physical volume of production and construction costs, on the prices of new and existing structures, and on the financing of real estate purchases. The following sections are devoted to an analysis of those problems.

EFFECTS ON THE VOLUME OF CONSTRUCTION

Since 1934, the principal objective of federal housing credit programs has been to increase the volume of construction. The months following October 1950, when Regulation X and related FHA and VA restrictions were in effect, are an exception; in the main, the object has been to induce a higher rate of construction than would otherwise have prevailed. How successful has this effort been?

Federal credit programs may stimulate construction in a number of ways, of which the three most important may be mentioned. First, the availability of loan insurance may increase the willingness of

[46] Based on data in *Loan Guaranty*, Veterans' Administration, December 1953, p. 69.

[47] Estimated from information supplied by the Veterans' Administration. Up to September 1, 1953, an amount equal to 4 percent of the guaranteed or insured portion of the loan, but not exceeding $160, was applied by VA to each veteran-borrower's loan account as an outright gift. The gratuities were discontinued by Public Law 149 (83rd Cong.) in 1953.

builders to undertake construction by reducing the equity they are required to invest in projects, and by raising their expectations as to the salability of the final product. Other things equal, the higher loan-to-value ratios of insured mortgages mean lower equity investment requirements. In some circumstances they could make equity investment altogether unnecessary, enabling a builder to "borrow out"—that is, to obtain by means of, say, an 80 percent loan an amount fully covering his out-of-pocket construction expense. When a loan was negotiated before, not after, construction, the maximum insurable mortgage might be determined according to the expected value of the land after improvement (rather than the amount paid for it) and according to estimated construction costs. If the value of the site with the physical improvement in place proved to be appreciably above its cost of acquisition and preparation, as it should, and if the builder was able to complete construction at less than the projected costs (without, of course, violating the insuring agency's construction standards), this increment in value and saving in cost might suffice as an equity; in some cases, apparently, the builder's permitted borrowing actually exceeded out-of-pocket costs. Naturally, the higher the permitted loan-to-value ratio, the greater the possibility that no equity would be required and the greater, other things equal, the willingness of builders to undertake construction projects.

Second, other things equal, one would expect the willingness of lenders to invest in mortgages, and thus to supply the necessary investment funds, to be increased by loan insurance. A complicating factor is that the maximum contractual interest rate may be fixed by the insuring or guaranteeing agency; where the rate is set below that available on alternative investments of equal or greater attractiveness, and especially if the loans can be sold at a discount only on terms onerous to the builder, the effect is to repel investible funds and to discourage construction. However, barring this possibility, which is not an essential feature of mortgage insurance, loan insurance should increase the availability of permanent mortgage financing and, what is especially important in the larger projects, indirectly increase the availability of construction credit. Even if these circumstances are not reflected in lower interest rates, and more especially if they are, one would expect them to stimulate building activity.

Finally, potential property owners, whether prospective owner-occupants of small dwellings or investors in multi-unit projects, are better able, other things equal, to make their demand effective if the available mortgage financing requires only a relatively small down payment and if carrying charges are low. By widening the market, loan insurance tends, of course, to produce higher levels of construction.

Two periods seem especially important for a study of whether the stimulative tendencies have actually been effective, namely the years immediately following the enactment of the National Housing Act in 1934, when a determined effort was made to revive the construction industry through credit programs, and the years following World War II, when a no less determined effort was made to increase construction by the provision of liberal mortgage credit.

Experience during recovery in the 1930's. The first of FHA's operations to get under way during the early thirties was the insurance of repair and modernization loans, which began on a small scale in 1934.

It is impossible to ascertain directly whether the Title I program caused a greater volume of repair and modernization credits to be extended, and thus of expenditures to be made, than would otherwise have occurred, but clearly the program was not an initiating factor in the recovery which, as measured by National Bureau reference dates, began in March 1933. In any case, other credit areas recovered earlier: total consumer installment sales credit began to rise as early as 1933,[48] and flotations of new corporate securities passed their low point in 1933, rose moderately in 1934 and fairly sharply in 1935, the first year of full-scale Title I operations.[49] Still other credit areas registered recovery concurrently with the expansion of repair and modernization loans, notably commercial bank lending as a whole. No data are available on the total volume of credit advanced by commercial banks, but the net change over six-month periods in the loan outstandings of all commercial banks turned from a decline to an increase in the second half of 1935, and increased at a rising rate until the second half of 1937.[50]

Nor can it be said that repair and modernization expenditures increased more rapidly than types of construction expenditures that lacked governmental aid. In fact, taking 1935 as a base, the opposite

[48] *Federal Reserve Bulletin*, December 1943, p. 1192.
[49] *Federal Reserve Bulletin*, January 1943, p. 68.
[50] *Banking and Monetary Statistics*, Board of Governors of the Federal Reserve System, 1943, Table 3, p. 19.

is the case. By 1937, average monthly expenditures on additions and alterations to private nonfarm residential properties stood at an index of 129, as compared with 208 for construction expenditures on new dwellings and 231 for private, nonresidential construction expenditures.[51] The output of construction materials, which would reflect construction activity generally, rose very little more than manufacturing output as a whole. Again on a 1935 base, the latter stood at 130 in 1937, as compared with 133 for lumber and lumber products production.

In short, one cannot say that the repair and modernization loan insurance program initiated either the general recovery of the economy or even the specific recovery of the construction industry, or that the rate of increase of repair and modernization expenditures, however much they were influenced by loan insurance, was any greater than that of expenditures not aided by federal credit programs. An earlier appraisal of the program concluded that increases in the mid-thirties in repair and modernization expenditures reflected the general recovery of the period, and could not be attributed wholly to the unique effect of Title I insurance.[52] This may be true, but it cannot be conclusively determined that expenditures might not have been lower without the program, and there is a strong presumption that they would have been. It seems fair to conclude, then, that while the program had little if any initiating influence on recovery, it contributed to some degree to the recovery movement once expansion was under way.

Turning now to the mortgage loan insurance program, and more specifically to the influence of home mortgage insurance under Section 203 of the National Housing Act, it is again clear that no initiating influence toward recovery was exerted, since the program did not reach significant dimensions until 1936. The question, then, is whether mortgage loan insurance produced a higher rate of mortgage lending, and thus of new construction, after 1935 than would otherwise have occurred.

Several facts suggest that it had some such stimulative effect, though probably a modest one. In the first place, as Table 66 shows, insured mortgage lending increased in 1935 against the trend in the volume of all mortgages made on one- to four family structures, increased in 1936 by more than all such lending combined, accounted

51 *Survey of Current Business, Business Statistics Supplement, 1951*, Department of Commerce, p. 30.
52 Coppock, *op.cit.*, p. 4.

TABLE 66

Volume of Home Mortgage Loans Made and of Section 203
Home Mortgages Insured, 1934–1941
(*in millions*)

YEAR	MORTGAGE LOANS MADE ON 1- TO 4-FAMILY HOMES—TOTAL		SECTION 203 HOME MORTGAGES INSURED	
	Amount	Net Change	Amount	Net Change
1934	$3,170	..	$ 0.0	..
1935	2,259	$—911	93.9	$ 93.9
1936	2,302	43	308.9	215.0
1937	2,588	286	424.4	115.5
1938	2,437	—151	473.2	48.8
1939	2,912	475	669.4	196.2
1940	3,510	598	736.5	67.1
1941	3,931	421	876.7	140.2

From *Estimated Home Mortgage Debt and Lending Activity 1950* (Home Loan Bank Board), July 1951, p. 3, and *Housing Statistics* (Housing and Home Finance Agency), January 1954, p. 35.

for about four-tenths of the combined rise in 1937, increased in 1938 while the total of home mortgages made was declining, and made up substantial percentages of the vjlume increases in the years 1939–1941.

Second, the growth in the volume of home mortgage credit granted, of which insured loans were so important a part, was less affected by the 1937–1938 recession than the volume of consumer installment sales credit granted,[53] where no direct benefit of federal loan insurance was felt.

It is impossible to determine whether the loans made on an insured basis would have been made in any case (that is, whether insured lending merely substituted for conventional loans), but there is a strong presumption that this would have been true in only a minority of cases; and even if it had been true in as many as half of the cases, the stimulative effect of insurance would have been substantial. It seems reasonable to conclude, therefore, that home mortgage insurance was an expansive factor in the recovery movement, but the strength of its effect cannot be ascertained precisely.

[53] See *Factors Affecting the Demand for Consumer Instalment Sales Credit*, by Avram Kisselgoff (Technical Paper 7, National Bureau of Economic Research, Financial Research Program, 1952), p. 61.

Experience after World War II. A more complex problem is whether the liberal home mortgage terms induced by loan insurance and guarantees after World War II produced a higher level of housing output than would otherwise have been achieved, or whether the force of the effort was spent mainly in raising construction costs and the prices of houses.

Perhaps the most effective way to get at this question is to compare residential building activity after World War II with the building boom of the 1920's, when special federal credit aids were absent. Specifically, was building activity greater in 1948–1950 than in 1923–1925, when measured against the underlying forces making for an expansion of residential construction—namely, changes in population and rates of family formation? This is admittedly an indirect test of the effect of federal credit aids on construction but is, perhaps, as direct a test as can be made.[54]

Though subject to many reservations, arising mainly from the data that must be employed, the analysis in terms of demographic changes clearly suggests that the building boom following World War II proceeded at a considerably lower rate, relatively, than the boom of the twenties. The salient facts are presented in Table 67. Referring first to the peak years, the ratios of new permanent housing starts to net family formation and to population increase were substantially higher in 1925 than in 1950; and they were higher in the full period 1923–1925 than for 1918–1950. Also, expenditures on new private residential construction (in 1929 dollars) per unit of increased population and per unit of family formation were substantially higher in 1925 than in 1950, and in 1923–1925 than in 1948–1950. However much the government-induced liberalization of mortgage financing stimulated building activity in the late forties, the fact is that it failed to produce a level of housing output even in the peak year 1950 which, considering the population factors at work, was as high as that achieved in the twenties without benefit of federal financing aids.

Two other relationships afford comparisons: the amount of build-

[54] Among available measures of building activity, none is altogether satisfactory for our purposes: the series used here are (a) new permanent nonfarm dwelling units started in the United States, and (b) the amount expended (in 1929 dollars) on privately financed nonfarm housekeeping units put in place in the United States. Measures of the demographic factors having the most immediate effect on housing demand, such as first births, are lacking, but rates of population increase and of net family formation will perhaps suffice, for comparison of residential building activity in the two periods.

TABLE 67

Selected Data Comparing Residential Building Activity with
Population Changes and Net Family Formation in
Nonfarm Areas, 1923–1925 and 1948–1950
(*number of units in thousands; dollar figures in millions*)

	1925	1923–25	1950	1948–50
Nonfarm dwelling units in housing stock, April 1a	22,100	..	39,075	..
New privately financed nonfarm residential construction				
Dwelling units startedb	937	2,701	1,352	3,255
Expenditures for housekeeping units (1929 dollars)c	$5,104	$13,853	$5,346	$12,461
Nonfarm populationd				
12-month increase to April 1	1,816	..	3,433	..
36-month increase to April 1	..	6,645	..	9,718
Nonfarm family groupse				
12-month increase to April 1	536	..	1,858	..
36-month increase to April 1	..	1,767	..	4,527
Ratio of nonfarm housing starts to:				
Housing stock	4.2%	12.2%f	3.5%	8.3%g
Increase in nonfarm population	51.6%	40.6%	39.4%	33.5%
Increase in nonfarm families	174.8%	152.9%	72.8%	71.9%
Expenditures for housekeeping units (1929 dollars) per unit of:				
Increase in nonfarm population	$2,811	$2,085	$1,557	$1,282
Increase in nonfarm family groups	$9,522	$7,840	$2,877	$2,753

a The estimate for 1925 was derived by backward projection and interpolation of decennial figures, from data on nonfarm dwelling units standing at the end of 1920–1929 in *American Housing*, by Miles L. Colean (Twentieth Century Fund, 1944; Table 35, p. 410), and from data on dwelling units built, converted, or demolished during 1920–1929 in *Residential Real Estate*, by David L. Wickens (National Bureau of Economic Research, 1941; Tables EM 5 and EM 9, pp. 54 and 60). The estimate for 1950 is a downward adjustment of the census figure (1950 *Census of Housing*, Vol. 1, General Characteristics, Part 1, Table F, p. xxv) by 550,000 units to correct for the broader definition of nonfarm residence as compared with that used in earlier censuses.

b Data are based on number of building permits issued for single family dwellings, supplemented for 1923–1925, by data of change in number of families; for 1948–1950, supplemented by BLS field surveys in non-permit-issuing places and adjusted for lapsed permits and for lag between permit issuance and start of construction. Source for the earlier period is *Non-Farm Residential Construction, 1920–1936*, by David L. Wickens and Ray R. Foster (National Bureau of Economic Research, Bulletin 65, September 1937), Table 1, p. 2; for the later years, *Handbook of Labor Statistics, 1950* (Bureau of Labor Statistics), Table I-1, p. 211.

(*continued on next page*)

TABLE 67 (continued)

c Represents value of new nonfarm residential housekeeping units put in place, deflated to 1929 price level by the Department of Commerce over-all average (converted to 1929 = 100) of the individual indexes of construction costs for various types of residential structures as prepared by E. H. Boeckh and Associates. Basic data are from *Construction and Building Materials*, Statistical Supplement May 1951 (Department of Commerce), Table 3, p. 6, and cost deflators (index of residential construction costs) from the same source, Table 10, p. 40; details of composition are given on pp. 1f. and 84.

d Data are as of April 1, from "Revised Estimates of the Farm Population of the United States, 1910 to 1950" (Bureau of the Census and Bureau of Agricultural Economics), Series Census-BAE, No. 16, March 1953, Table 1, p. 3, and include estimates of the armed forces overseas except for the period 1923–1925.

e Change during 1923–1925 is derived by linear interpolation from calendar year data in *Residential Building*, by Lowell J. Chawner (Industrial Committee of the National Resources Committee, Housing Monograph Series No. 1, 1939), Table 1, p. 2, which is also the source of the 1925 figure. Change during 1948–1950 is derived from estimates based on sample surveys conducted by the Bureau of the Census and published in the following series entitled "Current Population Reports," Population Characteristics, Series P-20: No. 11, February 1948; No. 17, May 1948; No. 21, December 1948; No. 26, January 1950; and No. 33, February 1951. Change from April 1, 1949 to April 1, 1950 is derived by inflating the eleven-month change to March 1950 (adjusted for revised definition of nonfarm residence in the 1950 census) by one-eleventh.

To provide comparability with the definition of family group used in 1923–1925, annual changes in "family groups" (i.e. families plus subfamilies as tabulated by the census) have been adjusted upward to make the sum of the yearly changes during 1947–1950 equal to the sum of the changes in "household groups" for that period.

f Expressed as a percent of the number of dwelling units in the housing stock as of April 1, 1925.

g Expressed as a percent of the number of dwelling units in the housing stock as of April 1, 1950.

ing relative to the stock of housing units, and building activity relative to the internal movement of population. With respect to the former, estimates place the stock of housing for 1925 and 1950 at 22.1 and 39.1 million units, respectively. Comparing these figures with the number of dwelling units started in 1925 and in 1950, and in the years 1923–1925 and 1948–1950, it is again apparent that the building boom after World War II was low compared to that following World War I (Table 67). In other words, if one takes into account the fact that our housing stock was very much greater in 1950 than in 1925, and that other things equal this would suggest a higher rate of new building, the boom of the late forties proves to be low in comparison with that of the twenties, despite the intervention in the former period of federal programs of credit aid.

Direct information on the internal migration of population is not available, but a derived measure may be constructed from state rates of population growth in the periods 1915–1925 and 1940–

1950.[55] The facts show that although the average rate of population growth was higher in 1915–1925 than in 1940–1950, differences in the rates of growth among the various states were somewhat greater in the recent than in the earlier period.[56] This is, of course, only presumptive evidence of a high degree of internal redistribution of population, but it does indicate a demographic factor favorable to the increase of housing demand and a further reason for having expected what actually was never realized, namely a higher relative rate of building activity in the post-World War II boom than in the twenties.

The results all suggest that despite efforts to promote building activity through easing mortgage credit terms, residential construction was actually less in the boom years following World War II than might have been expected in view of the trends in population and family formation. This is by no means conclusive proof, however, that the credit aids had no influence on the level of housing output; it may simply indicate that limitations on available labor and materials produced a lower response of housing output to differences in credit terms than characterized the twenties. In fact, in terms of credit expansion the two periods were roughly similar. Net nonfarm mortgage debt owed by individuals and noncorporate borrowers increased in 1923–1925 by $7.2 billion (51 percent) and in 1948–1950 by $20.6 billion (53.2 percent).[57] The somewhat greater relative increase in mortgage debt in the post-World War II boom than in the expansion of the twenties, compared with the lesser expansion that took place in housing output, suggests that the primary manifestation of the credit liberalization program must be found in con-

[55] Taking the forty-eight states and the District of Columbia as subdivisions, the percentage growth of population in the preceding decade is computed for each subdivision; then, the deviation of the growth rate for each subdivision from that for the nation as a whole (in percentage points) is weighted by the mean of the relative proportion of that subdivision's population in the total population at the initial and terminal dates of the decade, and weighted average deviations are computed for the two periods. The higher the weighted average deviation, the higher the presumed "turbulence" of the population, and the greater the presumed demand for new housing units.

[56] National population growth was 15.2 and 14.5 percent for the periods 1915–1925 and 1940–1950, respectively, while the weighted average deviation of state rates of growth from the national rate was 7.6 percent in 1915–1925 and 9.2 percent in 1940–1950. Data for 1915–1925 are intercensal estimates of the total population as of July 1 given in *Population Special Reports*, Series P-45, No. 9 (Bureau of the Census, October 1945). Data for 1940–1950 are actual enumerations of the total population as of April 1 given in the *1950 Census of Population*, Vol. 1.

[57] *Survey of Current Business* (Department of Commerce), September 1953, Table 1, p. 14, and October 1954, Table 1, p. 14.

struction costs and housing prices, which are examined in the following section.

It will be observed in Table 68 that construction costs moved roughly parallel with costs generally up to our entrance into World War II, and that the two continued to rise together without marked divergence through the war period. However, after the war and during the period of highest construction activity, construction costs rose significantly more than the costs of other types of output. It is evident, too, that the upward tendency of costs was more marked in residential construction than in total construction activity or in the more limited area of commercial and factory construction.

This cost trend was not due, apparently, to a tendency for average hourly earnings in building to outstrip those in manufacturing—actually, the reverse was the case; rather, the phenomenon seems to have been due to a more rapid rise in the prices of building materials, particularly of lumber, than of semimanufactured goods generally. The result was that the prices of houses increased more rapidly than the prices of consumer goods generally, and certainly of the prices of consumer durable goods. Thus, a considerable part of the effect of the federal housing credit programs during the post-World War II period would seem to have been to raise the costs of residential construction and the prices of homes above what would otherwise have prevailed.[58]

Experience during the twenties was quite different: with the low point of post-World War I prices and costs in 1922 taken as 100, the Department of Commerce composite index of construction costs stood at 107 in 1925 and at 109 in 1929; the Boeckh indexes of the cost of residential and commercial and factory construction both stood at 110 in 1925, and rose moderately further, to 114 and 113, respectively, in 1929. In short, there was an increase of only 10 percent, more or less in construction costs from trough to peak. Similarly, the prices of houses—using the same Washington, D.C. index—rose only 9 percent in 1922–1925, and in 1929 fell back to only 1 percent above the 1922 level. One cannot escape the sharp contrast between the two postwar periods: the period after World

---

[58] Compare the similar conclusion reached by Ernest M. Fisher in *Urban Real Estate Markets: Characteristics and Financing* (National Bureau of Economic Research, Financial Research Program, 1951), pp. 79–90.

TABLE 68

Indexes of Construction Costs and Selected Price
Movements, 1934–1950, Selected Years
(*1934 = 100*)

Index	1934	1937	1941	1946	1950
Index of construction costs					
Composite[a]	100	107	119	169	232
Boeckh—residential[b]	100	113	132	188	260
Boeckh—commercial and factory					
buildings[b]	100	114	127	172	239
Index of wholesale prices[c]					
Manufactured goods	100	112	114	149	201
Building materials	100	110	120	154	239
Semimanufactured articles	100	117	119	152	214
Lumber	100	118	145	211	387
Index of average hourly earnings[d]					
Building construction	100	114	127	186	255
Manufacturing	100	117	137	204	275
Index of prices of consumer					
durable goods[e]	100	104	114	166	196
Index of median asking price of					
existing single family houses—					
Washington, D.C.[f]	100	111	116	212	237

[a] Computed from the Department of Commerce composite index of construction costs (1939 = 100) given in *Construction and Building Materials*, Statistical Supplement May 1951, Table 10, p. 40; for details of composition, see p. 36.

[b] Computed from the Department of Commerce unweighted arithmetic average (1939 base = 100) of individual indexes for twenty cities for each of ten types of buildings, further consolidated into unweighted averages for three types of buildings, i.e. (1) residential, (2) commercial and factory buildings, and (3) apartments, hotels, and office buildings, given in the supplement just cited, Table 10, p. 40; see also p. 37. The individual indexes are prepared by E. H. Boeckh and Associates.

[c] Computed from Department of Labor indexes (1926 = 100) given in the *Business Statistics Supplement, 1951* of the *Survey of Current Business* (Department of Commerce), pp. 26f., and in the 1942 Supplement, p. 18. For details of composition, see the 1951 source, pp. 201f. (footnotes 1 and 3 of pp. 26 and 27), and the 1942 source, pp. 180f. (footnote 1, p. 18).

[d] Computed from data on average hourly earnings of all manufacturing industries and of the contract building construction industry compiled by the Department of Labor and given in *Handbook of Labor Statistics, 1947* (Bureau of Labor Statistics), Table C-1, pp. 54 and 84, and the handbook for 1950, Table C-1, pp. 57–59. For details of composition, see the latter, pp. 52–53.

[e] Computed from the Department of Commerce price index (1939 = 100) as given in *National Income Supplement, 1951, Survey of Current Business*, Table B, p. 146, where details of composition are also given.

[f] Computed from data on the median asking prices for existing single family houses in Washington, D.C. presented in *Prices of Single-Family Houses*, a special release of the National Housing Agency, Construction and Housing Division, Washington, D.C. area study, except that the index for 1950 was supplied by the Housing and Home Finance Agency.

War I, lacking the urgent stimulation of liberalized home mortgage credit, not only produced relatively more housing but did so virtually without cost and price inflation, though building costs rose slightly in what was a period of sagging price levels for the economy generally; the post-World War II expansion, on the other hand, which was relatively modest as compared with the demographic trends of the period, was characterized by a marked inflation of building costs and housing prices.

OTHER EFFECTS ON CONSTRUCTION

It would be interesting to know whether loan insurance has affected the character and quality of housing produced since 1934, but no reliable basis for judgment exists. It is known, however, that average construction cost per dwelling unit started—in constant dollars—has fallen since the beginning of the century, except for relatively brief periods, and that there has been no noticeable change in the general downward trend since the introduction of loan insurance in 1934.[59] Thus, average construction expenditures per dwelling unit started, deflated to a 1929 dollar level, were over $6,000 in the late 1890's, around $5,800 in the late twenties, and around $4,000 in 1950. This may be due in part to improvements in productivity, but the primary factor has doubtless been a change in the character of the construction. This does not necessarily mean a decline in quality; on the contrary, the standards of construction and land use imposed on builders who propose to use insured mortgage financing have probably resulted in higher quality. A more likely explanation is that the average size and room count of dwelling units have fallen, changes which can probably be attributed in large part to urbanization and to the decline in average family size.

It is possible also that the terms of loan insurance, which differ somewhat according to the type and character of the dwelling units involved, may have given special encouragement to the production of certain types of housing and to housing in certain price classes. An example is the FHA program which offers more liberal financing terms for multi-unit projects developed on a cooperative ownership basis than for those sold under a normal leasehold arrangement. It is still too early to judge how substantial the effect of the difference in terms will be, but present indications are that it will cause

[59] David M. Blank, *The Volume of Residential Construction, 1889–1950* (National Bureau of Economic Research, Technical Paper 9, 1954), Chart E, p. 18, and Table 19, p. 70.

more resources to be pulled into the cooperative type of development than would otherwise be the case.

Finally, the availability of advance commitments to insure mortgages has probably had an important effect on the organization of the construction industry. By giving the builder assurance that the mortgages he generates will (provided all standards of construction, land use, credit, etc., are satisfied) be insured, and thus virtually guaranteeing the financing (except where there is a general shortage of mortgage money), this system encourages the planning and construction of very large developments on a "speculative" basis; that is, without prior assurance of sale. Large projects, in turn, have made possible the application of methods of production organization that have doubtless lowered costs in the building industry.

EFFECTS ON CREDIT TERMS

The cost of borrowing. We may turn now to the effects of federal programs of credit aid on urban mortgage financing; first, to their effect on the costs of borrowing. One of the avowed objects of federal housing credit programs has been to lower borrowing costs, and in general one would expect loan insurance to produce a somewhat lower level of interest rates than would otherwise prevail. This would certainly be true if the insurance premium charged were less than the risk premium that private lenders would, on the average, incorporate in the financing cost of an uninsured loan. Such a differential would almost certainly exist if the insurance premium failed to cover a reasonable estimate of the full cost of the service, but it might also exist, without pricing on a partial-cost basis, if the cost of carrying the risks were lower for the federal agency than it would be for a private lender, which is a reasonable expectation in view of the wider diversification of risks and greater volume of activity of the insuring agency. Quite apart from that effect, one would expect loan insurance to lower interest rates by attracting investment funds that would not otherwise be available and also by improving competitive lending conditions through reducing rate differentials vis-à-vis other parts of the money market. It is of interest to inquire whether such cost-reducing effects can be detected.

By setting maximum rates on the mortgages eligible for insurance, and by making only downward adjustments in the rates from the beginning of loan insurance in 1934 until the upward adjustment in 1953, federal agencies exerted a more or less persistent downward pressure on the interest rates charged on conventional financing. However, money market conditions were being eased during much of the period to 1953, and the reduction in interest rates on conventionally financed mortgage loans may have been due in part to that development. It is pertinent, therefore, to compare the movement in the rates charged on conventional loans with the yields on corporate bonds and the rates charged for business loans at commercial banks.

The requisite data for the years 1934 to 1946 are presented in Table 69; unfortunately, the analysis cannot be carried beyond that date for lack of information on conventional loans. It will be observed that the percentage decline in interest rates charged on conventional loans was actually less than that registered by Aaa and Baa corporate bonds and in the rates charged on business loans made by commercial banks. To isolate the elements in the changed money-cost situation that should be attributed to the federal housing credit programs as distinct from the changes in money market conditions generally is not possible, but it would seem fair to conclude from the given evidence that the fall in mortgage interest rates must be attributed in large part to the latter. In any event, the historical relationship between mortgage rates and bond yields has not changed, namely, that the two tend to move in the same direction, but with mortgage rates varying somewhat less than bond yields.

The regional pattern of interest rates. One would expect insurance to reduce regional differentials in interest rates, if not to eliminate them altogether, by making the residential mortgage loan a more fungible investment medium and giving it greater liquidity through a broader market. This question is illuminated in Table 70, where the average interest rates charged by various mortgage lending institutions—life insurance companies, commercial banks, and savings and loan associations—on conventional loans secured by one- to four-family dwellings in three broad (though overlapping) regions of the United States are compared with the business loan rates charged by commercial banks in cities in the same general regions.

A number of observations may be made from the table. First, it is evident that regional differentials in home mortgage interest rates have always been of minor importance in loans made by the major life insurance companies. Interestingly enough, the differentials are

349

TABLE 69

Contract Interest Rates on Conventional Nonfarm Mortgage Loans of Life Insurance Companies, Commercial Banks, and Savings and Loan Associations, Compared with Corporate Bond Yields and Commercial Bank Interest Rates on Business Loans, 1934–1946

| | CONVENTIONAL NONFARM MORTGAGE LOANS[a] | | | | | CORPORATE BONDS[b] | | COMMERCIAL BANK BUSINESS LOANS[c] |
| | 1- to 4-Family Dwellings | | | All Other Property | | | | |
YEAR	Life Insurance Companies	Commercial Banks	Savings and Loan Associations	Life Insurance Companies	Commercial Banks	Aaa	Baa	
1934	5.7%	6.1%	6.4%	5.1%	4.2%	4.00%	6.32%	3.45%
1935	5.4	5.8	6.4	4.8	4.3	3.60	5.75	2.93
1936	5.2	5.6	6.3	5.0	4.1	3.24	4.77	2.68
1937	5.2	5.4	6.2	4.9	5.1	3.26	5.03	2.59
1938	5.1	5.3	6.1	5.0	5.1	3.19	5.80	2.53
1939	5.0	5.2	5.9	4.5	4.2	3.01	4.96	2.78
1940	4.8	5.0	5.8	4.4	4.1	2.84	4.75	2.63
1941	4.7	4.9	5.7	4.4	3.9	2.77	4.33	2.54
1942	4.6	4.8	5.7	4.4	4.3	2.83	4.28	2.61
1943	4.6	4.7	5.5	4.2	4.1	2.73	3.91	2.72
1944	4.4	4.6	5.4	4.0	4.1	2.72	3.61	2.59
1945	4.3	4.6	5.3	4.2	4.0	2.62	3.29	2.39
1946	4.2	4.6	5.2	4.3	4.0	2.53	3.05	2.34

(continued on next page)

TABLE 69 (*continued*)

a Based on NBER sample surveys of loans made after January 1, 1920 by 24 leading life insurance companies, 116 commercial banks, and 92 savings and loan associations. Represents three-year moving average of original contract interest rates weighted by original loan amounts. Includes only straight mortgage loans; excludes loans for which requisite data were unavailable.

b Data for 1934–1941 are from *Banking and Monetary Statistics* (Board of Governors of the Federal Reserve System) 1943, Table 128, p. 468; for 1942–1946, from *Federal Reserve Bulletin*, May 1945, p. 457, and October 1947, p. 1279. The yields represent unweighted arithmetic averages of yield for individual bonds based on closing prices, as compiled by Moody's Investor Service. Each rating grade originally included 30 bonds divided equally among industrial, railroad, and public utility bond groups. In 1941 Aaa grade includes 4 industrial, 5 railroad, and 10 public utility bonds; in 1942–43, it includes 5 industrial, 5 railroad, and 10 public utility bonds, and in 1944–1946, it includes 5 industrial, 6 railroad, and 10 public utility bonds.

c Data for 1934–1938 are from *Banking and Monetary Statistics* (cited above), Table 125, p. 464; for 1939–1946, from *Federal Reserve Bulletin*, July 1948, p. 839. The percentages represent averages of rates charged customers by banks in New York City, seven other northern and eastern cities, and eleven southern and western cities. Before 1939 averages were computed from monthly data; thereafter, from quarterly data reported on a basis not strictly comparable with the method used for the monthly series.

almost identical for the three periods, 1920–1924, 1930–1934, and 1940–1947. This merely reflects the fact that a national lending institution follows a policy of nearly standard rates for all sections of the country and that the principal development since 1920 has been a lowering of the entire structure of rates, with little change in the regional pattern.

Second, regional differences in mortgage interest rates have, in each of the periods studied, been greater among loans made by savings and loan associations than among those made by commercial banks. This reflects a widely recognized fact, namely, that the savings and loan group is the most narrowly localized of all institutional mortgage lenders.

Third, regional differentials in the rates charged on home mortgage loans by commercial banks and by savings and loan associations were substantially less in 1940–1947 than in 1920–1924. Indeed, they were not appreciably greater in 1940–1947 than those for the leading life insurance companies. The picture that emerges in the period 1930–1934 is a somewhat different one: its main features, especially as concerns commercial bank loans, are perhaps best explained by the unsettled credit conditions of the time.

These facts clearly indicate the emergence of a more uniform national pattern of home mortgage rates; and to know whether the change is attributable to federal loan insurance, one must determine

TABLE 70

Regional Comparison of Average Interest Rates on Conventional
Nonfarm Home Mortgage Loans and on Commercial Bank
Business Loans, Selected Periods, 1920–1947

	MORTGAGE LOANS			COMMERCIAL BANK BUSINESS LOANS
REGION OR CITY[a]	Life Insurance Companies	Commercial Banks	Savings and Loan Associations	
1920–1924				
Eastern states	5.87%	5.97%	6.00%	..
Northern and eastern states	5.92	6.05	6.55	..
Southern and western states	6.04	6.41	8.78	..
New York City	..	..	..	5.49%
7 other northern and eastern cities	..	..	..	5.92
11 southern and western cities	..	..	..	6.31
1930–1934				
Eastern states	5.88	5.32	5.87	..
Northern and eastern states	5.93	5.79	6.27	..
Southern and western states	6.05	6.44	7.68	..
New York City	..	..	..	3.66
7 other northern and eastern cities	..	..	..	4.42
11 southern and western cities	..	..	..	4.97
1940–1947				
Eastern states	4.45	4.87	5.09	..
Northern and eastern states	4.67	4.67	5.23	..
Southern and western states	4.63	4.63	5.65	..
New York City	..	..	..	2.01
7 other northern and eastern cities	..	..	..	2.55
11 southern and western cities	..	..	..	3.04

Average interest rates on mortgage loans are based on National Bureau of Economic Research sample surveys of loans made after January 1, 1920 by 24 leading life insurance companies, 116 commercial banks, and 92 savings and loan associations, and represent rates for conventional straight mortgage loans secured by one- to four-family dwellings, exclusive of loans for which year made or geographic region was not available or for which data necessary for the calculation of rates were inadequate. Rates are weighted by original loan amounts.

Business loan interest rates are simple arithmetic averages of annual weighted averages computed by the Board of Governors of the Federal Reserve System. For 1920–1934 they were compiled from *Banking and Monetary Statistics* (published by the board in 1943), Tables 124 and 125, pp. 463f.; for 1940–1947, from the *Federal Reserve Bulletin*, July 1948, p. 839. Before 1928 the business loan classification includes, besides commercial loans, other types of customer loans. The

(*continued on next page*)

TABLE 70 (continued)

average rates for 1940–1947 were derived from quarterly data and are not strictly comparable with the earlier averages, which were compiled from monthly statistics.

ᵃ Regional classification is based on census divisions, regrouped to approximate a similarity with the areas used in the survey of commercial bank business loan rates. The divisions are grouped as follows: *Eastern states*—Middle Atlantic (New York, New Jersey, and Pennsylvania); *northern and eastern states*—Middle Atlantic, New England (Connecticut, Maine, Massachusetts, New Hampshire, Rhode Island, and Vermont), and East North Central (Illinois, Indiana, Michigan, Ohio, and Wisconsin); *southern and western states*—South Atlantic (Delaware, Florida, Georgia, Maryland, North Carolina, South Carolina, Virginia, West Virginia, and District of Columbia), West North Central (Iowa, Kansas, Minnesota, Missouri, Nebraska, North Dakota, and South Dakota), West South Central (Arkansas, Louisiana, Oklahoma, and Texas), and Pacific (California, Oregon, and Washington).

The areas covered by the Federal Reserve Board survey of business loan rates include banks in the following cities: *seven other northern and eastern cities*— Boston, Buffalo, Chicago, Cleveland, Detroit, Philadelphia, and Pittsburgh; *eleven southern and western cities*—Atlanta, Baltimore, Dallas, Kansas City, Missouri, Los Angeles, Minneapolis, New Orleans, Richmond, St. Louis, San Francisco, and Seattle.

whether it is a development unique to the home mortgage market or one that has characterized the money market generally. A general test of the question is not easily made; but it would appear from the data in Table 70 that the regional pattern of commercial bank business loan rates is not more uniform now than it was in the period 1920–1924. This would suggest that the standardizing trend has made greater progress in the mortgage market than elsewhere and is therefore perhaps largely attributable to the federal programs of loan insurance.

Other terms of borrowing. One of the principal avowed purposes of federal housing credit programs has been to improve lending practices by discouraging the short-maturity loan, by substituting a more liberal first mortgage for a combination of conservative first mortgage and costly secondary financing, and by encouraging the regular retirement of debt through prescheduled amortization payments. We should examine, therefore, changes in the average maturity or contract length of loans made, the ratio of the amount loaned to the appraised value of the property, and the requirement that the loan be fully repaid by maturity. Again the effects of the federal credit programs are difficult to determine, but one can trace the changes in terms that have occurred in the insured mortgage field and can compare them with developments in the area of conventional lending.

Information bearing on this range of questions is brought together in Table 71. It will be seen there that the average duration

TABLE 71

Average Contract Length (in Years) of FHA-Insured Loans and of Conventional Nonfarm Mortgage Loans Made by Private Lending Institutions, 1935–1946

| | FHA-INSURED LOANS[a] | | CONVENTIONAL NONFARM MORTGAGE LOANS[b] | | | | |
| | | | 1- to 4-Family Dwellings | | | All Other Property | |
YEAR	New Homes	Existing Homes	Life Insurance Companies	Commercial Banks	Savings and Loan Associations	Life Insurance Companies	Commercial Banks
1935	17.6	16.0	12.6	4.4	11.6	9.6	c
1936	17.7	16.2	15.2	3.8	11.0	10.6	6.2
1937	18.4	16.5	15.5	5.3	12.2	12.2	4.2
1938	21.4	16.3	16.3	5.4	12.7	10.8	4.5
1939	22.0	16.9	16.0	6.2	12.4	12.1	7.8
1940	23.0	17.5	17.3	6.3	14.2	13.9	8.5
1941	23.3	17.8	17.5	6.4	13.2	13.6	6.2
1942	23.5	18.1	16.5	5.3	12.7	13.2	7.7
1943	24.6	18.3	15.8	5.2	12.1	13.5	6.6
1944	24.7	18.0	14.9	5.5	12.4	12.1	5.8
1945	24.6	18.3	15.9	6.5	13.2	11.7	8.8
1946	21.0	18.9	17.2	7.4	12.3	16.7	4.7

a Data for 1935–1939 are annual averages for mortgages on one- to four-family homes accepted for insurance under Section 203, from the *Seventh Annual Report* of the Federal Housing Administration, December 31, 1940, Table 33, p. 68. For 1940–1946, only single family home mortgages insured under Section 203 (or under Section 603 as noted below) are included; the data are from the *Thirteenth Annual Report of the FHA, 1946*, Tables 11 and 33, pp. 36 and 61. (During 1940–1946 single family homes accounted for nearly all Section 203 insured mortgage loans made on new homes, and for 93 percent or more of those on existing homes.) The 1943–1945 averages for new homes refer

Section 203 mortgages in those years were secured by existing homes, and as a result no statistical information was compiled by the FHA for new-home mortgages insured under Section 203; see page 35 of the *Thirteenth Annual Report.*

b Based on National Bureau of Economic sample surveys of loans made after January 1, 1920 by 24 leading life insurance companies, 116 commercial banks, and 92 savings and loan associations. Represents average contract lengths on conventional straight mortgage loans for which requisite data were available. Averages are weighted by original loan amounts.

c Less than ten loans included.

of FHA-insured mortgages secured by new dwellings has increased from 17.6 years in 1935 to 21.0 years in 1946. The increase for loans secured by existing homes was from 16.0 years to 18.9 years. In contrast, conventional loans made by life insurance companies in 1935 on one- to four-family dwellings had an average duration of 12.6 years, and by 1946 the average had increased to 17.2 years. The average length of comparable loans made by commercial banks was substantially less, but increased, possibly owing to the competition of the insured mortgage market, from 4.4 to 7.4 years over the period. Conventional mortgage loans made by life insurance companies on the security of other than one- to four-family properties showed a marked increase of average contract length between 1935 and 1946. The comparable loans of commercial banks have traditionally been made for shorter terms, but even they increased in average duration.

Savings and loan associations are shown to have undergone less change in lending policy than the other lenders. The average length of the home mortgage loans made by such associations increased very little between 1935 and 1946; indeed the 1946 average was not much greater than that for 1921 (12.3 as against 10.6 years.)[60]

The facts are not easily interpreted. They show that at least as regards lending by life insurance companies the period since 1934 had witnessed a substantial lengthening in the maturities of home mortgage loans; because the change followed a period during which average maturities were roughly constant,[61] it seems reasonable to attribute it in large part to the competition of insured mortgage lending. Yet the general liberalization of credit which took place during the period may also have had a prominent part in producing the result.

As will be seen in Table 72, there has been some liberalization in loan-to-value ratios since 1935, though the change has not been very great. The fact that it occurred to some degree even with loans secured by income-producing properties (commercial structures, and dwellings larger than four-family size), an area in which the direct competition of insured lending has been somewhat less intense than in the financing of single family homes, suggests that the change can be traced in part to factors other than loan insurance.

[60] J. E. Morton, *Urban Mortgage Lending: Comparative Markets and Experience* (Princeton University Press for the National Bureau of Economic Research, 1956), Table C-6, p. 174.
[61] *Loc.cit.*

TABLE 72

Average Loan-to-Value Ratios of FHA-Insured Loans and of Conventional Nonfarm Mortgage Loans Made by Private Lending Institutions, 1935–1946

| | FHA-INSURED LOANS[a] | | CONVENTIONAL NONFARM MORTGAGE LOANS[b] | | | | |
| | | | 1- to 4-Family Dwellings | | | All Other Property | |
YEAR	New Homes	Existing Homes	Life Insurance Companies	Commercial Banks	Savings and Loan Associations	Life Insurance Companies	Commercial Banks
1935	73.0%	69.0%	51.2%	53.3%	58.9%	48.2%	c
1936	73.9	70.4	56.0	54.6	61.4	45.9	52.0%
1937	75.3	73.7	58.4	52.9	60.7	56.0	33.1
1938	82.4	73.9	59.5	46.7	62.5	46.2	40.8
1939	83.7	74.4	59.1	53.2	63.8	48.4	43.1
1940	84.8	75.3	60.1	52.7	67.2	57.2	54.6
1941	85.8	75.9	61.2	51.3	66.5	53.5	46.5
1942	86.7	77.9	61.5	53.4	66.5	57.3	50.0
1943	89.8	78.2	57.9	53.3	67.2	52.9	50.6
1944	89.7	78.9	59.7	53.7	70.6	52.6	52.0
1945	89.3	79.1	59.6	55.1	69.2	59.5	49.6
1946	84.1	78.6	59.3	54.5	67.5	55.3	62.8

a Data for 1935–1939 are annual averages for mortgages on one- to four-family homes accepted for insurance under Section 203, from the *Seventh Annual Report* of the Federal Housing Administration, December 31, 1940, Table 34, p. 69, and Table 66. For 1940–1946, only single family home mortgages insured under Section 203 (or under Section 603 as noted below) are included; the data are from the *Thirteenth Annual Report* of the FHA, 1946, Tables 11 and 33, pp. 36 and 61. (During 1940–1946 single family homes accounted for nearly all Section 203 insured mortgage loans made on new homes, and for 93 percent or more of those on existing homes.) The 1943–1945 averages

tion 603; virtually all Section 203 mortgages in those years were secured by existing homes, and as a result no statistical information was compiled by the FHA for new-home mortgages insured under Section 203; see page 35 of the *Thirteenth Annual Report*.

b Based on National Bureau of Economic Research sample surveys of loans made after January 1, 1920 by 24 leading life insurance companies, 116 commercial banks, and 92 savings and loan associations. Represents average loan-to-value ratios on conventional straight mortgage loans for which requisite data were available. Averages are weighted by original loan amounts.

c **Less than ten loans included.**

Finally, there can be no doubt that one of the effects of the federal credit programs in the housing field has been to encourage the practice of regular and full amortization. It would be a mistake, however, to conclude that this was an innovation of the federal programs; as will be seen in Table 73, savings and loan associations have always made the bulk of their loans on an amortized basis, and even as early as 1920–1924 more than three-quarters of the urban mortgage loans made by life insurance companies were either partially or fully amortized—mainly partially. Commercial banks made a much higher percentage of their loans without amortization, and they too used partial oftener than full amortization.

Nonamortized loans seem to have been somewhat more frequent in 1925–1929 than before, and then to have become relatively less frequent in 1930–1934 than in the late twenties. The 1930–1934 period also shows some tendency for a lesser frequency of partially amortized loans relative to the fully amortized type. By the period 1940–1947, however, very considerable changes had become evident: for both commercial banks and life insurance companies, the nonamortized loan had declined in relative importance and fully amortized loans had become markedly more widespread, particularly among the home loans of life insurance companies. The practice of writing home mortgage loans on a regularly amortized basis doubtless would have increased in any case after the heavy foreclosure experience of the early thirties, but it seems not unreasonable to attribute a considerable share of the responsibility for the rapid spread of the practice after 1934 to the example set by the federal loan insurance program.

EFFECTS ON THE VOLUME OF MORTGAGE DEBT
AND ITS INSTITUTIONAL DISTRIBUTION

Since 1935 there has been a great transformation in the composition of the nonfarm mortgage debt. By the end of 1953, FHA-insured and VA-guaranteed loans constituted about 43 percent of the home mortgage debt and 34 percent of the mortgage debt on all types of properties, reflecting the fact that since 1935 the volume of insured lending has grown more rapidly than the volume of mortgage lending as a whole.[62] But the influence of federal loan insurance on the size of the nonfarm mortgage debt is more difficult to determine. One test of it is to compare the movement of home mortgage debt

[62] *Op.cit.*, Table 6, p. 25.

TABLE 73

Distribution of Conventional Nonfarm Mortgage Loans Made by Life Insurance Companies, Commercial Banks, and Savings and Loan Associations by Type of Loan within Indicated Period, 1920–1947

TYPE OF LOAN	1-TO 4-FAMILY DWELLINGS			ALL OTHER PROPERTY	
	Life Insurance Companies	Commercial Banks	Savings and Loan Associations[a]	Life Insurance Companies	Commercial Banks
1920–1924[b]					
Fully amortized	27.5%	15.5%	94.4%	1.7%	5.8%
Partially amortized	56.2	42.4	}	77.6	40.7
Nonamortized	16.2	42.1	5.6	20.7	53.5
Total	100.0	100.0	100.0	100.0	100.0
1925–1929					
Fully amortized	18.9	16.2	b	6.3	10.7
Partially amortized	58.9	37.9	b	66.1	43.4
Nonamortized	22.2	45.9	b	27.6	45.9
Total	100.0	100.0	b	100.0	100.0
1930–1934					
Fully amortized	33.4	17.1	94.1	3.8	10.3
Partially amortized	50.4	38.1	}	69.8	39.7
Nonamortized	16.2	44.8	5.9	26.4	50.0
Total	100.0	100.0	100.0	100.0	100.0
1940–1947[c]					
Fully amortized	90.6	48.8	99.8	53.1	51.9
Partially amortized	8.4	41.3	}	44.1	37.3
Nonamortized	1.0	9.8	0.2	2.8	10.8
Total	100.0	100.0	100.0	100.0	100.0

Based on National Bureau of Economic Research sample surveys of loans made after January 1, 1920 by 24 leading life insurance companies, 116 commercial banks, and 92 savings and loan associations. Excludes loans for which requisite information was not available.

a Includes 219 loans (about 5 percent of the total) secured by other than one-to-four-family [. . .]

ings. Amortized loans include direct reduction loans as well as loans made under share accumulation and cancel and endorse plans.

b Savings and loan association loans made during 1925–1929 are included with those made in 1920–1924.

c For savings and loan associations the distribution [. . .]

(where the insured component bulks largest) with debt totals in areas of the economy where no loan insurance facilities have been available.

Perhaps the most direct and significant comparison is between consumer installment sales credit and home mortgage credit extended annually. The former increased by about 50 percent between 1935 and 1937 and the latter by about 15 percent; FHA insurance, on the other hand, increased by around four and one-half times.[63] The FHA figure is of dubious significance, however, since it represents growth from the beginning of the program and because to whatever degree the insured credit would have been forthcoming without insurance it would not represent an increase in the over-all volume of mortgage lending.

Similarly, the amount of FHA-insured loans outstanding rose more rapidly from 1935 until 1941, and also during 1946–1953, than home mortgage debt as a whole, or all nonfarm mortgage debt, reflecting the rising importance of the insured loan in the total. However, the urban mortgage debt, whether defined in the limited sense of debt on small dwellings or on urban properties generally, did not increase as rapidly as consumer nonmortgage debt.[64] It must be concluded, therefore, that, while the availability of federal loan insurance tended to cause urban mortgage debt to be cast in insured form, it did not exert a sufficiently stimulative effect on mortgage credit to cause the total amount outstanding to rise as rapidly as the mainly uninsured credit extended to consumers on a non-real-estate basis.

The tendency for home mortgage debt to grow only moderately over the period 1935–1941, and at a lesser rate than consumer credit, was probably affected by trends in the frequency and intensity of use of mortgage credit. Census data reveal that the percentage of owner-occupied nonfarm dwellings that were mortgaged increased from 28 in 1890 to 45 in 1940 and fell back very slightly to 44 in 1950.[65] However, the percentage mortgaged had already risen to 40 by 1920, and no very marked increase in the frequency of recourse to mortgage financing took place during the thirty years from then to 1950.

63 Kisselgoff, *op.cit.*, p. 61; and Table 61, above.
64 For FHA-insured outstandings, see Appendix Table A-17; for nonfarm mortgage debt and consumer nonmortgage debt, *Survey of Current Business* (Department of Commerce, September 1953), Tables 6 and 7, pp. 18f.
65 Morton, *op.cit.*, Table 4, p. 22.

On the intensity with which homeowners utilize mortgage financing, census data indicate that the average ratio of debt to value on owner-occupied nonfarm homes was 39.8 percent in 1890, 42.6 percent in 1920, and 52.4 in 1940,[66] and that in 1950 the median ratio was about 43 percent and the average (judging by the frequency distribution) about 45 percent. The following table shows the situation as of 1950 in more detail; it will be observed that the debt-to-value ratio is very much higher on properties carrying a federally insured or guaranteed loan than on properties financed conventionally, and that the ratio is highest where VA-guaranteed second mortgages have been used.

	Total Outstanding Debt on Owner-Occupied, One-Family Dwellings as a Percentage of Market Value, 1950a (medians)
Total mortgaged properties	43%
No second mortgage	40
Second mortgage	77
FHA-insured first mortgage	62
No second mortgage	49
VA-guaranteed second mortgage	87
Conventional second mortgage	75
VA-guaranteed first mortgage	70
No second mortgage	70
Conventional second mortgage	77
Conventional first mortgage	35
No second mortgage	34
Conventional second mortgage	57

a Data are from the *1950 Census of Housing*, Vol. 4, Residential Financing, Part 1, Chapter 3, Table 3, p. 163.

The over-all ratio of outstanding mortgage debt to the value of the mortgaged properties is affected, through time, by changes in the rate of repayments and in current real estate values. In the period of rising incomes reflected in the 1950 data, both factors—high repayments and inflated property values—were operating to lower the debt-value ratio. Thus while the influence of the federal insurance and guaranty programs has been to encourage higher ratios of original loan amounts to the value of the mortgaged properties, so far it has not raised average debt-to-value ratios substantially above what they were thirty years ago. At the same time, there has been no substantial change in the frequency of use of mortgage credit.

[66] Fisher, *op.cit.*, Table 9, p. 63.

Participation in insured mortgage lending varies in some degree from one type of lending institution to another; savings and loan associations, for example, are notable for their relatively minor participation in the FHA program, whereas insurance companies and mortgage companies have placed an increasing and relatively high proportion of their mortgage holdings on an FHA-insured or VA-guaranteed basis. Accordingly, if there were some special advantage to the insured loan one might expect the latter agencies to have grown as mortgage lenders, relatively more than others. This seems not to have been the case. The proportion of home mortgage debt held by savings and loan associations has remained roughly constant since 1935.[67] There have been shifts in the relative importance of mutual savings banks, commercial banks, and life insurance companies, but consisting of little more than an increase in the proportion held by the last two named, at the expense of that held by mutual savings banks. Broadly speaking, it would appear that federal programs of loan insurance have exerted little, if any, influence on the institutional distribution of home mortgage debt. The shift in the relative position of mutual savings banks, which is also but less strikingly evident when one considers mortgage debt on multi-family dwellings and commercial properties, seems to be due more to the decrease in the share of those institutions in total investible resources than to any changes induced by the federal credit programs.

Furthermore, there is no evidence that the major private lending institutions have committed a larger proportion of their total resources to mortgage lending than they did before the inauguration of the federal insurance programs. In fact, the proportion of resources so committed by the major lender groups is somewhat lower now than it was in the late twenties (only for commercial banks about the same), a shift that reflects mainly the increasing importance of federal debt as an outlet for institutional funds in the period following 1940 and not necessarily a decline in the interest of lenders in the mortgage as an investment medium.[68]

In general, therefore, the influence of the loan insurance and guarantee programs on the volume and institutional distribution of home mortgage debt would seem to have been slight, though the programs have succeeded in causing an increasing proportion of such debt to be cast in the insured or guaranteed form. In the financial

[67] Morton, op.cit., Chart 3, Panel B, p. 44.
[68] Ibid., Table 21, p. 55.

sphere, their effect is evident in such matters as the wider practice of full amortization and the liberalization of lending terms; but even in those areas the influence of generally easier credit conditions, more or less characteristic of all money markets after 1934, must be credited with responsibility for part of the observed results.

APPENDIXES

APPENDIX A

Summary Tables

TABLE A-1

Credit Extended by Federal Agencies, by Type of Financial Aid, 1918–1953

(*in thousands*)

| | VOLUME DURING YEAR | | | OUTSTANDINGS AT YEAR END | | |
YEAR	Direct Loans	Loan Insurance or Guarantees	Stock Purchases	Direct Loans	Loan Insurance or Guarantees	Stock Purchases
1918	$ 136,475	..	..	$ 34,214	..	..
1919	241,271	..	..	101,264	..	..
1920	666,028	..	..	684,367	..	..
1921	287,743	..	..	827,603	..	..
1922	281,895	..	..	662,637	..	..
1923	144,894	..	..	587,973	..	..
1924	42,571	..	..	495,545	..	..
1925	12,608	..	..	387,097	..	..
1926	11,383	..	..	352,554	..	..
1927	13,683	..	..	236,312	..	..
1928	18,301	..	..	152,687	..	..
1929	47,821	..	..	195,582	..	..
1930	399,990	..	..	439,494	..	..
1931	633,027	..	..	718,060	..	..
1932	1,905,954	..	..	2,072,611	..	..

(*continued on next page*)

TABLE A-1 (continued)
(in thousands)

YEAR	VOLUME DURING YEAR			OUTSTANDINGS AT YEAR END		
	Direct Loans	Loan Insurance or Guarantees	Stock Purchases	Direct Loans	Loan Insurance or Guarantees	Stock Purchases
1933	$1,840,740	..	$268,740	$2,854,651	..	$268,582
1934	3,891,650	$ 31,575	697,716	5,577,318	$ 31,513	893,442
1935	1,556,412	322,667	161,539	6,187,015	310,445	986,287
1936	691,447	559,948	132,069	5,929,135	705,134	868,263
1937	445,261	496,110	98,378	5,553,324	1,023,352	848,148
1938	819,340	729,138	39,818	5,207,082	1,545,464	832,953
1939	1,090,106	984,519	27,906	5,294,086	2,233,883	772,823
1940	1,395,154	1,034,244	45,977	5,434,714	3,078,736	726,372
1941	1,435,751	1,205,560	3,399	5,604,722	3,744,043	645,146
1942	1,203,797	2,172,845	14,519	5,599,097	5,081,518	592,002
1943	934,664	5,122,473	563	5,032,695	6,335,060	459,743
1944	753,070	4,300,637	16	4,512,151	6,332,584	374,266
1945	703,352	2,609,938	269	3,792,117	5,517,565	307,859
1946	1,499,278	2,392,010	..	4,436,113	6,097,340	206,565
1947	1,603,909	3,680,900	5,000	5,317,819	8,238,784	160,469
1948	1,243,416	4,466,798	..	6,181,249	11,166,088	134,696
1949	1,652,058	4,737,171	3,000	7,010,730	14,317,517	116,314
1950	2,165,619	6,179,633	..	7,583,272	18,600,515	102,971
1951	2,224,080	6,816,885	..	8,773,078	22,876,391	84,344
1952	2,647,853	7,186,812	..	9,979,664	25,737,086	46,776
1953	2,837,651	7,859,747	..	10,513,814	29,326,600	41,539

Based on data shown in Tables A-3 and A-5 to A-8. A-33. Types of financial aid are defined, as to amounts
For greater detail see Tables A-9 to A-24 and A-27 to included, in Chapter 2, footnote 1.

TABLE A-2

Credit Extended by Federally Sponsored Agencies, by Type of Financial Aid, 1917–1953

(in thousands)

| | VOLUME DURING YEAR | | OUTSTANDINGS AT YEAR END | |
| | Direct Loans | Stock Purchases | Direct Loans | Stock Purchases |
YEAR				
1917	$ 39,112	..	$ 38,800	..
1918	118,130	..	156,214	..
1919	144,987	..	293,595	..
1920	66,985	..	349,843	..
1921	91,030	..	432,870	..
1922	224,301	..	639,863	..
1923	236,969	..	842,601	..
1924	282,737	..	991,098	..
1925	281,086	..	1,088,411	..
1926	308,780	..	1,174,420	..
1927	278,544	..	1,237,753	..
1928	239,375	..	1,285,188	..
1929	202,508	..	1,290,044	..
1930	266,945	..	1,339,441	..
1931	310,009	..	1,312,786	..
1932	269,231	..	1,251,496	..
1933	437,765	$ 2,430	1,448,807	$ 2,430
1934	1,116,777	89,405	2,237,815	90,086
1935	774,717	11,999	2,457,862	77,017
1936	643,629	3,895	2,523,809	75,038
1937	701,269	4,824	2,605,222	76,146
1938	659,708	2,419	2,553,518	75,788
1939	675,932	2,558	2,455,823	75,370
1940	783,039	1,301	2,447,710	61,445
1941	996,943	21,464	2,458,245	81,498
1942	1,129,327	1,920	2,243,345	81,621
1943	1,381,886	621	2,054,839	76,090
1944	1,427,758	538	1,796,109	63,587
1945	1,460,500	596	1,672,174	55,491
1946	1,766,148	292	1,734,354	46,034
1947	2,147,955	225	1,946,615	34,918
1948	2,397,843	30	2,124,791	29,139
1949	2,210,826	115	2,091,773	22,296
1950	2,807,950	965	2,633,573	15,728
1951	3,192,420	1,015	2,875,279	11,371
1952	3,309,383	100	3,046,164	7,596
1953	3,258,486	640	3,101,541	4,946

Based on data shown in Tables A-4 to A-6. For greater detail see Tables A-25 to A-27 inclusive. Types of financial aid are defined, as to amounts included, in Chapter 2, footnote 1.

TABLE A-3

Credit Extended to Agriculture by Federal Agencies, by Type of Financial Aid, 1918–1953

(in thousands)

YEAR	VOLUME DURING YEAR				OUTSTANDINGS AT YEAR END			
	Direct Loans		Loan Insurance or Guarantees(c)	Stock Purchases(d)	Direct Loans		Loan Insurance or Guarantees(c)	Stock Purchases(d)
	Real Estate(a)	Non-Real-Estate(b)			Real Estate(a)	Non-Real-Estate(b)		
1918	...	$ 8,504	...	...	...	$ 3,079	...	...
1919	...	3,524	...	...	...	5,660	...	...
1920	...	1	...	...	...	4,731	...	...
1921	...	84,924	...	...	...	86,408	...	...
1922	...	187,623	...	...	...	151,577	...	...
1923	...	18,135	...	...	...	72,560	...	...
1924	...	10,286	...	...	...	42,782	...	...
1925	...	937	...	...	...	17,796	...	...
1926	...	599	...	...	...	9,771	...	...
1927	...	178	...	...	...	3,654	...	...
1928	...	126	...	...	...	2,700	...	...
1929	...	20,582	...	...	...	22,647	...	...
1930	...	353,892	...	...	...	242,761	...	...
1931	...	574,121	...	...	...	487,581	...	...
1932	...	319,268	...	...	...	583,993	...	...
1933	$ 70,812	338,678	...	...	$ 70,738	581,333	...	...
1934	553,136	239,501	...	...	616,825	371,492	...	...
1935	196,395	200,814	...	...	794,752	419,117	...	...
1936	77,258	79,593	...	...	837,274	451,347	...	...
1937	40,020	92,815	...	$29	815,001	450,012	...	...
1938	39,670	195,372	...	5	767,985	564,398	...	$29
1939	53,993	245,775	...	...	732,661	708,787	...	34

(continued on next page)

(in thousands)

| | VOLUME DURING YEAR | | | | OUTSTANDINGS AT YEAR END | | | |
| | Direct Loans | | Loan Insurance or Guarantee c | Stock Purchased d | Direct Loans | | Loan Insurance or Guarantee c | Stock Purchased d |
YEAR	Real Estate a	Non-Real-Estate b			Real Estate a	Non-Real-Estate b		
1940	$76,377	$205,096	..	..	$728,486	$752,142	..	$34
1941	98,196	232,289	..	..	732,284	864,262	..	34
1942	59,964	240,077	..	..	693,183	923,659	..	34
1943	59,495	230,409	..	..	600,656	910,070	..	34
1944	60,120	128,303	..	..	526,604	848,508	..	34
1945	58,113	157,520	$1,238	..	426,297	847,653	e	34
1946	61,937	264,384	29,853	..	343,627	952,219	$30,654	34
1947	46,906	320,159	36,634	..	309,524	1,124,608	64,531	34
1948	21,500	373,582	21,533	..	273,921	1,358,506	80,644	..
1949	17,907	439,708	17,291	..	254,246	1,666,045	91,550	..
1950	46,640	402,301	25,602	..	264,927	1,891,929	109,068	..
1951	47,356	379,035	21,929	..	273,120	2,067,089	119,022	..
1952	50,914	408,935	13,771	..	289,159	2,281,042	122,566	..
1953	33,234	425,063	12,114	..	292,852	2,497,577	124,097	..

a Covers Federal Farm Mortgage Corporation "Commissioner" loans and Farmers Home Administration farm-ownership and farm housing loans. Volume figures for 1942, 1944, and 1945 are partially estimated. For sources of the components of these totals, see Tables A-15 and A-24.

b Covers non-real-estate loans made by the Farmers Home Administration and loans made by the Electric Home and Farm Authority, the Agricultural Marketing Act Revolving Fund, the Emergency Crop and Feed Loan Division of the Farm Credit Administration, the Farmers Seed Loan Office, the Reconstruction Finance Corporation, the regional agricultural credit corporations, the Rural Electrification Administration, the Tennessee Valley Associated Cooperatives, Inc., the Virgin Islands Corporation, and the War Finance Corporation. Volumes series for 1918–1923, 1934–1942, and 1944–1946, and outstandings for 1918–1934 and 1946–1947, are partially estimated. Advances on loans made by the Farmers Home Administration in 1934–1937 and by the Virgin Islands Corpora-

tion in 1949–1953 are excluded because annual data are lacking. Outstandings of the Emergency Crop and Feed Loan Division are not available for 1918, and those of the Electric Home and Farm Authority from 1942 on are carried in the RFC business loan series in Table A-9. For sources of the components of these totals, see Tables A-9, A-12, A-15, and A-21 to A-24.

c Refers to amount of commitments under loan insurance and guarantees written by the Farmers Home Administration and the Veterans' Administration. Volume series for 1945–1946 and all year-end outstandings are partially estimated. For sources of the components of these totals, see Tables A-10 and A-15.

d Represents purchases of stock of agricultural cooperative associations by the Tennessee Valley Associated Cooperatives, Inc. For sources, see Table A-23.

e Data not available.

TABLE A-4

Credit Extended to Agriculture by Federally Sponsored Agencies, by Type of Financial Aid, 1917–1953

(in thousands)

| YEAR | VOLUME DURING YEAR | | | OUTSTANDINGS AT YEAR END | | |
| | Direct Loans | | | Direct Loans | | |
	Real Estate a	Non-Real Estate b	Stock Purchases c	Real Estate a	Non-Real Estate b	Stock Purchases c
1917	$ 39,112	..	..	$ 38,800	..	..
1918	118,130	..	..	156,214	..	..
1919	144,987	..	..	293,595	..	..
1920	66,985	..	..	349,843	..	..
1921	91,030	..	..	432,870	..	..
1922	224,301	..	..	639,863	..	..
1923	192,083	$ 44,886	..	799,869	$ 42,732	..
1924	165,510	117,227	..	928,831	62,267	..
1925	127,355	153,731	..	1,008,359	80,052	..
1926	131,318	177,462	..	1,081,986	92,434	..
1927	140,384	138,160	..	1,161,838	75,915	..
1928	102,236	137,139	..	1,203,911	81,277	..
1929	64,253	138,255	..	1,213,953	76,091	..
1930	47,971	218,974	..	1,209,431	130,010	..
1931	42,015	267,994	..	1,192,918	119,868	..
1932	27,570	240,823	..	1,158,274	92,384	..
1933	151,634	196,099	$ 2,430	1,268,441	94,924	$ 2,430
1934	730,367	832,850	89,405	1,959,106	178,517	90,086

(continued on next page)

TABLE A-4 (continued)
(in thousands)

YEAR	VOLUME DURING YEAR			OUTSTANDINGS AT YEAR END		
	Direct Loans		Stock Purchases c	Direct Loans		Stock Purchases c
	Real Estate a	Non-Real Estate b		Real Estate a	Non-Real Estate b	
1935	248,671	438,437	11,999	2,126,117	196,566	77,017
1936	109,170	432,683	3,895	2,133,192	219,864	75,038
1937	63,092	509,994	4,824	2,119,018	265,950	76,146
1938	51,418	519,832	2,419	2,072,262	265,069	75,788
1939	51,582	525,764	2,558	2,002,061	258,766	75,370
1940	64,275	581,692	1,301	1,955,616	281,450	61,445
1941	65,068	758,580	21,464	1,879,901	348,561	81,498
1942	53,974	907,859	1,920	1,717,697	382,309	81,621
1943	61,900	1,102,796	621	1,456,334	477,905	76,090
1944	70,275	1,097,848	538	1,214,801	446,851	63,587
1945	92,986	1,075,723	596	1,086,488	388,819	55,491
1946	130,162	1,303,309	292	985,477	454,868	46,034
1947	138,764	1,648,816	225	898,417	611,239	34,918
1948	150,514	1,871,722	30	878,586	730,194	29,139
1949	182,357	1,768,802	115	916,862	739,304	22,296
1950	205,933	1,920,730	965	959,789	855,195	15,728
1951	214,220	2,527,568	1,015	1,007,695	1,056,960	11,371
1952	254,581	2,437,796	100	1,086,289	1,091,765	7,596
1953	289,772	2,219,173	640	1,185,781	962,305	4,946

a Represents mortgage loans made by the federal land banks. Outstandings cover regular and purchase money mortgages and real estate sales contracts. The volume series, however, exclude purchase money mortgages and sales contracts because annual data are lacking. Outstandings for 1917 are estimated. For sources, see Table A-26.

b Covers loans made by the Central Bank for Coopera-tives and the twelve district banks, and by the federal intermediate credit banks. For sources of the components of these totals, see Table A-25.

c Represents purchases of Class A stock of the produc-tion credit associations by the production credit corpora-tions. For source, see Table A-26.

TABLE A-5

Credit Extended to Business Enterprises by Federal and Federally Sponsored Agencies, by Type of Financial Aid, 1918–1953

(in thousands)

| | FEDERAL AGENCIES | | | | FEDERALLY SPONSORED AGENCIES | |
| | Volume during Year | | Year-End Outstandings | | Volume | Outstandings |
YEAR	Direct Loans^a	Loan Insurance or Guarantees^b	Direct Loans^a	Loan Insurance or Guarantees^b	Direct Loans^c	Direct Loans^c
1918	$ 122,792	..	$ 29,629	..	..	..
1919	237,667	..	93,928	..	..	..
1920	665,959	..	679,577	..	..	..
1921	201,119	..	740,443	..	..	..
1922	92,016	..	506,229	..	..	..
1923	122,950	..	507,773	..	..	..
1924	26,850	..	441,690	..	..	..
1925	4,760	..	353,351	..	..	..
1926	2,146	..	320,775	..	..	..
1927	3,162	..	203,579	..	..	..
1928	5,471	..	112,580	..	..	..
1929	6,729	..	119,977	..	..	..
1930	20,384	..	125,110	..	..	..
1931	28,705	..	140,088	..	..	..
1932	335,130	..	450,197	..	..	..
1933	174,203	..	532,776	..	..	..
1934	158,582	$ 1,124	689,482	$ 1,062	$14,884	$13,589

(continued on next page)

TABLE A-5 (continued)
(in thousands)

YEAR	FEDERAL AGENCIES				FEDERALLY SPONSORED AGENCIES	
	Volume during Year		Year-End Outstandings		Volume	Outstandings
	Direct Loans[a]	Loan Insurance or Guarantees[b]	Direct Loans[a]	Loan Insurance or Guarantees[b]	Direct Loans[c]	Direct Loans[c]
1935	143,163	2,810	738,251	2,630	28,479	32,493
1936	96,486	2,752	616,498	3,819	8,519	25,526
1937	52,321	871	618,177	3,748	4,932	20,216
1938	159,167	35,508	710,090	34,193	6,500	17,345
1939	147,616	30,183	754,809	46,910	3,805	13,683
1940	245,088	8,265	842,403	34,898	2,860	9,152
1941	234,598	19,141	902,048	38,078	15,695	10,337
1942	439,420	1,037,618	1,082,192	726,820	68,032	14,126
1943	396,138	4,179,307	1,159,453	1,715,309	60,265	10,532
1944	456,768	3,410,386	1,142,991	1,564,191	20,381	3,894
1945	433,679	1,854,434	916,122	537,414	14,043	1,995
1946	1,106,963	471,339	1,795,552	394,640	3,445	554
1947	1,026,830	224,532	2,581,153	381,310	9,296	1,387
1948	531,902	93,030	3,110,901	290,445	15,994	995
1949	424,526	85,987	3,242,186	245,511	4,005	2,178
1950	456,080	51,053	3,198,782	191,380	6,530	2,632
1951	485,015	1,362,533	3,324,506	732,923	27,656	4,687
1952	683,919	2,352,091	3,477,466	928,948	31,193	3,921
1953	821,117	1,996,178	3,755,378	765,162	22,009	1,900

(continued on next page)

TABLE A-5 (continued)

a Covers loans made by the Departments of Army and Navy, the Director General of Railroads and the Interstate Commerce Commission, the Export-Import Bank of Washington, the Housing and Home Finance Agency, the Public Works Administration, the Maritime Administration, the Reconstruction Finance Corporation, the Smaller War Plants Corporation, the Virgin Islands Corporation, and the War Finance Corporation. All yearly data on outstandings and data on volume for 1919–1937, 1942–1944, and 1950–1952 are partially estimated. Annual volume data are unavailable for the Maritime Administration in 1921–1923, and the Virgin Islands Corporation in 1950–1953; end-of-year outstandings are unavailable for the Director General in 1919, and the Public Works Administration in 1933 and 1951–1953. For sources of the components of these totals, see Tables A-9, A-12, A-13, A-14, A-16, A-18, A-21, A-27, A-30, and A-32.

b Refers to amount of commitments under loan guarantees written by the Veterans' Administration, and by the War and Navy Departments and the U.S. Maritime Commission under Regulation V, and by the Department of Defense, the Department of Commerce, the Atomic Energy Commission, and the General Services Administration under the Defense Production Act of 1950; also to ship mortgage insurance, and commitments to insure, written by the Maritime Administration; and to commitments under deferred participations made by the Reconstruction Finance Corporation. Outstandings for 1939–1953 and data on volume for 1939–1946, 1949, and 1951–1953 are partially estimated. Information is unavailable for outstanding amounts of VA guarantees in 1945 and for volume of guarantees made by the Defense Department in 1950 and the Atomic Energy Commission in 1951–1953. For sources of the components of these totals, see Tables A-9, A-10, A-16, A-30, A-32, and A-33.

c Data, supplied by the Board of Governors of the Federal Reserve System, represent Federal Reserve Bank loans, and participations in loans of private financing institutions, to business firms under Section 13b of the Federal Reserve Act.

TABLE A-6

Credit Extended to Financial Institutions by Federal and Federally Sponsored Agencies, by Type of Financial Aid, 1918–1953

(in thousands)

YEAR	FEDERAL AGENCIES				FEDERALLY SPONSORED AGENCIES	
	Volume during Year		Year-End Outstandings		Volume	Outstandings
	Direct Loans^a	Stock Purchases^b	Direct Loans^a	Stock Purchases^b	Direct Loans^c	Direct Loans^c
1918	$ 5,179	…	$ 1,506	…	…	…
1919	80	…	1,676	…	…	…
1920	9	…	…	…	…	…
1921	…	…	…	…	…	…
1922	…	…	…	…	…	…
1923	…	…	…	…	…	…
1924	…	…	…	…	…	…
1925	…	…	…	…	…	…
1926	…	…	…	…	…	…
1927	…	…	…	…	…	…
1928	…	…	…	…	…	…
1929	…	…	…	…	…	…
1930	…	…	…	…	…	…
1931	1,119,419	…	831,432	…	$ 838	$ 838
1932	758,614	$268,740	1,035,208	$268,582	90,032	85,442
1933	460,961	697,716	841,676	893,442	38,676	86,603
1934						
1935	138,328	161,539	519,628	986,287	59,130	102,686
1936	68,223	132,069	322,854	868,263	93,257	145,227
1937	41,865	98,378	249,961	848,148	123,251	200,038
1938	30,442	39,789	208,541	832,924	81,958	198,842
1939	15,764	27,901	171,207	772,789	94,781	181,313

(continued on next page)

TABLE A-6 (*continued*)
(*in thousands*)

| | FEDERAL AGENCIES | | | | FEDERALLY SPONSORED AGENCIES | |
| | Volume during Year | | Year-End Outstandings | | Volume | Outstandings |
YEAR	Direct Loans^a	Stock Purchases^b	Direct Loans^a	Stock Purchases^b	Direct Loans^c	Direct Loans^c
1940	45,063	45,977	172,353	726,338	134,212	201,492
1941	4,640	3,399	117,537	645,112	157,600	219,446
1942	29,097	14,519	111,076	591,968	99,462	129,213
1943	8,409	563	80,103	459,709	156,925	110,068
1944	260	16	29,921	374,232	239,254	130,563
1945	3,274	269	25,418	307,825	277,748	194,872
1946	..	..	21,841	206,531	329,232	293,455
1947	..	5,000	887	160,435	351,079	435,572
1948	..	..	344	134,696	359,613	515,016
1949	..	3,000	29	116,314	255,662	433,429
1950	..	..	27	102,971	674,757	815,957
1951	..	..	26	84,344	422,976	805,937
1952	..	..	24	46,776	585,813	864,189
1953	..	..	24	41,539	727,532	951,555

a Covers loans made by the Federal Housing Administration, the Reconstruction Finance Corporation, and the War Finance Corporation. Outstandings for 1918 (estimated) and for 1919 are as of November 30. For sources of the components of these totals, see Tables A-9, A-12, and A-17.

b Refers to purchases of, and loans on, preferred stock of banks and insurance companies, and purchases of capital notes and debentures of banks, by the Reconstruction Finance Corporation; purchases of shares of insured federal and state savings and loan associations by the Home Owners' Loan Corporation; and purchases of shares of federal savings and loan associations by the Treasury Department. For sources of the components of these totals, see Tables A-9, A-11, and A-19.

c Data, from Housing Statistics (Housing and Home Finance Agency, January 1954, p. 43), represent advances made by the federal home loan banks to financial institutions which are members of the Federal Home Loan Bank system.

TABLE A-7

Credit Extended for Housing by Federal Agencies, by Type of Financial Aid, 1933–1953

(*in thousands*)

	VOLUME DURING YEAR		OUTSTANDINGS AT YEAR END	
YEAR	Direct Loansa	Loan Insurance or Guaranteesb	Direct Loansa	Loan Insurance or Guaranteesb
1933	$ 141,604	..	$ 141,520	..
1934	2,240,162	$ 30,451	2,366,463	$ 30,451
1935	602,822	319,857	2,903,275	307,815
1936	168,298	557,196	2,806,510	701,315
1937	86,036	495,239	2,474,317	1,019,604
1938	233,258	693,630	2,314,216	1,511,271
1939	311,107	954,336	2,253,708	2,135,846
1940	253,761	1,025,979	2,227,147	2,795,975
1941	170,236	1,186,419	2,089,872	3,502,923
1942	138,745	1,135,227	1,917,050	4,095,955
1943	124,550	943,166	1,549,255	4,394,416
1944	90,564	890,251	1,279,275	4,542,369c
1945	30,734	754,266	931,837	4,750,933
1946	18,243	1,890,818	694,081	5,438,327
1947	134,854	3,419,734	651,423	7,567,442
1948	232,487	4,352,235	746,314	10,576,342
1949	698,964	4,633,893	1,244,404	13,759,829

(*continued on next page*)

TABLE A-7 (continued)
(in thousands)

YEAR	VOLUME DURING YEAR		OUTSTANDINGS AT YEAR END	
	Direct Loansa	Loan Insurance or Guaranteesb	Direct Loansa	Loan Insurance or Guaranteesb
1950	1,090,538	6,102,978	1,543,468	17,886,064
1951	828,449	5,432,523	2,160,521	21,218,521
1952	653,907	4,820,950	2,637,953	23,618,324
1953	723,412	5,851,455	3,003,134	26,504,388

a Covers loans made by the Defense Homes Corporation, the Federal Housing Administration, the Federal National Mortgage Association, the Home Owners' Loan Corporation, the Housing and Home Finance Agency, the RFC Mortgage Company, and the Veterans' Administration. Volume figures for 1935–1937, 1941–1944, and 1947–1948, and data on outstandings for 1934 and 1947, are partially estimated. Data for 1945–1946 on volume and for 1945–1947 on outstandings exclude VA loans because annual figures are unavailable. Outstandings of the Defense Homes Corporation from 1947 on are carried in the RFC business loan series in Table A-9. For sources of the components of these totals, see Tables A-10, A-11, A-14, A-17, A-28, and A-30.

b Refers to amount of commitments under loan insurance and guarantees written by the Federal Housing Administration and the Veterans' Administration. Volume data for 1944–1945 and outstandings for 1934–1953 are partially estimated. For sources, see Tables A-10 and A-17.

c Excludes outstanding guarantees on VA-guaranteed loans.

TABLE A-8

Credit Extended to Minor Governmental Units and for Miscellaneous Purposes by Federal Agencies, by Type of Financial Aid, 1920–1953

(in thousands)

| | MINOR GOVERNMENTAL UNITS | | | MISCELLANEOUS PURPOSES[c] | |
| | Direct Loans[a] | | Loan Guarantees[b] | Direct Loans | |
YEAR	Volume	Outstandings	Outstandings	Volume	Outstandings
1920	..	..	..	$ 59	$ 59
1921	$ 890	d	..	810	752
1922	..	$ 2,150	..	2,256	2,681
1923	..	1,918	..	3,809	5,722
1924	..	1,198	..	5,435	9,875
1925	..	1,101	..	6,911	14,849
1926	60	1,073	..	8,578	20,935
1927	15	861	..	10,328	28,218
1928	12	823	..	12,692	36,584
1929	5	828	..	20,505	52,130
1930	5	793	..	25,709	70,830
1931	..	731	..	30,201	89,660
1932	95,704	96,347	..	36,433	110,642
1933	323,446	368,620	..	33,383	124,456
1934	211,080	561,428	..	28,228	129,952
1935	252,165	675,255	..	22,725	136,737
1936	180,842	755,236	d	20,747	139,416
1937	98,597	790,241	d	33,607	155,615
1938	132,241	478,324	d	29,190	163,528
1939	276,341	495,515	$ 51,127	39,510	177,399
1940	541,046	532,535	247,863	28,723	179,648
1941	673,795	723,127	203,042	21,997	175,592
1942	280,276	711,046	258,743	16,218	160,891
1943	99,546	584,038	225,335	16,117	149,120
1944	5,396	543,852	226,024	11,659	141,000

(continued on next page)

TABLE A-8 (continued)

(in thousands)

| YEAR | MINOR GOVERNMENTAL UNITS | | | MISCELLANEOUS PURPOSE[c] | |
| | Direct Loans[a] | | Loan Guarantees[b] | Direct Loans | |
	Volume	Outstandings	Outstandings	Volume	Outstandings
1945	9,247	512,517	229,218	10,785	132,273
1946	32,467	499,602	233,719	15,284	129,191
1947	55,301	520,046	225,501	19,859	130,178
1948	57,618	547,169	218,657	26,327	144,094
1949	38,463	442,625	220,627	32,490	161,195
1950	132,640	502,511	414,003	37,420	181,628
1951	433,883	738,288	805,925	50,342	209,528
1952	800,639	1,061,464	1,067,248	49,539	232,556
1953	763,869	689,891	1,932,953	70,956	274,958

a Covers loans made by the Bureau of Community Facilities, the Housing and Home Finance Agency, the Inland Waterways Corporation, the Public Housing Administration, the Public Works Administration, the Reconstruction Finance Corporation, and the Tennessee Valley Authority. Data on volume for 1933–1953 are partially estimated. Advances made by the Bureau of Community Facilities are excluded because annual data are lacking. Year-end outstandings for 1922–1923 and 1934–1953 are partially estimated, and the relatively small amounts of outstandings on loans by the Inland Waterways Corporation in 1921 and the Public Works Administration in 1933 are excluded for lack of information. For sources of the components of these totals, see Tables A-9, A-13, A-14, A-20, and A-29.

b Refers to amount of commitments under loan guarantees written by the Public Housing Administration. Annual volume figures are not available. For details see Table A-20.

c Covers loans made by the Federal Security Agency, the Bureau of Indian Affairs of the Department of the Interior, Prencinradio, Inc., the Reconstruction Finance Corporation, the Housing and Home Finance Agency, the Disaster Loan Corporation, the Puerto Rico Reconstruction Administration, the Treasury Department, the Small Business Administration, and the Veterans' Administration. The volume series excludes advances made by the Puerto Rico Reconstruction Administration, because annual data are lacking. Volume series for 1934–1953 are partially estimated. Data for the Bureau of Indian Affairs are unavailable on year-end outstandings before 1936 and on volume before 1934; outstandings for Prencinradio, Inc. are unavailable for 1943 and 1944. For sources of the components of these totals, see Tables A-9, A-10, A-14, A-19, A-21, and A-31.

d Data not available.

TABLE A-9

Reconstruction Finance Corporation Lending and Loan Guaranteeing Activity, 1932–1953

(in thousands)

YEAR	DIRECT LOANS					LOAN GUARANTEES	STOCK PURCHASES
	Agricul- turea	Businessb	Financial Institu- tionsc	Minor Gov- ernmental Unitsd	Miscella- neous Pur- posese	Businessf	Financial Institutionsg
			VOLUME DURING YEAR				
1932	$ 1,440	$284,312	$1,119,419	$ 95,704	..	..	..
1933	11,475	109,789	758,614	273,425	$2,761	..	$268,722
1934	18,448	60,684	460,961	96,937	5,859	$ 1,124	687,009
1935	5,277	77,412	138,203	99,908	1,169	2,810	103,118
1936	2,508	63,153	68,207	75,217	1,624	2,752	26,294
1937	560	44,571	41,865	60,023	570	871	17,379
1938	20,073	140,567	30,442	61,447	19	35,508	30,868
1939	7,161	93,916	15,764	70,028	..	29,208	23,516
1940	..	149,788	45,063	56,222	..	7,915	44,257
1941	2	117,798	4,640	150,813	..	12,841	1,786
1942	..	385,706	29,097	12,275	..	109,118	13,921
1943	..	287,849	8,409	3,773	..	132,242	563
1944	..	198,883	260	1,896	..	95,386	16
1945	..	227,895	3,274	1,123	82	127,524	269
1946	..	53,871	..	12,796	61	351,952	..
1947	..	200,038	..	18,419	518	177,188	5,000
1948	..	102,996	..	13,806	2,259	71,683	..
1949	..	239,726	..	7,060	2,509	74,119	3,000
1950	..	246,680	..	1,624	655	42,481	..
1951	..	181,074	..	1,909	10,342	10,586	..
1952	..	171,577	..	8,167	7,579	5,068	..
1953	..	154,472	..	11,079	2,195	5,308	..

(continued on next page)

TABLE A-9 (continued)
(in thousands)

YEAR	DIRECT LOANS					LOAN GUARANTEES	STOCK PURCHASES
	Agriculture^b	Business^b	Financial Institutions^c	Minor Governmental Units^d	Miscellaneous Purposes^e	Business^f	Financial Institutions^g
			OUTSTANDINGS AT YEAR END				
1932	$ 1,325	$272,472	$ 831,432	$ 95,704	...	...	...
1933	10,389	337,087	1,035,208	368,002	$ 2,692	...	$268,564
1934	19,434	388,340	841,676	425,083	8,272	$ 1,062	882,717
1935	22,246	442,568	519,518	485,837	9,157	2,630	917,168
1936	1,369	414,261	322,836	546,319	8,722	3,819	693,651
1937	991	434,735	249,959	591,807	6,401	3,748	593,622
1938	20,743	547,161	208,541	268,089	2,481	34,193	571,070
1939	856	581,296	171,207	170,346	1,668	45,935	521,657
1940	490	596,570	172,353	126,878	1,234	33,631	505,326
1941	434	616,087	117,537	132,433	1,027	30,596	448,661
1942	339	794,888	111,076	136,044	936	88,718	422,109
1943	57	775,876	80,103	97,670	656	109,348	389,539
1944	55	718,136	29,921	79,167	509	80,523	336,192
1945	55	486,924	25,418	62,982	1,464	102,069	284,422
1946	55	393,689	21,841	55,955	940	326,162	190,189
1947	55	458,160	887	68,990	1,178	291,029	151,817
1948	47	450,495	344	77,836	3,034	196,385	128,566
1949	44	572,941	29	18,766	4,745	156,690	114,362
1950	44	527,018	27	13,623	4,090	107,767	102,557
1951	...	532,426	26	12,780	13,112	66,683	84,344
1952	...	542,743	24	18,442	17,130	40,942	46,776
1953	...	528,574	24	26,956	16,022	28,058	41,539

Data are from the *Quarterly Reports* of, and material supplied by, the Reconstruction Finance Corporation. Outstanding amounts of loans to business and to minor governmental units in 1947 are partially estimated.

(continued on next page)

TABLE A-9 (continued)

a Covers loans for financing exports of agricultural surpluses, livestock marketing, and the storage and marketing of agricultural commodities, except those made to the Commodity Credit Corporation.

b Covers loans to railroads; loans, and immediate participations in loans, to business enterprises (including those engaged in defense production); loans to business enterprises through mortgage loan companies and banks; loans to the fishing industry, to mining, milling and smelting companies (including those engaged in defense production), and to processors or distributors of farm products subject to processing taxes; loans, and immediate participations in loans, to manufacturers of prefabricated housing, as authorized under Sec. 102 of the Housing Act of 1948 and Sec. 4(a)(1) of the RFC Act as amended; loans on rationed articles and commodities; Contract Settlement Act loans; loans and purchases of participations in connection with the transfer of certain functions of the Smaller War Plants Corporation to the RFC, effective January 28, 1946; loans under Sections 302 and 714 of the Defense Production Act of 1950; and loans under Section 409 of the Federal Civil Defense Act. Outstanding amounts of loans to business and mining enterprises in 1947 are estimated by linear interpolation of repayments for the period July 1, 1947 to March 31, 1948.

c Represents loans to banks and trust companies, to closed banks through mortgage loan companies, and to livestock credit corporations; loans on assets of closed banks; loans to trustees, liquidating agents, and conservators of closed banks and trust companies; and loans to insurance companies, building and loan associations, mortgage loan companies, credit unions, joint stock land banks, and agricultural and livestock credit corporations.

d Covers construction loans to public agencies for defense and non-defense projects; loans to drainage, levee, and similar districts; loans to establish state funds for securing repayment of deposits of public moneys in banks and other depositories; loans to refinance obligations of public school districts; and loans for payment of teachers' salaries, for self-liquidating public works, and for relief and work relief under the Emergency Relief and Construction Act of 1932 as amended. Outstanding amounts of construction loans to public agencies in 1947 are estimated by linear interpolation of repayments for the period July 1, 1947 to March 31, 1948.

e Represents loans to repair damage caused by floods and other catastrophes.

f Refers to amounts authorized and commitments outstanding under agreements to participate with private lenders on a deferred basis in loans to business enterprises (including those engaged in defense production), to transportation companies other than railroads, and to manufacturers of prefabricated housing. The (deferred) participations made through blanket agreements are included, as are those connected with Contract Settlement Act loans; with loans made in connection with the transfer of certain functions of the Smaller War Plants Corporation to the RFC, effective January 28, 1946; with loans under Sections 302 and 714 of the Defense Production Act of 1950; and with loans under Section 409 of the Federal Civil Defense Act.

g Covers loans on, and subscriptions for, preferred stock of insurance companies and of banks and trust companies; and purchases of capital notes and debentures of banks.

TABLE A-10

Veterans' Administration Loan Guaranteeing and Direct Lending Activity,
1920–1953
(*in thousands*)

| YEAR | Miscellaneous Purposes^a | Housing | | Loan Insurance or Guarantees | | |
		Vendee Accts.^b	Rural Areas^c	Agricultural^d	Business^e	Housing
			VOLUME DURING YEAR			
1920	$ 59	..	..	..	..	..
1921	810	..	..	..	..	..
1922	2,256	..	..	..	..	..
1923	3,809	..	..	..	..	..
1924	5,435	..	..	..	..	..
1925	6,911	..	..	..	..	..
1926	8,578	..	..	..	..	..
1927	10,328	..	..	..	..	..
1928	12,692	..	..	..	..	..
1929	20,505	..	..	..	..	..
1930	25,709	..	..	..	..	..
1931	30,201	..	..	..	..	..
1932	36,433	..	..	..	..	..
1933	30,622	..	..	..	..	..
1934	22,230	..	..	..	..	..
1935	21,351	..	..	..	..	..
1936	18,779	..	..	..	..	..
1937	24,390	..	..	..	..	..
1938	24,728	..	..	..	..	..
1939	23,461	..	..	..	..	..
1940	22,614	..	..	..	..	..
1941	18,783	..	..	..	..	..
1942	12,883	..	..	..	..	..
1943	11,157	..	..	..	..	..
1944	9,294	..	..	..	..	..
1945	9,470	..	..	..	..	$ 1,568
1946	13,832	..	..	$ 1,238	$ 3,910	71,181
1947	17,127	$ 130g	..	29,853	49,387	1,092,891
1948	22,161	1,133	..	36,634	47,344	1,558,700
1949	27,742	3,111	..	18,561	21,347	927,580
				7,564	9,468	726,004
1950	33,792	6,716	$ 6,342	7,970	8,572	1,663,721
1951	37,347	12,191	103,095	5,930	14,968	2,124,245
1952	34,851	12,082	67,522	2,615	11,199	1,588,885
1953	42,594	11,877	113,899	1,641	5,882	1,781,450

(*continued on next page*)

TABLE A-10 (*continued*)

(*in thousands*)

	DIRECT LOANS			LOAN INSURANCE OR GUARANTEES		
		Housing				
	Miscel-laneous	Vendee	Rural	Agricul-	Busi-	
YEAR	Purposes[a]	Accts.[b]	Areas[c]	tured[d]	ness[e]	Housing[f]
	OUTSTANDINGS AT YEAR END					
1920	$ 59	..	..	..	..	..
1921	752	..	..	..	..	..
1922	2,681	..	..	..	..	..
1923	5,722	..	..	..	..	..
1924	9,875	..	..	..	..	..
1925	14,849	..	..	..	..	..
1926	20,935	..	..	..	..	..
1927	28,218	..	..	..	..	..
1928	36,584	..	..	..	..	..
1929	52,130	..	..	..	..	..
1930	70,830	..	..	..	..	..
1931	89,660	..	..	..	..	..
1932	110,642	..	..	..	..	..
1933	121,764	..	..	..	..	..
1934	121,680	..	..	..	..	..
1935	127,580	..	..	..	..	..
1936	128,560	..	..	..	..	..
1937	138,468	..	..	..	..	..
1938	147,426	..	..	..	..	..
1939	149,663	..	..	..	..	..
1940	150,645	..	..	..	..	..
1941	151,206	..	..	..	..	..
1942	144,762	..	..	..	..	..
1943	133,415	..	..	..	..	..
1944	123,125	..	..	..	..	h
1945	116,379	h	..	h	h	$ 250,000
1946	114,506	h	..	$30,654	$51,024	1,200,000
1947	115,554	h	..	64,531	88,098	2,600,000
1948	125,562	$ 1,239	..	77,736	92,876	3,300,000
1949	139,676	4,173	..	79,154	85,657	3,800,000
1950	157,270	10,453	$ 6,342	79,709	80,636	5,100,000
1951	175,238	21,633	108,000	75,938	83,106	6,750,000
1952	188,637	31,891	167,000	70,967	82,542	7,700,000
1953	208,002	41,111	274,684	65,562	67,780	8,980,000

Data were supplied by the Veterans' Administration or compiled from *Finance, Guaranty of Loans* (Office of Assistant Administrator, Veterans' Administration, 1946–50 Supplement, pp. 28–32), *Housing Statistics Handbook* (Housing and Home Finance Agency, 1948, p. 130) and the *Sixth Annual Report*, Housing and Home Finance Agency, (1952, p. 145).

Volume of loan guarantees for agriculture and for business was estimated for 1945 by deducting from the cumulative amount of guarantees through January 1946 an estimate of the amount guaranteed in January, and for 1946 by adding the January 1946 estimate to the

(*continued on next page*)

APPENDIX A

TABLE A-10 (continued)

February–December amount. Volume of loan guarantees for housing in 1944 and 1945 was estimated by assuming that the amount guaranteed from November 1944 through March 1945 was evenly distributed over the period. All data on outstanding amounts of guarantees 1945–1953 were estimated. For the agricultural and business sectors, estimates were obtained by deducting cumulated amount of guarantees-paid-in-full loans, plus the cumulated amount of net claims paid, from the cumulated amount of guarantees or insurance on loans closed. Estimates of outstanding guarantees on housing loans were prepared by the Veterans' Administration.

a Represents loans to holders of United States Government and National Service Life Insurance policies based on the amount of paid-up insurance. Excludes loans arising from federal guarantees of premiums on commercial private life insurance policies held by servicemen as provided under the Soldiers' and Sailors' Civil Relief Act. As of June 30, 1953 outstandings on such loans were less than $500,000.

b Covers purchase money mortgages and real estate sales contracts made in connection with the term sale of properties acquired through foreclosure of VA-guaranteed business, farm, and home loans.

c Represents direct loans to veterans for purchase or construction of housing in small towns and rural areas and for construction or improvement of farm houses as authorized under the Housing Act of 1950.

d Refers to the amount of VA's commitments on loans made by private financing institutions to veterans for purchase or improvement of farm properties and guaranteed (or insured) under Title III, Sections 502 and 507 of the Servicemen's Readjustment Act of 1944.

e Refers to the amount of VA's commitments on loans made by private lending institutions to veterans for the establishment or expansion of business enterprises and guaranteed (or insured) under Title III, Sections 503 and 507 of the Servicemen's Readjustment Act.

f Refers to the amount of VA's commitments on home mortgage loans guaranteed (or insured) under Title III, Sections 501, 505, and 507 of the Servicemen's Readjustment Act.

g Cumulative from 1945 through February 29, 1948.

h Data not available.

TABLE A-11

Home Owners' Loan Corporation Lending Activity, 1933–1950

(*in thousands*)

	VOLUME DURING YEAR		OUTSTANDINGS AT YEAR END	
	Direct Loans	*Stock Purchases*	*Direct Loans*	*Stock Purchases*
YEAR	*Housing*a	*Financial Institutions*b	*Housing*a	*Financial Institutions*b
1933	$ 141,604	..	$ 141,520	..
1934	2,240,162	..	2,366,463	..
1935	596,631	$ 19,846	2,897,162	$ 19,846
1936	128,533	105,775	2,765,098	125,621
1937	33,703	80,999	2,397,646	206,475
1938	109,135	8,921	2,168,100	214,801
1939	203,196	4,385	2,035,716	211,453
1940	166,448	1,720	1,955,572	194,264
1941	84,323	1,613	1,776,918	175,167
1942	53,838	598	1,566,971	152,311
1943	73,534	..	1,338,102	63,286
1944	41,816	..	1,091,363	34,551
1945	5,314	..	852,319	21,421
1946	1,896	..	636,463	15,192
1947	2,065	..	485,909	8,063
1948	2,050	..	368,908	5,883
1949	2,097	..	230,623	1,952
1950	868	..	9,592	414

a Data, supplied by the Home Owners' Loan Corporation, cover loans to refinance defaulted or otherwise distressed mortgages of home owners and to finance the sale of properties acquired through foreclosure. The volume series for 1935–1937 includes estimates for credit sales of foreclosed properties derived by adding estimated yearly repayments to annual net change in amounts outstanding. Outstandings for 1934 were estimated by assuming repayments in 1934 to be six-sevenths of repayments from July 1, 1934 through January 31, 1935 and subtracting these from the sum of outstandings as of June 30, 1934 and disbursements from July 31 to December 31, 1934.

b Data were supplied by the Federal Savings and Loan Insurance Corporation of the Housing and Home Finance Agency, and represent HOLC's investments in shares of insured federal and state savings and loan associations. Responsibility for administering these investments was vested in the Federal Home Loan Bank Board by Section 5(j) of the Home Owners' Loan Act of 1933.

TABLE A-12

War Finance Corporation Lending Activity, 1918–1939
(in thousands)

| | VOLUME DURING YEAR | | | OUTSTANDINGS AT YEAR END | | |
| | Direct Loans | | | Direct Loans | | |
YEAR	Agricul- turea	Businessb	Financial Institu- tionsc	Agricul- turea	Businessb	Financial Institu- tionsc
1918	$ 6,403	$122,792	$5,179	$ 3,079	$ 29,629	$1,506
1919	1,424	171,826	80	1,459	93,928	1,676
1920	1	45,348	9	793	116,934	..
1921	82,967	28,639	..	82,997	104,680	..
1922	186,143	10,015	..	148,692	29,533	..
1923	18,135	..	..	70,201	28,204	..
1924	9,872	..	..	40,269	16,945	..
1925	937	..	..	15,589	16,945	..
1926	355	..	..	7,670	16,745	..
1927	178	..	..	1,362	1,030	..
1928	126	..	..	454	190	..
1929	..	..	..	161	170	..
1930	..	..	..	59	170	..
1931	..	..	..	45	170	..
1932	..	..	..	14	170	..
1933	..	..	..	13	138	..
1934	..	..	..	9	119	..
1935	..	..	..	8	..	..
1936	..	..	..	7	..	..
1937	..	..	..	4	..	..
1938	..	..	..	3	..	..
1939	..	..	..	..	..	..

a Covers loans made in 1918–1923 to cattle raisers under Section 9 of the War Finance Corporation Act of 1918 and loans made in 1921–1924 to banks and other financial institutions, livestock loan companies, and cooperative marketing associations for agricultural and livestock purposes under Section 24 of the Agricultural Credits Act of August 24, 1921. Data were compiled from the Annual Reports of the War Finance Corporation, and the Liquidation of the War Finance Corporation (Treasury Department, 1943). Volume data for 1918–1920, and the part for 1921–1923 representing loans to cattle raisers, are for fiscal years ending November 30, (1920 having been estimated); volume after 1924 represents expense advances incident to the liquidation of the Corporation's assets. Outstandings in 1918–1920, and the part in 1921–1925 concerning loans to cattle raisers, are for November 30. Outstandings for 1918 were prorated among the agricultural, business, and financial sectors according to the sectors' respective shares in the year's volume.

b Data are from the Annual Reports of the War Finance Corporation and refer to loans through banks to public utilities, industrial corporations, railroads, and canning firms under Section 9 of the War Finance Corporation Act, and export advances under Sections 21 and 22 of the Agricultural Credits Act of 1921. Volume figures in 1921 are for January 1–November 30, and in 1922 for the fiscal year ending November 30. Data on outstandings in 1918–1928 are as of November 30 (estimated for 1918 as explained above).

c Data are from the Annual Reports of the War Finance Corporation and represent loans to commercial and savings banks, and building and loan associations, under Sections 7 and 8 of the War Finance Corporation Act. Outstandings are as of November 30 (estimated for 1918 as indicated in note a).

TABLE A-13

Public Works Administration Lending Activity, 1933–1953

(*in thousands*)

| | VOLUME DURING YEAR | | OUTSTANDINGS AT YEAR END | |
| | Direct Loans | | Direct Loans | |
YEAR	Business[a]	Minor Gov't Units[b]	Business[a]	Minor Gov't Units[b]
1933	$39,864	$ 50,021	c	c
1934	93,615	113,929	$133,478	$135,655
1935	55,113	151,728	148,780	188,290
1936	12,233	104,900	57,107	207,115
1937	150	36,251	50,731	186,230d
1938	..	40,921	46,506	175,574
1939	..	66,679	22,011	197,380
1940	.. ⁄	33,471	13,548	215,531
1941	..	14,947	11,696	218,857
1942	..	6,973	10,877	204,869
1943	..	270	10,188	160,635
1944	..	..	9,457	152,030
1945	..	..	7,839	147,986
1946	..	..	5,990	134,738
1947	..	..	3,035	133,383
1948	..	..	3,035	147,001e
1949	..	..	2,123	102,899
1950	..	..	2,123	100,457
1951	..	..	f	92,108
1952	..	..	f	89,825
1953	..	..	f	88,366

Volume of loans to business was estimated from the records of the Federal Works Agency: 1933 by linear interpolation of fiscal year data and 1934–1937 by obtaining estimates on a semiannual basis using data on outstandings and repayments. Volume of loans to minor governmental units is from records of the Federal Works Agency and *Financial Statements of Certain Government Agencies* (S. Doc. 172, Part 2, 76th Cong., 3rd sess., 1940, pp. 860 and 871) except that the amounts for 1941–1943 were estimated by linear interpolation of fiscal year data, and those for 1933–1936 include estimates for loans to limited dividend housing corporations. The latter were obtained by computing net change in outstandings between fiscal year ends and then combining on a calendar year basis by linear interpolation (in fiscal 1935 repayments were added to net change before interpolating).

Outstandings were estimated from Senate Document Number 172, pp. 860 and 871, the *Daily Statements* of the Treasury Department, and records of the Reconstruction Finance Corporation and the Federal Works Agency. For business loans, in 1934–1937 they reflect the par value of securities held by PWA plus the par value of securities purchased from PWA and held by the RFC (in 1935, estimated from outstandings, repayments, and disbursements for 1936); after 1937, the estimated par value of securities held by the RFC. For loans to minor

(*continued on next page*)

APPENDIX A

TABLE A-13 (*continued*)

governmental units, in 1934–1953 they reflect the par value of securities held by PWA plus the par value (estimated for 1937–1953) of securities purchased from PWA and held by the RFC.

a Represents loans to railroads for operational and maintenance purposes.

b Represents net payments (bonds purchased less bonds canceled in lieu of grant payments) on loans to states, municipalities, other public agencies, and private corporations for the construction of community facilities and low-cost housing projects; and net payments on loans to limited dividend housing corporations.

c Data not available.

d Excludes $10,142,400 outstanding on loans to limited dividend housing corporations. As of November 1, 1937 this account was transferred to the U.S. Housing Authority, the predecessor of the Public Housing Administration.

e Includes $13,900,000 in revenue bonds transferred in 1948 from the Department of the Interior pursuant to Executive Order 9839 of April 14, 1947.

f Probably extinguished.

TABLE A-14

Housing and Home Finance Agency Lending Activity, 1945–1953

(*in thousands*)

	DIRECT LOANS			
YEAR	Businessa	Housingb	Minor Governmental Unitsc	Miscellaneous Purposesd
		VOLUME DURING YEAR		
1945	..	..	$ 6,624	..
1946	..	..	18,271	..
1947	..	..	12,282	..
1948	..	..	6,812	..
1949	..	..	6,403	..
1950	$ 9,500e	$1,594f	7,216g	..
1951	11,390	3,742	9,174	$ 85h
1952	4,983	6,577	19,072	5,339
1953	8,837	5,839	25,490	23,498
		OUTSTANDINGS AT YEAR END		
1945	..	..	$ 6,624	..
1946	..	..	24,625	..
1947	..	..	35,425	..
1948	..	..	33,884	..
1949	..	..	33,246	..
1950	$21,917	$ 1,594	34,203	..
1951	30,425	5,274	37,228	$ 85
1952	13,893	10,748	51,504	5,414
1953	12,918	11,863	62,041	28,887

Data supplied by the Housing and Home Finance Agency, Office of the Administrator.

a Covers loans to prefabricated housing manufacturers for the production, distribution, sale, or erection of such units as authorized under Section 102 of the Housing Act of 1948, Section 4(a)(1) of the RFC Act as amended, and Public Law 139. Loans prior to 1950, when the program was administered by the RFC, are included in the RFC business loan series given in Table A-9.

b Represents loans to the Alaska Housing Authority, as authorized by the Alaska Housing Act of 1949 (Public Law 52, approved April 23, 1949), for residential construction and property improvement.

c Covers advances to state and local governments for the planning of public works as authorized under Title V of the War Mobilization and Reconversion Act of 1944, and under Public Law 352 approved October 13, 1949; advances under Title I of the Housing Act of 1949 (Public Law 171, approved July 15, 1949) to communities and local public agencies to assist in planning urban development projects, in acquiring land for their construction, and in financing such urban redevelopment and slum clearance projects; and loans to communities in critical defense areas to assist in providing necessary community facilities as authorized under Title III, Section 313(a) of the Defense Housing and Community Facilities and Services Act (Public Law 139, approved September 1, 1951).

d Covers loans to institutions of higher learning, as authorized under Title IV of the Housing Act of 1950 (Public Law 475, April 20, 1950), for provision of housing facilities for students and faculty.

e Computed by subtracting from the total disbursements on active loans reported by HHFA through December 31, 1950 ($26.4 million), the outstanding loan balances as of September 7, 1950 reported by RFC as transferred to the HHFA ($16.9 million).

f Cumulative from April 23, 1949.

g Includes data for the second half of 1949 for the Slum Clearance and Urban Redevelopment (P.L. 171) and Second Advance Planning (P.L. 352) programs.

h Cumulative from April 20, 1950.

TABLE A-15

Farmers Home Administration Lending and Loan Insuring Activity, 1934–1953
(in thousands)

| YEAR | VOLUME DURING YEAR | | | OUTSTANDINGS AT YEAR END | | |
| | Direct Farm Loans | | Farm Loan Insurance[c] | Direct Farm Loans | | Farm Loan Insurance[c] |
	Real Estate[a]	Non-Real-Estate[b]		Real Estate[a]	Non-Real-Estate[b]	
1934	..	d	..	..	$ 5,600	..
1935	..	d	..	..	62,900	..
1936	..	d	..	..	131,600	..
1937	..	d	..	..	121,685	..
1938	$10,275	$ 80,692	..	$ 10,275	173,171	..
1939	26,576	111,746	..	32,301	249,173	..
1940	39,713	95,426	..	66,286	296,724	..
1941	60,663	114,188	..	116,610	337,385	..
1942	31,430	172,108	..	160,258	403,912	..
1943	28,998	122,869	..	174,946	375,272	..
1944	25,103	65,510	..	179,840	332,230	..
1945	28,651	73,763	..	185,060	300,105	..
1946	46,902	112,766	..	194,622	301,175	..
1947	36,300	93,271	..	200,185	279,553	..
1948	21,483	87,781	$ 2,972	194,035	266,162	$ 2,908
1949	17,888	111,547	9,727	193,902	290,607	12,396
1950	46,615	128,342	17,632	219,503	292,494	29,359
1951	47,298	137,110	15,899	239,161	283,924	43,084
1952	50,873	180,340	11,156	264,294	330,656	51,599
1953	33,194	197,042	10,473	274,455	381,020	58,535

Volume data were supplied by the Farmers Home Administration except that the amount for real estate loans in 1942 was obtained by deducting cumulative loan advances through 1941 (*Agricultural Statistics, 1950*, Department of Agriculture, Tables 720 and 733, pp. 672 and 690) from cumulative advances through 1942 (FHA). Real estate loans for 1944–1945 were partially estimated by linear interpolation of data for the preceding and following half years; and data on non-real-estate loans in 1944 include estimates for certain quarters based on linear interpolation of the available quarterly figures.

Data on outstandings were supplied by the FHA except that those for 1934 through 1936 were compiled from *Agricultural Finance Review* (Department of Agriculture, Bureau of Agricultural Economics, Vol. 12, Supplement May 1950, Table 17, p. 25).

a Represents loans made from federal funds and state rural rehabilitation corporation trust funds to tenants, sharecroppers, and farm laborers for the purchase, enlargement, and development of family-type farms; loans or construction or repair of farm houses and buildings; and receivables from individuals purchasing surplus real property of rural rehabilitation projects.

b Covers operating and production loans to farmers and stockmen; loans to cooperative associations for rehabilitation purposes; water facilities loans to farmers, ranchers, and co-operatives; production disaster loans; and loans authorized July 14, 1953 under the Special Livestock and Emergency Loan Programs. Lending under the first two broad categories became a function of the Resettlement Administration in 1935 (when the functions of the Rural Rehabilitation Division of the Federal Emergency Relief Administration were transferred) and was continued by its successors, the Farm Security Administration and the Farmers Home Administration. Data prior to 1943 exclude loans made in the territorial possessions. Annual data on loan advances during 1934–1937 are not available, but as of December 31, 1937 the volume of loans made totaled approximately $160,000,000.

c Refers to amount of commitments under FHA insurance of loans made by private lenders to tenants, sharecroppers, and farm laborers for the purchase, enlargement, and development of family-type farms.

d Data not available.

TABLE A-16

Lending and Loan Insuring Activity of the Maritime Administration
and its Predecessors, 1921–1953

| | VOLUME DURING YEAR | | OUTSTANDINGS AT YEAR END | |
| | Direct Business Loans[a] | Business Loan Insurance[b] | Direct Business Loans[a] | Business Loan Insurance[b] |
YEAR				
1921	c	..	$ 67,291	..
1922	c	..	38,752	..
1923	c	..	45,188	..
1924	$ 400	..	41,906	..
1925	4,760	..	28,699	..
1926	2,146	..	39,232	..
1927	3,162	..	50,003	..
1928	5,471	..	43,736	..
1929	6,729	..	61,062	..
1930	20,384	..	77,573	..
1931	28,705	..	100,484	..
1932	50,818	..	138,851	..
1933	24,550	..	157,454	..
1934	483	..	133,093	..
1935	338	..	111,688	..
1936	..	..	97,292	..
1937	..	..	85,081	..
1938	..	..	59,993	..
1939	..	$ 975	56,116	$ 975
1940	..	350	71,205	1,267
1941	..	6,300	62,952	7,482
1942	..	500	68,872	5,628
1943	..	65	123,780	4,443
1944	..	..	100,762	1,630
1945	..	..	111,435	..
1946	..	..	126,356	..
1947	..	..	131,877	..
1948	..	..	502,075	..
1949	..	2,400	471,266	2,400
1950	..	..	412,081	2,313
1951	80,401	..	448,775	553
1952	21,600	..	405,909	446
1953	..	..	355,717	371

Volume of direct loans refers to fiscal years ending June 30 and was compiled from *United States Shipping Board*, by D. H. Smith and P. V. Betters (Brookings Institution, Service Monograph No. 63, 1931, p. 285), the *Annual Reports* of the U.S. Shipping Board, and material supplied by the Maritime Administration. Volume of loan insurance, compiled from the *Annual Reports* of the U.S. Maritime Commission, refers to fiscal years ending October 25, 1939; September 30, 1940 and 1941; and June 30, 1942, 1943, and 1949.

(*continued on next page*)

TABLE A-16 *(continued)*

Outstanding amounts of direct loans for 1921–1933 and 1947–1953 are given as of June 30 (estimated in 1922–1927 and 1929–1933) and for 1934–1946 as of December 31, and were compiled from the *Annual Reports* of the U.S. Shipping Board, the *Annual Reports* and the *Daily Statements* of the Treasury Department, and from material supplied by the Treasury and the Maritime Administration. In 1947, outstandings on ship sales notes as of March 31 are included. Outstanding amounts of loan insurance were compiled from *Annual Reports* of the U.S. Maritime Commission and material supplied by the Maritime Administration, and refer to the following dates: October 31, 1939; September 30, 1940 and 1941; June 30, 1942 through 1953.

a Covers construction loans to American shipowners as authorized by Section 11 of the Merchant Marine Act of 1920; and outstandings also cover advances made to finance the sale of government-owned ships. The volume series, however, excludes mortgage loans made in 1921–1950 in connection with the sale of government-owned ships, because annual data are lacking.

b Refers to insurance of, and commitments to insure, mortgage loans to American shipowners, as authorized by the Merchant Marine Act of 1936.

c Data not available.

TABLE A-17

Federal Housing Administration Lending and Loan Insuring Activity, 1934–1953
(*in thousands*)

	VOLUME DURING YEAR			OUTSTANDINGS AT YEAR END		
YEAR	Direct Housing Loans[a]	Housing Loan Insurance[b]	Direct Loans to Financial Institutions[c]	Direct Housing Loans[a]	Housing Loan Insurance[b]	Direct Loans to Financial Institutions[c]
1934	..	$ 30,451	..	..	$ 30,451	..
1935	$ 447	319,857	$125	$ 408	307,815	$110
1936	5,885	557,196	16	5,286	701,315	18
1937	6,938	495,239	..	9,137	1,019,604	2
1938	6,641	693,630	..	11,623	1,511,271	..
1939	6,006	954,336	..	13,855	2,135,846	..
1940	13,123	1,025,979	..	23,174	2,795,975	..
1941	14,468	1,186,419	..	32,948	3,502,923	..
1942	15,655	1,135,227	..	41,016	4,095,955	..
1943	7,494	943,166	..	41,127	4,394,416	..
1944	3,473	888,683	..	32,342	4,542,369	..
1945	7,927	683,085	..	31,935	4,500,933	..
1946	13,599	797,927	..	37,630	4,238,327	..
1947	8,855	1,861,034	..	38,379	4,967,442	..
1948	15,299	3,424,655	..	45,576	7,276,342	..
1949	21,543	3,907,889	..	58,601	9,959,829	..
1950	30,723	4,439,257	..	76,914	12,786,064	..
1951	32,112	3,308,278	..	97,603	14,468,521	..
1952	29,854	3,232,065	..	114,727	15,918,324	..
1953	49,340	4,070,005	..	148,310	17,524,388	..

Housing loan data, volume of housing loans insured, and estimates of insured loans outstanding were supplied by the Federal Housing Administration, except that the insurance outstandings in 1934–1938 were estimated by the National Bureau of Economic Research as follows: Data on Title I loans for 1934 were estimated by assuming no terminations or amortization, leaving the volume of loans insured equal to outstandings at the end of the year; for 1935–1938, by subtracting repayments during the second half of each year (which were estimated to be one-third of the amount outstanding as of June 30), from the sum of outstandings on June 30 and loans insured during the second half of each year. Also included are amounts for mortgages insured under Section 203 (estimated by linear interpolation of the ratio between estimated insurance outstanding and cumulated mortgages insured at fiscal year ends 1935–1938 so as to apply that ratio to the cumulated volume figures at calendar year ends) and under Section 207 (obtained by assuming insurance in force equal to insurance outstanding, a relationship which existed at fiscal year ends 1935–1938).

Data on loans to financial institutions are from the *Annual Reports* of the Federal Housing Administration and the report of the Joint Committee on Reduction of Nonessential Federal Expenditures, *Federal Lending 1934–1948* (S. Doc. 103, 80th Cong., 1st sess., 1947, p. 37).

a Refers to mortgage loans to individuals to finance the sales of properties acquired through foreclosure of FHA-insured mortgages; claims paid on defaulted Title I notes acquired by FHA; and the amounts of debentures and cash adjustments on insured mortgages assigned to

(*continued on next page*)

TABLE A-17 *(continued)*

FHA. Volume data for assigned mortgages represent annual net changes in the amounts of debentures and cash adjustments covered by mortgage notes on hand at year end.

b Covers insurance of property improvement loans (Section 2, Class 1 and 2 of the National Housing Act), mortgage loans on new and existing one- to four-family dwellings (Class 3 of Section 2, and Sections 8, 203, and 603), loans on site-fabricated houses (Section 611), mortgage loans on cooperative housing projects (Section 213), mortgage loans on rental housing projects (Sections 207, 207-10, and 608), short-term loans to finance the production of prefabricated houses (Section 609), mortgage loans on publicly constructed housing (Sections 603-10 and 608-10), loans to finance construction of housing for military and civilian employees of U.S. military posts (Section 803), and loans to finance housing in critical defense areas (Sections 903 for one- and two-family dwellings and 908 for rental projects of twelve or more units). Data are based on original face amount of loans insured.

c Represents loans, as authorized under Section 3 of the National Housing Act, to financial institutions which are insured under Section 2. Section 3 was repealed by the amendment of April 3, 1936.

TABLE A-18

Export-Import Bank Lending Activity, 1934–1953

(*in thousands*)

| | VOLUME DURING YEAR | | OUTSTANDINGS AT YEAR END | |
| | Direct Business Loans | | Direct Business Loans | |
YEAR	Regular Lending[a]	Other[b]	Regular Lending[a]	Other[b]
1934	$ 3,800	..	..	..
1935	10,300	..	$ 4,300	..
1936	21,100	..	17,600	..
1937	7,600	..	17,400	..
1938	18,600	..	26,200	..
1939	53,700	..	65,200	..
1940	95,300	..	131,000	..
1941	116,800	..	186,100	..
1942	50,500	..	181,500	..
1943	51,000	..	200,200	..
1944	47,500	..	217,700	..
1945	79,600	..	245,300	..
1946	1,036,500	..	1,241,700	..
1947	824,500	..	1,970,700	..
1948	428,900	..	2,138,500	..
1949	184,800	..	2,179,600	..
1950	199,900	..	2,219,500	..
1951	204,100	..	2,289,000	..
1952	478,200	$ 217	2,496,100	$ 188
1953	647,000	7,674	2,833,300	7,863

Data for 1934–1945 were supplied by the Export-Import Bank of Washington; for 1946–1953, were compiled from the *Semi-Annual Reports* of the Export-Import Bank. Amounts for regular lending (i.e. under the Export-Import Bank Act of 1945 as amended) are rounded to one-tenth of a million.

a Covers direct loans to finance exports and imports and to assist in reconstruction, development, and stabilization of foreign economies, and loans in connection with lend lease terminations. Also included, because the annual data do not permit separate treatment, are loans for similar purposes made by commercial banks and other private lenders under Export-Import Bank guaranty (the so-called agency agreements under which the lender, usually a commercial bank, is protected against nonpayment by an Export-Import Bank guarantee to reimburse the bank upon demand). Of the total advanced under Export-Import Bank risk through December 31, 1953 ($311.6 million) $300.5 million or 97 percent was disbursed before the end of 1946. Outstandings on such loans have represented a declining share of total year-end outstandings since the end of 1946 (from 15 percent in 1946 to 1 percent in 1953).

b Represents loans (including participations in loans) to private business enterprises for the expansion, development, and production of essential materials where such operations are conducted in foreign countries, as authorized under Section 302 of the Defense Production Act of 1950.

TABLE A-19

Treasury Department Lending Activity, 1933–1953

(in thousands)

YEAR	VOLUME DURING YEAR		OUTSTANDINGS AT YEAR END	
	Direct Loans	*Stock Purchases*	*Direct Loans*	*Stock Purchases*
	Miscellaneous Purposes[a]	*Financial Institutions*[b]	*Miscellaneous Purposes*[a]	*Financial Institutions*[b]
1933	..	$ 18	..	$ 18
1934	..	10,707	..	10,725
1935	..	38,575	..	49,273
1936	..	..	..	48,991
1937	..	..	..	48,051
1938	..	..	..	47,053
1939	..	..	..	39,679
1940	..	..	..	26,748
1941	..	..	..	21,284
1942	$ 800	..	$ 800	17,548
1943	900	..	701	6,884
1944	200	..	..	3,489
1945	..	..	..	1,982
1946	..	..	..	1,150
1947	..	..	..	555
1948	..	..	..	247
1949	..	..	..	..
1950	..	..	..	..
1951	..	..	..	..
1952	..	..	..	..
1953	1,900	..	1,900	..

Volume of direct loans in 1942–1944 was estimated from fiscal year data in the report of the Joint Committee on Reduction of Nonessential Federal Expenditures, *Federal Lending 1934–1948* (S. Doc. 103, 80th Cong., 1st sess. 1947, Table 1); volume in 1953 and outstandings throughout were supplied by the Treasury Department.

Data on stock purchases were supplied by the Federal Savings and Loan Insurance Corporation.

a Represents loans to the District of Columbia for civilian defense and other purposes during 1942–1944 and for construction of public works in 1953 (pursuant to Public Law 533 of June 2, 1950).

b Refers to purchases of shares of federal savings and loan associations. Responsibility for administering these investments was vested in the Federal Home Loan Bank Board by Section 5(j) of the Home Owners' Loan Act of 1933.

TABLE A-20

Public Housing Administration Lending and Loan Guaranteeing
Activity, 1937–1953

	VOLUME DURING YEAR	OUTSTANDINGS AT YEAR END	
YEAR	Direct Loans to Minor Governmental Units[a]	Direct Loans, Minor Gov.[a]	Loan Guarantees, Minor Gov.[b]
1937	$ 1,500	$ 10,024	[c]
1938	29,000	31,604	[c]
1939	138,500	122,755	$ 51,127
1940	450,500	185,519	247,863
1941	507,900	367,410	203,042
1942	261,000	365,808	258,743
1943	95,500	318,364	225,335
1944	3,500	304,711	226,024
1945	1,500	285,706	229,218
1946	1,400	278,300	233,719
1947	24,600	277,632	225,501
1948	37,000	285,406	218,657
1949	25,000	285,489	220,627
1950	123,800	352,319	414,003
1951	422,800	594,665	805,925
1952	773,400	900,316	1,067,248
1953	727,300	511,433	1,932,953

Volume data (rounded to one-tenth millions) were estimated by linear interpolation of fiscal year data for 1937–1945 from the report of the Joint Committee
on Reduction of Nonessential Federal Expenditures, *Federal Lending 1934–1948*
(S. Doc. 103, 80th Cong., 1st sess., 1947, Table 1) and for 1946–1953 from material
supplied by the Housing and Home Finance Agency.

Outstandings are from the *Daily Statements* of, and material supplied by, the
Treasury Department.

a Represents loans to local housing authorities for the construction and operation of low-rent housing and slum clearance projects, as authorized by the Housing
Act of 1937 (Public Law 412), by Public Law 671 (enacted as a war emergency
measure), and by the Housing Act of 1949 (Public Law 171), and advances in
fiscal 1939 on loans to limited dividend housing corporations which were made
originally by the Public Works Administration during 1933–1937. Outstandings
from 1937 on also include outstanding balances on PWA loans to limited dividend
housing corporations transferred to PHA as of November 1, 1937. At time of
transfer, balance of such loans totaled $10,142,182.

b Refers to outstanding commitments of PHA in connection with temporary
financing obtained by local housing authorities through private sources for which
PHA holds escrow notes, and with long-term obligations issued by local authorities to private investors and secured by annual contributions contracts of the
local authorities with PHA. Annual volume data of such guarantees are not
available.

c Data not available.

TABLE A-21

Lending Activity of the Small Business Administration, 1953,
and the Virgin Islands Corporation, 1949–1953
(*in thousands*)

	SMALL BUSINESS ADMINISTRATION [a]		VIRGIN ISLANDS CORPORATION [b]			
	Direct Loans for Miscellaneous Purposes		*Direct Loan Volume*		*Outstandings at Year End*	
YEAR	*Volume*	*Outstandings*	*Agric.*	*Bus.*	*Agric.*	*Bus.*
1949	..	..	c	..	$4	..
1950	..	..	c	c	4	$ 3
1951	..	..	c	c	4	87
1952	..	..	c	c	9	15
1953	$4	$4	c	c	1	33

a Data were supplied by the Small Business Administration. Represents loans to victims of floods or other catastrophes. The Small Business Administration was established under the Small Business Act of 1953 for the primary purpose of making loans to small business concerns. As of December 31, 1953 no disbursements on business loans had been made.

b Data were supplied by the Treasury Department and refer to loans to aid agriculture and business enterprises in the Virgin Islands.

c Data not available.

TABLE A-22

Lending Activity of the Agricultural Marketing Act Revolving Fund,
1929–1952, and the Emergency Crop and Feed Loan Division,
1918–1953
(*in thousands*)

	AGRICULTURAL MARKETING ACT REVOLVING FUND[a]		EMERGENCY CROP AND FEED LOAN DIVISION[b]	
	Direct Farm Loans		Direct Farm Loans	
YEAR	*Volume during Year*	*Outstandings at Year End*	*Volume during Year*	*Outstandings at Year End*
1918	..	..	$ 2,101	c
1919	..	..	2,100	$ 4,201
1920	..	..	..	3,938
1921	..	..	1,957	3,411
1922	..	..	1,480	2,885
1923	..	..	..	2,359
1924	..	..	414	2,513
1925	..	..	..	2,207
1926	..	..	244	2,101
1927	..	..	..	2,292
1928	..	..	..	2,246
1929	$ 14,823	$ 14,510	5,759	7,976
1930	348,552	233,756	5,340	8,946
1931	516,821	436,254	55,787	49,769
1932	229,026	466,501	64,205	90,353
1933	46,711	334,092	57,376	90,863
1934	9,555	146,911	70,471	111,238
1935	7,402	115,859	96,382	172,863
1936	20,450	121,762	16,135	165,369
1937	5,936	98,971	31,815	172,701
1938	7,911	91,183	19,648	171,489
1939	1,214	87,207	15,080	168,330
1940	3,094	16,461	19,517	168,438
1941	3,990	16,914	18,346	164,974
1942	5,017	12,551	19,698	156,675
1943	1,417	7,351	18,699	147,650
1944	809	3,067	18,444	139,541
1945	660	2,693	16,465	130,505
1946	975	2,232	16,972	118,120
1947	1,400	2,603	—2[d]	106,259
1948	1,000	1,315	..	90,240
1949	700	1,365	..	71,341
1950	700	1,309	—2[d]	53,347
1951	700	1,451	..	38,235
1952	375	905	..	27,955
1953	..	..	..	19,976

(*continued on next page*)

TABLE A-22 (*continued*)

a Compiled from the *Loans and Discounts Reports* and the *Annual Reports* of the Farm Credit Administration. Covers loans to farmers' cooperatives for marketing and operating purposes, for construction or purchase of physical facilities, and for refinancing debt incurred in acquiring such facilities, and loans to stabilization corporations to support farm commodity prices.

b Covers operating loans to farmers to relieve distress conditions caused by drought and flood in United States and possessions. Loans were made from 1918 to 1933 under the Department of Agriculture and thereafter (May 27, 1933 to October 1946) under the Farm Credit Administration. Also included are drought relief loans made in 1934–1935 and orchard rehabilitation loans made since 1942. The program is now being liquidated by the Farmers Home Administration.

Data were supplied by the Farm Credit Administration and the Farmers Home Administration. Volume for 1918 and 1919 was estimated by dividing equally the total of loans made in the two years; data for 1946 represent advances through October 31, 1946. Outstandings for 1919 represent total amount advanced in 1918 and 1919 without adjustment for repayments; 1920–1922 data represent estimates of the outstanding balances as of June 30 of each year; 1923–1930 data are for the year ending June 30.

c Data not available.

d Represent adjustments for noncash advances, etc., made after the lending program was discontinued.

Lending Activity of the Electric Home and Farm Authority, 1934–1942, the Farmers Seed Loan Office, 1931–1953, the Regional Agricultural Credit Corporations, 1932–1953, and the Tennessee Valley Associated Cooperatives, Inc., 1934–1947

(in thousands)

YEAR	ELECTRIC HOME AND FARM AUTHORITY[a] Direct Farm Loans		FARMERS SEED LOAN OFFICE[b] Direct Farm Loans		REGIONAL AGRICULTURAL CREDIT CORPORATIONS[c] Direct Farm Loans		TENNESSEE VALLEY ASSOCIATED COOPERATIVES, INC. Direct Farm Loans[d]		Stock Purchases[e]	
	Volume	Out-standings	Volume	Out-standings	Volume	Out-standings	Volume	Out-standings	Volume	Out-standings
1931	..	..	$1,513	$1,513	..	..	..	..	..	..
1932	..	..	..	1,427	$24,597	$24,373	..	..	..	..
1933	..	..	..	1,340	223,116	144,636	..	..	..	..
1934	$386	$116	..	1,009	140,589	87,102	$52	$73	..	..
1935	1,009	986	..	678	90,656	43,400	78	167	..	..
1936	2,426	1,913	..	570	34,667	25,288	79	131	..	..
1937	4,804	5,092	..	482	18,604	15,592	97	179	..	..
1938	7,211	7,871	..	454	5,719	11,081	111	262	$29	$29
1939	10,106	11,228	..	439	4,665	8,005	49	256	5	34
1940	13,013	14,305	..	362	4,804	5,855	7	258	..	34
1941	10,306	15,934	..	306	6,759	5,531	1	253	..	34
1942	3,203	..	..	295	7,759	3,991	1	252	..	34
1943	..	..	..	279	73,253	32,047	..	242	..	34
1944	..	..	..	254	15,666	12,195	..	236	..	34
1945	..	..	..	203	9,647	6,151	14	253	..	34
1946	..	..	..	124	1,470	2,560	13	131	..	34
1947	..	..	..	100	77	1,862	..	41	..	34
1948	..	..	..	88	77	1,522	..	..	..	..
1949	..	..	..	88	130	1,273	..	..	..	..
1950	..	..	..	88	9	1,236	..	..	..	..
1951	..	..	..	88	..	868	..	..	..	..
1952	..	..	..	88	..	656	..	..	..	..
1953	..	..	..	84	..	501	..	..	..	..

(continued on next page)

APPENDIX A

TABLE A-23 (*continued*)

a The series refer to discounts of dealers' paper originating in the sale or installation of electrical and gas appliances and equipment. Outstanding accounts were transferred to the Reconstruction Finance Corporation in 1942 for liquidation and are included in the RFC business loan series in Table A-9. Volume for 1934–1941 refers to amount of contracts accepted, estimated by linear interpolation of fiscal year data in the *Annual Reports* of the Electric Home and Farm Authority; 1942 volume refers to estimated amount disbursed, from the *U.S. Treasury Bulletin,* August 1942. Although the Electric Home and Farm Authority operated for a few weeks in 1933, contracts accepted in that year are included in the data for 1934. Data on year-end outstandings are from the *Daily Statements* of, and material supplied by, the Treasury Department.

b Data refer to loans made in 1931 to farmers and stockmen for purchase of stock in agricultural credit corporations and livestock loan companies, and were compiled from *Annual Reports* of, and material supplied by, the Farm Credit Administration, and from material supplied by the Farmers Home Administration. On the assumption that no repayments were made during 1931, outstandings as of the end of that year are based on loan volume during the year; data for 1932 and 1934 are estimated by linear interpolation between the outstandings at the preceding and following year ends (but the 1933 figure is for November 30); for 1946 and 1947, by linear interpolation of change in outstandings 1945–1948. The program is now being liquidated by the Farmers Home Administration.

c Compiled from the *Annual Reports* of the Farm Credit Administration, the *Agricultural Finance Review* (Department of Agriculture, Bureau of Agricultural Economics, Vol. 12, November 1949, Table 13), and material supplied by the Farmers Home Administration. Represents short-term production loans to farmers and stockmen made by the twelve regional agricultural credit corporations, including loans for regular operating and marketing purposes; loans to fruit growers in Washington; World War II food production loans (including those made under Section 2 of the Department of Agriculture Appropriation Act of 1944); and fur loans. The program is now being liquidated by the Farmers Home Administration.

d Calendar year data on volume were estimated by linear interpolation of semi-annual information taken from the report of the Joint Committee on Reduction of Nonessential Federal Expenditures, *Federal Lending, 1934–1948* (S. Doc. 103, 80th Cong., 1st sess., 1947, Table 1). Data on year-end outstandings are from the *Daily Statements* of, and material supplied by, the Treasury Department. The series cover loans to cooperatives in the Tennessee Valley to assist in their development and thereby improve the economic welfare of the area's inhabitants. Liquidation of the program was begun in September 1947; the corporation was dissolved in December 1948, assets being transferred to the Treasury.

e Refers to purchases of stock of agricultural cooperatives and canning associations. Volume data are from the *Report on the Audit of the Tennessee Valley Associated Cooperatives, Inc.* (H. Doc. 234, 81st Cong., 1st sess., 1949); year-end outstandings are from the *Daily Statements* of the Treasury Department.

TABLE A-24

Lending Activity of the Federal Farm Mortgage Corporation, 1933–1953, and the Rural Electrification Administration, 1935–1953

(*in thousands*)

YEAR	FEDERAL FARM MORTGAGE CORPORATION[a] Direct Real Estate Loans Volume during Year	Outstandings at Year End	RURAL ELECTRIFICATION ADMINISTRATION[b] Direct Non-Real-Estate Loans Volume during Year	Outstandings at Year End
1933	$ 70,812	$ 70,738	..	..
1934	553,136	616,825	..	..
1935	196,395	794,752	$ 10	$ 10
1936	77,258	837,274	3,328	3,338
1937	40,020	815,001	30,999	34,315
1938	29,395	757,710	54,007	88,141
1939	27,417	700,360	95,754	183,293
1940	36,664	662,200	69,235	249,249
1941	37,533	615,674	78,697	322,531
1942	28,534	532,925	32,291	345,644
1943	30,497	425,710	14,171	347,172
1944	35,017	346,764	27,874	360,930
1945	29,462	241,237	56,971	407,688
1946	15,035	149,005	132,188	527,822
1947	10,606	109,339	225,413	734,135
1948	17	79,886	284,724	999,132
1949	19	60,344	327,331	1,301,323
1950	25	45,424	273,252	1,543,407
1951	58	33,959	241,225	1,742,519
1952	41	24,865	228,220	1,920,773
1953	40	18,397	228,021	2,095,995

a Data were compiled from the *Loans and Discounts Reports* of, and material supplied by, the Farm Credit Administration, and cover first and second farm mortgage loans made by the Land Bank Commissioner in the United States and possessions. Outstandings also include purchase money mortgages and real estate sales contracts, which are excluded from the volume series because annual data are lacking.

b Data, supplied by the Rural Electrification Administration, represent self-liquidating loans made in the United States and possessions to local enterprises (cooperatives, public power districts, local government authorities, and private power companies) for construction of electric facilities and for purchase and installation of electric appliances and plumbing; also loans for the construction and operation of new, and the expansion and improvement of existing, telephone facilities in rural areas. Volume data represent net advances after the return of unused loan funds; outstandings are cumulative net advances less principal repayments.

TABLE A-25

Lending Activity of the Central and Regional Banks for Cooperatives, 1933–1953, and the Federal Intermediate Credit Banks, 1923–1953

| | CENTRAL & REGIONAL BANKS FOR COOPERATIVES[a] | | FEDERAL INTERMEDIATE CREDIT BANKS[b] | | | |
| | Direct Loans, Agric. | | Volume during Year | | Year-End Outstandings | |
YEAR	Volume during Year	Outstandings at Year End	Loans to Farmers' Cooperatives[c]	Other Agric. Loans[d]	Loans to Farmers' Cooperatives[c]	Other Agric. Loans[d]
1923	..	..	$ 35,519	$ 9,367	$33,627	$ 9,105
1924	..	..	83,223	34,004	43,507	18,760
1925	..	..	100,243	53,488	53,780	26,272
1926	..	..	103,941	73,521	52,704	39,730
1927	..	..	51,039	87,121	31,991	43,924
1928	..	..	53,571	83,568	36,174	45,103
1929	..	..	43,588	94,667	26,073	50,018
1930	..	..	109,927	109,047	64,377	65,633
1931	..	..	145,127	122,867	45,177	74,691
1932	..	..	89,245	151,578	9,866	82,518
1933	$ 27,144	$ 18,697	27,910	141,045	15,211	61,016
1934	40,371	27,851	57,369	235,110	33,969	116,697
1935	66,348	50,013	44,509	327,580	2,731	143,822
1936	81,294	69,647	3,755	347,634	1,641	148,576
1937	97,584	87,633	5,129	407,281	1,813	176,504
1938	94,945	87,496	2,668	422,219	920	176,653
1939	83,361	76,252	4,156	438,247	1,835	180,679
1940	101,231	74,741	4,593	475,868	1,490	205,219
1941	181,569	113,444	5,651	571,360	2,152	232,965
1942	252,380	144,644	9,397	646,082	2,000	235,665
1943	398,581	235,174	5,000	699,215	2,000	240,731
1944	363,637	212,835	3,402	730,809	700	233,316
1945	333,702	157,545	4,032	737,989	2,042	229,232
1946	399,769	181,550	11,579	891,961	4,151	269,167
1947	530,248	274,777	14,128	1,104,440	4,000	332,420
1948	494,678	304,684	13,639	1,363,405	4,709	420,801
1949	382,617	301,887	9,900	1,376,285	2,400	435,017
1950	402,176	344,978	9,044	1,509,510	3,233	506,984
1951	568,961	423,952	15,176	1,943,431	4,000	629,008
1952	528,118	418,504	8,000	1,901,678	2,000	671,261
1953	497,016	372,110	4,000	1,718,157	500	589,695

[a] Compiled from the *Loans and Discounts Reports* of the Farm Credit Administration; refers to loans made by the Central Bank for Cooperatives and the twelve district banks to farmers' groups for general farm operating purposes, the marketing of agricultural commodities, and construction or acquisition of marketing facilities.

[b] Data were supplied by the Farm Credit Administration, and are exclusive of loans to, and discounts for, regional agricultural credit corporations (1933 through 1935) and the central and regional banks for cooperatives.

[c] Represents loans to farmers' groups for production and general farm operating purposes.

[d] Represents loans to, and discounts of agricultural and livestock paper for, production credit associations, agricultural and livestock credit corporations organized under state laws, and commercial banks. Renewals are included.

TABLE A-26

Lending Activity of the Federal Land Banks, 1917–1953,
and the Production Credit Corporations, 1933–1953
(*in thousands*)

YEAR	FEDERAL LAND BANKS[a]		PRODUCTION CREDIT CORPORATIONS[b]	
	Direct Farm Real Estate Loans		Stock Purchases for Farm Production Credit	
	Volume during Year	*Outstandings at Year End*	*Volume during Year*	*Outstandings at Year End*
1917	$ 39,112	$ 38,800	..	..
1918	118,130	156,214	..	..
1919	144,987	293,595	..	..
1920	66,985	349,843	..	..
1921	91,030	432,870c	..	..
1922	224,301	639,863	..	..
1923	192,083	799,869	..	..
1924	165,510	928,831	..	..
1925	127,355	1,008,359	..	..
1926	131,318	1,081,986	..	..
1927	140,384	1,161,838	..	..
1928	102,236	1,203,911	..	..
1929	64,253	1,213,953	..	..
1930	47,971	1,209,431	..	..
1931	42,015	1,192,918	..	..
1932	27,570	1,158,274	..	..
1933	151,634	1,268,441	$ 2,430	$ 2,430
1934	730,367	1,959,106	89,405	90,086
1935	248,671	2,126,117	11,999	77,017
1936	109,170	2,133,192	3,895	75,038
1937	63,092	2,119,018	4,824	76,146
1938	51,418	2,072,262	2,419	75,788
1939	51,582	2,002,061	2,558	75,370
1940	64,275	1,955,616	1,301	61,445
1941	65,068	1,879,901	21,464	81,498
1942	53,974	1,717,697	1,920	81,621
1943	61,900	1,456,334	621	76,090
1944	70,275	1,214,801	538	63,587

(*continued on next page*)

TABLE A-26 (continued)

YEAR	FEDERAL LAND BANKS[a] Direct Farm Real Estate Loans		PRODUCTION CREDIT CORPORATIONS[b] Stock Purchases for Farm Production Credit	
	Volume during Year	Outstandings at Year End	Volume during Year	Outstandings at Year End
1945	$ 92,986	$1,086,488	$ 596	$55,491
1946	130,162	985,477	292	46,034
1947	138,764	898,417	225	34,918
1948	150,514	878,586	30	29,139
1949	182,357	916,862	115	22,296
1950	205,933	959,789	965	15,728
1951	214,220	1,007,695	1,015	11,371
1952	254,581	1,086,289	100	7,596
1953	289,772	1,185,781	640	4,946

a Volume data were compiled from the *Annual Reports* and the *Loans and Discounts Reports* of the Farm Credit Administration. Outstandings for 1917 are based on loans made through that year less the amount estimated to have been repaid during December; other outstandings data were compiled from the above-mentioned reports and from material supplied by the FCA. Both series cover regular mortgage loans made in the United States and Puerto Rico. Outstandings also include purchase money mortgages and real estate sales contracts, which are excluded from the volume series because annual data are lacking. For Land Bank Commissioner loans, see Table A-24.

b Data, supplied by the Farm Credit Administration, represent purchases by the production credit corporations of Class A stock of the production credit associations.

c Includes outstandings as of November 30 for purchase money mortgages and real estate sales contracts.

TABLE A-27

Lending Activity of the Director General of the Railroads and the
Interstate Commerce Commission, 1919–1953, the Federal Home Loan Banks,
1932–1953, and the Federal Reserve Banks, 1934–1953
(*in thousands*)

YEAR	DIRECTOR GEN'L OF RAILROADS AND ICC[a] *Direct Business Loans*		FEDERAL HOME LOAN BANKS[b] *Direct Loans to Financial Institutions*		FEDERAL RESERVE BANKS[c] *Direct Business Loans*	
	Volume	*Outstandings*	*Volume*	*Outstandings*	*Volume*	*Outstandings*
1919	$ 65,841	d	..	..	..	..
1920	620,611	$562,643	..	..	..	..
1921	172,480	568,472	..	..	..	..
1922	82,001	437,944	..	..	..	..
1923	122,950	434,381	..	..	..	..
1924	26,450	382,839	..	..	..	..
1925	..	307,707	..	..	..	..
1926	..	264,798	..	..	..	..
1927	..	152,546	..	..	..	..
1928	..	68,654	..	..	..	..
1929	..	58,745	..	..	..	..
1930	..	47,367	..	..	..	..
1931	..	39,434	..	..	..	..
1932	..	38,704	$ 838	$ 838	..	..
1933	..	38,097	90,032	85,442	..	..
1934	..	34,452	38,676	86,603	$14,884	$13,589
1935	..	30,915	59,130	102,686	28,479	32,493
1936	..	30,238	93,257	145,227	8,519	25,526
1937	..	30,230	123,251	200,038	4,932	20,216
1938	..	30,230	81,958	198,842	6,500	17,345
1939	..	30,186	94,781	181,313	3,805	13,683
1940	..	30,080	134,212	201,492	2,860	9,152
1941	..	25,213	157,600	219,446	15,695	10,337
1942	..	25,213	99,462	129,213	68,032	14,126
1943	..	25,121	156,925	110,068	60,265	10,532
1944	..	21,598	239,254	130,563	20,381	3,894
1945	..	21,598	277,748	194,872	14,043	1,995
1946	..	21,598	329,232	293,455	3,445	554
1947	..	11,964	351,079	435,572	9,296	1,387
1948	..	11,929	359,613	515,016	15,994	995
1949	..	11,805	255,662	433,429	4,005	2,178
1950	..	11,805	674,757	815,957	6,530	2,632
1951	..	11,805	422,976	805,937	27,656	4,687
1952	..	6,019	585,813	864,189	31,193	3,921
1953	..	5,759	727,532	951,555	22,009	1,900

(*continued on next page*)

TABLE A-27 (*continued*)

ᵃ The series represent operating loans to railroads made by the Director General as authorized under Section 7 of the Federal Control Act of 1918, equipment trust notes taken by him in connection with the transfer of railroad equipment to private hands at the cessation of federal control, operating loans to railroads by the Treasury Department upon certification by the Interstate Commerce Commission, as authorized under Section 210 of the Transportation Act of 1920, and loans to the carriers by the Director General, as authorized under Section 207 of the Transportation Act of 1920. Outstandings also include securities accepted in the reorganization of railroads pursuant to Executive Order 8533 of September 6, 1940. Loans made by the Director General under Section 12 of the Federal Control Act are excluded for lack of annual data. The total advanced under Section 12 was $62,103,453.

Volume figures were estimated from data in the *Annual Reports* of the Director General of Railroads and of the Secretary of the Treasury. In 1919 they represent purchases of equipment trust notes, estimated as one-fifth of the outstanding balance of June 30, 1920. In 1920 they include estimates constructed as follows: Section 7 loans were assumed to equal their amount outstanding as of June 30, 1920; Section 210 loans at year end were estimated as equal to outstandings at December 31 (estimated by linear interpolation between fiscal year dates); equipment trust notes were estimated by subtracting 1919 data from data on total advances. In 1921–1924 they were estimated from fiscal year data for Section 210 loans by assuming a constant monthly volume and then combining monthly data on a calendar year basis.

Year-end outstandings were compiled from the *Annual Reports* of and materials supplied by, the Treasury Department. For years before 1935, they were estimated by linear interpolation of outstandings for June 30 of the preceding and following years; in 1920 they exclude outstandings on Section 207 loans; and in 1944–1952 they include outstandings on securities received in the reorganization of certain carriers (in 1947–1951, $5,785,872 face value of bonds and script of Seaboard Air Line Railroad accepted and held by the RFC is included, but common and preferred stock also received in reorganization are excluded from the estimates, there being no valuation of these items).

ᵇ Data are from *Housing Statistics*, Housing and Home Finance Agency, January 1954, p. 43, and cover advances to savings and loan, building and loan, and homestead associations, to savings and cooperative banks, and to insurance companies which are members of the Federal Home Loan Bank system; outstandings are as at year ends.

ᶜ Data were supplied by the Board of Governors of the Federal Reserve System and represent loans, and participations in loans, to industrial and commercial businesses under Section 13b of the Federal Reserve Act as amended; outstandings are year-end figures.

ᵈ Data not available.

TABLE A-28

Lending Activity of the Federal National Mortgage Association, 1938–1953,
and the RFC Mortgage Company, 1935–1953

(*in thousands*)

YEAR	FEDERAL NATIONAL MORTGAGE ASSOCIATION[a] Direct Housing Loans Volume during Year	Outstandings at Year End	RFC MORTGAGE COMPANY[b] Direct Housing Loans Volume during Year	Outstandings at Year End
1935	..	..	$ 5,744	$ 5,705
1936	..	..	33,880	36,126
1937	..	..	45,395	67,534
1938	$ 82,166	$ 80,266	35,316	54,227
1939	74,081	146,760	27,824	57,377
1940	48,042	181,101	26,148	67,300
1941	42,321	206,840	29,034	73,036
1942	23,178	210,928	45,646	97,578
1943	1,502	64,487	41,625	104,634
1944	200	52,423	45,048	102,211
1945	57	7,442	17,436	39,240
1946	33	5,591	2,715	13,610
1947	60	4,420	123,744	122,715
1948	197,945	199,295	16,060	131,296
1949	672,213	828,354	..	122,653
1950	1,044,295	1,346,664	..	91,909
1951	677,309	1,849,534	..	78,477
1952	537,872	2,241,667	..	71,920
1953	542,457	2,461,637	..	65,529

a Data were supplied by the Federal National Mortgage Association and the Reconstruction Finance Corporation, or are from the *Semi-Annual Reports* of FNMA. They cover purchases of housing project and home mortgage loans insured by the Federal Housing Administration under Titles I, II, VI, VIII, and IX of the National Housing Act of 1934 or guaranteed by the Veterans' Administration under Title III of the Servicemen's Readjustment Act of 1944; also direct mortgage loans, made by FNMA under FHA insurance, on Alaskan properties as authorized by the Alaska Housing Act of 1949; and direct, FHA-insured loans on rental properties.

b Data were supplied by the Reconstruction Finance Corporation. Volume in 1947 and 1948 was partially estimated by assuming a constant monthly volume from October 1947 through March 1948; outstandings for 1947 were derived from estimated disbursements and repayments during the year. Both series cover the following: purchases of large-scale housing and home mortgage loans insured by the Federal Housing Administration under Titles I, II, and VI of the National Housing Act, and of VA-guaranteed home mortgage loans; loans on, and purchases of, mortgages secured by new and existing income-producing properties; loans to holders of mortgage bonds and certificates of deposit on such properties, in adverse circumstances; a loan for purchase of property and for building construction; and refunding loans to owners of business properties adversely affected by war conditions. The operations of the RFC Mortgage Company were discontinued in June 1947, but disbursements under previously approved commitments continued through 1948.

TABLE A-29

Lending Activity of the Bureau of Community Facilities, 1942–1953,
the Inland Waterways Corporation, 1921–1953,
and the Tennessee Valley Authority, 1934–1951
(*in thousands*)

| | DIRECT LOANS TO MINOR GOVERNMENTAL UNITS | | | | |
| | Bureau of Community Facilitiesa | Inland Waterways Corporationb | | Tennessee Valley Authorityc | |
YEAR	Outstandings	Volume	Outstandings	Volume	Outstandings
1921	..	$890	d		
1922	..	..	$2,150	..	..
1923	..	..	1,918	..	..
1924	..	..	1,198	..	..
1925	..	..	1,101	..	..
1926	..	60	1,073	..	..
1927	..	15	861	..	..
1928	..	12	823	..	..
1929	..	5	828	..	..
1930	..	5	793	..	..
1931	..	..	731	..	..
1932	..	..	643	..	..
1933	..	..	618	..	..
1934	..	..	594	$ 214	$ 96
1935	..	38	604	491	524
1936	..	..	576	725	1,226
1937	..	..	547	823	1,633
1938	..	..	514	873	2,543
1939	..	..	456	1,134	4,578
1940	..	..	435	853	4,172
1941	..	..	409	135	4,018
1942	$ 324	..	390	28	3,611
1943	3,711	..	363	3	3,295
1944	4,663	..	343	..	2,938
1945	6,477	..	314	..	2,428
1946	4,996	..	264	..	724
1947	4,294	..	224	..	98
1948	2,784	..	189	..	69
1949	1,940	..	271	..	14
1950	1,681	..	219	..	9
1951	1,319	..	185	..	3
1952	1,268	..	109	..	..
1953	1,022	..	73	..	..

(*continued on next page*)

TABLE A-29 *(continued)*

a Year-end data, from the *Daily Statements* of, and material supplied by, the Treasury Department; represents loans for the construction of community facilities in defense production areas as authorized under Title II of the Lanham Act. Annual loan volume is not available; the total advanced under Title II was approximately $8,115,000. Data for the First and Second Advance Planning Programs (P.L. 458 and 352) are included in Table A-14.

b Data represent loans to states, municipalities, and transportation companies for the construction of terminal facilities as authorized under Section 201(c) of the Transportation Act of 1920. The volume series excludes approximately $385,000 in loans to private companies for which annual data are lacking. Year-end outstandings in 1953 exclude a $9 million mortgage received from the sale of the corporation's property and operating equipment.

Information on volume was compiled from *Public Aids to Transportation* (Federal Coordinator of Transportation, Vol. 3, Part 2, pp. 229 and 262f.) and on year-end outstandings, from the *Annual Reports* of the Inland and Coastwise Waterways Service and of the Inland Waterways Corporation, and from the *Daily Statements* of, and material supplied by, the Treasury Department. Outstandings for 1922 were estimated by linear interpolation between June 30 data for 1922 and 1923; 1923 data were estimated by computing monthly average change in outstandings between June 30, 1923 and December 31, 1924 and subtracting the average change for the six months after June 30, 1923. Outstandings for 1945 and 1947–1952 are for November 30.

c Data, supplied by the Tennessee Valley Authority, refer to loans under Section 12a of the Tennessee Valley Authority Act to municipalities and cooperative wholesale power distribution companies for acquisition and operation of power plants and distribution facilities. The figures for 1948–1950 exclude the amounts of the outstanding loan balance in connection with the sale of Norris Village on June 15, 1948. Outstandings are as at calendar year ends. Volume figures were estimated by linear interpolation of fiscal year data.

d Data not available.

TABLE A-30

Lending Activity of the Defense Homes Corporation, 1941–1946,
the Smaller War Plants Corporation, 1942–1946,
and the War and Navy Departments and U.S. Maritime Commission, 1942–1953
(*in thousands*)

YEAR	DEFENSE HOMES CORPORATION[a] Direct Housing Loans		SMALLER WAR PLANTS CORPORATION[b] Direct Business Loans		WAR & NAVY DEPTS. AND U.S. MARITIME COMM.[c] Business Loan Guarantees	
	Volume	Outstandings	Volume	Outstandings	Volume	Outstandings
1941	$ 90	$130	..	..	..	..
1942	428	557	$ 3,090	$ 774	$ 928,000	$ 632,474
1943	395	905	46,686	14,519	4,047,000	1,601,518
1944	27	936	167,767	35,756	3,315,000	1,482,038
1945	..	901	120,794	28,500	1,723,000	435,345
1946	..	787	12,183	..	70,000	17,454
1947	..	..	..	..	..	2,183
1948	..	..	..	..	..	1,184
1949	..	..	..	..	..	764
1950	..	..	..	..	..	664
1951	..	..	..	..	..	664
1952	..	..	..	..	..	636
1953	..	..	..	..	..	613

a Data represent mortgage loans for construction of housing in defense production areas. The program was transferred to the Reconstruction Finance Corporation for liquidation in March 1947; outstandings on unpaid loans are included in the RFC business loan series in Table A-9.

Volume estimates were made by linear interpolation of fiscal year data in the report of the Joint Committee on Reduction of Nonessential Federal Expenditures, *Federal Lending 1934–1948* (S. Doc. 103, 80th Cong., 1st sess., 1947, Table 1); outstandings as at calendar year ends were supplied by the Treasury Department.

b Data refer to loans, and participations in loans, to small business concerns engaged in the production of war and essential civilian goods. The accounts were transferred to the Reconstruction Finance Corporation for liquidation in January 1946; outstandings on unpaid loans are included in the RFC business loan series in Table A-9.

The volume data were supplied by the Reconstruction Finance Corporation; those for 1942–1944 were estimated by reducing approved authorizations by the proportion of the cumulative net amount authorized to the cumulated amount of applications approved by December 31, 1944. Year-end outstandings are from the *Daily Statements* of the Treasury Department.

c The estimates concern amounts of guarantees on loans to war contractors made by private financing institutions and guaranteed by the War Department, the Navy Department, or the U.S. Maritime Commission under Regulation V.

Volume was estimated from data in *A Statistical Study of Regulation V Loans*, by Susan S. Burr and Elizabeth B. Sette (Board of Governors of the Federal Reserve System, 1950, Tables 2 and 17, pp. 14 and 47) by reducing the principal amount of authorizations by the weighted average ratio of amount guaranteed to principal amount authorized. Year-end outstandings are from the *Federal Reserve Bulletin*, May 1949, p. 535, and from data supplied by the Board of Governors of the Federal Reserve System.

TABLE A-31

Lending Activity of the Bureau of Indian Affairs, 1934–1953, the Disaster Loan Corporation, 1937–1945, the Federal Security Agency, 1942–1953, Prencinradio, Inc., 1943–1948, and the Puerto Rico Reconstruction Administration, 1936–1953

(in thousands)

| | | | DIRECT LOANS FOR MISCELLANEOUS PURPOSES | | | | | | |
| | Bureau of Indian Affairs[a] | | Disaster Loan Corporation[b] | | Federal Security Agency[c] | | Prencinradio, Inc.[d] | | Puerto Rico Reconstruction Adm.[e] |
YEAR	Vol.	Outst.	Vol.	Outst.	Vol.	Outst.	Vol.	Outst.	Outst.
1934	$139	f							..
1935	205	f							
1936	344	$ 179							$1,955
1937	1,076	849	$ 7,571	$ 5,907					3,990
1938	1,461	2,091	2,982	6,932					4,598
1939	1,073	2,624	14,976	19,302					4,142
1940	665	2,648	5,444	20,905					4,216
1941	619	2,788	2,595	16,290					4,281
1942	775	2,700	1,108	6,876	$ 652	$ 652			4,165
1943	875	2,569	603	2,677	2,468	3,125	$114	f	5,977
1944	1,011	5,879	848	1,735	209	3,044	97	f	6,708
1945	1,019	5,576	188			2,698	26	$119	6,037
1946	1,381	5,808				2,273	10	76	5,588
1947	2,214	6,132				1,871		25	5,418
1948	1,907	6,952				1,577		10	6,959
1949	2,239	7,537				1,329			7,908
1950	2,973	9,984				1,154			9,130
1951	2,568	11,197				1,018			8,878
1952	1,770	11,693				924			8,758
1953	765	11,208				837			8,098

(continued on next page)

TABLE A-31 (continued)

a Covers loans to Indians to promote industry and self-support made under yearly appropriations beginning in 1911, loans for educational purposes, as authorized under the Act of June 18, 1934, loans to Indians and Indian organizations such as tribes, credit associations, and cooperatives from a revolving fund established under the Acts of June 18, 1934 and June 28, 1936, and loans for emergency relief and rehabilitation made during 1935–1937. The volume series was estimated by linear interpolation of fiscal year data from the report of the Joint Committee on Reduction of Nonessential Federal Expenditures, *Federal Lending, 1934–1948* (S. Doc. 103, 80th Cong., 1st sess., 1947, Table 1) and from material supplied by the Bureau of Indian Affairs. Annual data on loans to promote industry are available only since 1934 and for education loans since 1939. Advances for 1911–1933 for the former totaled $5,441,000. Volume figures for emergency relief loans are also excluded for lack of annual data. Year-end outstandings are from the *Daily Statements* of, and material supplied by, the Treasury Department. For loans to promote industry and for education loans they are available only since 1944.

b Represents loans to victims of floods and other catastrophes occurring after January 1, 1936. The corporation was dissolved June 30, 1945; outstanding loan balances were transferred to the RFC and are included in the RFC miscellaneous loan series in Table A-9. Volume data, supplied by the RFC, represent annual withdrawals from funds held by the RFC for the Disaster Loan Corporation; as such they overstate somewhat the annual volume of loan disbursements. Outstandings as at year ends were supplied by the Treasury Department.

c Represents loans made by the Office of Education to students enrolled in accelerated courses during the war emergency period. In 1953 the Federal Security Agency was dissolved and its activities transferred to the Department of Health, Education, and Welfare. Volume data were estimated by linear interpolation of fiscal year data in the *Annual Reports* of the Federal Security Agency, except the 1942 figure, which was assumed to equal outstandings at December 31. Year-end outstandings are from the *Daily Statements* of, and material supplied by, the Treasury Department.

d Volume data were estimated by linear interpolation of fiscal year data from Senate Document 103 cited above. Year-end outstandings were supplied by the Treasury Department. The figures represent loans to radio stations in Uruguay and advances to Mexican motion picture producers, made through the Banco de Mexico as trustee, to finance the purchase of motion picture production equipment.

e Year-end outstandings, from the *Daily Statements* of, and material supplied by, the Treasury Department, refer to loans to farmers, farm tenants, laborers, and stockmen, and to cooperative associations and farm partnerships, for rural rehabilitation. Annual loan volume is not available. Liquidation of PRRA by February 14, 1955 was approved on August 15, 1953.

f Data not available.

TABLE A-32

Lending and Loan Guaranteeing Activity of the Department of Defense,
1942–1953

(*in thousands*)

| | VOLUME DURING YEAR | | OUTSTANDINGS AT YEAR END | |
| | *Direct Busi-* | *Business Loan* | *Direct Busi-* | *Business Loan* |
YEAR	*ness Loans*a	*Guarantees*b	*ness Loans*a	*Guarantees*b
1942	$ 124	c	$ 118	c
1943	10,603	c	9,769	c
1944	42,618	c	39,582	c
1945	5,390	c	14,526	c
1946	4,409	c	6,219	c
1947	2,292	..	5,417	c
1948	6	..	4,867	c
1949	..	..	4,451	c
1950	..	d	4,335	c
1951	8,050	$1,179,310d	11,988	$543,868
1952	7,342	2,223,924	12,599	703,338
1953	3,134	1,935,284	11,214	568,655

Compiled from material supplied by the Department of Defense and the Treasury Department.

a Covers direct loans to war contractors made by the War Department in 1943–1945, purchases of guaranteed portions of principal balances of loans guaranteed by the Navy and War Departments under Regulation V of World War II, and purchases of guaranteed portions of principal balances of loans guaranteed by the Army and Navy under Section 301 of the Defense Production Act of 1950.

b Refers to amount of commitments under loan guarantees written by the Departments of Army, Navy, and Airforce under Section 301 of the Defense Production Act of 1950. Guarantees on loans disbursed by the Reconstruction Finance Corporation are excluded, since covered in the RFC activity shown in Table A-9. Volume figures were estimated by reducing the total annual loan disbursements by yearly averages of percentage guaranteed on loans authorized.

c Data for guaranteeing activity of the Navy and War Departments under Regulation V are reported on a combined basis in Table A-30.

d The relatively small amount of activity in 1950 is included in the 1951 figure.

TABLE A-33

Loan Guaranteeing Activity of the Atomic Energy Commission, the General Services Administration, and the Department of Commerce, 1951–1953

(*in thousands*)

YEAR	BUSINESS LOAN GUARANTEES		
	*Atomic Energy Commission*a	*General Services Administration*b	*Department of Commerce*a
	VOLUME DURING YEAR		
1951	c	$157,129	$540
1952	c	111,517	383
1953	c	49,614	90
	OUTSTANDINGS AT YEAR END		
1951	$163	$ 37,374	$540
1952	512	100,470	85
1953	370	99,191	124

Volume data were supplied by General Services Administration and the Department of Commerce; outstandings, by the Treasury Department.

a Represents the amount of commitments on loans guaranteed under Section 301 of the Defense Production Act of 1950.

b Refers to amount of commitments on loans guaranteed under Section 301 of the Defense Production Act of 1950; and the amounts covered by letters of credit issued by GSA (and its predecessor, the Defense Materials Procurement Agency) as authorized under Section 303 of the Defense Production Act of 1950 to finance the overseas procurement of commodities. Excludes guarantees on Defense Production Act loans disbursed by the Reconstruction Finance Corporation, since they are included under RFC activity in Table A-9. The volume data were estimated by reducing total annual disbursements by yearly averages of percentage guaranteed on loans authorized.

c Data not available.

An Analysis of the Business Loans
of the
Reconstruction Finance Corporation,
1934-1951

PART of the research undertaken in preparing this volume was a detailed analysis of the business loans of the Reconstruction Finance Corporation. Only a few tabulations of RFC business loan data appear in the foregoing chapters, and in order that the statistics concerning this excursion of the federal government into the business credit market may be available in detail, the analysis as a whole is included here.

Objects of the Study

Of all federal lending agencies, the Reconstruction Finance Corporation had probably the most complex history. Its influence, from 1932 up to its termination in 1953 was pervasive; posed difficult problems of public policy; and drew more congressional attention than perhaps any other federal enterprise.

The business loan program was only one category of RFC activity. Begun in the early thirties as an anti-depression measure, it never reached the dimensions of the RFC programs for defense plant financing and construction, rubber and tin production, and stockpiling. Yet by its nature and continuity, the business loan program probably was the most controversial of RFC's operations.

LEADING ISSUES

Among the issues posed by RFC business lending were these: Should the federal government continuously operate an agency for the financing of private business? What functions could a federal source of business credit perform? Were there "gaps" in private finance which only a government agency could fill? If such gaps were not always present, did they emerge in time of war or deep economic depression? Was RFC needed in times of high employment as a stand-by source of credit? What effect did the program have upon the efficiency with which economic resources were utilized? Upon the vigor of private enterprise? Upon private financial institutions and markets?

A description of the business loans made by RFC during the seventeen-year period from mid-1934 through 1951 and comparisons of them, where practicable, with term loans to businesses by commercial banks will make it possible:

(1) To assess the magnitude of RFC business credit in relation to the total amount of business term credit.

(2) To compare the characteristics of businesses that borrowed money from RFC with those of businesses that were customers of private financial institutions.

(3) To compare the characteristics of RFC business loans with those of loans made by private lending agencies.

(4) To show what changes occurred in the business loans of RFC over its history.

(5) To contrast the record of repayment, default, and loss on RFC loans with that for business loans made by private institutions.

(6) To ascertain the types of RFC loans on which experience was favorable and the types that did not turn out well.

A number of questions also arise in connection with RFC's cooperation with commercial banks in lending money to business. Did "participation" loans perform a unique economic function, or did they merely transfer to a public agency risks which private banks would otherwise have borne? In particular,

(1) What types of businesses borrowed under RFC-bank participation agreements, and how did they compare with firms which borrowed directly from banks or from the RFC?

(2) How did the characteristics of participation loans compare with those of nonparticipation credits?

(3) What kind of commercial banks participated with RFC in business lending, and in what respects did banks participating frequently differ from banks which participated on only one occasion?

(4) What were the reasons for bank participation?

The importance of the policy questions involved was not diminished by the 1953 action of Congress in replacing RFC with a Small Business Administration. The basic issues remain, and a systematic analysis of RFC business loan experience can help to solve them.

SOURCES OF DATA AND METHODS OF STUDY

RFC was required by law to make monthly reports to Congress stating the name and address of each borrower and the amount of the loan authorized. For national security reasons these reports were discontinued in World War II. RFC also made quarterly and annual reports to Congress summarizing the number and amounts of loans authorized, canceled, disbursed, repaid, and outstanding. Another source of information about the Corporation's business loans are the reports of investigating committees of Congress. Supplementing published reports of RFC, these records give data on number of loans (by size and industry), loans in default, and losses. Detailed information about methods of appraising credit and servicing business loans was also assembled. Finally, the reports of the Comptroller General contain analyses of the costs of RFC business lending.

Despite all of this, comprehensive data on all RFC loans to business, giving details on the characteristics of loans and of the borrowing firms, have been lacking. To fill this gap, two special studies were undertaken by the National Bureau of Economic Research during 1952 with the cooperation of RFC. The first was a sample study of nonparticipation loans authorized by RFC through June 30, 1951 and disbursed before the end of 1951; the second, an analysis of participation loans authorized up to July 1, 1947. The account of RFC business lending which follows is based mainly on these data.

Even with comprehensive loan information, the account is not exhaustive. Being confined to a description of loans authorized or disbursed by RFC, it does not adequately describe the influence exercised by the Corporation in handling thousands of loan applications, in contacts with banks in behalf of borrowers, and in its mere existence as a "court of last resort" for business credit.

A brief review of the original purposes of Congress in granting to the Corporation powers to make direct loans to business enterprises, of subsequent alterations in those powers, and of the organization of operations precedes the analysis of loans, lending experience, and costs.

Evolution of RFC's Statutory Power to Make Business Loans

The Reconstruction Finance Corporation Act of 1932 was an antidepression measure intended to aid agriculture, commerce, and industry by strengthening the national credit structure.[1] On the assumption that the rehabilitation of banking institutions and the restoration of confidence in them would promote recovery, the lending powers of RFC were originally confined to the relief of financial institutions,[2] primarily commercial banks, insurance companies, and mortgage institutions. Direct loans to commercial and industrial firms were not contemplated.

[1] P.L. 2, 72nd Cong., January 22, 1932.
[2] The one exception was the railroad industry. For analysis of RFC activities in aid of railroads and financial institutions, see *The Reconstruction Finance Corporation, 1932–41*, by James B. Eckert (unpublished dissertation, Cornell University, 1947). See also *Fifty Billion Dollars: My Thirteen Years with the RFC (1932–1945)*, by Jesse H. Jones with Edward Angly (Macmillan, 1951), Chaps. I–XI.

By 1934 the financial crisis had been surmounted, but economic recovery was incomplete. Hearings held then by the House Committee on Banking and Currency indicated that RFC had not succeeded in helping small businesses, and a bill was introduced in the Senate designed to make the credit facilities of the Federal Reserve Banks available for industrial purposes. An amendment to the original bill extended the same power to the RFC.[3]

THE ACTS OF 1934 THROUGH 1938

The business lending activities of RFC began with the approval, in June 1934, of "An act relating to direct loans for industrial purposes by the Federal Reserve Banks, and for other purposes."[4] This authorized RFC to make loans to any industrial or commercial enterprise established before January 1, 1934. Such loans could be made by RFC alone or in cooperation with banks or other lending institutions.

The dominant purpose of the act was to maintain and increase employment by making RFC loans available to solvent business enterprises unable to obtain credit through normal channels. Loans were to be subject to such terms, conditions, and restrictions as the Board of Directors of the RFC might determine. The statute placed specific limitations upon the maturity, collateral security, and volume of loans to be made. The maximum maturity of business loans was five years; all loans were to be adequately secured; the aggregate outstanding amount was limited to $300 million and the aggregate amount for any one borrower to $500,000. The power to make loans under the act was to terminate on or before January 31, 1935. The act specifically authorized loans to the fishing and mining industries, subject to the same terms, conditions, and limitations.

Although severe limitations were imposed by the 1934 law, Congress was disappointed that a large volume of loans did not develop. In a letter to the President dated January 17, 1935, RFC chairman Jesse Jones stated that few business loans had been made because most of the businesses that needed help were unable to comply with the requirements of the law. Consequently, Congress passed on January 31, 1935, "An Act to extend the functions of the RFC for two years, and for other purposes."[5]

The original law had required that loans be adequately secured, and RFC interpreted this to mean that the current market value of collateral must be at least equal to the principal amount of a loan. The 1935 act provided merely that "loans shall be so secured as reasonably to assure repayment."

[3] *Loans to Industry*, H. Rept. 1719 to accompany S. 3487, 73rd Cong., 2nd sess., May 21, 1934.
[4] P.L. 417, 73rd Cong., June 19, 1934.
[5] P.L. 1, 74th Cong., January 31, 1935.

Secondly, whereas the 1934 statute had provided that all disbursements must be made within one year from the date of commitment, the 1935 act permitted disbursements at any time up to January 31, 1936 on commitments made before the new act. This change gave recognition to the fact that in many instances, especially in the case of receivers' loans, it was impossible to make disbursement within one year.

Thirdly, in order to avoid strain on the borrower resulting from a requirement of rapid repayment, the 1935 act provided that advances, renewals, or extensions of loans were to mature at such time as the RFC might determine, but not later than January 31, 1945. Since the previous maturity limit had been February 1, 1940, the effect was to extend the maximum maturity of RFC loans from five years to ten.

Fourth, the 1935 act struck out the provision that the aggregate of loans to any one borrower must be limited to $500,000.

The 1935 act also expanded the list of industries or operations specifically mentioned as eligible for RFC credit. Thus, it authorized loans to "any institution, now or hereafter established, financing principally the sale of electrical, plumbing, or air conditioning appliances or equipment or other appliances, both urban and rural"; and loans in the field of mining, milling, or smelting ores could be made for the development of sources of gold, silver, or tin ore as well as to producing firms.

The concern of Congress—that the direct lending powers of RFC were granted temporarily on an emergency basis to supply credit not otherwise available—was clearly indicated by the act of January 26, 1937 "to continue the functions of the RFC, and for other purposes."[6] This provided that the President might suspend any RFC lending activity when it was shown that any class of authorized borrowers had credit sufficiently available from private sources, upon fair terms and rates, to meet its legitimate demands. By that means the act intended to facilitate a withdrawal of the credit functions of the RFC during the two-year extension of its lending authority that was provided; but events moved in an unexpected direction.

Early in 1938 it became apparent that the nation was again in the throes of economic recession and a variety of corrective measures were prepared. One of these was an act, approved in April 1938, designed to liberalize the requirements relating to RFC business loans.[7] The act authorized RFC to purchase the securities and obligations of any business enterprise, thus enabling the Corporation to provide credit *and* capital when either was not otherwise available on reasonable terms and conditions from private sources. In accordance with this new provision, the collateral security requirements of the law were expanded to provide that

[6] P.L. 2, 75th Cong., January 26, 1937.
[7] P.L. 479, 75th Cong., April 13, 1938.

all purchases of securities and loans were to be of such sound value or so secured as to reasonably assure retirement of repayment. The limitation on maturities was removed and RFC authorized to set maturity dates by administrative decision.

DEFENSE LOAN POWERS IN 1940 AND THEREAFTER

The national defense and war programs brought further expansions of RFC's business lending powers. The first law relating to the wartime activities of RFC, approved in June 1940, authorized RFC to make loans to, or to purchase the capital stock of, any corporation for the purpose of developing and producing strategic and critical materials; for plant construction, expansion, and equipment; and for working capital, "to be used by the corporation in the manufacture of equipment and supplies necessary to the national defense."[8] Important nonlending functions were added: RFC was authorized to organize subsidiary corporations to produce or to aid in the production of critical materials, to purchase and lease land and other property for producing war materials, and to lease such property to private corporations.[9] All such activities were to be subject to such terms and conditions as the RFC might determine.

Although RFC had possessed authority to make loans for mineral development for some time, the acute shortage of certain critical minerals indicated that more definite legislation was needed. Accordingly, an act of September 1940 authorized the Corporation "to make loans for the development of deposits of strategic and critical minerals which, in the opinion of the Corporation, would be of value to the United States in time of war."[10] As before, loans were not to exceed $10,000,000 in the aggregate, and the total of loans to any one borrower was limited to $20,000, except that an additional $20,000 might be advanced if the borrower had expended funds previously obtained from RFC in such a manner as to justify another loan.

A further liberalization of the wartime powers of RFC occurred under an act approved in June 1941, which made a *carte blanche* extension of the emergency powers of the Corporation by authorizing *any* action which, in the opinion of the President and the Federal Loan Administrator, might

[8] P.L. 664, 76th Cong., June 25, 1940.

[9] This power was extended by P.L. 506, 77th Cong., March 27, 1942, which authorized the RFC to acquire real estate by purchase, lease, condemnation, or otherwise, in order to carry out the provisions of the law relating to the authority of subsidiary corporations created pursuant to Section 5(d) of the RFC Act as amended.

The Defense Plant Corporation, the Metals Reserve Company, the Rubber Reserve Company, and the Defense Supplies Corporation created by an act of June 25, 1940 were dissolved by a joint resolution approved June 30, 1945 (P.L. 109, 79th Cong.), and the power of the RFC to create such corporations was removed in 1947 by joint resolution (P.L. 132, 80th Cong., June 30, 1947).

[10] P.L. 784, 76th Cong., September 16, 1940.

expedite the defense program. The aggregate amount of funds authorized to be outstanding in carrying out the provision was limited to $200,000,000.[11]

Finally, the wartime role of RFC was enlarged by the passage on June 11, 1942 of "An act to mobilize the productive facilities of small business in the interests of successful prosecution of the war, and for other purposes." This authorized RFC to make loans to, to purchase the obligations of, and to subscribe to the capital stock of any business enterprise for any purpose deemed by the Corporation to be advantageous to the national defense, subject to such terms and conditions as the Corporation might determine. The act also authorized the War and Navy Departments to participate in or to guarantee any loan made by the RFC pursuant to the above provision.[12]

THE 1947 CHARTER AND THE 1948 ACT

Up to the end of World War II the business lending powers of RFC were successively widened by a series of amendments to the RFC Act. The life of the Corporation itself—originally conceived to be a temporary agency—was extended from time to time. In 1947 Congress approved a joint resolution repealing most of the existing legislation affecting RFC, and provided a new charter for the Corporation.[13] The law was designed to codify the functions of the RFC, to terminate most of its war powers, and to maintain it with greatly diminished powers as a government financial agency whose activities could be expanded should circumstances require.

As to the maturity and the collateral security of business loans the 1947 charter made no change; but in order to compel the liquidation of some outstanding loans and security holdings, the aggregate of loans, purchases, investments, and commitments authorized to be outstanding at any one time under all programs was limited to $2 billion. The requirement that loans and other commitments could be made only if private credit was not available on reasonable terms and conditions was retained; in fact, it was strongly emphasized in a House committee report that no loans or other commitment should be made unless the RFC had tangible evidence that credit was not otherwise available on reasonable terms.[14] The report also made clear that RFC should extend credit only on such terms and conditions as would not have the practical effect of making the Corporation a competitive source of business credit.

The congressional investigation that was largely responsible for these changes was still in process on June 30, 1947, the date previously set for the expiration of the Corporation. The joint resolution of 1947

11 P.L. 108, 77th Cong., June 10, 1941.
12 P.L. 603, 77th Cong., June 11, 1942.   13 P.L. 132, 80th Cong., June 30, 1947.
14 *Reconstruction Finance Corporation Act*, House Report No. 626, Committee of the Whole House on the State of the Union, 80th Cong., 1st sess., June 21, 1947.

therefore extended the succession and powers of the RFC for only one additional year. When the hearings were concluded and the final report of the investigations committee was submitted in 1948, a plenary revision of the statutes relating to the RFC was undertaken. In May 1948 a new RFC act became law.[15]

Senate debates reveal that the May 25, 1948 act was a turning point in the congressional view of RFC's business lending purposes and methods.[16] The committee on banking and currency concluded that four basic considerations should thereafter govern RFC's operations: (1) RFC should not compete with private sources of credit, (2) loans should be made only when the public interest was served thereby, (3) all lending activities should be self-sustaining as far as possible, and (4) the activities of the Corporation should be sharply curtailed in times of inflation. The committee apparently was of the opinion that the normal decline of applications in good times would automatically tend to reduce RFC's activity; it also advocated a limit on outstandings, and regular congressional review of operations. Under the 1948 act the aggregate of investments, loans, purchases, and commitments outstanding under all programs after June 30, 1947 was not to exceed $1.5 billion (later increased), and the Corporation was required to report regularly to Congress each direct loan of $100,000 or more to any one borrower, each loan in which the Corporation had a participation, and each investment of $100,000 or more in securities.

In accordance with the foregoing basic principles, the 1948 act continued the business lending powers and functions of the RFC subject to certain limitations: First, no loan or other commitment was to be made unless credit was not otherwise available on reasonable terms from private sources. Secondly, all securities or other obligations purchased by the Corporation, and all loans made by it, were to be of such sound value or so secured as to reasonably assure retirement or repayment. Thirdly, a ten-year maturity limitation was applied to loans, excepting that any loan made before July 1, 1947 might be renewed or extended in the interest of national defense or to aid in its orderly liquidation, and loans made for the purpose of construction of industrial facilities could have a maturity of ten years *plus* such additional period as might be required to complete the construction. Fourthly, in the case of deferred participation agreements, participation by the RFC was limited to 70 percent of the balance of the loan outstanding at the time of the disbursement in those cases where the total amount borrowed was $100,000, or less, and to 60 percent where the amount exceeded $100,000.

[15] P.L. 548, 80th Cong., May 25, 1948.
[16] Senate Report 974, 80th Cong., 2nd sess., March 1948. Committee on Banking and Currency, *Report on the Operations of the Reconstruction Finance Corporation* to accompany S. 2287.

Special statutory authority to make loans to particular types of business had been conferred on RFC by previous legislation, but experience had clearly shown that supplying credit on special terms resulted in extensive losses.[17] The 1948 act granted no such special authority.[18]

The capital stock of the RFC held by the U.S. Treasury was reduced to $100,000,000. Since all funds in excess of authorized capital stock and of accumulated surplus above $250,000,000 were to be paid by RFC into the Treasury, the effect was to compel RFC to pay interest thereafter on most of the funds used in conducting its operations.

In late 1950 RFC was directed to give priority under its regular lending programs to loans that would promote national defense; and in 1951 and 1952 it was given special lending powers to aid defense production.

Administration of the Business Loan Program

CENTRAL ORGANIZATION

The management of RFC was vested by law in its board of directors. For many years the Corporation functioned without a president or general manager. Jesse H. Jones served as chief executive while holding the office of Chairman of the Board of Directors (and later the office of Federal Loan Administrator) up to his resignation in 1945. The Corporation continued to operate with a five-member board of directors under a succession of chairmen up to May 1951, when, under Reorganization Plan 1 of 1951, the board of directors was replaced by an Administrator and a Loan Policy Board (responsible for basic lending policies) composed of the Secretaries of the Treasury and of Commerce, the RFC Administrator, and the RFC Deputy Administrator. The reorganization plan also established a Board of Review within the Corporation, composed of five loan examiners, to which all loan applications were referred. The Administrator could act contrary to the recommendation of the Board of

17 During the war RFC had expanded its program of assistance for mineral development purposes: many loans were not repaid.

18 On August 10, 1948, one special provision was added by P.L. 901 (80th Cong.). In order to aid in housing construction, the RFC was authorized to make loans to and purchase the obligations of any business enterprise for the purpose of providing financial assistance for the production of prefabricated houses or prefabricated housing components, or for large-scale modernized site construction. Terms, maturities, and conditions were to be such as the Corporation might determine. To the extent that the proceeds of such loans or purchases were used for the purchase of plant and equipment or machinery, the principal obligation was not to exceed 75 percent of the purchase price. The total authorized to be made available under this act was limited to $50,000,000 outstanding at any one time; and it was stipulated that no aid under the act was to be forthcoming unless it was not otherwise available on reasonable terms. As of September 7, 1950, this power was transferred to the Housing and Home Finance Agency by Reorganization Plan 23 of 1950.

Review, but only if he placed in the record a statement of his reasons for so doing.[19]

As of June 30, 1945 the activities of the Corporation were organized into the following divisions: Agency Division; Examining Division; Self-Liquidating [Loan] Division; Railroad Division; Legal Division; Treasurer's Office; Auditing Division; Statistical and Economic Division; Secretary's Office; Division of Personnel; Division of Information; Warehousing Division; Real Estate Division. During 1946 the office of Controller was established within the Corporation. It will be observed that the primary basis of RFC's internal organization was functional, the only exceptions being the divisions responsible for self-liquidating and railroad loans. One consequence of this is that the cost of administering any single program is difficult to determine.

FIELD OFFICE ORGANIZATION AND FUNCTIONS

Not long after RFC began operations in 1932, field offices or "loan agencies" were set up throughout the United States. During most of the period covered by business loan operations, RFC had 31 such agencies. So great was the volume of business, and so urgent were the loan applications, that the Board of Directors delegated to the managers of loan agencies authority to make final decisions on loans within certain limits. The extent of this delegation of authority varied from time to time, depending on the Board's view of the relative importance of policy uniformity and speed; in general, the administration after the early years and through World War II provided for a large measure of decentralization of the lending process.

As described in Senate hearings during 1947,[20] the procedure was that all business loan applications were filed initially with a loan agency. Agency managers were authorized to make direct loans up to $100,000, and participation loans up to $350,000 (provided a bank took at least a 25 percent participation) without prior Board approval. Applications recommended by the agency for decline were forwarded to Washington for a final decision.

Direct loan applications were assigned at once to an examiner. He determined the loan's eligibility (whether it would promote employment, was affected with a public interest, etc.), ascertained whether the borrower could obtain a loan through normal banking channels (by communicating with the applicant's banker), and analyzed the nature of the applicant's

[19] *Annual Report and Financial Statements*, Reconstruction Finance Corporation, 1951, p. 4.

[20] *Hearings* before a Subcommittee of the Committee on Banking and Currency, U.S. Senate, 80th Cong., 1st sess., on S. Res. 132, "A Resolution for an Inquiry into the Operation of the Reconstruction Finance Corporation and Its Subsidiaries"; Part 1, December 1947, pp. 32f., 219.

business, his managerial record and methods, his credit standing, and the security offered for the loan. The examiner's report and recommendation, if favorable, suggested terms and conditions.

The examiner's report was next reviewed by the agency review committee, composed of the senior credit examiners of the agency, and then submitted to the agency manager along with the committee's recommendations. If a loan of less than $50,000 was recommended, the agency manager could act finally, if affirmatively. If the proposed loan exceeded $50,000, it was reviewed by the agency advisory committee, consisting of experienced businessmen and bankers in the community. Agency managers were free to accept or reject the advice of the advisory committee.

A loan application that involved a larger credit than the agency office could approve, or one that was viewed negatively by the agency manager, was forwarded to Washington, along with the local examiner's report and the agency manager's recommendation. There it was assigned to another examiner, who obtained supplemental information, if necessary, and made his own report. This report, along with the entire loan file, was examined by the Washington review committee, whose chairman submitted the application finally to the RFC Board with the committee's recommendation.

Thus managers of loan agencies had final authority to act on the large majority of separate applications for direct or participation loans; and under the blanket participation program announced in March 1945[21] their powers, though subject to Board approval of the agreement with each bank, were considerable. This program provided, in effect, for an automatic guaranty by RFC of up to 75 percent of a loan made by an approved bank to a business enterprise which met the requirements of a blanket participation agreement between the bank and RFC. Each such agreement was subject to approval of the RFC Board; and with respect to each loan made under such an agreement, loan agency managers had power to approve of the reasonableness of the salaries and compensation paid to officers and key executives of the borrowing firm—a statutory requirement for all RFC direct or participation loans. As will be shown later, a very large volume of bank lending developed under such blanket participation agreements.

Appreciable divergence of lending practices among the agencies was possible, despite review in Washington of all large and all rejected loan applications. Partly because of congressional criticism, as of May 1951 RFC Administrator Symington withdrew from the loan agencies authority to approve of any loans, excepting disaster loans, and returned this authority to the Washington office. The result was a more uniform loan policy throughout the nation, but at the cost of slower processing of applications.

21 RFC Circular No. 25, *Information Regarding Blanket Participation in Loans Made by Banks to Business Enterprises*, March 1945.

Any attempt to appraise the quality of administration of the business loan program confronts the difficulty that the criteria ordinarily applicable to the management of a business enterprise were inapplicable in the case of RFC. RFC did not seek to maximize profit in any sense; nor, indeed, to realize any profit at all. It necessarily took risks which led to abnormally high ratios of losses to funds disbursed. Congress charged it with the duty of making many loans which, by their nature, were bound to end in loss. One is therefore forced to rely upon qualitative factors in judging the administration of RFC's business programs. Were its personnel able and experienced? Were its policies and procedures designed to give a searching review of the salient features of loan applications?

RFC attracted an unusually large number of experienced and competent financial men during the thirties, because alternative opportunities were limited. The wide range of financial operations undertaken by RFC during World War II also attracted men of ability.[22] During the post-World War II period, disclosures of "influence" and political favoritism in the administration of certain business loans suggest that there was some deterioration at that time in the quality of RFC personnel.

A reading of a large number of business loan files in the Corporation's hands reveals that investigations of loan applicants were characteristically conducted with thoroughness, that judgments of collateral values—though not infallible—reflected a careful weighing of the evidence, and that normally every precaution was taken to assure the repayment of sums advanced.

Characteristics of RFC Direct Business Loans

The course of RFC's business lending and loan guaranteeing activity over the full period of the Corporation's existence and including all types of programs is shown in Chart B-1, quarterly through 1950 and annually thereafter. Outstanding balances of direct loans cover those made under regular and wartime powers, and include RFC's share in immediate participation loans made with commercial banks. Commitments outstanding distinguish between two classes of deferred participations: those authorized under both regular and wartime powers where each loan was separately appraised by RFC, and those authorized under the blanket participation program that began in 1945 and continued in slightly restricted form after 1947 as the small loan participation program.

The long-term sweep of RFC business credit activity is seen in the chart as a rising trend, with commitments under deferred participations always a material fraction of the total except in the earliest years. Yet

---

[22] Although perhaps not fully representative, the list of "Some RFC Alumni Who Have Done Well" given by Jesse H. Jones is illustrative of the high caliber of personnel obtained by RFC. See *Fifty Billion Dollars* (cited in footnote 2), p. 602ff.

CHART B-1
RFC Business Lending and Loan Guaranteeing:
Amounts Outstanding Quarterly 1934–1953

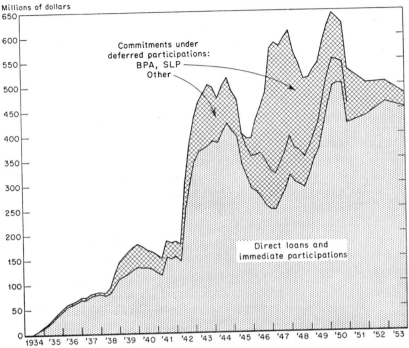

Covers loans and guarantee commitments (deferred participations) under both regular and wartime powers. Through June 30, 1947 data are from "Quarterly Reports" of the RFC; thereafter from records supplied by that agency, with adjustment of direct loans 1951–1953 to exclude outstanding railroad loans (from "Daily Statements" of the Treasury Department).

outstandings did not rise above $200 million until 1942; during the war period they rose sharply, to more than $500 million in 1944. After a brief decline, the entry of the BPA program in the reconversion period brought total outstandings to still higher levels by the end of 1946, and they remained above $500 million through 1952. Apart from the blanket participation programs the marked decline after 1944 continued until late 1946, but steep rises followed, especially in direct lending. Even at the highest, however, RFC direct loan outstandings would appear but small in comparison with commercial bank term lending: in 1946 the bank outstandings totaled $4.6 billion.[23]

For a summary of RFC activity in terms of number of loans, somewhat

[23] Duncan McC. Holthausen, "Term Lending to Business by Commercial Banks in 1946," *Federal Reserve Bulletin*, May 1947, Table 1, p. 499.

less comprehensive figures are available. From the beginning in June 1934 through mid-1951 approximately 47,000 business loans were authorized out of about 88,000 applications, totals that cover direct loans under both regular and wartime powers and also participation loans except under the BPA program. Of the 47,000, not quite half (about 23,100) were regular loans made solely by RFC. Of these, at least 5,900 were canceled, so that funds were disbursed on perhaps 17,000. To them the analysis now turns, reserving the participation programs to a later section.

The development of the business lending operations of RFC as sole lender and under peacetime laws may logically be studied in the following series of phases corresponding to strategic changes in the authority of the Corporation:

(1) *June 1934 to January 1935* marked the beginning of business lending operations, under rather restrictive statutory powers.

(2) *February 1935 to April 1938* began with the relaxation of RFC's statutory authority to omit the requirement of 100 percent collateralization of loans, to extend maximum term from 5 to 10 years, and to remove the limit of $500,000 to any one borrower.

(3) *May 1938 to May 1940* was marked by a further liberalization of RFC lending powers, notably by enabling the Corporation to purchase securities and obligations of any business.

(4) *June 1940 to February 1945*, during which RFC was empowered to make loans to or purchase securities of businesses engaged in national defense operations, without restrictions as to collateral, maturity, or use of proceeds; relatively little lending was done under the regular programs.

(5) *March 1945 to January 1947*, a period of postwar reconversion.

(6) *February 1947 to May 1948*, beginning with a new charter for RFC repealing its war powers and requiring it to have tangible evidence that a borrower could not obtain credit elsewhere.

(7) *June 1948 to June 1951*, beginning with enactment of a new RFC act specifying that RFC should not compete with private sources of credit, that loans should serve the public interest, and that activities should be curtailed in times of inflation.

Table B-1 presents estimates of the number and amount of direct business loans disbursed by RFC during each phase of the Corporation's program through 1951.[24] Over the entire seventeen-year period, the Corporation is estimated to have disbursed nearly $1.2 billion on the more than

[24] The analysis of RFC direct business loans in this chapter and the next is based on a sample survey, made by the National Bureau of Economic Research, of all such loans authorized by the RFC under its regular lending authority from the beginning of the program in June 1934 through June 1951. Besides loans to firms generally classified as manufacturing and merchandising enterprises, those to mining companies, transportation companies other than railroads, and housing

TABLE B-1

Estimated Number and Amount of RFC Direct Business Loans Disbursed 1934–1951, by Periods of the Business Lending Program

PERIOD OF LOAN AUTHORIZATION	NUMBER	AMOUNT (THOUSANDS)	PERCENTAGE DISTRIBUTION	
			Number	Amount
June 1934 to January 1935	389	$ 20,947	2.4%	1.8%
February 1935 to April 1938	1,118	87,609	7.0	7.6
May 1938 to May 1940	2,140	106,277	13.3	9.2
June 1940 to February 1945	600	67,279	3.7	5.8
March 1945 to January 1947	2,792	191,752	17.4	16.5
February 1947 to May 1948	2,397	120,256	14.9	10.4
June 1948 to June 1951	6,607	565,520	41.2	48.8
Total	16,043	$1,159,640	100.0%	100.0%

From the National Bureau of Economic Research survey of RFC direct business loans. The sample includes 2,851 loans and covers disbursements through December 1951 on loans authorized through June 30, 1951, exclusive of participation loans and national defense loans.

16,000 loans authorized through mid-1951. It is apparent that apart from the excluded national defense loans the program was of comparatively small dimensions until the postwar years 1945 and thereafter. Nearly three-quarters of the loans, by number and by amount, were made after February 1945; not far from half during the period beginning in June 1948. This acceleration shows that RFC credit to business was not used as a counter-cyclical measure after 1940. On the contrary, it expanded during a period of general economic prosperity and price inflation.

In the detailed analysis that follows, tabulations will usually cover the full seventeen-year span, with comment in the text on significant changes within the shorter periods.

CHARACTERISTICS OF THE LOANS

RFC regular business loans were predominantly in the middle size brackets, in comparison with the term loans held by commercial banks. A size classification of RFC loans made over the years 1934–1951 and of term loans made by Federal Reserve member banks in the year preceding November 20, 1946 discloses that 65 percent of the bank loans were in original amounts under $5,000, whereas only 28 percent of RFC loans

construction and manufacturing firms are included. From a total of about 17,000 net authorizations, a sample of 2,851 loans was drawn covering all loans of $500,-000 or more and a random selection of the smaller loans: roughly 10 percent of the loans of $100,000 or less, and nearly half the loans in the intermediate range. Before tabulating the results, the data for each size stratum below $500,000 were inflated by the reciprocal of the sampling ratios to obtain estimated full coverage. Tested against complete totals by region, industry, size of loan authorization, and year authorized, the estimates appeared representative of the population sampled.

were of such small amount (Table B-2).[25] Obviously, the RFC direct loan program cannot be described as filling a "gap" in the private financial markets for small term loans, because commercial banks had penetrated far more extensively into that market by 1946. The Corporation was not as well geared as were commercial banks to serve very small businesses. Higher up the loan-size scale, RFC had noticeably higher percentages of the number of its term loans to business in the $10,000 to $100,000 brackets than did commercial banks. As regards the amounts of funds disbursed, both RFC and commercial banks had nearly half their funds in loans of $1 million or over.

There were three periods, however, during which RFC shifted noticeably into smaller loans. Between May 1938 and May 1940 about 50 percent of the loans disbursed were under $10,000. Again, in 1945 and 1946 more than two-thirds of the loans, and during 1947 and up to May 1948 more than one-half, were under this amount. During mid-1948 through mid-1951, however, there was a marked shift toward loans of larger amount, possibly as a result of price inflation. Since 1935 it had consistently been true, nevertheless, that upwards of three-quarters of the funds disbursed to business by RFC represented loans of $100,000 or more.

Because of the widespread complaints of businessmen during the thirties, special interest attaches to the maturity terms of RFC loans. Commercial banks traditionally made business loans maturing in one year or less; only during the past fifteen years or so have they engaged actively in the extension of term credits. The Federal Reserve survey of the business loans held by member banks on November 20, 1946 revealed that, of an estimated 673,000 business loans aggregating $13.2 billion held by member banks at that date, 144,400 loans aggregating $4.6 billion had an original maturity in excess of one year. That is, 22 percent of the number and 34 percent of the amount of business loans of commercial banks were term loans.[26] In contrast, RFC operated almost exclusively in the field of term credit. Of its loans made during 1934–1951, less than half of one percent of the number and one percent of the amount had a term to maturity of under one year.

A comparison of the term loans made by RFC with those made by commercial banks, though inexact because of nonuniform class intervals, indicates that the RFC credit was of much longer duration. Of the term loans made by banks during the year ending November 20, 1946, no less

[25] The comparison somewhat understates the amounts disbursed by banks, because the size distribution refers to amounts outstanding in November 1946 (i.e. exclusive of amounts repaid twelve months or less after origination); but repayments within so short a period could scarcely affect the great contrast shown.

[26] Cf. Albert R. Koch, "Business Loans of Member Banks," *Federal Reserve Bulletin*, March 1947, Table 1, p. 255, and Holthausen, *op.cit.*, Table 13, p. 511.

TABLE B-2

Distributions by Size of Loan and Term to Maturity for RFC Direct Business
Loans Disbursed 1934–1951 and for Commercial Bank Term Loans to
Business Made in 1946

LOAN CHARACTERISTICS	NUMBER OF LOANS		AMOUNT OF LOANS	
	RFC 1934–1951	Member Banks 1946	RFC 1934–1951	Member Banks 1946
SIZE OF LOAN[a]				
Under $1,000	2.0%	19.7%	b	0.4%
$1,000–4,999	26.3	45.6	1.0%	3.8
5,000–9,999	14.5	13.9	1.3	3.2
10,000–24,999	21.7	10.7	4.2	5.1
25,000–49,999	13.2	4.1	5.7	4.2
50,000–99,999	12.0	2.5	9.8	5.0
100,000–499,999	8.2	2.4	19.0	16.3
500,000–999,999	1.1	0.6	9.5	12.4
1 million and over	1.0	0.5	49.5	49.8
TERM TO MATURITY[c]				
1 year	8.1%	} 45.2%	8.5%	} 18.3%
2 yrs.	11.6		7.4	
3, 4 yrs.	28.5	34.3	12.8	27.4
5–9 yrs.	43.9	17.5	41.3	47.5
10 yrs. and over	6.3	3.0	28.5	6.8
Other[d]	1.6	..	1.5	..
Total	100.0%	100.0%	100.0%	100.0%

RFC data are based on the National Bureau of Economic Research survey of RFC direct business loans exclusive of participations and national defense loans; for number and amount of loans, see Table B-1. Bank data are from a sample survey by the Board of Governors of the Federal Reserve System covering 2,000 member banks, and represent an estimated 119,900 term loans to industrial and commercial businesses made between November 1, 1945 and November 20, 1946 and still outstanding (to an estimated amount of $3.2 billion) on the latter date; see "Term Lending to Business by Commercial Banks in 1946," by Duncan McC. Holthausen, *Federal Reserve Bulletin*, May 1947, Tables 6 and 14, pp. 505 and 513.

a Size classes, for FRC loans, refer to amount authorized; for bank loans, to amount outstanding.

b Less than 0.05 percent.

c The class intervals differ for the two samples as follows:

RFC	Member Banks
7–18 mos. }	12–24 mos.
19–30	
31–54	25–60
55–114	61–120
115 and over	121 and over

d Includes loans with terms of six months or less, and a few loans payable "on demand" or whose term to maturity was unknown.

than 45 percent of the number and 18 percent of the amount had an original maturity of two years or less. Only a fifth of the commercial bank term loans, accounting for 54 percent of the total amount, had original maturities of over five years. In contrast, fully half of RFC loans, accounting for nearly 70 percent of the amount disbursed from 1934 through 1951, had original maturities of five years and over (Table B-2). Clearly, a salient distinction between RFC and commercial banking term credit has been the greater length of RFC terms.

Tabulations (not shown) of the maturity distribution of RFC loans made at different periods indicate that a smaller than usual proportion of the loans made during the war and immediate postwar periods—30 to 40 percent—had maturities of five years and over; up to 1940, and again from mid-1948 on, the proportion ranged from about half to three-quarters. As to amount, the longer-term loans consistently accounted for more than half of RFC credit disbursed. In fact, from 1935 through 1946, more than 80 percent of the credit was for terms of five years or more; and in 1945 and 1946 nearly three-fourths of the amount advanced was for ten years or more. The record reveals more stability than change, five to nine years being the modal maturity except from 1945 to mid-1948, when about one-third of the loans were made with terms of three to four years.

RFC was required by statute to lend money in support of employment and production, an injunction that was broadly interpreted to mean that it could lend to prevent reductions in production and employment. This made it possible to approve loans to refund outstanding debt. However, the principal use of loans by borrowers was to augment working capital: just under 34 percent of the number of loans, accounting for 38 percent of the amount of credit disbursed, were of this type (Table B-3). Re-

TABLE B-3

Distribution by Borrower's Use of Proceeds, for RFC Direct
Business Loans Disbursed 1934–1951

Principal Use of Proceeds	Number	Amount Disbursed
Construction of plant	11.0%	11.8%
Purchase of equipment	27.5	12.4
Repayment or retirement of debt	21.2	35.5
Addition to working capital	33.9	38.4
Purchase of land and buildings	3.6	0.8
Purchase of existing business	2.6	0.9
Not available	0.2	0.2
Total	100.0%	100.0%

From the National Bureal of Economic Research survey of RFC direct business loans exclusive of participations and national defense loans; for number and amount of loans, see Table B-1.

payment of outstanding loans, federal taxes, trade debt, and other obligations was the principal use of 21 percent of the loans, accounting for 36 percent of the amount of credit disbursed. Another frequent principal purpose of RFC loans was to purchase machinery and equipment, this being the dominant motive behind 28 percent of the number and 12 percent of the amount of credit. These three principal purposes jointly accounted for 83 percent of the number and 86 percent of the amount of funds disbursed by RFC. Construction of plant, purchase of business assets, and purchase of existing enterprises were comparatively unimportant as principal uses of RFC funds, although they may have constituted secondary uses in many loan transactions.

An analysis of the term loans to business firms held by a sample of commercial banks about June 30, 1941 indicates that retirement of outstanding obligations, increase of working capital, and purchase of machinery and equipment have also been the dominant uses of commercial bank term credit.[27] Apparently, businesses have used RFC credit for about the same purposes as they have used bank term loans.

Older, established enterprises tended to use the proceeds of RFC loans predominantly to augment their working capital, whereas new and recently established firms tended to use the funds primarily to purchase machinery and equipment. This is an interesting divergence, which may help to explain the comparative default and loss experience of RFC in its loans to enterprises of various ages, to which reference is made subsequently.

CHARACTERISTICS OF THE BORROWING BUSINESSES

We may now turn to the characteristics of RFC's borrowing enterprises, especially their size, age, industry, and region.

Table B-4 presents percentage distributions by size of borrowing business for RFC loans disbursed during 1934–1951. Table B-5 compares that information with a similar distribution for business term loans held by Federal Reserve member banks late in 1946. It is apparent that nearly three-quarters of the number of bank term credits went to businesses with assets of under $50,000, whereas only about half of the RFC loans went to such small firms. At the other end of the scale, a considerably higher proportion of the amount of bank term loans than of RFC loans went to firms with assets of $5 million or more. Evidently, RFC found the market for its credit services to business relatively largest among the medium-sized firms, with assets between $50,000 and $5 million. The notion that RFC mainly provided credit to "small business" is clearly without foundation in the comparative sense; for although RFC did extend credit to many

27 Neil H. Jacoby and R. J. Saulnier, *Term Lending to Business* (National Bureau of Economic Research, Financial Research Program, 1942), pp. 51f.

TABLE B-4

Business Size Distribution
of RFC Direct Business Loans Disbursed 1934–1951

Size of Business[a]	Number	Amount Disbursed
Less than $5,000	7.2%	0.3%
$5,000–24,999	18.7	1.5
25,000–49,999	14.2	2.3
50,000–99,999	13.0	4.2
100,000–249,999	13.0	8.8
250,000–499,999	7.4	7.2
500,000–749,999	3.1	5.7
750,000–999,999	1.5	4.0
1–4.9 million	3.2	19.7
5–49.9 million	0.8	18.5
50 million and over	0.1	11.8
Not available	17.7	16.0
Total	100.0%	100.0%

From the National Bureau of Economic Research survey of RFC direct business loans exclusive of participations and national defense loans; for number and amount of loans, see Table B-1.

[a] Based on total assets of borrowers at time of loan application.

TABLE B-5

Business Size Distributions of RFC Direct Business Loans Disbursed
1934–1951 and Commercial Bank Term Loans to
Business Outstanding November 20, 1946

	NUMBER OF LOANS		AMOUNT OF LOANS	
SIZE OF BUSINESS (TOTAL ASSETS)	Made by RFC[a] 1934–1951	Held by Member Banks,[a] 1946	Made by RFC[a] 1934–1951	Held by Member Banks,[a] 1946
Under $50,000	48.7%	74.0%	4.9%	7.9%
$50,000–249,999	31.6	17.1	15.5	8.6
250,000–749,999	12.8	3.7	15.4	5.3
750,000–4,999,999	5.8	2.2	28.2	11.6
5,000,000 and over	1.1	3.0	36.0	66.6
Total	100.0%	100.0%	100.0%	100.0%

RFC data are from the National Bureau of Economic Research survey of RFC direct business loans exclusive of participations and national defense loans; for number and amount of loans, see Table B-1. The underlying bank data are estimates from a nationwide survey of 2,000 member banks and cover 144,400 term loans to commercial and industrial businesses, totaling $4.6 billion, that were outstanding November 20, 1946; see "Term Lending to Business by Commercial Banks in 1946," by Duncan McC. Holthausen, *Federal Reserve Bulletin*, May 1947, Table 7, p. 506.

[a] Excludes loans unclassified by business size of borrower.

small firms with assets under $50,000, the concentration of commercial bank term loans in that field was much greater, both in number and amount.[28]

As its business loan program progressed, the percentages of RFC loans made to small and medium-sized borrowers combined were quite stable; but the proportion of loans to the smaller firms of that group increased. Firms with assets between $50,000 and $1 million received about three times as many loans, up to 1938, as did smaller firms; but from May 1938 through May 1948 the greater number went to the small firms, after which the situation again reversed. In amount, the small firms' share never exceeded 6 percent, and the principal shift for the other size groups was a greatly increased share for large firms during the war— June 1940 through February 1945—perhaps because smaller borrowers were being served through the defense loans of RFC, which are not included among the loans analyzed here.

As to age of borrowing firm: Only one-seventh of the business loans made by the RFC from 1934 to mid-1951 were for financing the establishment of new business ventures (Table B-6). The proportion varied markedly within the period. Relatively few loans to establish new businesses were made up to World War II; from June 1940 through February 1945, such loans formed only 6 percent of the small number of nondefense loans covered by the sample; but during 1945 and 1946 nearly half the loans went to businesses just starting. In amount such loans were never an important part of the total, even in 1945 and 1946 ac-

TABLE B-6

Distribution by Year Borrowing Firm Was Established, for
RFC Direct Business Loans Disbursed 1934–1951

Year Borrower Established	Number	Amount Disbursed
Before 1931	25.2%	40.2%
1931–1942	20.2	31.6
1943–1949	36.3	24.5
1950–1951	2.3	1.1
Newly forming at time of loan	14.3	1.5
Not available	1.7	1.1
Total	100.0%	100.0%

From the National Bureau of Economic Research survey of RFC direct business loans exclusive of participations and national defense loans; for number and amount of loans, see Table B-1.

[28] Nearly a fifth of bank term loans to businesses with total assets under $50,000 are unsecured, "character" loans, a type of loan RFC was forbidden to make.

counting for less than 4 percent. As to the proportion going to new businesses in a broader sense—that is, to firms organized within three years or less before date of loan as well as to newly forming ventures— Table B-9, below, gives information covering the full period. About 36 percent of RFC direct loans, accounting for 11 percent of the amount disbursed, went to such firms. Unfortunately, these data are not commensurable with the available information on commercial bank term loans.[29]

Taking the period 1934–1951 as a whole, the conclusion is inescapable that RFC business loans were heavily concentrated in the manufacturing segment of business (Table B-7). Nearly two-thirds of operating businesses in the American economy in 1946 were in retail trade (43 percent of the total) and service (21 percent—mostly small ventures not generally using institutional credit. Nevertheless, over half of the business term loans held by Federal Reserve member banks in November 1946 had been made to those groups (retail trade, 37 percent; services, 17 percent). Of RFC business loans made during 1934–1951 only three-tenths went to the retail and service groups (about 15 percent each). On the other hand, manufacturing firms, which comprised less than 10 percent of the business population and were accountable for about 15 percent of the business term loans outstanding in commercial banks in 1946, received about 45 percent of RFC business loans made through mid-1951.

In dollar amount the contrasts are equally striking, with retail and service firms accounting for larger shares of bank outstandings than of RFC loans made, and with three-quarters of RFC credit extended to manufacturing firms, as against somewhat more than half of the bank outstandings. Even more striking is the heavy concentration of RFC credit in the metals group of manufacturing firms. Two out of every five dollars advanced to business by RFC went to that group; but of the amount of bank holdings, only about one-sixth was owed by manufacturers in the metals industry. Presumably such firms were particularly subject to business cycle fluctuations and often found it comparatively difficult to obtain credit from private sources. Also notable are the relatively heavier concentrations of bank holdings in the groups including petroleum, coal, chemicals, rubber, and transportation, communications, utilities; and of RFC credit in the textiles, apparel, leather group and in miscellaneous manufacturing—lumber, stone, clay, glass, paper and printing, etc.

In all subperiods, metals and machinery producers were important among RFC borrowers. Through May 1938 they received about one-fourth of the loans and three-tenths of the amount disbursed. Thereafter only about a seventh of the loans went to the metals industry, but its share

[29] Of member bank term loans outstanding November 20, 1946, 44 percent of the number and 9 percent of the amount were obligations of firms three years old or less on that date (Holthausen, op.cit., Table 4, p. 504).

Industry Distributions of RFC Direct Business Loans Disbursed
1934–1951, of Commercial Bank Business Term Loans Outstanding in 1946,
and of All Operating Businesses in 1946

		NUMBER OF LOANS		AMOUNT OF LOANS	
INDUSTRY	NUMBER OF OPERATING BUSINESSES SEPT. 1946	Made by RFC 1934–1951	Held by Member Banks Nov. 1946	Made by RFC 1934–1951	Held by Member Banks Nov. 1946
Total manufacturing and mining[a]	9.4%	48.0%	14.6%	76.2%	52.0%
Food, liquor, and tobacco	1.0	8.2	1.8	6.5	8.6
Textiles, apparel, and leather	1.3	5.4	1.0	7.9	2.2
Metals and metal products[b]	1.8	13.8	4.2	40.3	15.6
Petroleum, coal, chemicals and rubber	0.8	3.0	1.6	5.6	16.6
Other[c]	4.5	17.6	5.9	15.9	9.0
Retail trade	43.4	15.5	37.3	2.8	9.0
Wholesale trade	5.0	4.6	6.8	1.4	4.9
Construction	7.0	6.3	5.3	3.0	1.4
Transportation, communications, and public utilities[d]	4.6	8.3	11.7	8.1	21.1
Services	21.4	14.6	16.7	3.0	5.1
Finance, insurance, and real estate[e]	9.2	0.5	0.2	5.1	1.6
All other[f]	g	2.1	7.4	0.4	4.9
Total	100.0%	100.0%	100.0%	100.0%	100.0%

Bank data are from Table 2 of "Term Lending to Business by Commercial Banks in 1946," by Duncan McC. Holthausen, *Federal Reserve Bulletin*, May 1947, p. 502. The underlying figures—144,400 loans totaling $4.6 billion—are estimates of outstanding term loans of all member banks to commercial and industrial businesses on November 20, 1946 and were developed from a nationwide sample survey of business loans held by almost 2,000 member banks.

RFC data are based on the National Bureau of Economic Research survey of RFC direct business loans exclusive of participations and national defense loans; for number and amount of loans, see Table B-1.

Data for the business population cover all firms outside of agriculture, forestry, fishing, and the professional services which were in operation on September 30, 1946 and are from the *Survey of Current Business* (Department of Commerce), June 1949, p. 21. A firm is defined as a business organization under one management and includes self-employed persons provided they have one or more employees or an established place of business.

a Mining companies represent just under one percent of all business firms in operation in late 1946, and among RFC borrowers account for only 3 percent of both the number and amount of loans disbursed. A breakdown of the combined total owed to banks by manufacturing and mining firms is not available.

b Besides metal mining the series for all operating businesses includes coal mining companies, but these two types combined formed less than 0.3 percent of the business population. Metal mining firms obtained under one percent of both the number and amount of loans made by the RFC.

c Covers lumber and lumber products; paper and allied products or industries, such as printing; stone, clay, and glass products (including nonmetallic mining or quarrying), and other miscellaneous manufactured products.

d Data for the RFC exclude railroads.

e For member banks, includes only sales finance companies.

f For the RFC, covers farming and fishing; for member banks, includes forestry, fishing, and real estate as well as a few cases for which type of business was unknown.

g Not covered in the Department of Commerce estimates of the business population.

of the funds did not diminish except briefly, and increased to 45 percent during 1945–1951; in the reconversion years, 1945 and 1946, such firms received over 70 percent of RFC disbursements. Manufacturers of textiles, apparel, and leather goods, a group which in the mid-thirties received about a fifth of the number and amount of loans, had a steadily decreasing share thereafter—only about one-twentieth during 1945–1951. Producers of lumber, furniture, paper, stone, clay, and glass received about a third of the amount disbursed up to mid-1938 and a fourth of the number of loans until 1944, but then their share declined, to roughly one-seventh of the number and amount of loans made in 1945–1951. In the war period, transportation, communications, and public utility firms were heavy borrowers, judging by the nondefense loans covered here, receiving about a tenth of the loans and 37 percent of the funds disbursed. Retail and service enterprises, inconspicuous among RFC borrowers in the early years, became more important after the thirties as to number of loans, so much that during 1945–1951 their share equaled that of all manufacturers combined, roughly one-third of all loans; presumably many of these retail and service credits were in aid of small businesses owned by veterans, for in amount they were less than a tenth of the total. Similar ventures in local trucking may explain the high frequency and small average amount of loans to transportation firms during 1945 and 1946.

Table B-8, comparing the distribution of RFC loans by location of the borrowing firm with the distribution of all operating businesses, affords an indication of the direction in which RFC affected the regional flow of credit. It is clear that firms in highly industrialized states—California and the Middle Atlantic and East North Central groups—received a relatively small share of RFC loans: only about 25 percent, whereas they included more than 50 percent of the nation's business population in 1948. Conversely, relatively large numbers of RFC loans were made in states whose business population was small, for instance in the southern and far western sections of the country. Firms in Texas obtained nearly 14 percent of all RFC loans, although only 5 percent of the nation's business firms were located there. Oklahoma, Arkansas, Tennessee, Georgia, and Florida show similar disparities. For Washington and Oregon, too, the percentage share of RFC loans was about three times their share of the business population. Altogether, the states mentioned accounted for nearly half of all RFC loans, but for only about 15 percent of the business population.

The differences in the regional distribution of public and private loans probably reflect a somewhat lesser sufficiency of private banking facilities, at least in places of smaller population, in the areas where RFC was relatively most active, and some tendency for these areas to have a more

TABLE B-8

Geographic Distribution of RFC Direct Business Loans
Disbursed 1934–1951, of Business Loans Held by Commercial
Banks in 1941 and 1951, and of All Operating Businesses in 1948

REGION AND STATE	OPERATING FIRMS IN CONTINENTAL U.S., 1948a	RFC LOANS, 1934–1951 Number	RFC LOANS, 1934–1951 Amount	OUTSTANDINGS ON COMMERCIAL BANK LOANS June 30, 1951	OUTSTANDINGS ON COMMERCIAL BANK LOANS Dec. 31, 1941
New England	6.91%	3.61%	5.78%	6.06%	6.94%
Maine	0.74	0.11	0.61	0.28	0.30
New Hampshire	0.44	0.19	0.14	0.17	0.16
Vermont	0.28	0.14	0.11	0.09	0.14
Massachusetts	3.44	2.20	3.19	4.17	4.16
Rhode Island	0.55	0.12	0.10	0.51	0.47
Connecticut	1.46	0.85	1.63	0.84	0.71
Middle Atlantic	22.86	10.17	18.44	41.82	43.91
New York	13.07	5.27	9.93	32.86	35.10
New Jersey	3.61	1.56	3.22	1.64	1.62
Pennsylvania	6.18	3.34	5.29	7.32	7.19
East North Central	20.66	10.30	21.19	16.42	17.85
Ohio	4.91	2.19	4.92	3.54	3.79
Indiana	2.50	1.18	1.29	1.03	1.02
Illinois	6.75	2.64	3.28	8.67	9.86
Michigan	4.00	3.45	10.47	1.91	1.78
Wisconsin	2.50	0.85	1.23	1.27	1.40
West North Central	9.91	5.58	3.71	6.33	6.48
Minnesota	2.01	1.13	0.42	1.53	1.63
Iowa	1.92	0.54	0.50	0.74	0.78
Missouri	2.77	1.94	2.06	2.75	3.02
North Dakota	0.37	0.33	0.24	0.09	0.08
South Dakota	0.44	0.19	0.02	0.12	0.08
Nebraska	0.97	0.83	0.28	0.52	0.44
Kansas	1.43	0.62	0.19	0.58	0.45
South Atlantic	11.07	15.13	13.55	6.14	6.47
Delaware	0.23	0.06	0.07	0.27	0.28
Maryland	1.27	1.16	5.08	0.57	0.75
District of Columbia	0.58	0.06	0.29	0.57	0.48
Virginia	1.66	0.70	1.13	0.92	1.05
West Virginia	0.96	0.22	0.22	0.25	0.37
North Carolina	1.78	1.18	1.20	1.16	1.00
South Carolina	0.88	0.27	0.28	0.30	0.32
Georgia	1.62	5.11	2.58	1.29	1.39
Florida	2.09	6.37	2.69	0.81	0.83
East South Central	4.97%	10.52%	4.98%	2.85%	2.97%
Kentucky	1.33	2.24	0.84	0.70	0.86
Tennessee	1.50	4.54	2.40	1.29	1.30
Alabama	1.33	2.77	1.08	0.59	0.62
Mississippi	0.81	0.97	0.66	0.27	0.19

(*continued on next page*)

TABLE B-8 (continued)

REGION AND STATE	OPERATING FIRMS IN CONTINENTAL U.S., 1948a	RFC LOANS, 1934–1951		OUTSTANDINGS ON COMMERCIAL BANK LOANS	
		Number	Amount	June 30, 1951	Dec. 31, 1941
West South Central	8.78	23.54	9.01	7.49	5.68
Arkansas	1.00	3.97	1.53	0.24	0.21
Louisiana	1.23	0.83	0.40	0.95	1.05
Oklahoma	1.38	4.83	0.95	0.98	0.97
Texas	5.17	13.91	6.13	5.32	3.45
Mountain	3.40	6.55	2.16	1.62	1.17
Montana	0.46	1.08	0.35	0.14	0.10
Idaho	0.39	1.18	0.33	0.18	0.10
Wyoming	0.21	0.14	0.05	0.08	0.05
Colorado	0.92	2.39	0.83	0.51	0.43
New Mexico	0.40	0.61	0.26	0.17	0.09
Arizona	0.48	0.33	0.07	0.23	0.12
Utah	0.39	0.59	0.22	0.27	0.25
Nevada	0.15	0.23	0.05	0.04	0.03
Pacific	11.46	13.69	20.50	10.71	8.52
Washington	1.71	6.50	2.51	1.38	1.39
Oregon	1.21	3.68	2.19	0.89	0.61
California	8.54	3.51	15.80	8.44	6.52
Possessions	..	0.91	0.68	0.56	0.01
Total	100.00%	100.00%	100.00%	100.00%	100.00%

RFC data are from the National Bureau of Economic Research survey of RFC direct business loans exclusive of participations and national defense loans; for number and amount of loans, see Table B-1. Bank series, which refer to commercial and industrial loans held by insured commercial banks at the end of 1941 and by all operating banks in mid-1951, were computed from data in *Assets and Liabilities of Operating Insured Banks* (Federal Deposit Insurance Corporation), December 31, 1941, Report No. 16, pp. 4–28, and *Assets, Liabilities, and Capital Accounts . . . Commercial and Mutual Savings Banks, id.,* June 30, 1951, Report No. 35, p. 8. Numbers of business firms in operation in March 1948 are from *Survey of Current Business,* December 1949, Table 6, p. 14.

proportionate share of new firms and of firms in new industries. Whatever, the reason, relatively large numbers of RFC loans were made in capital deficit areas, and relatively small numbers in areas of capital surplus.

The amounts of RFC credit advanced to businesses in the different states over the period 1934–1951 may also be compared, in Table B-8, with the amounts of commercial and industrial loans held by banks at mid-1951 and at the end of 1941. It appears that the regional pull of RFC loan disbursements was similar to that noted above in terms of the number of firms aided, though in a few states differences between public and private lending are traceable to a few very large RFC loans. Thus the number of California firms receiving RFC aid was, as noted previously, disproportionately small, but those firms received nearly 16 percent of RFC credit, whereas banks in California held only 8 percent of the national total of commercial and industrial loans in mid-1951. The various loans to Henry Kaiser enterprises centered in this state no doubt explain the disparity. Similarly, the loan to the Kaiser-Fraser Company in Michigan helps explain why that state received 10 percent of all RFC credit and yet had not quite 2 percent of commercial and industrial loans held by banks in mid-1951.

Up to mid-1938 firms in the Middle Atlantic region obtained about three-tenths of the number and one-fourth the amount of loans, and together with the East North Central states accounted for about half of the RFC credit totals. After 1938, firms in more recently industrializing regions—notably the East South Central, West South Central, and Pacific areas—tended to obtain increasing shares. Because these were areas of rapid economic growth, it may be inferred that RFC tended, through time, to engage in venture financing in regions where the capital demand was high in relation to supply and investment opportunities were comparatively large. It is notable that over the entire seventeen-year period, nearly 24 percent of the number of loans were made in the West South Central area (mainly Texas), aggregating only 9 percent of the amount disbursed in the nation. Evidently a comparatively large number of smaller-than-average loans were made in this area. The Pacific area obtained 14 percent of the number and about 20 percent of the amount of loans disbursed—also larger figures than the relative economic importance of the region would suggest.

The majority of firms that borrowed from RFC—probably not less than seven out of every ten—received only one loan. But 20 percent of all RFC loans during the full period 1934–1951 went to repeat borrowers, and these repeat loans were of very large size, accounting for more than half of the total amount disbursed. During the period June 1940 through February 1945 (a period of few loans, in the present sample, because those made under wartime powers are excluded) the proportion of repeat loans rose to 38 percent by number and 64 percent by amount. In short, a substantial part of the RFC credit volume was generated by firms which had used such aid before. In some cases the borrowing firm had not been financially rehabilitated by the first loan and remained unable to raise credit from private sources. In other cases, the firm's credit requirements increased after the first loan, and RFC increased the size of its commitment by a new loan.

FINANCIAL STRENGTH AND CREDIT RATINGS OF RFC BORROWERS

Under its regular programs RFC had authority to lend to business firms only when they were unable to procure credit on reasonable terms

445

from customary sources, and the most frequent reason why businesses are unable to obtain funds from commercial banks is that they lack the requisite financial strength. Special interest therefore attaches to a study of the creditworthiness of RFC borrowers. In the present investigation creditworthiness was measured by trends in sales, in net income, in net worth, and in the current ratios of borrowing firms during the three years preceding the loan authorization. Indexes for the year last preceding the negotiation of the loan were also utilized: the current ratio, the ratio of net worth to debt, and the credit rating assigned by Dun & Bradstreet.

Did RFC tend to finance firms whose sales trends during the three years prior to their loan applications were strongly upward, horizontal, or declining? Of the number of loans disbursed over the whole period 1934–1951, 23 percent were to firms with strong or moderate uptrends in sales prior to loan authorization, 20 percent were to firms with horizontal or mixed trends, and 9 percent were to firms with moderate or strong down-trends; 36 percent were to firms so recently established as to have no data for judging sales trend, and the remainder to established firms for which no data were available (Table B-9). With respect to amount, 45 percent of the credit went to businesses with horizontal or mixed sales trends, 27 percent to firms with rising sales, 12 percent to firms with falling sales, and the balance to firms for which data were lacking or inadequate.

Thus the striking feature of the record, besides the numerous loans to new and young enterprises, is the extent to which RFC funds were concentrated in financing firms with apparently stable business volumes. However, in 1934 about 30 percent of RFC credit went to depression-hit businesses with sharply declining sales. During 1935 through April 1938 over a third of both the number and amount of RFC loans went to firms with strong uptrends in sales, and very little went to firms with sales declines. During the period of war and postwar readjustment, especially the latter, a much increased fraction of the number of loans went to new firms without sales records sufficient to show trends (in fact, 69 percent during March 1945 through mid-1948). Though firms with horizontal sales trends received relatively fewer loans, as did other categories of established firms, by amount their share nevertheless increased.

The over-all distribution of RFC loans by three-year net income trend of borrower resembles that by sales trend, except that firms with sharp declines appear more important here, receiving about a tenth of the loans and a fifth of the amount (Table B-9). Numerous loans to new businesses, and a preponderance of funds going to firms with stable or mixed net income trends, stand out.

Time changes in the distribution by net income trend also resemble

446

TABLE B-9

Distributions of RFC Direct Business Loans Disbursed 1934–1951, by Trends in Borrower's Sales, Net Income, Net Worth, and Current Ratio during Three Fiscal Years Prior to Loan Authorization

NATURE OF TREND IN BORROWER'S FINANCIAL CONDITION[a]	NUMBER OF LOANS				AMOUNT DISBURSED			
	Sales	Net Income	Net Worth	Current Ratio	Sales	Net Income	Net Worth	Current Ratio
Sharply upward	18.0%	16.1%	4.6%	3.8%	22.0%	17.6%	16.3%	11.5%
Moderately upward	5.4	1.4	3.1	1.5	4.5	0.7	6.6	7.0
Horizontal or mixed	20.4	23.1	8.6	8.4	44.7	43.9	24.2	27.5
Moderately downward	5.2	1.8	3.2	2.7	4.5	1.6	7.6	5.7
Sharply downward	4.2	10.8	1.9	4.2	7.6	19.7	5.4	8.1
New businesses[b]	35.8	35.8	35.8	35.8	10.6	10.6	10.6	10.7
Records not available	11.0	10.9	42.7	43.5	6.1	5.9	29.3	29.5
Total	100.0%	100.0%	100.0%	100.0%	100.0%	100.0%	100.0%	100.0%

From the National Bureau of Economic Research survey of RFC direct business loans exclusive of participations and national defense loans; for number and amount of loans, see Table B-1.

a "Sharply" upward or downward refers to average annual expansion or contraction of 20.5 percent or more; "moderately," to expansions or contractions averaging between 5.5 and 20.5 percent. "Horizontal" refers to average annual contractions or expansions less than 5.5 percent, and the class includes movements of divergent direction.

b Includes firms newly organizing at time of loan or too young to have calculable trends.

those observed for sales trend. Until mid-1940 the percentages of both the number and amount of loans that went to firms with favorable profit trends were quite substantial: about 25 to 30 percent, even in the earliest year. During the immediate postwar period, with the greatly increased share of loans to new firms, a smaller share went to established firms; but, as in the past, firms with apparently stable profit trends received the major portion of all disbursements.

The trend of net worth measures the growth or erosion of owners' equity in an enterprise, and often reflects the profitability of the business. Besides the many loans to newly forming or young firms, loans to other firms not supplying records bulk large in the distribution by net worth trend, so that among loans to firms old enough to show trends (64 percent of the total), for only one-third (21 percent of the total) were the requisite data available (Table B-9). By amount the coverage is better, with information available for two-thirds of the credit extended to firms old enough to show trends. As to the businesses with known trends, again there was a preponderance of credit for those with stable or mixed trends over the three years preceding the loan. Also notable is the large share of credit going to firms with sharply rising net worth: over one-fourth of the amount disbursed to established firms supplying figures.

The deficiencies of the data forbid detailed comparison between subperiods, but there is reliable evidence on several points. During the thirties most of the RFC credit went to firms with stable or declining net worths. After World War II, while most of the loans went to new businesses, most of the credit went to established firms with expanding net worths. Thus during the period of postwar inflation the shift toward financing new firms was accompanied by a shift also toward growing firms.

The trend in the current ratio normally reveals whether a firm has become more or less liquid. As with net worth, current ratios were unavailable for many borrowers in addition to those too new to have calculable trends (Table B-9). Where the history is known, again the firms with stable or mixed trends are seen to have received the largest share of RFC credit. Somewhat larger proportions of the number of RFC loans went to firms with declining than with expanding current ratio trends, but they involved less credit than the loans to firms with expanding trends.

Up to about 1940, loans to firms with adverse current ratio trends bulked large in the aggregate number and amount of RFC credit. Thereafter, this group became relatively small, while loans to new firms or firms with no records became quite important—a finding that bears out the observations made previously regarding a fundamental change in the financial condition of RFC borrowers about 1940.

So far, creditworthiness has been weighed in terms of three-year trends in the borrowing firms' financial conditions. A somewhat sharper measure of financial strength is afforded by the values of the current ratio, the net worth to debt ratio, and the Dun & Bradstreet credit rating based on the borrower's financial statement for the fiscal year immediately preceding loan authorization.

Nearly half of the number of loans, involving more than half of the amount of the credit, were made to businesses whose current ratios in the last fiscal year preceding authorization were less than 2/1 (Table B-10).

TABLE B-10

Distributions of RFC Direct Business Loans Disbursed 1934–1951, by Borrower's Current Ratio, Net Worth to Debt Ratio, and Credit Rating during Fiscal Year Preceding Loan Authorization

Borrower's Financial Condition	Number	Amount
CURRENT RATIO		
Less than 1.00	22.2%	19.1%
1.00–1.49	15.4	19.1
1.50–1.99	9.0	16.1
2.00–2.99	9.7	14.5
3.00–4.99	5.7	7.5
5.00 and over	5.0	5.0
Not availablea	33.0	18.6
NET WORTH/TOTAL DEBT		
Less than 0.5	7.2%	16.5%
0.5–0.9	13.5	18.4
1.0–1.9	20.5	25.6
2.0–3.9	15.4	10.2
4.0–9.9	9.2	4.1
10 and over	4.7	3.7
Debt under $500	10.2	1.0
Negative ratiob	0.5	3.6
Not availablea	18.7	16.9
CREDIT RATING		
High	3.2%	9.7%
Good	41.3	55.4
Fair	23.0	14.0
Limited	3.7	2.2
Not availablec	28.7	18.7
Total	100.0%	100.0%

From the National Bureau of Economic Research survey of RFC direct business loans exclusive of participations and national defense loans; for number and amount of loans, see Table B-1.

a Includes firms just forming at time of loan, and other firms not supplying information.

b Liabilities in excess of assets.

c Loans to firms for which Dun & Bradstreet had credit reports but assigned no rating were included here unless the RFC file contained additional information that permitted assigning them to one of the rating classes. Also included are loans to firms for which credit reports were entirely lacking (firms just organizing, and others), and a very few loans rated "high to good," "fair to high," or "limited to fair."

Since the current ratio is an important gauge of liquidity, and private bankers usually decline to lend money to firms whose current ratio is less than 2/1, it appears that RFC did supply credit to many enterprises ordinarily unacceptable to private term lenders. Moreover, this situation appears to have obtained throughout nearly all periods of the RFC business loan program. An exception is the postwar period 1945–1948, when the proportions of loans made to businesses with subnormal current ratios fell sharply and there was an increase in the proportions of loans going to firms for which no data on current ratio were available (probably because of loans to newly organized ventures). Otherwise the distribution of borrowers according to current ratio during the last fiscal year preceding loan authorization did not change appreciably.

RFC tended to finance businesses whose indebtedness was large in relation to their equity. The ratio of net worth to debt of a business is usually taken to be a significant measure of the extent to which the firm is "trading on the equity," is exposed to the risk of default, and is worthy of additional credit. For the nation's businesses as a whole, net worth has averaged about twice total debt.[30] For the business loans of RFC over the whole seventeen-year period, about a fifth of the number, involving more than one-third of the amount, went to firms with a net worth to debt ratio of less than 1/1; 41 percent of the loans, comprising 61 percent of the credit, went to firms whose ratio was less than 2/1 (Table B-10). Clearly, RFC's borrowing clientele consisted largely of firms with more slender margins of equity than the average for all businesses. That such a large proportion of the firms borrowing from commercial banks would have subnormal ratios of net worth to debt is highly improbable. The condition held true of all periods of RFC lending to business, excepting the initial period June 1934 to January 1935, when a very strict statute resulted in few loans going to borrowers with ratios under 2/1, and the period March 1945 through 1946.

The credit ratings assigned by Dun & Bradstreet are widely used by private bankers and commercial creditors as a guide to the creditworthiness of businesses. Ratings or similar credit information were available in RFC files for about seven out of every ten loans in the sample. About 41 percent of the loans, comprising 55 percent of the amount of money disbursed, went to firms rated "good"; 23 percent of the number and 14 percent of the amount went to firms rated "fair" (Table B-10). Relatively few loans were made to borrowers with "high" credit ratings—as would be expected for a lending agency required to restrict its loans to firms unable to procure private credit. This situation appears to have obtained throughout all phases of RFC lending activity.

[30] Neil H. Jacoby and R. J. Saulnier, *Business Finance and Banking* (National Bureau of Economic Research, Financial Research Program, 1947), p. 33.

Experience on RFC Direct Business Loans

Study of the loans that fell short of contract performances during RFC's extensive lending experience, and comparisons of them with the loans that turned out well, should reveal something as to the sources of loss in business lending and may help guide business lending policies in the future. We shall consider in turn the frequency of default, of foreclosure, and of loss, and finally the extent of the losses incurred.

DELINQUENCY STATUS OF LOANS OUTSTANDING
AT THE END OF 1951

Our information on the frequency with which breach of contract in some respect was encountered by RFC is derived from the group of about 5,700 direct business loans outstanding at the end of 1951. Most of these loans were of rather recent origin and stemmed from the period of greatest RFC business lending activity. Approximately two-fifths of the number and one-half of the amount of all RFC loans made during 1934–1951 originated between June 1948 and June 1951, and such loans comprised upwards of four-fifths of the number and amount of all outstanding loans at December 31, 1951.

About 87 percent of the active loans (by amount, 90 percent) were classified by RFC as being in good standing (Table B-11). Of the 13 percent that were in distress, about one-third had become delinquent rather recently, most were "problem" loans with more serious default, and a few were "in liquidation" (that is, proceedings for termination at the lender's option were being prepared). These three groups will be

TABLE B-11

Delinquency Status of RFC Direct Business Loans
Outstanding December 31, 1951
(*dollar figures in thousands*)

| | | | PERCENTAGE DISTRIBUTION | |
| | NUMBER | AMOUNT | | |
STATUS	OF LOANS	DISBURSED	Number	Amount
In good standing	4,946	$406,923	86.8%	90.4%
Delinquent 2–6 months	242	9,185	4.2	2.0
"Problem" loans	435	27,673	7.6	6.2
Loans in liquidation	77	6,054	1.4	1.4
All loans	5,700	$449,925	100.0%	100.0%

From the National Bureau of Economic Research survey of RFC direct business loans exclusive of participations and national defense loans. Amounts cover disbursements through December 31, 1951 on loans authorized up to June 30 of that year and outstanding at year end.

combined in the analysis, without further regard to differences in degree of delinquency. It is not possible to compare the indicated quality of the RFC business loan portfolio directly with that of the business term loans held by commercial banks. However, it is known that of the total loans and discounts held by all insured commercial banks and appraised by bank examiners during the calendar year 1951, 99 percent of the amount was "not criticized" and less than 1 percent was classified as "substandard" in quality.[31] Assuming that currently delinquent loans held by RFC would surely have been classified as substandard by bank examiners, it follows that the quality of the RFC business loan portfolio was considerably lower than that of the loan and discount portfolios of commercial banks.

Surprisingly, no significant relationship appeared between the delinquency status of loans and their size, except in the over-all sense that loans in default averaged smaller than loans in good standing ($57,000 as against $82,300; Table B-11). Few loans of less than $1,000 were outstanding in 1951, as Table B-12 shows. And although there are reasons for expecting the proportion of delinquent loans to move inversely with size, the several classes above $1,000 show default ratios deviating rather moderately from the average, in an erratic pattern.

There was a decreasing frequency of delinquency for loan groups with successively longer maturities (Table B-12). The extremely high percentage of delinquency among loans maturing within a year should be regarded with some caution because of the small number of loans to judge by; but the distinct and regular improvement along the scale of increasing contract lengths is significant. A comparison of the ratios by amount with those by number shows that among loans in the two-year class it was the smaller ones that were relatively more often delinquent.

There were sharp differences in default ratios as between industry groups of RFC loans (Table B-13). The transportation, communications, and public utilities group had the highest percentage of delinquency—about one loan in five—and the status for loans to producers of consumer goods such as textiles and foods was not much better. In the groups including transportation and textile firms, delinquent loans averaged distinctly smaller than those in good standing within the same industry class. Less than average delinquency is shown for the following groups: metals and metal products; petroleum, coal, chemicals, rubber; miscellaneous manufacturing; construction; wholesale trade, and service. For the construction group, delinquent loans were of notably larger original size, on the average, than those in good standing.

Among regions, the South Atlantic states had the highest ratio of

[31] *Annual Report of the Federal Deposit Insurance Corporation*, 1951, Table 108, p. 154.

TABLE B-12

Relation of Loan Size and Term to Maturity to Proportion of
Outstanding RFC Direct Business Loans in Default

LOAN CHARACTERISTICS	RATIO OF LOANS IN DEFAULT TO ALL ACTIVE LOANS		DISTRIBUTION OF ACTIVE LOANS	
	Number	Amount	Number	Amount
AMOUNT AUTHORIZED				
Less than $500	..	..	..	..
$500–999	50.0%	50.0%	0.5%	a
1,000–4,999	11.5	8.1	13.6	0.5%
5,000–9,999	13.9	14.0	13.2	1.1
10,000–24,999	11.4	12.0	27.6	4.7
25,000–49,999	15.9	16.2	16.5	6.4
50,000–99,999	14.1	16.7	16.8	12.5
100,000–499,999	12.4	15.2	9.8	19.8
500,000–999,999	12.7	9.0	1.1	10.4
1 million and over	9.6	3.8	0.9	44.5
TERM TO MATURITY				
Less than six months	..	..	..	..
1 year	43.3%	42.3%	1.5%	1.8%
2 yrs.	18.8	1.9	4.2	6.4
3, 4 yrs.	15.7	7.9	24.9	13.3
5–9 yrs.	11.5	11.2	57.5	54.2
10 yrs. and over	9.9	6.1	11.3	24.0
Payable on demand	..	..	..	..
Not available	20.0	30.5	0.6	0.3
All loans	13.2%	9.6%	100.0%	100.0%

From the National Bureau of Economic Research survey of RFC direct business
loans exclusive of participations and national defense loans; for number and
amount of loans, see Table B-11.
a Less than 0.05 percent.

delinquent loans (17 percent), with the percentage for the East South
Central and Mountain states also worse than average. The conspicuously
low ratios are those for the West North Central and West South Central
regions.

Default ratios were about twice as large where borrowing firms used
the proceeds of loans principally to pay debt or to increase working
capital as for loans used mainly to construct or purchase plants, and were
half again as large as for loans used chiefly to purchase machinery and
equipment. Among the few outstanding loans used to purchase an existing
business delinquency was very high, about one loan in four.

The somewhat better than average record for loans to most size classes
of borrowing firms from the smallest up to the $250,000 level, and for
those to firms of unknown size (mainly, but not entirely, new ventures),
is noteworthy. Three of the size classes, however—$25,000 to $50,000
assets, $250,000 to $500,000, and one to five million—showed about one

TABLE B-13

Relation of Borrower's Industry, Region, and Use of Proceeds to Proportion of Outstanding RFC Direct Business Loans in Default

BORROWER CHARACTERISTICS	RATIO OF LOANS IN DEFAULT TO ALL ACTIVE LOANS		DISTRIBUTION OF ACTIVE LOANS	
	Number	Amount	Number	Amount
INDUSTRY				
Manufacturing and mining[a]	13.3%	8.9%	43.7%	72.6%
Food, liquor, and tobacco	17.0	18.7	10.0	8.9
Textiles, apparel, leather	16.9	4.4	3.2	5.7
Metals and metal products	11.8	6.0	12.9	34.7
Petroleum, coal, chemicals, rubber	10.6	4.2	3.2	10.1
Other[b]	11.7	15.7	14.4	13.2
Retail trade	13.9	19.0	16.9	3.7
Wholesale trade	11.2	9.4	4.8	1.9
Construction	10.0	20.1	6.2	4.0
Transportation, communications, public utilities[c]	20.4	8.4	5.8	4.6
Services	12.0	18.2	20.2	4.9
Finance, insurance, and real estate	0	0	0.4	7.8
All other[d]	15.7	21.2	1.9	0.5
REGION[e]				
New England	13.6	4.5	4.8	5.3
Middle Atlantic	12.2	10.4	7.0	17.2
East North Central	12.8	2.9	10.3	24.8
West North Central	9.4	7.8	5.6	3.0
South Atlantic	17.4	8.0	11.8	14.3
East South Central	14.0	7.4	13.7	8.4
West South Central	11.1	15.1	24.3	13.4
Mountain	15.1	41.7	6.3	2.3
Pacific	13.4	22.0	14.8	10.9
Possessions	19.2	15.5	1.4	0.4
PRINCIPAL USE OF PROCEEDS				
Construction of plant	6.6	4.9	17.0	16.3
Purchase of equipment	11.2	7.8	20.4	19.7
Retirement of debt	16.8	14.2	27.0	23.9
Addition to working capital	15.6	10.0	27.2	37.4
Purchase of land or bldgs.	6.5	2.2	6.1	1.5
Purchase of existing business	28.7	5.5	2.3	1.3
Not available	..	..	..	..
All loans	13.2%	9.6%	100.0%	100.0%

From the National Bureau of Economic Research survey of RFC direct business loans exclusive of participations and national defense loans; for number and amount of loans, see Table B-11.

[a] Mainly manufacturing.

[b] Covers lumber and lumber products; paper and allied products or industries, such as printing; stone, clay, and glass products (including nonmetallic mining or quarrying), and other miscellaneous manufactured products.

[c] Excludes railroads.

[d] Mainly fisheries and farming (fruit, poultry, truck, etc.).

[e] For states included in the regions, see Table B-8.

loan delinquent in every five, where most other groups showed about one in eight (Table B-14).

Loans to firms just organizing at time of loan had remarkably little delinquency: about one loan in twenty. Nearly 70 percent of the newly forming businesses referred to were started between mid-1948 and mid-1951, as is known by the loan dates. Thus their record may be considered alongside that of loans to another group of businesses organized at that time—firms established before date of loan but as recently as 1950 and 1951. The latter showed a higher delinquency percentage: nearly one loan in six. Taken together, the default ratios and the distribution of outstandings suggest that as a combined group the brand-new and very young firms indebted to RFC as of 1951 were fulfilling their loan contracts as frequently as older firms were, and perhaps somewhat more so, a point on which further evidence will be added.

TABLE B-14

Relation of Borrower's Asset Size, and of Year Business Established, to Proportion of Outstanding RFC Direct Business Loans in Default

BORROWER CHARACTERISTICS	RATIO OF LOANS IN DEFAULT TO ALL ACTIVE LOANS		DISTRIBUTION OF ACTIVE LOANS	
	Number	Amount	Number	Amount
TOTAL ASSETS[a]				
Less than $5,000	11.1%	3.6%	3.5%	0.1%
$5,000–24,999	12.0	8.7	15.3	1.1
25,000–49,999	17.4	22.0	18.1	3.0
50,000–99,999	11.1	14.0	17.7	5.2
100,000–249,999	12.3	11.0	17.3	11.2
250,000–499,999	20.7	19.1	8.5	9.1
500,000–999,999	11.6	19.2	3.9	8.6
1–4.9 million	18.7	11.6	2.9	21.4
5–49.9 million	4.5	2.8	0.4	14.0
50 million and over	0	0	0.1	19.3
Not available	8.1	8.4	12.3	7.0
YEAR BUSINESS ESTABLISHED				
Before 1931	14.0	6.9	15.3	34.4
1931–1942	13.6	17.6	19.7	21.3
1943–1949	13.9	7.9	50.0	39.6
1950–1951	15.9	8.5	5.8	2.6
Newly forming at time of loan	4.4	3.7	8.8	1.9
Not available	46.8	1.0	0.3	0.2
All loans	13.2%	9.6%	100.0%	100.0%

From the National Bureau of Economic Research survey of RFC direct business loans exclusive of participations and national defense loans; for number and amount of loans, see Table B-11.

a At time of loan application.

We have some evidence as to whether trends in the financial condition of borrowing firms before their applications for loans had a predictive value concerning default. The data are assembled in Table B-15.

One out of every four outstanding loans to firms with declining sales trends was delinquent, but no more than one in nine for firms that had stable or rising sales over the three years before loan authorization. A similar contrast, but considerably less marked, shows in the default ratios by net income trend. Businesses that were newly forming at time of loan authorization, together with those whose date of organization showed they were too young at time of loan to have calculable trends, had somewhat less than average delinquency—12.8 percent, as against 13.2 percent for all outstanding loans at the end of 1951. Among loans to older firms not supplying the requisite information the default ratio was higher than average: about 15 percent. In assessing such differences, it should be remembered that there was a considerable range of discretionary action open to RFC, both in classifying a loan as "in good standing" or "in default" and also in changing the status of a delinquent loan by rewriting the loan agreement; hence, the status at any given point of time is in many cases somewhat arbitrary.

Much more than with sales or profit trends, lack of information affects the figures relating the net worth and current ratio trends to delinquency status. Here, as elsewhere in Table B-15, it is observable that in almost all categories delinquent loans averaged smaller than those in good standing. But the reverse was true among loans to firms whose trend in financial condition was unknown.

In so far as the loan sample produced sufficient evidence, it appears that for RFC's comparatively high-risk portfolio the three-year trends in borrower's financial condition before loan authorization were serviceable at least in a general way as indicators of the probability of default. Similar comparisons focusing on the borrower's financial condition in the year preceding the loan, while they show, as would be expected, high default ratios for firms whose current liabilities exceeded their current assets, are otherwise unpatterned (Table B-16).

FREQUENCY OF FORECLOSURE AMONG EXTINGUISHED LOANS

From observing the default status of loans outstanding near the end of RFC's lending activity, we turn to the record of extinguished loans. It is estimated that of some 16,000 business loans on which $1,160 million were disbursed by RFC from June 1934 to the end of 1951, about 10,300 loans, involving disbursements of $710 million, had been extinguished by December 31, 1951. The overwhelming majority of them—78 percent of the number and 73 percent of the amount—were extinguished by the borrower's full repayment of principal and interest (Table B-17). Eight percent of the number and 12 percent of the amount of all loans extin-

TABLE B-15

Relation of Three-Year Trends in Borrower's Financial Condition before
Loan Authorization to Proportion of Outstanding RFC Direct
Business Loans in Default

NATURE OF TREND IN BORROWER'S FINANCIAL CONDITION a	RATIO OF LOANS IN DEFAULT TO ALL ACTIVE LOANS		DISTRIBUTION OF ACTIVE LOANS	
	Number	Amount	Number	Amount
NET SALES				
Sharply upward	11.9%	6.7%	21.3%	26.9%
Moderately upward	6.3	8.6	5.0	3.8
Horizontal or mixed	10.1	8.1	21.2	38.5
Moderately downward	24.3	16.4	5.6	4.8
Sharply downward	26.5	14.4	4.9	9.2
New business b	12.8	9.3	31.3	13.3
Not available	14.6	27.1	10.7	3.4
NET INCOME				
Sharply upward	12.2	7.5	17.1	17.6
Moderately upward	3.0	7.6	1.3	1.0
Horizontal or mixed	12.8	8.6	24.6	43.9
Moderately downward	16.3	17.3	2.4	1.3
Sharply downward	15.0	10.0	13.3	19.8
New business b	12.8	9.3	31.3	13.3
Not available	15.5	29.3	10.0	3.4
NET WORTH				
Sharply upward	11.4	4.5	5.6	25.6
Moderately upward	0	0	3.3	8.8
Horizontal or mixed	10.3	10.5	5.8	21.2
Moderately downward	13.7	9.2	1.3	3.1
Sharply downward	41.1	9.4	1.8	5.9
New business b	12.8	9.3	31.3	13.3
Not available	13.9	18.6	50.9	22.1
CURRENT RATIO				
Sharply upward	8.1	4.9	3.4	17.5
Moderately upward	9.6	0.7	1.4	15.0
Horizontal or mixed	5.4	5.8	5.1	19.7
Moderately downward	31.2	22.4	1.8	5.2
Sharply downward	16.5	13.5	3.9	6.4
New business b	12.8	9.3	31.3	13.3
Not available	13.8	18.3	53.1	22.8
All loans	13.2%	9.6%	100.0%	100.0%

From the National Bureau of Economic Research survey of RFC direct business
loans exclusive of participations and national defense loans; for number and
amount of loans, see Table B-11.

a "Strongly" upward or downward refers to average annual expansion or contraction of 20.5 percent or more; "moderately," to expansions or contractions
averaging between 5.5 and 20.5 percent. "Horizontal" refers to average annual
contractions or expansions less than 5.5 percent, and the class includes movements
of divergent direction.

b Includes firms newly organizing at time of loan or too young to have calculable
trends.

TABLE B-16

Relation of Borrower's Financial Condition at Time of Loan
Authorization to Proportion of Outstanding RFC Direct
Business Loans in Default

BORROWER'S FINANCIAL CONDITION	RATIO OF LOANS IN DEFAULT TO ALL ACTIVE LOANS		DISTRIBUTION OF ACTIVE LOANS	
	Number	Amount	Number	Amount
CURRENT RATIO				
Less than 1.00	17.8%	17.5%	30.9%	20.8%
1.00–1.49	12.0	11.4	15.8	17.8
1.50–1.99	14.5	8.6	8.2	14.1
2.00–2.99	11.9	2.0	9.6	23.5
3.00–4.99	13.9	8.0	5.4	10.9
5.00 and over	7.5	11.9	5.5	3.7
Not available[a]	9.5	9.5	24.6	9.3
NET WORTH/TOTAL DEBT				
Less than 0.5	13.8	16.2	7.8	15.6
0.5–0.9	14.8	8.6	16.8	23.1
1.0–1.9	12.5	3.2	21.9	35.9
2.0–3.9	20.1	23.5	15.5	9.4
4.0–9.9	7.5	3.3	10.5	2.9
10 and over	15.8	14.9	5.9	3.5
Debt under $500	11.7	22.2	8.2	1.1
Negative ratio[b]	27.4	18.5	0.5	1.3
Not available[a]	7.7	8.2	12.8	7.1
CREDIT RATING				
High	4.3	0.5	3.9	11.4
Good	14.0	5.0	33.6	45.5
Fair	15.2	16.9	27.2	20.5
Limited	11.9	20.5	3.3	3.8
Not available[c]	12.0	15.8	31.9	18.8
All loans	13.2%	9.6%	100.0%	100.0%

From the National Bureau of Economic Research survey of RFC direct business loans exclusive of participations and national defense loans; for number and amount of loans, see Table B-11.

[a] Includes firms just forming at time of loan, and other firms not supplying information.

[b] Liabilities in excess of assets.

[c] Loans to firms for which Dun & Bradstreet had credit reports but assigned no rating were included here unless the RFC file contained additional information that permitted assigning them to one of the rating classes. Also included are loans to firms for which credit reports were entirely lacking (firms just organizing, and others), and a very few loans rated "high to good" and "fair to good."

guished were terminated by RFC making another loan to enable the borrower to repay the debt due under a previous loan. RFC terminated 13 percent of the number and 9 percent of the amount of its business loans by foreclosing on the borrower's collateral security or otherwise

TABLE B-17

Method of Extinguishment for RFC Direct Business Loans, 1934–1951
(dollar figures in thousands)

METHOD OF EXTINGUISHMENT	NUMBER OF LOANS	AMOUNT DISBURSED	PERCENTAGE DISTRIBUTION	
			Number	Amount
Repaid in full	8,099	$514,344	78.3%	72.5%
Repaid by means of RFC refunding loan	850	88,088	8.2	12.4
Terminated by foreclosurea	1,338	60,895	13.0	8.6
Transferred to other lending institutions	56	46,388	0.5	6.5
Total	10,343	$709,715	100.0%	100.0%

From the National Bureau of Economic Research sample survey of RFC direct business loans exclusive of participations and national defense loans.
a Or by other liquidation proceedings at lender's option.

exercising its claim on the borrower's assets. The remainder was terminated by transfer to banks or to the Housing and Home Finance Agency.

The frequency measure chosen for analyzing the liquidated loans is the "foreclosure rate," here defined as the number (or amount) of loans foreclosed or otherwise liquidated at the option of RFC as a percentage of the number (or amount) of all loans disbursed during the entire period 1934–1951. Comprehensively, the estimates for loans terminated at the lender's option—1,338 in number, $60,895,000 in amount—yield foreclosure rates of 8.3 percent by number and 5.3 percent by amount. Adequate comparative data are not available on the foreclosure rates of privately made term loans to business. But it is clear that private lending agencies do not foreclose on as much as one loan of every twelve they make or one dollar in every twenty dollars loaned.

The foreclosure rates on RFC business loans were unusually high for loans up to $10,000 in amount and for loans for less than five years' term to maturity (Table B-18); within the latter group, comparison of the data by number and amount shows that among the loans of shortest contract length it was the originally larger ones that more often went into foreclosure, whereas with maturities of two to four years it was mainly the smaller loans. Foreclosure rates were high on loans to manufacturers of metal and metal products and to transportation enterprises borrowing small amounts (Table B-19). Borrowers in the East North Central and Mountain regions had high foreclosure rates by both number and amount. The relatively numerous foreclosures in the South Atlantic and West South Central regions evidently arose mainly from the smaller loans; in the West North Central states and especially in the territorial possessions, although foreclosures were relatively few, they

TABLE B-18

Foreclosure Rates on RFC Direct Business Loans, by Size of Loan
and Term to Maturity

LOAN CHARACTERISTICS	RATIO OF FORECLOSED LOANS TO ALL LOANS DISBURSED	
	Number	*Amount*
AMOUNT AUTHORIZED		
Less than $1,000	9.3%	9.1%
$1,000–4,999	12.7	14.4
5,000–9,999	11.2	10.9
10,000–24,999	5.1	5.3
25,000–49,999	6.7	6.8
50,000–99,999	5.4	5.0
100,000–499,999	5.0	5.7
500,000–999,999	4.9	4.1
1 million and over	6.4	4.8
TERM TO MATURITY		
Less than six months	5.3	45.1
1 year	9.6	21.0
2 yrs.	13.8	3.2
3, 4 yrs.	12.1	4.2
5–9 yrs.	4.4	4.1
10 yrs. and over	4.9	1.5
Payable on demand	51.6	41.5
Not available	14.6	17.1
PREVIOUS ACTION		
Repeat loan	6.7	6.4
Initial loan	8.7	3.9
All loans	8.3%	5.3%

From the National Bureau of Economic Research survey of RFC direct business loans exclusive of participations and national defense loans. Based on records of disbursements and of extinguishments through December 1951 on loans authorized from June 1934 through June 1951; see Tables B-1 and B-17 for number and amount of loans.

occurred with loans in which RFC's original investment had been larger than the average for all the extinguished loans within the region. High foreclosure rates are also found on loans to firms with assets under $25,000; to enterprises established during 1943–1949, those just organizing at time of loan application, and those on which age data were unavailable; and to businesses with a moderately downward net income trend, and firms too young to have calculable trends (Tables B-20 and B-21). Firms with a current ratio at time of loan application of less than 1.00 had high foreclosure rates, and the results for loans classified by borrower's credit rating are mixed, with a relatively bad record for firms rated "good" or "limited" at time of loan authorization (Table B-22). The over-all foreclosure rate fluctuated widely for various phases of

TABLE B-19

Industrial and Regional Differences in Foreclosure Rates
on RFC Direct Business Loans

BORROWER CHARACTERISTICS	RATIO OF FORECLOSED LOANS TO ALL LOANS DISBURSED	
	Number	*Amount*
INDUSTRY		
Manufacturing and mining[a]	7.8%	5.2%
Food, liquor, and tobacco	5.5	3.7
Textiles, apparel, and leather	6.8	6.5
Metals and metal products	9.1	7.4
Petroleum, coal, chemicals, rubber	8.7	4.4
Other[b]	7.9	5.2
Retail trade	6.9	4.0
Wholesale trade	2.0	1.4
Construction	8.1	2.4
Transportation, communications, and public utilities[c]	18.4	1.6
Services	7.9	2.9
Finance, insurance, and real estate	0	0
All other[d]	11.2	4.7
REGION[e]		
New England	4.6	2.0
Middle Atlantic	6.5	4.6
East North Central	9.5	11.6
West North Central	6.1	7.5
South Atlantic	10.4	2.6
East South Central	7.9	1.9
West South Central	9.3	4.3
Mountain	12.1	6.5
Pacific	5.5	1.6
Possessions	5.8	34.9
All loans	8.3%	5.3%

From the National Bureau of Economic Research survey of RFC direct business loans exclusive of participations and national defense loans. Based on records of disbursements and of extinguishments through December 1951 on loans authorized from June 1934 through June 1951; see Tables B-1 and B-17 for number and amount of loans.

a Mainly manufacturing; loans to mining companies form only 3 percent of the number and amount of all loans made.

b Covers lumber and lumber products; paper and allied products or industries, such as printing; stone, clay, and glass products (including nonmetallic mining or quarrying), and other miscellaneous manufactured products.

c Excludes railroads.

d Mainly fisheries and farming (fruit, poultry, truck, etc.).

e For states included in the regions, see Table B-8.

TABLE B-20

Relation of Borrower's Asset Size and of Year Business Established to Foreclosure Rates on RFC Direct Business Loans

BORROWER CHARACTERISTICS	RATIO OF FORECLOSED LOANS TO ALL LOANS DISBURSED	
	Number	Amount
TOTAL ASSETS[a]		
Less than $5,000	20.0%	27.6%
$5,000–24,999	9.9	11.3
25,000–49,999	3.6	3.5
50,000–99,999	4.7	4.4
100,000–249,999	6.5	7.3
250,000–499,999	5.0	5.6
500,000–749,999	7.5	4.9
750,000–999,999	4.9	5.1
1–4.9 million	3.0	3.7
5–49.9 million	5.1	10.5
50 million and over	0	0
Not available	12.7	3.3
YEAR BUSINESS ESTABLISHED		
Before 1931	6.3	3.1
1931–42	4.1	2.9
1943–49	8.8	10.8
1950–51	0	0
Newly forming at time of loan	16.6	13.0
Not available	21.3	22.6
All loans	8.3%	5.3%

From the National Bureau of Economic Research survey of RFC direct business loans exclusive of participations and national defense loans. Based on records of disbursements and of extinguishments through December 1951 on loans authorized from June 1934 through June 1951; see Tables B-1 and B-17 for number and amount of loans.

[a] At time of loan application.

RFC's business lending operations. Foreclosures were relatively frequent on loans made during the earlier period—June 1934 to April 1938—fell considerably with economic recovery in 1939 and with the onset of World War II; rose again after the war and during the period of postwar reconversion; and dropped during the inflationary boom of June 1948–June 1951.

FREQUENCY OF LOSS

It is estimated that 1,338 RFC business loans foreclosed or otherwise terminated at the lender's option during 1934–1951, 959 were extinguished with some loss to RFC or were still in process of settlement at the end of 1951 with loss anticipated (Table B-23). Among all loans made and extinguished during 1934–1951, those eventuating in some loss comprised

TABLE B-21

Foreclosure Rates on RFC Direct Business Loans, by Three-Year
Trends in Borrower's Financial Condition before Loan
Authorization

NATURE OF TREND IN BORROWER'S FINANCIAL CONDITIONa	RATIO OF FORECLOSED LOANS TO ALL LOANS DISBURSED	
	Number	*Amount*
SALES		
Sharply upward	3.3%	3 2%
Moderately upward	3.1	3.3
Horizontal or mixed	3.8	2.1
Moderately downward	7.3	6.8
Sharply downward	4.9	2.8
New businessb	14.2	5.4
Not available	10.2	39.0
NET INCOME		
Sharply upward	2.8	1.5
Moderately upward	3.4	4.6
Horizontal or mixed	4.7	2.9
Moderately downward	9.1	12.5
Sharply downward	3.6	2.8
New businessb	14.2	5.4
Not available	10.3	40.1
NET WORTH		
Sharply upward	1.1	0.4
Moderately upward	1.7	3.0
Horizontal or mixed	7.6	3.5
Moderately downward	9.2	4.5
Sharply downward	11.4	4.0
New businessb	14.2	5.4
Not available	4.6	10.2
CURRENT RATIO		
Sharply upward	4.8	3.0
Moderately upward	3.4	0.5
Horizontal or mixed	6.2	2.3
Moderately downward	5.1	4.9
Sharply downward	8.0	4.7
New businessb	14.2	5.4
Not available	4.7	10.2
All loans	8.3%	5.3%

From the National Bureau of Economic Research survey of RFC direct business
loans exclusive of participations and national defense loans. Foreclosure rates
are based on records of disbursements and of extinguishments through December
1951 on loans authorized from June 1934 through June 1951; see Tables B-1 and
B-17 for number and amount of loans.

a "Sharply" upward or downward refers to average annual expansion or contraction of 20.5 percent or more; "moderately," to expansions or contractions
averaging between 5.5 and 20.5 percent. "Horizontal" refers to average annual
contractions or expansions less than 5.5 percent, and the class includes movements
of divergent direction.

b Includes firms newly organizing at time of loan or too young to have calculable
trends.

TABLE B-22

Foreclosure Rates on RFC Direct Business Loans, by Borrower's Financial Condition at Time of Loan Authorization

BORROWER CHARACTERISTICS	RATIO OF FORECLOSED LOANS TO ALL LOANS DISBURSED	
	Number	*Amount*
CURRENT RATIO		
Less than 1.00	8.3%	15.8%
1.00–1.49	5.4	3.7
1.50–1.99	4.5	2.4
2.00–2.99	3.6	1.0
3.00–4.99	5.2	1.7
5.00 and over	4.9	2.7
Not available a	13.2	3.9
NET WORTH/TOTAL DEBT		
Less than 0.5	7.8	4.9
0.5–0.9	7.7	3.0
1.0–1.9	5.4	2.6
2.0–3.9	6.9	3.8
4.0–9.9	5.0	1.9
10 and over	3.3	3.2
Debt under $500	12.7	8.1
Negative ratio b	29.1	54.8
Not available a	13.4	3.4
CREDIT RATING		
High	0.4	0.4
Good	12.4	7.0
Fair	4.5	2.3
Limited	9.9	8.3
Not available c	6.3	4.5
All loans	8.3%	5.3%

From the National Bureau of Economic Research survey of RFC direct business loans exclusive of participations and national defense loans. Foreclosure rates are based on records of disbursements and of extinguishments through December 1951 on loans authorized from June 1934 through June 1951; see Tables B-1 and B-17 for number and amount of loans.

a Includes firms just forming at time of loan, and other firms not supplying information.

b Liabilities in excess of assets.

c Includes loans to firms for which Dun & Bradstreet rating or similar information was lacking, and a few loans rated "high to good" and the like.

9.3 percent of the number and 7.4 percent of the amount disbursed. These percentages illustrate the "loss-loan ratio" which will be used to compare the frequency of loss on RFC loans grouped by salient characteristics of loan and of borrower. Information is lacking for the application of such a measure to commercial bank business term loans, but it is unlikely that so high a frequency of loss would be found there as one loan in every

TABLE B-23

RFC Direct Business Loans Extinguished with
and without Loss, to December 31, 1951
(*dollar figures in thousands*)

	Number	Amount Disbursed
Extinguished with loss	959	$ 52,618
Extinguished without loss	9,384	657,097
Total	10,343	$709,715
Ratio of loss loans to all extinguished loans	9.3%	7.4%

From the National Bureau of Economic Research sample survey of RFC direct business loans exclusive of participations and national defense loans. The records cover disbursements and extinguishments through December 1951 on loans authorized from June 1934 through June 1951. Foreclosed loans in process of settlement at the end of 1951 on which loss was anticipated are classified as loss loans.

eleven that were made and extinguished. RFC had a relatively unfavorable experience with its business loans, notwithstanding that it was more patient than most private bankers in dealing with defaulting firms. However, this result is not unexpected in view of the less creditworthy group of firms with which RFC dealt.

The ratios of loss loans to total loans extinguished varied significantly among the different periods of RFC business lending activity. On loans made up to mid-1938 frequency of loss was more than average, yet only moderately so (Table B-24). The record for loans made from May 1938

TABLE B-24

Period of Lending Activity and Proportion of RFC Direct Business
Loans Extinguished with Loss

PERIOD LOAN MADE	RATIO OF LOSS LOANS TO ALL EXTINGUISHED LOANS		DISTRIBUTION OF EXTINGUISHED LOANS	
	Number	Amount	Number	Amount
June 1934–January 1935	10.7%	10.5%	3.8%	2.9%
February 1935–April 1938	9.9	9.7	10.8	12.2
May 1938–May 1940	4.1	3.7	20.7	15.0
June 1940–February 1945	1.2	0.2	5.8	9.4
March 1945–January 1947	16.6	6.8	23.8	23.2
February 1947–May 1948	13.0	6.5	18.3	10.6
June 1948–June 1951	3.3	12.1	16.8	26.7
All loans	9.3%	7.4%	100.0%	100.0%

From the National Bureau of Economic Research survey of RFC direct business loans exclusive of participations and national defense loans; for number and amount of extinguished loans, 1934–1951, see Table B-23.

through February 1945—from which our sample excludes those made under special wartime powers—shows up as very much better than average. The highest loss-loan ratio came in 1945 and 1946, with one out of every six loans extinguished having involved some loss to RFC; as is shown by comparing the ratio by amount with that by number, trouble occurred mainly with the smaller of the loans in original amount. The next years of lending, through mid-1948, brought similar results. Just the reverse is true for the three last years covered, with loss infrequent and occurring mainly with the larger of the loans. Partly the high loss frequency for the immediate postwar years resulted from the many GI business loans which turned out unfavorably. The record may also reflect variations in the rigor with which loan agreements were policed by RFC.

The proportion of loans involving loss was significantly higher for loans in the $1,000 to $10,000 range than for any other size class of loan, about one out of every nine loans of this size having been extinguished with loss, as compared with one out of eleven for loans of all sizes (Table B-25). Because small loans were ordinarily made to rela-

TABLE B-25

Relation of Loan Size and Term to Maturity to Proportion of
RFC Direct Business Loans Extinguished with Loss

LOAN CHARACTERISTICS	RATIO OF LOSS LOANS TO ALL EXTINGUISHED LOANS	
	Number	Amount
AMOUNT AUTHORIZED		
Less than $1,000	5.1%	3.7%
$1,000–4,999	10.8	12.3
5,000–9,999	12.7	12.8
10,000–24,999	7.8	7.6
25,000–49,999	7.0	7.2
50,000–99,999	6.9	6.6
100,000–499,999	7.3	7.9
500,000–999,999	5.7	5.5
1 million and over	9.6	7.4
TERM TO MATURITY		
Less than six months	5.3	45.1
1 year	7.9	21.0
2 yrs.	11.6	2.1
3, 4 yrs.	12.8	5.0
5–9 yrs.	5.2	7.1
10 yrs. and over	13.5	2.3
Payable on demand	51.6	41.5
Not available	6.4	12.2
All loans	9.3%	7.4%

From the National Bureau of Economic Research survey of RFC direct business loans exclusive of participations and national defense loans; for number and amount of extinguished loans, 1934–1951, see Table B-23.

tively small businesses, and the risks of failure for small firms were definitely larger than for medium or large firms, this result is understandable; but contrary to expectation there was no clear tendency for the loss-loan ratio to increase with original term to maturity. In fact, the highest ratios were for the relatively few loans payable on demand.

Industrially, the highest frequency of loss appears among the extinguished loans that had been made to transportation, communications, and public utility firms; and their low loss-loan ratio by amount indicates (as other information, not shown, does also) that it was principally small loans during 1945 and 1946, probably in aid of veterans' trucking businesses, that accounted for the high over-all loss frequency in that loan group. Of the four industrial divisions in which RFC made the most loans, two show higher than average frequency of loss: metal and metal products manufacturing, and services (Table B-26). Loans to retail trade and miscellaneous manufacturing firms (stone, clay, glass, lumber, paper) were also numerous, but had less than average frequency of loss. Among divisions where RFC loans were few but sufficient for measurement, two show above-average loss-loan ratios—manufacturing firms in the fuel, chemicals, and rubber field; and fishing and farming—and the others (wholesale trade and construction) show smaller than average ratios. Loans to manufacturers of consumer goods such as textiles and foods also had less than average frequency of loss. The loss-loan ratios by amount are usually lower than the ratios by number, and when higher are not extremely so; that is, loss loans averaged smaller in total amount disbursed than other extinguished loans within most industry groups as well as when compared for the sample as a whole.

Regionally, among extinguished loans the highest frequency of loss was that in the Mountain states, where one loan in seven (against a national average of one in eleven) brought some loss to RFC; next worst are the ratios for the East South Central region and the territorial possessions, roughly one loan in eight. The distinctly good records are those for the New England, Middle Atlantic, West North Central, and Pacific regions. Again, most of the ratios by amount show that loss loans averaged smaller in original size than other loans in the same group, but here the exceptions are more marked. In the territorial possessions, where the loans made averaged considerably smaller than the average size for all regions, loans on which losses occurred averaged larger in original amount than other extinguished loans. In the East North Central states, where the loans made were typically large, loss loans were also of large average size, even for that region.

Loss was relatively frequent where the major use of RFC credit was to purchase land, buildings, or equipment (Table B-27). Where borrowing firms used loan proceeds principally to construct plant or to acquire going concerns, the incidence of loss was comparatively low, roughly one

467

TABLE B-26

Industrial and Regional Differences in Proportion of RFC
Direct Business Loans Extinguished with Loss

BORROWER CHARACTERISTICS	RATIO OF LOSS LOANS TO ALL EXTINGUISHED LOANS	
	Number	Amount
INDUSTRY		
Manufacturing and mining[a]	8.8%	8.9%
Food, liquor, and tobacco	7.6	6.7
Textiles, apparel, and leather	7.2	8.3
Metals and metal products	11.4	10.3
Petroleum, coal, chemicals, and rubber	11.4	13.8
Other[b]	7.5	5.7
Retail trade	6.4	2.6
Wholesale trade	1.6	2.6
Construction	6.8	2.6
Transportation, communications, and public utilities[c]	19.2	1.5
Services	10.6	5.5
Finance, insurance, real estate	0	0
All other[d]	13.3	7.9
REGION[e]		
New England	5.6	1.4
Middle Atlantic	6.1	6.5
East North Central	9.9	20.6
West North Central	6.8	8.9
South Atlantic	10.3	2.5
East South Central	13.1	5.3
West South Central	9.2	7.6
Mountain	15.1	7.2
Pacific	6.6	1.2
Possessions	12.4	43.7
All loans	9.3%	7.4%

From the National Bureau of Economic Research survey of RFC direct business loans exclusive of participations and national defense loans; for number and amount of extinguished loans, 1934–1951, see Table B-23.

a Mainly manufacturing.

b Covers lumber and lumber products; paper and allied products or industries, such as printing; stone, clay, and glass products (including nonmetallic mining or quarrying), and other miscellaneous manufactured products.

c Excludes railroads.

d Mainly fisheries and farming (fruit, poultry, truck, etc.).

e For states included in the regions, see Table B-8.

loss loan in twenty loans extinguished; it was somewhat greater, but still below average, where the proceeds went mainly to augment working capital or to repay debt. The information-lacking group contains negligibly few loans, and the ratios by amount differ too little from those by number to occasion comment. In the breakdown of loans by the year the borrow-

TABLE B-27

Relation of Borrower's Use of Proceeds, and of Year Business
Established, to Proportion of RFC Direct Business
Loans Extinguished with Loss

BORROWER CHARACTERISTICS	RATIO OF LOSS LOANS TO ALL EXTINGUISHED LOANS	
	Number	Amount
PRINCIPAL USE OF PROCEEDS		
Construction of plant	4.3%	4.9%
Purchase of equipment	13.3	7.5
Retirement of debt	8.2	4.9
Addition to working capital	7.2	10.7
Purchase of land or buildings	16.1	14.7
Purchase of existing business	5.2	0.9
Not available	21.8	20.0
YEAR BUSINESS ESTABLISHED		
Before 1931	5.4	3.8
1931–1942	4.7	3.4
1943–1949	13.2	25.7
1950–1951	0	0
Newly forming at time of loan	14.2	16.8
Not available	16.7	22.3
All loans	9.3%	7.4%

From the National Bureau of Economic Research survey of RFC direct business loans exclusive of participations and national defense loans; for number and amount of extinguished loans, 1934–1951, see Table B-23.

ing firm was established, the notable figures are the high loss-loan ratios for businesses just organizing at time of loan, and for firms organized during 1943–1949.

In Table B-28, the data relating loss frequency to three-year trends in the borrower's sales and net income up to date of loan are the most reliable. It is shown that loans to firms too young to record trends had a high loss-loan ratio, over one loan in seven that had been extinguished. The ratio was also high for firms old enough to record trends but not supplying information. Among extinguished loans to firms with downward sales trends, about one in thirteen brought some loss, whereas for firms with stable or rising trends the ratio was better than one in twenty. Among the loans to young businesses, those on which loss was incurred averaged smaller in original size than others; but where, for other reasons, sales and profit performance were unknown, the reverse was true. Also notable are the high loss frequency where borrowers' net income trends were declining moderately, and the much lesser frequency of loss where the profit declines were sharp. The evidence provided by trends in net worth and current ratio must be regarded as unclear—with information-lacking loans (apart from those to young firms) comprising

TABLE B-28

Relation of Three-Year Trends in Borrower's Financial Condition before Loan Authorization to Proportion of RFC Direct Business Loans Extinguished with Loss

NATURE OF TREND IN BORROWER'S FINANCIAL CONDITION[a]	RATIO OF LOSS LOANS TO ALL EXTINGUISHED LOANS	
	Number	*Amount*
NET SALES		
Sharply upward	2.7%	4.1%
Moderately upward	4.6	5.0
Horizontal or mixed	4.5	2.7
Moderately downward	7.5	9.7
Sharply downward	6.5	4.6
New business[b]	15.1	8.2
Not available	11.3	46.6
NET INCOME		
Sharply upward	2.5	0.9
Moderately upward	5.0	9.9
Horizontal or mixed	5.3	4.0
Moderately downward	12.5	17.4
Sharply downward	4.1	4.2
New business[b]	15.1	8.2
Not available	11.1	47.1
NET WORTH		
Sharply upward	2.0	1.0
Moderately upward	0.3	6.2
Horizontal or mixed	6.0	4.1
Moderately downward	7.4	5.0
Sharply downward	13.4	6.1
New business[b]	15.1	8.2
Not available	5.7	12.8
CURRENT RATIO		
Sharply upward	4.7	5.4
Moderately upward	5.0	2.8
Horizontal or mixed	4.9	2.6
Moderately downward	4.4	7.4
Sharply downward	8.6	6.0
New business[b]	15.1	8.2
Not available	5.7	12.9
All loans	9.3%	7.4%

From the National Bureau of Economic Research survey of RFC direct business loans exclusive of participations and national defense loans; for number and amount of extinguished loans, 1934–1951, see Table B-23.

[a] "Sharply" upward or downward refers to average annual expansion or contraction of 20.5 percent or more; "moderately," to expansions or contractions averaging between 5.5 and 20.5 percent. "Horizontal" refers to average annual contractions or expansions less than 5.5 percent, and the class includes movements of divergent direction.

[b] Includes firms newly organizing at time of loan or too young to have calculable trends.

about 40 percent of all extinguished loans—even though the variations in the known cases are not particularly implausible.

Loss-loan ratios by indicators of the borrower's financial condition shortly before loan date show a clear-cut relationship between the current ratio and the frequency of loss (Table B-29). The proportion of loans extinguished with loss was almost one in every nine where the current ratio was less than one (a loss frequency nearly twice as high as where current assets equaled or exceeded current liabilities), and the loss loans

TABLE B-29

Relation of Borrower's Financial Condition at Time of Loan Authorization to Proportion of RFC Direct Business Loans Extinguished with Loss

BORROWER'S FINANCIAL CONDITION	RATIO OF LOSS LOANS TO ALL EXTINGUISHED LOANS	
	Number	Amount
CURRENT RATIO		
Less than 1.00	10.8%	25.0%
1.00–1.49	5.9	4.6
1.50–1.99	5.7	2.4
2.00–2.99	4.1	2.3
3.00–4.99	6.6	3.7
5.00 and over	6.5	3.5
Not available[a]	12.9	4.0
NET WORTH/TOTAL DEBT		
Less than 0.5	9.4	6.1
0.5–0.9	10.0	4.1
1.0–1.9	7.3	4.9
2.0–3.9	5.6	3.8
4.0–9.9	7.6	2.5
10 and over	2.3	4.3
Debt under $500	13.3	10.9
Negative ratio[b]	51.2	64.0
Not available[a]	12.3	3.4
CREDIT RATING		
High	0.7	0.7
Good	14.2	9.3
Fair	3.9	2.9
Limited	10.9	25.1
Not available[c]	6.0	6.0
All loans	9.3%	7.4%

From the National Bureau of Economic Research survey of RFC direct business loans exclusive of participations and national defense loans; for number and amount of extinguished loans, 1934–1951, see Table B-23.

[a] Includes firms just forming at time of loan, and other firms not supplying information.

[b] Liabilities in excess of assets.

[c] Includes loans to firms for which Dun & Bradstreet rating or similar information was lacking, and a few loans rated "high to good" and the like.

tended to average larger in original size than other loans in that group. Loss was most frequent where information on the current ratio was lacking; but in this case the trouble related more to the smaller of the loans. As regards the ratio of net worth to debt: Few loans were made to firms with liabilities in excess of assets, but they averaged exceptionally large in original amount, and over half of them brought loss. The next highest loss frequencies were those among loans where debt totaled less than $500—probably to small and new establishments—and where information was not supplied. Loans to firms whose debt exceeded their net worth had distinctly higher loss-loan ratios than where firms were less heavily indebted. The evidence from the borrower's credit rating is mixed.

EXTENT OF LOSS

On the loans made during 1934–1951 and foreclosed (or otherwise liquidated at the option of RFC) by the end of 1951, the sample indicates that losses totaled 37.5 percent of the amount originally disbursed, or about $14.6 million. This may be compared with $710 million that had been disbursed on all loans extinguished, to yield a loss ratio of about 2.1 percent. In other words, RFC lost about 2 cents and collected 98 cents of every dollar of principal originally disbursed or business loans extinguished up to December 31, 1951.

Comparable loss ratios are not reported by commercial banks for their business term loans, but the RFC figure is greatly in excess of that considered normal by private lending agencies. During 1951, all insured commercial banks reported losses, charge-offs, and transfers to reserve account of less than one-half of one percent of all loans and discounts held by them.[32] Considering that the weighted average term to maturity of these credits was probably under two years, this implies a loss ratio of under 1 percent of the amount of all loans and discounts extinguished during the year, and there is no evidence that term loans had a poorer record of loss than other commercial bank loans.

In studying the extent of loss according to different characteristics of RFC loans and borrowers, loss loans will be considered first as among other foreclosed loans, and then as among all extinguished loans and all loans made. Loss ratios on liquidated loans varied widely among industry groups of loans: for two of the divisions where our earlier materials showed that foreclosure was frequent—namely, with metal and metal products manufacturers, and for the petroleum, coal, chemicals, rubber group—losses on the foreclosed loans were very heavy (Table B-30). Regionally, the loss ratios were highest in the Middle Atlantic, Mountain, and Pacific regions, among which only the Mountain states showed high frequency of foreclosure. Relatively few loans maturing in ten years or

[32] *Annual Report of Federal Deposit Insurance Corporation*, 1951, pp. 154, 162.

TABLE B-30

Industrial and Regional Differences in Loss Rates on
Foreclosed RFC Direct Business Loans

BORROWER CHARACTERISTICS	REALIZED NET LOSS AS A PERCENTAGE OF AMOUNT DISBURSED ON FORECLOSED LOANS	DISTRIBUTION OF FORECLOSED LOANS	
		Number	*Amount*
INDUSTRY			
Manufacturing and mining[a]	40.6%	44.5%	86.8%
Food, liquor, and tobacco	35.7	5.4	7.3
Textiles, apparel, and leather	33.1	4.4	15.2
Metals and metal products	50.4	14.8	32.3
Petroleum, coal, chemicals, and rubber	61.6	3.1	7.4
Other[b]	27.3	16.8	24.6
Retail trade	6.9	12.9	3.3
Wholesale trade	22.9	1.1	0.6
Construction	18.8	6.2	2.2
Transportation, communications, and public utilities[c]	25.2	18.5	3.9
Services	16.1	14.0	2.6
Finance, insurance, real estate	..	..	..
All other[d]	26.6	2.8	0.6
REGION[e]			
New England	27.5	2.0	3.4
Middle Atlantic	47.7	8.0	25.3
East North Central	35.5	11.4	16.7
West North Central	13.6	4.1	8.4
South Atlantic	19.7	18.9	10.5
East South Central	32.4	10.1	2.8
West South Central	28.1	26.3	11.6
Mountain	73.8	9.5	4.2
Pacific	47.1	9.1	10.0
Possessions	48.3	0.6	7.1
All loans	37.5%	100.0%	100.0%

From the National Bureau of Economic Research survey of RFC direct business loans exclusive of participations and national defense loans; for number and amount of foreclosed loans, 1934–1951, see Table B-17. Foreclosed loans whose settlement record was not complete are included, with losses to December 31, 1951, excepting six large ones where substantial recoveries on collateral security were anticipated.

a Mainly manufacturing.

b Covers lumber and lumber products; paper and allied products or industries, such as printing; stone, clay, and glass products (including nonmetallic mining or quarrying), and other miscellaneous manufactured products.

c Excludes railroads.

d Mainly fisheries and farming (fruit, poultry, truck, etc.).

e For states included in the regions, see Table B-8.

more were foreclosed, but of the original investment in the loans foreclosed, half had to be written off; the same is true, but with losses not quite so heavy, for the five- through nine-year range (Table B-31). Loans of $500,000 and over had better than average records as to frequency of foreclosure, but worse than average loss records on liquidated loans, with over half of RFC's original investment lost. Similarly heavy losses were incurred on foreclosed loans in the $10,000 to $25,000 range.

As to size of borrower, heavy losses were sustained on the foreclosed loans to firms with assets of $25,000 to $50,000 and of $1 million and over (Table B-32). Both those groups had relatively low frequency of foreclosure. In the $5,000 to $25,000 range, there was above-average

TABLE B-31

Loss Rates on Foreclosed RFC Direct Business Loans,
by Size of Loan and Term to Maturity

LOAN CHARACTERISTICS	REALIZED NET LOSS AS A PERCENTAGE OF AMOUNT DISBURSED ON FORECLOSED LOANS	DISTRIBUTION OF FORECLOSED LOANS Number	Amount
AMOUNT AUTHORIZED			
Less than $1,000	20.0%	2.3%	0.1%
$1,000–4,999	16.9	40.3	4.2
5,000–9,999	33.8	19.6	4.2
10,000–24,999	57.1	13.4	6.8
25,000–49,999	14.2	10.7	11.5
50,000–99,999	32.3	7.8	14.7
100,000–499,999	35.3	5.0	32.0
500,000–999,999	61.6	0.6	11.7
1 million and over	44.8	0.3	14.8
TERM TO MATURITY			
Less than six months	..	..	..
1 year	19.7	9.2	9.6
2 yrs.	20.2	19.3	7.0
3, 4 yrs.	20.1	41.6	16.1
5–9 yrs.	43.3	23.3	50.4
10 yrs. and over	51.5	3.7	13.2
Payable on demand[a]	63.8	2.9	3.7
PREVIOUS ACTION			
Repeat loan	40.7	16.2	45.3
Initial loan	34.9	83.8	54.7
All loans	37.5%	100.0%	100.0%

From the National Bureau of Economic Research survey of RFC direct business loans exclusive of participations and national defense loans; for number and amount of foreclosed loans, 1934–1951, see Table B-17. Foreclosed loans whose settlement record was not complete are included, with losses to December 31, 1951, excepting six large ones where substantial recoveries on collateral security were anticipated.

[a] Includes loans of unknown term, on which losses were light.

frequency of foreclosure, with two-fifths of the amount of the disbursements finally written off.

Receipts on liquidated loans to businesses newly forming at time of loan, which had a poor record as to frequency of foreclosure, were better than average (Table B-32). The relatively heavy losses on foreclosed loans came with firms established during 1931–1942, comparatively few of whose loans went into foreclosure. Firms with moderately declining net income trends up to loan date, which had the worst foreclosure rate so far as trends were known, also apparently had a very poor loss record on foreclosed loans, with RFC receiving less than four dollars out of every ten originally invested.

Loss rates relating the amount of RFC losses to the total amount of extinguished loans and of all loans made are given for different classes of loan and of borrower in Tables B-33, B-34, and B-35.

Manufacturing firms, it may be recalled, received most of the credit extended by RFC, by far the largest share going to metal and metal products manufacturers (40 percent of the RFC total), and the second largest share to the miscellaneous group (lumber, paper, stone, clay, glass; 16 percent). Loans in the metals group had high foreclosure rates, high incidence of loss, and poor receipts on liquidated loans as compared to RFC's average experience. Yet their loss rate, by either of the measures shown, differed little from the over-all average (Table B-33). The explanation is that while the average size of loans to metals firms was large (about $211,000, as against an over-all average of $72,300), trouble arose mainly from the smaller of them, and the good performance of many large loans improved the loss rates for the group. Loss rates for the miscellaneous manufacturing group, also close to the over-all averages, are not surprising in view of the experience data given earlier.

The worst loss rates among industries are those for the petroleum, coal, chemicals, rubber division. Those for the textile, apparel, leather group are also high. Relatively low loss rates appear for construction, for trade, and for service; also for the transportation, communications, public utility group, notwithstanding a high frequency of distress among the smaller of the loans. Loans in the insurance, real estate, financial group were very few and brought no losses in the period covered.

Almost three-quarters of the total credit extended by RFC was concentrated in four regions: the East North Central and Pacific, each with one-fifth, and the Middle Atlantic and South Atlantic with smaller but sizable shares. Three of the four had relatively low loss rates: the East North Central, where loss-loan frequency was somewhat high and involved loans in which RFC's original investment had been large, but where receipts on liquidated loans were better than average; the Pacific, where such receipts were poor but foreclosure and loss infrequent and pertaining unusually to the smaller of the loans; and the South Atlantic,

TABLE B-32

Loss Rates on Foreclosed RFC Direct Business Loans, by Borrower's Asset Size, Year Established, Net Income Trend, and Current Ratio

BORROWER CHARACTERISTICS	REALIZED NET LOSS AS A PERCENTAGE OF AMOUNT DISBURSED ON FORECLOSED LOANS	DISTRIBUTION OF FORECLOSED LOANS Number	Amount
TOTAL ASSETS[a]			
Less than $5,000	22.4%	17.4%	2.3%
$5,000–24,999	40.7	22.4	5.0
25,000–49,999	49.5	6.2	2.4
50,000–99,999	25.1	7.3	5.5
100,000–249,999	39.6	10.2	19.4
250,000–499,999	21.5	4.5	12.2
500,000–749,999	18.1	2.8	8.3
750,000–999,999	19.5	0.9	6.0
1 million and over	44.4	1.3	23.3
Not available	58.3	27.1	15.5
YEAR BUSINESS ESTABLISHED			
Before 1931	34.7	19.1	36.6
1931–1942	46.3	9.9	27.7
1943–1949	16.2	38.1	22.1
1950–1951	..	..	..
Newly forming at time of loan	29.4	28.6	5.9
Not available	87.0	4.2	7.7
NET INCOME TREND[b]			
Sharply upward	12.1	5.5	7.6
Moderately upward	42.2	0.6	1.0
Horizontal or mixed	34.7	13.0	37.8
Moderately downward	63.7	2.0	5.8
Sharply downward	31.9	4.6	11.5
New business[c]	28.7	61.2	17.1
Not available	56.1	13.1	19.2
CURRENT RATIO[a]			
Less than 1.00	38.5	21.8	33.6
1.00–1.49	27.0	10.1	20.9
1.50–1.99	12.2	4.9	11.7
2.00–2.99	39.6	4.2	4.5
3.00–4.99	44.3	3.5	3.7
5.00 and over	82.0	3.0	4.1
Not available[d]	50.1	52.5	21.5
All loans	37.5%	100.0%	100.0%

From the National Bureau of Economic Research survey of RFC direct business loans exclusive of participations and national defense loans; for number and amount of foreclosed loans, 1934–1951, see Table B-17. Foreclosed loans whose settlement record was not complete are included, with losses to December 31, 1951, excepting six large ones where substantial recoveries on collateral security were anticipated.

a At time of loan application.

b During three fiscal years prior to loan authorization. For classification used, see Table B-28.

c Firms newly forming at time of loan or too young to have calculable trend.

d Includes firms just forming at time of loan, and other firms not supplying information.

TABLE B-33

Loss Rates on RFC Direct Business Loans Made, and on Extinguished Loans, by Borrower's Industry, Region, and Year Established

BORROWER CHARACTERISTICS	REALIZED NET LOSS AS A PERCENTAGE OF AMOUNT DISBURSED	
	On All Loans Made	On Extin- guished Loans
INDUSTRY		
Manufacturing and mining[a]	1.6%	2.5%
Food, liquor, and tobacco	1.3	2.9
Textiles, apparel, and leather	2.1	3.0
Metals and metal products[b]	1.4	2.0
Petroleum, coal, chemicals, and rubber	2.7	9.2
Other[c]	1.4	2.1
Retail trade	0.3	0.5
Wholesale trade	0.3	0.7
Construction	0.5	0.9
Transportation, communications, and public utilities[d]	0.4	0.5
Services	0.5	1.3
Finance, insurance, real estate	0	0
All Other[e]	1.3	2.6
REGION[f]		
New England	0.5	0.8
Middle Atlantic	2.2	3.5
East North Central[b]	0.9	1.7
West North Central	1.0	1.5
South Atlantic	0.5	0.9
East South Central	0.6	1.8
West South Central	1.2	2.9
Mountain	4.8	3.0
Pacific	0.8	1.0
Possessions	16.9	21.1
YEAR BUSINESS ESTABLISHED		
Before 1931	1.1	1.6
1931–1942	1.4	1.8
1943–1949[b]	0.5	1.3
1950–1951	0	0
Newly forming at time of loan	3.8	7.5
Not available	19.7	20.8
All loans	1.3%	2.1%

From the National Bureau of Economic Research sample survey of RFC direct business loans exclusive of participations and national defense loans. The record covers disbursements and losses through December 1951 on loans authorized from June 1934 through June 1951; for number and amount of loans made and loans extinguished, see Tables B-1 and B-17.

a Mainly manufacturing. Loans to mining companies account for 3 percent of the number and amount of loans disbursed.

b Loss on six loans in process of settlement at the end of 1951 is excluded.

c Covers lumber and lumber products; paper and allied products or industries, such as printing; stone, clay, and glass products (including nonmetallic mining or quarrying), and other miscellaneous manufactured products.

d Excludes railroads.

e Mainly fisheries and farming (fruit, poultry, truck, etc.).

f For states included in the regions, see Table B-8.

where slightly higher than average foreclosure and loss frequency concerned mainly small loans, and where receipts on liquidated loans were very good.

The very high loss rates for the territorial possessions—where loans were few and usually small—reflect bad experience with a small number of loans much larger than others in the group. The Mountain states, another area of small loans as compared to the RFC average, show high loss rates accordant with their high frequency of foreclosure and loss and their poor record of receipts on liquidated loans. They also show a high loss frequency of default among loans still outstanding at the end of 1951. The West South Central states, a rapidly developing region to which RFC made a large share of its loans (nearly one-fourth of the total number), but where, again, loan size averaged relatively small, had a loss rate somewhat above average as measured by total extinguishments but somewhat below average as measured by the amount of all loans made—a difference explained by the good record of receipts on liquidated loans. The delinquency status for loans still active in 1951 in the West South Central region was also good as compared to RFC loans elsewhere.

Loans to newly forming enterprises (which received less than 2 percent of the total amount of RFC credit) brought very high loss rates. Differences in the loss experience with established firms dating from the forties, the thirties, and before are not striking. Firms established during 1931–1942 had the least good record. Delinquency among loans still active in 1951 was slightly less frequent for that group than for the other two, but concerned the larger of its loans as to original amount.

Earlier measures of experience showed rather irregular patterns for size classes of RFC loans, except that frequency of foreclosure was worse than average for loans below $10,000 size and better than average for the groups above that amount. The irregularity reappears when extent of loss is measured (Table B-34). It may be worth noting that among loans still active in 1951 (hence not includable in the loss measures) the highest default ratios appeared for the size classes that show up best as to loss rates on all loans made ($25,000 to $100,000) and a better than average default ratio for one of the poorer groups as to loss rates ($10,000 to $25,000). On the record of extinguishments through 1951, the extremely low loss rates for very large loans, $1 million and over, stand out; and the default status of that group among loans still active in 1951 was also good. Half of all RFC credit extended during 1934–1951 went into loans of $1 million or over; thus their comparatively good record counts heavily in the over-all loss rates on RFC business lending.

Among the loss rates by term to maturity, those for loans of unknown term, or payable on demand or in less than six months, concern very few cases. The loan group with 5- through 9-year contract lengths, where 41 percent of RFC business credit was concentrated, brought losses

478

roughly twice as high, in proportion to the amount of loans made, as those of the other considerable groups (Table B-34). Loans still active in 1951, it may be recalled, showed lower frequency of default the longer the term to maturity. The opposite pattern appears in the extent of loss on extinguished loans, except for the relatively good record of those with maturities of 10 years and over.

In general, the loss rates on RFC loans were worse the smaller the asset size of the borrower; but firms in the $100,000 to $250,000 range are an exception, with loss rates higher than any other loan group except those to businesses with assets of less than $25,000 (Table B-35).

RFC credit to firms that were old enough to have three-year net income trends before date of loan yet failed to supply information was not negligible in amount (6 percent of the total) and brought heavy losses. Loans to businesses too young to have calculable profit trends had loss rates worse than the RFC average, yet not extremely so. Since that group of firms received 11 percent of total RFC credit, and since only about one-seventh of their share represented loans to enterprises just organizing at time of loan, the loss rates for "new" businesses given in Table B-35 pertain mainly to young rather than to brand-new enterprises. Heavy losses were sustained on the less than 2 percent of RFC credit that went to firms with moderately declining net income trends, and distinctly above-average losses on the still smaller amount that went to firms with moderate rises. Eleven percent of the number and 20 percent of the amount of RFC loans went to firms with sharply downward profit trends, and brought smaller than average loss rates—better than those for the large share of RFC credit (44 percent) that went to firms with stable or mixed trends. As would be expected from the other measures of loan performance, borrowers with current liabilities exceeding current assets at time of loan produced a poor loss record.

Analysis of RFC Participation Loans

A large part of RFC's credit activity in the business loan field involved commercial banks. From the beginning of its business lending operations, RFC stood ready to participate with a commercial bank on either an "immediate" or a "deferred" basis. Immediate participation occurred when the RFC and a bank each advanced a specified part of the funds under a single loan agreement, initiated either by the bank or by RFC. Deferred participation occurred when a bank advanced the total amount of a loan from its own funds and RFC agreed to take up any amount not exceeding a specified proportion of the loan upon demand by the bank, in effect guaranteeing to the bank repayment of that part of the loan. RFC charged the bank a fee on deferred participations, based upon the absolute amount and the proportion of the loan which it was committed to purchase. During most of the time, the deferred participation fee was

TABLE B-34

Loss Rates on RFC Direct Business Loans Made, and on
Extinguished Loans, by Size of Loan and Term to Maturity

	REALIZED NET LOSS AS A PERCENTAGE OF AMOUNT DISBURSED	
LOAN CHARACTERISTICS	On All Loans Made	On Extinguished Loans
AMOUNT AUTHORIZED		
Less than $1,000	1.9%	2.2%
$1,000–4,999	2.4	3.0
5,000–9,999	3.7	5.5
10,000–24,999	3.1	5.3
25,000–49,999	1.0	1.7
50,000–99,999	1.6	3.2
100,000–499,999	2.0	3.4
500,000–999,999	2.5	4.4
1 million and over[a]	0.4	0.7
PERIOD LOAN MADE		
June 1934–January 1935	3.1	3.1
February 1935–April 1938	4.3	4.4
May 1938–May 1940	2.3	2.3
June 1940–February 1945	0.2	0.2
March 1945–January 1947	2.8	3.3
February 1947–May 1948	1.6	2.6
June 1948–June 1951[a]	b	0.1
TERM TO MATURITY		
Less than six months[c]	0	0
1 year[d]	0.7	0.8
2 yrs.	0.6	1.0
3, 4 yrs.	0.9	1.4
5–9 yrs.	1.8	3.6
10 yrs. and over	0.8	1.2
Payable on demand	47.3	47.3
Not available	2.2	3.0
PREVIOUS ACTION		
Repeat loan[a]	1.2	1.8
Initial loan	1.4	2.3
All loans	1.3%	2.1%

From the National Bureau of Economic Research survey of RFC direct business loans exclusive of participations and national defense loans. The record covers disbursements and losses through December 1951 on loans authorized from June 1934 through June 1951; for number and amount of loans made and loans extinguished, see Tables B-1 and B-17.

[a] Loss on six loans in process of settlement at the end of 1951 is excluded.
[b] Less than 0.05 percent.
[c] Loss on four loans in process of settlement is excluded.
[d] Loss on two loans in process of settlement is excluded.

TABLE B-35

Loss Rates on RFC Direct Business Loans Made, and on
Extinguished Loans, by Financial Characteristics of
Borrower

BORROWER CHARACTERISTICS	REALIZED NET LOSS AS A PERCENTAGE OF AMOUNT DISBURSED	
	On All Loans Made	On Extinguished Loans
TOTAL ASSETS[a]		
Less than $5,000	6.2%	7.7%
$5,000–24,999	4.6	6.5
25,000–49,999	1.7	3.5
50,000–999,999	1.1	2.1
100,000–249,999	2.9	5.7
250,000–499,999	1.2	2.4
500,000–749,999	0.9	1.4
750,000–999,999	1.0	1.5
1 million and over[b]	0.7	1.2
Not available	1.9	2.3
NET INCOME TREND[c]		
Sharply upward	0.2	0.3
Moderately upward	2.0	4.2
Horizontal or mixed	1.0	1.6
Moderately downward	7.9	14.1
Sharply downward[d]	0.6	1.0
New business[e]	1.5	3.0
Not available[f]	6.1	7.7
CURRENT RATIO[a]		
Less than 1.00[b]	2.3	3.9
1.00–1.49	1.0	1.6
1.50–1.99	0.3	0.5
2.00–2.99	0.4	1.1
3.00–4.99	0.7	1.7
5.00 and over	2.2	3.1
Not available[g]	1.9	2.4
All loans	1.3%	2.1%

From the National Bureau of Economic Research survey of RFC direct business loans exclusive of participations and national defense loans. The record covers disbursements and losses through December 1951 on loans authorized from June 1934 through June 1951; for number and amount of loans made and loans extinguished, see Tables B-1 and B-17.

[a] At time of loan application.

[b] Loss on six loans in process of settlement at the end of 1951 is excluded.

[c] During three fiscal years prior to loan authorization. For classification used, see Table B-28.

[d] Loss on one loan in process of settlement is excluded.

[e] Firms newly forming at time of loan or too young to have calculable trend.

[f] Loss on five loans in process of settlement is excluded.

[g] Includes firms just forming at time of loan, and other firms not supplying information.

computed on the outstanding balance of RFC's portion of a loan: 1 percent when the bank's share was 10 to 25 percent; ¾ of 1 percent when the bank's share was 25 to 50 percent; and ½ of 1 percent when the bank's share was over 50 percent.

In March 1945 RFC extended the principle of participation by writing Blanket Participation Agreements with commercial banks. Under such an agreement, an approved bank was automatically assured of a deferred participation up to 75 percent of the amount of any business loan made by the bank which conformed to the statutory restrictions imposed upon RFC. The announced purpose of the BPA program was to "adequately and promptly care for the large volume of applications for loans which it is anticipated may develop during and subsequent to the period of reconversion from a wartime to a peacetime economy." Originally, banks were permitted to make eligible loans up to $250,000 to any one borrower (later increased to $350,000, and then reduced to $100,000) without prior approval. By making it possible for a bank to obtain a loan guarantee without prior appraisal by RFC of each individual loan, the BPA program greatly extended the range of RFC participations.

Although numerous banks availed themselves of BPA facilities, the program was criticized by some bankers on grounds of providing an unnecessary and untimely stimulus to credit expansion, of encouraging loose lending practices by banks, and of adding to the already heavy liabilities of the federal government.[33] On January 22, 1947 it was withdrawn by RFC, and was replaced by the Small Loan Participation program, which was in effect a simplified procedure for handling applications for deferred participation. SLP loans, with an RFC commitment up to 75 percent on business loans limited to $100,000 each, could be finally approved in RFC's field offices, provided the loan agency manager telegraphed a report to Washington on the solvency of the borrower and the value of his collateral, and received from the Secretary a telegraphed reply that solvency and collateral were satisfactory to the RFC Board.

The BPA and SLP programs involved special features and were operative only late in the period of RFC's activity. Chief attention will be focused upon the ordinary, ongoing types of participation loans made by RFC, with later comment on the characteristics of loans under blanket participation agreements.

DEVELOPMENT AND MAGNITUDE OF PARTICIPATION LENDING

Outstanding amounts that RFC was committed to extend on demand—or, in some cases, had extended—in participation loans always formed a considerable segment of the Corporation's total credit volume, and at times (from mid-1946 through mid-1947) exceeded the amount of its

[33] See *Proceedings* of American Bankers Association, Convention, Chicago, September 1946. Also *Wall Street Journal*, September 26, 1946.

direct lending.[34] Up to mid-1947 RFC authorized more than $1 billion as its share of immediate and deferred participations with commercial banks. Of this amount, $629 million consisted of the RFC share of ordinary participation loans, and the balance represented commitments under the BPA program (with a small amount under the SLP program begun in 1947). Among ordinary participation loans are included both the "regular" business loans, made under the authority and subject to the limitations of Section 5 (d) of the RFC Act of June 19, 1934, and the "national defense" loans, made under expanded statutory authority effective June 1940, which removed some of the restrictions as to purpose, maturity, and collateral security that otherwise applied.

Nearly all of the ordinary participations were made on a deferred basis (as were all of the BPA loans); only 12 percent of them involved the immediate extension of RFC funds. Thus we are dealing here largely with a loan guaranteeing function, and will use that terminology except if immediate participations alone are meant.

Table B-36 gives a summary of the number of participating banks, number of ordinary participation loans (exclusive of withdrawals and cancellations), gross amount authorized, and RFC share of the authorizations over the period June 1, 1934 to July 1, 1947, and for three sub-periods: the post-depression period June 1934 through December 1937; the recession and pre-World War II recovery period January 1938 through December 1941; and the war and postwar period January 1942 through June 1947. Mid-1947 was chosen as terminal date because it marked the end of the regular monthly reporting by RFC to Congress on which the study relied for information about participating banks.

Over the period as a whole, the gross amount of ordinary participation loans authorized was about $828 million, of which the RFC share was 76 percent. The average size of loan authorized was $70,100 in the case of immediate participations, of which the amount extended by RFC averaged $53,200. The average size of deferred participations was $148,300, with the share guaranteed by RFC averaging $112,600. Before World War II the average amount of loan authorizations was considerably smaller, and the RFC percentage share was less, than after the price inflation of the war and postwar periods. Yet RFC was consistently the major partner in participation loans, carrying two-thirds to three-quarters of the risk.

The deferred participation loans made during 1934–1947 averaged about twice the size of RFC's direct loans—$148,300 versus $72,300— and both were considerably larger than the average bank term loan made during 1946, which was somewhat over $27,000.[35] Thus, RFC's guaran-

[34] See Chart B-1, page 431, for quarterly outstandings from 1934 on, where the small amounts of immediate participations are included with direct loans and contrasted with the deferred participations (loan guarantees).

[35] Holthausen, op.cit., Table 6, p. 505; the estimates refer to term loans made from November 1945 to November 1946 and give the amount loaned less repayments during the year.

TABLE B-36

Summary of RFC Participation Loan Operations, 1934–1947

	June 1934 through Dec. 1937	Jan. 1938 through Dec. 1941	Jan. 1942 through June 1947	Total 1934– 1947
Number of participating banks	312	1,043	1,218	2,018a
Number of participation loans	395	1,891	3,679	5,965
Immediate	269	371	88	728
Deferred	126	1,520	3,591	5,237
Gross amount of loans authorized	$27,503,900	$148,107,100	$651,920,100	$827,531,10(
Immediate	17,550,100	17,999,600	15,506,000	51,055,70(
Deferred	9,953,800	130,107,500	636,414,100	776,475,40(
RFC share	$19,783,100	$ 98,110,400	$510,636,600	$628,530,10(
Immediate	12,576,100	12,672,100	13,513,300	38,761,50(
Deferred	7,207,000	85,438,300	497,123,300	589,768,60(
Average size of loans	$69,630	$78,322	$177,200	$138,73]
Immediate	65,242	48,516	176,204	70,13]
Deferred	78,998	85,597	177,225	148,267
Average RFC share	$50,084	$51,883	$138,798	$105,37(
Immediate	46,751	34,157	153,560	53,244
Deferred	57,198	56,209	138,436	112,61(
Average RFC percentage share	71.9%	66.2%	78.3%	76.0%
Immediate	71.7	70.4	87.1	75.9
Deferred	72.4	65.7	78.1	76.0

From the National Bureau of Economic Research compilation of all RFC participation loans to business except those made under blanket agreements; the few SLP loans made in 1947 are also excluded. Refers to net authorizations, i.e. exclusive of loans canceled in full before initial disbursement.

a Less than the sum of the numbers shown in each period because banks participating in more than one period are counted only once.

teeing of commercial bank loans occurred with respect to credits of considerably larger average amount than either banks or RFC were extending singly.

Participation loans appear to have functioned as a counter-cyclical factor before World War II and as a war financing measure after 1941 (Table B-37). They expanded through 1934 and 1935 and tapered off during 1936 as the Great Depression ended, falling to a very low point of activity during 1937. During 1938, RFC business lending programs were greatly accelerated to combat the sharp business recession; thereafter the pace of participation lending was slowed. After the United States' entry into World War II the number of ordinary participation loans authorized rose to an all-time peak, the high for the aggregate amount

TABLE B-37

Number and Amount of RFC Participation Loans Authorized Annually, 1934–1947
(*dollar figures in thousands*)

YEAR	PARTICIPATIONS		GROSS AMOUNT		RFC SHARE	
	No.	*Percent*	*Amount*	*Percent*	*Amount*	*Percent*
1934 (6 mo.)	51	0.9%	$ 3,243	0.4%	$ 2,419	0.4%
1935	201	3.4	11,855	1.4	8,552	1.4
1936	87	1.5	7,967	1.0	5,681	0.9
1937	56	0.9	4,440	0.5	3,131	0.5
1938	883	14.8	64,473	7.8	41,409	6.6
1939	525	8.8	45,361	5.5	31,985	5.1
1940	312	5.2	15,181	1.8	9,845	1.6
1941	171	2.9	23,092	2.8	14,871	2.4
1942	1,370	23.0	133,162	16.1	103,326	16.4
1943	856	14.4	167,139	20.2	134,930	21.4
1944	606	10.1	142,993	17.3	115,579	18.4
1945	357	6.0	96,362	11.6	74,758	11.9
1946	318	5.3	65,351	7.9	48,910	7.8
1947 (6 mo.)	172	2.9	46,912	5.7	33,135	5.3
Total	5,965	100.0%	$827,531	100.0%	$628,530	100.0%

From the National Bureau of Economic Research compilation of all RFC participation loans to business except those made under the BPA and SLP programs. Refers to net authorizations, i.e. exclusive of loans canceled in full before initial disbursement.

coming a year later. The volume remained high through 1944, and then declined substantially after the end of the war.

Viewing these movements over longer spans, it is seen that the volume of participation loans authorized rose at an accelerating rate. During the first 43 months of RFC's life only 395 loans aggregating $28 million were involved; during the succeeding 48 months (to the end of 1941), 1,891 loans aggregating $148 million were authorized; during the final 66 months (to mid-1947) no less than 3,679 loans amounting to $652 million were authorized, exclusive of loans in which RFC participated under the BPA program and which alone amounted to more than $525 million. Evidently, loan guaranteeing under participation arrangements was a practice of growing popularity and vitality, at least until the curtailment of RFC's functions in 1947 and 1948.

Of the 5,965 ordinary participation loans authorized during 1934–1947, not far from half were national defense credits (Table B-38). The defense loans averaged larger than the regular loans, and the RFC share in them was also higher, in dollar amount and percentagewise. Hence about 60 percent of the total RFC commitments to participation loans from 1934 to mid-1947 consisted of national defense loans made after June 1940 under wartime powers.

TABLE B-38

Regular vs. Defense, and Deferred vs. Immediate Participations
by RFC, 1934–1947

Type of Participation	Number	Gross Amount	RFC Share
Regular	54.5%	42.6%	39.5%
Immediate	11.0	4.4	4.1
Deferred	43.5	38.1	35.4
National Defense	45.5	57.4	60.5
Immediate	1.2	1.7	2.0
Deferred	44.3	55.7	58.4
Total	100.0%	100.0%	100.0%

From the National Bureau of Economic Research compilation of all RFC participation loans to business except those made under the BPA and SLP programs. Refers to net authorizations, i.e. exclusive of loans canceled in full before initial disbursement. For number and amount of loans, see Table B-36.

Among the national defense participations only a very few—about 3 percent by number and by amount—involved the immediate use of RFC funds (Table B-38). Among the regular participations, immediate extension of RFC loan funds was more frequent but nevertheless was far outweighed by deferred participations, which represented 80 percent by number and 90 percent by amount. Commercial bankers naturally preferred a loan under which the bank advanced the total amount of the funds and earned the interest thereon (less participation charges), with the RFC standing by to take up a major part of the loan upon demand, rather than to have the RFC share in the original advance and divide the interest income from the loan.

RFC participations were strongly concentrated around the 75 percent level (Table B-39). Other points of concentration were around the 50 percent and 90 percent levels. Altogether, about 70 percent of the loans and 76 percent of the gross amount authorized involved an RFC share of either 50, 75, or 90 percent; and over two-thirds of the amount of RFC commitments represented participations at the 75 and 90 percent levels. These facts suggest that if RFC had been limited by law to a maximum participation of 50 percent, the volume of its participation lending might have been considerably reduced.

CHARACTERISTICS OF PARTICIPATION LOANS
AND OF BORROWING FIRMS

The size distribution of bank loans made with RFC participation is as would be expected from the average size figures already given. Over half were in the over $10,000 to $100,000 range, and only 25 percent in amounts of $10,000 or less. Nearly three-quarters of the gross amount authorized represented loans of more than $200,000; in fact 43 percent

APPENDIX B

TABLE B-39

Distribution of Participation Loans by RFC
Percentage Share Authorized, 1934–1947

RFC Percentage Share	Number	Gross Amount	RFC Share
0–39.9	1.0%	0.9%	0.3%
40.0–47.4	0.9	0.4	0.2
47.5–52.4	16.2	12.6	8.3
52.5–60.8	3.2	2.5	1.9
60.9–72.4	8.4	6.4	5.7
72.5–77.4	32.5	35.6	35.1
77.5–82.4	12.2	6.4	6.7
82.5–87.4	3.6	4.8	5.4
87.5–92.4	20.9	27.8	33.0
92.5–99.9	0.6	1.4	1.7
100.0	0.4	1.3	1.7
Total	100.0%	100.0%	100.0%

From the National Bureau of Economic Research compilation of all RFC participation loans to business except those made under the BPA and SLP programs. Refers to net authorizations, i.e. exclusive of loans canceled in full before initial disbursement. For number and amount of loans, see Table B-36.

represented loans of over $1 million (Table B-40). A comparison of this material with the distributions given earlier for loans made independently by banks and by RFC (Table B-2), though hampered by differences in the class boundaries used, again clearly shows the essentially "middle size" character of the RFC business credit programs. Even more than

TABLE B-40

Size Distribution of RFC Participation Loans
Authorized 1934–1947

Size of Loan Authorized	Number	Gross Amount	RFC Share
$5,000 and under	11.1%	0.3%	0.3%
5,000–10,000	13.5	0.8	0.8
10,000–25,000	22.3	3.0	2.8
25,000–50,000	16.4	4.7	4.6
50,000–100,000	16.5	9.6	9.6
100,000–200,000	8.6	9.6	9.2
200,000–500,000	7.2	17.1	17.0
500,000–1,000,000	2.2	11.7	11.7
Over $1 million	2.1	43.2	44.1
Total	100.0%	100.0%	100.0%

From the National Bureau of Economic Research compilation of all RFC participation loans to business except those made under the BPA and SLP programs. Refers to net authorizations, i.e. exclusive of loans canceled in full before initial disbursement. For number and amount of loans, see Table B-36.

RFC's direct lending, its participation credit—largely in the deferred, or guarantee, form—was concentrated in loans of $50,000 to $500,000 size, whereas commercial bank loans made independently were concentrated more in the smallest and largest size classes.

As with direct lending, RFC's loan guaranteeing activity concentrated heavily in the manufacturing sector of business (Table B-41). Within that sector, again the metals and metal products division received the

TABLE B-41

Industrial and Regional Distributions of RFC Participation Loans Authorized 1934–1947

Borrower's Industry and Region[a]	Number	Gross Amount	RFC Share
Manufacturing and mining[b]	60.4%	71.7%	72.7%
Food, liquor, and tobacco	10.8	12.8	12.4
Textiles, apparel, and leather	6.0	5.5	5.2
Metals and metal products[c]	20.2	31.9	34.0
Petroleum, coal, chemicals, and rubber[c]	5.7	7.5	7.7
Other[d]	17.7	14.0	13.4
Retail trade	13.3	2.4	2.4
Wholesale trade	4.9	6.5	6.4
Construction	6.9	7.0	7.0
Transportation, communications, and public utilities[e]	6.1	3.4	3.3
Services	3.9	1.1	0.9
Finance, insurance, real estate	3.3	6.7	6.1
All other[f]	1.3	1.2	1.1
New England	6.7	4.1	4.2
Middle Atlantic	10.7	9.3	9.3
East North Central	16.3	14.2	14.1
West North Central	10.5	7.9	7.8
South Atlantic	16.1	16.6	16.8
East South Central	9.1	8.0	7.6
West South Central	12.4	12.5	12.4
Mountain	5.7	3.9	3.9
Pacific	12.2	23.2	23.7
Possessions	0.3	0.3	0.2
Total	100.0%	100.0%	100.0%

From the National Bureau of Economic Research compilation of all RFC participation loans to business except those made under the BPA and SLP programs. Refers to net authorizations, i.e. exclusive of loans canceled in full before initial disbursement. For number and amount of loans, see Table B-36.

a For states included in the regions, see Table B-8. Details of industry composition are given below.

b Mainly manufacturing; mining concerns account for 3.6 percent of the total number and less than 2 percent of the total gross amount authorized.

c Loans to mining companies form only a nominal fraction.

d Covers lumber and lumber products; paper and allied products or industries such as printing; stone, clay, and glass products (including nonmetallic mining and quarrying, with very few loans); and other miscellaneous manufactured products.

e Excludes railroads.

f Mainly fisheries and farming.

most loans (20 percent of loans to all industries) and the largest credit (32 percent of the gross amount authorized); loans to aircraft and aircraft parts makers, and to other manufacturers of transportation equipment (except automobiles)—industries which were expanding rapidly during the period under consideration—were particularly important within the metals group. In contrast, of bank term loans made during 1946 without RFC participation only 4 percent by number and 16 percent by amount went to the metals and metal products industry. But the fields where bank term loans were most numerous—retail trade, and services—were comparatively unimportant in bank lending under ordinary RFC guarantee.

The reasons for these differences are not definitely known. It is a plausible view, however, that the risks of term lending are, on the average, greater for firms in manufacturing than for firms of equal size in retail or service trades, because the term to maturity of the credit that is required is normally longer, the profitability of the investment fluctuates through a wider range, and technological and cyclical influences are more pronounced. Banks probably found relatively more numerous instances to request RFC participation in lending money to manufacturing firms.

Regionally, the pattern of participation lending departed significantly from the sizes of the business loan markets as measured by outstanding commercial and industrial loans made independently by commercial banks. The South Atlantic, West South Central, and Pacific regions had relatively large percentages of the amount of participation loans authorized (Tables B-41 and B-8). New England, the East North Central region, and especially the Middle Atlantic region had smaller shares of participation credit than ordinary bank loans. In the Pacific states, which received about 12 percent of the number and 23 percent of the amount of participation loans, average loan size was relatively large—$264,200 against $138,700 for the nation—and the portion guaranteed by RFC was correspondingly large (averaging about three-quarters of the gross amount, as elsewhere). These figures bear out an observation made subsequently in connection with the regional distribution of participating banks: participation credits were relatively heaviest in those states and regions which were in process of most rapid economic development. In this respect, RFC loan guaranteeing apparently tended to function as a support for venture capital.

CHARACTERISTICS OF BANKS UTILIZING
RFC PARTICIPATION FACILITIES

What kinds of commercial banks made the most frequent and extensive use of cooperative lending arrangements with RFC, particularly as regards their size, type of charter, location, and the population of the communities served?

APPENDIX B

There has been a general impression that, in sharing the risks of business loans, RFC mainly helped small commercial banks to meet the credit needs of their communities. The evidence shows, to the contrary, that medium-sized and large banks consistently used RFC participation facilities with relatively much greater frequency than did small institutions. During the years 1942–1947, banks with deposits of less than $5 million comprised 77 percent of the total number of insured banks in the United States, but they included only 32 percent of the number of insured banks utilizing RFC participation (Table B-42). At the other

TABLE B-42

City Size and Deposit Size Distributions of All Insured Banks and of Banks Using RFC Participation, and Corresponding Distribution of Participation Loans Authorized 1942–1947

BANK CHARACTERISTICS	ALL INSURED BANKS[a]	PARTICIPATING BANKS[b]	PARTICIPATION LOANS[b] Number	Gross Amount	RF Sh
SIZE OF CITY					
Less than 2,500	53.1%	17.1%	8.0%	2.2%	2.
2,500–4,999	13.0	8.1	5.1	1.5	1.
5,000–9,999	10.7	11.4	7.1	2.4	2.
10,000–24,999	9.1	16.7	11.8	7.7	7.
25,000–49,999	4.1	9.9	8.2	6.0	6.
50,000–99,999	2.8	9.3	15.0	12.3	12.
100,000–499,999	4.2	17.5	33.7	52.0	52.
500,000 and over	3.0	9.5	10.9	15.8	15.
Not available	..	0.5	0.2	c	c
DEPOSIT SIZE					
Under $250,000	0.7	..	..	..	..
$250,000–499,999	4.9	0.7	0.2	c	c
500,000–999,999	16.6	3.2	1.3	0.1	0.
1–1.9 million	26.1	8.3	4.0	0.9	0.
2–4.9 million	28.6	19.7	12.0	4.0	4.
5–9.9 million	11.7	21.5	14.4	7.1	7.
10–24.9 million	6.6	19.7	19.6	10.8	11.
25–49.9 million	2.2	9.8	10.6	10.9	11.
50–99.9 million	1.2	7.0	12.5	14.8	14.
$100 million and over	1.4	10.1	25.3	51.3	50.
Total	100.0%	100.0%	100.0%	100.0%	100.

a As of October 10, 1945; computed from *Annual Report* of the Federal Deposit Insura Corporation, 1945, Tables 41 and 45, pp. 74 and 78. The total number of insured banks inclu is 13,481. The deposit size classes differ from those used for participating banks, "$250,000 a under" forming the first group, and so on.

b From the National Bureau of Economic Research compilation of all RFC participat loans to business except those made under the BPA and SLP programs. Refers to net autho zations, i.e. exclusive of loans canceled in full before initial disbursement. The number of sured banks using RFC participation in 1942–1947 was 1,201; the number of participation loa 3,654; their gross amount, $650,737,000; and the RFC share authorized, $509,653,000.

c Less than 0.05 percent.

end of the size scale, large banks (deposits $10 million and over) formed only 11 percent of the total number of banks but included 47 percent of the participating banks. Clearly, the RFC participation program was not characteristically a small bank aid. To a much greater extent, medium-sized and large institutions tended to use a public guaranty in lending money to business. Nearly 70 percent of the participation loans authorized, and nearly 90 percent of their amount and of the RFC share, pertained to commercial banks with deposits of $10 million or more.

The banks which utilized RFC participation facilities characteristically were large-city institutions. This refutes the impression that RFC participation was mainly useful to the bank in the small community which was unable, because of legal limitations upon its lending powers or prudent diversification of its portfolio, to meet by itself the credit needs of its larger customers. The dominance of large-city banks in the RFC participation clientele persisted throughout the period 1934–1947, although it declined to some extent through time. During 1942–1947 only about 10 percent of all insured banks were located in cities with populations of 50,000 and over, but about 36 percent of all participating banks were located in these large centers (Table B-42). Only a very small fraction—about 3 percent—of banks in centers under 5,000 population utilized RFC guaranty in business lending; yet appreciable proportions of the institutions in larger centers did so. These findings are, of course, consistent with those regarding the distribution of participation loans by size of bank, because of the fairly strong positive correlation between the size of banks and the size of the communities in which they are situated.

Throughout the thirteen-year period 1934–1947, the banks utilizing RFC participation in business lending were to a relatively large extent members of the Federal Reserve System. During the years 1942–1947 member banks formed 46.8 percent of the American banking population, but they included no less than 74.5 percent of all participating banks (Table B-43). Because the larger institutions tend to hold national charters, or, if state-chartered, to hold membership in the Federal Reserve System, the figures substantiate the view that participation with RFC was characteristically most frequent with the larger and better-established banks of the nation.

Comparison of the regional distribution of participating banks with that for all banks shows that through 1937 the New England, Middle Atlantic, South Atlantic, and Pacific regions had disproportionately large numbers participating; relatively few banks in the East North Central, West North Central, and West South Central regions participated (Table B-44). Later, some of these regional disparities disappeared. But the Mountain region emerged as an area of relatively frequent use of RFC participation facilities and the South Atlantic and Pacific regions con-

TABLE B-43

Distributions by Type of Charter for All Banks and for Banks Using RFC Participation, and Corresponding Distribution of Participation Loans Authorized 1942–1947

TYPE OF BANK	ALL BANKS[a]	PARTICI-PATING BANKS[b]	PARTICIPATION LOANS[b] Number	PARTICIPATION LOANS[b] Gross Amount	PARTICIPATION LOANS[b] RFC Share
National	34.1%	53.9%	65.3%	77.3%	77.6%
Insured state member of Federal Reserve System	12.7	20.6	18.3	16.5	16.5
Other insured state	44.9	24.1	15.7	6.0	5.7
Noninsured state	8.3	1.4	0.7	0.2	0.2
Total	100.0%	100.0%	100.0%	100.0%	100.0%

a Covers all commercial and mutual savings banks in the United States and possessions (14,725) as of December 31, 1945; computed from the *Annual Report* of the Federal Deposit Insurance Corporation for that year, Table 102, p. 98. Includes 92 trust companies not regularly engaged in deposit banking: 1 national, 3 state members of the Federal Reserve system, 5 insured state nonmembers, and 83 noninsured.

b From the National Bureau of Economic Research compilation of all RFC participation loans to business except those made under the BPA and SLP programs (with information on type of bank from the source given above). Refers to net authorizations, i.e. exclusive of loans canceled in full before initial disbursement. Covers 1,218 participating banks; and 3,679 loans, whose gross amount was $651,920,000 and the RFC share authorized $510,637,000.

TABLE B-44

Regional Distributions of All Banks and of Banks Using RFC Participation, 1934–1937, 1938–1941, and 1942–1947

REGION[a]	1934–1937 All Banks	1934–1937 Participating Banks	1938–1941 All Banks	1938–1941 Participating Banks	1942–1947 All Banks	1942–1947 Participating Banks
New England	5.9%	8.7%	6.0%	5.6%	6.0%	8.2%
Middle Atlantic	15.6	22.1	15.5	15.6	15.1	12.6
East North Central	20.6	16.3	20.4	19.2	20.6	20.2
West North Central	22.6	12.5	22.5	13.6	22.3	12.0
South Atlantic	10.8	14.7	11.0	13.7	11.1	15.5
East South Central	7.5	8.0	7.5	7.2	7.5	7.2
West South Central	10.7	3.9	10.8	10.6	11.0	11.3
Mountain	3.2	3.5	3.3	5.8	3.3	6.0
Pacific	2.9	9.9	2.7	8.1	2.7	6.4
Possessions	0.2	0.3	0.2	0.6	0.3	0.5
Total	100.0%	100.0%	100.0%	100.0%	100.0%	100.0%
Number of banks	15,444	312	14,877	1,043	14,725	1,218
Ratio of participating to all banks		2.0%		7.0%		8.3%

Data for participating banks are from the National Bureau of Economic Research compilation of all RFC participation loans except those made under the BPA and SLP programs. Figures for all commercial and mutual savings banks are year-end data from *Annual Reports* of the Federal Deposit Insurance Corporation for 1937, 1941, and 1945 (pp. 73ff., 108f., and 98ff., respectively); the 1937 and 1941 data exclude all noninsured trust companies, and those for 1945 exclude such companies if not engaged in deposit banking.

a For states included in the regions, see Table B-8.

tinued so, while banks in the West North Central region—containing the predominantly agricultural states of Minnesota, Iowa, Missouri, the Dakotas, Nebraska, and Kansas—continued to use RFC guaranty comparatively seldom. Relatively most frequent participation was found in those regions which were developing economically with the greatest rapidity. Thus RFC's cooperation with banks in business lending tended to aid firms in developing areas rather than businesses in areas of less rapid development, as was seen also in the regional distribution of borrowing business concerns.

BANK CONCENTRATION OF PARTICIPATION LENDING

There was a high degree of concentration in the use of RFC participation facilities by banks. No less than 51 percent of the gross amount authorized under such arrangements over the years 1934–1947 was concentrated with 99 banks—about 5 percent of all participating banks— each of which utilized RFC guaranty (or, in some cases, immediate extension of RFC funds for part of the loan amount) in ten or more business loans (Table B-45). On the other hand, 1,109 participating banks—55 percent of the total number—used RFC guaranty only once. The 99 banks that were the most frequent users of RFC guaranty accounted for nearly twice as many participation loans, and for nearly seven times as much in gross amount of loan, as the 1,109 banks that made only one RFC

TABLE B-45

Distribution of RFC Participation Loans Authorized
1934–1947, and of the Participating Banks,
by Number of Participations per Bank

NUMBER OF PAR-TICIPATIONS PER BANK	BANKS USING RFC PARTICIPATION		PARTICIPATION LOANS		
	Number	Percent	Number	Gross Amount	RFC Share
1	1,109	55.0%	18.6%	7.4%	7.4%
2	369	18.3	12.4	7.8	7.4
3	160	7.9	8.0	6.8	6.5
4	95	4.7	6.4	4.5	4.6
5	71	3.5	5.9	5.2	5.1
6	39	1.9	3.9	4.2	4.1
7	35	1.7	4.1	4.1	4.2
8	22	1.1	3.0	4.8	5.0
9	19	0.9	2.9	4.3	4.6
10 and over	99	4.9	34.8	50.9	51.2
Total	2,018	100.0%	100.0%	100.0%	100.0%

From the National Bureau of Economic Research compilation of all RFC participation loans to business except those made under the BPA and SLP programs. Refers to net authorizations, i.e. exclusive of loans canceled in full before initial disbursement. For number and amount of loans, see Table B-36.

participation loan each. The average size of participation loans was very much greater for the frequent users than for banks with one, two, or three participations. Concentration in participation lending increased greatly both just before and during World War II, probably because of the exigencies of financing defense and war production.

Why did this high degree of concentration occur, and why did it tend to increase rather than to diminish? The answers are not clear. Such evidence as the data afford was gathered by comparing the distributions of multiple users and of all participating banks by various bank characteristics. The proportion of multiple users tended to be higher the larger the size class of bank. During 1938–1941, banks with deposits of $5 million and over, which formed 40 percent of all participating banks, constituted 62 percent of all multiple users, and this disproportion characterized each of five subclasses within the group, whereas for each smaller size class the reverse was true. A similar pattern, but with $10 million deposits as the dividing line, appeared for 1942–1947. Correspondingly, throughout the period 1934–1947 it was consistently true that multiple use of RFC guaranty was relatively more frequent among participating banks in the larger than in the smaller centers of population. Regionally, differences in the distribution of multiple users and of all participating banks were not striking, except that during 1938–1941 the East North Central region had few multiple users in relation to the number of banks participating, and the Pacific states, comparatively many.

PARTICIPATION AND THE LEGAL LENDING
LIMITATIONS ON BANKS

Did banks seek RFC cooperation in making business loans because the amounts of credit required in individual cases exceeded the amounts they could lawfully or prudently lend to a borrower? The states variously limit the amount of credit a bank may grant a single borrower to between 10 and 25 percent of the amount of capital and surplus, in order to compel banks to diversify their earning assets and to avoid the risk of crippling impairment of capital in the event of default of a very large loan. Furthermore, bank managements generally limit their commitments to individual borrowers to smaller amounts than the law permits. A knowledge of such management policies would be necessary before one could judge the extent to which RFC participation was sought for the purpose of enabling banks to make larger-than-usual loans without incurring what they would regard as undue risk through inadequate asset diversification.

It is possible, however, to state the relative frequency of participation loans whose amount exceeded the legal lending limitations on the participating banks, and thus could not have been made without the collaboration of RFC (or of other banks). One-quarter of them did exceed the statutory lending limitations on the banks making them (Table B-46). Bearing in mind that the policies of most banks frequently held the size of independently made loans even below the legal limit, the percentage of RFC participations sought by the banks in order to minimize the risks of departing from customary policies of portfolio diversification might be set appreciably higher: say, at one-half.

When the proportions of loans over and under legal loan limits were analyzed by size of lending bank, it was found, as might be expected, that the proportion of over-limit loans rose as size of bank diminished. In summary: RFC undoubtedly functioned as a risk-distributing agency, mainly for banks of medium size, with respect to a considerable part of these loans. It is natural that RFC should have performed such a function. The United States is increasingly characterized by large enterprises with great credit requirements; yet the dominant institutional pattern of banking is one of comparatively small-scale, unit institutions.

PARTICIPATION AND THE RISK POSITION OF BANKS

In addition to the risk element in larger than usual individual loans, the over-all risk position of a bank may have played a motivating role in the use of RFC participation facilities. The available evidence is given in Table B-47, which compares the ratio of risk assets to total assets for participating banks and for all banks, on selected dates near the close of given lending periods. Among member banks in the Federal Reserve system, the proportion of risk assets, was, in fact, higher for participating than for all banks; the same was true for nonmember banks after 1941,

TABLE B-46

Percentage of RFC Participation Loans Authorized
1934–1947 Whose Amount Exceeded the
Lending Bank's Legal Limit

LEGAL LENDING LIMIT[a]	NUMBER OF PARTICIPATION LOANS	PERCENTAGE OF LOANS WHOSE SIZE WAS:	
		Over Limit	Under Limit
10 percent	4,437	27.1%	72.9%
15	305	28.2	71.8
20	667	22.8	77.2
25	365	8.2	91.8
All banks	5,774	25.5%	74.5%

From the National Bureau of Economic Research compilation of all RFC participation loans to business except those made under the BPA and SLP programs. Refers to net authorizations (i.e. exclusive of loans canceled in full before initial disbursement) for which the necessary information was available.

a Defines maximum amount allowable per loan in terms of the lending bank's total capital and surplus.

TABLE B-47

Ratios of Risk Assets to Total Assets for Banks Using RFC Participation and for All Banks, 1934–1947, by Period of Participation

PERIOD AND TYPE OF BANK	RATIO OF RISK ASSETS TO TOTAL ASSETS[a]	
	Participating Banks	All Banks
Insured nonmember banks, 1934–1937[b]	57.2%	61.1%
Insured nonmember banks, 1938–1941[b]	52.0	52.0
Insured nonmember banks, 1942–1947[b]	25.6	23.2
National banks, 1934–1937	47.8	40.2
National banks, 1938–1941	39.3	37.8
All member banks, 1938–1941	35.5	27.2
All member banks, 1942–1947	23.0	21.8

[a] Risk assets were computed by subtracting cash and U.S. government securities (direct and guaranteed) from total assets. Ratios are as at the close of the periods, excepting for 1942–1947 (ratios as of 1945), for member banks 1938–1941 (as at end of 1942), and for national banks 1934–1937 (as at mid-1939). *Sources: Assets and Liabilities of Operating Insured Banks* (Federal Deposit Insurance Corporation), pp. 30 and 31 of the following issues: December 31, 1937, No. 8; December 31, 1941, No. 16; June 30, 1945, No. 23. *Annual Reports of Comptroller of the Currency,* 1939 and 1942, pp. 127 and 29 respectively. *Federal Reserve Bulletin,* July 1943, p. 676, and June 1946, p. 678.

[b] Excludes a few banks in the District of Columbia, Alaska, and the Virgin Islands and banks which either did not accept deposits or were liquidating their deposit business.

though not before. There is some basis for the view, therefore, that participating banks sought RFC assistance because they were in comparatively exposed positions, though the evidence is not conclusive. Before the relative amounts of risk carried by each group of banks could be known accurately, an analysis of the qualities of the assets held by participating and nonparticipating banks would be necessary. The true differences in risk positions are not unambiguously disclosed by the relationships between broad categories of assets.

SPECIAL FEATURES OF LOANS UNDER BLANKET PARTICIPATION AGREEMENTS

Having described the characteristics of the loans, of the borrowing business enterprises, and of the commercial banks participating in the regular participation program of RFC, it remains to observe the special features of the BPA credits to business which commenced during March 1945 and ended twenty-two months later on January 22, 1947.

The BPA program, in operation during the period of business reconversion following World War II, was administered energetically by

RFC. Blanket agreements for deferred RFC participation were made with no fewer than 5,253 banks, and loans under the agreements were actually made by 2,422 banks, about one-fifth of all operating commercial banks.[36] The BPA program brought many banks into cooperative credit relations with RFC over and above those which had participated under ordinary arrangements.

More than 11,000 separate loans to business firms were made under blanket agreements, with a total authorized amount of about $525 million. Thus the average size of loan under BPA arrangements was $48,000, only about a third as large as the average ordinary participation loan. Evidently, the automatic approval principle caused the RFC loan guaranty to reach loans of much smaller average amount than had theretofore been the case. Of the total amount of loans, the part guaranteed by RFC was $381 million, or 73 percent (about the same as in ordinary deferred participations, where it was 76 percent). When it is recalled that RFC guarantees under the ordinary participation program during the same two years totaled only $124 million, and even during the two years when their total was highest (1943 and 1944) only $251 million, it is apparent that the BPA arrangement vastly enlarged the scale of RFC participation and enormously increased the usage of governmental guarantee of business loans. This raised apprehensions among bankers, provoked criticism, and contributed to the ultimate withdrawal of the program.

Under the blanket agreements RFC first began to guarantee loans of comparatively small amount in large numbers, partly because there was a maximum size placed upon such loans. About 56 percent of the loans made under blanket agreements were of $25,000 size or less, whereas only 47 percent of ordinary participations were of similarly small size (Table B-48). In gross amount, loans of $25,000 or less constituted about 14 percent of credit authorized under BPA arrangements, but only 4 percent of ordinary participation credit. At the other end of the scale, only 29 percent of the gross amount of loans carrying a BPA guarantee comprised loans of over $200,000, whereas 72 percent of ordinary participation credit fell in that class.

The BPA program also brought the RFC into closer cooperation with banks located in small communities. Data are not available showing BPA loans classified by size of banks or by size of city, but the number of banks that entered into BPA agreements with the RFC, classified by size of city in which located, is known. Nearly half of the BPA banks were in small centers under 5,000 population, whereas only a quarter of the banks were located in such centers under the ordinary participation arrange-

[36] Sources of statistical information about operations under the BPA program are special tabulations prepared by the Research and Statistics Division and Economics Analysis Staff, Controller's Office, RFC.

TABLE B-48

Size Distributions of Loans Authorized under Blanket Participation
Agreements between RFC and Banks, 1945–1947, and of
Ordinary RFC Participations, 1934–1947

SIZE OF LOAN	LOANS UNDER BPA[a]		LOANS MADE WITH ORDINARY RFC PARTICIPATION[b]	
	Number	*Amount*	*Number*	*Amount*
$5,000 and under	11.7%	0.8%	11.1%	0.3%
5,000–10,000	15.6	2.7	13.5	0.8
10,000–25,000	28.3	10.8	22.3	3.0
25,000–50,000	21.1	17.0	16.4	4.7
50,000–100,000	13.2	21.3	16.5	9.6
100,000–200,000	5.8	18.4	8.6	9.6
Over 200,000	4.3	29.0	11.5	72.0
Total	100.0%	100.0%	100.0%	100.0%

[a] From an unpublished tabulation by the Research and Statistics Division, Office
of the Controller, Reconstruction Finance Corporation, August 22, 1947; covers
11,057 loans totaling $525,423,000. RFC participation under the BPA program was
always on a deferred basis.

[b] From the National Bureau of Economic Research compilation of all RFC
participation loans except those made under the BPA and SLP programs. Refers
to net authorizations, i.e. exclusive of loans canceled in full before initial disbursement.

ments made during 1942–1947 (Table B-49). Under the BPA program
RFC participation thus began to assume more of the character of a small-
town banking aid.

The industry distribution of loans made under BPA guarantee was
more like that of bank term loans made independently at about the same
time than was the industrial pattern of ordinary participation lending
from 1934 to mid-1947 (Table B-50 compared with Tables B-7 and
B-41). The greatest number of ordinary participation loans went to
manufacturers of metals and metal products, and of miscellaneous products
such as lumber, paper, clay, and glass—altogether, about 38 percent of
the total—whereas only 10 percent of bank term loans went to those two
divisions. The figure for BPA loans lay between: about 27 percent. Of
ordinary participation loans, 22 percent went to the retail trade, wholesale trade, and service divisions of industry; of BPA loans, 33 percent; of
bank loans, 61 percent. Still more in terms of amount is the closer resem-
blance of the BPA and the independent bank loan distributions apparent.
Of independently extended bank credit, 25 percent, and of BPA-
guaranteed credit, 28 percent went to the metals and miscellaneous manufacturing groups, as against 46 percent of ordinary participation credit.
And the percentage of BPA-guaranteed credit going to retail, wholesale,

TABLE B-49

City Size Distributions of Banks with RFC Blanket Participation
Agreements, 1945–1947, and of Banks Using Ordinary RFC
Participation Facilities, 1942–1947

	NUMBER OF BANKS		PERCENTAGE DISTRIBUTION	
		Participating		*Banks Partici-*
		with RCA under	*Banks*	*pating under*
	With	*Ordinary Ar-*	*with*	*Ordinary Ar-*
SIZE OF CITY	*BPA's*[a]	*rangements*[b]	*BPA's*	*rangements*
Under 5,000	2,604	314	49.6%	25.8%
5,000–9,999	701	139	13.3	11.4
10,000–24,999	730	202	13.9	16.6
25,000–49,999	332	119	6.3	9.8
50,000–99,999	253	113	4.8	9.3
100,000–199,999	187	101	3.5	8.3
200,000–499,999	224	110	4.3	9.0
500,000–999,999	103	48	2.0	3.9
1 million and over	119	66	2.3	5.4
Total	5,253	1,218[c]	100.0%	100.0%

[a] From an unpublished tabulation by the Research and Statistics Division, Office of the Controller, Reconstruction Finance Corporation, August 27, 1947.

[b] From the National Bureau of Economic Research compilation of all RFC participation loans except those made under the BPA and SLP programs.

[c] Includes a few banks in communities unclassified as to size, accounting for about 0.5 percent of the total.

and service firms—divisions relatively neglected in other RFC credit activities—actually exceeded the figure for independently extended bank credit (24 as against 19 percent). This is further evidence that banks tended to use the simplified form of government guarantee available under PBA to underwrite risks of a type that they had been assuming under their term lending programs.

Prices and Costs of Business Credit Supplied by RFC

Information is assembled in this section on the prices charged by the RFC for its business credit services, on the costs incurred, and on the relation between revenues and costs. Estimates are made of the amount of "subsidy" inherent in the Corporation's policies, and some comparisons are drawn between those policies and the business lending practices of commercial banks. Certain implications regarding the ability of the Corporation to carry credit risks, the incentives for business firms and banks to utilize RFC services, and the credit policies of commercial banks are pointed out.

THE STANDARD LOAN RATE POLICY OF RFC

The statutes governing RFC never specified the rate of interest to be charged by the Corporation for business loans; nor did they indicate an

TABLE B-50

Industry Distribution of Loans Authorized under Blanket Agreements between RFC and Banks, 1945–1947

Industry	Number	Gross Amount
Manufacturing	38.7%	45.4%
Food, liquor, and tobacco	8.4	11.4
Textiles, apparel, and leather	1.7	3.0
Metals and metal products	14.2	16.7
Petroleum, coal, chemicals and rubber	2.1	3.1
Other[a]	12.3	11.2
Mining	2.4	3.1
Retail trade	16.6	8.6
Wholesale trade	6.6	9.1
Construction	14.2	17.2
Transportation, communications, and public utilities	8.9	7.5
Services	10.1	6.4
Finance, insurance, real estate	0.7	1.5
Forestry, fishing, and farming	1.7	1.2
Total	100.0%	100.0%

From a special tabulation prepared by the Economic Analysis Staff, Office of the Controller, Reconstruction Finance Corporation.

[a] Covers lumber and lumber products; paper and allied products or industries such as printing; stone, clay, and glass products, and miscellaneous manufacturing.

average or a range of rates. Indeed, Congress did not even provide a broad directive to the management of RFC regarding its aggregate income from credit operations, or the relation of such income to the Corporation's costs. The management was free to operate at a profit or a loss, so far as the statute was concerned, either on its lending operations as a whole, or on its business loan activities in particular.[37]

The policy of the Board of Directors of RFC was to charge a single, standard rate of interest for each broad class of loans. When industrial and commercial lending was initiated in June 1934, the board established a rate of 6 percent per annum on the unpaid balance of a business loan, irrespective of its amount, term to maturity, or credit risk. In May 1935 the rate was lowered to 5 percent. On April 1, 1939, it was further reduced to 4 percent on all outstanding loans, as well as on loans made thereafter. Effective November 10, 1950, the board raised the rate back to 5 percent, apparently in response to congressional criticism that the Corporation was not covering its business lending costs at the 4 percent rate, and also to bring RFC rates into line with bank rates. RFC applied

[37] The circulars published by the RFC from time to time relative to loans to industry have contained only general statements such as "Interest shall be at prevailing rates for the character of loan applied for," or "interest shall be at such rates as may be fixed from time to time by this corporation."

the standard rate to its portion of loans made in cooperation with commercial banks (regardless of the bank's rate), as well as to the loans it made independently.

A comparison of the quarterly movement of commercial bank rates on short-term business loans in the $10,000 to $100,000 size bracket with the RFC rate for the period 1935–1951 appears in Chart B-2. The Federal Reserve series on short-term loan rates in the $10,000 to $100,000 bracket was chosen for comparison because the great majority of RFC loans fell into this size class.[38] The chart illustrates the relative insensitivity of the RFC rate to changes in money market conditions.

CHART B-2

Average Interest Rates on Short-Term Commercial Bank Business Loans of Size $10,000–99,999, Quarterly 1936–1953, Compared with RFC Business Loan Rate

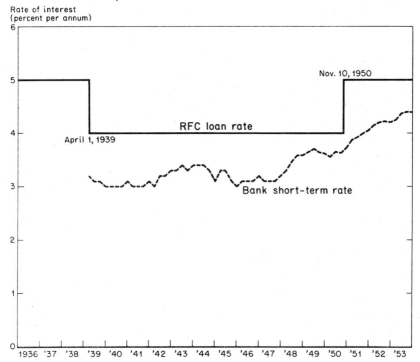

Bank data through 1948 are from "New Statistics of Interest Rates on Business Loans," by Richard Youngdahl, "Federal Reserve Bulletin," March 1949, Table 1, p. 231; after 1948, from various issues of the "Bulletin." They give estimated average rates on loans of one year or less made to businesses by banks in nineteen cities: New York, Boston, Buffalo, Philadelphia, Pittsburgh, Cleveland, Detroit, Chicago, Baltimore, Richmond, Atlanta, New Orleans, Dallas, St. Louis, Minneapolis, Kansas City, Seattle, San Francisco and Los Angeles.

[38] The relation between the levels of the two curves has no significance, because the bank curve reflects rates on short-term loans carrying limited credit

The attention of Congress was called to the propriety of RFC lending rates in June 1947 when the Comptroller General submitted his first report on the audit of RFC and its subsidiaries for the fiscal year ending mid-1945. Therein, he pointed out that the RFC act "has not contained the general requirement that the Corporation apply such interest rates to loans made by it as would be necessary to cover all of the costs of operation and all of the risks of loss."[39]

The interest rate policy of RFC was one of the principal points of inquiry during late 1947 by the subcommittee of the Senate Committee on Banking and Currency under the chairmanship of Senator Buck. Officials of RFC vigorously defended the policy of a standard rate of interest undifferentiated as between borrowers, and the adequacy of the 4 percent figure. They argued that it would be impracticable to vary the loan rate according to size, degree of risk. or maturity, because, as RFC Chairman Goodloe put it, "distinctions would be a matter of opinion which in most cases would satisfy neither the borrower nor anyone else."[40] They said that because RFC's funds were provided by the Treasury at a fixed rate of interest, the rate it charged for relending this money could not fairly be carried geographically. Concerning the adequacy of the 4 percent rate then current, Chairman Goodloe stated that "the differential between the rate of interest which RFC pays the Treasury and the rate which it charges borrowers should be sufficient to pay the Corporation's overhead and to set up reserves required by good accounting practices. Our present rate of 4 percent has, in the past, been sufficient to accomplish these purposes."[41]

The standard loan rate policy was not challenged by the Committee on Banking and Currency in its 1948 report to the Congress. The committee acknowledged that discriminatory pricing by RFC would probably encounter administrative difficulties and borrower dissatisfactions. It suggested that the advisory committees of bankers and businessmen appointed by RFC to advise the managers of each loan agency might be requested to establish loan rates for their particular areas, but left a decision on this matter up to the Board of Directors of RFC.

The committee did challenge Chairman Goodloe's assertion that the 4 percent rate had been adequate to cover all costs of business lending, pointing out that RFC accounting did not fully reflect the true cost of lending, and that the net result of each lending program could not be determined. It instructed RFC thereafter to maintain its accounts so that

risk whereas the RFC curve covers rates on term loans carrying higher risks. For loans having identical characteristics, bank rates would undoubtedly have exceeded the RFC rate.

[39] House Doc. 316, 80th Cong., 1st sess., June 11, 1947. Letter from the Comptroller General of the United States transmitting a *Report on the Audit of RFC and Affiliated Corporations* for the fiscal year ended June 30, 1945, p. 16.

[40] *Hearings* on S. Res. 132 (cited in footnote 20), Part I, p. 65.

[41] *Loc. cit.*

the financial results realized in the business lending field could be determined, and it recommended amendment of the RFC Act to require that loans should bear an interest rate "reasonably calculated to enable the Corporation to operate without loss," with a similar recommendation on fees charged for deferred participations.[42] The RFC Act of 1948, however, while providing for regular congressional review of operations, did not include any directive on interest rates or participation fees (see page 426 above).

The RFC loan rate policy was again subjected to close scrutiny during 1950 by the subcommittee on the Senate Committee on Banking and Currency headed by Senator Fulbright. One focal point of the subcommittee's attention was whether RFC lending operations had been conducted on a self-sustaining basis. It was brought out that RFC lending activities as a whole were conducted at a loss of about $6.5 million during the fiscal year 1949, if RFC were charged with the interest paid by the Treasury Department on the full amount of funds employed, whereas it earned its published profit of about $5.2 million on a basis of employment of some $600 million of "cost-free" capital and surplus.[43] Lending operations had been self-sustaining from the standpoint of RFC but they had not been self-sustaining from the standpoint of the taxpayer. Obviously, interest had to be paid by the Treasury Department on funds utilized by RFC in business loan operations, and this interest must be taken into account in calculating the full cost of RFC operations. RFC officials took the view that Congress had deliberately provided the Corporation with interest-free capital funds from the Treasury and in addition had permitted the Corporation to retain (interest-free) earned surplus from previous operations,[44] so that the program was self-sustaining if RFC merely earned sufficient income to cover its other costs of lending. RFC officials regarded the use of interest-free capital funds as a congressional subsidy to small borrowers enabling the Corporation to charge a lower rate. They argued that if Congress had intended otherwise, it should have said so.

To clear up this ambiguity in the statute, the Comptroller General had recommended in February 1950 that Congress enact legislation requiring RFC to pay interest at current costs to the Treasury on all funds used in loan operations, to pay that part of the government's costs of civil service retirement and disability benefits for RFC employees, and to pay

---

[42] Senate Report 974 (cited in footnote 16), pp. 14, 15, and 21.

[43] *Hearings* before a subcommittee of the Committee on Banking and Currency, 81st Cong., 2nd sess., May 8 and 9, 1950, on *A Study of the Operations of the Reconstruction Finance Corporation* pursuant to S. Res. 219. *Analysis of Income and Costs*, p. 3.

[44] The 1948 act limited the interest-free Treasury funds used by RFC to $100 million; originally, $500 million had been provided as capital stock, of which $175 million was retired in April 1941 as required by a previous enactment. Originally, there was no provision regarding earned surplus; the 1948 act provided that earned surplus in excess of $250 million be turned back to the Treasury.

"all other costs incurred by other governmental agencies for the Corporation's account or benefit where it is practicable and economically feasible to measure the benefits and related costs."[45]

RFC officials conceded before the Fulbright Subcommittee that the single, standard rate of charge for business loans meant that profits on a few big loans covered losses on many small loans, and they forecast higher rates on loans to small firms if this policy was changed. A member of the RFC Board of Directors said: "Ten percent of our loans carry the cost for ninety [percent]. That is the way it has always been, and that is the way it has to be if you are going to continue to make small loans."[46] Manifestly, it would be impossible for RFC or any other lending institution to put each individual loan on a self-sustaining basis. Yet RFC's officials failed to explain why it would not be feasible to classify loans into a limited number of groups with respect to amount or maturity, as is done by some commercial banks, and to vary the loan rate between groups. This would have avoided the subsidy effect of the single standard rate.

Senator Fulbright questioned the desirability of the standard rate policy, and reiterated the suggestion made in the Buck Subcommittee hearings, that loan rates might well vary with size of loan and as between Federal Reserve districts, and urged that RFC rates should be higher than comparable commercial bank rates to discourage business firms from applying to the RFC.[47] But up to the end, RFC persisted in the standard loan rate policy.

COMPARISON OF RFC AND COMMERCIAL
BANK LOAN RATES

The standard loan rate policy of RFC has been at variance with the business loan pricing policies of American commercial banks. In practice banks vary their rates with a number of factors, chief of which are (1) size of the loan, (2) term to maturity, and (3) size of the borrowing firm. Size of loan is important, because a large portion of the administrative expense of lending is fixed irrespective of the amount of a loan. Administrative expense per dollar falls rapidly as the amount of a loan rises, and administrative expense is a large component of the gross interest rate charged. Size of borrowing firm is another determinant of loan rate because of its positive correlation with the degree of risk. Other things being equal, a loan of given amount and maturity will carry more risk of nonrepayment if made to a small firm than if made to a large enter-

---

[45] House Doc. 468, 81st Cong., 2nd sess., February 1950. Letter from the Comptroller General of the United States transmitting the *Report on Audit of Reconstruction Finance Corporation and Subsidiaries* for the fiscal years ending June 30, 1946 and 1947, p. 9.

[46] *Analysis of Income and Costs* (cited in footnote 43), p. 71.

[47] *Hearings* before a subcommittee of the Committee on Banking and Currency, 81st Cong., 2nd sess., June–July 1950, on *A Study of the Operations of the Reconstruction Finance Corporation* pursuant to S. Res. 219. *Lending Policy*, p. 349ff.

prise, because the relative burden of the debt is greater to the smaller firm and the mortality rate of small enterprises is higher. Of the three factors, the amount of a loan is undoubtedly the most important single determinant of loan rate. Commercial banks therefore commonly scale their interest charges sharply upward, in successive brackets, as loan size falls.[48]

Available information concerning the size structure of commercial bank interest rates on business loans is computed on the basis of outstanding balances (as of November 1946) rather than by original amount, and, for that reason among others, does not afford a precise measure of differences between bank rates and the RFC standard loan rate from the standpoint of loan applicants. Nevertheless, Table B-51 is suggestive on that point. The RFC rate far undershot the bank rates on business term loans with $10,000 or less outstanding, and a classification by original amount would undoubtedly widen rather than diminish the difference shown. The figures show bank rates and the RFC standard 4 percent rate coinciding for term loan balances of about $50,000 size (Chart B-3); and since most RFC loans were less than that in original amount (in 1945 and 1946, for example, 90 percent of them), it is evident that, in general, RFC loans were made at rates well below those of commercial banks.

TABLE B-51

Average Interest Rates on Different Sizes of Outstanding Commercial Bank Loans to Business, November 20, 1946, Compared with RFC Business Loan Rate

SIZE OF LOAN BALANCE	MEMBER BANK AVERAGE RATE ON		DEVIATION OF RFC RATE OF 4% FROM AVERAGE BANK RATE	
	Short-Term Loans	Intermediate and Long-Term Loans	Short-Term Loans	Intermediate and Long-Term Loans
Less than $500	7.0%	8.9%	—3.0	—4.9
$500–999	6.5	7.7	—2.5	—3.7
1,000–4,999	5.5	5.9	—1.5	—1.9
5,000–9,999	4.8	5.1	—0.8	—1.1
10,000–24,999	4.3	4.6	—0.3	—0.6
25,000–49,999	3.9	4.2	0.1	—0.2
50,000–99,999	3.5	3.8	0.5	0.2
100,000–499,999	2.6	3.0	1.4	1.0
500,000–999,999	2.2	2.4	1.8	1.6
1,000,000 and over	1.8	2.1	2.2	1.9
All loans	3.0%	2.8%	1.0	1.2

From "The Structure of Interest Rates on Business Loans at Member Banks," by Richard Youngdahl, *Federal Reserve Bulletin*, July 1947, Table 16, p. 816.

[48] Cf. Richard Youngdahl, "The Structure of Interest Rates on Business Loans at Member Banks," *Federal Reserve Bulletin*, July 1947, pp. 803–819.

CHART B-3

Comparison of RFC Business Loan Rate with Average Interest Rates on Outstanding Commercial Bank Business Loans, 1946, by Size of Loan Balance

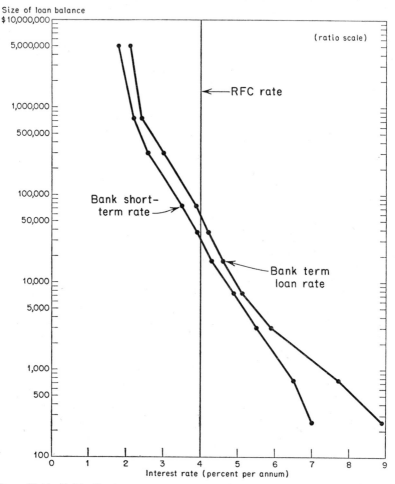

From Table B-51. Bank rate averages are plotted at midpoints of closed size classes and at $5 million for loans $1 million and over.

Remembering the high-risk character of RFC's portfolio, one would guess that on the average the RFC loans of sizes smaller than $50,000 were priced not only below bank loans of comparable size but also below the cost of RFC, so that the Corporation must either have sustained considerable loss or have met the losses on many small loans out of interest income from a relatively few large ones. This subsidy effect was testified to by the Controller of RFC before the Fulbright Subcommittee in 1950: "Our break-even point on a one-year loan is $150,000; on a 10-year loan it is $50,000. Since our average loan is around 5 years, our break-even point on the average would be between $75,000 and $100,000."[49] The break-even point would have been even higher if RFC had been required to pay interest on the full amount of funds employed in business lending operations.

DEFERRED PARTICIPATION FEES CHARGED BY RFC

As was the case with direct loan rates, the statutes were silent regarding the amount of RFC's participation fees. Initially, the fees charged for such credit insurance were graduated according to the duration of the Corporation's obligation. For agreements to purchase participations for periods up to one year, the fee was ½ of 1 percent of RFC's agreed participation for each quarter-year, or 2 percent per annum. For agreements running more than one year but not more than two years, the fee was 2 percent of RFC's agreed portion for the first year, plus 1 percent for the second year. Fees for agreements running more than two years were subject to negotiation.[50]

In May 1935 the fee schedule was altered by raising the charge on agreements running between one and two years from 1 percent for the second year to 2 percent of RFC's agreed participation.[51] This action, in effect, made RFC's charge a flat 2 percent per annum on the daily balances of the Corporation's outstanding commitment to purchase a participation in a disbursed loan, a rate maintained until 1938.[52]

In April 1938 the Corporation announced a new schedule of fees, graduated according to the proportion of an outstanding bank loan that it was obligated to purchase: if not more than 50 percent, the fee was 1 percent per annum of RFC's commitment; if more than 50 percent, but not over 75 percent, the fee was 1½ percent; if more than 75 percent, but not more than 90 percent, the fee was 2 percent.[53] That is, the new schedule reduced the charge made by RFC in all cases where the proportion of a loan guaranteed by RFC was 75 percent or less. In comparison with the former arrangements, it provided an inducement to commercial banks to carry a larger proportion of the risk on business loans. Clearly, the amount of risk of nonpayment carried by RFC varied directly with both the duration of its guaranty and the proportion of the loan guaranteed, so that a scientific schedule of premiums to be charged for carrying such risks should have reflected both factors. Yet the new fee schedule considered only the second.

[49] *Analysis of Income and Costs* (cited in footnote 43), pp. 150f.
[50] RFC Circular No. 15, August 1934, pp. 2–3.
[51] RFC Circular No. 15 (revised) May 1935, Sec. E, p. 3.
[52] RFC Circular No. 15 (revised) December 1936, p. 2, and (revised) April 1937, p. 2.
[53] RFC Circular No. 15 (revised) April 1938, p. 1.

As of September 1939, deferred participation fees were cut in half for each size of commitment specified in the 1938 schedule.

Another charge was made in March 1945, when RFC introduced blanket participation agreements. Under such agreements banks purchased protection at a charge of ¾ of 1 percent per annum of RFC's commitment if it covered more than 50 percent of an outstanding loan, and a charge of ½ of 1 percent per annum where RFC's commitment was less than 50 percent.[54] This represented a further reduction in the Corporation's loan guaranty rates. By 1945, fees were little more than one-third of those of ten years earlier.

The propriety of RFC's deferred participation fees was one of the issues posed for inquiry by the Buck Subcommittee in 1947. John D. Goodloe, Chairman of the Corporation, testified with respect to the BPA program: "Our experience leads me to believe that the participation fees collected under this program will more than cover expenses and losses. A survey of 500 such loans chosen at random shows that the collateral pledged averaged $1.83 per dollar loaned, and that 20 percent of all the loans were additionally secured by guarantees."[55] The small participation fees were attacked, however, not because they might fail to cover RFC costs, but because they provided a strong financial inducement to commercial banks to seek RFC participations rather than those of other banks.[56] They caused RFC to encroach upon credit functions formerly performed by private institutions. While the extent of encroachment was open to question, the existence of an inducement could not be doubted.

The Buck Subcommittee in its report to Congress did not condemn the BPA agreement or the principle of loan guaranty by RFC but did recom-

[54] RFC Circular No. 25, March 1945, p. 1.

[55] *Hearings* . . . on S. Res. 132, Part 1 (cited in footnote 20), p. 37.

[56] Henry T. Bodman, an RFC director, placed the following hypothetical illustration before the Buck Subcommittee: Consider a $100,000 loan by a bank at 4 percent interest, in which RFC takes a deferred participation of 75 percent of the amount for a ¾ of 1 percent annual fee:

Bank collects from borrower interest of	$4,000.00
Bank pays RFC "insurance" premium of	562.50
Leaving the bank a net interest income of	$3,437.50
Since the RFC guaranty is, in a broad sense, equivalent to a government obligation of $75,000, from the point of view of the bank, the yield of which is 1¼ percent or:	937.50
The balance is	$2,500.00

This balance represents an effective income of 10 percent per annum to the bank on the $25,000 it has risked on the credit of the borrower. If the lending bank had sold a 75 percent participation in the loan to another bank, the other bank would have been paid 75 percent of the interest income of $4,000, leaving only $1,000 to the lending bank, or 4 percent on its money risk. (*Hearings* . . . on S. Res. 132, 80th Cong., 1st sess., Part 2, January 1948, pp. 272 and 453.)

mend revisions of the RFC Act to require that "fees charged for deferred participations be at rates which will give reasonable assurance that those operations will be conducted without loss," and the RFC's interest in such participations be limited to 65 percent in loans of $100,000 or less, and to 50 percent in loans over $100,000.[57] The committee apparently concluded that if a bank carried a sufficiently large portion of the loan, it would not relax its ordinary credit standards. In any event, RFC abandoned the BPA program in January 1947, and the deferred participation fee schedule of September 1939 again became effective.

As of November 10, 1950, at the same time that the direct loan rate was raised from 4 to 5 percent, RFC sharply increased the fee for deferred participations to a flat 2 percent. The reasons for this action were probably the doubts expressed at the Fulbright Subcommittee inquiries about the self-sustaining character of the lower rates, objections to the encroachment of RFC activities upon those of commercial banks, and the rising structure of business loan rates during 1950. Thus by 1950 the course of participation fees had come full circle, and returned to the level at which they were originally set in 1934. Like direct loan rates, they had been cut from the original level, then restored; but the amplitude of the swing in participation fees had been much greater. The wide changes in prices of RFC credit insurance apparently did not reflect changes in costs, or even a systematic study of costs, a subject to which attention is now directed.

COSTS AND REVENUES OF RFC BUSINESS LENDING
AND LOAN GUARANTY OPERATIONS

The problem of costing a business lending operation is difficult at best. In fact, no accurate determination of the profitability of a lending operation may be made until after the operation has been wound up and all loans have been finally terminated. The problem of cost calculation becomes more complex when, as has been the case with RFC, the business lending operation is only one of a series of lending, purchasing, selling, and investing activities conducted by the same organization, requiring allocation of joint expenses to separate programs. A further complication arises from the fact—noted previously—that RFC was provided with cost-free capital on which the Treasury Department paid interest, and such interest has been a cost of RFC lending operations from the point of view of the public. Moreover, RFC did not maintain its records in a manner which permits ready comparison of the results of its lending operations with those of private banks.

[57] Senate Report 974 (cited in footnote 16), pp. 21f.

Nevertheless, the Fulbright Subcommittee's inquiry into RFC's costs of business lending during 1949–1950, and the Reports on Audit of the RFC by the General Accounting Office after 1945, produced data which permit useful estimates of costs for the fiscal years 1946 and thereafter. These data for five successive years during which the business lending program bulked large in the totality of RFC activities afford a basis for generalizations concerning the costs of RFC's lending.

RFC reported a net income from its combined lending programs in each year of the period 1946–1950, after provision for losses. Reported net income for the five years amounted to roughly $100 million, an average of about $20 million per annum. Deducting from the reported figures the estimated amounts of interest paid by the Treasury Department on cost-free funds employed by RFC, as well as the estimated amount paid by the Treasury as the government's contribution toward retirement income of RFC employees, the adjusted net income was found by the subcommittee to have been positive in three years and negative in two years. In amount, adjusted net income for the five-year period was estimated at approximately $21 million, or upwards of $4 million per annum. RFC apparently covered its full expenses and earned a small net income on its combined lending programs during the postwar period. The net income was negligible, however, in proportion to the resources employed, forming about 0.3 percent per annum of the average total—some $1.6 billion—of assets employed in all lending programs during the five-year period.

A special study made for the Fulbright Subcommittee provides a statement of the operating results of the business loan program for the fiscal year 1949 and the first nine months of the fiscal year 1950. During fiscal 1949, according to the subcommittee's estimates, if full expenses including interest on cost-free capital and surplus employed in business lending operations are charged against the gross income from business loans, RFC had a deficit of more than $8 million in its business lending operations, and during the first nine months of fiscal 1950 it had a deficit of $5.6 million (Table B-52).

The relation of costs to revenues was even less satisfactory for deferred participation loans than for direct loans during 1949–1950. Although with adjustment for the cost of Treasury funds both operations resulted in losses, relative to the gross revenue, the amount of the losses from deferred participation was much larger. On the basis of the subcommittee's estimates, the operating deficit for loan guaranty was 117 percent of the total income; for direct loans, only 38 percent of the total income. Deferred participation fees would have had to be about double those charged during the 1949 and 1950 fiscal years in order to make the operation break even. Fees of ½ of 1 percent to 1 percent per annum grossly under-

TABLE B-52

Estimated Income and Expense of RFC in Conducting Its Business Loan Program, 1949 and 1950

(in thousands)

	YEAR ENDED JUNE 30, 1949			NINE MONTHS ENDED MARCH 31, 1950		
	Direct Loans (Incl. Immediate Participations)	Deferred Participations	Total	Direct Loans (Incl. Immediate Participations)	Deferred Participations	Total
Income						
Interest & dividends	$11,759	$ 792	$12,551	$12,997	$ 684	$13,681
Other	17	1,322	1,340	..	784	784
Total income	11,777	2,114	13,891	12,997	1,468	14,465
Expense						
Interest at 1⅞% on money employed	5,572	351	5,923	6,082	318	6,400
Administration:						
Loan acquisition	4,708	1,147	5,855	3,903	679	4,582
Loan servicing	3,436	2,718	6,154	3,244	1,885	5,129
Total expense	13,716	4,216	17,932	13,229	2,882	16,111
NET INCOME BEFORE PROVISION FOR LOSSES [a]	(1,939)	(2,102)	(4,041)	(232)	(1,414)	(1,646)
Provision for losses	3,586	385	3,971	3,689	290	3,978
NET INCOME AFTER "FULL EXPENSE" [a]	(5,525)	(2,487)	(8,012)	(3,921)	(1,704)	(5,624)
Add: Allowance for interest-free capital and surplus	8,308	2,524	10,831	4,883	930	5,813
NET INCOME BEFORE ALLOWANCE FOR INTEREST-FREE FUNDS	2,783	37	2,820	962	(773)	189

From Fulbright Subcommittee hearings, 1950, *Analysis of Income and Costs* (cited in text footnote 43), pp. 145 and 148; with the order of items changed to reveal clearly the effect of employment of interest-free capital and surplus by RFC. Amounts do not always add to totals because of rounding.

[a] Figures in parentheses are negative.

priced RFC's loan guaranty services. The sharp increase of charges to 2 percent, effective in November 1950, approximately equated costs and revenues on this calculation.

In regard to direct loans, it appears from Table B-52 that over the twenty-one months covered, a gross income of $24,774,000 and a deficit of $9,446,000 was realized at the 4 percent loan rate. The gross income of $34,220,000 which would have been necessary to place direct business lending on a break-even basis according to the subcommittee's analysis could have been produced with a standard interest rate of between 5½ and 6 percent per annum on all outstanding loans, large and small.

COSTS AND REVENUES FOR RFC LOANS
OF DIFFERENT SIZES

Even if, as the Fulbright Subcommittee's analysis suggests, a standard loan rate of between 5.5 and 6 percent would have enabled RFC to break even on all direct loans to business firms during the fiscal years 1949 and 1950, there would have remained great disparities in operating results as between loans of different sizes. RFC did not maintain the records necessary for an accurate costing of loans of different sizes, but special studies for the subcommittee afford a basis for estimating the profit or loss realized by RFC on loans of different amounts.

During fiscal 1949 and 1950, RFC calculated its average cost of acquiring a direct business loan at $1,368, its average cost per annum of servicing a loan at $907, and the average annual provision for loss at 0.66 percent of loan disbursements.[58] Such costs undoubtedly varied to some extent with size of loan, but, lacking information, it is here assumed that they were constant. The principal element of variable cost was interest paid by the Treasury Department on money employed by RFC. The average Treasury borrowing rate during 1949–1950 was approximately 1⅞ percent, which may be adjusted upward to 2 percent in order to allow for contributions by the Treasury to the retirement fund for RFC employees. This information enables one to estimate roughly the total cost incurred by RFC on loans of different amounts. Gross revenues collected by RFC may be computed by applying the standard 4 percent rate to outstanding loan balances. The difference between gross revenue and total cost is net profit or loss per loan.

Estimates were made of the amount of profit or loss realized by RFC on loans of different amounts at the standard 4 percent rate, on the assumptions that all loans were fully amortized and matured in five years, that all expense and cost was payable at time of making the loan, and that simple interest was charged. On these simplifying assumptions, and without attempting adjustment for variability of cost as among different sizes of loan, it appears that RFC lost about $5,876 on each loan of

[58] *Analysis of Income and Costs* (cited in footnote 43), pp. 150f.

$1,000 it put on its books, and lost very little less than that on each loan of $5,000 (Table B-53).[59] With interest on capital and surplus figured among costs, not until loans reached about $200,000 did RFC avoid loss. As the amount rose above $200,000, the net profit per loan increased steadily. The profit of $21,000 on a loan of $1 million almost sufficed to cover losses on four loans of $5,000. The standard 4 percent rate clearly produced profits on the relatively few large loans sufficient to cover losses on many small loans.

On the assumptions that have been made, the break-even interest rate for a loan of $1,000 would have been unconscionable; even for a loan of $5,000 it would have been about 40 percent. A rate of interest of 3.5

TABLE B-53

Estimated Costs, Revenues, and Profit or Loss Realized by RFC on Business Loans of Different Sizes
(standard interest rate of 4 percent on a 5-year amortized loan)

Loan Size	Acquisition and Service Costs[a]	Interest Costs[b]	Provision for Losses[c]	Total Cost	Gross Revenue[d]	Profit or Loss
$1,000	$5,903	$ 60	$ 33	$ 5,996	$ 120	$—5,876
5,000	5,903	300	165	6,368	600	—5,768
10,000	5,903	600	330	6,833	1,200	—5,633
25,000	5,903	1,500	825	8,228	3,000	—5,228
50,000	5,903	3,000	1,650	10,553	6,000	—4,553
75,000	5,903	4,500	2,475	12,878	9,000	—3,878
100,000	5,903	6,000	3,300	15,203	12,000	—3,203
150,000	5,903	9,000	4,950	19,853	18,000	—1,853
200,000	5,903	12,000	6,600	24,503	24,000	—503
250,000	5,903	15,000	8,250	29,153	30,000	847
300,000	5,903	18,000	9,900	33,803	36,000	2,197
400,000	5,903	24,000	13,200	43,103	48,000	4,897
500,000	5,903	30,000	16,500	52,403	60,000	7,597
1,000,000	5,903	60,000	33,000	98,903	120,000	21,097

Basic information on acquisition and service costs and loss provision from Fulbright Subcommittee hearings, *Analysis of Income and Costs* (cited in text footnote 43), pp. 150f., relating to the twenty-one-month period ending March 31, 1950. Acquisition and service cost data are averages for all loans, and are here applied equally to each size of loan since information on variability of costs with loan size is lacking.

a Acquisition cost of $1,368 plus annual service cost of $907 times five (five years being the modal maturity of RFC business loans). For simplicity, all costs are assumed to be incurred at date of making the loan.

b Calculated at rate of 2 percent per annum on average outstanding loan balance.

c Calculated at rate of 3.3 percent of original loan amount.

d Calculated at standard rate of 4 percent per annum on average outstanding loan balance.

59 This startling result is borne out by testimony of RFC director Harvey Gunderson: "There is no way for a corporation which operates with our checks and balances to make a $1,500 GI loan and make any money on it. I am sure we would be better off if we just wrote them a check and called it a day." *Ibid.*, p. 84.

percent would have been sufficient to cover costs for loans of over $400,-000 in amount. Because costs per dollar could not fall below the basic Treasury borrowing rate, adjusted for retirement fund payments by the Treasury on behalf of RFC, 2 percent would have formed a floor below which loan rates could not fall.

SOME IMPLICATIONS OF RFC BUSINESS
CREDIT CHARGES

What have been the major economic effects and implications of RFC's credit pricing policies? One effect has been to provide a stronger inducement to business firms to obtain RFC loans, and to commercial banks to obtain RFC guarantees of their business loans, than would have existed if RFC had pursued a policy of full-cost pricing of its credit services. Although the Corporation sought vigorously to place loans and loan participations with private institutions, and to avoid lending that could have been undertaken privately, these efforts were counteracted to some extent by its own pricing policies.

The standard rate policy subsidized small firms at the expense of larger firms, and offered a stronger inducement to the marginal small business to seek RFC credit than was offered to the medium or large firm. This result appears to have been recognized and deliberately sought by the management of RFC.

An inflexible rate policy had the effect of making RFC credit relatively more attractive at times when loan rates from private agencies were high and firm than when private rates were relatively low. Because high and rising money rates are ordinarily associated with periods of prosperity, and falling rates with contractions in business, the inflexible interest rate policy of RFC had the effect of tending to expand governmental credit to business at times when counter-cyclical policy would have contracted it, and vice versa. One essential instrument for coordination of federal credit programs with other policies for economic stabilization would be a loan rate flexible through time.

The Business Loan Guaranty and Insurance Program of the Veterans' Administration, 1945-1955

Origin and Purpose

THE Veterans' Administration was authorized to guarantee home, farm, and business loans to veterans by Title III of the Servicemen's Readjustment Act of 1944, popularly known as the GI Bill of Rights.[1] Under this statute, far-reaching benefits were conferred upon men and women who had served in the armed forces of the United States during World War II, and a later law included veterans of the Korean conflict.[2] Loan guarantees were but one part of a vast program of public aids to veterans. By mid-1955 VA had guaranteed over four million home, farm, and business loans in original principal amounts totaling $30 billion; VA-guaranteed home loans were a major factor in the postwar housing market.

The dominant purpose of the Servicemen's Readjustment Act, expressed in public and congressional discussions, was to aid the civil re-establishment of returning veterans, whether disabled or not. The principal motives underlying other federal business credit programs—such as assistance to small businesses, reduction of secular or cyclical unemployment, closure of gaps in the structure of private finance, aid to depressed industries, areas, or economic groups—were not at the forefront of the VA loan program, although they may have been in the background. Approximately sixteen million young men and women were to be re-established in civilian life, after service to the nation in time of crisis. It was believed that a complete program of benefits should be provided to them in the public interest, because the destiny of the nation was inseparable from their welfare.[3]

The great range of benefits provided is seen in reviewing the several titles of the Servicemen's Readjustment Act. Title I provided hospitalization and domiciliary care, and payment of disability claims and pensions. Title II granted educational and vocational training benefits. Title III—with which this study is concerned—made available governmental loan guarantees for the purchase or construction of homes, farms, and business. Title IV created rights and services for the placement of veterans in

---

[1] P.L. 346, 78th Cong., June 22, 1944.
[2] Veterans Readjustment Assistance Act of 1952 (P.L. 550, 82nd Cong., July 16, 1952).
[3] *Annual Report* of the Administrator of Veterans' Affairs, 1944, p. 1.

employment. Title V granted weekly cash readjustment allowances to unemployed veterans.

As these benefits were extended, the aggregate expenditures of the Veterans' Administration for all purposes rose from $828 million during the fiscal year 1944 to a peak of $9.8 billion during fiscal 1950, after which they fell to between $5 billion and $6 billion annually through June 30, 1954.[4] Outlays from 1944 to that date totaled over $60 billion. Over the same period the VA assumed contingent liabilities totaling nearly $13 billion on loans to veterans of about $24 billion.[5] Net expenditures by VA on lenders' claims paid under those guarantees totaled only $21 million up to mid-1954.[6] Business loans were far outweighed by home loans; cumulatively to mid-1954, they formed only about 1.2 percent of the amount of liability assumed by VA on home, farm, and business loans combined.

The business loan guaranty plan in the GI Bill of Rights apparently was based upon a belief that, without support, the creditworthiness of many veterans desiring to acquire businesses would be inadequate. It was designed to support the credit of persons who, through long service at military pay, had been deprived of an opportunity to accumulate substantial amounts of savings or to establish credit or employment records. It was also expected to facilitate the postwar flow of private capital into private enterprise.[7]

VA business credit aid was confined to guarantees or insurance and did not include the power to make loans directly. An early version of the Servicemen's Readjustment Act, passed by the Senate, did include that power. It directed VA upon approval of another federal agency to lend veterans up to $1,000 for the purpose of making "the usual required downpayment" in connection with home, farm, or business financing; VA would have had no discretion in approving or disapproving loans. Later, the present plan—partial guaranty by VA of loans made by other lenders —was substituted;[8] the guaranty was thus intended to take the place of what was normally required as a down payment.[9] The record of congressional discussions is not explicit on the reasons for omitting the direct lending power, but they may perhaps be inferred from considering, for the business program alone, what could have been entailed by a direct loan program. Under a power to lend for business purposes to

[4] *Annual Report* of the Administrator of Veterans' Affairs, 1954, p. 283.
[5] *Ibid.*, p. 97.   [6] *Ibid.*, p. 99.
[7] Cf. *GI Loans—The First Ten Years*, Decennial of the Loan Guaranty Program, Veterans' Administration, June 22, 1954, p. 2.
[8] In 1950 the agency received authority to make direct loans for home purchase or construction, or for construction or improvement of a farm house, if credit was unavailable through private channels.
[9] Cf. Report of Committee on World War Veterans Legislation, H.R. 1418, 78th Cong., 2nd sess., May 5, 1944.

veterans "unable to obtain necessary credit from private sources on reasonable terms"—the formula usually applied to government lending agencies—VA could have been plunged into the banking business on a national scale. The number of loan applications could conceivably have been vastly greater than was ever before handled by a federal business lending agency. Unprecedentedly in federal lending to business firms, VA would have been concerned with a very large number of very small enterprises, and in time might have become through foreclosure the proprietor of numerous firms. The VA was unequipped with personnel, facilities, or experience to become a banker for business. The preferable course was to utilize existing banking facilities, and through VA guaranty or insurance, to stimulate the supply of private business credit to veterans.

The business loan program of VA differs from its farm and home programs in making no charge for the guaranty or insurance service. The public subsidy implied in that feature of the law had two purposes: to reduce the cost of credit to veterans; and to induce lenders to make funds available to veterans that they would not otherwise supply. Congress believed that credit should be available to a veteran who aspired to entrepreneurship and who had a reasonable prospect of success. At the time the act was formulated, fear of postwar unemployment was strong, adding to the desire that veterans be helped to establish their own businesses.

Though but small in terms of the total liabilities and expenditures of the Veterans' Administration credit programs, the guaranty or insurance of business loan is a novel undertaking, of interest for the particular segment of the business population reached—that is, new and very small firms—and for its effect on the practices of business financing institutions.

Statutory Provisions

Rather than trace in detail the numerous amendments of the law under which the VA business credit program operated, we summarize the provisions in effect about the end of 1954, noting the principal changes up to that time.[10]

ELIGIBILITY

Veterans of World War II honorably discharged after having served for ninety days or more after September 16, 1940 and before July 25, 1947,[11] and veterans of the Korean conflict who served after June 27, 1950

---

[10] Major amendments to the Servicemen's Readjustment Act of 1944 were made by Public Law 268, 79th Congress, approved September 4, 1946, and numerous changes have been enacted in a series of laws approved during 1947 and 1948. See Veterans' Administration, *Lenders Handbook*, VA Pamphlet 4-3, especially the December 1948 revision.

[11] The original act referred to the "termination of the war." This was established as July 25, 1947 by Public Law 239, 80th Congress, approved on the same day. In cases where a veteran has been discharged because of service-incurred disability, the period of service can be less than ninety days.

and before a date to be determined by Presidential proclamation or concurrent resolution of Congress, are eligible for loan guaranty benefits.[12] An eligible veteran who applies for a loan within ten years after the official end of the conflict in which he participated is entitled to have it automatically guaranteed by the government in an amount not exceeding 50 percent of the loan, provided that the guaranteed amount does not exceed $4,000 in the case of loans secured by real estate or $2,000 in the case of other loans.[13] Veterans going into joint ventures may pool their guarantees.

The authority given VA in 1950 to guarantee secondary loans need not be considered here, since in practice it affected the home loan, not the business loan part of the program.

PURPOSES

A business loan may be guaranteed if the proceeds "are to be used for the purpose of engaging in business or pursuing a gainful occupation, or for the cost of acquiring for such purpose land, buildings, supplies, equipment, machinery, tools, inventory, stock in trade, or for the cost of the construction, repair, alterations or improvement of any realty or personalty used for such purposes or to provide the funds needed for working capital." The proceeds of business loans may also be used to refinance business indebtedness (but, as a general rule, only if that indebtedness is delinquent) or to pay delinquent taxes or assessments on business property.

Besides specifying the purposes as above, the law requires (1) that the property in question be "useful in and reasonably necessary for the efficient and successful pursuit of the business"; (2) that the "ability and experience of the veteran and the conditions under which he proposes to pursue such business or occupation are such that there is reasonable likelihood that he will be successful"; and (3) that "the purchase price paid or to be paid by the veteran for such property or the cost of construction, alterations, or improvements, does not exceed the reasonable value thereof as determined by proper appraisal made by an appraiser designated by the Administrator."[14]

[12] For veterans of World War II who served again after June 27, 1950, whatever entitlement benefit remained from earlier service was canceled by the law extending coverage to Korean veterans (P.L. 550, 82nd Cong., July 16, 1952) and a new guaranty privilege granted.

[13] The original act required that application for loan benefits must be made within two years after separation from military service or after termination of the war, whichever was the later. The time span for application was lengthened by amendment during 1946. The guaranty maxima for home loans were raised to 60 percent and $7,500 by the Housing Act of 1950, but these loans require prior approval by the Administrator.

[14] See *Lender's Handbook* (VA Pamphlet 4-3, revised December 1948), p. 3.5f., citing 38 USE 694c. "Reasonable value" is interpreted by regulation to mean

It is apparent that the proceeds of a VA-guaranteed loan may be used for almost any business purpose, in contrast to loans of the RFC, Federal Reserve Banks, or other federal business loan agencies, which limit purposes in various ways. Nevertheless, the law does not leave wide open the privilege of obtaining a VA-guaranteed loan for business purposes. The limitations set—that "a reasonable likelihood" of success in business should be shown, and that property expenditures should not exceed "reasonable values" for the assets acquired—are more accurately described as conditions of eligibility than as "credit standards." A veteran who meets those conditions is entitled to a loan guarantee by the Administrator, provided that he can find a lender willing to make a loan within the maximum interest rates specified by the law. He must still convince a lender of his ability to repay the loan.

TERM TO MATURITY

The law left the term to maturity of a guaranteed business loan up to the lender and the veteran, within general limits of thirty years for loans secured by realty (other than farm realty) and ten years for other loans.[15] VA regulations impose the additional limitation that the maximum maturity may not exceed the economic life of the property securing the loan. Any loan for a term in excess of five years must be amortized in accordance with established procedures. Regulations require at least an annual payment against the outstanding loan balance, and a final payment not more than twice the average of preceding installment payments, excepting in the case of construction loans or extended loans. Loans may be repaid before maturity without penalty. As a loan is repaid, the amount of the VA guaranty is reduced proportionately to the remaining loan balance outstanding.

COLLATERAL SECURITY

Real estate loans (except those for repairs or improvements) must be secured by a first lien on the realty. Loans for purchase, alteration, improvement, repair, or production of tangible personal property must be secured "to the extent legal and practicable," and a loan for working capital or other capital, merchandise, or good will or other intangible assets may be made without a lien. Loans of $1,000 or less for alteration, repair, or improvement of real property need not be secured. If over $1,000, such loans must be secured by a first or second lien, and if the

market prices current at time of acquisition of property. The original law had referred to "reasonable normal value" which was construed by many appraisers to indicate pre-World War II price levels, and therefore proved to be unduly restrictive. Cf. *GI Loans—the First 10 Years, op.cit.*, p. 4.

15 The Housing Act of 1950 increased the maximum term for GI business loans secured by real estate from twenty-five years to thirty.

expenditures on property exceed 40 percent of its reasonable prior value, the security must be a first lien. Because loans may be as much as 100 percent of the appraised value of the property offered as security—a loan ratio much beyond the usual standards of prudence—the VA must place a major reliance for repayment of sums borrowed upon the moral character and business ability of the veteran.

INTEREST RATES

The original legislation prescribed a maximum rate of interest of 4 percent per annum on the unpaid principal balance of all VA-guaranteed loans. However, this was found to be too low and inflexible a limit to make many loans attractive to banks and other lenders, particularly under conditions of active demand for credit and rising money rates. An amendment effective December 17, 1947 permitted the interest rate on insured non-real-estate loans to rise to a maximum of 3 percent discount on the original amount of one-year notes payable in equal monthly installments, or 5.7 percent per annum on the unpaid balance of an interest-bearing note. An amendment of August 10, 1948 also permitted the Administrator, with the approval of the Secretary of the Treasury, to approve of rates up to 4½ percent per annum on guaranteed loans, "if he finds that the loan market demands it."[16] This amendment represented an interesting deviation from the customary federal policy of prescribing an inflexible maximum loan rate.[17] It was due to the inability of VA to make direct loans to veterans on its own initiative, and its need for finding private lenders willing to carry that part of the risk of nonrepayment which was not assumed by VA. The interest rate on guaranteed real estate loans remained at 4 percent until May 5, 1953 when, with credit stringent in the mortgage loan markets in most sections of the country, the Administrator of Veterans Affairs authorized an increase to 4½ percent. Up until September 1, 1953 the VA paid to the lender a "gratuity" equal to 4 percent of the guaranteed or insured portion of each loan, but not exceeding $160, which amount was credited to the veteran's loan account. It was believed that the VA should prepay approximately the first year's interest due on the part of a loan for which it was responsible, as an additional aid to the veteran.

PROCEDURE IN CASE OF DEFAULT

In the event of default or to avoid imminent default, the terms of repayment of any VA-guaranteed business loan may be extended by written agreement between the lender and the veteran-borrower, without the

---

[16] P.L. 901, 80th Cong.

[17] Statutory *maxima* for interest rates under some of the titles of the National Housing Act have been fixed at 5 or 6 percent, but actual rates have been adjusted from time to time at various points below the maxima.

approval of the VA. If an extension is proposed for some other reason, or if the extension will result in the release of an obligor, the prior approval of VA must be obtained.

Failing extension of maturity, when a default has continued (a) 60 days in nonpayment of an installment, (b) 90 days in failure to comply with some obligation other than periodic payment, or (c) 180 days in nonpayment of taxes, the lender is required to file a notice of default with VA within the next 45 days.

A claim for guaranty may be submitted at any time after default has continued for three months (in the case of an extended loan or a term loan, after one month). A claim for insurance may be submitted after three months' default, provided the holder has established the net loss by liquidating all of the available security. It is important to distinguish between a claim for insurance, which represents the net amount due the holder after the property has been sold, from the guaranty claim, which may be filed before sale of the property.

Before the holder forecloses or liquidates security for a guaranteed or insured loan, VA must be notified. The notice may be given at any time after default has continued for three months, and action may be taken thirty days after notification. If the property has been abandoned, waste is occurring, or other circumstances warrant immediate action, the holder may act without advance notice but must report to VA within ten days the action taken and the reasons for it.

Within thirty days after receiving notice of default, notice of intention to foreclose, or a claim for the guaranty, the VA may require the lender to assign the loan and the security therefor to the VA or to another lender designated by the VA, upon paying the original lender the full amount of the outstanding loan balance. If the VA does not exercise this right, the usual result is a sale of the property by the lender. Because the rights of VA are subordinate to those of the lender, the lender has first claim against the proceeds of sale for the satisfaction of the unguaranteed portion of the unpaid loan balance.

To illustrate, suppose a default and property sale in the following circumstances: VA has guaranteed the legal maximum of 50 percent of a loan, the proceeds of which were used to purchase property appraised at 100 percent of the amount expended (i.e. the loan/value ratio was also at the legal maximum); and no repayment whatever has been made by the debtor before default. Even if the property sells for as little as one-half of its original appraised value, plus liquidation expenses, the lender will still have recovered all of the unguaranteed portion of his loan. In other words, the effect of the VA guarantee from the point of view of the lender would essentially be to reduce the maximum loan-value ratio from 100 percent to 50 percent, which brings such loans within the range of the credit standards ordinarily applied in mortgage lending. Hence it appears that for the institutions advancing the funds the potential losses on VA-guaranteed business loans are greatest with respect to non-real-estate loans, particularly where loans for working capital or to acquire intangible business assets are unsecured or are secured by property with low resale value.

LOAN INSURANCE

The original law of 1944 provided only for loan guaranty. An important amendment effective December 28, 1945 (P.L. 268, 79th Cong.) permitted supervised lenders to elect VA insurance against losses in lieu of loan guaranty. By agreement between a lender and VA, the lender may be insured against loss up to 15 percent of the aggregate amount of eligible loans made by him. Purchased loans meeting the conditions of eligibility are also insurable if, with the loan report, the lender submits to the Administrator evidence of an agreement, made before the loan was closed, to purchase such loans subject to their being insured by VA. The VA maintains a current account in the name of each insured lender, crediting it with the appropriate amounts available for the payment of losses on insured loans made or purchased, and debiting it with the appropriate amounts on account of transfers to other lenders, or payment of losses. The pattern of FHA Title I loan insurance was followed. The 15 percent premium necessarily represented an estimate of the amount needed for reserve, rather than an actuarial calculation.[18]

The loan insurance provision greatly expanded potential operations under Title III, and in the business loan part of the program was widely used. It enlarged the amount of government-supported credit available to any one veteran, and also made the extension of such credit more attractive to lenders. It permitted a veteran to obtain several loans up to a total—in the case of non-real-estate credits—of $13,333, before he had used up the $2,000 maximum legal VA guarantee, whereas previously $4,000 was the maximum obtainable[19] (15 percent of $13,333 equaling $2,000, which is the amount of the available guaranty.) Under it the lender was in a position to recover 100 percent of any loan subsequently defaulting or resulting in a loss instead of the previous maximum of 50 percent covered by VA guarantee, if his insurance account was adequate. The insurance provision was especially attractive to lenders making a large volume of VA loans, because the probabilities were then high that their insurance accounts would have sufficient credits to repay the bank in full for any losses. In effect, a large number of good loans could carry the full amount of a small number of bad loans in a lender's portfolio.[20]

[18] The reserve originally called for in FHA loan insurance, 20 percent of the loan amount, was found excessive and reduced to 10 percent.

[19] Cf. *Banking*, July 1946, p. 37.

[20] It has been shown algebraically that an insured mortgage affords the lender

The reduction of the balance amount of an insured loan by installment payments, or the final payment of a loan, does not reduce a lending institution's reservoir of insurance credit. Hence institutions doing a large volume of insured lending to veterans may in the course of time accumulate insurance coverage equivalent to 100 percent or more of the unpaid balance of all loans in their portfolios.

It should be emphasized that even under the most favorable conditions, loan insurance does not enable a lender to recover *all* of the costs incurred in connection with a bad loan, although reasonable foreclosure costs are recoverable along with unpaid principal and interest. Even if the insurance account of a lender enabled the VA to repay 100 percent of the principal and interest, the lender must still incur administrative expense in arranging for loan extensions, attempting to collect sums due, reducing its claim to judgment, and foregoing interest on the amount of the unpaid balance during the period elapsing between the sale of the property securing the loan and the payment of the claim. Hence it is vitally important to lenders that loans be set up soundly at the start, and 100 percent loan insurance by no means obviates this need.

AUTOMATIC GUARANTEE AND PRIOR APPROVAL LOANS

Originally, VA-loan guarantees were available only to lenders who had referred loan applications to the Administrator for prior approval, but the very large number of applications received after demobilization began in 1945 resulted in delays in granting credits to veterans. By amendment to the law in 1946, lenders subject to examination and supervision of an agency of a federal or state government (such as commercial banks and insurance companies) were empowered to make loans with an automatic guarantee *without* prior reference to the VA. Nonsupervised lenders (such as individuals, or commercial finance companies in some states) continue to require prior approval.[21] Because supervised lenders must bear the risk of ineligibility of a loan, many of them, despite the availability of automatic guarantee, have continued to seek the Administrator's

---

more protection than a guaranteed mortgage up to $8,000, provided portfolio defaults do not exceed 30 percent. In addition, as amortization proceeds, insured mortgages will absorb still higher percentages of defaults at an increasingly faster rate (e.g. after 17 percent amortization has taken place, insured mortgages are preferable unless defaults exceed 35 percent). Moreover, business and other loans may be merged into a common insurance account for the lender, which is desirable in helping to underwrite the (usually) more hazardous business loans. See the article by Julian R. Fleischman, "Guaranteed vs. Insured GI Loans," *Savings and Loan News*, August 1946, p. 7. In fact, the number of business loans made on a guaranteed basis up to mid-1955 was considerably smaller than the number insured. Insured loans comprised 60.8 percent of all business loans closed up to that date (*Loan Guaranty*, June 1955, p. 57).

21 On home loans guaranteed under Section 501(b), which permit the higher guarantee, prior approval by VA is also required.

approval before making loans.[22] However, the proportion of business loans made with prior approval fell from 35 percent in 1946 to less than 10 percent in 1952.

A SECONDARY MARKET FOR VA REAL ESTATE LOANS

The attractiveness of VA-guaranteed home loans to commercial banks, savings and loan associations, and other lenders was materially increased by the secondary market supports initiated in 1946. As of August of that year the RFC was authorized to purchase VA-insured or -guaranteed loans, either directly or through a subsidiary,[23] and in 1948 the Federal National Mortgage Association was given power to purchase VA-protected mortgage loans.[24] It is noteworthy that this legislation applied only to home and farm loans and did not provide secondary markets for business loans to veterans, even if secured by real estate. Thus the further legislative measures taken by Congress in that connection need not concern us here.

Administration

ORGANIZATION OF THE VETERANS' ADMINISTRATION

The business loan insurance and guaranty program was administered during most of the period under study by the Finance Office of VA, one of the agency's major operating divisions.[25] The Finance Office handled payments of all benefits to veterans and their dependents, made disbursements for services and supplies furnished, paid all VA administrative expenses, and administered guarantees and insurance of loans. Each major function of the Finance Office was assigned to a director, loan insurance and guaranty being the responsibility of the Director of the Loan Guaranty Service. In turn, division chiefs were in charge, respectively, of home, farm, and business loans.

After the Servicemen's Readjustment Act became effective on June 22, 1944, regulations were drafted and forms were designed and printed. In November 1944, four field offices were equipped with loan guaranty divisions to serve the entire United States. As demobilization of the armed forces proceeded during 1945, a flood of applications for loan

[22] *Annual Report of the Veterans' Administration*, 1946, p. 42, and *Finance, Guaranty of Loans*, December 1952, p. 71.

[23] P.L. 656, 79th Cong., August 7, 1946.

[24] P.L. 864, 80th Cong., July 1, 1948.

[25] On June 30, 1953 the Executive Office of the President authorized the VA to proceed with a plan for reorganization of its central office along "major purpose" lines in lieu of the "functional line" type of organization previously in effect. Three major departments were established: the Department of Medicine and Surgery, the Department of Insurance, and the Department of Veterans Benefits. Loan guaranty and insurance operations were assigned to the last-named department. *Annual Report of the Administrator of Veterans' Affairs*, 1953, p. 4.

guaranty benefits made apparent a need for decentralization of authority in order to reduce the time elapsing between receipt of an application and disbursement of a guaranteed loan, and for a large number of additional field offices with facilities for processing applications.

Between November 1944 and June 30, 1945, loan guarantee divisions were established in 22 additional field offices, making a total of 26 offices so equipped at mid-1945.[26] In addition, revised administrative procedures for expediting action on applications were first tested, and then installed. The aim was to process loan applications within forty-eight hours of receipt, excluding an additional four or five days required for verification of eligibility at the New York office.[27] The number of field offices equipped for loan guaranty service was further increased to 74 by mid-1946. By mid-1947 the new standard administrative procedures had been installed in all field offices, and the time required for processing loan applications had been reduced by as much as 25 percent.[28] The 1946 amendment extending to supervised lenders automatic guaranty (without prior referral of loan applications to VA) further accelerated loan disbursements. It was said that "Under this new arrangement, a loan can be completely processed in a week at the maximum, or if the veteran is known to the bank, the loan can be granted on the spot. Prior to the 'automatic guarantee' procedure, a month might elapse between application and disbursement."[29]

Field offices equipped with loan guaranty service have full authority to approve or disapprove of most applications for loan guaranty or insurance without reference to Washington. Because veterans move from one region to another and may apply for loan guaranty benefits at different locations and for different purposes, it is necessary for the Veterans' Administration to maintain at a single location a record of each veteran's available but unused benefits under the Servicemen's Readjustment Act, known as the veteran's "entitlement." All entitlement records for the nation are maintained at the Readjustment Accounting Control Division (RACD) of VA located in New York City. Field offices obtained from RACD a statement of a veteran's entitlement before issuing certificates of eligibility to lenders.

APPLICATION FOR AND ORIGINATION OF LOANS

Applications for business loan guaranty or insurance where the prior approval of VA is required or sought are made jointly by the veteran and the lender. On a single form, the veteran applies to the lender for a loan,

[26] *Annual Report of the Administrator of Veterans' Affairs*, 1945, p. 28. See also *Banking*, April 1946, p. 63.
[27] *Annual Report of the Administrator of Veterans' Affairs*, 1946, p. 43.
[28] *Annual Report of the Administrator of Veterans' Affairs*, 1947, p. 57.
[29] Cf. *Banking*, July 1946, p. 37.

and both then apply to the Administrator of Veterans Affairs for insurance or guaranty. The standard form of application requires the following information: (1) general purpose, amount, and terms of the proposed loan; (2) description of prior lien, if any, on the property to be acquired; (3) estimated disbursements of the loan for various purposes, along with expected total cost to the veteran of business property to be acquired, and sources of other funds to finance its acquisition; (4) description of the security offered for repayment; (5) statement of business experience and plans of the veteran applicant, including an estimate of business income and expense for the next twelve months, if the loan is to be used to establish a new business, or a recent balance sheet and operating statement, if the loan is to be used to expand or refinance an existing business. Credit reports and financial data are submitted to the regional office of VA, so that it may determine whether there is a reasonable prospect of repayment.

In the case of loans processed on an automatic basis, the credit function is performed by the lending institution and reported to VA. The same information is given as for prior approval loans, excepting that in lieu of (5) above, the lender certifies to VA that the conditions of eligibility for guaranty have been met by the veteran. Obviously, the lender assumes a greater risk and responsibility with automatic than with prior approval loans. However, once the evidence of guaranty or insurance is issued, it is incontestable except for fraud or material misrepresentation.

The changes in procedure adopted in December 1945, which greatly expedited the credit process, are shown by the following comparative summary of steps:

Original Procedure: Veteran discusses loan with bank officer. Veteran and bank fill out form of application for certificate of eligibility for the veteran and send it to the regional office of the VA. Certificate of eligibility is returned to the bank, and enclosed with it is the name of a qualified appraiser who is to appraise the real property involved. The bank obtains a credit rating report on the veteran from an approved credit rating agency. The bank completes arrangements to make the loan and applies to the VA for a certificate of guaranty. The VA sends the guaranty certificate to the bank. The funds may then be paid out to the veteran.

Revised Procedure: Veteran discusses loan with bank officer. Bank may accept the veteran's honorable discharge certificate as verification of eligibility for loan. Bank proceeds with credit appraisal, and requests the VA to assign an appraiser. After receiving appraiser's report, bank may pay out loan. After making the loan, the bank sends to VA the veteran's honorable discharge certificate, the note or evidence of debt signed by the veteran, the appraiser's report, and the loan closing statement of the bank. VA endorses the discharge certificate with the amount of the loan made and the portion of the guaranty right used and remaining for the veteran. VA endorses the note, indicating the guaranty reserve covering the loan, and returns to the bank the discharge certificate and the note, retaining the appraiser's report and the closing statement. The discharge certificate is returned to the veteran.

Loans may originate in a number of ways, but it is the standing instruction of VA to the veteran that he "find his own lender." While the loan guaranty and insurance offered to lenders without charge was designed to help veterans obtain credit, it may not be sufficient inducement to lenders to advance funds at the maximum interest charges specified by the law. VA does not assume responsibility for finding a lender nor assure a veteran desiring a loan that he will obtain one. Nevertheless, it assists veterans coming initially to its field offices, by supplying application forms advising the veteran how to make his loan application a bankable proposition. VA has recommended the following steps in arranging for a loan:[30] "(1) find the property you want, (2) go to a bank or other lending agency, (3) present your plan and original discharge papers, (4) property is checked by an approved appraiser,[31] (5) certificate of reasonable value goes to lender, (6) if loan is approved, you get the money."

On occasion, VA offices have suggested banks or other lending institutions which might be disposed to consider a veteran's application. When competition among lenders for VA-guaranteed or -insured loans has been active (as appears to have been the case at times during 1945 and 1946) the VA offices have refrained from directing veterans to particular lenders, in order to avoid the criticism of putting other lenders under a competitive handicap. But at other times VA has not hesitated to direct them. In some instances VA offices referred veterans to government lending agencies; RFC, for example, made a number of VA-guaranteed business loans to veterans unable to get credit from private sources. The ability of VA itself to advance funds, when it could be established that private credit was not available at the specified rates of interest, applied only to loans for home purchase or construction, or for construction or improvement of a farmhouse, not to business loans.

The VA has been flexible in assenting to different procedures of loan origination. For example, a large proportion of business loans—especially in the Pacific Coast region—have been utilized by veterans to purchase automobiles or trucks for business purposes. In many such cases, the automotive dealers making the sales have supplied veterans with application forms, and, acting as authorized agents of the lender (the bank or

---

[30] Veterans' Administration, *Guaranteed Loans for Veterans*, Pamphlet 4-1, (revised), November 1949.

[31] Officers of banks and other supervised lending institutions are frequently designated as appraisers of assets other than real estate, so that with personal property loans it is usually the lending officer who makes the appraisal.

commercial finance company acquiring their installment receivable paper), have completed applications for VA-protected loans jointly with veterans. Where the lender involved was a supervised institution utilizing the automatic guaranty provision, a loan might be closed without any personal contact of the lender or the VA with the veteran.[32]

It would be useful to know what percentage of veterans seeking VA business loans have been unable to obtain them because they were deemed by lenders to lack experience or reasonable likelihood of success in business. The VA offices do not prejudge the creditworthiness of a veteran nor deter any veteran from applying for a loan, although they may later reject formal applications on the ground that legal requirements including likelihood of success have not been met. A considerable number of veterans have desired business loans which never reached the stage of formal application—and therefore do not appear in VA statistical records —because they could not find a lender willing to extend credit. The fact that some veterans have obtained VA business loans from the RFC indicates that VA loan guaranty or insurance was not a sufficient inducement to private lenders in all cases. One large bank reported that its officers deterred many veterans from borrowing to go into business, in order to prevent them from dissipating their own savings, as well as public funds, in trying to operate businesses which probably would have turned out unsuccessfully.

PARTICIPATION OF PRIVATE LENDERS

The success of VA loan guaranty or insurance in aiding veterans was heavily dependent upon the cooperation of commercial banks and other lending institutions. The VA was a passive agency in the credit process; private lenders were to be the makers of loans. Did private lenders enter into the program actively?

There is strong evidence that commercial banks and other lending institutions were aggressive in seeking and making VA loans during the initial years of the program, when good will toward returning servicemen was high and there was a strong, general disposition to aid them in their re-establishment in civilian life. The Federal Reserve survey of business loans held by member banks at November 20, 1946 indicated that although

[32] Similarly, in connection with loans to purchase homes in residential real estate tracts under development, it may be the tract developer instead of the lender who completes with the veteran an application for a VA-protected loan, as part of the total plan for financing purchase of a new home. Ordinarily the tract developer first obtains a "certificate of reasonable value" from VA based upon an appraisal of the prices fixed for the homes, and he also obtains from a lender a commitment to purchase from him VA-guaranteed or -insured loans. He is then able to proceed; but the lender or the VA must still pass upon the borrower's credit rating, ability to pay, and eligibility.

VA-protected loans were but a small fraction of the total, their occurrence was widespread: "Guaranteed or insured lending to G.I.'s for business purposes was general among the member banks in all Federal Reserve Districts. About a third of all of the member banks had some of these business loans. A substantial proportion of the banks in each size group engaged in this type of lending, although it appeared to be more common among the large than among the small banks."[33] During 1945 the American Bankers Association organized a Committee on Service for War Veterans.[34] This committee prepared and circulated a *Manual of Procedure for Making GI Loans*, conducted questionnaire surveys of bankers' attitudes toward such loans, and sought amendments to the law designed to augment the volume of insured and guaranteed loans, for example, the automatic guaranty of VA loans and the provision of a secondary market for them. It conferred frequently with officials of the VA, and sought procedures for obtaining more uniform appraisals, which, during 1946, was said to be "the most troublesome factor in the veterans' credit situation."[35]

Many commercial banks established separate loan offices staffed by specialists in VA loans. In various cities—for example, Philadelphia, Rochester, Houston—banks jointly established centers where veterans could discuss their plans and make loan applications, in some instances staffed to provide information and counsel on housing, business, job placement, and other matters as well as loans. These actions[36] illustrate the receptiveness of commercial bankers to the VA credit program during the demobilization period. Profit was certainly not the only, or even the major, motive of bank extension of VA business loans, considering the relatively long risks, high administrative costs per dollar of credit, and limited interest return. A desire to cultivate public good will and help veterans re-establish themselves was equally important.

After 1946, there was some diminution of banking interest in VA business loans. Even from the start there were certain rural areas in which local bankers were reluctant to make them. Business loans were generally more hazardous than home or farm loans; most of them did not have a first lien on realty, and therefore had no secondary market. In many small communities local bankers had been accustomed to charging 6 to 8 percent or more on small business loans, and were not attracted by credits offering a maximum of 5.7 percent, even when the VA insured the loans or guaranteed half of their amount. For small banks in small communities, the

[33] Cf. Tynan Smith, "Security Pledged on Member Bank Loans to Business," *Federal Reserve Bulletin*, June 1947, pp. 676f.
[34] Cf. *Banking*, October 1946, p. 56. [35] Cf. *Banking*, November 1946, pp. 117f.
[36] See *Banking*, September 1945, p. 62; February 1946, p. 39; March 1946, p. 36; July 1946, p. 36; and August 1946, pp. 47, 89.

number of VA business loans that might be developed was insufficient to make the VA loan insurance device attractive.

Savings and loan associations, although active in the home loan part of the program, scarcely participated in VA-protected business lending because only a small fraction of the loans were eligible for negotiation or purchase by them.

By late 1947, RFC had made a total of 3,924 GI business loans aggregating $16,483,000, instances where veterans had been unable to find private sources of credit in their communities. In a study covering 2,910 business loans authorized by RFC from June 1946 through September 1947 after they had been declined by banks—of which 1,852 were GI loans—the agency found that in 22 percent of the cases, or about one-third of those concerning veterans, the bank's refusal resulted from a stated policy not to make GI loans.[37]

EVOLUTION OF BANK CREDIT STANDARDS

Commercial banks made the great majority of all VA business loans. To most commercial banks the veteran's business loan posed a new type of credit problem, namely, the making of term loans to new or very small businesses that would be amortized out of earnings. This is a fact that deserves great emphasis. Since 1935, commercial banks have developed a large volume of term loans to medium-sized and large business enterprises.[38] They have traditionally made numerous small short-term business loans maturing within a year and based primarily on the personal credit or collateral security of the small businessman rather than upon an estimate of the earning power of the enterprise.[39] Most banks regarded these loans essentially as personal rather than business loans. VA business loans were novel in applying the term-loan principle to very small enterprises, including new as well as established firms.[40]

Faced with a new type of credit problem, commercial banks gradually evolved procedures and credit standards as a result of experimentation and observation. The law and regulations of VA did not go beyond the general criteria that the borrower show experience and reasonable like-

[37] Hearings before a Subcommittee of the Committee on Banking and Currency, U.S. Senate, 80th Cong., 1st sess., on S. Res. 132, "A Resolution for an Inquiry into the Operation of the Reconstruction Finance Corporation and Its Subsidiaries"; Part 1, December 11, 1947, p. 34.

[38] For descriptions of the development of bank term lending, see Term Lending to Business (1942) and Business Finance and Banking (1947), by Neil H. Jacoby and R. J. Saulnier (National Bureau of Economic Research, Financial Research Program).

[39] Cf. Charles H. Schmidt, "Member Bank Loans to Small Business," Federal Reserve Bulletin, August 1947, p. 963.

[40] From the standpoint of the lender, the difference between new and established firms in the very small business field is not important, because the fortunes of the enterprise are so heavily determined by the single owner-manager.

lihood of success in business. It was up to the banks to interpret these general requirements in terms of specific rules and standards.

During the initial phase of the VA program, which lasted from 1945 up to about mid-1947, commercial banks did not have well-formulated credit standards for veterans' business loans, and were inclined to be liberal in making them. Because many young veterans had not had any business experience, loans were often made to men who had only a technical proficiency in a certain trade or occupation. For example, a young veteran who acquired skill as a radio technician in the army, would be considered to have sufficient experience to obtain a loan to open a radio repair shop. His skill in repairing radios, however, may not have been matched by business acumen in purchasing parts, maintaining records, marketing his services, and controlling expenses. Many VA business loans were made to enable veterans to purchase Army surplus trucks for the purpose of entering the commercial trucking business. These appeared to be sound loans, especially since many veterans had learned truck operation and repair in military service and the trucks were purchased at apparently low prices. Experience showed, however, that commercial trucking was a business requiring talents additional to those of truck driver and mechanic; also, military vehicles were ill-adapted to many commercial transportation needs. Hence, many of these loans turned out unfortunately for the bank, the VA, and the veteran.

At the beginning, banks also lacked experience with respect to the amount of the veteran's own funds that he should be expected to invest in a business. Certain banks advanced nearly the entire amount of money required by a veteran for equipment, stock of goods, and working capital. If the venture did not immediately succeed, a veteran could simply "walk away" from it after the working capital had been exhausted, leaving the bank with a liquidation problem, though the veteran would remain liable to the VA in the event it had to pay a claim by the bank.

Another question was the maturity of loans. The law permitted maturities up to ten years for non-real-estate loans, provided the loan was amortized. During the initial phase of the program, many banks set up business loans on a five-year basis, or for even longer periods. Repayment experience however, was often unfavorable on business loans of such long terms.

Through trial and error, banks gradually learned what credit standards should be met in order to make VA business loans bankable. One banker, writing from considerable experience, recommended the following rules:[41]

(1) Insist on a down-payment by the veteran out of his own resources of about 10 percent of the property purchased with a loan, so that the

[41] Earl R. Parsons, "We're Learning a Lot about GI Loans," *Banking*, July 1946, pp. 36f.

veteran will have an equity of his own to protect. (2) Set up an amortization schedule for repayment of the loan as soon as possible—within two or three years. Veterans may always apply for new loans, after the initial loan has been repaid, if they have unused benefits left. (3) Make sure the veteran has enough working capital for business operations and funds for personal and family living expense before granting a loan to purchase business equipment. Loans to provide both equipment and working capital are unsound. (4) Be certain the veteran is physically able to carry on the business for which he requests a loan. If he is receiving a disability compensation, get a signed statement from him permitting the VA to show you his service record. (5) Be certain that the veteran does not exaggerate the true profit potentialities of his business, and study the business periodically to provide him with management counsel. (6) Limit loans to veterans with business experience in the type of enterprise they plan to enter, or to those whose background indicates they will succeed.

About mid-1947, after the initial flood of loan applications arising from demobilization had passed and as experience with VA business loans developed, there is evidence that bank credit standards were generally raised, and loan applications were more critically scrutinized by banks and VA offices. This change was not solely the product of repayment difficulties, but also reflected the rise in alternative loan opportunities open to banks. In addition, some bankers felt they had perfected the technique of making small business term loans profitably, and preferred to do so without VA participation; for a loan properly set up they considered VA guaranty or insurance unnecessary. In many cases, banks could charge a higher interest rate on nonguaranteed loans than the 5.7 percent maximum under the GI statute; the veteran was often willing to pay a higher rate in order to conserve his guaranty benefits for a home loan, to avoid payment of appraisal fees, or to obtain funds more rapidly with less red tape.[42]

One large branch-system bank with extensive experience in VA business lending came to apply the same credit standards to its VA business loans as to other small term loans to business. Its requirements of any small business term borrower were: (1) He must invest in the enterprise an amount equal to the loan of the bank, thus insuring that the bank would not be, in effect, the senior "partner" in the enterprise. (2) He must have had business experience as well as technical proficiency in the trade or mechanical art used in the business. (3) The loan must be amortized within a maximum period of three years.

[42] Public Law 139, effective September 1, 1951, permitted a veteran to deduct guaranty or insurance entitlement used for business or farm loans from the $7,500 maximum home loan guaranty, with the remainder available for a home loan guaranteed under Section 501(b) of the Servicemen's Readjustment Act.

A Statistical Summary, 1945–1955

BUSINESS LOANS IN THE TOTAL VETERANS'

ADMINISTRATION LOAN PROGRAM

Table C-1 presents a cumulative summary of the number, original amount of loans, and original amount of the VA liability on loans, for home, farm, and business loans combined, and for business loans separately, by fiscal years ending June 30, 1945 through 1955. The relatively small role of business loans in the total veterans' credit program is apparent. Through mid-1955 business loans formed only 5.3 percent of the number of loans closed, and only 2.0 percent of the original cumulated amount of loans closed, and only 1.1 percent of the cumulative amount of

TABLE C-1

Cumulative Summary of Home, Farm, and Business Loans Made with VA Guaranty or Insurance in Fiscal Years 1945–1955

| FISCAL YEAR ENDING JUNE 25 | NUMBER OF LOANS CLOSED | ORIGINAL AMOUNT (000) | ORIGINAL VA LIABILITY | | AVERAGE SIZE OF LOAN | AVERAGE VA LIABILITY PER LOAN |
			Amount (000)	As % of Amount of Loans		
		CUMULATIVE TOTALS—HOME, FARM, AND BUSINESS LOANS				
1945	12,228	$ 55,209	$ 19,645	35.6%	$4,515	$1,607
1946	188,417	872,276	393,978	45.2	4,629	2,091
1947	823,548	4,458,034	2,077,608	46.6	5,413	2,523
1948	1,343,642	7,420,871	3,487,292	47.0	5,523	2,595
1949	1,622,873	8,773,513	4,170,185	47.5	5,406	2,570
1950	2,020,603	10,938,750	5,248,360	48.0	5,414	2,597
1951	2,558,613	14,630,906	7,370,093	50.4	5,718	2,881
1952	2,983,267	17,943,871	9,266,056	51.6	6,015	3,106
1953	3,299,949	20,723,544	10,870,824	52.5	6,280	3,294
1954	3,632,518	23,947,972	12,726,702	53.1	6,593	3,504
1955	4,203,668	30,001,134	16,153,207	53.8	7,137	3,843
		CUMULATIVE TOTALS—BUSINESS LOANS				
1945	738	a	a	a	a	a
1946	16,215	$ 47,820	$ 20,300	42.5%	$2,949	$1,252
1947	68,172	213,106	81,384	38.2	3,126	1,194
1948	94,455	299,433	114,538	38.3	3,170	1,213
1949	107,244	337,629	127,130	37.7	3,148	1,185
1950	119,316	369,155	134,942	36.6	3,094	1,131
1951	136,836	410,718	145,168	35.5	3,002	1,064
1952	190,767	514,407	162,898	31.7	2,697	854
1953	205,450	552,365	169,578	30.7	2,689	825
1954	214,544	577,685	174,092	30.1	2,693	811
1955	221,014	598,723	178,114	29.7	2,709	806

Data for 1945–1954 are from *Annual Reports* of the Administrator of Veterans' Affairs, and for 1955 from *Loan Guaranty*, June 1955, p. 57.

a Not available.

VA liability. Earlier, the percentages for business loans were somewhat higher, though not large; through mid-1947, about 8 percent by number, 5 percent by amount of loan, and 4 percent by amount of VA liability. But the great diversity of small business ventures posed specially difficult tasks of credit appraisal and administration, both for lenders and for the VA, which made business loans more important in the administration of the whole program than the ratios suggest.

Up to mid-1955 a cumulative total of about 221,000 VA business loans had been disbursed in an aggregate original amount of nearly $600 million. The average original amount of the loans made over the preceding ten and one-half years was about $2,700 and the average original amount of the VA liability was about 30 percent thereof, or $810. Business loans in comparison to all loans were of smaller average size, and VA's liability on them covered lesser fractions of the loan amount (Table C-1); and the contrast increased through time. Business loans made in fiscal years through 1949 averaged between 56 and 64 percent as large as all loans combined, but after mid-1951, less than one-third as large. The portion of the loan amount for which VA carried liability averaged between 29 and 39 percent through 1949, then less than 20 percent after 1950 (Table C-6). The smaller average size of business loans reflects the legal limitation of $2,000 on the amount of the VA guarantee on non-real-estate loans (most business loans were of that type), whereas the limit was $4,000 on real estate loans until 1950 when it was raised to $7,500 for home loans. The smaller portion of the loan amount for which VA protection was utilized by veterans obtaining business loans reflects the relatively wider use of insurance (where VA's protection could not cover more than 15 percent of the loan amount) rather than guaranty in that part of the program.

For business loans and for all loans combined, the VA credit program expanded rapidly during the fiscal years 1945–1947 as demobilization and veteran readjustment to civilian life proceeded. It advanced at a slower rate in fiscal 1948 and at a still slower pace in fiscal 1949 when business activity underwent a mild recession. Then the combined program gained new momentum, especially during fiscal 1951 as economic activity increased after the outbreak of hostilities in Korea. The expansion of the combined credit program during fiscal 1948–1951 was greater than that of the business loan program by itself, the cumulative original amount of all loans combined doubling between mid-1948 and mid-1951, whereas the amount for business loans rose by only 40 percent. This reflected the strong demand of veterans for homes, the availability (until repeal by the Housing Act of 1950) of VA-guaranteed secondary loans while the primary loan was insured by FHA, and the establishment of a 100 percent secondary market for VA-guaranteed real estate loans, as well as a more ample supply of low-cost housing.[43] Again between 1951 and 1955 the cumulative loan amount of the combined program doubled, whereas for business loans the amount rose by only 23 percent. The comparatively small demand for business loans may reflect veterans' preferring to use their VA entitlements for home loans, and increased availability of business credit without VA participation.

A summary of the default and loss experience up to mid-1955 on home, farm, and business loans guaranteed or insured by the VA clearly indicates the much greater hazard inherent in lending to small business enterprises than was present in home and farm loans, nearly all of which are secured by marketable real estate (Table C-2). Of the more than 3.9 million home loans reported closed, the VA had paid claims on about 22,300 loans, or 0.57 percent of the number; and the amount of claims paid formed less than one-tenth of one percent of the original amount of all loans closed. The record was somewhat less favorable for farm loans and strikingly unfavorable for business loans. Up to June 1955 the VA had paid claims on 12,600 of the 221,000 business loans closed, or 5.71 percent of the number; and the amount of those claims was 1.65 percent of the original amount of all such loans closed. Because business loans had a much shorter average maturity than home loans, it is undoubtedly true that the critical period for repayment of home loans has not yet arrived. However, the percentage of the number of outstanding loans in default (including loans awaiting payment of the lenders' claims) at mid-1955 affords a limited preview of relative losses in the future; and the default ratio for home loans was just under 1.1 percent whereas it stood at nearly 10 percent for business loans.[44]

The loan insurance principle was applied much more extensively to VA business loans than to VA home or farm loans, because of the smaller average size of business loans and the infrequency with which they were secured by real estate. Through May 1951 less than one-half of 1 percent of home loans were insured, about 7.0 percent of farm loans, and nearly 40 percent of business loans (Table C-3). Although the number and dollar volume of home loans far outweighed business loans, nearly two-thirds of the initial amounts of insurance credits on the books of the VA at May 25, 1951 were on account of business loans. This appears to indicate that the loan insurance principle finds its widest application in a credit field marked by large numbers of small loans, with respect to each of which risks and uncertainties are considerable.

43 Cf. T. B. King, "The Revival of the GI Loan," *Savings and Loan News*, November 1950, p. 27.

44 A more significant comparison would lie between the default and claim experience on GI business loans and the portfolio experience of lenders with conventional small business term loans. Requisite data are not available, but a few banks which have had extensive experience with small business term loans report a more favorable experience with conventional than with GI loans.

TABLE C-2

Summary of Default and Loss Experience on Home, Farm, and Business Loans Guaranteed or Insured by VA, to June 25, 1955

(dollar figures in millions)

TYPE OF LOAN	CUMULATIVE NUMBER			CUMULATIVE AMOUNT				LOANS OUTSTANDING, JUNE 25, 1955		
	Loans Closed	Claims Paid		Loans Closed	Claims Paid			Total Number	In Default[a]	
		Number	Percent		Amount	Percent			Number	Percent
Home	3,914,535	22,285	0.57%	$29,136	$17.5	0.06%		3,202,177	34,514	1.08%
Farm	68,119	2,110	3.10	267	1.5	0.55		25,751	699	2.71
Business	221,014	12,621	5.71	599	9.9	1.65		43,771	4,260	9.73
Total	4,203,668	37,016	0.88%	$30,001	$28.8	0.10%		3,271,699	39,473	1.21%

Computed from *Loan Guaranty*, Veterans' Administration, June 1955, p. 57.

[a] Also includes loans on which payment of lender's claim was pending.

TABLE C-3

Relative Importance of Insured Loans among Home, Farm, and
Business Loans Made with VA Credit Support, to Mid-1951
(*dollar figures in thousands*)

| LOAN PROGRAM | CUMULATIVE TO MAY 25, 1951 | | | INITIAL INSURANCE CREDITS | |
| | Number of Loans Closed | Loans Insured | | | |
		Number	Percent	Amount	Percent
Home	2,328,961	8,960	0.38%	$ 8,488	29.6%
Farm	60,657	3,943	6.50	1,356	4.7
Business	134,290	52,966	39.44	18,798	65.6
Total	2,523,908	65,869	2.61%	$28,642	100.0%

Numbers of loans closed and loans insured are from *Finance, Guaranty of Loans,*
Veterans' Administration, May 1951, p. 81. Other data, from a special tabulation
supplied by the Veterans' Administration.

The preceding observation is borne out by an analysis of the insured
loan accounts of both active and inactive lenders that were on the books
of the VA at May 25, 1951. Although information is lacking on the total
number of lending institutions participating in the VA loan programs, it
is apparent that only a minor fraction of them (696) utilized loan insurance at all, and that only about 40 percent of this number were active
lenders (Table C-4). These 273 active lending institutions accounted for
more than nine-tenths of the insurance credits outstanding on the books
of the VA. Hence, the data bear out the a priori expectations—that VA
business loan insurance proved to be attractive to a relatively small num-

TABLE C-4

Number of Private Lenders Participating in the VA Business
Loan Insurance Program through May 25, 1951 and
Amount of Their Outstanding Insurance Credits

| | LENDING INSTITUTIONS | | INSURANCE CREDITS OUTSTANDING | |
	Number	Percent	Amount (000)	Percent
Active lenders	273	39.2%	$21,565	90.9%
Inactive lenders	423	60.8	2,159	9.1
Lenders reporting	696	100.0%	$23,724	100.0%

From a special tabulation by the Veterans' Administration, June 18, 1952.
"Active lenders" are defined as lenders who made one or more new loans during
the preceding six months.

ber of lending institutions with relatively large individual loan volumes. Only when a lender could develop a considerable volume of VA business loans would the amount of his insurance reserve expand to provide ample protection against loss. Although the largest number of banks participating in insured loans were institutions with total assets under $25 million, by far the largest proportion of credit was disbursed by a few large banks each with assets of $100 million or more.[45]

ANNUAL VOLUME OF VA BUSINESS LOAN OPERATIONS

Up to mid-1955, a cumulative total of 235,320 applications for business loans had been received by VA offices, of which 221,950 or 94 percent were approved. Of the number of loan applications approved, 221,014 loans were reported closed and disbursed (Table C-5). The high percentage of approvals is indicative of the careful screening of applications by commercial banks and other lenders.

By mid-1955 nearly 165,000 loans, or 75 percent of those disbursed, had been repaid in full. An additional 12,621 loans, representing 5.7 percent of the number disbursed, had been terminated by payment of a claim by the VA. The balance of 43,771 loans, representing not quite 20 percent of the total number disbursed, were outstanding at mid-1955.

TABLE C-5

Applications for VA-Guaranteed or -Insured Business Loans, and Loans Made, Extinguished, and Outstanding, 1945–1955

				LOANS TERMINATED		
CALENDAR YEAR	APPLICATIONS RECEIVED	APPLICATIONS APPROVED	LOANS CLOSED AND DISBURSED	By Repayment in Full	By Payment of Claim by VA	LOANS OUTSTANDING AT YEAR END
1945	3,871	3,312	} 44,485	} 2,231	{ 379	a
1946	51,106	44,764				41,875
1947	39,508	37,534	38,889	9,764	2,028	68,972
1948	17,393	16,596	17,817	15,763	2,604	68,422
1949	13,271	12,695	11,995	14,914	2,057	63,446
1950	13,448	11,699	11,819	11,451	1,161	62,653
1951	48,566	42,789	42,491	10,319	589	94,236
1952	25,618	29,961	30,638	13,317	791	110,766
1953	11,853	12,213	12,473	41,798	1,339	80,102
1954	7,262	7,113	7,157	29,464	1,180	56,615
1955b	3,424	3,274	3,250	15,601	493	43,771
Total	235,320	221,950	221,014	164,622	12,621	..

Computed from data in *Finance, Guaranty of Loans* (Veterans' Administration), 1946–1950 Supplement, and from December issues of *Loan Guaranty*, 1951–1954, and the June 1955 issue.
a Not available. b To June 25.

[45] Data provided by letter from the Veterans' Administration, April 23, 1953.

Applications received reached a peak of 51,100 during the calendar year 1946; applications approved reached their peak of 44,764 during the same year. Terminations by payment of lenders' claims were most numerous in 1948, whereas repayments of loans in full were highest during 1953, following the 1951 increase in lending mentioned below. By the beginning of 1948, it appears that the VA business loan program had reached a plateau, with between 60,000 and 70,000 loans outstanding at year ends through 1950, and the annual number of new loans closed just about offsetting the number of loans terminated (Table C-5). A sharp increase occurred in number of loan applications during 1951, apparently resulting from veterans' efforts to get longer credit terms for the purchase of automobiles than were available elsewhere, under Federal Reserve restriction of consumer credit by means of Regulation W. During the ten months ended May 25, 1952, some 47,634 VA business loans were closed, of which no less than 43,446 loans, or 91.2 percent of the total, were auto loans.[46]

Tables C-6 and C-7 give annual dollar amounts and average size of loan and of VA liability for the business credit program through 1954 and part of 1955, for all loans closed and for loans repaid. The average size of loans closed decreased by more than one-sixth in 1949, and again, more sharply, in 1951; then rose in 1953 and later. The smaller average size of loans during the middle years may be attributed in part to greater caution on the part of lenders as experience with GI loans developed, and also to changes in the business purposes for which loans were made, especially in 1951–1952 when Regulation W was operative. The average amount of liability assumed by VA also decreased in 1949 and again in 1951, representing less than 20 percent of the amounts of loans made from 1951 through 1954. Primarily the decreasing percentages of VA liability reflect a relative increase in use of VA insurance, under which the public liability was limited to 15 percent of the aggregate amount of a lender's loans, whereas in loan guaranteeing it could cover as much as 50 percent of the amount of a loan.

DEFAULT AND LOSS EXPERIENCE

The proportion of outstandings loans that were in default (or on which payment of claims was pending) rose from 1.4 percent at the end of 1946 to 6.0 percent at the end of 1949, during three years when defaults were numerous and many loans terminated with loss, as evidenced by VA's payment of a lender's claim (Tables C-8 and C-9). The sharp rise in the default ratio in 1953 and 1954 reflects mainly the decrease in number of outstandings as many loans were repaid.

Up to mid-1955 the cumulative number of business loans for which

[46] Special tabulation provided by the Veterans' Administration, June 18, 1952.

APPENDIX C

TABLE C-6

VA-Guaranteed or -Insured Business Loans Made, 1945–1955: Number, Original Amount, and Amount of VA Liability

YEAR ENDING DEC. 25	NUMBER	ORIGINAL AMOUNT (000)	ORIGINAL VA LIABILITY		AVERAGE SIZE OF LOAN	AVERAGE VA LIABILITY PER LOAN
			Amount (000)	Percent		
1946a	44,485	$136,049	$ 53,297	39.2%	$3,058	$1,198
1947	38,889	126,045	47,344	37.6	3,241	1,217
1948	17,817	58,450	21,347	36.5	3,281	1,198
1949	11,995	32,290	9,468	29.3	2,692	789
1950	11,819	32,351	8,572	26.5	2,737	725
1951	42,491	82,729	14,968	18.1	1,947	352
1952	30,638	64,855	11,199	17.3	2,117	366
1953	12,473	33,646	5,882	17.5	2,698	472
1954	7,157	21,316	3,870	18.2	2,978	541
1955b	3,250	10,991	2,166	19.7	3,382	667
Total	221,014	$598,723	$178,114	29.7%	$2,709	$ 806

Computed from data in *Finance, Guaranty of Loans* (Veterans' Administration), 1946–1950 Supplement, and from December issues of *Loan Guaranty*, 1951–1954, and the June 1955 issue.
a Cumulative from the beginning of the program.
b To June 25.

TABLE C-7

VA-Guaranteed or -Insured Business Loans Repaid in Full, 1945–1955: Number, Original Amount, and Amount of VA Liability

YEAR ENDING DEC. 25	NUMBER	ORIGINAL AMOUNT (000)	ORIGINAL VA LIABILITY		AVERAGE SIZE OF LOAN	AVERAGE VA LIABILITY PER LOAN
			Amount (000)	Percent		
1946a	2,231	$ 4,664	$ 1,962	42.1%	$2,091	$ 879
1947	9,764	20,926	8,182	39.1	2,143	838
1948	15,763	36,185	13,722	37.9	2,296	871
1949	14,914	38,921	14,638	37.6	2,610	981
1950	11,451	34,051	12,887	37.8	2,974	1,125
1951	10,319	32,929	12,343	37.5	3,191	1,196
1952	13,317	36,109	11,867	32.9	2,712	891
1953	41,798	95,686	19,752	20.6	2,289	473
1954	29,464	62,293	13,089	21.0	2,114	444
1955b	15,601	35,336	7,337	20.8	2,265	470
Total	164,622	$397,101	$115,778	29.2%	$2,412	$ 703

Computed from data in *Finance, Guaranty of Loans* (Veterans' Administration), 1946–1950 Supplement, and from December issues of *Loan Guaranty*, 1951–1954, and the June 1955 issue.
a Cumulative from the beginning of the program.
b To June 25.

TABLE C-8

Default Experience on VA-Guaranteed and -Insured Business Loans, 1945–1955

| YEAR ENDING DEC. 25 | DEFAULTS DURING YEAR | | | | LOANS OUTSTANDING AT YEAR END | | |
| | Reported in Default | Cured or Withdrawn | Ratio of Cured Defaults to Reported | | | In Default[a] | |
			Annual	Cumulative	Total	Number	Percent
1946	1,105[b]	122[b]	11.0%[b]	11.0%	41,875	586	1.4%
1947	6,231	1,628	26.1	23.9	68,972	3,076	4.5
1948	7,345	3,727	50.7	37.3	68,422	3,936	5.8
1949	5,427	3,347	61.7	43.9	63,446	3,797	6.0
1950	3,082	2,476	80.3	48.7	62,653	3,153	5.0
1951	3,439	2,042	59.4	50.1	94,236	3,900	4.1
1952	4,976	2,988	60.0	51.7	110,766	5,038	4.5
1953	4,408	2,027	46.0	51.0	80,102	6,024	7.5
1954	2,989	2,706	90.5	54.0	56,615	5,076	9.0
1955[c]	612	922	150.7	55.5	43,771	4,260	9.7
Total	39,614	21,985	55.5%	..	..	..	..

Computed from the 1946–1950 Supplement and various monthly issues of *Finance, Guaranty of Loans* (Veterans' Administration; now titled *Loan Guaranty*).

a Also includes loans on which payment of lender's claim was pending at year end.
b Cumulative from the beginning of the program.
c To June 25.

TABLE C-9

VA-Guaranteed or -Insured Business Loans Terminated by Payment of Lender's Claim, 1945–1955

| YEAR ENDING DEC. 25 | CLAIMS FILED AFTER DEFAULT[a] | CLAIMS PAID | RATIO OF CLAIMS PAID TO FILED | | NET AMOUNT PAID (000) | AVERAGE SIZE OF CLAIM PAYMENT |
			Annual	Cumulative		
1946[b]	474	379	80.0%	80.0%	$ 311	$ 821
1947	2,563	2,028	79.1	79.3	2,088	1,030
1948	2,855	2,604	91.2	85.0	2,847	1,093
1949	2,008	2,057	102.4	89.5	2,049	996
1950	1,049	1,161	110.7	92.0	706	608
1951	596	589	98.8	92.4	194	329
1952	924	791	85.6	91.8	301	380
1953	1,412	1,339	94.8	92.1	563	420
1954	1,158	1,180	101.9	93.0	593	503
1955[c]	640	493	77.0	92.3	210	426
Total	13,679	12,621	92.3%	..	$9,862	$ 781

Computed from the 1946–1950 Supplement and various monthly issues of *Finance, Guaranty of Loans* (Veterans' Administration; now titled *Loan Guaranty*).

a Includes claim subsequently withdrawn.
b Cumulative from the beginning of the program.
c To June 25.

defaults were reported to VA offices was 39,614, or 17.9 percent of the 221,014 loans closed and disbursed up to that time. In other words, perhaps as many as one out of every six loans made became delinquent in some respect.[47] More than half of the defaulting loans were later removed from default status (Table C-8). A cumulative total of 17,629 loans, or 8 percent of the cumulative number disbursed, had remained delinquent, most of which were terminated before mid-1955 by payment of lenders' claims, with 4,260 still outstanding in default or in process of claim payment. The ratio of loans withdrawn from default status to the number reported in default rose substantially during the first five years of the program, so that by the end of 1950 the number of defaulted loans reinstated to current status was nearly half as large as the total number of defaults reported up to that date. Presumably, this reflected an improvement in administrative technique by the VA and by lenders, and an increasing disposition to work out modifications and extensions of original loans which got into difficulties.

Up to mid-1955, 13,679 claims against the VA had been filed by lenders after default, and claims had been paid on 12,621 loans or 92 percent of those originally filed (Table C-9). The remainder had either been withdrawn or were still pending payment as of that date. During the early years of the program, VA processing of claims lagged materially behind claims filed,[48] giving rise to complaints from lenders. Beginning in 1949 VA offices processed and paid more claims than were filed, and by 1951 they had worked off most of the backlog. A comparison, annually, of the average size of claim payments on loans ending in loss with the average amount of VA's liability on loans that were fully repaid is of interest (Tables C-9 and C-7). In the early years, losses occurred where liability was comparatively heavy; after 1949, the reverse was usually true.

Up to June 25, 1955, claims had been paid on 5.7 percent of all loans closed and disbursed up to that time, and for every claim paid there were 13 loans that had been paid in full up to the same date. The total amount of claims paid was $9,862,000, which was 1.6 percent of the $598,723,000 original amount of loans disbursed. VA statistical records show only the original amounts of loans repaid in full, so that it is necessary to estimate the total amount of repayments up to June 25, 1955.[49]

[47] The statement is only approximate, because repeated delinquencies of the same loan are not taken into account.

[48] Note that part of the difference, in Table C-9, between claims filed and claims paid would be accounted for by claims withdrawn.

[49] Loans fully repaid amounted to $397.1 million by mid-1955. Assuming that loss loans averaged equal in size to loans repaid in full, the total original amount of the 12,621 loans on which claims had been paid by that date would be about $30.4 million, and the total original amount of loans terminated, $428 million. Subtracting that amount from the cumulative amount of all loans closed and disbursed, $599 million, gives an estimate for the total original amount of loans still

Repayments may be estimated roughly at about $480 million, so that the ratio of the amount of claims paid to the total amount of repayments was about 2 percent. It would be desirable to compare the default and loss ratios for VA business loans with those for small business loans made by private lending institutions, but adequate data for the latter are not available. Fragmentary evidence suggests that defaults and losses on VA business loans were relatively higher than those on conventional small business term loans.[50] The hazards involved in extending small term loans to very small and new business enterprises were undoubtedly larger than those which commercial banks had previously been accustomed to carry.

VA LOANS IN THE SMALL BUSINESS LOAN MARKET

The slight importance of VA activity—from the quantitative standpoint—in the small business credit market can be gauged by means of the commercial and industrial loan survey conducted by the Board of Governors of the Federal Reserve System among member banks in November 1946. (Reliable data for nonmember banks and other lenders to small business are lacking.) The Federal Reserve study embraced a nationwide sample of 2,000 member banks, each of which submitted detailed information on a sample of its business loans outstanding.[51] For purposes of the survey, small businesses were defined as manufacturing and mining concerns with total assets under $750,000; wholesale trade concerns with total assets under $250,000; and retail trade, service, construction, public utility, transportation, and other concerns with total assets under $50,000.

On that definition, loans to small firms were estimated to number 514,-000, or three-fourths of all outstanding member bank loans to business. Their total amount was estimated at $2.9 billion, or 22 percent of the business loans held by member banks at the end of 1946, and the average balance outstanding at $5,600. VA-guaranteed or -insured business loans, of which there were an estimated 16,000 totaling $54 million,[52] formed about 3 percent of the number, and just under 2 percent of the outstanding

---

outstanding in mid-1955, $171 million. Then, assuming that on the average, half of the indebtedness on the outstanding loans had been paid off, $85.6 million of such payments may be added to the $397.1 million of loans repaid in full to give the estimate for total repayments up to mid-1955: some $480 million.

50 For example, a large bank that made many thousands of small term loans to business, all under $10,000 in amount, during the period covered by the VA business loan program, found that its ratio of losses charged off to the amount of repayments was well under 1.0 percent. Its delinquency ratio (ratio of amount of loans in default to amount of loans outstanding) was about 3 percent, despite a definition of delinquency more rigorous than that used by the VA.

51 Cf. Charles H. Schmidt, "Member Bank Loans to Small Business," *Federal Reserve Bulletin*, August 1947, pp. 963ff.

52 "Security Pledged on Member Bank Loans to Business," by Tynan Smith, *Federal Reserve Bulletin*, June 1947, p. 665.

amount, of member bank loans to small business. The importance of the VA business credit program lies in the particular segment of the market— new and extremely small enterprises—into which it extended the use of term loans, rather than in its size.

Characteristics of the Loans

The distinguishing characteristics of VA-protected business loans are thrown into relief by comparing them with loans of commercial banks to small business enterprises, to the extent that different categories of analysis in the available data allow. Commercial banks are undoubtedly the most important institutional source of credit for very small businesses. Moreover, banks were the preponderant makers of VA business loans, as Table C-10 shows.

Commercial banks made nearly 95 out of every 100 VA business loans during the three and a half years ending in mid-1951, and advanced more than 90 percent of the credit provided. Savings and loan associations, real estate and mortgage companies, mutual savings banks, and life insurance companies made comparatively insignificant numbers of guaranteed business loans, but those they made were larger on the average than those of commercial banks—in the case of all but the savings and loan associations, about twice as large. Next to commercial banks in importance stood individual lenders, who collectively accounted for 2.8 percent of the loans and for 5.1 percent of the amount of credit advanced. Such VA business loans as were made by commercial finance companies presumably are included in this small volume of credits.

TABLE C-10

Number and Amount of VA-Guaranteed or -Insured Business Loans
Closed from 1948 through Mid-1951, by Type of Lender

TYPE OF LENDER	NUMBER OF LOANS	AMOUNT OF LOANS	PERCENTAGE DISTRIBUTIONS	
			Number	Amount
Commercial banks	51,947	$134,451	94.3%	90.1%
Savings and loan associations	489	1,464	0.9	1.0
Real estate and mortgage companies	523	2,771	0.9	1.9
Mutual savings banks	563	2,678	1.0	1.8
Insurance companies	32	242	0.1	0.2
Individuals and other lenders	1,521	7,574	2.8	5.1
Total	55,075	$149,180	100.0%	100.0%

From a special tabulation provided by the Loan Guaranty Service of the Veterans' Administration. The exact period covered is from December 25, 1947 through June 25, 1951.

APPENDIX C

Information on the size distribution of VA loans by original amount is not available. The best approximation is a distribution by purchase price of the business property financed by the loan, available for a five-month period in late 1947.[53] For the great majority of loans made up to the end of 1947 the loan financed 90 percent or more of the purchase price; use of purchase price therefore overstates only moderately the original amount of loans (excepting loans over $5,000 in amount, for which the ratio of original amount of loan to purchase price fell well below 90 percent).

In comparison with the generality of member bank loans to small business outstanding in November 1946, VA-protected loans show a much greater concentration within the range of $1,000 to $5,000 (Table C-11). The explanation is obvious. On loans not secured by real estate VA's guarantee, by law, could not exceed $2,000 or 50 percent of the loan amount; most VA-protected loans were of that type, hence tended toward amounts close to or below $4,000.

TABLE C-11

Size Distributions of Business Loans Guaranteed or Insured by VA, 1947, and of Outstanding Member Bank Loans to Small Businesses, 1946

	NUMBER OF LOANS		PERCENTAGE DISTRIBUTIONS	
SIZE OF LOAN[a]	*VA-Protected*	*Member Bank*	*VA-Protected*	*Member Bank*
Less than $1,000	2,051	143,300	13.2%	27.9%
$1,000–4,999	10,219	228,800	65.6	44.5
5,000–9,999	2,384	66,700	15.3	13.0
10,000–24,999	849	48,200	5.5	9.4
25,000 and over	61	27,300	0.4	5.3
All loans	15,564	514,300	100.0%	100.0%

VA data refer to business loans closed during five months of 1947 (those ending May 25, June 25, August 25, September 25, and October 25) with VA guarantee or insurance, from a special tabulation by the Veterans' Administration. Bank data refer to loans to small businesses outstanding on November 20, 1946, from "Member Bank Loans to Small Business," by Charles H. Schmidt, *Federal Reserve Bulletin*, August 1947, Table 6, p. 970.

a For VA-protected loans, refers to purchase price of assets acquired; for member bank loans, to original amount.

53 The succeeding materials on contract length, type of security, and repayment method for VA-protected loans also refer to limited periods in 1947. No doubt the pattern of loan size underwent some change over time, and terms to maturity may have tended to shorten in later years; but the available data are believed representative for the broad comparisons with bank loans to small business that are possible.

MATURITY

Perhaps the most significant distinguishing characteristics of VA business loans was their relatively long term of final maturity. More than three-quarters of the member bank loans to small business were written to mature within one year or less or were payable on demand; in contrast, only about one out of a hundred VA-protected business loans had a maturity of less than ten months (Table C-12). Looking at the maturity scale from the opposite direction, only 22 percent of the small business loans held by banks had maturities over twelve months, whereas 99 percent of VA business loans called for final payments ten months or more in the future.

It should be recognized that the actual maturities of loans may differ considerably from their original maturities because of extensions and renewals, and that a considerable number of demand or short-term bank loans to small businesses were term loans in practice. However, the term of the formal loan contract is not incidental. The making of a term loan compels lender and borrower to estimate the long-term earning and debt-repaying capacity of the firm at the outset, and requires a different method of credit appraisal than the making of a short-term loan. The VA program brought banks into a relatively new type of credit operation—term lending to new and very small enterprises. Probably for this reason, commercial banks as well as other lenders wrote VA business loans for terms well within the statutory maximum. Whereas the Servicemen's Readjustment Act permitted amortized loans to run as long as ten years even if unsecured, and for twenty years (currently, thirty years) if secured by real estate, it is noteworthy that 74 percent of all VA loans made during the three-month sample period matured within less than five years.

TYPE OF SECURITY

Nearly three-quarters of VA business loans in the sample period were secured by chattel mortgages or conditional sales contracts on the personal property purchased with the proceeds of the loan (Table C-13). About one-sixth were secured by real estate. Less than 10 percent were otherwise secured, or unsecured. The distribution for member bank loans to small businesses outstanding in November 1946 shows, in contrast, a preponderance of unsecured loans (38 percent) and of loans secured by inventory, or various types of claim, or endorsement (32 percent).

Veterans were, of course, in the great majority of cases unable to offer any other collateral security than the property they purchased with the proceeds of a loan, and, lacking a record of successful experience in operating the business they were entering, they were rarely eligible for unsecured personal credit. Although the law permitted VA guarantee on certain types of unsecured loans, it required that veterans using a loan

TABLE C-12

Distributions by Term to Maturity for Business Loans Guaranteed or Insured by VA, 1947, and for Outstanding Member Bank Loans to Small Businesses, 1946

| | NUMBER OF LOANS | | | PERCENTAGE DISTRIBUTIONS | | |
| | Member Bank | | | | | |
TERM TO MATURITY[a]	VA-Protected	All Loans	Term Loans	VA-Protected	All Loans	Term Loans
Payable on demand	..	64,800	..	..	12.6%	..
1 year and less	101	335,200	..	1.0%	65.2	..
1–3 years	4,252	69,300	69,300	40.7	13.5	60.6%
3–5 years	3,374	21,800	21,800	32.4	4.2	19.1
5–10 years	1,411	19,700	19,700	13.5	3.8	17.2
Over 10 years	1,295	3,500	3,500	12.4	0.7	3.1
Total	10,433	514,300	114,300	100.0%	100.0%	100.0%

VA data refer to business loans closed during three months of 1947 (those ending May 25, July 25, and August 25) with VA guarantee or insurance, from a special tabulation by the Veterans' Administration. Bank data, referring to loans to small businesses outstanding on November 20, 1946, were compiled from "Member Bank Loans to Small Business," by Charles H. Schmidt, *Federal Reserve Bulletin*, August 1947, Tables 8 and 14, pp. 972 and 975.

[a] Class intervals for VA-protected and for member bank loans differ as follows:

VA	Banks
Less than 10 months	12 months and less
10–30 months	12–36 months
30–60 months	36–60 months
60–120 months	60–120 months
120 months and over	Over 120 months

TABLE C-13

Distributions by Type of Security for Business Loans Guaranteed or Insured by VA, 1947, and for Outstanding Member Bank Loans to Small Businesses, 1946

TYPE OF SECURITY	VA-Protected Loans	TYPE OF SECURITY	Member Bank Loans
Land sale contract	0.2%	Unsecured	38.1%
Real estate mortgage	16.7		
		Plant & real property	10.8
Chattel mortgage	72.2	Equipment	18.8
Conditional sales contract, personal property	1.4	Government guarantee[a]	0.3
Other and nonreported	9.5	Other[b]	32.0
Total	100.0%	Total	100.0%

VA data refer to 6,569 business loans closed during two months of 1947 (those ending June 25 and July 25) with VA guarantee or insurance, from a special tabulation by the Veterans' Administration. Bank data refer to an estimated 514,300 loans to small businesses outstanding on November 20, 1946, from "Member Bank Loans to Small Business," by Charles H. Schmidt, *Federal Reserve Bulletin*, August 1947, Table 16, p. 977.

[a] Covers loans involving deferred participation by RFC or the Federal Reserve Banks, or VA guarantee or insurance, where the federal protection was the primary security; otherwise such loans were classified according to major collateral.

[b] Refers to loans secured by stocks and bonds, life insurance, inventories, accounts receivable, assignment of claims, endorsement or co-maker, and miscellaneous other security.

to purchase an interest in real property pledge real estate, and that loans to purchase or improve personal property be secured "to the extent legal and practicable." Lenders did acquire liens on the business property in the great majority of cases. VA business loans were term loans,[54] unlike most of the traditional bank loans to small firms. The greater hazard of nonrepayment involved in distant maturities naturally would have led lenders to take whatever collateral was available, irrespective of the legal injunction.

METHOD OF REPAYMENT

VA business loan agreements have overwhelmingly called for repayments in equal monthly installments: that was the method in more than 94 out of every 100 VA-protected loans made in the sample period (Table C-14). Since the law required amortization only for loans in excess of five years' maturity and the regulation specified a payment "at least once annually," this probably reflects the favorable experience of lenders with monthly installment payments against FHA Title I loans and consumer

[54] That is, loans maturing in more than one year. The VA has customarily used the phrase "term loan" to designate a "straight" or unamortized loan in distinction from an amortized or serial-payment loan.

TABLE C-14

Distributions by Repayment Method for Business Loans Guaranteed or Insured
by VA, 1947, and for Outstanding Member Bank Term Loans
to Small Businesses, 1946

METHOD OF REPAYMENT	VA-Protected Loans	METHOD OF REPAYMENT	Member Bank Term Loans
Monthly installments	94.3%	Equal installments	86.8%
Quarterly installments	1.1	Unequal installments	4.3
Semiannual installments	1.3	Serial notes	2.4
Annual installments	2.2	Several notes	0.2
Unamortized	0.8	Single payment	6.1
Not reported	0.2	Unclassified	0.2
Total	100.0%	Total	100.0%

VA data refer to 6,569 business loans closed during two months of 1947 (those ending
June 25 and July 25) with VA guarantee or insurance, from a special tabulation by the
Veterans' Administration. Bank data refer to an estimated 114,300 term loans to small busi-
nesses outstanding on November 20, 1946, from "Member Bank Loans to Small Business," by
Charles H. Schmidt, *Federal Reserve Bulletin*, August 1947, Table 8, p. 972.

credits. The monthly payment has become a deep-seated convention in
consumer financing. The available information on repayment provisions
in the generality of bank term loans to small business is of interest as
showing the extent to which regular amortization of credits extending
more than one year had become common banking practice by 1946, but
does not make clear whether monthly, quarterly, or annual payments predominate.

Characteristics of the Borrowing Businesses and of the Business Population

What were the probable effects of the VA business loan program upon
the business population of the country, its aggregate size, its geographical
distribution, and its type-of-business composition?

SIZE OF THE BUSINESS POPULATION

Between March 31, 1944 and March 31, 1949 there was a net increase
of 913,000 in the total number of operating firms in the nation.[55] This
30 percent rise during a five-year period was due to the previous wartime
shrinkage in the business population and to generally favorable business
profits and opportunities during the postwar years. From the beginning
of VA credit activity (June 1944) through March 1949 a total of 104,000
VA-protected business loans were closed; and data for the latter half
of 1947 and the calendar year 1948 indicate that perhaps one-third, or
35,000 of the 104,000, were used by veterans to establish new enterprises

[55] See Table C-16, below.

(Table C-15). On the extreme assumption that none of these veterans would have established a new business without VA credit, the indicated ratio of new enterprises financed under VA loan guaranty or insurance to the increase in the business population would be only 3.8 percent. Evidently, the impact of the VA program upon the aggregate size of the business population was slight.[56] In view of the fact that many veterans were in the age group that normally accounts for a large proportion of new enterprise formations, it is likely that far more veterans established new businesses without VA loans than did so with them.

Evidence of the fact that many veterans intended to, and probably did, enter business (i.e., purchase, resume, or start a business) without VA loan benefits is provided by the results of a questionnaire survey of a sample of 20,000 officers and enlisted men made by the Army Service Forces during mid-1944.[57] Eleven percent of the men had fairly definite plans to enter business by themselves or with a relative, and more than 80 percent of them had experience in the line they intended to enter. Most planned to invest not more than $4,000, and about 60 percent stated they possessed at least half of the necessary capital. Only one-sixth stated they planned to borrow from banks and loan companies, and one-tenth from friends. Bearing in mind the fact that this sample covered a soldier

TABLE C-15

Distribution by Purpose for Business Loans
Guaranteed or Insured by VA, 1947, 1948

BUSINESS PURPOSE	FIVE MONTHS OF 1947		CALENDAR YEAR 1948	
	Number of Loans	Percent	Number of Loans	Percent
Establish new business	5,415	35.0%	5,170	26.9%
Purchase going concern	4,108	26.6	4,401	22.9
Repairs to equipment	164	1.1	139	0.7
Purchase equipment and other assets for going concerns	5,767	37.3	9,525	49.5
Total	15,454	100.0%	19,235	100.0%

From special tabulations by the Veterans' Administration for months ending May 25, June 25, August 25, September 25, and October 25, 1947; and for the period December 25, 1947 through December 25, 1948.

[56] Table C-15 suggests that the proportion of VA-protected loans used for starting a new business may have been higher in earlier than in later years; but even assuming a proportion as high as two-fifths for the period through March 1949, the ratio of new firms financed under the VA program to the increase in the business population would be only 4.6 percent.

[57] Cf. D'Alton B. Myers, "Postwar Business Plans of G.I.'s," *Domestic Commerce*, January 1945, p. 11.

population of about 14 million, it appears that entry into business was contemplated by some 1.5 million men. If even as few as one-quarter of them actually did follow their plans, it would mean that up to March 1949 three veterans entered businesses without VA assistance for every one who entered with VA loan aid.

In 1947 and 1948 (and probably later, as well) the majority of VA-protected business loans were used by veterans to purchase going concerns or to buy equipment, inventory, and other assets for businesses they already operated. The latter purpose was the most frequent, motivating 37 percent of the loans in five months of 1947 and half of the loans in 1948.

LINES OF TRADE

Over 40 percent of the operating business firms in the United States in 1944 and 1949 were engaged in retail trade, and over 20 percent in the service trades (Table C-16). If the count were confined to small firms, probably those two industry groups would bulk even larger. They also were the groups in which most of the net increase in the total number of firms between 1944 and 1949 occurred: 33 percent in retail trade, 22 percent in services, with a large increase also in construction firms— 19 percent of the total increase—though in 1944 that group had represented only 5 percent of the business population.

TABLE C-16

Industry Distributions of the Number of Operating Businesses, 1944 and 1949, and of the Increase in That Period

TYPE OF BUSINESS	NUMBER OF OPERATING FIRMS (IN THOUSANDS)			PERCENTAGE DISTRIBUTIONS		
	March 31, 1944	March 31, 1949	Increase 1944–1949	1944	1949	Increase 1944–1949
Manufacturing	242.0	308.1	66.1	8.0%	7.8%	7.2%
Wholesale trade	143.1	202.4	59.3	4.7	5.1	6.5
Retail trade	1,379.8	1,684.7	304.9	45.7	42.8	33.4
Service industries	647.6	849.0	201.4	21.4	21.6	22.1
Contract construction	149.1	323.4	174.3	4.9	8.2	19.1
Transportation, finance, and all others[a]	460.6	567.7	107.1	15.2	14.4	11.7
Total	3,022.2	3,935.3	913.1	100.0%	100.0%	100.0%

Computed from Table 7 in "State Estimates of the Business Population," by Betty C. Churchill and Murray F. Foss, *Survey of Current Business*, December 1949, pp. 15f.

[a] Includes mining and quarrying, communications and other public utilities, and insurance and real estate firms.

Among member bank loans to small business outstanding in November 1946, those that had been made under VA protection were distributed industrially about as the foregoing census would suggest, with 63 percent in the retail and service groups combined (Table C-17). A disproportionately large fraction of the generality of the bank loans went to manufacturing firms, whereas the fraction of VA-protected loans going to that industry group corresponded more closely to its proportion in the business population and in the net number of new firms. VA loans to service industries (21 percent of the total) matched that group's importance in the population and in the increase during the postwar years, whereas only 12 percent of the generality of member bank small business loans went to such firms. A disproportionately large fraction of VA loans, on the other hand, appears in the combined groups "utilities, transportation" and "all other," probably reflecting numerous loans to aid veterans' local trucking enterprises. Neither the proportion of the bank loans generally nor of the VA-protected bank loans going to construction firms matched that group's increase of population during the postwar years.

The industry distribution for loans by all types of lender that were made under VA protection during 1949 and 1950 shows an even greater concentration in the retail and service groups than was observed for VA-protected member bank loans outstanding in 1946 (Table C-17); but differences in the classification systems make the comparison doubtful.

GEOGRAPHICAL DISTRIBUTION

Areas where the share of the business loans made up to mid-1949 under VA guaranty or insurance was larger than the fraction of the business population they included were: northern New England (Maine, New Hampshire, Vermont); Minnesota and the Dakotas; and most of the Mountain states (Montana, Wyoming, Utah, Colorado, Arizona, New Mexico). Areas where the share of VA business loans was small in relation to the business population were: most of the southeast (North Carolina and Tennessee; Louisiana, Mississippi, Alabama, and Florida); also Illinois; Ohio and West Virginia; and New Jersey. The geographical distribution of VA-protected business loans to mid-1949 was not apparently related to differing rates of gain in business population (Table C-18). For example, of seventeen states where the number of firms increased between 1944 and 1949 by 39 percent or more (against a national average of 30 percent), only three (Arizona, New Mexico, Oregon) received a fraction of VA-protected loans that was markedly larger than their share of the business population. The rest had shares of VA loans that either were low compared to the business population or were not much out of line (North Carolina, Georgia, Florida, Alabama, Louisiana, Kentucky, Arkansas, Texas; California, Washington, Idaho, Nevada). Nor, apparently, does the distribution of the veteran population account

TABLE C-17

Industry Distributions of Outstanding Member Bank Loans to Small Businesses, 1946, of Such Loans Carrying VA Guaranty or Insurance, and of Business Loans Guaranteed or Insured by VA during 1949-1950

INDUSTRY	NUMBER OF LOANS			AMOUNT		
	Held by Member Banks, 1946a		Guaranteed or Insured by VA, 1949-1950b	Outstanding in Member Banks, 1946a		Loans Guaranteed or Insured by VA, 1949-1950b
	All Loans	VA-Protected		All Loans	VA-Protected	
Manufacturing and mining	19.6%	8.3%	3.6%	46.0%	14.6%	4.6%
Wholesale trade	14.1	5.1	2.5	24.2	5.1	3.3
Retail trade	38.2	42.0	48.0	16.2	35.8	46.1
Services	11.9	21.0	30.8	5.0	16.1	33.2
Construction	5.2	5.1	4.5	3.0	4.8	4.1
Public utilities and transportation	5.3	13.4	9.5	2.4	8.3	7.5
All other	5.7	5.1	1.1	3.3	15.3	1.2
Total	100.0%	100.0%	100.0%	100.0%	100.0%	100.0%

a Data for "all loans" cover an estimated 514,300 loans to small businesses, with outstandings totaling $2.9 million, from "Member Bank Loans to Small Business," by Charles H. Schmidt, *Federal Reserve Bulletin*, August 1947, Table 3, p. 967. Distribution for the VA loans among them—an estimated 16,000, with unpaid balances of $54 million—was computed from data on number of loans and average size by industry group, from "Security Pledged on Member Bank Loans to Business," by Tynan Smith, *Federal Reserve Bulletin*, June 1947, Table 15, p. 676.

b Based on a special tabulation by the Veterans' Administration covering loans closed—approximately 24,000 for $64.5 million—with VA guarantee or insurance, during the two years ending December 25, 1950.

The industry classification differed from that of the bank data, and certain groups were combined, as follows: Sales agents, brokers, and jobbers (27 percent of the total by number, 18 percent by amount) were assigned to retail trade, though some may belong in wholesale trade. To the service category were added recreations and amusements (less than 2 percent, by number and amount); professional and semiprofessional (about 11 percent); and trade crafts (about 4 percent), though part may belong with construction.

TABLE C-18

Distributions by Region and State for Number of Business Loans Made to Mid-1949 with VA Guaranty or Insurance, and for Number of Businesses in 1948, with Percentage Change in Number of Businesses, 1944–1949

STATE AND REGION	PERCENTAGE INCREASE IN NUMBER OF OPERATING FIRMS, 1944–1949	PERCENTAGE DISTRIBUTION OF OPERATING FIRMS IN U.S., MARCH 1948	VA-PROTECTED BUSINESS LOANS CLOSED TO JUNE 25, 1949	
			Number	Percent
New England	*24.1%*	*6.91%*	*9,933*	*9.32%*
Connecticut	24.9	1.46	1,150	1.08
Maine	22.9	0.74	1,471	1.38
Massachusetts	23.4	3.44	4,557	4.27
New Hampshire	21.5	0.44	1,407	1.32
Rhode Island	29.0	0.55	765	0.72
Vermont	25.8	0.28	583	0.55
Middle East	*23.9*	*25.90*	*29,050*	*27.19*
Delaware	20.9	0.23	150	0.14
District of Columbia	9.5	0.58	1,518	1.42
Maryland	23.6	1.27	1,152	1.08
New Jersey	22.4	3.61	1,328	1.24
New York	22.3	13.07	17,850	16.71
Pennsylvania	27.2	6.18	6,483	6.07
West Virginia	44.6	0.96	569	0.53
South East	*43.0*	*15.23*	*11,751*	*10.98*
Alabama	39.1	1.33	917	0.86
Arkansas	45.0	1.00	1,104	1.03
Florida	70.9	2.09	1,142	1.07
Georgia	41.3	1.62	1,885	1.76
Kentucky	43.4	1.33	1,208	1.13
Louisiana	41.8	1.23	892	0.83
Mississippi	39.2	0.81	451	0.42
North Carolina	41.6	1.78	917	0.86
South Carolina	36.1	0.88	1,073	1.00
Tennessee	32.6	1.50	720	0.67
Virginia	36.8	1.66	1,442	1.35
South West	*48.7*	*7.44*	*7,817*	*7.31*
Arizona	67.3	0.48	1,137	1.06
New Mexico	46.8	0.40	685	0.64
Oklahoma	33.9	1.38	1,238	1.16
Texas	47.4	5.17	4,757	4.45
Central	*20.3*	*27.36*	*26,216*	*24.54*
Illinois	12.2	6.75	5,049	4.73
Indiana	23.8	2.50	2,260	2.12
Iowa	20.1	1.92	2,841	2.66
Michigan	24.3	4.00	3,711	3.47
Minnesota	21.1	2.01	3,340	3.13
Missouri	13.9	2.77	3,441	3.22
Ohio	28.6	4.91	2,580	2.41
Wisconsin	26.0	2.50	2,994	2.80

(*continued on next page*)

TABLE C-18 (continued)

STATE AND REGION	PERCENTAGE INCREASE IN NUMBER OF OPERATING FIRMS, 1944–1949	PERCENTAGE DISTRIBUTION OF OPERATING FIRMS IN U.S., MARCH 1948	VA-PROTECTED BUSINESS LOANS CLOSED TO JUNE 25, 1949 Number	VA-PROTECTED BUSINESS LOANS CLOSED TO JUNE 25, 1949 Percent
North West	*27.4%*	*5.58%*	*8,900*	*8.33%*
Colorado	28.7	0.92	1,552	1.45
Idaho	40.0	0.39	412	0.39
Kansas	20.9	1.43	1,918	1.80
Montana	24.1	0.46	887	0.83
Nebraska	20.4	0.97	994	0.93
North Dakota	18.1	0.37	1,161	1.09
South Dakota	23.6	0.44	996	0.93
Utah	36.9	0.39	655	0.61
Wyoming	36.1	0.21	325	0.30
Far West	*56.0*	*11.61*	*13,177*	*12.34*
California	59.2	8.54	9,176	8.59
Nevada	44.9	0.15	169	0.16
Oregon	46.1	1.21	1,763	1.65
Washington	48.6	1.71	2,069	1.94
United States	*30.2%*	*100.00%*	*106,844*	*100.00%*

VA data from Annual Report of the *Administrator of Veterans Affairs*, 1949, Table 88, p. 236; other data from "State Estimates of the Business Population," by Betty C. Churchill and Murray F. Foss, *Survey of Current Business*, December 1949, pp. 14ff. (change in business population refers to March 31 dates).

for the disproportions in the distributions of VA loans and of the business population. Partly, no doubt, the geographical pattern of VA loans reflects differences in the availability of private banking services and the willingness of banks to make such loans.

Effects on the Amount and Cost of Credit

The primary objectives of the VA business credit program were, first, to lower the price of credit to every veteran desiring to enter business for himself and possessing a reasonable likelihood of success, and, secondly, to obtain for veterans more liberal credit terms, such as credit with smaller-than-normal equity on the part of the borrower. One important criterion for judging the success of the program is therefore the extent to which the program actually succeeded in (a) increasing the number of veterans able to obtain business credit, and (b) reducing the cost of business credit to veterans who would have been able to negotiate loans without VA assistance.

How high an interest rate would veterans have had to pay for loans of the sizes, maturities, collateral security, and other characteristics of VA business loans, without VA guaranty or insurance? One need merely recall the observed characteristics of VA business loans to realize that, up to the time of the VA program, very small term loans to new and small enterprises were not generally available from commercial banks. Neither were they generally available from commercial finance companies, which dealt with many small enterprises, but not with many firms as small as those into which veterans entered. It follows that the program did succeed in increasing materially the number of veterans able to obtain business credit from financial institutions. VA guaranty of up to 50 percent of the amount of a loan (and later VA insurance of up to 100 percent of individual loans where the lender had sufficient insurance credit in his account), combined with the desire of banks to aid returning veterans, did induce banks to make many loans which were formerly considered beyond the pale of sound banking practice, and to make them at a moderate rate of interest, as prescribed by the law.

Analysis of the probable effects of VA guaranty or insurance upon the cost of business credit to veterans requires an understanding of the components of interest rates charged by banks for business credit. In theory, three important components enter into the gross interest rate charged for a business loan: (1) pure interest on riskless assets, (2) costs of administration of a loan, which rise rapidly per dollar loaned as loan sizes diminish, (3) risk premium to compensate for the hazard of nonrepayment of principal and interest and to provide a reserve out of which losses may be met. VA loan guaranty or insurance served to reduce the third component; it did not affect the other two. If the amounts of pure interest and of costs of administration may be estimated roughly, it will be possible to calculate the importance of VA guaranty in reducing the total interest rate charged on a loan. A loan of $3,000 maturing in three years may be considered as representative of VA business loans during 1946 and 1947, the most active years of the program.[58]

"Pure interest" on riskless assets, judged by yields of government securities with three-year maturities, was about $1\frac{1}{2}$ percent per annum during 1946 and 1947. Scattered information suggests that the average cost of administering VA loans of $3,000 was at least $2\frac{1}{2}$ percent per annum. The sum of these two items, 4 percent, may be taken as the minimum basic return to a commercial bank, without allowance for risk premium; the risk premium may be regarded as the difference between the interest rate charged and 4 percent per annum.

A small business loan to a veteran at 6 percent would involve a 2 percent risk premium component. If VA guaranteed repayment of half the loan, it would reduce the appropriate risk premium by at least one-half, or to 1 percent, and in the case of a lender who had built up an adequate insurance reserve it might reduce it by 100 percent, or be the

[58] See Tables C-6 and C-12, above.

equivalent of a 2 percent annual rate of interest. A bank might therefore be expected to make guaranteed or insured loans at 5 percent which it would not have made without guaranty except at 6 or 7 percent. Similarly, an 8 percent unguaranteed loan would have a risk premium component of 4 percent, and VA guaranty would reduce the bank's loan rate by at least half this amount, or 2 percent. The bank would be expected to make the same loan on a guaranteed basis at 6 percent that it would have made without guaranty at 8 to 10 percent. It is noteworthy that the relative reduction in loan rate caused by VA guaranty rises as the risk-premium component rises. VA guaranty provided a relatively larger incentive to banks toward riskier than toward safer loans.

An indication of the amount of reduction in loan rate caused by VA guaranty is provided by a consideration of interest rates charged on member bank term loans to business that were outstanding in late 1946. The average interest rate charged varied according to the amount of the loan and the size of the borrowing firm; for three size classes of small firms, the averages were as follows:[59]

	AVERAGE RATE FOR BORROWERS WITH TOTAL ASSETS OF		
LOAN SIZE[a]	*Less than* *$50,000*	*$50,000–* *249,999*	*$250,000–* *749,999*
Less than $500	9.0%	6.9%	6.8%
$500–999	7.8	6.0	4.9
1,000–4,999	6.0	5.6	5.0
5,000–9,999	5.2	5.0	4.3
10,000–24,999	4.8	4.5	4.3
25,000–49,999	4.5	4.3	4.2
50,000–99,999	..	4.2	4.0
100,000–499,999	..	4.3	3.9
500,000–999,999	..	..	3.8
Loans of all sizes	5.4%	4.4%	4.0%

a Size of loan refers to unpaid balance; hence the results somewhat understate the differences between rates on loans of larger and smaller original amount.

Since the enterprises of VA borrowers by and large were of smaller size and subject to greater risk than those included in the smallest size class of bank term borrowers, it seems likely that the charge on three-year loans of $3,000 to very small firms, if banks had made them without guaranty, would have been at least 10 percent per annum.[60] On the

59 From "The Structure of Interest Rates on Business Loans at Member Banks," by Richard Youngdahl, *Federal Reserve Bulletin*, July 1947, Table 16, p. 816.
60 On small amortized business term loans, banks ordinarily quote rates of discount on the borrower's note. Thus 5 percent discount on a loan maturing within three years and repayable in equal monthly installments would be equivalent to approximately 9½ percent interest.

assumptions made previously, regarding administrative cost and pure interest, such loans would have about a 6 percent risk-premium component. VA guaranty would have reduced this by one-half, or 3 percent, enabling a bank to make a loan at 7 percent with VA guaranty for which it would have charged 10 percent without it. However, the law limited the bank's charges (on insured non-real-estate loans) to 5.7 percent. This limitation undoubtedly made numerous VA loans unattractive as bank portfolio holdings, even with VA insurance, and was a restrictive factor in the program to enlist broad banking participation in making business credit available to veterans. The statutory differential of 1.7 percent between the maximum charge for real estate loans and that for non-real-estate business loans understated the true difference in costs and risks.

Index of Authors

Index of Subjects